W9-BUP-934

ANTHROPOLOGY 98/99

Twenty-First Edition

_____

_____

_____

_____

_____

Editor

Elvio Angeloni

Pasadena City College

Elvio Angeloni received his B.A. from UCLA in 1963, his M.A. in anthropology from UCLA in 1965, and his M.A. in communication arts from Loyola Marymount University in 1976. He has produced several films, including *Little Warrior,* winner of the Cinemedia VI Best Bicentennial Theme, and *Broken Bottles,* shown on PBS. He most recently served as an academic adviser on the instructional television series *Faces of Culture.*

Annual Editions

A Library of Information from the Public Press

Dushkin/McGraw·Hill

Sluice Dock, Guilford, Connecticut 06437

Visit us on the Internet—http://www.dushkin.com/annualeditions

PEOPLES DISCUSSED IN *ANNUAL EDITIONS: ANTHROPOLOGY 98/99*

Map Location Number	People	Article Number
1.	Yąnomamö	1, 11, 21, 40
2.	Punjabi	2
3.	!Kung-Kalahari Desert	3, 21
4.	Tiv	9
5.	Eskimo (Inupiaq)	10
	Koyukon Indians	10
6.	Eskimo (Inuit)	4, 21, 41
7.	Masai (Maasai)	12, 25
8.	Kaliai	13
9.	Simbu	14
10.	Tibetans	16
11.	Dobe San-Kalahari Desert	21
	Hadza-Tanzania	21
	Tiwi-Northeast coast of Australia	21
12.	Laguna Pueblo	22
13.	Bundu	24
14.	Mbuti Pygmies	28
15.	Fore-Papua New Guinea	38
16.	Maori	15

The Annual Editions Series

ANNUAL EDITIONS, including GLOBAL STUDIES, consist of over 70 volumes designed to provide the reader with convenient, low-cost access to a wide range of current, carefully selected articles from some of the most important magazines, newspapers, and journals published today. ANNUAL EDITIONS are updated on an annual basis through a continuous monitoring of over 300 periodical sources. All ANNUAL EDITIONS have a number of features that are designed to make them particularly useful, including topic guides, annotated tables of contents, unit overviews, and indexes. For the teacher using ANNUAL EDITIONS in the classroom, an Instructor's Resource Guide with test questions is available for each volume. GLOBAL STUDIES titles provide comprehensive background information and selected world press articles on the regions and countries of the world.

VOLUMES AVAILABLE

ANNUAL EDITIONS

Abnormal Psychology
Accounting
Adolescent Psychology
Aging
American Foreign Policy
American Government
American History, Pre-Civil War
American History, Post-Civil War
American Public Policy
Anthropology
Archaeology
Astronomy
Biopsychology
Business Ethics
Canadian Politics
Child Growth and Development
Comparative Politics
Computers in Education
Computers in Society
Criminal Justice
Criminology
Developing World
Deviant Behavior
Drugs, Society, and Behavior
Dying, Death, and Bereavement

Early Childhood Education
Economics
Educating Exceptional Children
Education
Educational Psychology
Environment
Geography
Geology
Global Issues
Health
Human Development
Human Resources
Human Sexuality
International Business
Macroeconomics
Management
Marketing
Marriage and Family
Mass Media
Microeconomics
Multicultural Education
Nutrition
Personal Growth and Behavior
Physical Anthropology
Psychology
Public Administration
Race and Ethnic Relations

Social Problems
Social Psychology
Sociology
State and Local Government
Teaching English as a Second
    Language
Urban Society
Violence and Terrorism
Western Civilization, Pre-Reformation
Western Civilization, Post-Reformation
Women's Health
World History, Pre-Modern
World History, Modern
World Politics

GLOBAL STUDIES

Africa
China
India and South Asia
Japan and the Pacific Rim
Latin America
Middle East
Russia, the Eurasian Republics, and
    Central/Eastern Europe
Western Europe

Cataloging in Publication Data
Main entry under title: Annual Editions: Anthropology. 1998/99.
    1. Anthropology—Periodicals. I. Angeloni, Elvio, *comp*. II. Title: Anthropology.
ISBN 0–697–39124–8   ISSN 1091–613X   301.2   74–84595

Twenty-First Edition

Cover: A traditional Solomon Island initiation ceremony for boys. Photo by Irv DeVore/Anthro-Photo.

Printed in the United States of America

Printed on Recycled Paper

Editors/Advisory Board

Members of the Advisory Board are instrumental in the final selection of articles for each edition of ANNUAL EDITIONS. Their review of articles for content, level, currentness, and appropriateness provides critical direction to the editor and staff. We think that you will find their careful consideration well reflected in this volume.

EDITOR

Elvio Angeloni
Pasadena City College

ADVISORY BOARD

Staff

Ian A. Nielsen, Publisher

To the Reader

In publishing ANNUAL EDITIONS we recognize the enormous role played by the magazines, newspapers, and journals of the *public press* in providing current, first-rate educational information in a broad spectrum of interest areas. Many of these articles are appropriate for students, researchers, and professionals seeking accurate, current material to help bridge the gap between principles and theories and the real world. These articles, however, become more useful for study when those of lasting value are carefully *collected, organized, indexed,* and *reproduced* in a *low-cost format,* which provides easy and permanent access when the material is needed. That is the role played by ANNUAL EDITIONS. Under the direction of each volume's *academic editor,* who is an expert in the subject area, and with the guidance of an *Advisory Board,* each year we seek to provide in each ANNUAL EDITION a current, well-balanced, carefully selected collection of the best of the public press for your study and enjoyment. We think that you will find this volume useful, and we hope that you will take a moment to let us know what you think.

The twenty-first edition of *Annual Editions: Anthropology* contains a variety of articles on contemporary issues in social and cultural anthropology. In contrast to the broad range of topics and minimum depth typical of standard textbooks, this anthology provides an opportunity to read firsthand accounts by anthropologists of their own research. In allowing scholars to speak for themselves about the issues on which they are expert, we are better able to understand the kind of questions anthropologists ask, the ways in which they ask them, and how they go about searching for answers. Indeed, where there is disagreement among anthropologists, this format allows the readers to draw their own conclusions.

Given the very broad scope of anthropology—in time, space, and subject matter—the present collection of highly readable articles has been selected according to certain criteria. The articles have been chosen from both professional and nonprofessional publications for the purpose of supplementing the standard textbook in cultural anthropology that is used in introductory courses. Some of the articles are considered classics in the field, while others have been selected for their timely relevance.

Included in this volume are a number of features designed to make it useful for students, researchers, and professionals in the field of anthropology. While the articles are arranged along the lines of broadly unifying themes, the *topic guide* can be used to establish specific reading assignments tailored to the needs of a particular course of study. Other useful features include the *table of contents* abstracts, which summarize each article and present key concepts in italics, and a comprehensive *index*. In addition, each unit is preceded by an overview, which provides a background for informed reading of the articles, emphasizes critical issues, and presents *challenge questions.*

New to this edition are *World Wide Web* sites that can be used to further explore the topics. These sites will be cross-referenced by number in the topic guide.

Annual Editions: Anthropology 98/99 will continue to be updated annually. Those involved in producing this volume wish to make the next one as useful and effective as possible. Your criticism and advice are welcomed. Please fill out the article rating form on the last page of the book and let us know your opinions. Any anthology can be improved. This continues to be—annually.

Elvio Angeloni
Editor
(E-mail address: *evangeloni@paccd.cc.ca.us*)

Contents

World Map   ii
To the Reader   vi
Topic Guide   4
Selected World Wide Web Sites   6

Overview   8

UNIT 1

Anthropological Perspectives

Five selections examine the role of anthropologists in studying different cultures. The innate problems in developing productive relationships between anthropologists and exotic cultures are considered by reviewing a number of fieldwork experiences.

1. **Doing Fieldwork among the Yąnomamö,** Napoleon A. Chagnon, from *Yąnomamo: The Fierce People,* Holt, Rinehart & Winston, 1992.   10
Although an anthropologist's first experience may involve **culture shock,** Napoleon Chagnon reports that the long process of **participant observation** may transform personal hardship and frustration into confident understanding of exotic cultural patterns.

2. **Doctor, Lawyer, Indian Chief,** Richard Kurin, *Natural History,* November 1980.   22
In transforming an anthropologist into one of their own, villagers of Punjab say, "You never really know who a man is until you know who his grandfather and his ancestors were." In this way, Richard Kurin finds, selecting a village for **fieldwork** is a matter of mutual acceptance and mutual **economic** benefit.

3. **Eating Christmas in the Kalahari,** Richard Borshay Lee, *Natural History,* December 1969.   27
Anthropologist Richard Borshay Lee gives an account of the misunderstanding and confusion that often accompany the **cross-cultural experience.** In this case, he violated a basic principle of the !Kung Bushmen's social relations—**food sharing.**

4. **The Challenge of Cultural Relativism,** James Rachels, from *The Elements of Moral Philosophy,* McGraw–Hill Inc., 1993.   31
From the perspective of **cultural relativism,** many of our behaviors and **values** are situational, products of cultural circumstance. As valuable as this insight may be, says the author, it fails to take into account the fact that there are also some values that all human beings must adhere to and that are, therefore, **universal.**

5. **The Lost Man,** Douglas Preston, *The New Yorker,* June 16, 1997.   37
Recent findings indicate that the **first Americans** might not be who we think they are. Before the evidence could be adequately assessed, however, the U.S. government withheld it, Native Americans have been wanting to rebury it, and archaeologists have gone to court to retrieve it. In the process, issues of **race** and **ethnicity** have been brought to a steaming head.

The concepts in bold italics are developed in the article. For further expansion please refer to the Topic Guide and the Index.

UNIT 2

Culture and Communication

Four selections discuss communication as an element of culture. Ingrained social and cultural values have a tremendous effect on an individual's perception or interpretation of both verbal and nonverbal communication.

Overview   46

6. **Language, Appearance, and Reality: Doublespeak in 1984,**   48
   William D. Lutz, *Et Cetera,* Winter 1987.
   When *language* is used to alter our perception of reality, its main function—that of *communication* between people and social groups—is in grave danger.

7. **Why Don't You Say What You Mean?** Deborah Tannen,   54
   New York Times Magazine, August 28, 1994.
   As fundamental elements in human *communication, directness* is not necessarily logical or effective, and *indirectness* is not necessarily manipulative or insecure. Each has its place in the broader scheme of things, depending upon the culture and the relationship between the speakers.

8. **Teaching in the Postmodern Classroom,** Conrad Phillip Kot-   58
   tak, from *General Anthropology,* American Anthropological Association, 1994.
   Anthropologists do not always travel to exotic locales to find unique patterns of *culturally conditioned behavior.* They may even find it in their own *classrooms.*

9. **Shakespeare in the Bush,** Laura Bohannan, *Natural History,*   61
   August/September 1966.
   It is often claimed that great literature has *cross-cultural* significance. In this article, Laura Bohannan describes the difficulties she encountered and the lessons she learned as she attempted to relate the story of *Hamlet* to the Tiv of West Africa in their own *language.*

UNIT 3

The Organization of Society and Culture

Six selections discuss the influence of the environment and culture on the organization of the social structure of groups.

Overview   66

10. **Understanding Eskimo Science,** Richard Nelson, *Audubon,*   68
September/October 1993.
The traditional **hunters'** insights into the world of **nature** may be different, but they are as extensive and profound as those of modern science.

11. **The Yanomami Keep on Trekking,** Kenneth Good, *Natural*   71
History, April 1995.
Lacking a more balanced range of crops and domesticated food animals, the Yąnomami must get their meat and fat from the wild animals of the forest. **Trekking for game** thus helps to fulfill nutritional needs and maintain **social bonds** through the sharing of scarce commodities.

12. **Mystique of the Masai,** Ettagale Blauer, *The World & I,*   76
March 1987.
Living in the midst of tourist traffic and straddling two nations struggling to modernize, the Masai have retained their **traditional culture** longer than virtually every other group of people in East Africa.

13. **Too Many Bananas, Not Enough Pineapples, and No Wa-**   83
termelon at All: Three Object Lessons in Living with Reci-
procity, David Counts, from *The Humbled Anthropologist:*
Tales from the Pacific, Wadsworth Publishing, 1990.
Among the lessons to be learned regarding **reciprocity** is that one may not demand a gift or refuse it. Yet, even without a system of record-keeping or money involved, there is a long-term balance of mutual benefit.

14. *From Shells to Money,* Karl F. Rambo, *The World & I,* May   87
1989.
High in the mountains of New Guinea, the once-secluded Simbu have increasingly adopted **money** as a medium of exchange. Still, the **economic strategy** of maximizing **social relationships** rather than individual wealth remains intact.

15. **Continental Divides,** Jared Diamond, *The Sciences,* March/   93
April 1997.
Not all continents are equal, even though their inhabitants are. Differing circumstances, says Jared Diamond, will explain why some parts of the world remained cultural backwaters, while others enabled people to develop their **technologies** to exert their **dominance.**

The concepts in bold italics are developed in the article. For further expansion please refer to the Topic Guide and the Index.

UNIT 4

Other Families, Other Ways

Five selections examine some of the influences on the family structure of different cultures. The strength of the family unit is affected by both economic and social pressures.

Overview   **98**

16. **When Brothers Share a Wife,** Melvyn C. Goldstein, *Natural History,* March 1987.   **100**
    While the custom of *fraternal polyandry* relegated many Tibetan women to spinsterhood, this unusual *marriage* form promoted personal security and economic well-being for its participants.

17. **On the Streets of America,** Mark S. Fleisher, *Natural History,* July/August 1997.   **104**
    Born and raised in *fragile families* with weak social ties, some American teenagers seek companionship and *personal security* on the streets. Even prison is seen as a refuge for *survival.*

18. **Death without Weeping,** Nancy Scheper-Hughes, *Natural History,* October 1989.   **108**
    In the shantytowns of Brazil, the seeming indifference of mothers who allow some of their *children* to die is a *survival strategy* geared to circumstances in which only a few may live.

19. **Arranging a Marriage in India,** Serena Nanda, from *The Naked Anthropologist,* Wadsworth Publishing, 1992.   **113**
    Arranging a marriage in India is far too serious a business for the young and inexperienced. Instead, the parents make decisions on the basis of both families' social position, reputation, and ability to get along.

20. **Who Needs Love! In Japan, Many Couples Don't,** Nicholas D. Kristof, *New York Times,* February 11, 1996.   **117**
    Paradoxically, *Japanese families* seem to survive not because husbands and wives love each other more than do American couples, but rather because they perhaps love each other less. And as *love marriages* increase, with the compatibility factor becoming more important in the decision to marry, the *divorce rate* is rising.

The concepts in bold italics are developed in the article. For further expansion please refer to the Topic Guide and the Index.

UNIT 5

Gender and Status

Five selections discuss some of the sex roles prescribed by the social, economic, and political forces of a culture.

Overview   120

21. **Society and Sex Roles,** Ernestine Friedl, *Human Nature,* April   122
1978.
Ernestine Friedl relates the extent of *male domination* over *women*
to the degree to which men control the exchange of valued goods
with people outside the family. As women gain increasing access to
positions of power in industrial society, they may regain the *equality*
that seems to have been prevalent among our foraging ancestors.

22. **Yellow Woman and a Beauty of the Spirit,** Leslie Marmon   127
Silko, *Los Angeles Times Magazine,* December 19, 1993.
The traditional Pueblo societies were *communal* and strictly *egalitarian. Beauty* was manifested in behavior and in one's relationship
with other living things. It was as much a feeling of *harmony* as it
was a visual, aural, or sensual effect.

23. **Status, Property, and the Value on Virginity,** Alice Schlegel,   131
from *The Other Fifty Percent: Multicultural Perspectives on Gender Relations,* Waveland Press, 1993.
Wherever brides' families use *marital alliances* to maintain or enhance their *social status,* there is a strong emphasis upon *biological
paternity* and the value of *virginity.*

24. **Bundu Trap,** Memuna M. Sillah, *Natural History,* August   137
1996.
In discussing her childhood experiences in Sierra Leone, Memuna
Sillah provides us with a glimpse of what it is like for a young girl
to anticipate her own *circumcision ceremony.* In the "Afterword,"
Asha Samad summarizes the various perpectives regarding this controversial issue.

25. **The Initiation of a Maasai Warrior,** Tepilit Ole Saitoti, from   143
The Worlds of a Maasai Warrior, Random House, 1986.
In virtually every society, certain rites and ceremonies are used to
signify adulthood. This article describes the Masai (Maasai) circumcision ceremony that *initiates an individual* into *adulthood.*

The concepts in bold italics are developed in the article. For further expansion please refer to the Topic Guide and the Index.

UNIT 6

Religion, Belief, and Ritual

Nine selections examine the role of ritual, religion, and belief in a culture. The need to develop a religion is universal among societies.

Overview   148

26. **A Different Drummer,** Michael Harner, *Natural History,* March 1997.   150
Although he entered the *spirit worlds of the shamans* in pursuit of anthropological research, Michael Harner came away with a new mission—restoring shamanism to the Western world.

27. **Psychotherapy in Africa,** Thomas Adeoye Lambo, *Human Nature,* March 1978.   152
Despite the technological advances and material benefits of *modern medicine, traditional healing* methods are found to cope more effectively with the psychological and social aspects of illness. When the old and the new forms of treatment are combined, the consequences are beneficial for both the individual and society.

28. **The Mbuti Pygmies: Change and Adaptation,** Colin M. Turnbull, from *The Mbuti Pygmies: Change and Adaptation,* Holt, Rinehart & Winston, 1983.   157
Although informal in appearance, the *ritual* life of the Mbuti Pygmies provides individuals with deep feelings of personal security, individual responsibility, and overall *social equality.*

29. *Real* **Men** *Don't* **Eat Deer,** Katharine Milton, *Discover,* June 1997.   160
Beyond the specific reasons for *food taboos* in particular cultures, there is one overriding factor common to them all, according to Katharine Milton: they serve as a constant reminder of *tribal identity* and the behavior expected of "true" humans.

30. **The Secrets of Haiti's Living Dead,** Gino Del Guercio, *Harvard Magazine,* January/February 1986.   163
In seeking scientific documentation of the existence of zombies, anthropologist Wade Davis found himself looking beyond the stereotypes and mysteries of *voodoo* and directly into a cohesive system of *social control* in rural Haiti.

31. **Rituals of Death,** Elizabeth D. Purdum and J. Anthony Paredes, from *Facing the Death Penalty: Essays on a Cruel and Unusual Punishment,* Temple University Press, 1989.   167
In a parallel manner, *capital punishment* in the United States and *human sacrifice* among the Aztecs have a similar social function: to assure citizens that society is not out of control and that God is indeed in his heaven.

32. **Body Ritual among the Nacirema,** Horace Miner, *American Anthropologist,* June 1956.   173
The *ritual* beliefs and *taboos* of the Nacirema provide us with a test case of the objectivity of ethnographic description and show us the extremes to which human behavior can go.

33. **The Tnevnoc Cult,** David G. Bromley and Anson D. Shupe Jr., from *Sociological Analysis,* Volume 40, Number 4, 1979.   176
By comparing the *socialization practices* of the nineteenth-century Tnevnoc cult with modern-day religious *cults,* the authors not only demonstrate the remarkable similarities but show that it is the *legitimacy* accorded a group rather than its practices that shape public reactions and definitions.

34. **Baseball Magic,** George Gmelch, *Dushkin/McGraw-Hill Inc.,* 1998.   180
Professional baseball players, like Trobriand Islanders, often resort to *magic* in *situations of chance and uncertainty.* As irrational as it may seem, magic creates confidence, competence, and control in the practitioner.

The concepts in bold italics are developed in the article. For further expansion please refer to the Topic Guide and the Index.

UNIT 7

Sociocultural Change: The Impact of the West

Seven articles examine the influence that the developed world has had on primitive culture. Exposure to the industrial West often has disastrous effects on the delicate balance of a primitive society.

Overview   186

35. **Why Can't People Feed Themselves?** Frances Moore Lappé   188
and Joseph Collins, from *Food First: Beyond the Myth of Scarcity*, Random House, 1977.
When *colonial* governments force the conversion of *subsistence* farms to *cash crop* plantations, peasants are driven into marginal lands or into a large pool of cheap labor. In either case, the authors maintain, they are no longer able to feed themselves.

36. **The Arrow of Disease**, Jared Diamond, *Discover*, October   193
1992.
The most deadly weapon *colonial Europeans* carried to other continents was their germs. The most intriguing question to answer here is why the flow of *disease* did not move in the opposite direction.

37. **A Pacific Haze: Alcohol and Drugs in Oceania**, Mac Marshall, *Contemporary Pacific Societies: Studies in Development and Change*, Prentice Hall, 1993.   200
The relatively benign use of *psychoactive drugs*, such as betel and kava in the Pacific Islands, is deeply rooted in *cultural traditions* and patterns of social interaction. Today, as a result of new drugs and disruptive *social and economic changes* introduced from the outside, a haze hangs over Oceania.

38. **Growing Up as a Fore**, E. Richard Sorenson, *Smithsonian*,   207
May 1977.
In the context of a bountiful *subsistence system,* Fore *children* were taught spontaneous expression and exploratory freedom. Hidden within this receptive character, however, was an Achilles' heel, for it permitted the willing adoption of a *cash crop economy* and a consequent reformulation of the identity and practices of the Fore.

39. **Academic Scholarship and Sikhism: Conflict or Legitimization**, Arthur W. Helweg, from *The Transmission of Sikh Heritage in the Diaspora*, New Delhi: Manohar Publications, 1996.   212
When two groups interact but perceive the situation from different *cultural systems,* as in this case involving *Western science* and *South Asian Sikhism*, misunderstanding and tension will result.

40. **New Spirits for Old**, Shoefoot (Bautista Cajicuwa), *Natural History*, March 1997.   218
Malaria runs rampant, food is scarce, and vengeance raids are a fact of life. It is in this troubled context that a *Yąnomami shaman* reveals his sense of failure and, in an attempt to help his people, exchanges *old spirits for new*.

41. **Grounded on Ice**, Eric P. Olsen, *The World & I*, March 1997.   220
As the *Inuit* prepare to assume *political autonomy* in the newly created province of Nunavut, it remains to be seen whether their *survival skills* will be relevant to the modern world or will be relegated to the status of museum relics.

Index   225
Article Review Form   228
Article Rating Form   229

The concepts in bold italics are developed in the article. For further expansion please refer to the Topic Guide and the Index.

Topic Guide

This topic guide suggests how the selections in this book relate to topics of traditional concern to students and professionals involved with the study of anthropology. It is useful for locating articles that relate to each other for reading and research. The guide is arranged alphabetically according to topic. Articles may, of course, treat topics that do not appear in the topic guide. In turn, entries in the topic guide do not necessarily constitute a comprehensive listing of all the contents of each selection. **In addition, relevant Web sites, which are annotated on pages 6 and 7, are noted in bold italics under the topic articles.**

TOPIC AREA	TREATED IN	TOPIC AREA	TREATED IN
Acculturation	14. From Shells to Money 15. Continental Divides 20. Who Needs Love! 22. Yellow Woman 26. Different Drummer 29. *Real* Men *Don't* Eat Deer 33. Tnevnoc Cult 37. Pacific Haze 38. Growing Up as a Fore 40. New Spirits for Old 41. Grounded on Ice *(2, 6, 8, 12, 14, 27, 29)*	**Cultural Diversity (cont.)** **Cultural Identity**	40. New Spirits for Old 41. Grounded on Ice *(8, 9, 10, 11, 12, 13, 14, 15, 16, 18)* 5. Lost Man 12. Mystique of the Masai 17. On the Streets of America 22. Yellow Woman 24. Bundu Trap 26. Different Drummer 29. *Real* Men *Don't* Eat Deer 33. Tnevnoc Cult 39. Academic Scholarship and Sikhism 40. New Spirits for Old 41. Grounded on Ice *(12, 13, 14, 15, 18, 21, 22, 23, 29)*
Aggression and Violence	17. On the Streets of America 31. Rituals of Death 36. Arrow of Disease *(2, 5, 7, 14, 18, 21, 22)*		
Children and Child Care	8. Teaching in the Postmodern Classroom 17. On the Streets of America 18. Death without Weeping 22. Yellow Woman 24. Bundu Trap 28. Mbuti Pygmies *(5, 16, 18, 19)*	**Cultural Relativity and Ethnocentrism**	1. Doing Fieldwork among the Yąnomamö 3. Eating Christmas in the Kalahari 4. Challenge of Cultural Relativism 7. Why Don't You Say What You Mean? 19. Arranging a Marriage in India 24. Bundu Trap 32. Body Ritual among the Nacirema 39. Academic Scholarship and Sikhism *(5, 6, 7, 16, 17, 23)*
Cooperation, Sharing, and Altruism	3. Eating Christmas in the Kalahari 13. Too Many Bananas 14. From Shells to Money 22. Yellow Woman *(1, 2, 5, 12, 13, 14, 15, 18)*	**Culture Shock, Ecology, and Society**	1. Doing Fieldwork among the Yąnomamö 10. Understanding Eskimo Science 11. Yąnomami Keep on Trekking 12. Mystique of the Masai 14. From Shells to Money 15. Continental Divides 16. When Brothers Share a Wife 21. Society and Sex Roles 29. *Real* Men *Don't* Eat Deer 35. Why Can't People Feed Themselves? 36. Arrow of Disease 41. Grounded on Ice *(2, 5, 12, 13, 14, 15, 16, 17, 22, 27, 28, 29)*
Cross-Cultural Experience	1. Doing Fieldwork among the Yąnomamö 2. Doctor, Lawyer, Indian Chief 3. Eating Christmas in the Kalahari 7. Why Don't You Say What You Mean? 9. Shakespeare in the Bush 10. Understanding Eskimo Science 13. Too Many Bananas 18. Death without Weeping 19. Arranging a Marriage in India 26. Different Drummer 29. *Real* Men *Don't* Eat Deer 39. Academic Scholarship and Sikhism 40. New Spirits for Old 41. Grounded on Ice *(2, 5, 6, 10, 11)*		
		Economic and Political Systems	2. Doctor, Lawyer, Indian Chief 11. Yąnomami Keep on Trekking 12. Mystique of the Masai 13. Too Many Bananas 14. From Shells to Money 15. Continental Divides 16. When Brothers Share a Wife 18. Death without Weeping 21. Society and Sex Roles 22. Yellow Woman 23. Status, Property, and the Value on Virginity
Cultural Diversity	4. Challenge of Cultural Relativism 7. Why Don't You Say What You Mean? 15. Continental Divides 19. Arranging a Marriage in India 22. Yellow Woman 23. Status, Property, and the Value on Virginity 39. Academic Scholarship and Sikhism		

4

TOPIC AREA	TREATED IN	TOPIC AREA	TREATED IN
Economic and Political Systems (cont.)	29. *Real* Men *Don't* Eat Deer 35. Why Can't People Feed Themselves? 36. Arrow of Disease 41. Grounded on Ice *(2, 3, 5, 6, 7, 16, 17, 23, 27, 28, 29)*	Patriarchy	20. Who Needs Love! 21. Society and Sex Roles 23. Status, Property, and the Value on Virginity 24. Bundu Trap *(16, 17, 18, 19, 22)*
Ethnographic Fieldwork	1. Doing Fieldwork among the Yąnomamö 2. Doctor, Lawyer, Indian Chief 3. Eating Christmas in the Kalahari 13. Too Many Bananas 26. Different Drummer *(2, 3, 5, 6, 7, 23)*	Poverty	17. On the Streets of America 18. Death without Weeping 35. Why Can't People Feed Themselves? *(17, 27)*
Gender/Sexuality	16. When Brothers Share a Wife 20. Who Needs Love! 21. Society and Sex Roles 22. Yellow Woman 23. Status, Property, and the Value on Virginity 24. Bundu Trap *(16, 17, 18, 19, 20, 22)*	Rituals	14. From Shells to Money 24. Bundu Trap 25. Initiation of a Maasai Warrior 26. Different Drummer 27. Psychotherapy in Africa 28. Mbuti Pygmies 30. Secrets of Haiti's Living Dead 31. Rituals of Death 32. Body Ritual among the Nacirema 33. Tnevnoc Cult 34. Baseball Magic 40. New Spirits for Old *(2, 12, 13, 14, 23, 24, 25, 26, 28)*
Health and Welfare	17. On the Streets of America 18. Death without Weeping 24. Bundu Trap 27. Psychotherapy in Africa 32. Body Ritual among the Nacirema 35. Why Can't People Feed Themselves? 36. Arrow of Disease 37. Pacific Haze *(1, 2, 3, 4, 16, 17, 27, 28)*	Social, Cultural, and Industrial Change	14. From Shells to Money 15. Continental Divides 20. Who Needs Love! 27. Psychotherapy in Africa 35. Why Can't People Feed Themselves? 36. Arrow of Disease 37. Pacific Haze 38. Growing Up as a Fore 39. Academic Scholarship and Sikhism 40. New Spirits for Old 41. Grounded on Ice *(1, 2, 3, 12, 13, 14, 15, 16, 23, 27)*
Hunter-Collectors	10. Understanding Eskimo Science 28. Mbuti Pygmies *(12, 13, 14, 15, 23)*	Social Equality	7. Why Don't You Say What You Mean? 14. From Shells to Money 20. Who Needs Love! 22. Yellow Woman 23. Status, Property, and the Value on Virginity 28. Mbuti Pygmies *(8, 9, 11, 12, 13, 14, 15)*
Language	6. Language, Appearance, and Reality 7. Why Don't You Say What You Mean? 9. Shakespeare in the Bush *(8, 9, 10, 11)*		
Marriage, Kinship, and Family Systems	14. From Shells to Money 16. When Brothers Share a Wife 17. On the Streets of America 18. Death without Weeping 19. Arranging a Marriage in India 20. Who Needs Love! 21. Society and Sex Roles 22. Yellow Woman 23. Status, Property, and the Value on Virginity 24. Bundu Trap *(2, 12, 13, 14, 15, 18, 21)*	Social Relationships	1. Doing Fieldwork among the Yąnomamö 2. Doctor, Lawyer, Indian Chief 3. Eating Christmas in the Kalahari 8. Teaching in the Postmodern Classroom 13. Too Many Bananas 14. From Shells to Money 17. On the Streets of America 19. Arranging a Marriage in India 20. Who Needs Love! 22. Yellow Woman 23. Status, Property, and the Value on Virginity 24. Bundu Trap 28. Mbuti Pygmies 29. *Real* Men *Don't* Eat Deer 30. Secrets of Haiti's Living Dead 33. Tnevnoc Cult *(1, 2, 3, 4, 5, 6, 7, 8, 10, 12, 14, 16, 17, 18, 21, 23, 24, 25, 26)*
Medicine and Healing	27. Psychotherapy in Africa 32. Body Ritual among the Nacirema 40. New Spirits for Old *(23, 24, 26, 27, 28, 29)*		
Participant Observation	1. Doing Fieldwork among the Yąnomamö 2. Doctor, Lawyer, Indian Chief 3. Eating Christmas in the Kalahari 9. Shakespeare in the Bush 13. Too Many Bananas *(5, 7, 8, 12, 13, 14, 15)*		

Selected World Wide Web Sites for *Annual Editions: Anthropology*

All of these Web sites are hot-linked through the *Annual Editions* home page: *http://www.dushkin.com/annualeditions* (just click on a book). In addition, these sites are referenced by number and appear where relevant in the Topic Guide on the previous two pages.

Some Web sites are continually changing their structure and content, so the information listed may not always be available.

General Sources

1. Library of Congress—*http://www.loc.gov/*—Examine this extensive Web site to learn about resource tools, library services/resources, exhibitions, and databases in many different subfields of anthropology.

2. Anthropology Resources on the Internet—*http://www.socsciresearch.com/r7.html*—This site provides extensive links to Internet resources that are directly and primarily of anthropological relevance, including Web servers in different fields, e-mail discussion groups, and gopher servers. *The Education Index* rated it "one of the best education-related sites on the Web."

3. American Anthropologist—*http://www.ameranthassn.org/*—Check out this site—the home page of the American Anthropology Association—for general information about the field of anthropology as well as access to a wide variety of articles. It can also lead you to a number of AAA publications, services, and resources.

4. Anthropology, Archaeology, and American Indian Sites on the Internet—*http://dizzy.library.arizona.edu:80/users/jlcox/first.html*—This Web page points out a number of Internet sites of interest to different kinds of anthropologists. Visit this page for links to electronic journals and more.

Anthropological Perspectives

5. Anthropology Fieldstudy—*http://www.truman.edu/academics/ss/faculty/tamakoshil/index.html*—Don't miss this fascinating site, which gives a detailed report on how to prepare for and conduct fieldwork. Laura Zimmer Tamakoshi's fieldwork experience in Papua New Guinea is must reading for any anthropologist planning to do research in the field.

6. Institute of Social and Cultural Anthropology—*http://www.rsl.ox.ac.uk/isa/CASSnotes.html*—Consult this site of the Institute of Social and Cultural Anthropology to learn about ways to use the computer as an aid in conducting anthropological fieldwork, methodology, and analysis.

7. Introduction to Anthropological Fieldwork and Ethnography—*http://web.mit.edu/dumit/www/syl-anth.html*—This class outline can serve as an invaluable resource for conducting anthropological fieldwork. Addressing such topics as The Interview and Power Relations in the Field, the site identifies many important books and articles for further reading.

Culture and Communication

8. Hypertext and Ethnography—*http://www.umanitoba.ca/anthropology/tutor/aaa_presentation.html*—Presented by Brian Schwimmer of the University of Manitoba, this site will be of great value to people who are interested in culture and communication. He addresses such topics as multivocality and complex symbolization, among many others.

9. Showcase—*http://www.usc.edu/dept/v-lib/showcase.html*—Examples of documents that make innovative use of the Web as a tool for "an anthropology of the future"—one consisting of multimedia representations in a nonlinear and interactive form—are provided on this Web site. An example of the links available is Noun Classification in Swahili.

10. GMU Anthropology Department—*http://www.gmu.edu/departments/anthro/*—Look over this George Mason University site for current listings of scientific papers dealing with anthropological studies. The site provides a number of interesting links.

11. CAM Cultural Anthropology Methods—*http://www.lawrence.edu/~bradleyc/cam.html*—This home page of the *Cultural Anthropology Methods* journal provides diverse yet helpful information about conducting anthropological fieldwork, such as using computer software for taking notes in the field and choosing field informants. One link will be of particular value to those creating dictionaries in the field.

The Organization of Society and Culture

12. Smithsonian Institution Web Site—*http://www.si.edu/*—Looking through this site, which provides access to many of the enormous resources of the Smithsonian, will give a sense of the scope of anthropological inquiry today.

13. Society for Economic Anthropology—*http://www.lawrence.edu/~peregrip/seahome.html*—This is the home page of the Society for Economic Anthropology, an association that strives to understand diversity and change in the economic systems of the world and, hence, in the organization of society and culture.

14. Culture Tour—*http://www.pic.net/~willep/culturetour.html*—This site, currently being developed, promises to be an exciting way to learn more about anthropology. The creator describes it as a CD-ROM anthropology textbook under construction, in which he will look at human nature through space and time.

15. The Seven Money Personalities—*http://www.bitnik.com/PPP/personality.html*—For a change of pace, look at this site devoted to analyzing "money personalities" in the United States. To what extent might these "personalities" affect sociocultural behavior?

Other Families, Other Ways

16. Sex and Marriage: Patrilocal Residence to Polyandry—*http://www.palomar.edu/more/beh_sci/marriage/mar_104.htm*—Explore this site's extensive glossary of terms related to family structure. It describes rules of marriage and residence and provides a variety of links for further study.

17. ARD-Information about ARD—*http://wings.buffalo.edu/anthropology/ ARD/info.html*—Consult this newly created Anthropology Review Database—still under expansion—for useful reviews of anthropology films, books, videos, audio recordings, software, multimedia, and online resources.

Gender and Status

18. Reflections on Sinai Bedouin Women—*http://www.sherryart.com/women/bedouin.html*—Social anthropologist Ann Gardner tells something of her culture shock while first living with a Sinai Bedouin family as a teenager. She provides links to a number of sites having to do with organization of society and culture, particularly with regard to women.

19. Bonobo Sex and Society—*http://soong.club.cc.cmu.edu/~julie/bonobos.html*—This site, accessed through Carnegie Mellon University, includes a *Scientific American* article discussing a primate's behavior that challenges traditional assumptions about male supremacy in human evolution. Guaranteed to generate spirited debate.

20. OMIM Home Page-Online Mendelian Inheritance in Man—*http://www3.ncbi.nlm.nih.gov/omim/*—This National Center for Biotechnology Information database is a catalog of human genes and genetic disorders. It contains text, pictures, and reference information of great interest to students of physical anthropology.

21. Patterns of Variability: The Concept of Race—*http://www.as.ua.edu/ant/bindon/ant101/syllabus/race/race1.htm*—A handy, at-a-glance reference to the prevailing concepts of race and the causes of human variability since ancient times is available on this Web site. It can serve as a valuable starting point for research and understanding into the concept of race.

22. American Scientist—*http://www.amsci.org/amsci/amsci.html*—Investigating this site will help students of anthropology to access a variety of articles and to explore issues and concepts related to race and gender.

Religion, Belief, and Ritual

23. Philosophy of Religion: Magic, Ritual, and Symbolism—*http://www.kcmetro.cc.mo.us/longview/socsci/philosophy/religion/magic.htm*—This site presents course notes for a Philosophy of Religion class in which the roles of magic, ritual, and symbolism are examined. Links to many helpful reading options are provided.

24. Anthropology Resources Page—*http://www.usd.edu/anth/*—Many topics can be accessed from this University of South Dakota Web site. Repatriation and reburial are just a few examples of the variety of information available.

25. Yahoo: Society and Culture: Death—*http://www.yahoo.com/Society_and_Culture/death/*—This Yahoo site has an extensive index to diverse issues related to death and how different people approach or regard it, such as beliefs about euthanasia, reincarnation, and burial.

26. Mask Links—*http://www.masks.org/*—Masks have been an important part of many cultures' burial and death rituals. Visit this site to look at an exhibition center showing the work of maskmakers from around the world and to locate mask information published on the Web.

Sociocultural Change:
The Impact of the West

27. Human Rights and Humanitarian Assistance—*http://info.pitt.edu/~ian/resource/human.htm*—Through this site, part of the World Wide Web Virtual Library, you can conduct research into a number of human rights topics in order to gain a greater understanding of the issues affecting indigenous peoples in the modern era. The site also provides links to many other subjects related to anthropology.

28. Nicole's AnthroPage—*http://www.wsu.edu/~i9248809/anthrop.html*—Access this handy site to find current news having to do with the field of anthropology and numerous related links.

29. Archaeology and Anthropology: The Australian National University— *http://online.anu.edu.au/AandA/*—Browse through this home page of the Anthropology and Archaeology Departments of the Australian National University for information about the impact of the West on indigenous cultures (e.g., the Aborigines). The site provides extensive links to other universities and resource centers.

We highly recommend that you review our Web site for expanded information and our other product lines. We are continually updating and adding links to our Web site in order to offer you the most usable and useful information that will support and expand the value of your Annual Editions. You can reach us at: *http://www.dushkin.com/annualeditions/*.

Anthropological Perspectives

For at least a century, the goals of anthropology have been to describe societies and cultures throughout the world and to compare the differences and similarities among them. Anthropologists study in a variety of settings and situations, ranging from small hamlets and villages to neighborhoods and corporate offices of major urban centers throughout the world. They study hunters and gatherers, peasants, farmers, labor leaders, politicians, and bureaucrats. They examine religious life in Latin America as well as revolutionary movements.

Wherever practicable, anthropologists take on the role of "participant observer." Through active involvement in the lifeways of people, they hope to gain an insider's perspective without sacrificing the objectivity of the trained scientist. Sometimes the conditions for achieving such a goal seem to form an almost insurmountable barrier, but anthropologists call on persistence, adaptability, and imagination to overcome the odds against them.

The diversity of focus in anthropology means that it is earmarked less by its particular subject matter than by its perspective. Although the discipline relates to both the biological and social sciences, anthropologists know that the boundaries drawn between disciplines are highly artificial. For example, while in theory it is possible to examine only the social organization of a family unit or the organization of political power in a nation-state, in reality it is impossible to separate the biological from the social, from the economic, from the political. The explanatory perspective of anthropology, as the articles in this unit demonstrate, is to seek out interrelationships among all these factors. The first three articles in this section illustrate varying degrees of difficulty an anthropologist may encounter in taking on the role of the participant observer. Napoleon Chagnon's essay, "Doing Fieldwork among the Yąnomamö," for instance, shows the hardships imposed by certain physical conditions, the unwillingness of the people to provide needed information, and the vast differences in values and attitudes to be bridged by the anthropologist just to get along.

Richard Kurin, in "Doctor, Lawyer, Indian Chief," and Richard Lee, in "Eating Christmas in the Kalahari," apparently had few problems with the physical conditions and the personalities of the people they were studying. However, they were not completely accepted by the communities until they modified their behavior to conform to the expectations of their hosts and found ways to participate as equals in the socioeconomic exchange systems.

The final two articles in this unit deal with matters of great controversy. "The Challenge of Cultural Relativism" goes to the heart of one of the key issues in anthropology: How does one maintain the objectivity of cultural relativism while not becoming a party to the violation of human rights? In "The Lost Man," however, we find anthropologists being charged with the violation of human rights while trying to proceed with their tasks in an atmosphere of free inquiry.

Much is at stake in these discussions, since the purpose of anthropology is not only to describe and explain, but also to develop a special vision of the world in which cultural alternatives (past, present, and future) can be measured against one another and used as guides for human action.

Looking Ahead: Challenge Questions

What is culture shock?

How can anthropologists who become personally involved with a community through participant observation maintain their objectivity as scientists?

In what ways do the results of fieldwork depend on the kinds of questions asked?

In what sense is sharing intrinsic to egalitarianism?

How can we avoid the pitfalls of cultural relativism and ethnocentrism in dealing with what we think of as harmful practices in other cultures?

Should anthropologists have access to Kennewick Man for scientific analysis? Should the bones be repatriated instead? Support your response.

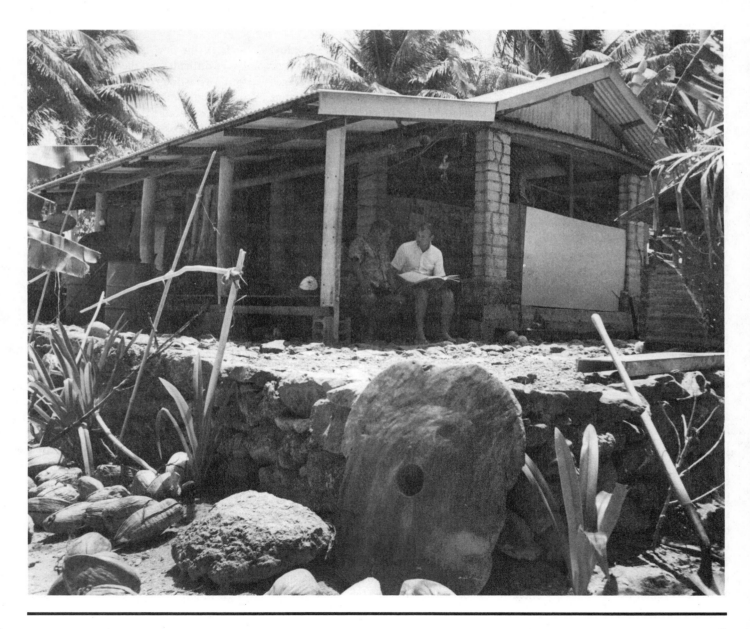

Doing Fieldwork among the Yąnomamö[1]

Napoleon A. Chagnon

VIGNETTE

The Yąnomamö are thinly scattered over a vast and verdant tropical forest, living in small villages that are separated by many miles of unoccupied land. They have no writing, but they have a rich and complex language. Their clothing is more decorative than protective. Well-dressed men sport nothing more than a few cotton strings around their wrists, ankles, and waists. They tie the foreskins of their penises to the waist string. Women dress about the same. Much of their daily life revolves around gardening, hunting, collecting wild foods, collecting firewood, fetching water, visiting with each other, gossiping, and making the few material possessions they own: baskets, hammocks, bows, arrows, and colorful pigments with which they paint their bodies. Life is relatively easy in the sense that they can 'earn a living' with about three hours' work per day. Most of what they eat they cultivate in their gardens, and most of that is plantains—a kind of cooking banana that is usually eaten green, either roasted on the coals or boiled in pots. Their meat comes from a large variety of game animals, hunted daily by the men. It is usually roasted on coals or smoked, and is always well done. Their villages are round and open—and very public. One can hear, see, and smell almost everything that goes on anywhere in the village. Privacy is rare, but sexual discreetness is possible in the garden or at night while others sleep. The villages can be as small as 40 to 50 people or as large as 300 people, but in all cases there are many more children and babies than there are adults. This is true of most primitive populations and of our own demographic past. Life expectancy is short.

The Yąnomamö fall into the category of Tropical Forest Indians called 'foot people'. They avoid large rivers and live in interfluvial plains of the major rivers. They have neighbors to the north, Carib-speaking Ye'kwana, who are true 'river people': They make elegant, large dugout canoes and travel extensively along the major waterways. For the Yąnomamö, a large stream is an obstacle and can be crossed only in the dry season. Thus, they have traditionally avoided larger rivers and, because of this, contact with outsiders who usually come by river.

They enjoy taking trips when the jungle abounds with seasonally ripe wild fruits and vegetables. Then, the large village—the *shabono*—is abandoned for a few weeks and everyone camps out for from one to several days away from the village and garden. On these trips, they make temporary huts from poles, vines, and leaves, each family making a separate hut.

Two major seasons dominate their annual cycle: the wet season, which inundates the low-lying jungle, making travel difficult, and the dry season—the time of visiting other villages to feast, trade, and politic with allies. The dry season is also the time when raiders can travel and strike silently at their unsuspecting enemies. The Yąnomamö are still conducting intervillage warfare, a phenomenon that affects all aspects of their social organization, settlement pattern, and daily routines. It is not simply 'ritualistic' war: At least one-fourth of all adult males die violently in the area I lived in.

Social life is organized around those same principles utilized by all tribesmen: kinship relationships, descent from ancestors, marriage exchanges between kinship/descent groups, and the transient charisma of distinguished headmen who attempt to keep order in the village and whose responsibility it is to determine the village's relationships with those in other villages. Their positions are largely the result of kinship and marriage patterns; they come from the largest kinship groups within the village. They can, by their personal wit, wisdom, and charisma, become autocrats, but most of them are largely 'greaters' among equals. They, too, must clear gardens, plant crops, collect wild foods, and hunt. They are simultaneously peacemakers and valiant warriors. Peacemaking often requires the threat or actual use of force, and most headmen have an acquired reputation for being *waiteri:* fierce.

The social dynamics within villages are involved with giving and receiving marriageable girls. Marriages are arranged by older kin, usually men, who are brothers, uncles, and the father. It is a political process, for girls are promised in marriage while they are young, and the men who do this attempt to create alliances with other men via marriage exchanges. There is a shortage of women due in part to a sex-ratio imbalance in the younger age categories, but also complicated by the fact that some men have multiple wives. Most fighting within the village stems from sexual affairs or failure to deliver a promised woman—or out-and-out seizure of a married woman by some other man. This can lead to internal fighting and conflict of such an intensity that villages split up and fission, each group then becoming a new village and, often, enemies to each other.

But their conflicts are not blind, uncontrolled violence. They have a series of graded forms of violence that ranges from chest-pounding and club-fighting duels to out-and-out shooting to kill. This gives them a good deal of flexibility in settling disputes without immediate resort to lethal violence. In addition, they have developed patterns of alliance and friendship that serve to limit violence—trading and feasting with others in order to become friends. These alliances can, and often do, result in intervillage exchanges of marriageable women, which leads to additional amity between villages. No good thing lasts forever, and most alliances crumble. Old friends become hostile and, occasionally, treacherous. Each village must therefore be keenly aware that its neighbors are fickle and must behave accordingly. The thin line between friendship and animosity must be traversed by the village leaders, whose political acumen and strategies are both admirable and complex.

Each village, then, is a replica of all others in a broad sense. But each village is part of a larger political, demographic, and ecological process, and it is difficult to attempt to understand the village without knowing something of the larger forces that affect it and it's particular history with all its neighbors.

COLLECTING THE DATA IN THE FIELD

I have now spent over 60 months with Yąnomamö, during which time I gradually learned their language and, up to a point, submerged myself in their culture and way of life.[2] As my research progressed, the thing that impressed me most was the importance that aggression played in shaping their culture. I had the opportunity to witness a good many incidents that expressed individual vindictiveness on the one hand and collective bellicosity on the other hand. These ranged in seriousness from the ordinary incidents of wife beating and chest pounding to dueling and organized raids by parties that set out with the intention of ambushing and killing men from enemy villages. One of the villages was raided approximately twenty-five times during my first 15 months of fieldwork—six times by the group among whom I was living. And, the history of every village I investigated, from 1964 to 1991, was intimately bound up in patterns of warfare with neighbors that shaped its politics and determined where it was found at any point in time and how it dealt with its current neighbors.

The fact that the Yąnomamö have lived in a chronic state of warfare is reflected in their mythology, ceremonies, settlement pattern, political behavior, and marriage practices. Accordingly, I have organized this case study in such a way that students can appreciate the effects of warfare on Yąnomamö culture in general and on their social organization and political relationships in particular.

I collected the data under somewhat trying circumstances, some of which I will describe to give a rough idea of what is generally meant when anthropologists speak of 'culture shock' and 'fieldwork.' It should be borne in mind, however, that each field situation is in many respects unique, so that the problems I encountered do not necessarily exhaust the range of possible problems other anthropologists have confronted in other areas. There are a few problems, however, that seem to be nearly universal among anthropological fieldworkers, particularly those having to do with eating, bathing, sleeping, lack of privacy, loneliness, or discovering that the people you are living with have a lower opinion of you than you have of them or you yourself are not as culturally or emotionally 'flexible' as you assumed.

The Yąnomamö can be difficult people to live with at times, but I have spoken to colleagues who have had difficulties living in the communities they studied. These things vary from society to society, and probably from one anthropologist to the next. I have also done limited fieldwork among the Yąnomamö's northern neighbors, the Carib-speaking Ye'kwana Indians. By contrast to many experiences I had among the Yąnomamö, the Ye'kwana were very pleasant and charming, all of them anxious to help me and honor bound to show any visitor the numerous courtesies of their system of etiquette. In short, they approached the image of 'primitive man' that I had conjured up in my mind before doing fieldwork, a kind of 'Rousseauian' view, and it was sheer pleasure to work with them. Other anthropologists have also noted sharp contrasts in the people they study from one field situation to another. One of the most startling examples of this is in the work of Colin Turnbull, who first studied the Ituri Pygmies (1965, 1983) and found them delightful to live with, but then studied the Ik (1972) of the desolate outcroppings of the Kenya/Uganda/ Sudan border region, a people he had difficulty coping with intellectually, emotionally, and physically. While it is possible that the anthropologist's reactions to a particular people are personal and idiosyncratic, it nevertheless remains true that there are enormous differences between whole peoples, differences that affect the anthropologist in often dramatic ways.

Hence, what I say about some of my experiences is probably equally true of the experiences of many other fieldworkers. I describe some of them here for the benefit of future anthropologists—because I think I could have profited by reading about the pitfalls and field problems of my own teachers. At the very least I might have been able to avoid some of my more stupid errors. In this regard there is a growing body of excellent descriptive work on field research. Students who plan to make a career in anthropology should consult these works, which cover a wide range of field situations in the ethnographic present.[3]

The Longest Day: The First One

My first day in the field illustrated to me what my teachers meant when they spoke of 'culture shock.' I had traveled in a small, aluminum rowboat propelled by a large outboard motor for two and a half days. This took me from the territorial capital, a small town on the Orinoco River, deep into Yąnomamö country. On the morning of the third day we reached a small mission settlement, the field 'headquarters' of a group of Americans who were working in two Yąnomamö villages. The missionaries had come out of these villages to hold their annual conference on the progress of their mission work and were conducting their meetings when I arrived. We picked up a passenger at the mission station, James P. Barker, the first non-Yąnomamö to make a sustained, permanent contact with the tribe (in 1950). He had just returned from a year's furlough in the United States, where I had earlier visited him before leaving for Venezuela. He agreed to accompany me to the village I had selected for my base of operations to introduce me to the Indians. This village was also his own home base, but he had not been there for over a year and did not plan to join me for another three months. Mr. Barker had been living with this particular group about five years.

We arrived at the village, Bisaasi-teri, about 2:00 P.M. and docked the boat along the muddy bank at the terminus of the path used by Yąnomamö to fetch their drinking water. It was hot and muggy, and my clothing was soaked with perspiration. It clung uncomfortably to my body, as it did thereafter for the remainder of the work. The small biting gnats, *bareto*, were out in astronomical numbers, for it was the begin-

ning of the dry season. My face and hands were swollen from the venom of their numerous stings. In just a few moments I was to meet my first Yąnomamö, my first primitive man. What would he be like? I had visions of entering the village and seeing 125 social facts running about altruistically calling each other kinship terms and sharing food, each waiting and anxious to have me collect his genealogy. I would wear them out in turn. Would they like me? This was important to me; I wanted them to be so fond of me that they would adopt me into their kinship system and way of life. I had heard that successful anthropologists always get adopted by their people. I had learned during my seven years of anthropological training at the University of Michigan that kinship was equivalent to society in primitive tribes and that it was a moral way of life, 'moral' being something 'good' and 'desirable.' I was determined to work my way into their moral system of kinship and become a member of their society—to be 'accepted' by them.

How Did They Accept You?

My heart began to pound as we approached the village and heard the buzz of activity within the circular compound. Mr. Barker commented that he was anxious to see if any changes had taken place while he was away and wondered how many of them had died during his absence. I nervously felt my back pocket to make sure that my notebook was still there and felt personally more secure when I touched it.

The entrance to the village was covered over with brush and dry palm leaves. We pushed them aside to expose the low opening to the village. The excitement of meeting my first Yąnomamö was almost unbearable as I duck-waddled through the low passage into the village clearing.

I looked up and gasped when I saw a dozen burly, naked, sweaty, hideous men staring at us down the shafts of their drawn arrows! Immense wads of green tobacco were stuck between their lower teeth and lips making them look even more hideous, and strands of dark-green slime dripped or hung from their

nostrils—strands so long that they clung to their pectoral muscles or drizzled down their chins. We arrived at the village while the men were blowing a hallucinogenic drug up their noses. One of the side effects of the drug is a runny nose. The mucus is always saturated with the green powder and they usually let it run freely from their nostrils. My next discovery was that there were a dozen or so vicious, underfed dogs snapping at my legs, circling me as if I were to be their next meal. I just stood there holding my notebook, helpless and pathetic. Then the stench of the decaying vegetation and filth hit me and I almost got sick. I was horrified. What kind of welcome was this for the person who came here to live with you and learn your way of life, to become friends with you? They put their weapons down when they recognized Barker and returned to their chanting, keeping a nervous eye on the village entrances.

We had arrived just after a serious fight. Seven women had been abducted the day before by a neighboring group, and the local men and their guests had just that morning recovered five of them in a brutal club fight that nearly ended in a shooting war. The abductors, angry because they had lost five of their seven new captives, vowed to raid the Bisaasi-teri. When we arrived and entered the village unexpectedly, the Indians feared that we were the raiders. On several occasions during the next two hours the men in the village jumped to their feet, armed themselves, nocked their arrows and waited nervously for the noise outside the village to be identified. My enthusiasm for collecting ethnographic facts diminished in proportion to the number of times such an alarm was raised. In fact, I was relieved when Barker suggested that we sleep across the river for the evening. It would be safer over there.

As we walked down the path to the boat, I pondered the wisdom of having decided to spend a year and a half with these people before I had even seen what they were like. I am not ashamed to admit that had there been a diplomatic way out, I would have ended my fieldwork then and there. I did not look forward to the next day—and months—

when I would be left alone with the Yąnomamö; I did not speak a word of their language, and they were decidedly different from what I had imagined them to be. The whole situation was depressing, and I wondered why I ever decided to switch from physics and engineering in the first place. I had not eaten all day, I was soaking wet from perspiration, the *bareto* were biting me, and I was covered with red pigment, the result of a dozen or so complete examinations I had been given by as many very pushy Yąnomamö men. These examinations capped an otherwise grim day. The men would blow their noses into their hands, flick as much of the mucus off that would separate in a snap of the wrist, wipe the residue into their hair, and then carefully examine my face, arms, legs, hair, and the contents of my pockets. I asked Barker how to say, 'Your hands are dirty'; my comments were met by the Yąnomamö in the following way: They would 'clean' their hands by spitting a quantity of slimy tobacco juice into them, rub them together, grin, and then proceed with the examination.

Mr. Barker and I crossed the river and slung our hammocks. When he pulled his hammock out of a rubber bag, a heavy disagreeable odor of mildewed cotton and stale wood smoke came with it. 'Even the missionaries are filthy,' I thought to myself. Within two weeks, everything I owned smelled the same way, and I lived with that odor for the remainder of the fieldwork. My own habits of personal cleanliness declined to such levels that I didn't even mind being examined by the Yąnomamö, as I was not much cleaner than they were after I had adjusted to the circumstances. It is difficult to blow your nose gracefully when you are stark naked and the invention of hankerchiefs is millenia away.

Life in the Jungle: Oatmeal, Peanut Butter, and Bugs

It isn't easy to plop down in the Amazon Basin for a year and get immediately into the anthropological swing of things. You have been told about horrible diseases, snakes, jaguars, electric eels, little spiny fish that will swim up your urine into your penis, quicksand, and getting lost. Some of the dangers are real, but your imagination makes them more real and threatening than many of them really are. What my teachers never bothered to advise me about, however, was the mundane, nonexciting, and trivial stuff—like eating, defecating, sleeping, or keeping clean. These turned out to be the bane of my existence during the first several months of field research. I set up my household in Barker's abandoned mud hut, a few yards from the village of Bisaasi-teri, and immediately set to work building my own mud/thatch hut with the help of the Yąnomamö. Meanwhile, I had to eat and try to do my 'field research.' I soon discovered that it was an enormously time-consuming task to maintain my own body in the manner to which it had grown accustomed in the relatively antiseptic environment of the northern United States. Either I could be relatively well fed and relatively comfortable in a fresh change of clothes and do very little fieldwork, or I could do considerably more fieldwork and be less well fed and less comfortable.

It is appalling how complicated it can be to make oatmeal in the jungle. First, I had to make two trips to the river to haul the water. Next, I had to prime my kerosene stove with alcohol to get it burning, a tricky procedure when you are trying to mix powdered milk and fill a coffee pot at the same time. The alcohol prime always burned out before I could turn the kerosene on, and I would have to start all over. Or, I would turn the kerosene on, optimistically hoping that the Coleman element was still hot enough to vaporize the fuel, and start a small fire in my palm-thatched hut as the liquid kerosene squirted all over the table and walls and then ignited. Many amused Yąnomamö onlookers quickly learned the English phrase 'Oh, Shit!', and, once they discovered that the phrase offended and irritated the missionaries, they used it as often as they could in their presence. I usually had to start over with the alcohol. Then I had to boil the oatmeal and pick the bugs out of it. All my supplies, of course, were carefully stored in rat-proof, moisture-proof, and insect-proof containers, not one of which ever served its purpose adequately. Just taking things out of the multiplicity of containers and repacking them afterward was a minor project in itself. By the time I had hauled the water to cook with, unpacked my food, prepared the oatmeal, milk, and coffee, heated water for dishes, washed and dried the dishes, repacked the food in the containers, stored the containers in locked trunks, and cleaned up my mess, the ceremony of preparing breakfast had brought me almost up to lunch time!

Eating three meals a day was simply out of the question. I solved the problem by eating a single meal that could be prepared in a single container, or, at most, in two containers, washed my dishes only when there were no clean ones left, using cold river water, and wore each change of clothing at least a week to cut down on my laundry problem—a courageous undertaking in the tropics. I reeked like a jockstrap that had been left to mildew in the bottom of some dark gym locker. I also became less concerned about sharing my provisions with the rats, insects, Yąnomamö, and the elements, thereby eliminating the need for my complicated storage process. I was able to last most of the day on *café con leche,* heavily sugared espresso coffee diluted about five to one with hot milk. I would prepare this in the evening and store it in a large thermos. Frequently, my single meal was no more complicated than a can of sardines and a package of soggy crackers. But at least two or three times a week I would do something 'special' and sophisticated, like make a batch of oatmeal or boil rice and add a can of tuna fish or tomato paste to it. I even saved time by devising a water system that obviated the trips to the river. I had a few sheets of tin roofing brought in and made a rain water trap; I caught the water on the tin surface, funneled it into an empty gasoline drum, and then ran a plastic hose from the drum to my hut. When the drum was exhausted in the dry season, I would get a few Yąnomamö boys to fill it with buckets of water from the river, 'paying' them with crackers, of which they grew all too fond all too soon.

I ate much less when I traveled with the Yąnomamö to visit other villages.

Most of the time my travel diet consisted of roasted or boiled green plantains (cooking bananas) that I obtained from the Yąnomamö, but I always carried a few cans of sardines with me in case I got lost or stayed away longer than I had planned. I found peanut butter and crackers a very nourishing 'trail' meal, and a simple one to prepare. It was nutritious and portable, and only one tool was required to make the meal: a hunting knife that could be cleaned by wiping the blade on a convenient leaf. More importantly, it was one of the few foods the Yąnomamö would let me eat in relative peace. It looked suspiciously like animal feces to them, an impression I encouraged. I referred to the peanut butter as the feces of babies or 'cattle'. They found this disgusting and repugnant. They did not know what 'cattle' were, but were increasingly aware that I ate several canned products of such an animal. Tin cans were thought of as containers made of 'machete skins', but how the cows got inside was always a mystery to them. I went out of my way to describe my foods in such a way as to make them sound unpalatable to them, for it gave me some peace of mind while I ate: They wouldn't beg for a share of something that was too horrible to contemplate. Fieldworkers develop strange defense mechanisms and strategies, and this was one of my own forms of adaptation to the fieldwork. On another occasion I was eating a can of frankfurters and growing very weary of the demands from one of the onlookers for a share in my meal. When he finally asked what I was eating, I replied: 'Beef.' He then asked: 'Shaki![4] What part of the animal are you eating?' To which I replied, 'Guess.' He muttered a contemptuous epithet, but stopped asking for a share. He got back at me later, as we shall see.

Meals were a problem in a way that had nothing to do with the inconvenience of preparing them. Food sharing is important to the Yąnomamö in the context of displaying friendship. 'I am hungry!' is almost a form of greeting with them. I could not possibly have brought enough food with me to feed the entire village, yet they seemed to overlook this logistic fact as they begged for my food. What became fixed in their minds was the fact that I did not share my food with whomsoever was present—usually a small crowd—at each and every meal. Nor could I easily enter their system of reciprocity with respect to food. Every time one of them 'gave' me something 'freely', he would dog me for months to 'pay him back', not necessarily with food but with knives, fishhooks, axes, and so on. Thus, if I accepted a plantain from someone in a different village while I was on a visit, he would most likely visit me in the future and demand a machete as payment for the time that he 'fed' me. I usually reacted to these kinds of demands by giving a banana, the customary reciprocity in their culture—food for food—but this would be a disappointment for the individual who had nursed visions of that single plantain growing into a machete over time. Many years after beginning my fieldwork. I was approached by one of the prominent men who demanded a machete for a piece of meat he claimed he had given me five or six years earlier.

Despite the fact that most of them knew I would not share my food with them at their request, some of them always showed up at my hut during mealtime. I gradually resigned myself to this and learned to ignore their persistent demands while I ate. Some of them would get angry because I failed to give in, but most of them accepted it as just a peculiarity of the subhuman foreigner who had come to live among them. If or when I did accede to a request for a share of my food, my hut quickly filled with Yąnomamö, each demanding their share of the food that I had just given to one of them. Their begging for food was not provoked by hunger, but by a desire to try something new and to attempt to establish a coercive relationship in which I would accede to a demand. If one received something, all others would immediately have to test the system to see if they, too, could coerce me.

A few of them went out of their way to make my meals downright unpleasant—to spite me for not sharing, especially if it was a food that they had tried before and liked, or a food that was part of their own cuisine. For example, I was eating a cracker with peanut butter and honey one day. The Yąnomamö will do almost anything for honey, one of the most prized delicacies in their own diet. One of my cynical onlookers—the fellow who had earlier watched me eating frankfurters—immediately recognized the honey and knew that I would not share the tiny precious bottle. It would be futile to even ask. Instead, he glared at me and queried icily, 'Shaki! What kind of animal semen are you pouring onto your food and eating?' His question had the desired effect and my meal ended.

Finally, there was the problem of being lonely and separated from your own kind, especially your family. I tried to overcome this by seeking personal friendships among the Yąnomamö. This usually complicated the matter because all my 'friends' simply used my confidence to gain privileged access to my hut and my cache of steel tools and trade goods—and looted me when I wasn't looking. I would be bitterly disappointed that my erstwhile friend thought no more of me than to finesse our personal relationship exclusively with the intention of getting at my locked up possessions, and my depression would hit new lows every time I discovered this. The loss of the possessions bothered me much less than the shock that I was, as far as most of them were concerned, nothing more than a source of desirable items. No holds were barred in relieving me of these, since I was considered something subhuman, a non-Yąnomamö.

The hardest thing to learn to live with was the incessant, passioned, and often aggressive demands they would make. It would become so unbearable at times that I would have to lock myself in my hut periodically just to escape from it. Privacy is one of our culture's most satisfying achievements, one you never think about until you suddenly have none. It is like not appreciating how good your left thumb feels until someone hits it with a hammer. But I did not want privacy for its own sake; rather, I simply had to get away from the begging. Day and night for almost the entire time I lived with the Yąnomamö. I was plagued by such demands as: 'Give me a knife, I am poor!'; 'If you don't take me with you on your next trip to

Widokaiyateri, I'll chop a hole in your canoe!'; 'Take us hunting up the Mavaca River with your shotgun or we won't help you!'; 'Give me some matches so I can trade with the Reyaboböwei-teri, and be quick about it or I'll hit you!'; 'Share your food with me, or I'll burn your hut!'; 'Give me a flashlight so I can hunt at night!'; 'Give me all your medicine, I itch all over!'; 'Give me an ax or I'll break into your hut when you are away and steal all of them!' And so I was bombarded by such demands day after day, month after month, until I could not bear to see a Yąnomamö at times.

It was not as difficult to become calloused to the incessant begging as it was to ignore the sense of urgency, the impassioned tone of voice and whining, or the intimidation and aggression with which many of the demands were made. It was likewise difficult to adjust to the fact that the Yąnomamö refused to accept 'No' for an answer until or unless it seethed with passion and intimidation—which it did after a few months. So persistent and characteristic is the begging that the early 'semiofficial' maps made by the Venezuelan Malaria Control Service (*Malarialogía*) designated the site of their first permanent field station, next to the village of Bisaasi-teri, as *Yababuhii:* 'Gimme.' I had to become like the Yąnomamö to be able to get along with them on their terms: somewhat sly, aggressive, intimidating, and pushy.

It became indelibly clear to me shortly after I arrived there that had I failed to adjust in this fashion I would have lost six months of supplies to them in a single day or would have spent most of my time ferrying them around in my canoe or taking them on long hunting trips. As it was, I did spend a considerable amount of time doing these things and did succumb often to their outrageous demands for axes and machetes, at least at first, for things changed as I became more fluent in their language and learned how to defend myself socially as well as verbally. More importantly, had I failed to demonstrate that I could not be pushed around beyond a certain point, I would have been the subject of far more ridicule, theft, and practical jokes than was the actual case. In short, I had to acquire a certain proficiency in their style of interpersonal politics and to learn how to imply subtly that certain potentially undesirable, but unspecified, consequences might follow if they did such and such to me. They do this to each other incessantly in order to establish precisely the point at which they cannot goad or intimidate an individual any further without precipitating some kind of retaliation. As soon as I realized this and gradually acquired the self-confidence to adopt this strategy, it became clear that much of the intimidation was calculated to determine my flash point or my 'last ditch' position—and I got along much better with them. Indeed, I even regained some lost ground. It was sort of like a political, interpersonal game that everyone had to play, but one in which each individual sooner or later had to give evidence that his bluffs and implied threats could be backed up with a sanction. I suspect that the frequency of wife beating is a component in this syndrome, since men can display their *waiteri* (ferocity) and 'show' others that they are capable of great violence. Beating a wife with a club is one way of displaying ferocity, one that does not expose the man to much danger—unless the wife has concerned, aggressive brothers in the village who will come to her aid. Apparently an important thing in wife beating is that the man has displayed his presumed potential for violence and the intended message is that other men ought to treat him with circumspection, caution, and even deference.

After six months, the level of Yąnomamö demand was tolerable in Bisaasi-teri, the village I used for my base of operations. We had adjusted somewhat to each other and knew what to expect with regard to demands for food, trade goods, and favors. Had I elected to remain in just one Yąnomamö village for the entire duration of my first 15 months of fieldwork, the experience would have been far more enjoyable than it actually was. However, as I began to understand the social and political dynamics of this village, it became patently obvious that I would have to travel to many other villages to determine the demographic bases and political histories that lay behind what I could understand in the village of Bisaasi-teri. I began making regular trips to some dozen neighboring Yąnomamö villages as my language fluency improved. I collected local genealogies there, or rechecked and cross-checked those I had collected elsewhere. Hence, the intensity of begging was relatively constant and relatively high for the duration of my fieldwork, for I had to establish my personal position in each village I visited and revisited.

For the most part, my own 'fierceness' took the form of shouting back at the Yąnomamö as loudly and as passionately as they shouted at me, especially at first, when I did not know much of the language. As I became more fluent and learned more about their political tactics, I became more sophisticated in the art of bluffing and brinksmanship. For example, I paid one young man a machete (then worth about $2.50) to cut a palm tree and help me make boards from the wood. I used these to fashion a flooring in the bottom of my dugout canoe to keep my possession out of the water that always seeped into the canoe and sloshed around. That afternoon I was working with one of my informants in the village. The long-awaited mission supply boat arrived and most of the Yąnomamö ran out of the village to see the supplies and try to beg items from the crew. I continued to work in the village for another hour or so and then went down to the river to visit with the men on the supply boat. When I reached the river I noticed, with anger and frustration, that the Yąnomamö had chopped up all my new floor boards to use as crude paddles to get their own canoes across the river to the supply boat.[5] I knew that if I ignored this abuse I would have invited the Yąnomamö to take even greater liberties with my possessions in the future. I got into my canoe, crossed the river, and docked amidst their flimsy, leaky craft. I shouted loudly to them, attracting their attention. They were somewhat sheepish, but all had mischievous grins on their impish faces. A few of them came down to the canoe, where I proceeded with a spirited lecture that revealed my anger at their audacity and license. I explained that I had just that morning paid one of them a machete for bringing me the palmwood, how hard I had worked to shape each board and place it in the canoe, how carefully and painstakingly I had tied each one in with vines, how much I had perspired, how many *bareto* bites I had suffered, and so on. Then, with exaggerated drama and finality, I withdrew my hunting knife as their grins disappeared and cut each one of their canoes loose and set it into the strong current of the Orinoco River where it was immediately swept up and carried downstream. I left without looking back and huffed over to the other side of the river to resume my work.

They managed to borrow another canoe and, after some effort, recovered their dugouts. Later, the headman of the village told me, with an approving chuckle, that I had done the correct thing. Everyone in the village, except, of course, the culprits, supported and defended my actions—and my status increased as a consequence.

Whenever I defended myself in such ways I got along much better with the Yąnomamö and gradually acquired the respect of many of them. A good deal of their demeanor toward me was directed with the forethought of establishing the point at which I would draw the line and react defensively. Many of them, years later, reminisced about the early days of my fieldwork when I was timid and *mohode* ("stupid") and a little afraid of them, those golden days when it was easy to bully me into giving my goods away for almost nothing.

Theft was the most persistent situation that required some sort of defensive action. I simply could not keep everything I owned locked in trunks, and the Yąnomamö came into my hut and left at will. I eventually developed a very effective strategy for recovering almost all the stolen items: I would simply ask a child who took the item and then I would confiscate that person's hammock when he was not around, giving a spirited lecture to all who could hear on the antisociality of thievery as I stalked off in a faked rage with the thief's hammock slung over my shoulder. Nobody ever attempted to stop me from doing this, and almost all of them

told me that my technique for recovering my possessions was ingenious. By nightfall the thief would appear at my hut with the stolen item or send it over with someone else to make an exchange to recover his hammock. He would be heckled by his covillagers for having got caught and for being embarrassed into returning my item for his hammock. The explanation was usually, 'I just borrowed your ax! I wouldn't think of stealing it!'

Collecting Yąnomamö Genealogies and Reproductive Histories

My purpose for living among Yąnomamö was to systematically collect certain kinds of information on genealogy, reproduction, marriage practices, kinship, settlement patterns, migrations, and politics. Much of the fundamental data was genealogical—who was the parent of whom, tracing these connections as far back in time as Yąnomamö knowledge and memory permitted. Since 'primitive' society is organized largely by kinship relationships, figuring out the social organization of the Yąnomamö essentially meant collecting extensive data on genealogies, marriage, and reproduction. This turned out to be a staggering and very frustrating problem. I could not have deliberately picked a more difficult people to work with in this regard. They have very stringent name taboos and eschew mentioning the names of prominent living people as well as all deceased friends and relatives. They attempt to name people in such a way that when the person dies and they can no longer use his or her name, the loss of the word in their language is not inconvenient. Hence, they name people for specific and minute parts of things, such as 'toenail of sloth,' 'whisker of howler monkey,' and so on, thereby being able to retain the words 'toenail' or 'whisker' but somewhat handicapped in referring to these anatomical parts of sloths and monkeys respectively. The taboo is maintained even for the living, for one mark of prestige is the courtesy others show you by not using your name publicly. This is particularly true for men, who are much more competitive for status than women in this culture, and it is fascinating to

watch boys grow into young men, demanding to be called either by a kinship term in public, or by a teknonymous reference such as 'brother of Himotoma'. The more effective they are at getting others to avoid using their names, the more public acknowledgment there is that they are of high esteem and social standing. Helena Valero, a Brazilian woman who was captured as a child by a Yąnomamö raiding party, was married for many years to a Yąnomamö headman before she discovered what his name was (Biocca, 1970; Valero, 1984). The sanctions behind the taboo are more complex than just this, for they involve a combination of fear, respect, admiration, political deference, and honor.

At first I tried to use kinship terms alone to collect genealogies, but Yąnomamö kinship terms, like the kinship terms in all systems, are ambiguous at some point because they include so many possible relatives (as the term 'uncle' does in our own kinship system). Again, their system of kin classification merges many relatives that we 'separate' by using different terms: They call both their actual father and their father's brother by a single term, whereas we call one 'father' and the other 'uncle.' I was forced, therefore, to resort to personal names to collect unambiguous genealogies or 'pedigrees'. They quickly grasped what I was up to and that I was determined to learn everyone's 'true name', which amounted to an invasion of their system of prestige and etiquette, if not a flagrant violation of it. They reacted to this in a brilliant but devastating manner: They invented false names for everybody in the village and systematically learned them, freely revealing to me the 'true' identities of everyone. I smugly thought I had cracked the system and enthusiastically constructed elaborate genealogies over a period of some five months. They enjoyed watching me learn their names and kinship relationships. I naively assumed that I would get the 'truth' to each question and the best information by working in public. This set the stage for converting my serious project into an amusing hoax of the grandest proportions. Each 'informant' would try to outdo his peers by inventing a name even more preposterous or ridiculous than what I had been given by someone earlier, the explanations for discrepancies being 'Well, he has two names and this is the other one.' They even fabricated devilishiy improbable genealogical relationships, such as someone being married to his grandmother, or worse yet, to his mother-in-law, a grotesque and horrifying prospect to the Yąnomamö. I would collect the desired names and relationships by having my informant whisper the name of the person softly into my ear, noting that he or she was the parent of such and such or the child of such and such, and so on. Everyone who was observing my work would then insist that I repeat the name aloud, roaring in hysterical laughter as I clumsily pronounced the name, sometimes laughing until tears streamed down their faces. The 'named' person would usually react with annoyance and hiss some untranslatable epithet at me, which served to reassure me that I had the 'true' name. I conscientiously checked and rechecked the names and relationships with multiple informants, pleased to see the inconsistencies disappear as my genealogy sheets filled with those desirable little triangles and circles, thousands of them.

My anthropological bubble was burst when I visited a village about 10 hours' walk to the southwest of Bisaasi-teri some five months after I had begun collecting genealogies on the Bisaasi-teri. I was chatting with the local headman of this village and happened to casually drop the name of the wife of the Bisaasi-teri headman. A stunned silence followed, and then a villagewide roar of uncontrollable laughter, choking, gasping, and howling followed. It seems that I thought the Bisaasi-teri headman was married to a woman named "hairy cunt." It also seems that the Bisaasi-teri headman was called 'long dong' and his brother 'eagle shit.' The Bisaasi-teri headman had a son called "asshole" and a daughter called 'fart breath.' And so on. Blood welled up my temples as I realized that I had nothing but nonsense to show for my five months' of dedicated genealogical effort, and I had to throw away almost all the information I had collected on this the most basic set of data I had come there to get. I un-

derstood at that point why the Bisaasi-teri laughed so hard when they made me repeat the names of their covillagers, and why the 'named' person would react with anger and annoyance as I pronounced his 'name' aloud.

I was forced to change research strategy—to make an understatement to describe this serious situation. The first thing I did was to begin working in private with my informants to eliminate the horseplay and distraction that attended public sessions. Once I did this, my informants, who did not know what others were telling me, began to agree with each other and I managed to begin learning the 'real' names, starting first with children and gradually moving to adult women and then, cautiously, adult men, a sequence that reflected the relative degree of intransigence at revealing names of people. As I built up a core of accurate genealogies and relationships—a core that all independent informants had verified repetitiously—I could 'test' any new informant by soliciting his or her opinion and knowledge about these 'core' people whose names and relationships I was confident were accurate. I was, in this fashion, able to immediately weed out the mischievous informants who persisted in trying to deceive me. Still, I had great difficulty getting the names of dead kinsmen, the only accurate way to extend genealogies back in time. Even my best informants continued to falsify names of the deceased, especially closely related deceased. The falsifications at this point were not serious and turned out to be readily corrected as my interviewing methods improved (see below). Most of the deceptions were of the sort where the informant would give me the name of a living man as the father of some child whose actual father was dead, a response that enabled the informant to avoid using the name of a deceased kinsman or friend.

The quality of a genealogy depends in part on the number of generations it embraces, and the name taboo prevented me from making any substantial progress in learning about the deceased ancestors of the present population. Without this information, I could not, for example, document marriage pat-

terns and interfamilial alliances through time. I had to rely on older informants for this information, but these were the most reluctant informants of all for this data. As I became more proficient in the language and more skilled at detecting fabrications, any informants became better at deception. One old man was particularly cunning and persuasive, following a sort of Mark Twain policy that the most effective lie is a sincere lie. He specialized in making a ceremony out of false names for dead ancestors. He would look around nervously to make sure nobody was listening outside my hut, enjoin me never to mention the name again, become very anxious and spooky, and grab me by the head to whisper a secret name into my ear. I was always elated after a session with him, because I managed to add several generations of ancestors for particular members of the village. Others steadfastly refused to give me such information. To show my gratitude, I paid him quadruple the rate that I had been paying the others. When word got around that I had increased the pay for genealogical and demographic information, volunteers began pouring into my hut to 'work' for me, assuring me of their changed ways and keen desire to divest themselves of the 'truth'.

Enter Rerebawä: Inmarried Tough Guy
I discovered that the old man was lying quite by accident. A club fight broke out in the village one day, the result of a dispute over the possession of a woman. She had been promised to a young man in the village, a man named Rerebawä, who was particularly aggressive. He had married into Bisaasi-teri and was doing his 'bride service'—a period of several years during which he had to provide game for his wife's father and mother, provide them with wild foods he might collect, and help them in certain gardening and other tasks. Rerebawä had already been given one of the daughters in marriage and was promised her younger sister as his second wife. He was enraged when the younger sister, then about 16 years old, began having an affair with another young man in the village, Bäkotawä, making no attempt to conceal it. Rerebawä challenged Bäk-

otawä to a club fight. He swaggered boisterously out to the duel with his 10-foot-long club, a roof-pole he had cut from the house on the spur of the moment, as is the usual procedure. He hurled insult after insult at both Bäkotawä and his father, trying to goad them into a fight. His insults were bitter and nasty. They tolerated them for a few moments, but Rerebawä's biting insults provoked them to rage. Finally, they stormed angrily out of their hammocks and ripped out roof-poles, now returning the insults verbally, and rushed to the village clearing. Rerebawä continued to insult them, goading them into striking him on the head with their equally long clubs. Had either of them struck his head—which he held out conspicuously for them to swing at—he would then have the right to take his turn on their heads with his club. His opponents were intimidated by his fury, and simply backed down, refusing to strike him, and the argument ended. He had intimidated them into submission. All three retired pompously to their respective hammocks, exchanging nasty insults as they departed. But Rerebawä had won the showdown and thereafter swaggered around the village, insulting the two men behind their backs at every opportunity. He was genuinely angry with them, to the point of calling the older man by the name of his long-deceased father. I quickly seized on this incident as an opportunity to collect an accurate genealogy and confidentially asked Rerebawä about his adversary's ancestors. Rerebawä had been particularly 'pushy' with me up to this point, but we soon became warm friends and staunch allies: We were both 'outsiders' in Bisaasi-teri and, although he was a Yąnomamö, he nevertheless had to put up with some considerable amount of pointed teasing and scorn from the locals, as all inmarried 'sons-in-law' must. He gave me the information I requested of his adversary's deceased ancestors, almost with devilish glee. I asked about dead ancestors of other people in the village and got prompt, unequivocal answers: He was angry with everyone in the village. When I compared his answers to those of the old man, it was obvious that one of them was lying. I then challenged his

answers. He explained, in a sort of 'you damned fool, don't you know better?' tone of voice that everyone in the village knew the old man was lying to me and gloating over it when I was out of earshot. The names the old man had given to me were names of dead ancestors of the members of a village so far away that he thought I would never have occasion to check them out authoritatively. As it turned out, Rerebawä knew most of the people in that distant village and recognized the names given by the old man.

I then went over all my Bisaasi-teri genealogies with Rerebawä, genealogies I had presumed to be close to their final form. I had to revise them all because of the numerous lies and falsifications they contained, much of it provided by the sly old man. Once again, after months of work, I had to recheck everything with Rerebawä's aid. Only the living members of the nuclear families turned out to be accurate; the deceased ancestors were mostly fabrications.

Discouraging as it was to have to recheck everything all over again, it was a major turning point in my fieldwork. Thereafter, I began taking advantage of local arguments and animosities in selecting my informants, and used more extensively informants who had married into the village in the recent past. I also began traveling more regularly to other villages at this time to check on genealogies, seeking out villages whose members were on strained terms with the people about whom I wanted information. I would then return to my base in the village of Bisaasi-teri and check with local informants the accuracy of the new information. I had to be careful in this work and scrupulously select my local informants in such a way that I would not be inquiring about *their* closely related kin. Thus, for each of my local informants, I had to make lists of names of certain deceased people that I dared not mention in their presence. But despite this precaution, I would occasionally hit a new name that would put some informants into a rage, or into a surly mood, such as that of a dead 'brother' or 'sister'[6] whose existence had not been indicted to me by other informants. This usually terminated my

day's work with that informant, for he or she would be too touchy or upset to continue any further, and I would be reluctant to take a chance on accidentally discovering another dead close kinsman soon after discovering the first.

These were unpleasant experiences, and occasionally dangerous as well, depending on the temperament of my informant. On one occasion I was planning to visit a village that had been raided recently by one of their enemies. A woman, whose name I had on my census list for that village, had been killed by the raiders. Killing women is considered to be bad form in Yąnomamö warfare, but this woman was deliberately killed for revenge. The raiders were unable to bushwhack some man who stepped out of the village at dawn to urinate, so they shot a volley of arrows over the roof into the village and beat a hasty retreat. Unfortunately, one of the arrows struck and killed a woman, an accident. For that reason, her village's raiders *deliberately* sought out and killed a woman in retaliation—whose name was on my list. My reason for going to the village was to update my census data on a name-by-name basis and estimate the ages of all the residents. I knew I had the name of the dead woman in my list, but nobody would dare to utter her name so I could remove it. I knew that I would be in very serious trouble if I got to the village and said her name aloud, and I desperately wanted to remove it from my list. I called on one of my regular and usually cooperative informants and asked him to tell me the woman's name. He refused adamantly, explaining that she was a close relative—and was angry that I even raised the topic with him. I then asked him if he would let me whisper the names of *all* the women of that village in his ear, and he would simply have to nod when I hit the right name. We had been 'friends' for some time, and I thought I was able to predict his reaction, and thought that our friendship was good enough to use this procedure. He agreed to the procedure, and I began whispering the names of the women, one by one. We were alone in my hut so that nobody would know what we were doing and nobody could hear us.

I read the names softly, continuing to the next when his response was a negative. When I ultimately hit the dead woman's name, he flew out of his chair, enraged and trembling violently, his arm raised to strike me: 'You son-of-a-bitch!' he screamed. 'If you say her name in my presence again, I'll kill you in an instant!' I sat there, bewildered, shocked, and confused. And frightened, as much because of his reaction, but also because I could imagine what might happen to me should I unknowingly visit a village to check genealogy accuracy without knowing that someone had just died there or had been shot by raiders since my last visit. I reflected on the several articles I had read as a graduate student that explained the 'genealogical method,' but could not recall anything about its being a potentially lethal undertaking. My furious informant left my hut, never again to be invited back to be an informant. I had other similar experiences in different villages, but I was always fortunate in that the dead person had been dead for some time, or was not very closely related to the individual into whose ear I whispered the forbidden name. I was usually cautioned by one of the men to desist from saying any more names lest I get people 'angry'.[7]

Kaobawä: The Bisaasi-teri Headman Volunteers to Help Me

I had been working on the genealogies for nearly a year when another individual came to my aid. It was Kaobawä, the headman of Upper Bisaasi-teri. The village of Bisaasi-teri was split into two components, each with its own garden and own circular house. Both were in sight of each other. However, the intensity and frequency of internal bickering and argumentation was so high that they decided to split into two separate groups but remain close to each other for protection in case they were raided. One group was downstream from the other; I refer to that group as the 'Lower' Bisaasi-teri and call Kaobawä's group 'Upper' (upstream) Bisaasi-teri, a convenience they themselves adopted after separating from each other. I spent most of my time with the members of Kaobawä's group, some 200 people when I first arrived there. I did not have much contact with Kaobawä during the early months of my work. He was a somewhat retiring, quiet man, and among the Yạnomamö, the outsider has little time to notice the rare quiet ones when most everyone else is in the front row, pushing and demanding attention. He showed up at my hut one day after all the others had left. He had come to volunteer to help me with the genealogies. He was 'poor,' he explained, and needed a machete. He would work only on the condition that I did not ask him about his own parents and other very close kinsmen who had died. He also added that he would not lie to me as the others had done in the past.

This was perhaps the single most important event in my first 15 months of field research, for out of this fortuitous circumstance evolved a very warm friendship, and among the many things following from it was a wealth of accurate information on the political history of Kaobawä's village and related villages, highly detailed genealogical information, sincere and useful advice to me, and hundreds of valuable insights into the Yạnomamö way of life. Kaobawä's familiarity with his group's history and his candidness were remarkable. His knowledge of details was almost encyclopedic, his memory almost photographic. More than that, he was enthusiastic about making sure I learned the truth, and he encouraged me, indeed, *demanded that* I learn all details I might otherwise have ignored. If there were subtle details he could not recite on the spot, he would advise me to wait until he could check things out with someone else in the village. He would often do this clandestinely, giving me a report the next day, telling me who revealed the new information and whether or not he thought they were in a position to know it. With the information provided by Kaobawä and Rerebawä, I made enormous gains in understanding village interrelationships based on common ancestors and political histories and became lifelong friends with both. And both men knew that I had to learn about his recently deceased kin from the other one. It was one of those quiet understandings we all had but none of us could mention.

Once again I went over the genealogies with Kaobawä to recheck them, a considerable task by this time. They included about two thousand names, representing several generations of individuals from four different villages. Rerebawä's information was very accurate, and Kaobawä's contribution enabled me to trace the genealogies further back in time. Thus, after nearly a year of intensive effort on genealogies, Yạnomamö demographic patterns and social organization began to make a good deal of sense to me. Only at this point did the patterns through time begin to emerge in the data, and I could begin to understand how kinship groups took form, exchanged women in marriage over several generations, and only then did the fissioning of larger villages into smaller ones emerge as a chronic and important feature of Yạnomamö social, political, demographic, economic, and ecological adaptation. At this point I was able to begin formulating more sophisticated questions, for there was now a pattern to work from and one to flesh out. Without the help of Rerebawä and Kaobawä it would have taken much longer to make sense of the plethora of details I had collected from not only them, but dozens of other informants as well.

I spent a good deal of time with these two men and their families, and got to know them much better than I knew most Yạnomamö. They frequently gave their information in a way which related themselves to the topic under discussion. We became warm friends as time passed, and the formal 'informant/anthropologist' relationship faded into the background. Eventually, we simply stopped 'keeping track' of work and pay. They would both spend hours talking with me, leaving without asking for anything. When they wanted something, they would ask for it no matter what the relative balance of reciprocity between us might have been at that point. . . .

For many of the customary things that anthropologists try to communicate about another culture, these two men and their families might be considered to be 'exemplary' or 'typical'. For other things, they are exceptional in many regards, but the reader will, even knowing some of the exceptions, understand Yạnomamö culture more intimately by being familiar with a few examples.

Kaobawä was about 40 years old when I first came to his village in 1964. I say "about 40" because the Yąnomamö numeration system has only three numbers: one, two, and more-than-two. It is hard to give accurate ages or dates for events when the informants have no means in their language to reveal such detail. Kaobawä is the headman of his village, meaning that he has somewhat more responsibility in political dealings with other Yąnomamö groups, and very little control over those who live in his group except when the village is being raided by enemies. We will learn more about political leadership and warfare in a later chapter, but most of the time men like Kaobawä are like the North American Indian 'chief' whose authority was characterized in the following fashion: "One word from the chief, and each man does as he pleases." There are different 'styles' of political leadership among the Yąnomamö. Some leaders are mild, quiet, inconspicuous most of the time, but intensely competent. They act parsimoniously, but when they do, people listen and conform. Other men are more tyranical, despotic, pushy, flamboyant, and unpleasant to all around them. They shout orders frequently, are prone to beat their wives, or pick on weaker men. Some are very violent. I have met headmen who run the entire spectrum between these polar types, for I have visited some 60 Yąnomamö villages. Kaobawä stands at the mild, quietly competent end of the spectrum. He has had six wives thus far—and temporary affairs with as many more, at least one of which resulted in a child that is publicly acknowledged as his child. When I first met him he had just two wives: Bahimi and Koamashima. Bahimi had two living children when I first met her; many others had died. She was the older and enduring wife, as much a friend to him as a mate. Their relationship was as close to what we think of as 'love' in our culture as I have seen among the Yąnomamö. His second wife was a girl of about 20 years, Koamashima. She had a new baby boy when I first met her, her first child. There was speculation that Kaobawä was planning to give

Koamashima to one of his younger brothers who had no wife; he occasionally allows his younger brother to have sex with Koamashima, but only if he asks in advance. Kaobawä gave another wife to one of his other brothers because she was *beshi* ("horny"). In fact, this earlier wife had been married to two other men, both of whom discarded her because of her infidelity. Kaobawä had one daughter by her. However, the girl is being raised by Kaobawä's brother, though acknowledged to be Kaobawä's child.

Bahimi, his oldest wife, is about five years younger than he. She is his cross-cousin—his mother's brother's daughter. Ideally, all Yąnomamö men should marry a cross-cousin. . . . Bahimi was pregnant when I began my field work, but she destroyed the infant when it was born—a boy in this case—explaining tearfully that she had no choice. The new baby would have competed for milk with Ariwari, her youngest child, who was still nursing. Rather than expose Ariwari to the dangers and uncertainty of an early weaning, she chose to terminate the newborn instead. By Yąnomamö standards, this has been a very warm, enduring marriage. Kaobawä claims he beats Bahimi only 'once in a while, and only lightly' and she, for her part, never has affairs with other men.

Kaobawä is a quiet, intense, wise, and unobtrusive man. It came as something of a surprise to me when I learned that he was the headman of his village, for he stayed at the sidelines while others would surround me and press their demands on me. He leads more by example than by coercion. He can afford to be this way at his age, for he established his reputation for being forthright and as fierce as the situation required when he was younger, and the other men respect him. He also has five mature brothers or half-brothers in his village, men he can count on for support. He also has several other mature 'brothers' (parallel cousins, whom he must refer to as 'brothers' in his kinship system) in the village who frequently come to his aid, but not as often as his 'real' brothers do. Kaobawä has also given a number of his sisters to other men in

the village and has promised his young (8-year-old) daughter in marriage to a young man who, for that reason, is obliged to help him. In short, his 'natural' or 'kinship' following is large, and partially because of this support, he does not have to display his aggressiveness to remind his peers of his position.

Rerebawä is a very different kind of person. He is much younger—perhaps in his early twenties. He has just one wife, but they have already had three children. He is from a village called Karohi-teri, located about five hours' walk up the Orinoco, slightly inland off to the east of the river itself. Kaobawä's village enjoys amicable relationships with Rerebawä's, and it is for this reason that marriage alliances of the kind represented by Rerebawä's marriage into Kaobawä's village occur between the two groups. Rerebawä told me that he came to Bisaasi-teri because there were no eligible women from him to marry in his own village, a fact that I later was able to document when I did a census of his village and a preliminary analysis of its social organization. Rerebawä is perhaps more typical than Kaobawä in the sense that he is chronically concerned about his personal reputation for aggressiveness and goes out of his way to be noticed, even if he has to act tough. He gave me a hard time during my early months of fieldwork, intimidating, teasing, and insulting me frequently. He is, however, much braver than the other men his age and is quite prepared to back up his threats with immediate action—as in the club fight incident just described above. Moreover, he is fascinated with political relationships and knows the details of intervillage relationships over a large area of the tribe. In this respect he shows all the attributes of being a headman, although he has too many competent brothers in his own village to expect to move easily into the leadership position there.

He does not intend to stay in Kaobawä's group and refuses to make his own garden—a commitment that would reveal something of an intended long-term residence. He feels that he has adequately discharged his obligations to his wife's parents by providing them with fresh game, which he has done for several years. They should let him take his wife and return to his own village with her, but they refuse and try to entice him to remain permanently in Bisaasi-teri to continue to provide them with game when they are old. It is for this reason that they promised to give him their second daughter, their only other child, in marriage. Unfortunately, the girl was opposed to the marriage and ultimately married another man, a rare instance where the woman in the marriage had this much influence on the choice of her husband.

Although Rerebawä has displayed his ferocity in many ways, one incident in particular illustrates what his character can be like. Before he left his own village to take his new wife in Bisaasi-teri, he had an affair with the wife of an older brother. When it was discovered, his brother attacked him with a club. Rerebawä responded furiously: He grabbed an ax and drove his brother out of the village after soundly beating him with the blunt side of the single-bit ax. His brother was so intimidated by the thrashing and promise of more to come that he did not return to the village for several days. I visited this village with Kabawä shortly after this event had taken place; Rerebawä was with me as my guide. He made it a point to introduce me to this man. He approached his hammock, grabbed him by the wrist, and dragged him out on the ground: 'This is the brother whose wife I screwed when he wasn't around!' A deadly insult, one that would usually provoke a bloody club fight among more valiant Yąnomamö. The man did nothing. He slunk sheepishly back into his hammock, shamed, but relieved to have Rerebawä release his grip.

Even though Rerebawä is fierce and capable of considerable nastiness, he has a charming, witty side as well. He has a biting sense of humor and can entertain the group for hours with jokes and clever manipulations of language. And, he is one of few Yąnomamö that I feel I can trust. I recall indelibly my return to Bisaasi-teri after being away a year—the occasion of my second field trip to the Yąnomamö. When I reached Bisaasi-teri, Rerebawä was in his own village visiting his kinsmen. Word reached him that I had returned, and he paddled downstream immediately to see me. He greeted me with an immense bear hug and exclaimed, with tears welling up in his eyes, 'Shaki! Why did you stay away so long? Did you not know that my will was so cold while you were gone that I could not at times eat for want of seeing you again?' I, too, felt the same way about him—then, and now.

Of all the Yąnomamö I know, he is the most genuine and the most devoted to his culture's ways and values. I admire him for that, although I cannot say that I subscribe to or endorse some of these values. By contrast, Kaobawä is older and wiser, a polished diplomat. He sees his own culture in a slightly different light and seems even to question aspects of it. Thus, while many of his peers enthusiastically accept the 'explanations' of things given in myths, he occasionally reflects on them—even laughing at some of the most preposterous of them.... Probably more of the Yąnomamö are like Rerebawä than like Kaobawä , or at least try to be. ...

Notes

1. The word Yąnomamö is nasalized through its entire length, indicated by the diacritical mark ' , '. When this mark appears on any Yąnomamö word, the whole word is nasalized. The vowel ' ö ' represents a sound that does not occur in the English language. It is similar to the umlat ' ö ' in the German language or the 'oe' equivalent, as in the poet Goethe's name. Unfortunately, many presses and typesetters simply eliminate diacritical marks, and this has led to multiple spellings of the word Yąnomamö—and multiple mispronunciations. Some anthropologists have chosen to introduce a slightly different spelling of the word Yąnomamö since I began writing about them, such as Yąnomami, leading to additional misspellings as their diacriticals are characteristically eliminated by presses, and to the *incorrect* pronunciation 'Yąnomameee.' Vowels indicated as ' ä ' are pronounced as the 'uh' sound in the word 'duck'. Thus, the name Kaobawä would be pronounced 'cow-ba-wuh,' but entirely nasalized.

2. I spent a total of 60 months among the Yąnomamö between 1964 and 1991. The first edition of this case study was based on the first 15 months I spent among them in Venezuela. I have, at the time of this writing, made 20 field trips to the Yąnomamö and this edition reflects the new information and understandings I have acquired over the years. I plan to return regularly to continue what has now turned into a lifelong study.

3. See Spindler (1970) for a general discussion of field research by anthropologists who have worked in other cultures. Nancy Howell has recently written a very useful book (1990) on some of the medical, personal, and environmental hazards of doing field research, which includes a selected bibliography on other fieldwork programs.

4. They could not pronounce "Chagnon." It sounded to them like their name for a pesky bee, shaki, and that is what they called me: pesky, noisome bee.

5. The Yąnomamö in this region acquired canoes very recently. The missionaries would purchase them from the Ye'kwana Indians to the north for money, and then trade them to the Yąnomamö in exchange for labor, produce, or 'informant' work in translating. It should be emphasized that those Yąnomamö who lived on navigable portions of the Upper Orinoco River moved there recently from the deep forest in order to have contact with the missionaries and acquire the trade goods the missionaries (and their supply system) brought.

6. Rarely were there actual brothers or sisters. In Yąnomamö kinship classifications, certain kinds of cousins are classified as siblings. See Chapter 4.

7. Over time, as I became more and more 'accepted' by the Yąnomamö, they became less and less concerned about my genealogical inquiries and now, provide me with this information quite willingly because I have been very discrete with it. Now, when I revisit familiar villages I am called aside by someone who whispers to me things like, "Don't ask about so-and-so's father."

Doctor, Lawyer, Indian Chief

As Punjabi villagers say, "You never really know who a man is until you know who his grandfather and his ancestors were"

Richard Kurin

Richard Kurin is the Deputy Director of Folklife Programs at the Smithsonian Institution.

I was full of confidence when—equipped with a scholarly proposal, blessings from my advisers, and generous research grants—I set out to study village social structure in the Punjab province of Pakistan. But after looking for an appropriate fieldwork site for several weeks without success, I began to think that my research project would never get off the ground. Daily I would seek out villages aboard my puttering motor scooter, traversing the dusty dirt roads, footpaths, and irrigation ditches that crisscross the Punjab. But I couldn't seem to find a village amenable to study. The major problem was that the villagers I did approach were baffled by my presence. They could not understand why anyone would travel ten thousand miles from home to a foreign country in order to live in a poor village, interview illiterate peasants, and then write a book about it. Life, they were sure, was to be lived, not written about. Besides, they thought, what of any importance could they possibly tell me? Committed as I was to ethnographic research, I readily understood their viewpoint. I was a *babu log*—literally, a noble; figuratively, a clerk; and simply, a person of the city. I rode a motor scooter, wore tight-fitting clothing, and spoke Urdu, a language associated with the urban literary elite. Obviously, I did not belong, and the villagers simply did not see me fitting into their society.

The Punjab, a region about the size of Colorado, straddles the northern border of India and Pakistan. Partitioned between the two countries in 1947, the Punjab now consists of a western province, inhabited by Muslims, and an eastern one, populated in the main by Sikhs and Hindus. As its name implies—*punj* meaning "five" and *ab* meaning "rivers"—the region is endowed with plentiful resources to support widespread agriculture and a large rural population. The Punjab has traditionally supplied grains, produce, and dairy products to the peoples of neighboring and considerably more arid states, earning it a reputation as the breadbasket of southern Asia.

Given this predilection for agriculture, Punjabis like to emphasize that they are earthy people, having values they see as consonant with rural life. These values include an appreciation of, and trust in, nature; simplicity and directness of expression; an awareness of the basic drives and desires that motivate men (namely, *zan, zar, zamin*—"women, wealth, land"); a concern with honor and shame as abiding principles of social organization; and for Muslims, a deep faith in Allah and the teachings of his prophet Mohammed.

Besides being known for its fertile soils, life-giving rivers, and superlative agriculturists, the Punjab is also perceived as a zone of transitional culture, a region that has experienced repeated invasions of people from western and central Asia into the Indian subcontinent. Over the last four thousand years, numerous groups, among them Scythians, Parthians, Huns, Greeks, Moguls, Persians, Afghans, and Turks, have entered the subcontinent through the Punjab in search of bountiful land, riches, or power. Although Punjabis—notably Rajputs, Sikhs, and Jats—have a reputation for courage and fortitude on the battlefield, their primary, self-professed strength has been their ability to incorporate new, exogenous elements into their society with a minimum of conflict. Punjabis are proud that theirs is a multiethnic society in which diverse groups have been largely unified by a common language and by common customs and traditions.

Given this background, I had not expected much difficulty in locating a village in which to settle and conduct my research. As an anthropologist, I viewed myself as an "earthy" social scientist who, being concerned with basics, would have a good deal in common with rural Punjabis. True, I might be looked on as an invader of a sort; but I was benevolent, and sensing this, villagers were sure to incorporate me into their society with even greater ease than was the case for the would-be conquering armies that had preceded me. Indeed, they would welcome me with open arms.

I was wrong. The villages whom I approached attributed my desire to live with them either to neurotic delusions or nefarious ulterior motives. Perhaps, so the arguments went, I was really after women, land, or wealth.

On the day I had decided would be my last in search of a village, I was driving along a road when I saw a farmer running through a rice field waving me down. I stopped and he climbed on the scooter. Figuring I had nothing to lose, I began to explain why I wanted to live in a village. To my surprise and delight, he was very receptive, and after sharing a pomegranate milkshake at a roadside shop, he invited me to his home. His name was Allah Ditta, which means "God given," and I took this as a sign that I had indeed found my village.

"My" village turned out to be a settlement of about fifteen hundred people, mostly of the Nunari *qaum,* or "tribe." The Nunaris engage primarily in agriculture (wheat, rice, sugar cane, and cotton), and most families own small plots of land. Members of the Bhatti tribe constitute the largest minority in the village. Although traditionally a warrior tribe, the Bhattis serve in the main as the village artisans and craftsmen.

On my first day in the village I tried explaining in great detail the purposes of my study to the village elders and clan leaders. Despite my efforts, most of the elders were perplexed about why I wanted to live in their village. As a guest, I was entitled to the hospitality traditionally bestowed by Muslim peoples of Asia, and during the first evening I was assigned a place to stay. But I was an enigma, for guests leave, and I wanted to remain. I was also perceived as being strange, for I was both a non-Muslim and a non-Punjabi, a type of person not heretofore encountered by most of the villagers. Although I tried to temper my behavior, there was little I could say or do to dissuade my hosts from the view that I embodied the antithesis of Punjabi values. While I was able to converse in their language, Jatki, a dialect of western Punjabi, I was only able to do so with the ability of a four-year-old. This achievement fell far short of speaking the *t'et',* or "genuine form," of the villagers. Their idiom is rich with the terminology of agricultural operations and rural life. It is unpretentious, uninflected, and direct, and villagers hold high opinions of those who are good with words, who can speak to a point and be convincing. Needless to say, my infantile babble realized none of these characteristics and evoked no such respect.

Similarly, even though I wore indigenous dress, I was inept at tying my *lungi,* or pant cloth. The fact that my *lungi* occasionally fell off and revealed what was underneath gave my neighbors reason to believe that I indeed had no shame and could not control the passions of my *nafs,* or "libidinous nature."

This image of a doltish, shameless infidel barely capable of caring for himself lasted for the first week of my residence in the village. My inability to distinguish among the five varieties of rice and four varieties of lentil grown in the village illustrated that I knew or cared little about nature and agricultural enterprise. This display of ignorance only served to confirm the general consensus that the mysterious morsels I ate from tin cans labeled "Chef Boy-ar-Dee" were not really food at all. Additionally, I did not oil and henna my hair, shave my armpits, or perform ablutions, thereby convincing some commentators that I was a member of a species of subhuman beings, possessing little in the form of either common or moral sense. That the villagers did not quite grant me the status of a person was reflected by their not according me a proper name. In the Punjab, a person's name is equated with honor and respect and is symbolized by his turban. A man who does not have a name, or whose name is not recognized by his neighbors, is unworthy of respect. For such a man, his turban is said to be either nonexistent or to lie in the dust at the feet of others. To be given a name is to have one's head crowned by a turban, an acknowledgment that one leads a responsible and respectable life. Although I repeatedly introduced myself as "Rashid Karim," a fairly decent Pakistani rendering of Richard Kurin, just about all the villagers insisted on calling me *Angrez* ("Englishman"), thus denying me full personhood and implicitly refusing to grant me the right to wear a turban.

As I began to pick up the vernacular, to question villagers about their clan and kinship structure and trace out relationships between different families, my image began to change. My drawings of kinship diagrams and preliminary census mappings were looked upon not only with wonder but also suspicion. My neighbors now began to think there might be a method to my madness. And so there was. Now I had become a spy. Of course it took a week for people to figure out whom I was supposedly spying for. Located as they were at a crossroads of Asia, at a nexus of conflicting geopolitical interests, they had many possibilities to consider. There was a good deal of disagreement on the issue, with the vast majority maintaining that I was either an American, Russian, or Indian spy. A small, but nonetheless vocal, minority held steadfastly to the belief that I was a Chinese spy. I thought it all rather humorous until one day a group confronted me in the main square in front of the nine-by-nine-foot mud hut that I had rented. The leader spoke up and accused me of spying. The remainder of the group grumbled *jahsus! jahsus!* ("spy! spy!"), and I realized that this ad hoc committee of inquiry had the potential of becoming a mob.

To be sure, the villagers had good reason to be suspicious. For one, the times were tense in Pakistan—a national political crisis gripped the country and the populace had been anxious for months over the uncertainty of elections and effective governmental functions. Second, keenly aware of their history, some of the villagers did not have to go too far to imagine that I was at the vanguard of some invading group that had designs upon their land. Such intrigues, with far greater sophistication, had been played out before by nations seeking to expand their power into the Punjab. That I possessed a gold seal letter (which no one save myself could read) from the University of Chicago to the effect that I was pursuing legitimate studies was not enough to convince the crowd that I was indeed an innocent scholar.

I repeatedly denied the charge, but to no avail. The shouts of *jahsus! jahsus!* prevailed. Confronted with this I had no choice.

"Okay," I said. "I admit it. I am a spy!"

The crowd quieted for my long-awaited confession.

"I am a spy and am here to study this village, so that when my country attacks you we will be prepared. You see, we will not bomb Lahore or Karachi or Islamabad. Why should we waste our bombs on millions of people, on factories, dams, airports, and harbors? No, it is far more advantageous to bomb this strategic small village replete with its mud huts, livestock, Persian wheels, and one light bulb. And when we bomb this village, it is imperative that we know how Allah Ditta is related to Abdullah, and who owns the land near the well, and what your marriage customs are."

Silence hung over the crowd, and then one by one the assemblage began to disperse. My sarcasm had worked. The spy charges were defused. But I was no hero in light of my performance, and so I was once again relegated to the status of a nonperson without an identity in the village.

I remained in limbo for the next week, and although I continued my attempts to collect information about village life, I had my doubts as to whether I would ever be accepted by the villagers. And then, through no effort of my own, there was a breakthrough, this time due to another Allah Ditta, a relative of the village headman and one of my leading accusers during my spying days.

I was sitting on my woven string bed on my porch when Allah Ditta approached, leading his son by the neck. "Oh, *Angrez!*" he yelled, "this worthless son of mine is doing poorly in school.

He is supposed to be learning English, but he is failing. He has a good mind, but he's lazy. And his teacher is no help, being more intent upon drinking tea and singing film songs than upon teaching English. Oh son of an Englishman, do you know English?"

"Yes, I know English," I replied, "after all, I am an *Angrez.*"

"Teach him," Allah Ditta blurted out, without any sense of making a tactful request.

And so, I spent the next hour with the boy, reviewing his lessons and correcting his pronunciation and grammar. As I did so, villagers stopped to watch and listen, and by the end of the hour, nearly one hundred people had gathered around, engrossed by this tutoring session. They were stupefied. I was an effective teacher, and I actually seemed to know English. The boy responded well, and the crowd reached a new consensus. I had a brain. And in recognition of this achievement I was given a name—"Ustad Rashid," or Richard the Teacher.

Achieving the status of a teacher was only the beginning of my success. The next morning I awoke to find the village sugar vendor at my door. He had a headache and wanted to know if I could cure him.

"Why do you think I can help you?" I asked.

Bhai Khan answered, "Because you are a *ustad*, you have a great deal of knowledge."

The logic was certainly compelling. If I could teach English, I should be able to cure a headache. I gave him two aspirins.

An hour later, my fame had spread. Bhai Khan had been cured, and he did not hesitate to let others know that it was the *ustad* who had been responsible. By the next day, and in fact for the remainder of my stay, I was to see an average of twenty-five to thirty patients a day. I was asked to cure everything from coughs and colds to typhoid, elephantiasis, and impotency. Upon establishing a flourishing and free medical practice, I received another title, *hakim*, or "physician." I was not yet an anthropologist, but I was on my way.

A few days later I took on yet another role. One of my research interests

involved tracing out patterns of land ownership and inheritance. While working on the problem of figuring out who owned what, I was approached by the village watchman. He claimed he had been swindled in a land deal and requested my help. As the accused was not another villager, I agreed to present the watchman's case to the local authorities.

Somehow, my efforts managed to achieve results. The plaintiff's grievance was redressed, and I was given yet another title in the village—*wakil*, or "lawyer." And in the weeks that followed, I was steadily called upon to read, translate, and advise upon various court orders that affected the lives of the villagers.

My roles as teacher, doctor, and lawyer not only provided me with an identity but also facilitated my integration into the economic structure of the community. As my imputed skills offered my neighbors services not readily available in the village, I was drawn into exchange relationships known as *seipi*. *Seipi* refers to the barter system of goods and services among village farmers, craftsmen, artisans, and other specialists. Every morning Roshan the milkman would deliver fresh milk to my hut. Every other day Hajam Ali the barber would stop by and give me a shave. My next-door neighbor, Nura the cobbler, would repair my sandals when required. Ghulam the horse-cart driver would transport me to town when my motor scooter was in disrepair. The parents of my students would send me sweets and sometimes delicious meals. In return, none of my neighbors asked for direct payment for the specific actions performed. Rather, as they told me, they would call upon me when they had need of my services. And they did. Nura needed cough syrup for his children, the milkman's brother needed a job contact in the city, students wanted to continue their lessons, and so on. Through *seipi* relations, various neighbors gave goods and services to me, and I to them.

Even so, I knew that by Punjabi standards I could never be truly accepted into village life because I was not a member of either the Nunari or Bhatti tribe. As the villagers would say, "You never really know who a man is until you know who his grandfather and his ancestors were." And to know a person's grandfather or ancestors properly, you had to be a member of the same or a closely allied tribe.

The Nunari tribe is composed of a number of groups. The nucleus consists of four clans—Naul, Vadel, Sadan, and More—each named for one of four brothers thought to have originally founded the tribe. Clan members are said to be related by blood ties, also called *pag da sak*, or "ties of the turban." In sharing the turban, members of each clan share the same name. Other clans, unrelated by ties of blood to these four, have become attached to this nucleus through a history of marital relations or of continuous political and economic interdependence. Marital relations, called *gag da sak*, or "ties of the skirt," are conceived of as relations in which alienable turbans (skirts) in the form of women are exchanged with other, non-turban-sharing groups. Similarly, ties of political and economic domination and subordination are thought of as relations in which the turban of the client is given to that of the patron. A major part of my research work was concerned with reconstructing how the four brothers formed the Nunari tribe, how additional clans became associated with it, and how clan and tribal identity were defined by nomenclature, codes of honor, and the symbols of sharing and exchanging turbans.

To approach these issues I set out to reconstruct the genealogical relationships within the tribe and between the various clans. I elicited genealogies from many of the villagers and questioned older informants about the history of the Nunari tribe. Most knew only bits and pieces of this history, and after several months of interviews and research, I was directed to the tribal genealogists. These people, usually not Nunaris themselves, perform the service of memorizing and then orally relating the history of the tribe and the relationships among its members. The genealogist in the village was an aged and arthritic man named Hedayat, who in his later years was engaged in teaching the Nunari genealogy to his son, who would then carry out the traditional and hereditary duties of his position.

The villagers claimed that Hedayat knew every generation of the Nunari from the present to the founding brothers and even beyond. So I invited Hedayat to my hut and explained my purpose.

"Do you know Allah Ditta son of Rohm?" I asked.

"Yes, of course," he replied.

"Who was Rohm's father?" I continued.

"Shahadat Mohammad," he answered.

"And his father?"

"Hamid."

"And his?"

"Chigatah," he snapped without hesitation.

I was now quite excited, for no one else in the village had been able to recall an ancestor of this generation. My estimate was that Chigatah had been born sometime between 1850 and 1870. But Hedayat went on.

"Chigatah's father was Kamal. And Kamal's father was Nanak. And Nanak's father was Sikhu. And before him was Dargai, and before him Maiy. And before him was Siddiq. And Siddiq's father was Nur. And Nur's Asmat. And Asmat was of Channa. And Channa of Nau. And Nau of Bhatta. And Bhatta was the son of Koduk."

Hedayat had now recounted sixteen generations of lineal ascendants related through the turban. Koduk was probably born in the sixteenth century. But still Hedayat continued.

"Sigun was the father of Koduk. And Man the father of Sigun. And before Man was his father Maneswar. And Maneswar's father was the founder of the clan, Naul."

This then was a line of the Naul clan of the Nunari tribe, ascending twenty-one generations from the present descendants (Allah Ditta's son) to the founder, one of four brothers who lived perhaps in the fifteenth century. I asked Hedayat to recite genealogies of the other Nunari clans, and he did, with some blanks here and there, ending with Vadel, More, and Saddan, the other three brothers who formed the tribal nucleus. I then asked the obvious question, "Hedayat, who was the father of these four brothers? Who is the founding ancestor of the Nunari tribe?"

"The father of these brothers was not a Muslim. He was an Indian rajput [chief]. The tribe actually begins with the conversion of the four brothers," Hedayat explained.

"Well then," I replied, "who was this Indian chief?"

"He was a famous and noble chief who fought against the Moguls. His name was Raja Kurin, who lived in a massive fort in Kurinnagar, about twenty-seven miles from Delhi."

"What!" I asked, both startled and unsure of what I had heard.

"Raja Kurin is the father of the brothers who make up—"

"But his name! It's the same as mine," I stammered. "Hedayat, my name is Richard Kurin. What a coincidence! Here I am living with your tribe thousands of miles from my home and it turns out that I have the same name as the founder of the tribe! Do you think I might be related to Raja Kurin and the Nunaris?"

Hedayat looked at me, but only for an instant. Redoing his turban, he tilted his head skyward, smiled, and asked, "What is the name of your father?"

I had come a long way. I now had a name that could be recognized and respected, and as I answered Hedayat, I knew that I had finally and irrevocably fit into "my" village. Whether by fortuitous circumstances or by careful manipulation, my neighbors had found a way to take an invading city person intent on studying their life and transform him into one of their own, a full person entitled to wear a turban for participating in, and being identified with, that life. As has gone on for centuries in the region, once again the new and exogenous had been recast into something Punjabi.

Epilogue: There is no positive evidence linking the Nunaris to a historical Raja Kurin, although there are several famous personages identified by that name (also transcribed as Karan and Kurran). Estimated from the genealogy recited by Hedayat, the founding of the tribe by four brothers appears to have occurred sometime between 440 and 640 years ago, depending on the interval assumed for each generation. On that basis, the most likely candidate for Nunari progenitor (actual or imputed) is Raja Karan, ruler of Anhilvara (Gujerat), who was defeated by the Khilji Ala-ud-Din in 1297 and again in 1307. Although this is slightly earlier than suggested by the genealogical data, such genealogies are often telescoped or otherwise unreliable.

Nevertheless, several aspects of Hedayat's account make this association doubtful. Hedayat clearly identifies Raja Kurin's conquerors as Moguls, whereas the Gujerati Raja Karan was defeated by the Khiljis. Second, Hedayat places the Nunari ancestor's kingdom only twenty-seven miles from Delhi. The Gujerati Raja Karan ruled several kingdoms, none closer than several hundred miles to Delhi.

Other circumstances, however, offer support for this identification of the Nunari ancestor. According to Hedayat, Raja Kurin's father was named Kam Deo. Although the historical figure was the son of Serung Deo, the use of "Deo," a popular title for the rajas of the Vaghela and Solonki dynasties, does seem to place the Nunari fonder in the context of medieval Gujerat. Furthermore, Hedayat clearly identifies the saint (*pir*) said to have initiated the conversion of the Nunaris to Islam. This saint, Mukhdum-i-Jehaniyan, was a contemporary of the historical Raja Karan.

Also of interest, but as yet unexplained, is that several other groups living in Nunari settlement ares specifically claim to be descended from Raja Karan of Gujerat, who is said to have migrated northward into the Punjab after his defeat. Controverting this theory, the available evidence indicates that Raja Karan fled, not toward the Punjab, but rather southward to the Deccan, and that his patriline ended with him. It is his daughter, Deval Devi who is remembered: she is the celebrated heroine of "Ashiqa," a famous Urdu poem written by Amir Khusrau in 1316. She was married to Khizr Khan, the son of Karan's conqueror; nothing is known of her progeny.

Eating Christmas in the Kalahari

Richard Borshay Lee

Richard Borshay Lee is a full professor of anthropology at the University of Toronto. He has done extensive fieldwork in southern Africa, is coeditor of Man the Hunter *(1968) and* Kalahari Hunter-Gatherers *(1976), and author of* The !Kung San: Men, Women, and Work in a Foraging Society.

The !Kung Bushmen's knowledge of Christmas is thirdhand. The London Missionary Society brought the holiday to the southern Tswana tribes in the early nineteenth century. Later, native catechists spread the idea far and wide among the Bantu-speaking pastoralists, even in the remotest corners of the Kalahari Desert. The Bushmen's idea of the Christmas story, stripped to its essentials, is "praise the birth of white man's god-chief"; what keeps their interest in the holiday high is the Tswana-Herero custom of slaughtering an ox for his Bushmen neighbors as an annual goodwill gesture. Since the 1930's, part of the Bushmen's annual round of activities has included a December congregation at the cattle posts for trading, marriage brokering, and several days of trance-dance feasting at which the local Tswana headman is host.

As a social anthropologist working with !Kung Bushmen, I found that the Christmas ox custom suited by purposes. I had come to the Kalahari to study the hunting and gathering subsistence economy of the !Kung, and to accomplish this it was essential not to provide them with food, share my own food, or interfere in any way with their food-gathering activities. While liberal handouts of tobacco and medical supplies were appreciated, they were scarcely adequate to erase the glaring disparity in wealth between the anthropologist, who maintained a two-month inventory of canned goods, and the Bushmen, who rarely had a day's supply of food on hand. My approach, while paying off in terms of data, left me open to frequent accusations of stinginess and hard-heartedness. By their lights, I was a miser.

The Christmas ox was to be my way of saying thank you for the cooperation of the past year; and since it was to be our last Christmas in the field, I determined to slaughter the largest, meatiest ox that money could buy, insuring that the feast and trance-dance would be a success.

Through December I kept my eyes open at the wells as the cattle were brought down for watering. Several animals were offered, but none had quite the grossness that I had in mind. Then, ten days before the holiday, a Herero friend led an ox of astonishing size and mass up to our camp. It was solid black, stood five feet high at the shoulder, had a five-foot span of horns, and must have weighed 1,200 pounds on the hoof. Food consumption calculations are my specialty, and I quickly figured that bones and viscera aside, there was enough meat—at least four pounds—for every man, woman, and child of the 150 Bushmen in the vicinity of /ai/ai who were expected at the feast.

Having found the right animal at last, I paid the Herero £20 ($56) and asked him to keep the beast with his herd until Christmas day. The next morning word spread among the people that the big solid black one was the ox chosen by /ontah (my Bushman name; it means, roughly, "whitey") for the Christmas feast. That afternoon I received the first delegation. Ben!a, an outspoken sixty-year-old mother of five, came to the point slowly.

"Where were you planning to eat Christmas?"

"Right here at /ai/ai," I replied.

"Alone or with others?"

"I expect to invite all the people to eat Christmas with me."

"Eat what?"

"I have purchased Yehave's black ox, and I am going to slaughter and cook it."

"That's what we were told at the well but refused to believe it until we heard it from yourself."

"Well, it's the black one," I replied expansively, although wondering what she was driving at.

"Oh, no!" Ben!a groaned, turning to her group. "They were right." Turning back to me she asked, "Do you expect us to eat that bag of bones?"

"Bag of bones! It's the biggest ox at /ai/ai."

"Big, yes, but old. And thin. Everybody knows there's no meat on that old ox. What did you expect us to eat off it, the horns?"

Everybody chuckled at Ben!a's one-liner as they walked away, but all I could manage was a weak grin.

That evening it was the turn of the young men. They came to sit at our evening fire. /gaugo, about my age, spoke to me man-to-man.

"/ontah, you have always been square with us," he lied. "What has happened to change your heart? That sack of guts and bones of Yehave's will hardly feed one camp, let alone all the Bushmen around ai/ai." And he proceeded to enumerate the seven camps in the /ai/ai vicinity, family by family. "Perhaps you have forgotten that we are not few, but many. Or are you too blind to tell the difference between a proper cow and an old wreck? That ox is thin to the point of death."

"Look, you guys," I retorted, "that is a beautiful animal, and I"m sure you will eat it with pleasure at Christmas."

"Of course we will eat it; it's food. But it won"t fill us up to the point where we will have enough strength to dance. We will eat and go home to bed with stomachs rumbling."

That night as we turned in, I asked my wife, Nancy: "What did you think of the black ox?"

"It looked enormous to me. Why?"

"Well, about eight different people have told me I got gypped; that the ox is nothing but bones."

"What's the angle?" Nancy asked. "Did they have a better one to sell?"

"No, they just said that it was going to be a grim Christmas because there won't be enough meat to go around. Maybe I'll get an independent judge to look at the beast in the morning."

Bright and early, Halingisi, a Tswana cattle owner, appeared at our camp. But before I could ask him to give me his opinion on Yehave's black ox, he gave me the eye signal that indicated a confidential chat. We left the camp and sat down.

"/ontah, I'm surprised at you: you've lived here for three years and still haven't learned anything about cattle."

"But what else can a person do but choose the biggest, strongest animal one can find?" I retorted.

"Look, just because an animal is big doesn't mean that it has plenty of meat on it. The black one was a beauty when it was younger, but now it is thin to the point of death."

"Well I've already bought it. What can I do at this stage?"

"Bought it already? I thought you were just considering it. Well, you'll have to kill it and serve it, I suppose. But don't expect much of a dance to follow."

My spirits dropped rapidly. I could believe that Ben!a and /gaugo just might be putting me on about the black ox, but Halingisi seemed to be an impartial critic. I went around that day feeling as though I had bought a lemon of a used car.

In the afternoon it was Tomazo's turn. Tomazo is a fine hunter, a top trance performer... and one of my most reliable informants. He approached the subject of the Christmas cow as part of my continuing Bushman education.

"My friend, the way it is with us Bushmen," he began, "is that we love meat. And even more than that, we love fat. When we hunt we always search for the fat ones, the ones dripping with layers of white fat: fat that turns into a clear, thick oil in the cooking pot, fat that slides down your gullet, fills your stomach and gives you a roaring diarrhea," he rhapsodized.

"So, feeling as we do," he continued, "it gives us pain to be served such a scrawny thing as Yehave's black ox. It is big, yes, and no doubt its giant bones are good for soup, but fat is what we really crave and so we will eat Christmas this year with a heavy heart."

The prospect of a gloomy Christmas now had me worried, so I asked Tomazo what I could do about it.

"Look for a fat one, a young one... smaller, but fat. Fat enough to make us //gom ('evacuate the bowels'), then we will be happy."

My suspicions were aroused when Tomazo said that he happened to know of a young, fat, barren cow that the owner was willing to part with. Was Tomazo working on commission, I wondered? But I dispelled this unworthy thought when we approached the Herero owner of the cow in question and found that he had decided not to sell.

The scrawny wreck of a Christmas ox now became the talk of the /ai/ai water hole and was the first news told to the outlying groups as they began to come in from the bush for the feast. What finally convinced me that real trouble might be brewing was the visit from u!au, an old conservative with a reputation for fierceness. His nickname meant spear and referred to an incident thirty years ago in which he had speared a man to death. He had an intense manner; fixing me with his eyes, he said in clipped tones:

"I have only just heard about the black ox today, or else I would have come here earlier. /ontah, do you honestly think you can serve meat like that to people and avoid a fight?" He paused, letting the implications sink in. "I don't mean fight you, /ontah; you are a white man. I mean a fight between Bushmen. There are many fierce ones here, and with such a small quantity of meat to distribute, how can you give everybody a fair share? Someone is sure to accuse another of taking too much or hogging all the choice pieces. Then you will see what happens when some go hungry while others eat."

The possibility of at least a serious argument struck me as all too real. I had witnessed the tension that surrounds the distribution of meat from a kudu or gemsbok kill, and had documented many arguments that sprang up from a real or imagined slight in meat distribution. The owners of a kill may spend up to two hours arranging and rearranging the piles of meat under the gaze of a circle of recipients before handing them out. And I also knew that the Christmas feast at /ai/ai would be bringing together groups that had feuded in the past.

Convinced now of the gravity of the situation, I went in earnest to search for a second cow; but all my inquiries failed to turn one up.

The Christmas feast was evidently going to be a disaster, and the incessant complaints about the meagerness of the ox had already taken the fun out of it for me. Moreover, I was getting bored with the wisecracks, and after losing my temper a few times, I resolved to serve the beast anyway. If the meat fell short, the hell with it. In the Bushmen idiom, I announced to all who would listen:

"I am a poor man and blind. If I have chosen one that is too old and too thin, we will eat it anyway and see if there is enough meat there to quiet the rumbling of our stomachs."

On hearing this speech, Ben!a offered me a rare word of comfort. "It's thin," she said philosophically, "but the bones will make a good soup."

At dawn Christmas morning, instinct told me to turn over the butchering and cooking to a friend and take off with Nancy to spend Christmas alone in the bush. But curiosity kept me from retreating. I wanted to see what such a scrawny ox looked like on butchering and if there *was* going to be a fight, I wanted to catch every word of it. Anthropologists are incurable that way.

The great beast was driven up to our dancing ground, and a shot in the forehead dropped it in its tracks. Then, freshly cut branches were heaped around the fallen carcass to receive the meat. Ten men volunteered to help with the cutting. I asked /gaugo to make the breast bone cut. This cut, which begins the butchering process for most large game, offers easy access for removal of the viscera. But it also allows the hunter to spot-check the amount of fat on the animal. A fat game animal carries a white layer up to an inch thick on the chest, while in a thin one, the knife will quickly cut to bone. All eyes fixed on his hand as /gaugo, dwarfed by the great carcass, knelt to the breast. The first cut opened a pool of solid white in the black skin. The second and third cut widened and deepened the creamy white. Still no bone. It was pure fat; it must have been two inches thick.

"Hey /gau," I burst out, "that ox is loaded with fat. What's this about the ox being too thin to bother eating? Are you out of your mind?"

"Fat?" /gau shot back, "You call that fat? This wreck is thin, sick, dead!" And he broke out laughing. So did everyone else. They rolled on the ground, paralyzed with laughter. Everybody laughed except me; I was thinking.

I ran back to the tent and burst in just as Nancy was getting up. "Hey, the black ox. It's fat as hell! They were kidding about it being too thin to eat. It was a joke or something. A put-on. Everyone is really delighted with it!"

"Some joke," my wife replied. "It was so funny that you were ready to pack up and leave /ai/ai."

If it had indeed been a joke, it had been an extraordinarily convincing one, and tinged, I thought, with more than a touch of malice as many jokes are. Nevertheless, that it was a joke lifted my spirits considerably, and I returned to the butchering site where the shape of the ox was rapidly disappearing under the axes and knives of the butchers. The atmosphere had become festive. Grinning broadly, their arms covered with blood well past the elbow, men packed chunks of meat into the big cast-iron cooking pots, fifty pounds to the load, and muttered and chuckled all the while about the thinness and worthlessness of the animal and /ontah's poor judgment.

We danced and ate that ox two days and two nights; we cooked and distributed fourteen potfuls of meat and no one went home hungry and no fights broke out.

But the "joke" stayed in my mind. I had a growing feeling that something important had happened in my relationship with the Bushmen and that the clue lay in the meaning of the joke. Several days later, when most of the people had dispersed back to the bush camps, I raised the question with Hakekgose, a Tswana man who had grown up among the !Kung, married a !Kung girl, and who probably knew their culture better than any other non-Bushman.

"With us whites," I began, "Christmas is supposed to be the day of friendship and brotherly love. What I can't figure out is why the Bushmen went to such lengths to criticize and belittle the ox I had bought for the feast. The animal was perfectly good and their jokes and wisecracks practically ruined the holiday for me."

"So it really did bother you," said Hakekgose. "Well, that's the way they always talk. When I take my rifle and go hunting with them, if I miss, they laugh at me for the rest of the day. But even if I hit and bring one down, it's no better. To them, the kill is always too small or too old or too thin; and as we sit down on the kill site to cook and eat the liver, they keep grumbling, even with their mouths full of meat. They say things like, 'Oh this is awful! What a worthless animal! Whatever made me think that this Tswana rascal could hunt!' "

"Is this the way outsiders are treated?" I asked.

"No, it is their custom; they talk that way to each other too. Go and ask them."

/gaugo had been one of the most enthusiastic in making me feel bad about the merit of the Christmas ox. I sought him out first.

"Why did you tell me the black ox was worthless, when you could see that it was loaded with fat and meat?"

"It is our way," he said smiling. "We always like to fool people about that. Say there is a Bushman who has been hunting. He must not come home and announce like a braggard, 'I have killed a big one in the bush!' He must first sit down in silence until I or someone else comes up to his fire and asks, 'What did you see today?' He replies quietly, 'Ah, I'm no good for hunting. I saw nothing at all [pause] just a little tiny one.' Then I smile to myself," /gaugo continued, "because I know he has killed something big."

"In the morning we make up a party of four or five people to cut up and carry the meat back to the camp. When we arrive at the kill we examine it and cry out, 'You mean to say you have dragged us all the way out here in order to make us cart home your pile of bones? Oh, if I had known it was this thin I wouldn't have come.' Another one pipes up, 'People, to think I gave up a nice day in the shade for this. At home we may be hungry but at least we have nice cool water to drink.' If the horns are big, someone says, 'Did you think that somehow you

1 ❖ ANTHROPOLOGICAL PERSPECTIVES

were going to boil down the horns for soup?'

"To all this you must respond in kind. 'I agree,' you say, 'this one is not worth the effort; let's just cook the liver for strength and leave the rest for the hyenas. It is not too late to hunt today and even a duiker or a steenbok would be better than this mess.'

"Then you set to work nevertheless; butcher the animal, carry the meat back to the camp and everyone eats," /gaugo concluded.

Things were beginning to make sense. Next, I went to Tomazo. He corroborated /gaugo's story of the obligatory insults over a kill and added a few details of his own.

"But," I asked, "why insult a man after he has gone to all that trouble to track and kill an animal and when he is going to share the meat with you so that your children will have something to eat?"

"Arrogance," was his cryptic answer.
"Arrogance?"

"Yes, when a young man kills much meat he comes to think of himself as a chief or a big man, and he thinks of the rest of us as his servants or inferiors. We can't accept this. We refuse one who boasts, for someday his pride will make him kill somebody. So we always speak of his meat as worthless. This way we cool his heart and make him gentle."

"But why didn't you tell me this before?" I asked Tomazo with some heat.

"Because you never asked me," said Tomazo, echoing the refrain that has come to haunt every field ethnographer.

The pieces now fell into place. I had known for a long time that in situations of social conflict with Bushmen I held all the cards. I was the only source of tobacco in a thousand square miles, and I was not incapable of cutting an individual off for non-cooperation. Though my boycott never lasted longer than a few days, it was an indication of my strength. People resented my presence at the water hole, yet simultaneously dreaded my leaving. In short I was a perfect target for the charge of arrogance and for the Bushmen tactic of enforcing humility.

I had been taught an object lesson by the Bushmen; it had come from an unexpected corner and had hurt me in a vulnerable area. For the big black ox was to be the one totally generous, unstinting act of my year at /ai/ai, and I was quite unprepared for the reaction I received.

As I read it, their message was this: There are no totally generous acts. All "acts" have an element of calculation. One black ox slaughtered at Christmas does not wipe out a year of careful manipulation of gifts given to serve your own ends. After all, to kill an animal and share the meat with people is really no more than Bushmen do for each other every day and with far less fanfare.

In the end, I had to admire how the Bushmen had played out the farce—collectively straight-faced to the end. Curiously, the episode reminded me of the *Good Solider Schweik* and his marvelous encounters with authority. Like Schweik, the Bushmen had retained a thorough-going skepticism of good intentions. Was it this independence of spirit, I wondered, that had kept them culturally viable in the face of generations of contact with more powerful societies, both black and white? The thought that the Bushmen were alive and well in the Kalahari was strangely comforting. Perhaps, armed with that independence and with their superb knowledge of their environment, they might yet survive the future.

The Challenge of Cultural Relativism

*Morality differs in every society, and is a
convenient term for socially approved habits.*
RUTH BENEDICT, *PATTERNS OF CULTURE* (1934)

James Rachels

How Different Cultures Have Different Moral Codes

Darius, a king of ancient Persia, was intrigued by the variety of cultures he encountered in his travels. He had found, for example, that the Callatians (a tribe of Indians) customarily ate the bodies of their dead fathers. The Greeks, of course, did not do that—the Greeks practiced cremation and regarded the funeral pyre as the natural and fitting way to dispose of the dead. Darius thought that a sophisticated understanding of the world must include an appreciation of such differences between cultures. One day, to teach this lesson, he summoned some Greeks who happened to be present at his court and asked them what they would take to eat the bodies of their dead fathers. They were shocked, as Darius knew they would be, and replied that no amount of money could persuade them to do such a thing. Then Darius called in some Callatians, and while the Greeks listened asked them what they would take to burn their dead fathers' bodies. The Callatians were horrified and told Darius not even to mention such a dreadful thing.

This story, recounted by Herodotus in his *History,* illustrates a recurring theme in the literature of social science: different cultures have different moral codes. What is thought right within one group may be utterly abhorrent to the members of another group, and vice versa. Should we eat the bodies of the dead or burn them? If you were a Greek, one answer would seem obviously correct; but if you were a Callatian, the opposite would seem equally certain.

It is easy to give additional examples of the same kind. Consider the Eskimos. They are a remote and inaccessible people. Numbering only about 25,000, they live in small, isolated settlements scattered mostly along the northern fringes of North America and Greenland. Until the beginning of this century, the outside world knew little about them. Then explorers began to bring back strange tales.

Eskimo customs turned out to be very different from our own. The men often had more than one wife, and they would share their wives with guests, lending

them for the night as a sign of hospitality. Moreover, within a community, a dominant male might demand—and get —regular sexual access to other men's wives. The women, however, were free to break these arrangements simply by leaving their husbands and taking up with new partners—free, that is, so long as their former husbands chose not to make trouble. All in all, the Eskimo practice was a volatile scheme that bore little resemblance to what we call marriage.

But it was not only their marriage and sexual practices that were different. The Eskimos also seemed to have less regard for human life. Infanticide, for example, was common. Knud Rasmussen, one of the most famous early explorers, reported that he met one woman who had borne twenty children but had killed ten of them at birth. Female babies, he found, were especially liable to be destroyed, and this was permitted simply at the parents' discretion, with no social stigma attached to it. Old people also, when they became too feeble to contribute to the family, were left out in the snow to die. So there seemed to be, in this society, remarkably little respect for life.

JAMES RACHELS is University Professor of Philosophy at the University of Alabama at Birmingham. He is also the author of *The End of Life: Euthanasia and Morality* and *Created from Animals: The Moral Implications of Darwinism.*

From *The Elements of Moral Philosophy* by James Rachels, 1993, Second Edition, Chapter 2, pp. 15-29. © 1993 by McGraw-Hill, Inc. Reprinted by permission of The McGraw-Hill Companies, Inc.

To the general public, these were disturbing revelations. Our own way of living seems so natural and right that for many of us it is hard to conceive of others living so differently. And when we do hear of such things, we tend immediately to categorize those other peoples as "backward" or "primitive." But to anthropologists and sociologists, there was nothing particularly surprising about the Eskimos. Since the time of Herodotus, enlightened observers have been accustomed to the idea that conceptions of right and wrong differ from culture to culture. If we assume that *our* ideas of right and wrong will be shared by all peoples at all times, we are merely naive.

Cultural Relativism

To many thinkers, this observation—"Different cultures have different moral codes"—has seemed to be the key to understanding morality. The idea of universal truth in ethics, they say, is a myth. The customs of different societies are all that exist. These customs cannot be said to be "correct" or "incorrect," for that implies we have an independent standard of right and wrong by which they may be judged. But there is no such independent standard; every standard is culture-bound. The great pioneering sociologist William Graham Sumner, writing in 1906, put the point like this:

> The "right" way is the way which the ancestors used and which has been handed down. The tradition is its own warrant. It is not held subject to verification by experience. The notion of right is in the folkways. It is not outside of them, of independent origin, and brought to test them. In the folkways, whatever is, is right. This is because they are traditional, and therefore contain in themselves the authority of the ancestral ghosts. When we come to the folkways we are at the end of our analysis.

This line of thought has probably persuaded more people to be skeptical about ethics than any other single thing. *Cultural Relativism,* as it has been called, challenges our ordinary belief in the objectivity and universality of moral truth. It says, in effect, that there is no such thing as universal truth in ethics; there are only the various cultural codes, and nothing more. Moreover, our own code has no special status; it is merely one among many.

As we shall see, this basic idea is really a compound of several different thoughts. It is important to separate the various elements of the theory because, on analysis, some parts of the theory turn out to be correct, whereas others seem to be mistaken. As a beginning, we may distinguish the following claims, all of which have been made by cultural relativists:

1. Different societies have different moral codes.
2. There is no objective standard that can be used to judge one societal code better than another.
3. The moral code of our own society has no special status; it is merely one among many.
4. There is no "universal truth" in ethics—that is, there are no moral truths that hold for all peoples at all times.
5. The moral code of a society determines what is right within that society; that is, if the moral code of a society says that a certain action is right, then that action *is* right, at least within that society.
6. It is mere arrogance for us to try to judge the conduct of other peoples. We should adopt an attitude of tolerance toward the practices of other cultures.

Although it may seem that these six propositions go naturally together, they are independent of one another, in the sense that some of them might be true even if others are false. In what follows, we will try to identify what is correct in Cultural Relativism, but we will also be concerned to expose what is mistaken about it.

The Cultural Differences Argument

Cultural Relativism is a theory about the nature of morality. At first blush it seems quite plausible. However, like all such theories, it may be evaluated by subjecting it to rational analysis; and when we analyze Cultural Relativism we find that it is not so plausible as it first appears to be.

The first thing we need to notice is that at the heart of Cultural Relativism there is a certain *form of argument.* The strategy used by cultural relativists is to argue from facts about the differences between cultural outlooks to a conclusion about the status of morality. Thus we are invited to accept this reasoning:

1. The Greeks believed it was wrong to eat the dead, whereas the Callatians believed it was right to eat the dead.
2. Therefore, eating the dead is neither objectively right nor objectively wrong. It is merely a matter of opinion, which varies from culture to culture.

Or, alternatively:

1. The Eskimos see nothing wrong with infanticide, whereas Americans believe infanticide is immoral.
2. Therefore, infanticide is neither objectively right nor objectively wrong. It is merely a matter of opinion, which varies from culture to culture.

Clearly, these arguments are variations of one fundamental idea. They are both special cases of a more general argument, which says:

1. Different cultures have different moral codes.
2. Therefore, there is no objective "truth" in morality. Right and wrong are only matters of opinion, and opinions vary from culture to culture.

We may call this the *Cultural Differences Argument.* To many people, it is very persuasive. But from a logical point of view, is it a *sound* argument?

It is not sound. The trouble is that the conclusion does not really follow from the premise—that is, even if the premise is true, the conclusion still might be false. The premise concerns what people *believe:* in some societies, people believe one thing; in other societies, people believe differently. The conclusion, however, concerns *what really is the case.* The trouble is that this sort of conclusion does not follow logically from this sort of premise.

Consider again the example of the Greeks and Callatians. The Greeks believed it was wrong to eat the dead; the Callatians believed it was right. Does it follow, *from the mere fact that they disagreed,* that there is no objective truth in the matter? No, it does not follow; for it *could* be that the practice was objectively right (or wrong) and that one or the other of them was simply mistaken.

To make the point clearer, consider a very different matter. In some societies, people believe the earth is flat. In other societies, such as our own, people believe the earth is (roughly) spherical. Does it follow, *from the mere fact that they disagree,* that there is no "objective truth" in geography? Of course not; we would never draw such a conclusion because we realize that, in their beliefs about the world, the members of some societies might simply be wrong. There is no reason to think that if the world is round everyone must know it. Similarly, there is no reason to think that if there is moral truth everyone must know it. The fundamental mistake in the Cultural Differences Argument is that it attempts to derive a substantive conclusion about a subject (morality) from the mere fact that people disagree about it.

It is important to understand the nature of the point that is being made here. We are *not* saying (not yet, anyway) that the conclusion of the argument is false. Insofar as anything being said here is concerned, it is still an open question whether the conclusion is true. We *are* making a purely logical point and saying that the conclusion does not *follow from* the premise. This is important, because in order to determine whether the conclusion is true, we need arguments in its support. Cultural Relativism proposes this argument, but unfortunately the argument turns out to be fallacious. So it proves nothing.

The Consequences of Taking Cultural Relativism Seriously

Even if the Cultural Differences Argument is invalid, Cultural Relativism might still be true. What would it be like if it were true?

In the passage quoted above, William Graham Sumner summarizes the essence of Cultural Relativism. He says that there is no measure of right and wrong other than the standards of one's society: "The notion of right is in the folkways. It is not outside of them, of independent origin, and brought to test them. In the folkways, whatever is, is right."

Suppose we took this seriously. What would be some of the consequences?

1. *We could no longer say that the customs of other societies are morally inferior to our own.* This, of course, is one of the main points stressed by Cultural Relativism. We would have to stop condemning other societies merely because they are "different." So long as we concentrate on certain examples, such as the funerary practices of the Greeks and Callatians, this may seem to be a sophisticated, enlightened attitude.

However, we would also be stopped from criticizing other, less benign practices. Suppose a society waged war on its neighbors for the purpose of taking slaves. Or suppose a society was violently anti-Semitic and its leaders set out to destroy the Jews. Cultural Relativism would preclude us from saying that either of these practices was wrong. We would not even be able to say that a society tolerant of Jews is *better* than the anti-Semitic society, for that would imply some sort of transcultural standard of comparison. The failure to condemn *these* practices does not seem "enlightened"; on the contrary, slavery and anti-Semitism seem wrong *wherever* they occur. Nevertheless, if we took Cultural Relativism seriously, we would have to admit that these social practices also are immune from criticism.

2. *We could decide whether actions are right or wrong just by consulting the standards of our society.* Cultural Relativism suggests a simple test for determining what is right and what is wrong: all one has to do is ask whether the ac-

tion is in accordance with the code of one's society. Suppose a resident of South Africa is wondering whether his country's policy of *apartheid*—rigid racial segregation—is morally correct. All he has to do is ask whether this policy conforms to his society's moral code. If it does, there is nothing to worry about, at least from a moral point of view.

This implication of Cultural Relativism is disturbing because few of us think that our society's code is perfect—we can think of ways it might be improved. Yet Cultural Relativism would not only forbid us from criticizing the codes of *other* societies; it would stop us from criticizing our *own.* After all, if right and wrong are relative to culture, this must be true for our own culture just as much as for others.

3. *The idea of moral progress is called into doubt.* Usually, we think that at least some changes in our society have been for the better. (Some, of course, may have been changes for the worse.) Consider this example: Throughout most of Western history the place of women in society was very narrowly circumscribed. They could not own property; they could not vote or hold political office; with a few exceptions, they were not permitted to have paying jobs; and generally they were under the almost absolute control of their husbands. Recently much of this has changed, and most people think of it as progress.

If Cultural Relativism is correct, can we legitimately think of this as progress? Progress means replacing a way of doing things with a *better* way. But by what standard do we judge the new ways as better? If the old ways were in accordance with the social standards of their time, then Cultural Relativism would say it is a mistake to judge them by the standards of a different time. Eighteenth-century society was, in effect, a different society from the one we have now. To say that we have made progress implies a judgment that present-day society is better, and that is just the sort of transcultural judgment that, according to Cultural Relativism, is impermissible.

Our idea of social *reform* will also have to be reconsidered. A reformer such as Martin Luther King, Jr., seeks to change his society for the better. Within the constraints imposed by Cultural Relativism, there is one way this might be done. If a society is not living up to its own ideals, the reformer may be regarded as acting for the best: the ideals of the society are the standard by which we judge his or her proposals as worthwhile. But the "reformer" may not challenge the ideals themselves, for those ideals are by definition correct. According to Cultural Relativism, then, the idea of social reform makes sense only in this very limited way.

These three consequences of Cultural Relativism have led many thinkers to reject it as implausible on its face. It does make sense, they say, to condemn some practices, such as slavery and anti-Semitism, wherever they occur. It makes sense to think that our own society has made some moral progress, while admitting that it is still imperfect and in need of reform. Because Cultural Relativism says that these judgments make no sense, the argument goes, it cannot be right.

Why There Is Less Disagreement Than It Seems

The original impetus for Cultural Relativism comes from the observation that cultures differ dramatically in their views of right and wrong. But just how much do they differ? It is true that there are differences. However, it is easy to overestimate the extent of those differences. Often, when we examine what *seems* to be a dramatic difference, we find that the cultures do not differ nearly as much as it appears.

Consider a culture in which people believe it is wrong to eat cows. This may even be a poor culture, in which there is not enough food; still, the cows are not to be touched. Such a society would *appear* to have values very different from our own. But does it? We have not yet asked why these people will not eat cows. Suppose it is because they believe that after death the souls of humans inhabit the bodies of animals, especially

cows, so that a cow may be someone's grandmother. Now do we want to say that their values are different from ours? No; the difference lies elsewhere. The difference is in our belief systems, not in our values. We agree that we shouldn't eat Grandma; we simply disagree about whether the cow *is* (or could be) Grandma.

The general point is this. Many factors work together to produce the customs of a society. The society's values are only one of them. Other matters, such as the religious and factual beliefs held by its members and the physical circumstances in which they must live, are also important. We cannot conclude, then, merely because customs differ, that there is a disagreement about *values*. The difference in customs may be attributable to some other aspect of social life. Thus there may be less disagreement about values than there appears to be.

Consider the Eskimos again. They often kill perfectly normal infants, especially girls. We do not approve of this at all; a parent who did this in our society would be locked up. Thus there appears to be a great difference in the values of our two cultures. But suppose we ask *why* the Eskimos do this. The explanation is not that they have less affection for their children or less respect for human life. An Eskimo family will always protect its babies if conditions permit. But they live in a harsh environment, where food is often in short supply. A fundamental postulate of Eskimo thought is: "Life is hard, and the margin of safety small." A family may want to nourish its babies but be unable to do so.

As in many "primitive" societies, Eskimo mothers will nurse their infants over a much longer period of time than mothers in our culture. The child will take nourishment from its mother's breast for four years, perhaps even longer. So even in the best of times there are limits to the number of infants that one mother can sustain. Moreover, the Eskimos are a nomadic people—unable to farm, they must move about in search of food. Infants must be carried, and a mother can carry only one baby in her parka as she travels and goes

about her outdoor work. Other family members can help, but this is not always possible.

Infant girls are more readily disposed of because, first, in this society the males are the primary food providers— they are the hunters, according to the traditional division of labor—and it is obviously important to maintain a sufficient number of food gatherers. But there is an important second reason as well. Because the hunters suffer a high casualty rate, the adult men who die prematurely far outnumber the women who die early. Thus if male and female infants survived in equal numbers, the female adult population would greatly outnumber the male adult population. Examining the available statistics, one writer concluded that "were it not for female infanticide . . . there would be approximately one-and-a-half times as many females in the average Eskimo local group as there are food-producing males."

So among the Eskimos, infanticide does not signal a fundamentally different attitude toward children. Instead, it is a recognition that drastic measures are sometimes needed to ensure the family's survival. Even then, however, killing the baby is not the first option considered. Adoption is common; childless couples are especially happy to take a more fertile couple's "surplus." Killing is only the last resort. I emphasize this in order to show that the raw data of the anthropologists can be misleading; it can make the differences in values between cultures appear greater than they are. The Eskimos' values are not all that different from our values. It is only that life forces upon them choices that we do not have to make.

How All Cultures Have Some Values in Common

It should not be surprising that, despite appearances, the Eskimos are protective of their children. How could it be otherwise? How could a group survive that did *not* value its young? This suggests a certain argument, one which shows that all cultural groups must be protective of their infants:

1. Human infants are helpless and cannot survive if they are not given extensive care for a period of years.
2. Therefore, if a group did not care for its young, the young would not survive, and the older members of the group would not be replaced. After a while the group would die out.
3. Therefore, any cultural group that continues to exist must care for its young. Infants that are *not* cared for must be the exception rather than the rule.

Similar reasoning shows that other values must be more or less universal. Imagine what it would be like for a society to place no value at all on truth telling. When one person spoke to another, there would be no presumption at all that he was telling the truth—for he could just as easily be speaking falsely. Within that society, there would be no reason to pay attention to what anyone says. (I ask you what time it is, and you say "Four o'clock." But there is no presumption that you are speaking truly; you could just as easily have said the first thing that came into your head. So I have no reason to pay attention to your answer—in fact, there was no point in my asking you in the first place!) Communication would then be extremely difficult, if not impossible. And because complex societies cannot exist without regular communication among their members, society would become impossible. It follows that in any complex society there *must* be a presumption in favor of truthfulness. There may of course be exceptions to this rule: there may be situations in which it is thought to be permissible to lie. Nevertheless, these will be exceptions to a rule that *is* in force in the society.

Let me give one further example of the same type. Could a society exist in which there was no prohibition on murder? What would this be like? Suppose people were free to kill other people at will, and no one thought there was anything wrong with it. In such a "society," no one could feel secure. Everyone would have to be constantly on guard.

People who wanted to survive would have to avoid other people as much as possible. This would inevitably result in individuals trying to become as self-sufficient as possible—after all, associating with others would be dangerous. Society on any large scale would collapse. Of course, people might band together in smaller groups with others that they *could* trust not to harm them. But notice what this means: they would be forming smaller societies that *did* acknowledge a rule against murder. The prohibition of murder, then, is a necessary feature of all societies.

There is a general theoretical point here, namely, that *there are some moral rules that all societies will have in common, because those rules are necessary for society to exist*. The rules against lying and murder are two examples. And in fact, we do find these rules in force in all viable cultures. Cultures may differ in what they regard as legitimate exceptions to the rules, but this disagreement exists against a background of agreement on the larger issues. Therefore, it is a mistake to overestimate the amount of difference between cultures. Not *every* moral rule can vary from society to society.

What Can Be Learned from Cultural Relativism

At the outset, I said that we were going to identify both what is right and what is wrong in Cultural Relativism. Thus far I have mentioned only its mistakes: I have said that it rests on an invalid argument, that it has consequences that make it implausible on its face, and that the extent of cultural disagreement is far less than it implies. This all adds up to a pretty thorough repudiation of the theory. Nevertheless, it is still a very appealing idea, and the reader may have the feeling that all this is a little unfair. The theory *must* have something going for it, or else why has it been so influential? In fact, I think there *is* something right about Cultural Relativism, and now I want to say what that is. There are two lessons we should learn from the theory, even if we ultimately reject it.

1. Cultural Relativism warns us, quite rightly, about the danger of assuming that all our preferences are based on some absolute rational standard. They are not. Many (but not all) of our practices are merely peculiar to our society, and it is easy to lose sight of that fact. In reminding us of it, the theory does a service.

Funerary practices are one example. The Callatians, according to Herodotus, were "men who eat their fathers"—a shocking idea, to us at least. But eating the flesh of the dead could be understood as a sign of respect. It could be taken as a symbolic act that says: We wish this person's spirit to dwell within us. Perhaps this was the understanding of the Callatians. On such a way of thinking, burying the dead could be seen as an act of rejection, and burning the corpse as positively scornful. If this is hard to imagine, then we may need to have our imaginations stretched. Of course we may feel a visceral repugnance at the idea of eating human flesh in any circumstances. But what of it? This repugnance may be, as the relativists say, only a matter of what is customary in our particular society.

There are many other matters that we tend to think of in terms of objective right and wrong, but that are really nothing more than social conventions. Should women cover their breasts? A publicly exposed breast is scandalous in our society, whereas in other cultures it is unremarkable. Objectively speaking, it is neither right nor wrong—there is no objective reason why either custom is better. Cultural Relativism begins with the valuable insight that many of our practices are like this—they are only cultural products. Then it goes wrong by concluding that, because *some* practices are like this, *all* must be.

2. The second lesson has to do with keeping an open mind. In the course of growing up, each of us has acquired some strong feelings: we have learned to think of some types of conduct as acceptable, and others we have learned to regard as simply unacceptable. Occasionally, we may find those feelings challenged. We may encounter someone who claims that our feelings are mistaken. For example, we may have been taught that homosexuality is immoral,

and we may feel quite uncomfortable around gay people and see them as alien and "different." Now someone suggests that this may be a mere prejudice; that there is nothing evil about homosexuality; that gay people are just people, like anyone else, who happen, through no choice of their own, to be attracted to others of the same sex. But because we feel so strongly about the matter, we may find it hard to take this seriously. Even after we listen to the arguments, we may still have the unshakable feeling that homosexuals *must* somehow, be an unsavory lot.

Cultural Relativism, by stressing that our moral views can reflect the prejudices of our society, provides an antidote for this kind of dogmatism. When he tells the story of the Greeks and Callatians, Herodotus adds:

> For if anyone, no matter who, were given the opportunity of choosing from amongst all the nations of the world the set of beliefs which he thought best, he would inevitably, after careful consideration of their relative merits, choose that of his own country. Everyone without exception believes his own native customs, and the religion he was brought up in, to be the best.

Realizing this can result in our having more open minds. We can come to understand that our feelings are not necessarily perceptions of the truth—they may be nothing more than the result of cultural conditioning. Thus when we hear it suggested that some element of our social code is *not* really the best and we find ourselves instinctively resisting the suggestion, we might stop and remember this. Then we may be more open to discovering the truth, whatever that might be.

We can understand the appeal of Cultural Relativism, then, even though the theory has serious shortcomings. It is an attractive theory because it is based on a genuine insight—that many of the practices and attitudes we think so natural are really only cultural products. Moreover, keeping this insight firmly in view is important if we want to avoid arrogance and have open minds. These are important points, not to be taken lightly. But we can accept these points without going on to accept the whole theory.

A REPORTER AT LARGE

The Lost Man

Is it possible that the first Americans weren't who we think they were? And why is the government withholding Kennewick Man, who might turn out to be the most significant archeological find of the decade?

BY DOUGLAS PRESTON

On Sunday, July 28, 1996, in the middle of the afternoon, two college students who were watching a hydroplane race on the Columbia River in Kennewick, Washington, decided to take a shortcut along the river's edge. While wading through the shallows, one of them stubbed his toe on a human skull partly buried in the sand. The students picked it up and, thinking it might be that of a murder victim, hid it in some bushes and called the police.

Floyd Johnson, the Benton County coroner, was called in, and the police gave him the skull in a plastic bucket. Late in the afternoon, Johnson called James Chatters, a forensic anthropologist and the owner of a local consulting firm called Applied Paleoscience. "Hey, buddy, I got a skull for you to look at," Johnson said. Chatters had often helped the police identify skeletons and distinguish between those of murder victims and those found in Indian burial sites. He is a small, determined, physically powerful man of forty-eight who used to be a gymnast and a wrestler. His work occasionally involves him in grisly or spectacular murders, where the victims

are difficult to identify, such as burnings and dismemberments.

"When I looked down at the skull," Chatters told me, "right off the bat I saw it had a very large number of Caucasoid features"—in particular, a long, narrow braincase, a narrow face, and a slightly projecting upper jaw. But when Chatters took it out of the bucket and laid it on his worktable he began to see some unusual traits. The crowns of the teeth were worn flat, a common characteristic of prehistoric Indian skulls, and the color of the bone indicated that it was fairly old. The skull sutures had fused, indicating that the individual was past middle age. And, for a prehistoric Indian of what was then an advanced age, he or she was in exceptional health; the skull had, for example, all its teeth and no cavities.

As dusk fell, Chatters and Johnson went out to the site to see if they could find the rest of the skeleton. There, working in the dying light, they found more bones, lying around on sand and mud in about two feet of water. The remains were remarkably complete: only the sternum, a few rib fragments, and

some tiny hand, wrist, and foot bones were missing. The bones had evidently fallen out of a bank during recent flooding of the Columbia River.

The following day, Chatters and Johnson spread the bones out in Chatters's laboratory. In forensic anthropology, the first order of business is to determine sex, age, and race. Determining race was particularly important, because if the skeleton turned out to be Native American it fell under a federal law called the Native American Graves Protection and Repatriation Act, or NAGPRA. Passed in 1990, NAGPRA requires the government—in this case, the Army Corps of Engineers, which controls the stretch of the Columbia River where the bones were found—to ascertain if human remains found on federal lands are Native American and, if they are, to "repatriate" them to the appropriate Indian tribe.

Chatters determined that the skeleton was male, Caucasoid, from an individual between forty and fifty-five years old, and about five feet nine inches tall—much taller than most prehistoric Native Americans in the Northwest. In physical anthropology, the term "Caucasoid" does not necessarily mean "white" or "European"; it is a descriptive term applied to certain biological features of a diverse category that includes, for example, some south-Asian groups as well as Europeans. (In contrast, the term "Caucasian" is a culturally defined racial category.) "I thought maybe we had an early pioneer or fur trapper," he said. As he was cleaning the pelvis, he noticed a gray object embedded in the bone, which had partly healed and fused around it. He took the bone to be X-rayed, but the object did not show up, meaning that it was not made of metal. So he requested a CAT scan. To his surprise, the scan revealed the object to be part of a willow-leaf-shaped spear point, which had been thrust into the bone and broken off. It strongly resembled a Cascade projectile point—an Archaic Indian style in wide use from around nine thousand to forty-five hundred years ago.

The Army Corps of Engineers asked Chatters to get a second opinion. He put the skeleton into his car and drove it a hundred miles to Ellensburg, Washington, where an anthropologist named Catherine J. Mac Millan ran a forensic consulting business called the Bone-Apart Agency. "He didn't say anything," Mac Millan told me. "I examined the bones, and I said 'Male, Caucasian.' He said 'Are you sure?' and I said 'Yeah.' And then he handed me the pelvis and showed me the ancient point embedded in it, and he said, 'What do you think now?' And I said, 'That's extremely interesting, but it still looks Caucasian to me.'" "In her report to the Benton County coroner's office she wrote that in her opinion the skeleton was "Caucasian male."

Toward the end of the week, Chatters told Floyd Johnson and the Army Corps of Engineers that he thought they needed to get a radiocarbon date on Kennewick Man. The two parties agreed, so Chatters sent the left fifth metacarpal bone—a tiny bone in the hand—to the University of California at Riverside.

On Friday, August 23rd, Jim Chatters received a telephone call from the radiocarbon lab. The bone was between ninety-three hundred and ninety-six hundred years old. He was astounded. "It was just a phone call," he said. "I thought, Maybe there's been a mistake.

I had to see the report with my own eyes." The report came on Monday, in the form of a fax. "I got very nervous then," Chatters said. He knew that, because of their age, the bones on his worktable had to be one of the most important archeological finds of the decade. "It was just a tremendous responsibility." The following Tuesday, the coroner's office issued a press release on the find, and it was reported in the Seattle Times, and other local papers.

Chatters called in a third physical anthropologist, Grover S. Krantz, a professor at Washington State University. Krantz looked at the bones on Friday, August 30th. His report noted some characteristics common to both Europeans and Plains Indians but concluded that "this skeleton cannot be racially or culturally associated with any existing American Indian group." He also wrote, "The Native Repatriation Act has no more applicability to this skeleton than it would if an early Chinese expedition had left one of its members there."

Fifteen minutes after Krantz finished looking at the bones, Chatters received a call from Johnson. Apologetically, the coroner said, "I'm going to have to come over and get the bones." The Army Corps of Engineers had demanded that all study of the bones cease, and had required him to put the skeleton in the county sheriff's evidence locker. On the basis of the carbon date, the Corps had evidently decided that the skeleton was Native American and that it fell under NAGPRA.

"When I heard this, I panicked," Chatters said. "I was the only one who'd recorded any information on it. There were all these things I should have done. I didn't even have photographs of the postcranial skeleton. I thought, Am I going to be the last scientist to see these bones?"

On September 9th, the Umatilla Indians, leading a coalition of five tribes and bands of the Columbia River basin, formally claimed the skeleton under NAGPRA, and the Corps quickly made a preliminary decision to "repatriate" it. The Umatilla Indian Reservation lies just over the border, in northeastern Oregon, and the other tribes live in Washington and Idaho; all consider the Kennewick area part of their traditional

territories. The Umatillas announced that they were going to bury the skeleton in a secret site, where it would never again be available to science.

Three weeks later, the New York Times picked up the story, and from there it went to Time and on around the world. Television crews from as far away as France and Korea descended on Kennewick. The Corps received more than a dozen other claims for the skeleton, including one from a group known as the Asatru Folk Assembly, the California-based followers of an Old Norse religion, who wanted the bones for their own religious purposes.

On September 2nd, the Corps had directed that the bones be placed in a secure vault at the Pacific Northwest National Laboratory, in Richland, Washington. Nobody outside of the Corps has seen them since. They are now at the center of a legal controversy that will likely determine the course of American archeology.

WHAT was a Caucasoid man doing in the New World more than ninety-three centuries ago? In the reams of press reports last fall, that question never seemed to be dealt with. I called up Douglas Owsley, who is the Division Head for Physical Anthropology at the National Museum of Natural History, Smithsonian Institution, in Washington, D.C., and an expert on Paleo-American remains. I asked him how many well-preserved skeletons that old had been found in North America.

He replied, "Including Kennewick, about seven."

Then I asked if any others had Caucasoid features, and there was a silence that gave me the sense that I was venturing onto controversial ground.

He guardedly replied, "Yes."

"How many?"

"Well," he said, "in varying degrees, all of them."

Kennewick Man's bones are part of a growing quantity of evidence that the earliest inhabitants of the New World may have been a Caucasoid people. Other, tentative evidence suggests that these people may have originally come from Europe. The new evidence is fragmentary, contradictory, and controversial. Critical research remains to be done, and many studies are still unpublished. At the least, the new evidence calls into question the standard Beringian Walk theory, which holds that the first human beings to reach the New World were Asians of Mongoloid stock, who crossed from Siberia to Alaska over a land bridge. The new evidence involves three basic questions. Who were the original Americans? Where did they come from? And what happened to them?

"You're dealing with such a black hole," Owsley told me. "It's hard to draw any firm conclusions from such a small sample of skeletons, and there is more than one group represented. That's why Kennewick is so important."

KENNEWICK MAN made his appearance at the dawn of a new age in physical anthropology. Scientists are now able to extract traces of organic material from a person's bone and perform a succession of powerful biochemical assays which can reveal an astonishing amount of information about the person. In March, for example, scientists at Oxford University announced that they had compared DNA extracted from the molar cavity of a nine-thousand-year-old skeleton known as Cheddar Man to DNA collected from fifteen pupils and five adults from old families in the village of Cheddar, in Somersetshire. They had established a blood tie between Cheddar Man and a schoolteacher who lived just half a mile from the cave where the bones were found.

In the few weeks that Kennewick Man was in the hands of scientists, they discovered a great deal about him. Isotopic-carbon studies of the bones indicate that he had a diet high in marine food—that he may have been a fisherman who ate a lot of salmon. He seems to have been a tall, good-looking man, slender and well proportioned. (Studies have shown that "handsomeness" is largely the result of symmetrical features and good health, both of which Kennewick Man had.) Archeological finds of similar age in the area suggest that he was part of a small band of people who moved about, hunting, fishing, and gathering wild plants. He may have

lived in a simple sewn tent or mat hut that could be disassembled and carried. Some nearby sites contain large numbers of fine bone needles, indicating that a lot of delicate sewing was going on: Kennewick Man may have worn tailored clothing. For a person at that time to live so long in relatively good health indicates that he was clever or lucky, or both, or had family and close friends around him.

He appears to have perished from recurring infections caused by the stone point in his hip. Because of the way his bones were found, and the layer of soil from which they presumably emerged, it may be that he was not deliberately buried but died near the river and was swept away and covered up in a flood. He may have perished alone on a fishing trip, far from his family.

Chatters made a cast of the skull before the skeleton was taken from his office. In the months since, he has been examining it to figure out how Kennewick Man may have looked. He plans to work with physical anthropologists and a forensic sculptor to make a facial reconstruction. "On the physical characteristics alone, he could fit on the streets of Stockholm without causing any kind of notice," Chatters told me. "Or on the streets of Jerusalem or New Delhi, for that matter. I've been looking around for someone who matches this Kennewick gentleman, looking for weeks and weeks at people on the street, thinking, This one's got a little bit here, that one a little bit there. And then, one evening, I turned on the TV, and there was Patrick Stewart"—Captain Picard, of "Star Trek"—"and I said, 'My God, there he is! Kennewick Man!'"

IN September, following the requirements of NAGPRA, the Corps advertised in a local paper its intention of repatriating the skeleton secreted in the laboratory vault. The law mandated a thirty-day waiting period after the advertisements before the Corps could give a skeleton to a tribe.

Physical anthropologists and archeologists around the country were horrified by the seizure of the skeleton. They protested that it was not possible to demonstrate a relationship between

nine-thousand-year-old remains and any modern tribe of the area. "Those tribes are relatively new," says Dennis Stanford, the chairman of the Department of Anthropology at the Smithsonian's National Museum of Natural History. "They pushed out other tribes that were there." Both Owsley and Richard L. Jantz, a biological anthropologist at the University of Tennessee, wrote letters to the Army Corps of Engineers in late September saying that the loss to science would be incalculable if Kennewick Man were to be reburied before being studied. They received no response. Robson Bonnichsen, the director of the Center for the Study of the First Americans, at Oregon State University, also wrote to the Corps and received no reply. Three representatives and a United States senator from the state of Washington got in touch with the Corps, pleading that it allow the skeleton to be studied before reburial, or, at least, refrain from repatriating the skeleton until Congress could take up the issue. The Corps rebuffed them.

The Umatillas themselves issued a statement, which was written by Armand Minthorn, a tribal religious leader. Minthorn, a small, well-spoken young man with long braids, is a member of a new generation of Native American activists, who see religious fundamentalism—in this case, the Washat religion—as a road back to Native American traditions and values:

> Our elders have taught us that once a body goes into the ground, it is meant to stay there until the end of time.... If this individual is truly over 9,000 years old, that only substantiates our belief that he is Native American. From our oral histories, we know that our people have been part of this land since the beginning of time. We do not believe that our people migrated here from another continent, as the scientists do.... Scientists believe that because the individual's head measurement does not match ours, he is not Native American. Our elders have told us that Indian people did not always look the way we look today. Some scientists say that if this individual is not studied further, we, as Indians, will be destroying evidence of our history. We already know our history. It is passed on to us through

our elders and through our religious practices.

Despite the mounting protests, the Corps refused to reconsider its decision to ban scientific study of the Kennewick skeleton. As the thirty-day waiting period came to a close, anthropologists around the country panicked. Just a week before it ended, on October 23rd, a group of eight anthropologists filed suit against the Corps. The plaintiffs included Douglas Owsley, Robson Bonnichsen, and also Dennis Stanford. Stanford, one of the country's top Paleo-Indian experts, is a formidable opponent. While attending graduate school in New Mexico, he roped in local rodeos, and helped support his family by leasing an alfalfa farm. There's still a kind of laconic, frontier toughness about him. "Kennewick Man has the potential to change the way we view the entire peopling of the Americas," he said to me. "We had to act. Otherwise, I might as well retire."

The eight are pursuing the suit as individuals. Their academic institutions are reluctant to get involved in a lawsuit as controversial as this, particularly at a time when most of them are negotiating with tribes over their own collections.

In the suit, the scientists have argued that Kennewick Man may not meet the NAGPRA definition of "Native American" as being "of, or relating to, a tribe, people, or culture that is indigenous to the United States." The judge trying the case has asked both sides to be prepared to define the word "indigenous" as it is used in NAGPRA. This will be an interesting exercise, since no human beings are indigenous to the New World: we are all immigrants.

The scientists have also argued that the Corps had had no evidence to support its claim that the skeleton had a connection to the Umatillas. Alan Schneider, the scientists' attorney, says, "Our analysis of NAGPRA is that first you have to make a determination if the human remains are Native American. And then you get to the question of cultural affiliation. The Army Corps assumed that anyone who died in the continental United States prior to a certain date is automatically Native American."

The NAGPRA law appears to support the scientists' point of view. It says that when there are no known lineal descendants "cultural affiliation" should be determined using "geographical, kinship, biological, archeological, anthropological, linguistic, folkloric, oral traditional, historical," or other "relevant information or expert opinion" before human remains are repatriated. In other words, human remains must often be studied before anyone can say whom they are related to.

The Corps, represented by the Justice Department, has refused to comment on most aspects of the case. "It's really as if the government didn't want to know the truth about Kennewick Man," Alan Schneider told me in late April. "It seems clear that the government will *never* allow this skeleton to be studied, for any reason, unless it is forced to by the courts."

Preliminary oral arguments in the case were heard on June 2nd in the United States District Court for the District of Oregon. The scientists asked for immediate access to study the bones, and the Corps asked for summary judgment. Judge John Jelderks denied both motions, and said that he would have a list of questions for the Corps that it is to answer within a reasonable time. With the likelihood of appeals, the case could last a couple of years longer, and could ultimately go to the Supreme Court.

Schneider was not surprised that the Corps had sided with the Indians. "It constantly has a variety of issues it has to negotiate with Native American tribes," he told me, and he specified, among others, land issues, water rights, dams, salmon fishing, hydroelectric projects, and toxic-waste dumps. The Corps apparently decided, Schneider speculated, that in this case its political interests would be better served by supporting the tribes than by supporting a disgruntled group of anthropologists with no institutional backing, no money, and no political power. There are large constituencies for the Indians' point of view: fundamentalist Christians and liberal supporters of Indian rights. Fundamentalists of all varieties tend to object to scientific research into the origins of humankind, because the results usually contradict their various creation myths. A novel coalition of conservative Chris-

tians and liberal activists was important in getting NAGPRA through Congress.

KENNEWICK MAN, early as he is, was not one of the first Americans. But he could be their descendant. There is evidence that those mysterious first Americans were a Caucasoid people. They may have come from Europe and may be connected to the Clovis people of America. Kennewick may provide evidence of a connection between the Old World and the New.

The Clovis mammoth hunters were the earliest widespread culture that we know of in the Americas. They appeared abruptly, seemingly out of nowhere, all over North and South America about eleven thousand five hundred years ago—two thousand years before Kennewick. (They were called Clovis after a town in New Mexico near an early site—a campground beside an ancient spring which is littered with projectile points, tools, and the remains of fires.) We have only a few fragments of human bone from the Clovis people and their immediate descendants, the Folsom, and these remains are so damaged that nothing can be learned from them at present.

The oldest bones that scientists have been able to study are the less than a dozen human remains that are contemporaneous with Kennewick. They date from between eight thousand and nearly eleven thousand years ago—the transition period between the Paleo-Indian and the Archaic Indian traditions. Most of the skeletons have been uncovered accidentally in recent years, primarily because of the building boom in the West. (Bones do not survive well in the East: the soil is too wet and acidic.) Some other ancient skeletons, though, have been discovered gathering dust in museum drawers. Among these oldest remains are the Spirit Cave mummy and Wizard's Beach Willie, both from Nevada; the Hourglass Cave and Gordon's Creek skeletons, from Colorado; the Buhl Burial, from Idaho; and remains from Texas, California, and Minnesota.

Douglas Owsley and Richard Jantz made a special study of several of these ancient remains. The best-preserved specimen they looked at was a partial mummy from Spirit Cave, Nevada, which is more than nine thousand years old. Owsley and Jantz compared the Spirit Cave skull with thirty-four population samples from around the world, including ten Native American groups. In an as yet unpublished letter to the Nevada State Museum, they concluded that the Spirit Cave skull was "very different" from any historic-period Native American groups. They wrote, "In terms of its closest classification, it does have a 'European' or 'Archaic Caucasoid' look, because morphometrically it is most similar to the Ainu from Japan and a Medieval period Norse population." Additional early skeletons that they and others have looked at also show Caucasoid-like traits that, in varying degrees, resemble Kennewick Man's. Among these early skeletons, there are no close resemblances to modern Native Americans.

But, even though the skeletons do look Caucasoid, other evidence indicates that the concept of "race" may not be applicable to human beings of ten or fifteen thousand years ago. Recent studies have discovered that all Eurasians may have looked Caucasoid-like in varying degrees. In addition, some researchers believe that the Caucasoid type first emerged in Western Asia or the Middle East, rather than in Europe. The racial differences we see today may be a late (and trivial) development in human evolution. If this is the case, then Kennewick may indeed be a direct ancestor of today's Native Americans—an idea that some preliminary DNA and dental studies seem to support.

BIOLOGY, however, isn't the whole story. There is some archeological evidence that the Clovis people of America—Kennewick Man's predecessors—came from Europe, which could account for his Caucasoid features. When the Clovis people appeared in the New World, they possessed an advanced stone and bone technology, and employed it in hunting big game. (It is no small feat to kill a mammoth or a mastodon with a hand-held spear or an atlatl.) If the Clovis people—or their precursors—had migrated to North America from Asia, one would expect to find early forms of their distinctive tools, of the right age, in Alaska or eastern Siberia. We don't. But we do find such artifacts in Europe and parts of Russia.

Bruce Bradley is the country's leading expert on Paleo-Indian flaked-stone technology. In 1970, as a recent college graduate, Bradley spent time in Europe studying paleolithic artifacts, including those of the Solutrean people, who lived in southwestern France and Spain between twenty thousand and sixteen thousand years ago. During his stay in Europe, Bradley learned how to flake out a decent Solutrean point. Then he came back to America and started studying stone tools made by the Clovis people. He noticed not only striking visual similarities between the Old World Solutrean and the New World Clovis artifacts, as many researchers had before, but also a strikingly similar use of flaking technology.

"The artifacts don't just look identical," Bradley told me. "They are *made* the same way." Both the European Solutrean and the American Clovis stone tools are fashioned using the same complex flaking techniques. He went on, "As far as I know, overshot flaking is unique to Solutrean and Clovis, and the only diving flaking that is more than eleven thousand years old is that of Solutrean and Clovis."

To argue his case, he drove from Cortez, Colorado, where he lives, to see me, in Santa Fe, bringing with him a trunkful of Solutrean artifacts, casts of Clovis bone and stone tools, and detailed illustrations of artifacts, along with a two-pound chunk of gray Texas flint and some flaking tools.

Silently, he laid a piece of felt on my desk and put on it a cast of a Clovis knife from Blackwater Draw, New Mexico. On top of that, he put a broken Solutrean knife from Laugerie-Haute, in France. They matched perfectly—in size, shape, thickness, and pattern of flaking. As we went through the collection, the similarities could be seen again and again. "It isn't just the flaking as you see it on the finished piece that is the same," Bradley explained. "Both cultures had a very specific way of preparing the edge before striking it to get a very specific type of flake. I call these deep technologies. These are not mere resemblances—they are deep, complex, abstract concepts applied to the stone."

I remarked that according to other archeologists I had talked to the resemblances were coincidental, the result of two cultures—one Old World, the other New World—confronting the same problems and solving them in the same way. "Maybe," Bradley said. "But a lot of older archeologists were not trained with technology in mind. They see convergence of form or look, but they don't see the technology that goes into it. I'm not saying this is the final answer. But there is so much similarity that we cannot say, 'This is just coincidence,' and ignore it."

To show me what he meant, he brought out the piece of gray flint, and we went into the back yard. "This isn't just knocking away at a stone," he said, hefting the piece of flint and examining it from various angles with narrowed eyes. "After the initial flaking of a spear point, there comes a stage where you have almost limitless choices on how to continue." He squatted down and began to work on the flint with hammer stones and antler billets, his hands deftly turning and shaping the material—knapping, chipping, scraping, pressing, flaking. The pile of razor-sharp flakes grew bigger, and the chunk of flint began to take on a definite shape. Over the next ninety minutes, Bradley reduced the nodule to a five-inch-long Clovis spear point.

It was a revelation to see that making a Clovis point was primarily an intellectual process. Sometimes ten minutes would pass while Bradley examined the stone and mapped out the next flaking sequence. "After thirty years of intense practice, I'm still at the level of a mediocre Clovis craftsman," he said, wiping his bloodied hands and reviving himself with a cup of cocoa. "This is as difficult and complex as a game of chess."

Those are not the only similarities between the Old World Solutrean and the New World Clovis cultures. As we went through Bradley's casts of Clovis artifacts, he compared them with pictures of similar Solutrean artifacts. The Clovis people, for example, produced enigmatic bone rods that were bevelled on both ends and crosshatched; so did the Solutrean. The Clovis people fashioned distinctive spear points out of mammoth ivory; so did the Solutrean. Clovis and Solutrean shaft wrenches (tools thought to have been used for straightening spears) look almost identical. At the same time, there are significant differences between the Clovis and the Solutrean tool kits; the Clovis people fluted their spear points, for instance, while the Solutrean did not.

"To get to the kind of complexity you find in Clovis tools, I see a long technological development," Bradley said. "It isn't one person in one place inventing something. But there is no evolution in Clovis technology. It just appears, full blown, all over the New World, around eleven thousand five hundred years ago. Where's the evolution? *Where did that advanced Clovis technology come from?*"

When I mentioned the idea of a possible Old World Solutrean origin for the New World Clovis to Lawrence Straus, a Solutrean expert at the University of New Mexico, he said, "There are two gigantic problems with it—thousands of years of separation and thousands of miles of ocean." Pointing out that the Solutrean technology itself appeared relatively abruptly in the South of France, he added, "I think this is a fairly clear case of mankind's ability to reinvent things."

But Bradley and other archeologists have pointed out that these objections may not be quite so insurmountable. Recently, in southern Virginia, archeologists discovered a layer of non-Clovis artifacts beneath a Clovis site. The layer dates from fifteen thousand years ago—much closer to the late Solutrean period, sixteen thousand five hundred years ago. Only a few rough tools have been found, but if more emerge they might provide evidence for the independent development of Clovis—or provide a link to the Solutrean. The as yet unnamed culture may be precisely the precursor to Clovis which archeologists have been looking for since the nineteen-thirties. The gap between Solutrean and Clovis may be narrowing.

The other problem is how the Solutrean people—if they are indeed the ancestors of the Clovis—might have reached America in the first place. Al-

though most of them lived along riverbanks and on the seacoast of France and Spain, there is no evidence that they had boats. No Paleo-Indian boats have been found on the American side, either, but there is circumstantial evidence that the Paleo-Indians used boats. The ancestors of the Australian aborigines got to Australia in boats from the Indonesian archipelago at least fifty thousand years ago.

But the Solutrean people may not have needed boats at all: sixteen thousand years ago, the North Atlantic was frozen from Norway to Newfoundland. Seasonal pack ice probably extended as far south as Britain and Nova Scotia. William Fitzhugh, the director of the Arctic Studies Center, at the Smithsonian, points out that if human beings had started in France, crossed the English Channel, then hopped along the archipelago from Scotland to the Faeroes to Iceland to Greenland to Newfoundland, and, finally, Nova Scotia, the biggest distance between landfalls would have been about five hundred miles, which Fitzhugh says could have been done on foot over ice. It would still have been a stupendous journey, but perhaps not much more difficult than the Beringian Walk, across thousands of miles of tundra, muskeg, snow, and ice.

"For a long time, most archeologists have been afraid to challenge the Beringian Walk paradigm," Bradley said. "I don't want to try to convince anybody. But I do want to shake the bushes. You could put all the archeological evidence for the Asian-Clovis connection in an envelope and mail it for thirty-two cents. The evidence for a European-Clovis connection you'd have to send in a U.P.S. box, at least."

Robson Bonnichsen, the director of the Center for the Study of the First Americans, at Oregon State University, is another archeologist whose research is challenging the established theories. "There is a presumption, written into almost every textbook on prehistory, that Paleo-Americans such as Clovis are the direct ancestors of today's Native Americans," he told me. "But now we have a very limited number of skeletons from that early time, and it's not clear that that's true. We're getting some hints from people working with genetic data

that these earliest populations might have some shared genetic characteristics with latter-day European populations. A lot more research is needed to sort all this out. Now, for the first time, we have the technology to do this research, especially in molecular biology. Which is why we *must* study Kennewick."

This summer, Bonnichsen hopes to go to France and recover human hair from Solutrean and other Upper Paleolithic sites. He will compare DNA from that hair with DNA taken from naturally shed Paleo-American hair recovered from the United States to see if there is a genetic link. Human hair can survive thousands of years in the ground, and, using new techniques, Bonnichsen and his research team have been finding hair in the places where people worked and camped.

BONNICHSEN and most other archeologists tend to favor the view that if the ancestors of Clovis once lived in Europe they came to America via Asia—the Beringian Walk theory with somewhat different people doing the walking. C. Vance Haynes, Jr., the country's top Paleo-Indian geochronologist, who is a professor of anthropology at the University of Arizona, and is a plaintiff in the lawsuit, said to me, "When I look at Clovis and ask myself where in the world the culture was derived from, I would say Europe." In an article on the origins of Clovis, Haynes noted that there were extraordinary resemblances between New World Clovis and groups that lived in Czechoslovakia and Ukraine twenty thousand years ago. He noted at least nine "common traits" shared by Clovis and certain Eastern European cultures: large blades, end scrapers, burins, shaft wrenches, cylindrical bone points, knapped bone, unifacial flake tools, red ochre, and circumferentially chopped mammoth tusks. He also pointed out that an eighteen-thousand-year-old burial site of two children near Lake Baikal, in Central Asia, exhibits remarkable similarities to what appears to be a Clovis burial site of two cremated children in Montana. The similarities extend beyond tools and points buried with the remains: red ochre, a kind of iron oxide, was placed in both graves. This suggests a migratory group carrying its technology from Europe across Asia. "If you want to speculate, I see a band moving eastward from Europe through Siberia, and meeting people there, and having cultural differences," Haynes said to me. "Any time there's conflict, it drives people, and maybe it just drove them right across the Bering land bridge. And exploration could have been as powerful a driving force thirteen thousand years ago as it was in 1492."

ONCE the Clovis people or their predecessors reached the New World, what happened to them? This is the second—and equally controversial—half of the theory: that the Clovis people or their immediate successors, the Folsom people, may have been supplanted by the ancestors of today's Native Americans. In this scenario, Kennewick Man may have been part of a remnant Caucasoid population related to Clovis and Folsom. Dennis Stanford, of the Smithsonian, said to me, "For a long time, I've held the theory that the Clovis and the Folsom were overwhelmed by a migration of Asians over the Bering land bridge. It may not just have been a genetic swamping or a pushing aside. The north Asians may have been carrying diseases that the Folsom and the Clovis had no resistance to"—just as European diseases wiped out a large percentage of the Native American population after the arrival of Columbus. Stanford explained that at several sites the Paleo-Indian tradition of Clovis and Folsom was abruptly replaced by Archaic Indian traditions, which had advanced but very different lithic technologies. The abruptness of the transition and the sharp change in technology, Stanford feels, suggest a rapid replacement of Folsom by the Archaic cultural complex, rather than an evolution from one into the other. The Archaic spear point embedded in Kennewick Man's hip could even be evidence of an ancient conflict: the Archaic Indian tradition was just beginning to appear in the Pacific Northwest at the time of Kennewick Man's death.

OWSLEY and other physical anthropologists who have studied the skulls of the earliest Americans say that the living population they most closely match is the mysterious Ainu, the aboriginal inhabitants of the Japanese islands. Called the Hairy People by the Japanese, the Ainu are considered by some researchers to be a Causasoid group who, before mixing with the Japanese, in the late nineteenth and twentieth centuries, had European faces, wavy hair, thick beards, and a European-type distribution of body hair. Early travellers reported that some also had blue eyes. Linguists have not been able to connect the Ainu language with any other on earth. The American Museum of Natural History, in New York, has a collection of nineteenth-century photographs of pure-blood Ainu, which I have examined: they stare from the glass plates like fierce, black-bearded Norwegians.

Historically, the Ainu have been the "Indians" of Japan. After the ancestors of the Japanese migrated from the mainland a couple of thousand years ago, they fought the Ainu and pushed them into the northernmost islands of the Japanese archipelago. The Japanese later discriminated against the Ainu, forcing their children to attend Japanese schools, and suppressing their religion and their language. Today, most Ainu have lost their language and many of their distinct physical characteristics, although there has recently been a movement among them to recapture their traditions, their religion, their language, and their songs. Like the American Indians, the Ainu suffer high rates of alcoholism. The final irony is that the Ainu, like the American Indians for Americans, have become a popular Japanese tourist attraction. Many Ainu now make a living doing traditional dances and selling handicrafts to Japanese tourists. The Japanese are as fascinated by the Ainu as we are by the Indians. The stories are mirror images of each other, with only the races changed.

If the Ainu are a remnant population of those people who crossed into America thirteen or more millennia ago, then they are right where one might expect to find them, in the extreme eastern part of Asia. Stanford says, "That racial type goes all the way to Europe, and I suspect that originally they were the same racial group at both ends. At that point in time, this racial diversification hadn't developed. They could have come into the New World from two directions at once, east and west."

THERE is a suspicion among anthropologists that some of the people behind the effort to rebury Kennewick and other ancient skeletons are afraid that the bones could show that the earliest Americans were Caucasoid. I asked Armand Minthorn about this. "We're not afraid of the truth," he said calmly. "We already know our truth. We're not telling the scientists what *their* truth is."

The Umatillas were infuriated by the research that Chatters did on the skeleton before it was seized by the Corps. "Scientists have dug up and studied Native Americans for decades," Minthorn wrote. "We view this practice as desecration of the body and a violation of our most deeply-held religious beliefs." Chatters told me that he had received "vitriolic" and "abusive" telephone calls from tribe members, accusing him of illegalities and racism. (The latter was an odd charge, since Chatters's wife is of Native American descent.) A client of his, he said, received an unsigned letter from one of the tribes, telling the client not to work with Chatters anymore. "They're going to ruin my livelihood," the forensic consultant said.

In a larger sense, the anger of the Umatillas and other Native American tribes is understandable, and even justified. If you look into the acquisition records of most large, old natural-history museums, you will see a history of unethical, and even grisly, collecting practices. Fresh graves were dug up and looted, sometimes in the dead of night. "It is most unpleasant to steal bones from a grave," the eminent anthropologist Franz Boas wrote in his diary just around the turn of the century, "but what is the use, someone has to do it." Indian skulls were bought and sold among collectors like arrowheads and pots. Skeletons were exhibited with no regard for

ANTHROPOLOGY

Anthropologists 1, Army Corps 0

American anthropologists won a round in an important legal battle last week, when a U.S. District Court in Portland, Oregon, ordered the Army Corps of Engineers to reopen the case of 9300-year-old human skeleton found on federal land in Washington state. The corps, which has jurisdiction over the skeleton—one of the oldest in the Americas—had planned to turn it over to American Indian tribes for reburial last October under the 1990 Native American Graves Protection and Repatriation Act (NAGPRA). But scientists sued to prevent the handover until they had studied the bones.

Now, although the court stopped short of allowing study of the skeleton, it opened the door for future research by recognizing that the scientists have a legitimate claim that must be considered. "It's a landmark ruling," exulted Alan Schneider, the Portland attorney for the scientists. "This is the first case where a court has held that a third party like a scientist has standing to challenge a government agency's overenforcement of NAGPRA."

The male skeleton, known as "Kennewick Man" for the town where it was discovered in the bank of the Columbia River last summer, is a rare representative of the earliest people to inhabit the Americas. It also had a projectile point embedded in its pelvis and facial features that may be Caucasoid-like, offering clues about early Americans (Science, 11 October 1996, p. 172).

As soon as the skeleton was discovered, Smithsonian Institution skeletal biologist Douglas Owsley sought permission to study it, and a team at the University of California, Davis, extracted ancient DNA from a bit of its finger bone for analysis. Owsley and others say that without scientific study it's impossible to know whether the skeleton has a biological or cultural tie to any living people—knowledge needed to determine which tribe, if any, should receive it.

But Owsley says he was told by the corps "flat-out that there would be no scientific study." The corps ordered a halt to the DNA work as soon as it learned of it in October, and announced that it would hand over the skeleton to the Confederated Tribes of the Umatilla Indian Reservation under the auspices of NAGPRA, which requires remains or cultural objects to be given to a culturally affiliated tribe. It later rescinded that order but has kept the skeleton locked away and unavailable for study. Court documents suggest that corps officials were concerned about alienating the Indians. In an 18 September 1996 e-mail message, a corps official wrote: "All risk to us seems to be associated with not repatriating the remains."

In the new decision, U.S. District Court Magistrate John Jelderks invalidated all the corps' orders in the case and criticized the "flawed" procedures used by the agency, which he said "acted before it had all the evidence or fully appreciated the scope of the problem." Jelderks also asked the corps to report back to him with its decision on the case and to answer several questions, including whether repatriation under NAGPRA required a biological or cultural link between bones and living tribes, and how such a link would be determined.

Corps attorney Daria Zane declined to comment for the record. As for the scientists, although they still can't study the skeleton, they're pleased. "Hopefully, the Army Corps will come to its senses," says Owsley. "They are using government lawyers and taxpayers' dollars to argue against academic freedom."

—Ann Gibbons

tribal sensitivities. During the Indian wars, warriors who had been killed on the battlefield were sometimes decapitated by Army doctors so that scientists back in the East could study their heads. The American Museum of Natural History "collected" six live Inuits in Greenland and brought them to New York to study; four of them died of respiratory diseases, whereupon the museum macerated their corpses and installed the bones in its collection. When I worked at the museum, in the nineteen-eighties, entire hallways were lined with glass cases containing Indian bones and mummified body parts—a small fraction of the museum's collection, which includes an estimated twenty thousand or more human remains, of all races. Before NAGPRA, the Smithsonian had some thirty-five thousand sets of human remains in storage; around eighteen thousand of them were Native American.

Now angry Native Americans, armed with NAGPRA and various state reburial laws, are emptying such museums of bones and grave goods. Although most anthropologists agree that burials identified with particular tribes should be returned, many have been horrified to discover that some tribes are trying to get everything—even skeletons and priceless funerary objects that are thousands of years old.

An amendment that was introduced in Congress last January would tighten NAGPRA further. The amended law could have the effect of hindering much archeology in the United States involving human remains, and add to the cost of construction projects that inadvertently uncover human bones. (Or perhaps the law would merely guarantee that such remains would be quietly destroyed.)

Native Americans have already claimed and reburied two of the earliest skeletons, the Buhl Burial and the Hourglass Cave skeleton, both of which apparently had some Caucasoid characteristics. The loss of the Buhl Burial was particularly significant to anthropologists, because it was more than ten thousand years old—a thousand years older than Kennewick Man—and had been found buried with its grave goods. The skeleton, of a woman between eighteen and twenty years old, received, in the opinion of some anthropologists, inadequate study before it was turned over to the Shoshone-Bannock tribe. The Northern

Paiute have asked that the Spirit Cave mummy be reburied. If these early skeletons are all put back in the ground, anthropologists say, much of the history of the peopling of the Americas will be lost.

WHEN Darwin proposed his theory of natural selection, it was seized upon and distorted by economists, social engineers, and politicians, particularly in England: they used it to justify all sorts of vicious social and economic policies. The scientific argument about the original peopling of the Americas threatens to be distorted in a similar way. Some tabloids and radio talk shows have referred to Kennewick as a "white man" and have suggested that his discovery changes everything with respect to the rights of Native Americans in this country. James

Chatters said to me, "There are some less racially enlightened folks in the neighborhood who are saying, 'Hey, our ancestors were here first, so we don't owe the Indians anything.' "

This is clearly racist nonsense: these new theories cannot erase or negate the existing history of genocide, broken treaties, and repression. But it does raise an interesting question: If the original inhabitants of the New World were Europeans who were pushed out by Indians, would it change the Indians' position in the great moral landscape?

"No," Stanford said in reply to this question. "Whose ancestors are the people who were pushed out? And who did the pushing? The answer is that we're all the descendants of those folks. If you go back far enough, eventually we all have a common ancestor—*we're all the*

same. When the story is finally written, the peopling of the Americas will turn out to be far more complicated than anyone imagined. There have been a lot of people who came here, at many different times. Some stayed and some left, some made it and some didn't, some got pushed out and some did the pushing. It's the history of humankind: the tough guy gets the ground."

Chatters put it another way. "We didn't go digging for this man. He fell out—he was actually a volunteer. I think it would be wrong to stick him back in the ground without waiting to hear the story he has to tell. We need to look at things as human beings, not as one race or another. The message this man brings to us is one of unification: there may be some commonality in our past that will bring us together."

Culture and Communication

Anthropologists are interested in all aspects of human behavior and how they interrelate with each other. Language is a form of such behavior (albeit primarily verbal behavior) and, therefore, worthy of study. It is patterned and passed down from one generation to the next through learning, not instinct. In keeping with the idea that language is integral to human social interaction, it has long been recognized that human communication through language is by its nature different from the kind of communication found among other animals. Central to this difference is the fact that humans communicate abstractly, with symbols that have meaning independent of the immediate sensory experiences of either the sender or receiver of messages. Thus, for instance, humans are able to refer to the future and the past instead of just the here and now.

Recent experiments have shown that anthropoid apes can be taught a small portion of Ameslan (American Sign Language). It must be remembered, however, that their very rudimentary ability has to be tapped by painstaking human effort, and that the degree of difference between apes and humans serves only to emphasize the peculiarly human need for and development of language.

Just as the abstract quality of symbols lifts our thoughts beyond immediate sense perception, it also inhibits our ability to think about and convey the full meaning of our personal experience. No categorical term can do justice to its referents—the variety of forms to which the term refers. The degree to which this is an obstacle to clarity of thought and communication relates to the degree of abstraction in the symbols involved. The word "chair," for instance, would not present much difficulty, since it has objective referents. However, consider the trouble we have in thinking and communicating with words whose referents are not tied to immediate sense perception—words such as "freedom," "democracy," and "justice." At best, the likely result is symbolic confusion: an inability to think or communicate in objectively definable symbols. At worst, language may be used to purposefully obfuscate, as William Lutz shows in "Language, Appearance, and Reality: Doublespeak in 1984."

A related issue has to do with the fact that languages differ as to what is relatively easy to express within the restrictions of their particular vocabularies. Thus, although a given language may not have enough words to cope with a new situation or a new field of activity, the typical solution is to invent words or to borrow them. In this way, it may be said that any language can be used to teach anything. This point is illustrated by Laura Bohannan's attempt to convey the "true" meaning of Shakespeare's *Hamlet* to the West African Tiv (see "Shakespeare in the Bush"). Much of her task was devoted to finding the most appropriate words in the Tiv language to convey her Western thoughts. At least part of her failure was due to the fact that some of the words are just not there, and her inventions were unacceptable to the Tiv.

In a somewhat different manner, as Deborah Tannen, in "Why Don't You Say What You Mean?" points out, there are subtleties to language that cannot be found in a dictionary and whose meaning can only be interpreted in the context of the social situation.

In "Teaching in the Postmodern Classroom," Conrad Phillip Kottak draws upon his classroom teaching experience to show how television—the most pervasive and invasive communication form in the modern world—is affecting mass culture.

Taken collectively, the articles in this unit show how symbolic confusion may occur between individuals or groups. In addition, they demonstrate the tremendous potential of recent research to enhance effective communication among all of us.

Looking Ahead: Challenge Questions

What common strategies are used throughout the world to overcome linguistic barriers?

How can language restrict our thought processes?

Under what circumstances may indirectness convey more security and power than directness?

In what ways is communication difficult in a cross-cultural situation?

In what ways has television affected the way we communicate and relate to others?

What kinds of messages are transmitted through non-verbal communication?

How has this section enhanced your ability to communicate more effectively?

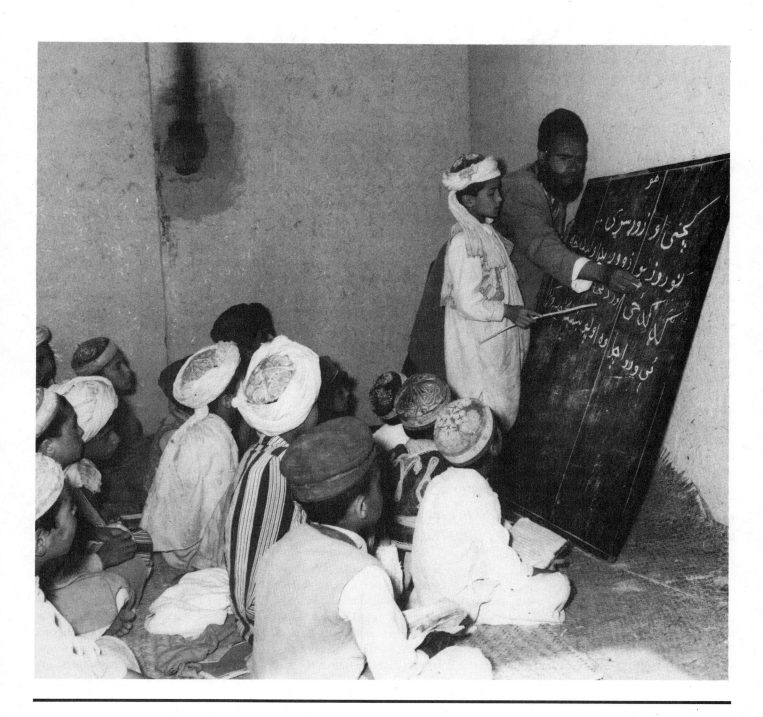

Language, Appearance, and Reality: Doublespeak in 1984

William D. Lutz

William D. Lutz, chair of the Department of English at Rutgers University, is also chair of the National Council of Teachers of English (NCTE) Committee on Public Doublespeak and editor of the Quarterly Review of Doublespeak.

There are at least four kinds of doublespeak. The first kind is the euphemism, a word or phrase that is designed to avoid a harsh or distasteful reality. When a euphemism is used out of sensitivity for the feelings of someone or out of concern for a social or cultural taboo, it is not doublespeak. For example, we express grief that someone has *passed away* because we do not want to say to a grieving person, "I'm sorry your father is dead." The euphemism *passed away* functions here not just to protect the feelings of another person but also to communicate our concern over that person's feelings during a period of mourning.

However, when a euphemism is used to mislead or deceive, it becomes doublespeak. For example, the U.S. State Department decided in 1984 that in its annual reports on the status of human rights in countries around the world it would no longer use the word *killing*. Instead, it used the phrase *unlawful or arbitrary deprivation of life*. Thus the State Department avoids discussing the embarrassing situation of the govern-

When a member of the group uses jargon to communicate with a person outside the group, and uses it knowing that the nonmember does not understand such language, then there is doublespeak.

ment-sanctioned killings in countries that are supported by the United States. This use of language constitutes doublespeak because it is designed to mislead, to cover up the unpleasant. Its real intent is at variance with its apparent intent. It is language designed to alter our perception of reality.

A second kind of doublespeak is jargon, the specialized language of a trade, profession, or similar group. It is the specialized language of doctors, lawyers, engineers, educators, or car mechanics. Jargon can serve an important and useful function. Within a group, jargon allows members of the group to communicate with each other clearly, efficiently, and quickly. Indeed, it is a mark of membership in the group to be able to use and understand the group's jargon. For example, lawyers speak of an *involuntary conversion* of property when discussing the loss or destruction of property through theft, accident, or condemnation When used by lawyers in a legal situation, such jargon is a legitimate use of language, since all members of the group can be expected to understand the term.

However, when a member of the group uses jargon to communicate with a person outside the group, and uses it knowing that the nonmember does not understand such language, then there is doublespeak. For example, a number of years ago a commercial airliner crashed on takeoff, killing three passengers, injuring twenty-one others, and destroying

From *Et Cetera (ETC)*, Winter 1987, pp. 383-391. Excerpted from *The Legacy of Language: A Tribute to Charlton Laird*, edited by Phillip C. Boardman. © 1987 by the University of Nevada Press. Reprinted by permission.

the airplane, a 727. The insured value of the airplane was greater than its book value, so the airline made a profit of three million dollars on the destroyed airplane. But the airline had two problems: it did not want to talk about one of its airplanes crashing and it had to account for the three million dollars when it issued its annual report to its stockholders. The airline solved these problems by inserting a footnote in its annual report explaining that this three million dollars was due to "the involuntary conversion of a 727." Note that airline officials could thus claim to have explained the crash of the airplane and the subsequent three million dollars in profit. However, since most stockholders in the company, and indeed most of the general public, are not familiar with legal jargon, the use of such jargon constitutes doublespeak.

A third kind of doublespeak is gobbledygook or bureaucratese. Basically, such doublespeak is simply a matter of piling on words, of overwhelming the audience with words, the bigger the better. For example, when Alan Greenspan was chairman of the President's Council of Economic Advisors, he made this statement when testifying before a Senate committee:

> It is a tricky problem to find the particular calibration in timing that would be appropriate to stem the acceleration in risk premiums created by falling incomes without prematurely aborting the decline in the inflation-generated risk premiums.

Did Alan Greenspan's audience really understand what he was saying? Did he believe his statement really explained anything? Perhaps there is some meaning beneath all those words, but it would take some time to search it out. This seems to be language that pretends to communicate but does not.

The fourth kind of doublespeak is inflated language. Inflated language designed to make the ordinary seem extraordinary, the common, uncommon; to make everyday things seem impressive; to give an air of importance to people, situations, or things that would not normally be considered important; to make the simple seem complex. With

this kind of language, car mechanics become *automotive internists,* elevator operators become members of the *vertical transportation corps,* used cars become not just *pre-owned* but *experienced cars.* When the Pentagon uses the phrase *preemptive counterattack* to mean that American forces attacked first, or when it uses the phrase *engage the enemy on all sides* to describe an ambush of American troops, or when it uses the phrase *tactical redeployment* to describe a retreat by American troops, it is using doublespeak. The electronics company that sells the television set with *nonmulticolor capability* is also using the doublespeak of inflated language.

Doublespeak is not a new use of language peculiar to the politics or economics of the twentieth century. Thucydides in *The Peloponnesian War* wrote that

> revolution thus ran its course from city to city.... Words had to change their ordinary meanings and to take those which were now given them. Reckless audacity came to be considered the courage of a loyal ally; prudent hesitation, specious cowardice; moderation was held to be a cloak for unmanliness; ability to see all sides of a question, inaptness to act on any. Frantic violence become the attribute of manliness; cautious plotting, a justifiable means of self-defense. The advocate of extreme measures was always trustworthy; his opponent, a man to be suspected.[1]

Caesar in his account of the Gallic Wars described his brutal conquest as "pacifying" Gaul. Doublespeak has a long history.

Military doublespeak seems always to have been with us. In 1947 the name of the War Department was changed to the more pleasing if misleading *Defense Department.* During the Vietnam War the American public learned that it was an *incursion,* not an invasion; a *protective reaction strike* or a *limited duration protective reaction strike* or *air support,* not bombing; and *incontinent ordinance,* not bombs and artillery shells, fell on civilians. This use of language continued with the invasion of Grenada, which was conducted not by the United States Army, Navy, or Air Force, but by the Caribbean Peace Keeping Forces.

Indeed, according to the Pentagon, it was not an invasion of Grenada, but a *predawn, vertical insertion.* And it wasn't that the armed forces lacked intelligence data on Grenada before the invasion, it was just that "we were not micromanaging Grenada intelligence-wise until about that time frame." In today's army forces, it's not a shovel but a *combat emplacement evacuator,* not a toothpick but a *wood interdental stimulator,* not a pencil but a *portable, hand-held communications inscriber,* not a bullet hole but a *ballistically induced aperture in the subcutaneous environment.*

Members of the military and politicians are not the only ones who use doublespeak. People in all parts of society use it. Take educators, for example. On some college campuses what was once the Department of Physical Education is now the *Department of Human Kinetics* or the *College of Applied Life Studies.* Home Economics is now the *School of Human Resources and Family Studies.* College campuses no longer have libraries but *learning resource centers.* Those are not desks in the classroom, they are *pupil stations.* Teachers—*classroom managers* who apply an *action plan* to a *knowledge base*—are concerned with the *basic fundamentals,* which are *inexorably linked to the education user's* (not student's) *time-on-task.* Students don't take tests; now it is *criterion referencing testing* which measures whether a student has achieved the *operational curricular objectives.* A school system in Pennsylvania uses the following grading system on report cards: "no effort, less than minimal effort, minimal effort, more than minimal effort, less than full effort, full effort, better than full effort, effort increasing, effort decreasing." Some college students in New York come from *economically nonaffluent* families, while the coach at a Southern university wasn't fired, "he just won't be asked to continue in that job." An article in a scholarly journal suggests teaching students three approaches to writing to help them become better writers: "concretization of goals, procedural facilitation, and modeling planning." An article on family relationships entitled "Familial Love and Intertemporal Optimality" observes that "an altruistic utility function promotes intertemporal efficiency. However, altruism creates an externality that implies that satisfying the condition for efficiency does not insure intertemporal optimality." A research report issued by the U.S. Office of Education contains this sentence: "In other words, feediness is the shared information between toputness, where toputness is at a time just prior to the inputness." Education contributes more than its share to current doublespeak.

The world of business has produced large amounts of doublespeak. If an airplane crash is one of the worst things that can happen to an airline company, a recall of automobiles because of a safety defect is one of the worst things that can happen to an automobile company. So a few years ago, when one of the three largest car companies in America had to recall two of its models to correct mechanical defects, the company sent a letter to all those who had bought those models. In its letter, the company said that the rear axle bearings of the cars "can deteriorate" and that "continued driving with a failed bearing could result in disengagement of the axle shaft and adversely affect vehicle control." This is the language of nonresponsibility. What are "mechanical deficiencies"—poor design, bad workmanship? If they do, what causes the deterioration? Note that "continued driving" is the subject of the sentence and suggests that it is not the company's poor manufacturing which is at fault but the driver who persists in driving. Note, too, "failed bearing," which implies that the bearing failed, not the company. Finally, "adversely affect vehicle control" means nothing more than that the driver could lose control of the car and get killed.

If we apply Hugh Rank's criteria for examining such language, we quickly discover the doublespeak here. What the car company should be saying to its customers is that the car the company sold them has a serious defect which should be corrected immediately—otherwise the customer runs the risk of being killed. But the reader of the letter must find this message beneath the doublespeak the company has used to disguise the harshness of its message. We will probably never know how many of the customers never brought their cars in for the necessary repairs because they did not think the problem serious enough to warrant the inconvenience involved.

When it comes time to fire employees, business has produced more than enough doublespeak to deal with the unpleasant situation. Employees are, of course, never fired. They are *selected out, placed out, non-retained, released, de-hired, non-renewed.* A corporation will *eliminate the redundancies in the human resources area,* assign *candidates for derecruitment* to a *mobility pool, revitalize the department* by placing executives on *special assignment, enhance the efficiency of operations, streamline the field sales organization,* or *further rationalize marketing efforts.* The reality behind all this doublespeak is that companies are firing employees, but no one wants the stockholders, public, or competition to know that times are tough and people have to go.

Recently the oil industry has been hard hit by declining sales and a surplus of oil. Because of *reduced demand for product,* which results in *spare refining capacity* and problems in *down-stream operations,* oil companies have been forced to *re-evaluate and consolidate their operations* and take *appropriate cost reduction actions,* in order to *enhance the efficiency of operations,* which has meant the *elimination of marginal outlets, accelerating the divestment program,* and the *disposition of low throughput marketing units.* What this doublespeak really means is that oil companies have fired employees, cut back on expenses, and closed gas stations and oil refineries because there's surplus of oil and people are not buying as much gas and oil as in the past.

One corporation faced with declining business sent a memorandum to its employees advising them that the company's "business plans are under revision and now reflect a more moderate approach toward our operating and capital programs." The result of this "more moderate approach" is a "surplus of professional/technical employees." To "assist in alleviating the surplus, selected professional and technical employees" have been "selected to participate" in a "Voluntary Program." Note that individuals were selected to "resign voluntarily." What this memorandum means, of course, is that expenses must be cut because of declining business, so employees will have to be fired.

It is rare to read that the stock market *fell.* Members of the financial community prefer to say that the stock market *retreated, eased, made a technical adjustment* or a *technical correction,* or perhaps that *prices were off due to profit taking,* or *off in light trading,* or *lost ground.* But the stock market never falls, not if stockbrokers have their say. As a side note, it is interesting to observe that the stock market never rises because of a *technical adjustment* or *correction,* nor does it ever *ease* upwards.

The business sections of newspapers, business magazines, corporate reports, and executive speeches are filled with words and phrases such as *marginal rates of substitution, equilibrium price,*

Most doublespeak is the product of clear thinking and is language carefully designed and constructed to appear to communicate when in fact it does not.

---

getting off margin, distribution coalition, non-performing assets, and *encompassing organizations.* Much of this is jargon or inflated language designed to make the simple seem complex, but there are other examples of business doublespeak that mislead, that are designed to avoid a harsh reality. What should we make of such expressions as *negative deficit* or *revenue excesses* for profit, *invest in* for buy, *price enhancement* or *price adjustment* for price increase, *shortfall* for a mistake in planning or *period of accelerated negative growth* or *negative economic growth* for recession?

Business doublespeak often attempts to give substance to wind, to make ordinary actions seem complex. Executives *operate* in *timeframes* within the *context* of which a *task force* will serve as the proper *conduit* for all the necessary *input* to *program a scenario* that, within acceptable *parameters,* and with the proper *throughput,* will *generate* the *maximum output* for a *print out* of *zero defect terminal objectives* that will *enhance the bottom line.*

There are instances, however, where doublespeak becomes more than amusing, more than a cause for a weary shake of the head. When the anesthetist turned the wrong knob during a Caesarean delivery and killed the mother and unborn child, the hospital called it a *therapeutic misadventure.* The Pentagon calls the neutron bomb "an efficient nuclear weapon that eliminates an enemy with a minimum degree of damage to friendly territory." The Pentagon also calls expected civilian casualties in a nuclear war *collateral damage.* And it was the Central Intelligence Agency which during the Vietnam War created the phrase *eliminate with extreme prejudice* to replace the more direct verb *kill.*

Identifying doublespeak can at times be difficult. For example, on July 27, 1981, President Ronald Reagan said in a speech televised to the American public: "I will not stand by and see those of you who are dependent on Social Security deprived of the benefits you've worked so hard to earn. You will continue to receive your checks in the full amount due you." This speech had been billed as President Reagan's position on Social Security, a subject of much debate at the time. After the speech, public opinion polls revealed that the great majority of the public believed that President Reagan had affirmed his support for Social Security and that he would not support cuts in benefits. However, five days after the speech, on July 31, 1981, an article in the *Philadelphia Inquirer* quoted White House spokesman David Gergen as saying that President Reagan's words had been "carefully chosen." What President Reagan did mean, according to Gergen, was that he was reserving the right to decide who was "dependent" on those benefits, who had "earned" them, and who, therefore, was "due" them.[2]

The subsequent remarks of David Gergen reveal the real intent of President Reagan as opposed to his apparent intent. Thus Hugh Rank's criteria for analyzing language to determine whether it is doublespeak, when applied in light of David Gergen's remarks, reveal the doublespeak of President Reagan. Here indeed is the insincerity of which Orwell wrote. Here, too, is the gap between the speaker's real and declared aim.

In 1982 the Republican National Committee sponsored a television advertisement which pictured an elderly, folksy postman delivering Social Security checks "with the 7.4% cost-of-living raise that President Reagan promised."

Doublespeak is insidious because it can infect and ultimately destroy the function of language, which is communication between people and social groups.

The postman then added that "he promised that raise and he kept his promise, in spite of those sticks-in-the-mud who tried to keep him from doing what we elected him to do." The commercial was, in fact, deliberately misleading. The cost-of-living increases had been provided automatically by law since 1975, and President Reagan tried three times to roll them back or delay them but was overruled by congressional opposition. When these discrepancies were pointed out to an official of the Republican National Committee, he called the commercial "inoffensive" and added, "Since when is a commercial supposed to be accurate? Do women really smile when they clean their ovens?"

Again, applying Hugh Rank's criteria to this advertisement reveals the doublespeak in it once we know the facts of past actions by President Reagan. Moreover, the official for the Republican National Committee assumes that all advertisements, whether for political candidates or commercial products, are lies, or in his doublespeak term, *inaccurate.* Thus, the real intent of the advertisement was to mislead while the apparent purpose was to inform the public of President Reagan's position on possible cuts in Social Security benefits. Again their is insincerity, and again there is a gap between the speaker's real and declared aims.

In 1981 Secretary of State Alexander Haig testified before congressional committees about the murder of three American nuns and a Catholic lay worker in El Salvador. The four women had been raped and shot at close range, and there was clear evidence that the crime had been committed by soldiers of the Salvadoran government. Before the House Foreign Affairs Committee, Secretary Haig said,

> I'd like to suggest to you that some of the investigations would lead one to believe that perhaps the vehicle the nuns were riding in may have tried to run a roadblock, or may accidentally have been perceived to have been doing so, and there'd been an exchange of fire and then perhaps those who inflicted the casualties sought to cover it up. And this could have been at a very low level of both competence and motivation in the context of the issue itself. But the facts on this are not clear enough for anyone to draw a definitive conclusion.

The next day, before the Senate Foreign Relations Committee, Secretary Haig claimed that press reports on his previous testimony were inaccurate. When Senator Claiborne Pell asked whether Secretary Haig was suggesting the possibility that "the nuns may have run through a roadblock." Secretary Haig replied, "You mean that they tried to violate . . . ? Not at all, no, not at all. My heavens! The dear nuns who raised me in my parochial schooling would forever isolate me from their affections and respect." When Senator Pell asked Secretary Haig, "Did you mean that the nuns were firing at the people, or what did 'exchange of fire' mean?" Secretary Haig replied, "I haven't met any pistol-packing nuns in my day, Senator. What I meant was that if one fellow starts shooting, then the next thing you know they all panic." Thus did the secretary of state of the United States explain official government policy on the murder of four American citizens in a foreign land.

Secretary Haig's testimony implies that the women were in some way responsible for their own fate. By using such vague wording as "would lead one to believe" and "may accidentally have been perceived to have been," he avoids any direct assertion. The use of "inflicted the casualties" not only avoids using the word *kill* but also implies that at the worst the killings were accidental or justifiable. The result of this testimony is that the secretary of state has become an apologist for murder. This is indeed language in defense of the indefensible; language designed to make lies sound truthful and murder respectable; language designed to give an appearance of solidity to pure wind.

These last three examples of doublespeak should make it clear that doublespeak is not the product of careless language or sloppy thinking. Indeed, most doublespeak is the product of clear thinking and is language carefully designed and constructed to appear to communicate when in fact it does not. It is language designed not to lead but to mislead. It is language designed to distort reality and corrupt the mind. It is not a tax increase but *revenue enhancement* or *tax base broadening,* so how can you complain about higher taxes? It is not acid rain, but *poorly buffered precipitation,* so don't worry about all those dead trees. That is not the Mafia in Atlantic City, New Jersey, those are *members of a career offender cartel,* so don't worry about the influence of organized crime in the city. The judge was not addicted to the pain-killing drug he was taking, it was just that the drug had "established an interrelationship with the body, such that if the drug is removed precipitously, there is a reaction," so don't worry that his decisions might have been influenced by his drug addiction. It's not a Titan II nuclear-armed, intercontinental ballistic missile with a warhead 630 times more powerful than the atomic bomb dropped on Hiroshima, it is just a *very large, potentially disruptive re-entry system,* so don't worry about the threat of nuclear destruction. It is not a neutron bomb but a *radiation enhancement device,* so

don't worry about escalating the arms race. It is not an invasion but a *rescue mission,* or a *predawn vertical insertion,* so don't worry about any violations of United States or international law.

Doublespeak has become so common in our everyday lives that we fail to notice it. We do not protest when we are asked to check our packages at the desk "for our convenience" when it is not for our convenience at all but for someone else's convenience. We see advertisements for *genuine imitation leather, virgin vinyl,* or *real counterfeit diamonds* and do not question the language or the supposed quality of the product. We do not speak of slums or ghettos but of the *inner city* or *substandard housing where the disadvantaged* live and thus avoid

---

Only by teaching respect for and love of language can teachers of English instill in students the sense of outrage they should experience when they encounter doublespeak.

---

talking about the poor who have to live in filthy, poorly heated, ramshackle apartments or houses. Patients do not die in the hospital; it is just *negative patient care outcome.*

Doublespeak which calls cab drivers *urban transportation specialists,* elevator operators *members of the vertical transportation corps,* and automobile mechanics *automotive internists* can be considered humorous and relatively harmless. However, doublespeak which calls a fire in a nuclear reactor building *rapid oxidation,* an explosion in a nuclear power plant an *energetic disassembly,* the illegal overthrow of a legitimate administration *destabilizing a government,* and lies *inoperative statements* is language which attempts to avoid responsibility, which attempts to make the bad seem good, the negative appear positive, something unpleasant appear attractive, and which seems to com-

municate but does not. It is language designed to alter our perception of reality and corrupt our minds. Such language does not provide us with the tools needed to develop and preserve civilization. Such language breeds suspicion, cynicism, distrust, and, ultimately, hostility.

Doublespeak is insidious because it can infect and ultimately destroy the function of language, which is communication between people and social groups. If this corrupting process does occur, it can have serious consequences in a country that depends upon an informed electorate to make decisions in selecting candidates for office and deciding issues of public policy. After a while we may really believe that politicians don't lie but only *misspeak,* that illegal acts are merely *inappropriate actions,* that fraud and criminal conspiracy are just *miscertification.* And if we really believe that we understand such language, then the world of *Nineteen Eighty-four* with its control of reality through language is not far away.

The consistent use of doublespeak can have serious and far-reaching consequences beyond the obvious ones. The pervasive use of doublespeak can spread so that doublespeak becomes the coin of the political realm with speakers and listeners convinced that they really understand such language. President Jimmy Carter could call the aborted raid to free the hostages in Tehran in 1980 an "incomplete success" and really believe that he had made a statement that clearly communicated with the American public. So, too, President Ronald Reagan could say in 1985 that "ultimately our security and our hopes for success at the arms reduction talks hinge on the determination that we show here to continue our program to rebuild and refortify our defenses" and really believe that greatly increasing the amount of money spent building new weapons will lead to a reduction in the number of weapons in the world.

The task of English teachers is to teach not just the effective use of language but respect for language as well. Those who use language to conceal or prevent or corrupt thought must be called to account. Only by teaching respect for and love of language can teachers of English instill in students the sense of outrage they should experience when they encounter doublespeak. But before students can experience that outrage, they must first learn to use language effectively, to understand its beauty and power. Only then will we begin to make headway in the fight against doublespeak, for only by using language well will we come to appreciate the perversion inherent in doublespeak.

In his book *The Miracle of Language,* Charlton Laird notes that

language is ... the most important tool man ever devised. ... Language is [man's] basic tool. It is the tool more than any other with which he makes his living, makes his home, makes his life. As man becomes more and more a social being, as the world becomes more and more a social community, communication grows ever more imperative. And language is the basis of communication. Language is also the instrument with which we think, and thinking is the rarest and most needed commodity in the world.[3]

In this opinion Laird echoes Orwell's comment that "if thought corrupts language, language can also corrupt thought."[4] Both men have given us a legacy of respect for language, a respect that should prompt us to cry "Enough!" when we encounter doublespeak. The greatest honor we can do Charlton Laird is to continue to have the greatest respect of language in all its manifestations, for, as Laird taught us, language is a miracle.

Notes and References

1. Thucydides, *The Peloponnesian Way,* 3.82.
2. David Hess, "Reagan's Language on Benefits Confused, Angered Many," *Philadelphia Inquirer,* July 31, 1981, p. 6-A.
3. Charlton Laird, *The Miracle of Language* (New York: Fawcett, Premier Books, 1953), p. 224.
4. Orwell, *The Collected Essays,* 4:137.

Why Don't You Say What You Mean?

Directness is not necessarily logical or effective. Indirectness is not necessarily manipulative or insecure.

Deborah Tannen

Deborah Tannen is University Professor of Linguistics at Georgetown University.

A university president was expecting a visit from a member of the board of trustees. When her secretary buzzed to tell her that the board member had arrived, she left her office and entered the reception area to greet him. Before ushering him into her office, she handed her secretary a sheet of paper and said: "I've just finished drafting this letter. Do you think you could type it right away? I'd like to get it out before lunch. And would you please do me a favor and hold all calls while I'm meeting with Mr. Smith?"

When they sat down behind the closed door of her office, Mr. Smith began by telling her that he thought she had spoken inappropriately to her secretary. "Don't forget," he said. *"You're* the president!"

Putting aside the question of the appropriateness of his admonishing the president on her way of speaking, it is revealing—and representative of many Americans' assumptions—that the indirect way in which the university president told her secretary what to do struck him as self-deprecating. He took it as evidence that she didn't think she had the right to make demands of her sec-

retary. He probably thought he was giving her a needed pep talk, bolstering her self-confidence.

I challenge the assumption that talking in an indirect way necessarily reveals powerlessness, lack of self-confidence or anything else about the character of the speaker. Indirectness is a fundamental element in human communication. It is also one of the elements that varies most from one culture to another, and one that can cause confusion and misunderstanding when speakers have different habits with regard to using it. I also want to dispel the assumption that American women tend to be more indirect than American men. Women and men are both indirect, but in addition to differences associated with their backgrounds—regional, ethnic and class—they tend to be indirect in different situations and in different ways.

At work, we need to get others to do things, and we all have different ways of accomplishing this. Any individual's ways will vary depending on who is being addressed—a boss, a peer or a subordinate. At one extreme are bald commands. At the other are requests so indirect that they don't sound like requests at all, but are just a statement of need or a description of a situation. People with direct styles of asking others to do things perceive indirect requests—if

they perceive them as requests at all—as manipulative. But this is often just a way of blaming others for our discomfort with their styles.

The indirect style is no more manipulative than making a telephone call, asking "Is Rachel there?" and expecting whoever answers the phone to put Rachel on. Only a child is likely to answer "Yes" and continue holding the phone—not out of orneriness but because of inexperience with the conventional meaning of the questions. (A mischievous adult might do it to tease.) Those who feel that indirect orders are illogical or manipulative do not recognize the conventional nature of indirect requests.

Issuing orders indirectly can be the prerogative of those in power. Imagine, for example, a master who says "It's cold in here" and expects a servant to make a move to close a window, while a servant who says the same thing is not likely to see his employer rise to correct the situation and make him more comfortable. Indeed, a Frenchman raised in Brittany tells me that his family never gave bald commands to their servants but always communicated orders in indirect and highly polite ways. This pattern renders less surprising the finding of David Bellinger and Jean Berko Gleason that fathers' speech to their

From *The New York Times Magazine*, August 28, 1994, pp. 46–49. Adapted from *Talking 9 to 5: How Women's and Men's Conversational Styles Affect Who Gets Heard, Who Gets Credit, and What Gets Done at Work* by Deborah Tannen, Ph.D. © 1994 by Deborah Tannen, Ph.D. Reprinted by permission of William Morrow & Company, Inc.

young children had a higher incidence than mothers' of both direct imperatives like "Turn the bolt with the wrench" *and* indirect orders like "The wheel is going to fall off."

The use of indirectness can hardly be understood without the cross-cultural perspective. Many Americans find it self-evident that directness is logical and aligned with power while indirectness is akin to dishonesty and reflects subservience. But for speakers raised in most of the world's cultures, varieties of indirectness are the norm in communication. This is the pattern found by a Japanese sociolinguist, Kunihiko Harada, in his analysis of a conversation he recorded between a Japanese boss and a subordinate.

The markers of superior status were clear. One speaker was a Japanese man in his late 40's who managed the local branch of a Japanese private school in the United States. His conversational partner was Japanese-American woman in her early 20's who worked at the school. By virtue of his job, his age and his native fluency in the language being taught, the man was in the superior position. Yet when he addressed the woman, he frequently used polite language and almost always used indirectness. For example, he had tried and failed to find a photography store that would make a black-and-white print from a color negative for a brochure they were producing. He let her know that he wanted her to take over the task by stating the situation and allowed her to volunteer to do it: (This is a translation of the Japanese conversation.)

On this matter, that, that, on the leaflet? This photo, I'm thinking of changing it to black-and-white and making it clearer. . . . I went to a photo shop and asked them. They said they didn't do black-and-white. I asked if they knew any place that did. They said they didn't know. They weren't very helpful, but anyway, a place must be found, the negative brought to it, the picture developed.

Harada observes, "Given the fact that there are some duties to be performed and that there are two parties present,

the subordinate is supposed to assume that those are his or her obligation." It was precisely because of his higher status that the boss was free to choose whether to speak formally or informally, to assert his power or to play it down and build rapport—an option not available to the subordinate, who would have seemed cheeky if she had chosen a style that enhanced friendliness and closeness.

The same pattern was found by a Chinese sociolinguist, Yuling Pan, in a meeting of officials involved in a neighborhood youth program. All spoke in ways that reflected their place in the hierarchy. A subordinate addressing a superior always spoke in a deferential way, but a superior addressing a subordinate could either be authoritarian, demonstrating his power, or friendly, establishing rapport. The ones in power had the option of choosing which style to use. In this spirit, I have been told by people who prefer their bosses to give orders indirectly that those who issue bald commands must be pretty insecure; otherwise why would they have to bolster their egos by throwing their weight around?

I am not inclined to accept that those who give orders directly are really insecure and powerless, any more than I want to accept that judgment of those who give indirect orders. The conclusion to be drawn is that ways of talking should not be taken as obvious evidence of inner psychological states like insecurity or lack of confidence. Considering the many influences on conversational style, individuals have a wide range of ways of getting things done and expressing their emotional states. Personality characteristics like insecurity cannot be linked to ways of speaking in an automatic, self-evident way.

Those who expect orders to be given indirectly are offended when they come unadorned. One woman said that when her boss gives her instructions, she feels she should click her heels, salute, and say "Yes, Boss!" His directions strike her as so imperious as to border on the militaristic. Yet I received a letter from a man telling me that indirect orders were a fundamental part of his military training: He wrote:

Many years ago, when I was in the Navy, I was training to be a radio technician. One class I was in was taught by a chief radioman, a regular Navy man who had been to sea, and who was then in his third hitch. The students, about 20 of us, were fresh out of boot camp, with no sea duty and little knowledge of real Navy life. One day in class the chief said it was hot in the room. The student didn't react, except to nod in agreement. The chief repeated himself: "It's hot in this room." Again there was no reaction from the students.

Then the chief explained. He wasn't looking for agreement or discussion from us. When he said that the room was hot, he expected us to do something about it—like opening the window. He tried it one more time, and this time all of us left our workbenches and headed for the windows. We had learned. And we had many opportunities to apply what we had learned.

This letter especially intrigued me because "It's cold in here" is the standard sentence used by linguists to illustrate an indirect way of getting someone to do something—as I used it earlier. In this example, it is the very obviousness and rigidity of the military hierarchy that makes the statement of a problem sufficient to trigger corrective action on the part of subordinates.

A man who had worked at the Pentagon reinforced the view that the burden of interpretation is on subordinates in the military—and he noticed the difference when he moved to a position in the private sector. He was frustrated when he'd say to his new secretary, for example, "Do we have a list of invitees?" and be told, "I don't know; we probably do" rather than "I'll get it for you." Indeed, he explained, at the Pentagon, such a question would likely be heard as a reproach that the list was not already on his desk.

The suggestion that indirectness is associated with the military must come as a surprise to many. But everyone is indirect, meaning more than is put into words and deriving meaning from words that are never actually said. It's a matter of where, when and how we each tend to be indirect and look for hidden meanings. But indirectness has a built-in liability. There is a risk that the other will either miss or choose to ignore your meaning.

On Jan. 13, 1982, a freezing cold, snowy day in Washington, Air Florida Flight 90 took off from National Airport, but could not get the lift it needed to keep climbing. It crashed into a bridge linking Washington to the state of Virginia and plunged into the Potomac. Of the 79 people on board all but 5 perished, many floundering and drowning in the icy

---

The co-pilot repeatedly called attention to dangerous conditions, but the captain didn't get the message.

---

water while horror-stricken by-standers watched helplessly from the river's edge and millions more watched, aghast, on their television screens. Experts later concluded that the plane had waited too long after de-icing to take off. Fresh buildup of ice on the wings and engine brought the plane down. How could the pilot and co-pilot have made such a blunder? Didn't at least one of them realize it was dangerous to take off under these conditions?

Charlotte Linde, a linguist at the Institute for Research on Learning in Palo Alto, Calif., has studied the "black box" recordings of cockpit conversations that preceded crashes as well as tape recordings of conversations that took place among crews during flight simulations in which problems were presented. Among the black box conversations she studied was the one between the pilot and co-pilot just before the Air Florida crash. The pilot, it turned out, had little experience flying in icy weather. The co-pilot had a bit more, and it became heartbreakingly clear on analysis that he

had tried to warn the pilot, but he did so indirectly.

The co-pilot repeatedly called attention to the bad weather and to ice building up on other planes:

Co-pilot: Look how the ice is just hanging on his, ah, back, back there, see that? . . .
Co-pilot: See all those icicles on the back there and everything?
Captain: Yeah.

He expressed concern early on about the long waiting time between de-icing:

Co-pilot: Boy, this is a, this is a losing battle here on trying to de-ice those things, it [gives] you a false feeling of security, that's all that does.

Shortly after they were given clearance to take off, he again expressed concern:

Co-pilot: Let's check these tops again since we been setting here awhile.
Captain: I think we get to go here in a minute.

When they were about to take off, the co-pilot called attention to the engine instrument readings, which were not normal:

Co-pilot: That don't seem right, does it? [three-second pause] Ah, that's not right. . . .
Captain: Yes, it is, there's 80.
Co-pilot: Naw, I don't think that's right. [seven-second pause] Ah, maybe it is.
Captain: Hundred and twenty.
Co-pilot: I don't know.

The takeoff proceeded, and 37 seconds later the pilot and co-pilot exchanged their last words.

The co-pilot had repeatedly called the pilot's attention to dangerous conditions but did not directly suggest they abort the takeoff. In Linde's judgment, he was expressing his concern indirectly, and the captain didn't pick up on it—with tragic results.

That the co-pilot was trying to warn the captain indirectly is supported by evidence from another airline accident— a relatively minor one—investigated by

Linde that also involved the unsuccessful use of indirectness.

On July 9, 1978, Allegheny Airlines Flight 453 was landing at Monroe County Airport in Rochester, when it overran the runway by 728 feet. Everyone survived. This meant that the captain and co-pilot could be interviewed. It turned out that the plane had been flying too fast for a safe landing. The captain should have realized this and flown around a second time, decreasing his speed before trying to land. The captain said he simply had not been aware that he was going too fast. But the co-pilot told interviewers that he "tried to warn the captain in subtle ways, like mentioning the possibility of a tail wind and the slowness of flap extension." His exact words were recorded in the black box. The cross-hatches indicate words deleted by the National Transportation Safety Board and were probably expletives:

Co-pilot: Yeah, it looks like you got a tail wind here.
Yeah.
[?]: Yeah [it] moves awfully # slow.
Co-pilot: Yeah the # flaps are slower than a #.
Captain: We'll make it, gonna have to add power.
Co-pilot: I know.

The co-pilot thought the captain would understand that if there was a tail wind, it would result in the plane going too fast, and if the flaps were slow, they would be inadequate to break the speed sufficiently for a safe landing. He thought the captain would then correct for the error by not trying to land. But the captain said he didn't interpret the co-pilot's remarks to mean they were going too fast.

Linde believes it is not a coincidence that the people being indirect in these conversations were the co-pilots. In her analyses of flight-crew conversations she found it was typical for the speech of subordinates to be more mitigated—polite, tentative or indirect. She also found that topics broached in a mitigated way were more likely to fail, and that captains were more likely to ignore hints from their crew members than the other way around. These findings are evidence that not only can indirectness and other forms of mitigation be misunderstood, but they are also easier to ignore.

In the Air Florida case, it is doubtful that the captain did not realize what the co-pilot was suggesting when he said, "Let's check these tops again since we been setting here awhile" (though it seems safe to assume he did not realize the gravity of the co-pilot's concern). But the indirectness of the co-pilot's phrasing certainly made it easier for the pilot to ignore it. In this sense, the captain's response, "I think we get to go here in a minute," was an indirect way of saying, "I'd rather not." In view of these patterns, the flight crews of some airlines are now given training to express their concerns, even to superiors, in more direct ways.

The conclusion that people should learn to express themselves more directly has a ring of truth to it—especially for Americans. But direct communication is not necessarily always preferable. If more direct expression is better communication, then the most direct-speaking crews should be the best ones. Linde was surprised to find in her research that crews that used the most mitigated speech were often judged the best crews. As part of the study of talk among cockpit crews in flight simulations, the trainers observed and rated the performances of the simulation crews. The crews they rated top in performance had a higher rate of mitigation than crews they judged to be poor.

This finding seems at odds with the role played by indirectness in the examples of crashes that we just saw. Linde concluded that since every utterance functions on two levels—the referential (what is says) and the relational (what it implies about the speaker's relationships), crews that attend to the relational level will be better crews. A similar explanation was suggested by Kunihiko Harada. He believes that the secret of successful communication lies not in teaching subordinates to be more direct, but in teaching higher-ups to be more sensitive to indirect meaning. In other words, the crashes resulted not only because the co-pilots tried to alert the captains to danger indirectly but also because the captains were not attuned to the co-pilots' hints. What made for successful performance among the best crews might have been the ability—or willingness—of listeners to pick up on hints, just as members of families or longstanding couples come to understand each other's meaning without anyone being particularly explicit.

It is not surprising that a Japanese sociolinguist came up with this explanation; what he described is the Japanese system, by which good communication is believed to take place when meaning is gleaned without being stated directly—or at all.

While Americans believe that "the squeaky wheel gets the grease" (so it's best to speak up), the Japanese say, "The nail that sticks out gets hammered back in" (so it's best to remain silent if you don't want to be hit on the head). Many Japanese scholars writing in English have tried to explain to bewildered Americans the ethics of a culture in which silence is often given greater value than speech, and ideas are believed to be best communicated without being explicitly stated. Key concepts in Japanese give a flavor of the attitudes toward language that they reveal—and set in relief the strategies that Americans encounter at work when talking to other Americans.

Takie Sugiyama Lebra, a Japanese-born anthropologist, explains that one of the most basic values in Japanese culture is *omoiyari*, which she translates as "empathy." Because of *omoiyari*, it should not be necessary to state one's meaning explicitly; people should be able to sense each other's meaning intuitively. Lebra explains that it is typical for a Japanese speaker to let sentences trail off rather than complete them because expressing ideas before knowing how they will be received seems intrusive. "Only an insensitive, uncouth person needs a direct, verbal, complete message," Lebra says.

Sasshi, the anticipation of another's message through insightful guesswork, is considered an indication of maturity.

Considering the value placed on direct communication by Americans in general, and especially by American business people, it is easy to imagine that many American readers may scoff at such conversational habits. But the success of Japanese businesses makes it impossible to continue to maintain that there is anything inherently inefficient about such conversational conventions. With indirectness, as with all aspects of conversational style, our own habitual style seems to make sense—seems polite, right and good. The light cast by the habits and assumptions of another culture can help us see our way to the flexibility and respect for other styles that is the only best way of speaking.

Teaching in the Postmodern Classroom

Conrad Phillip Kottak

New culture patterns related to television's penetration of the American home have emerged since the 1950s. As technology, television affects collective behavior, as people duplicate, in many areas of their lives, habits developed while watching TV. Television content also influences mass culture because it provides widely shared common knowledge, beliefs, and expectations. (Conrad Kottak, Prime-Time Society: An Anthropological Analysis of Television and Culture.)

As the millennium approaches, linkages in the world system have both enlarged and erased old boundaries and distinctions. Arjun Appadurai[1] characterizes today's world as a "translocal" "interactive system" that is "strikingly new." Whether as refugees, migrants, tourists, pilgrims, proselytizers, laborers, business people, development agents, employees of nongovernmental organizations (NGOs), politicians, soldiers, sports figures, students, reporters, or media-borne images, people travel more than ever.

Postmodernity describes our time and situation—today's world in flux, these media-saturated people on-the-move who must manage new, shifting, and multiple identities depending on place and context. In its most general sense, *postmodern* refers to the blurring and breakdown of established rules, standards, categories, distinctions, and boundaries.[2] In multiple guises, postmodernity has invaded the classroom, as traditional roles, boundaries, and canons of behavior are contested, challenged, opened up, and broken down. The electronic mass media, especially television, have played a major role in this process. I shall draw on my own experience in showing how.

I have taught introductory anthropology at the University of Michigan since 1968. I teach the course, which enrolls 550–600 students, in a large auditorium. A microphone is necessary if the perennial instructor wants to avoid cancer of the larynx. Each fall, I stand on a platform in front of these massed undergraduates. In 13–14 weeks of lecturing I survey the subfields of general anthropology.

Among the first courses taken at the University of Michigan, Anthropology 101 carries social science distribution credit. It also satisfies our new Diversity requirement (a course dealing with race or ethnicity). Few of the students in it plan to major in anthropology, and many will never take another anthropology course. For these reasons, the lecturer must work hard to keep students' attention, and my evaluations usually give me good marks for making the course interesting. In this setting students perceive a successful lecturer not simply as a teacher, but as something of an entertainer. The combination of large auditorium, huddled masses, and electronic amplification transforms this assembly from a mere class into an audience. Although these conditions have remained fairly constant since I began teaching in 1968, there have been noticeable changes in student behavior, particularly in their less formal classroom comportment. Indeed, my observation of Anthropology 101 students helped turn my attention to the influence of the electronic mass media on human behavior (as elaborated in my 1990 book *Prime-Time Society: An Anthropological Analysis of Television and Culture*).

My students have never known a world without TV. The tube has been as much a fixture in their homes as mom or dad. Considering how common divorce has become, the TV even outlasts the father in many homes. American kids devote 22 to 30 hours to television each week. By the end of high school, they will have spent 22,000 hours in front of the set, versus only 11,000 in the classroom.[3] Such prolonged exposure must affect their behavior in observable ways.

I've discussed the behavior modification I see in my classroom with university colleagues; many report similar observations. The point I'm making here differs from familiar pronouncements about television's effects on human behavior. Other researchers have found, or asserted, links between exposure to media content (e.g., violence) and individual behavior (hyperactivity, aggression, "acting out"). Like them, I believe that content may affect behavior. But I make a more basic claim: The very habit of watching TV has modified the behavior of Americans who have grown up with television.

Anyone who has been to a movie house (or to an annual meeting of the American Anthropological Association) lately has seen examples of TV-conditioned behavior—*teleconditioning*. Audience members talk, babies gurgle and cry, people file out and in, getting snacks and going to the bathroom. Students act similarly in college courses. In the "golden age" before teleconditioning (the pre-postmodern world), there was always an isolated student who did such things. What is new is a behavior pattern characteristic of a group rather than an individual. This cultural pattern is becoming more pronounced, and I think it's linked to all those hours of "watching television." Stated simply, the pattern, which I call teleconditioning, is this: Televiewing causes people to duplicate in many areas of their lives styles of behavior developed while watching television, and this fuels the culture of postmodernity.

Remembering that *postmodern* refers to the blurring and breakdown of established canons, categories, and boundaries, some examples of teleconditioning in the postmodern classroom are in order. Almost nothing bothers a professor more than having someone read a newspaper in class. Lecturers are understandably perturbed when a student shows more interest in a sports column or *Doonesbury* than in the lecture content. I don't often get newspapers in class, but one day I noticed a student sitting in the front row reading a paperback novel. Irritated by her audacity, I stopped lecturing and asked "Why are you reading a book in my class?" Her answer: "Oh, I'm not in your class. I just came in here to read my book."

How is this wildly improbable response to be explained? Why would someone take the trouble to migrate into a lecture hall to read? The answer, I think, is this: after years of televiewing (plus rock music), many young Americans have trouble reading unless they have background noise. Research confirms that most Americans do something else while watching television. Often they read. Even I do it. It's not unusual for me to get home, turn on the TV, sit down in a comfortable chair and go through the mail or read the newspaper.

Research on television's impact confirms that televiewing evolves through certain stages. The first stage, when sets are introduced, is rapt attention, gazes glued to the screen. Some of us can remember from the late 1940s or early 1950s sitting in front of our first TV, dumbly watching even test patterns. Later, as the novelty diminishes, viewers become less attentive. Televiewers in Brazil, whom I began studying systematically in 1983, had already moved past the first stage, but they were still much more attentive than Americans. A study done in São Paulo illustrates the contrast. The study shocked Rede Globo, Brazil's dominant network, when it revealed that half the viewers weren't paying full attention to commercials. Worried about losing advertising revenue, Rede Globo challenged the research. (American sponsors, by contrast, are so accustomed to inattention and, nowadays, remote control tune-outs, that it would delight them if even half the audience stayed put.)

The student who came to my class to read a novel was simply an extreme example of a culture pattern derived from exposure to the mass media. Because of her lifelong TV dependency, she had trouble reading without background noise. It didn't matter to her whether the hum came from a stereo, a TV set, or a live professor. Accustomed to machines that don't talk back, she probably was amazed I noticed her at all. My questioning may even have prompted her to check inside her set that night to see if someone real was lurking there.

Another effect of televiewing is students' increasing tendency to enter and leave classrooms at will. Of course, individual students do occasionally get sick or have a dentist's appointment. But here again I'm describing a group pattern rather than individual circumstances or idiosyncrasies. During the past few years I've regularly observed students getting up in mid-lecture, leaving the room for a few minutes, then returning. Sometimes they bring back a canned soft drink or coffee and doughnuts (which campus groups have started selling in classroom buildings).

I don't think these ambulatory students mean to be disrespectful; rather, the rules and boundaries they recognize differ from those of students past. They are transferring a home-grown pattern of informality, including snack and bathroom breaks, from family (TV) room to classroom. They perceive nothing unusual in acting the same way in front of a live speaker and fellow students as they do when they watch television. (A few students manage to remain seated for only 10–15 minutes, then get up and leave. They are exhibiting a less flattering pattern. Either they have diarrhea, as one student told me he did, or they have decided to turn off the "set" or "change channels.")

Nowadays, almost all Americans talk while watching TV. Talking is getting more common in the classroom, just as in the movie house, and this also illustrates television's effects on our collective behavior. Not only do my students bring food and drink to class, some lie down on the floor if they arrive too late to get a seat. I've seen couples kissing and caressing just a few rows away. New examples of postmodern expectations and/or teleconditioning pop up all the time. In two recent semesters, students requested that I say, publicly, "Happy Birthday" to a friend in the class. They perceived me as a professorial analogue of Willard Scott, the NBC "Today Show" weather caster who offers birthday greetings (to people 100 and over). Long ago I put into my syllabus injunctions against reading newspapers and eating crunchy foods in class. Now I feel compelled to announce "I don't do birthdays."

In response to all this, I've modified my lecture style, trying to enhance students' attention, interest, and, I hope, learning. In search of ways of dealing with teleconditioning and post-modernity, I subscribed to a newsletter called *The Teaching Professor* (Magna Publications). I've heeded some of its advice for more effective teaching—"Don't stand passively at the front of the room and lecture." "Don't let yourself be chained to a chalkboard, lectern, podium, overhead projector, or microphone." "Move around and show your students you own the entire classroom."

These lessons led me to adopt the technology of the current television age to instruct students who have been teleconditioned. Now, like the TV talk-show host Phil Donahue, I use a remote microphone, which allows me to roam the lecture hall at will. A teaching assistant sits at the overhead projector in front and writes down terms and notes as I walk and talk. Unlike Phil, whose studio layout promotes his elicitation of comments from audience members (into whose faces Donahue regularly pushes his microphone), my mobility and personal encounters (student "feedback," "participation," or "empowerment") are constrained by an auditorium that is very wide and lacks a center aisle. Unlike Phil and Oprah (Winfrey), I can't rush up and down the center aisle asking probing questions like "What do you think of serial monogamy?" or "Should Americans adopt bifurcate collateral kinship terminology?" I have to confine my striding to the front, sides, and back of the auditorium, occasionally moving a few seats into a row (sometimes activating the Boundary Recognition and Response System of students who have failed to recognize the reciprocal implications of postmodernity).

Student attention shifts between me, the peripatetic lecturer, and the front of the auditorium, where my vigilant TA scribe works at the overhead and where loudspeakers broadcast my voice. Wandering from time to time to the rear of the room, I occasionally challenge the anonymity of a somnolent or notetaking young man in the last row (where only male students sit). Sometimes, I let a student ask a question into the microphone. Often, if I see someone about to leave during lecture, my remote mike allows me to head in that direction. I believe that my roaming, which permits me to mingle with students more than I used to, inhibits the teleconditioned behavior that used to bother me (and that increasingly perturbs my colleagues who teach the same class without circumambulating). If you can't lick it, join it.

My students grow accustomed to my style and generally pay attention, but the supply of postmodern manifestations seems endless. Thus, students "empowered" by campus email send me questions, comments, poems, stories, even pictures of MTV's Beavis and Butthead. (The Dean of the College and the President of the University get some of the same mail.)

As Fall 1993 progressed, I started noticing a young male student who perpetually arrived late and greeted me with a friendly wave. One day he extended his hand and gave me what seemed to be a secret shake. Another day, as I began my lecture at the front of the auditorium, he and two friends walked up to me, shook hands, and sat down in the front row. My most memorable encounter with this, my most postmodern student, came one day on the University of Michigan "Diag." He approached me on a bike, stopped, stuck out his hand, and said "Gimme five, Connie, baby." Conditioned by my own teen-aged son to do that without pause, I matched him, high and low, and continued my trek across campus. If Franz Boas were alive today to witness such behavior, he would, as they say, turn over in his grave.

Notes

1. "Disjuncture and Difference in the Global Cultural Economy," *Public Culture*, vol. 2, no. 2, pp. 1–24, 1990.
2. The word is taken from *postmodernism*—a style and movement in architecture that succeeded modernism, beginning in the 1970s. Postmodern architecture rejected the rules, geometric order, and austerity of modernism. Modernist buildings were expected to have a clear and functional design. Postmodern design is "messier" and more playful. It draws on a diversity of styles from different times and places—including popular, ethnic, and nonwestern cultures. Postmodernism extends "value" well beyond classic, elite, and western cultural forms. *Postmodern* is now used to describe comparable developments in music, literature, and visual art.
3. "Too Much TV Time Linked to Obesity in Children, Teens," *Ann Arbor News*, May 6, 1985.

Shakespeare in the Bush

Laura Bohannan

Laura Bohannan is a former professor of anthropology at the University of Illinois, at Chicago.

Just before I left Oxford for the Tiv in West Africa, conversation turned to the season at Stratford. "You Americans," said a friend, "often have difficulty with Shakespeare. He was, after all, a very English poet, and one can easily misinterpret the universal by misunderstanding the particular."

I protested that human nature is pretty much the same the whole world over; at least the general plot and motivation of the greater tragedies would always be clear—everywhere—although some details of custom might have to be explained and difficulties of translation might produce other slight changes. To end an argument we could not conclude, my friend gave me a copy of *Hamlet* to study in the African bush: it would, he hoped, lift my mind above its primitive surroundings, and possibly I might, by prolonged meditation, achieve the grace of correct interpretation.

It was my second field trip to that African tribe, and I thought myself ready to live in one of its remote sections—an area difficult to cross even on foot. I eventually settled on the hillock of a very knowledgeable old man, the head of a homestead of some hundred and forty people, all of whom were either his close relatives or their wives and children. Like the other elders of the vicinity, the old man spent most of his time performing ceremonies seldom seen these days in the more accessible parts of the tribe. I was delighted. Soon there would be three months of enforced isolation and leisure, between the harvest that takes place just before the rising of the swamps and the clearing of new farms when the water goes down. Then, I thought, they would have even more time to perform ceremonies and explain them to me.

I was quite mistaken. Most of the ceremonies demanded the presence of elders from several homesteads. As the swamps rose, the old men found it too difficult to walk from one homestead to the next, and the ceremonies gradually ceased. As the swamps rose even higher, all activities but one came to an end. The women brewed beer from maize and millet. Men, women, and children sat on their hillocks and drank it.

People began to drink at dawn. By midmorning the whole homestead was singing, dancing, and drumming. When it rained, people had to sit inside their huts: there they drank and sang or they drank and told stories. In any case, by noon or before, I either had to join the party or retire to my own hut and my books. "One does not discuss serious matters when there is beer. Come, drink with us." Since I lacked their capacity for the thick native beer, I spent more and more time with *Hamlet*. Before the end of the second month, grace descended on me. I was quite sure that *Hamlet* had only one possible interpretation, and that one universally obvious.

Early every morning, in the hope of having some serious talk before the beer party, I used to call on the old man at his reception hut—a circle of posts supporting a thatched roof above a low mud wall to keep out wind and rain. One day I crawled through the low doorway and found most of the men of the homestead sitting huddled in their ragged cloths on stools, low plank beds, and reclining chairs, warming themselves against the chill of the rain around a smoky fire. In the center were three pots of beer. The party had started.

The old man greeted me cordially. "Sit down and drink." I accepted a large calabash full of beer, poured some into a small drinking gourd, and tossed it down. Then I poured some more into the same gourd for the man second in seniority to my host before I handed my calabash over to a young man for further distribution. Important people shouldn't ladle beer themselves.

"It is better like this," the old man said, looking at me approvingly and plucking at the thatch that had caught in my hair. "You should sit and drink with us more often. Your servants tell me that when you are not with us, you sit inside your hut looking at a paper."

The old man was acquainted with four kinds of "papers": tax receipts, bride price receipts, court fee receipts, and letters. The messenger who brought him letters from the chief used them

From *Natural History,* August/September 1966. © 1966 by Laura Bohannan. Reprinted by permission.

mainly as a badge of office, for he always knew what was in them and told the old man. Personal letters for the few who had relatives in the government or mission stations were kept until someone went to a large market where there was a letter writer and reader. Since my arrival, letters were brought to me to be read. A few men also brought me bride price receipts, privately, with requests to change the figures to a higher sum. I found moral arguments were of no avail, since in-laws are fair game, and the technical hazards of forgery difficult to explain to an illiterate people. I did not wish them to think me silly enough to look at any such papers for days on end, and I hastily explained that my "paper" was one of the "things of long ago" of my country.

"Ah," said the old man. "Tell us."

I protested that I was not a storyteller. Story telling is a skilled art among them; their standards are high, and the audiences critical—and vocal in their criticism. I protested in vain. This morning they wanted to hear a story while they drank. They threatened to tell me no more stories until I told them one of mine. Finally, the old man promised that no one would criticize my style "for we know you are struggling with our language." "But," put in one of the elders, "you must explain what we do not understand, as we do when we tell you our stories." Realizing that here was my chance to prove *Hamlet* universally intelligible, I agreed.

The old man handed me some more beer to help me on with my storytelling. Men filled their long wooden pipes and knocked coals from the fire to place in the pipe bowls; then, puffing contentedly, they sat back to listen. I began in the proper style, "Not yesterday, not yesterday, but long ago, a thing occurred. One night three men were keeping watch outside the homestead of the great chief, when suddenly they saw the former chief approach them."

"Why was he no longer their chief?"

"He was dead," I explained. "That is why they were troubled and afraid when they saw him."

"Impossible," began one of the elders, handing his pipe on to his neighbor, who interrupted, "Of course it wasn't

the dead chief. It was an omen sent by a witch. Go on."

Slightly shaken, I continued. "One of these three was a man who knew things"—the closest translation for scholar, but unfortunately it also meant witch. The second elder looked triumphantly at the first. "So he spoke to the dead chief saying, 'Tell us what we must do so you may rest in your grave,' but the dead chief did not answer. He vanished, and they could see him no more. Then the man who knew things—his name was Horatio—said this event was the affair of the dead chief's son, Hamlet."

There was a general shaking of heads round the circle. "Had the dead chief no living brothers? Or was this son the chief?"

"No," I replied. "That is, he had one living brother who became the chief when the elder brother died."

The old men muttered: such omens were matters for chiefs and elders, not for youngsters; no good could come of going behind a chief's back; clearly Horatio was not a man who knew things.

"Yes, he was," I insisted, shooing a chicken away from my beer. "In our country the son is next to the father. The dead chief's younger brother had become the great chief. He had also married his elder brother's widow only about a month after the funeral."

"He did well," the old man beamed and announced to the others, "I told you that if we knew more about Europeans, we would find they really were very like us. In our country also," he added to me, "the younger brother marries the elder brother's widow and becomes the father of his children. Now, if your uncle, who married your widowed mother, is your father's full brother, then he will be a real father to you. Did Hamlet's father and uncle have one mother?"

His question barely penetrated my mind; I was too upset and thrown too far off balance by having one of the most important elements of *Hamlet* knocked straight out of the picture. Rather uncertainly I said that I thought they had the same mother, but I wasn't sure—the story didn't say. The old man told me severely that these genealogical details made all the difference and that

when I got home I must ask the elders about it. He shouted out the door to one of his younger wives to bring his goatskin bag.

Determined to save what I could of the mother motif, I took a deep breath and began again. "The son Hamlet was very sad because his mother had married again so quickly. There was no need for her to do so, and it is our custom for a widow not to go to her next husband until she has mourned for two years."

"Two years is too long," objected the wife, who had appeared with the old man's battered goatskin bag. "Who will hoe your farms for you while you have no husband?"

"Hamlet," I retorted without thinking, "was old enough to hoe his mother's farms himself. There was no need for her to remarry." No one looked convinced. I gave up. "His mother and the great chief told Hamlet not to be sad, for the great chief himself would be a father to Hamlet. Furthermore, Hamlet would be the next chief: therefore he must stay to learn the things of a chief. Hamlet agreed to remain, and all the rest went off to drink beer."

While I paused, perplexed at how to render Hamlet's disgusted soliloquy to an audience convinced that Claudius and Gertrude had behaved in the best possible manner, one of the younger men asked me who had married the other wives of the dead chief.

"He had no other wives," I told him.

"But a chief must have many wives! How else can he brew beer and prepare food for all his guests?"

I said firmly that in our country even chiefs had only one wife, that they had servants to do their work, and that they paid them from tax money.

It was better, they returned, for a chief to have many wives and sons who would help him hoe his farms and feed his people; then everyone loved the chief who gave much and took nothing—taxes were a bad thing.

I agreed with the last comment, but for the rest fell back on their favorite way of fobbing off my questions: "That is the way it is done, so that is how we do it."

I decided to skip the soliloquy. Even if Claudius was here thought quite right to marry his brother's widow, there remained the poison motif, and I knew they would disapprove of fratricide. More hopefully I resumed, "That night Hamlet kept watch with the three who had seen his dead father. The dead chief again appeared, and although the others were afraid, Hamlet followed his dead father off to one side. When they were alone, Hamlet's dead father spoke."

"Omens can't talk!" The old man was emphatic.

"Hamlet's dead father wasn't an omen. Seeing him might have been an omen, but he was not." My audience looked as confused as I sounded. "It *was* Hamlet's dead father. It was a thing we call a 'ghost.' " I had to use the English word, for unlike many of the neighboring tribes, these people didn't believe in the survival after death of any individuating part of the personality.

"What is a 'ghost?' An omen?"

"No, a 'ghost' is someone who is dead but who walks around and can talk, and people can hear him and see him but not touch him."

They objected. "One can touch zombis."

"No, no! It was not a dead body the witches had animated to sacrifice and eat. No one else made Hamlet's dead father walk. He did it himself."

"Dead men can't walk," protested my audience as one man.

I was quite willing to compromise. "A 'ghost' is the dead man's shadow."

But again they objected. "Dead men cast no shadows."

"They do in my country," I snapped.

The old man quelled the babble of disbelief that arose immediately and told me with that insincere, but courteous, agreement one extends to the fancies of the young, ignorant, and superstitious, "No doubt in your country the dead can also walk without being zombis." From the depths of his bag he produced a withered fragment of kola nut, bit off one end to show it wasn't poisoned, and handed me the rest as a peace offering.

"Anyhow," I resumed, "Hamlet's dead father said that his own brother, the one who became chief, had poisoned him. He wanted Hamlet to avenge him. Hamlet believed this in his heart, for he did not like his father's brother." I took

another swallow of beer. "In the country of the great chief, living in the same homestead, for it was a very large one, was an important elder who was often with the chief to advise and help him. His name was Polonius. Hamlet was courting his daughter, but her father and her brother . . . [I cast hastily about for some tribal analogy] warned her not to let Hamlet visit her when she was alone on her farm, for he would be a great chief and so could not marry her."

"Why not?" asked the wife, who had settled down on the edge of the old man's chair. He frowned at her for asking stupid questions and growled, "They lived in the same homestead."

"That was not the reason," I informed them. "Polonius was a stranger who lived in the homestead because he helped the chief, not because he was a relative."

"Then why couldn't Hamlet marry her?"

"He could have," I explained, "but Polonius didn't think he would. After all, Hamlet was a man of great importance who ought to marry a chief's daughter, for in his country a man could have only one wife. Polonius was afraid that if Hamlet made love to his daughter, then no one else would give a high price for her."

"That might be true," remarked one of the shrewder elders, "but a chief's son would give his mistress's father enough presents and patronage to more than make up the difference. Polonius sounds like a fool to me."

"Many people think he was," I agreed. "Meanwhile Polonius sent his son Laertes off to Paris to learn the things of that country, for it was the homestead of a very great chief indeed. Because he was afraid that Laertes might waste a lot of money on beer and women and gambling, or get into trouble by fighting, he sent one of his servants to Paris secretly, to spy out what Laertes was doing. One day Hamlet came upon Polonius's daughter Ophelia. He behaved so oddly he frightened her. Indeed"—I was fumbling for words to express the dubious quality of Hamlet's madness—"the chief and many others had also noticed that when Hamlet talked one could understand the words but not what they meant. Many

people thought that he had become mad." My audience suddenly became much more attentive. "The great chief wanted to know what was wrong with Hamlet, so he sent for two of Hamlet's age mates [school friends would have taken long explanation] to talk to Hamlet and find out what troubled his heart. Hamlet, seeing that they had been bribed by the chief to betray him, told them nothing. Polonius, however, insisted that Hamlet was mad because he had been forbidden to see Ophelia, whom he loved."

"Why," inquired a bewildered voice, "should anyone bewitch Hamlet on that account?"

"Bewitch him?"

"Yes, only witchcraft can make anyone mad, unless, of course, one sees the beings that lurk in the forest."

I stopped being a storyteller, took out my notebook and demanded to be told more about these two causes of madness. Even while they spoke and I jotted notes, I tried to calculate the effect of this new factor on the plot. Hamlet had not been exposed to the beings that lurk in the forests. Only his relatives in the male line could bewitch him. Barring relatives not mentioned by Shakespeare, it had to be Claudius who was attempting to harm him. And, or course, it was.

For the moment I staved off questions by saying that the great chief also refused to believe that Hamlet was mad for the love of Ophelia and nothing else. "He was sure that something much more important was troubling Hamlet's heart."

"Now Hamlet's age mates," I continued, "had brought with them a famous storyteller. Hamlet decided to have this man tell the chief and all his homestead a story about a man who had poisoned his brother because he desired his brother's wife and wished to be chief himself. Hamlet was sure the great chief could not hear the story without making a sign if he was indeed guilty, and then he would discover whether his dead father had told him the truth."

The old man interrupted, with deep cunning, "Why should a father lie to his son?" he asked.

I hedged: "Hamlet wasn't sure that it really was his dead father." It was impossible to say anything, in that language, about devil-inspired visions.

"You mean," he said, "it actually was an omen, and he knew witches sometimes send false ones. Hamlet was a fool not to go to one skilled in reading omens and divining the truth in the first place. A man-who-sees-the-truth could have told him how his father died, if he really had been poisoned, and if there was witchcraft in it; then Hamlet could have called the elders to settle the matter."

The shrewd elder ventured to disagree. "Because his father's brother was a great chief, one-who-sees-the-truth might therefore have been afraid to tell it. I think it was for that reason that a friend of Hamlet's father—a witch and an elder—sent an omen so his friend's son would know. Was the omen true?"

"Yes," I said, abandoning ghosts and the devil; a witch-sent omen it would have to be. "It was true, for when the storyteller was telling his tale before all the homestead, the great chief rose in fear. Afraid that Hamlet knew his secret he planned to him killed."

The stage set of the next bit presented some difficulties of translation. I began cautiously. "The great chief told Hamlet's mother to find out from her son what he knew. But because a woman's children are always first in her heart, he had the important elder Polonius hide behind a cloth that hung against the wall of Hamlet's mother's sleeping hut. Hamlet started to scold his mother for what she had done."

There was a shocked murmur from everyone. A man should never scold his mother.

"She called out in fear, and Polonius moved behind the cloth. Shouting, 'A rat!' Hamlet took his machete and slashed through the cloth." I paused for dramatic effect. "He had killed Polonius!"

The old men looked at each other in supreme disgust. "That Polonius truly was a fool and a man who knew nothing! What child would not know enough to shout, 'It's me!'" With a pang, I remembered that these people are ardent hunters, always armed with bow, arrow, and machete; at the first rustle in the grass an arrow is aimed and ready, and the hunter shouts "Game!" If no human voice answers immediately, the arrow

speeds on its way. Like a good hunter Hamlet had shouted, "A rat!"

I rushed in to save Polonius's reputation. "Polonius did speak. Hamlet heard him. But he thought it was the chief and wished to kill him earlier that evening. . . ." I broke down, unable to describe to these pagans, who had no belief in individual afterlife, the difference between dying at one's prayers and dying "unhousell'd, disappointed, unaneled."

This time I had shocked my audience seriously. "For a man to raise his hand against his father's brother and the one who has become his father—that is a terrible thing. The elders ought to let such a man be bewitched."

I nibbled at my kola nut in some perplexity, then pointed out that after all the man had killed Hamlet's father.

"No," pronounced the old man, speaking less to me than to the young men sitting behind the elders. "If your father's brother has killed your father, you must appeal to your father's age mates; *they* may avenge him. No man may use violence against his senior relatives." Another thought struck him. "But if his father's brother had indeed been wicked enough to bewitch Hamlet and make him mad that would be a good story indeed, for it would be his fault that Hamlet, being mad, no longer had any sense and thus was ready to kill his father's brother."

There was a murmur of applause. *Hamlet* was again a good story to them, but it no longer seemed quite the same story to me. As I thought over the coming complications of plot and motive, I lost courage and decided to skim over dangerous ground quickly.

"The great chief," I went on, "was not sorry that Hamlet had killed Polonius. It gave him a reason to send Hamlet away, with his two treacherous mates, with letters to a chief of a far country, saying that Hamlet should be killed. But Hamlet changed the writing on their papers, so that the chief killed his age mates instead." I encountered a reproachful glare from one of the men whom I had told undetectable forgery was not merely immoral but beyond human skill. I looked the other way.

"Before Hamlet could return, Laertes came back for his father's funeral. The

great chief told him Hamlet had killed Polonius. Laertes swore to kill Hamlet because of this, and because his sister Ophelia, hearing her father had been killed by the man she loved, went mad and drowned in the river."

"Have you already forgotten what we told you?" The old man was reproachful. "One cannot take vengeance on a madman; Hamlet killed Polonius in his madness. As for the girl, she not only went mad, she was drowned. Only witches can make people drown. Water itself can't hurt anything. It is merely something one drinks and bathes in."

I began to get cross. "If you don't like the story, I'll stop."

The old man made soothing noises and himself poured me some more beer. "You tell the story well, and we are listening. But it is clear that the elders of your country have never told you what the story really means. No, don't interrupt! We believe you when you say your marriage customs are different, or your clothes and weapons. But people are the same everywhere; therefore, there are always witches and it is we, the elders, who know how witches work. We told you it was the great chief who wished to kill Hamlet, and now your own words have proved us right. Who were Ophelia's male relatives?"

"There were only her father and her brother." *Hamlet* was clearly out of my hands.

"There must have been many more; this also you must ask of your elders when you get back to your country. From what you tell us, since Polonius was dead, it must have been Laertes who killed Ophelia, although I do not see the reason for it."

We had emptied one pot of beer, and the old men argued the point with slightly tipsy interest. Finally one of them demanded of me, "What did the servant of Polonius say on his return?"

With difficulty I recollected Reynaldo and his mission. "I don't think he did return before Polonius was killed."

"Listen," said the elder, "and I will tell you how it was and how your story will go, then you may tell me if I am right. Polonius knew his son would get into trouble, and so he did. He had many fines to pay for fighting, and debts from gambling. But he had only two ways of getting money quickly. One was to marry off his sister at once, but it is difficult to find a man who will marry a woman desired by the son of a chief. For if the chief's heir commits adultery with your wife, what can you do? Only a fool calls a case against a man who will someday be his judge. Therefore Laertes had to take the second way: he killed his sister by witchcraft, drowning her so he could secretly sell her body to the witches."

I raised an objection. "They found her body and buried it. Indeed Laertes jumped into the grave to see his sister once more—so, you see, the body was truly there. Hamlet, who had just come back, jumped in after him."

"What did I tell you?" The elder appealed to the others. "Laertes was up to no good with his sister's body. Hamlet prevented him, because the chief's heir,

like a chief, does not wish any other man to grow rich and powerful. Laertes would be angry, because he would have killed his sister without benefit to himself. In our country he would try to kill Hamlet for that reason. Is this not what happened?"

"More or less," I admitted. "When the great chief found Hamlet was still alive, he encouraged Laertes to try to kill Hamlet and arranged a fight with machetes between them. In the fight both the young men were wounded to death. Hamlet's mother drank the poisoned beer that the chief meant for Hamlet in case he won the fight. When he saw his mother die of poison, Hamlet, dying, managed to kill his father's brother with his machete."

"You see, I was right!" exclaimed the elder.

"That was a very good story," added the old man, "and you told it with very few mistakes. There was just one more error, at the very end. The poison Hamlet's mother drank was obviously meant for the survivor of the fight, whichever it was. If Laertes had won, the great chief would have poisoned him, for no one would know that he arranged Hamlet's death. Then, too, he need not fear Laertes' witchcraft; it takes a strong heart to kill one's only sister by witchcraft.

"Sometime," concluded the old man, gathering his ragged toga about him, "you must tell us some more stories of your country. We, who are elders, will instruct you in their true meaning, so that when you return to your own land your elders will see that you have not been sitting in the bush, but among those who know things and who have taught you wisdom."

The Organization of Society and Culture

Human beings do not interact with one another or think about their world in random fashion. Instead, they engage in both structured and recurrent physical and mental activities. In this section, such patterns of behavior and thought—referred to here as the organization of society and culture—may be seen in a number of different contexts, from the hunting tactics of the Inupiaq Eskimos of the Arctic ("Understanding Eskimo Science") to the cattle-herding Masai of East Africa ("Mystique of the Masai") to the Yąnomami of Amazonia (see "The Yąnomami Keep on Trekking").

Of special importance are the ways in which people make a living—in other words, the production, distribution, and consumption of goods and services. It is only by knowing the basic subsistence systems that we can hope to gain insight into the other levels of social and cultural phenomena, for, as anthropologists have found, they are all inextricably bound together.

Noting the various aspects of a sociocultural system in harmonious balance, however, does not imply an anthropological seal of approval. To understand infanticide (killing of the newborn) in the manner that it is practiced among some peoples is neither to condone nor condemn it. The adaptive patterns that have been in existence for a great length of time, such as many of the patterns of hunters and gatherers, probably owe their existence to their contributions to long-term human survival.

Anthropologists, however, are not content with the data derived from individual experience. On the contrary, personal descriptions must become the basis for sound anthropological theory. Otherwise, they remain meaningless, isolated relics of culture in the manner of museum pieces. Thus, in "Too Many Bananas, Not Enough Pineapples, and No Watermelon at All: Three Object Lessons in Living with Reciprocity," David Counts provides us with ground rules for reciprocity that were derived from his own particular field experience and yet are cross-culturally applicable. Karl Rambo, in "From Shells to Money," shows that the adoption of money as a medium of exchange does not in itself create a market mentality, especially if a people's basic subsistence system remains intact. Finally, "Continental Divides" by Jared Diamond expresses that constant striving in anthropology to develop a general perspective from particular events by showing how environmental circumstances and shifts in technology may result in marked changes in lifestyle and centralization of political power.

While the articles in this unit are to some extent descriptive, they also serve to challenge both academic and commonsense notions about why people behave and think as they do. They remind us that assumptions are never really safe. Any time anthropologists can be kept on their toes, their field as a whole is the better for it.

Looking Ahead: Challenge Questions

What traditional Inuit (Eskimo) practices do you find contrary to values professed in your society but important to Eskimo survival under certain circumstances?

What can contemporary hunter-collector societies tell us about the quality of life in the prehistoric past?

Why do the Simbu value money as a medium of ceremonial exchange rather than as a means to accumulate personal wealth?

Under what circumstances do social stratification and centralization of power appear in human societies?

What are the rules of reciprocity?

Why have wealth and power been distributed in favor of people of European descent over most other people in the world?

UNIT 3

Understanding Eskimo Science

Traditional hunters' insights into the natural world are worth rediscovering.

Richard Nelson

Just below the Arctic Circle in the boreal forest of interior Alaska; an amber afternoon in mid-November; the temperature −20°; the air adrift with frost crystals, presaging the onset of deeper cold.

Five men—Koyukon Indians—lean over the carcass of an exceptionally large black bear. For two days they've traversed the Koyukuk River valley, searching for bears that have recently entered hibernation dens. The animals are in prime condition at this season but extremely hard to find. Den entrances, hidden beneath 18 inches of powdery snow, are betrayed only by the subtlest of clues—patches where no grass protrudes from the surface because it's been clawed away for insulation, faint concavities hinting of footprint depressions in the moss below.

Earlier this morning the hunters took a yearling bear. In accordance with Koyukon tradition, they followed elaborate rules for the proper treatment of killed animals. For example, the bear's feet were removed first, to keep its spirit from wandering. Also, certain parts were to be eaten away from the village, at a kind of funeral feast. All the rest would be eaten either at home or at community events, as people here have done for countless generations.

Koyukon hunters know that an animal's life ebbs slowly, that it remains aware and sensitive to how people treat its body. This is especially true for the potent and demanding spirit of the bear.

The leader of the hunting group is Moses Sam, a man in his 60s who has trapped in this territory since childhood. He is known for his detailed knowledge of the land and for his extraordinary success as a bear hunter. "No one else has that kind of luck with bears," I've been told. "Some people are born with it. He always takes good care of his animals—respects them. That's how he keeps his luck."

Moses pulls a small knife from his pocket, kneels beside the bear's head, and carefully slits the clear domes of its eyes. "Now," he explains softly, "the bear won't see if one of us makes a mistake or does something wrong."

Contemporary Americans are likely to find this story exotic, but over the course of time episodes like this have been utterly commonplace, the essence of people's relationship to the natural world. After all, for 99 percent of human history we lived exclusively as hunter-gatherers; by comparison, agriculture has existed only for a moment and urban societies scarcely more than a blink.

From this perspective, much of human experience over the past several million years lies beyond our grasp. Probably no society has been so deeply alienated as ours from the community of nature, has viewed the natural world from a greater distance of mind, has lapsed into a murkier comprehension of its connections with the sustaining environment. Because of this, we have great difficulty understanding our rootedness to earth, our affinities with nonhuman life.

I believe it's essential that we learn from traditional societies, especially those whose livelihood depends on the harvest of a wild environment—hunters, fishers, trappers, and gatherers. These people have accumulated bodies of knowledge much like our own sciences. And they can give us vital insights about responsible membership in the community of life, insights founded on a wisdom we'd long forgotten and now are beginning to rediscover.

Since the mid-1960s I have worked as an ethnographer in Alaska, living intermittently in remote northern communities and recording native traditions centered around the natural world. I spent about two years in Koyukon Indian villages and just over a year with Inupiaq Eskimos on the Arctic coast—traveling by dog team and snowmobile, recording traditional knowledge, and learning the hunter's way.

Eskimos have long inhabited some of the harshest environments on earth, and they are among the most exquisitely adapted of all human groups. Because plant life is so scarce in their northern terrain, Eskimos depend more than any other people on hunting.

Eskimos are famous for the cleverness of their technology—kayaks, harpoons, skin clothing, snow houses, dog

This article originally appeared in *Audubon* magazine, September/October 1993, pp. 102-109. Adapted from *Biophilia* by Richard Nelson, 1993. Published by Island Press. © 1993 by Richard Nelson. Reprinted by permission of Susan Bergholz Literary Services, New York. All rights reserved.

teams. But I believe their greatest genius, and the basis of their success, lies in the less tangible realm of the intellect—the nexus of mind and nature. For what repeatedly struck me above all else was their profound knowledge of the environment.

Several times, when my Inupiaq hunting companion did something especially clever, he'd point to his head and declare: "You see—Eskimo scientist!" At first I took it as hyperbole, but as time went by I realized he was speaking the truth. Scientists had often come to his village, and he saw in them a familiar commitment to the empirical method.

Traditional Inupiaq hunters spend a lifetime acquiring knowledge—from others in the community and from their own observations. If they are to survive, they must have absolutely reliable information. When I first went to live with Inupiaq people, I doubted many things they told me. But the longer I stayed, the more I trusted their teachings.

The Inupiaq hunter possesses as much knowledge as a highly trained scientist in our own society.

For example, hunters say that ringed seals surfacing in open leads—wide cracks in the sea ice—can reliably forecast the weather. Because an unexpected gale might set people adrift on the pack ice, accurate prediction is a matter of life and death. When seals rise chest-high in the water, snout pointed skyward, not going anywhere in particular, it indicates stable weather, the Inupiaq say. But if they surface briefly, head low, snout parallel to the water, and show themselves only once or twice, watch for a sudden storm. And take special heed if you've also noticed the sled dogs howling incessantly, stars twinkling erratically, or the current running strong from the south. As time passed, my own experiences with seals and winter storms affirmed what the Eskimos said.

Like a young Inupiaq in training, I gradually grew less skeptical and started to apply what I was told. For example, had I ever been rushed by a polar bear, I would have jumped away to the animal's *right* side. Inupiaq elders say polar bears are left-handed, so you have a slightly better chance to avoid their right paw, which is slower and less accurate. I'm pleased to say I never had the chance for a field test. But in judging assertions like this, remember that Eskimos have had close contact with polar bears for several thousand years.

During winter, ringed and bearded seals maintain tunnel-like breathing holes in ice that is many feet thick. These holes are often capped with an igloo-shaped dome created by water sloshing onto the surface when the animal enters from below. Inupiaq elders told me that polar bears are clever enough to excavate around the base of this dome, leaving it perfectly intact but weak enough that a hard swat will shatter the ice and smash the seal's skull. I couldn't help wondering if this were really true; but then a younger man told me he'd recently followed the tracks of a bear that had excavated one seal hole after another, exactly as the elders had described.

In the village where I lived, the most respected hunter was Igruk, a man in his 70s. He had an extraordinary sense of animals—a gift for understanding and predicting their behavior. Although he was no longer quick and strong, he joined a crew hunting bowhead whales during the spring migration, his main role being that of adviser. Each time Igruk spotted a whale coming from the south, he counted the number of blows, timed how long it stayed down, and noted the distance it traveled along the open lead, until it vanished toward the north. This way he learned to predict, with uncanny accuracy, where hunters could expect the whale to resurface.

I believe the expert Inupiaq hunter possesses as much knowledge as a highly trained scientist in our own society, although the information may be of a different sort. Volumes could be written on the behavior, ecology, and utilization of Arctic animals—polar

bear, walrus, bowhead whale, beluga, bearded seal, ringed seal, caribou, musk ox, and others—based entirely on Eskimo knowledge.

Comparable bodies of knowledge existed in every Native American culture before the time of Columbus. Since then, even in the far north, Western education and cultural change have steadily eroded these traditions. Reflecting on a time before Europeans arrived, we can imagine the whole array of North American animal species—deer, elk, black bear, wolf, mountain lion, beaver, coyote, Canada goose, ruffed grouse, passenger pigeon, northern pike—each known in hundreds of different ways by tribal communities; the entire continent, sheathed in intricate webs of knowledge. Taken as a whole, this composed a vast intellectual legacy, born of intimacy with the natural world. Sadly, not more than a hint of it has ever been recorded.

Like other Native Americans, the Inupiaq acquired their knowledge through gradual accretion of naturalistic observations—year after year, lifetime after lifetime, generation after generation, century after century. Modern science often relies on other techniques—specialized full-time observation, controlled experiments, captive-animal studies, technological devices like radio collars—which can provide similar information much more quickly.

Yet Eskimo people have learned not only *about* animals but also *from* them. Polar bears hunt seals not only by waiting at their winter breathing holes, but also by stalking seals that crawl up on the ice to bask in the spring warmth. Both methods depend on being silent, staying downwind, keeping out of sight, and moving only when the seal is asleep or distracted. According to the elders, a stalking bear will even use one paw to cover its conspicuous black nose.

Inupiaq methods for hunting seals, both at breathing holes and atop the spring ice, are nearly identical to those of the polar bear. Is this a case of independent invention? Or did ancestral Eskimos learn the techniques by watching polar bears, who had perfected an adaptation to the sea-ice-environment long before humans arrived in the Arctic?

The hunter's genius centers on knowing an animal's behavior so well he can turn it to his advantage. For instance, Igruk once saw a polar bear far off across flat ice, where he couldn't stalk it without being seen. But he knew an old technique of mimicking a seal. He lay down in plain sight, conspicuous in his dark parka and pants, then lifted and dropped his head like a seal, scratched the ice, and imitated flippers with his hands. The bear mistook his pursuer for prey. Each time Igruk lifted his head the animal kept still; whenever Igruk "slept" the bear crept closer. When it came near enough, a gunshot pierced the snowy silence. That night, polar bear meat was shared among the villagers.

"Each animal knows way more than you do," a Koyukon Indian elder was fond of telling me.

A traditional hunter like Igruk plumbs the depths of his intellect—his capacity to manipulate complex knowledge. But he also delves into his animal nature, drawing from intuitions of sense and body and heart: feeling the wind's touch, listening for the tick of moving ice, peering from crannies, hiding as if he himself were the hunted. He moves in a world of eyes, where everything watches—the bear, the seal, the wind, the moon and stars, the drifting ice, the silent waters below. He is beholden to powers we have long forgotten or ignored.

In Western society we rest comfortably on our own accepted truths about the nature of nature. We treat the environment as if it were numb to our presence and blind to our behavior. Yet despite our certainty on this matter, accounts of traditional people throughout the world reveal that most of humankind has concluded otherwise. Perhaps our scientific method really does follow the path to a single, absolute truth. But there may be wisdom in accepting other possibilities and opening ourselves to different views of the world.

I remember asking a Koyukon man about the behavior and temperament of the Canada goose. He described it as a gentle and good-natured animal, then added: "Even if [a goose] had the power to knock you over, I don't think it would do it."

For me, his words carried a deep metaphorical wisdom. They exemplified the Koyukon people's own restraint toward the world around them. And they offered a contrast to our culture, in which possessing the power to overwhelm the environment has long been sufficient justification for its use.

We often think of this continent as having been a pristine wilderness when the first Europeans arrived. Yet for at least 12,000 years, and possibly twice that long, Native American people had inhabited and intensively utilized the land; had gathered, hunted, fished, settled, and cultivated; had learned the terrain in all its details, infusing it with meaning and memory; and had shaped every aspect of their life around it. That humans could sustain membership in a natural community for such an enormous span of time without profoundly degrading it fairly staggers the imagination. And it gives strong testimony to the adaptation of mind—the braiding together of knowledge and ideology—that linked North America's indigenous people with their environment.

A Koyukon elder, who took it upon himself to be my teacher, was fond of telling me: "Each animal knows way more than you do." He spoke as if it summarized all that he understood and believed.

This statement epitomizes relationships to the natural world among many Native American people. And it goes far in explaining the diversity and fecundity of life on our continent when the first sailing ship approached these shores.

There's been much discussion in recent years about what biologist E. O. Wilson has termed "biophilia"—a deep, pervasive, ubiquitous, all-embracing affinity for nonhuman life. Evidence for this "instinct" may be elusive in Western cultures, but not among traditional societies. People like the Koyukon mani-

fest biophilia in virtually all dimensions of their existence. Connectedness with nonhuman life infuses the whole spectrum of their thought, behavior, and belief.

It's often said that a fish might have no concept of water, never having left it. In the same way, traditional peoples might never stand far enough outside themselves to imagine a generalized concept of biophilia. Perhaps it would be impossible for people to intimately bound with the natural world, people who recognize that all nature is our own embracing community. Perhaps, to bring a word like *biophilia* into their language, they would first need to separate themselves from nature.

In April 1971 I was in a whaling camp several miles off the Arctic coast with a group of Inupiaq hunters, including Igruk, who understood animals so well he almost seemed to enter their minds.

Onshore winds had closed the lead that migrating whales usually follow, but one large opening remained, and here the Inupiaq men placed their camp. For a couple of days there had been no whales, so everyone stayed inside the warm tent, talking and relaxing. The old man rested on a soft bed of caribou skins with his eyes closed. Then, suddenly, he interrupted the conversation: "I think a whale is coming, and perhaps it will surface very close. . . ."

To my amazement everyone jumped into action, although none had seen or heard anything except Igruk's words. Only he stayed behind, while the others rushed for the water's edge. I was last to leave the tent. Seconds after I stepped outside, a broad, shining back cleaved the still water near the opposite side of the opening, accompanied by the burst of a whale's blow.

Later, when I asked how he'd known, Igruk said, "There was a ringing inside my ears." I have no explanation other than his; I can only report what I saw. None of the Inupiaq crew members even commented afterward, as if nothing out of the ordinary had happened.

The Yanomami Keep on Trekking

In Amazonia, a break from gardening makes for a balanced diet

Kenneth Good

Kenneth Good went to Venezuela with plans to study the Yanomami of Hasupi-wetëri for fifteen months and ended up staying with them for twelve years. His personal odyssey is detailed in his book, coauthored with David Chanoff, Into the Heart: One Man's Pursuit of Love and Knowledge among the Yanomama *(New York: Simon and Schuster, 1991). Good is now an assistant professor of anthropology at Jersey City State College.*

Bë kuami! "They are not home!" I remember my disappointment as I arrived at empty village after empty village on my month-long expedition. I had started out from the Yanomami community of Hasupiwëteri, on the upper Orinoco River in the Venezuelan Amazon, with the goal of reaching the banks of the Parakeet River, thirty-five miles to the south. It was 1976, the second of twelve consecutive years that I would live with the Hasupiwëteri at their changing locales. I and five of their strongest young men had set off with food, gear, and gifts to contact the scattered inland villages. No nonindigenous outsider had ever made this trip overland, through the hilly terrain covered with dense forest, although one group in the area had been visited once by helicopter. None of the Yanomami from my community had penetrated that far either, although some had reached the closest villages and knew by word of mouth of the others.

We had spent three days pushing along little-used trails barely visible to the inexperienced eye. One day out, we had visited the first village, but after that we had encountered no one. The third day had been especially difficult, as we chopped and hacked our way through an old, abandoned garden during a torrential downpour. I realized then why the Yanomami are "pioneering horticulturists," always planting their gardens in virgin forest. Who would want to reclear this snake-infested tangle of thorny brush? Beyond the garden we began the last of numerous ascents in the rolling hills to the community of Ashitowëteri. As we neared our destination, my excitement peaked. My guides told me we had reached the last stream before we would arrive, and as is the Yanomami custom when visiting another village, we stopped to bathe.

After a brief, refreshing dip we hurried down the trail until we arrived at the village gardens. Bananas and plantains in various stages of growth made up about nine-tenths of the well-tended vegetation. Off to one side we saw a few *ohina* root and manioc plants. Some cotton bushes and a couple of avocado trees were the only other visible crops. After several hundred yards, we were out of the gardens and standing before one of the largest and best-constructed communal shelters I had seen. But it was empty.

The Yanomami are what anthropologists call horticulturists, or gardeners. Although a large and important part of their diet consists of foods from hunting and gathering, they also grow plantains and bananas, using simple tools and a clearing technique known as slash-and-burn. Their crops enable them to live a more sedentary life than full-time hunter-gatherers, who have to follow their food as it becomes available in the forest. Their communities are larger and their homes and personal possessions are more elaborate. So where were the horticultural Yanomami of Ashitowëteri when I arrived to pay my respects?

I realized that there was only one thing they could be doing: they were on a *wayumi,* a trek in which the entire community packs up its possessions, abandons the communal shelter, and takes to the forest in one or several groups to hunt and gather wild foods. I already knew about the treks. It takes at most a few months' residence with the Yanomami to become familiar with them. But I could not contain my frustration at finding no one at home, and my feelings were shared by my Hasupi-wëteri friends. While I wailed, "Why do they have to go trekking now?" my guides heaped scorn on our absent hosts, calling them peccaries for spending their days foraging in the forest.

Another frustration of arriving at an empty village is missing out on a good meal. When one travels long distances across the forest, the intermittent stops are critical for keeping up energy levels. Now we were forced to take what we could from the garden and pay for it another day. While the other men checked the trails to determine when the resi-

Ripe plantains, the Yanomami's main cultivated crop, are peeled for a feast.

dents had left and in which direction, Karisi and I collected food from the Ashitowëteri gardens. Fortunately, on our way back after visiting several other empty villages, we came across the Ashitowëteri at one of their temporary camps. We showered them with our gifts—machetes, knives, and other desirable items—more than reciprocating for the food we had taken. It was the first of my several stays with this previously uncontacted community over the next ten years.

Not long after we returned to Hasupiwëteri, that community also determined to go trekking. While we had been away, the able-bodied men had gone on a hunt. They were planning to invite another village to a funeral ceremony, and meat was a major requirement for the event. The hunt had failed, as many of them do, and after our return they made a second attempt. They returned with white-lipped peccaries and some small game. The hunters were happy to bring back such a quantity of smoked meat, even though out of a herd of more than fifty peccaries, a force of thirty-two hunters succeeded in bringing down only three.

When I awakened the morning after the feast was over, preparations for the trek were already under way. While the last few mature plantains from the garden roasted on the family hearth, men and women were packing all their pos-

sessions in bundles. Using a tumpline, the women bear the burden of portage, sometimes carrying loads of more than 100 pounds—plantains, aluminum pots, axes, hammocks, and even a child. Quickly I got out of my hammock and began organizing my own equipment and necessities (many supplies could be left behind, stashed in locked trunks). Fortunately, I could arrange for four young men to help carry my possessions.

While the women were still packing, the men marched out of the village, anxious to start down the trails before the animals were scared off by the larger group. Most carried little more than their bows and arrows, so they would be unencumbered for any hunting opportunity. Burdened as they are, the women and children move very slowly and rarely cover more than a mile in a day. The men periodically stop and wait for them to catch up.

After only a few hours, still before noon, the men began to make camp for the night. Each cleared a small area, and in no more than half an hour erected a simple frame for the family shelter. Most then disappeared into the forest to hunt. When the women arrived, they cut *platanillo* leaves and covered the roof frames prepared by their husbands. After setting up house by hanging their hammocks, gourds, and other belongings,

they took to the streams to crab or to the forest to gather wild foods.

Our trek lasted five weeks. If there was a large stand of food near a campsite or if hunting proved productive, the community would spend several nights there. Otherwise, they would pack up their belongings at daybreak, bundle the leaves from the roofs, and move on to another site. Men, women, and children, the old and the infirm moved through the forest, exploiting Amazonia's varied wild foods. In addition to the skill with which the Yanomami hunted and gathered, the ease with which they trekked reinforced my view that this was an ancient pattern of livelihood.

As I accompanied this trek and many more over the years, I kept detailed records of the Yanomami's activities, especially those related to food and nutrition, the subject of my research. The same thought was always on my mind: "Why do they trek?" Probably underlying my question was the ethnocentric notion that social progress consists of having a settled life, and that trekking is a kind of enforced hardship to acquire food in lean times. The Yanomami see it differently, however. For them the trek is a welcome event, one that raises the spirits. Trekking takes the community to fresh, cool forest areas that have not been exploited for a long period, perhaps not within living memory. Nevertheless, the question remains: Do the Yanomami really need to go trekking?

At first glance, the reason the Yanomami trek seems to be that they run out of mature plantains from their gardens. Plantains and bananas were most likely introduced into the New World by the conquistadors. Scientists generally believe that in pre-Columbian times, the Yanomami were hunters and gatherers and that they continue to trek because their forager culture has failed to make maximum use of agriculture. So why don't they just grow more plantains?

Decades ago, anthropologist Robert Carneiro, of the American Museum of Natural History, demonstrated that there is no environmental limitation in Amazonia on growing sufficient crops for a village to remain sedentary. My own studies of forest areas around the Yanomami communities confirm that there is almost always land suitable for expansion of cultivation. The men, who do all of the garden work, spend an average of less than two hours per day preparing the gardens. They could easily double that time without significantly changing their other activities. But they don't.

Instead, the Yanomami apparently take into consideration that they will trek and, therefore, plant no more than necessary for several months' supply. In fact they spend an average of 40 percent of the time in the forest trekking, and in some cases as much as 60 percent. The underlying practical reason seems to be that plantains (or manioc, in the case of other Amazonian tribes, such as the Kayapó) are rich in vitamins and minerals but have very little protein. Lacking a more balanced range of crops and domesticated food animals, the Yanomami must get their meat and fat as they have always done, from the wild animals of the forest.

Amazonian game species are relatively small and elusive, and hunters often fail in their quests. Even with this poor hunting record, when a village stays in one place for a long period of time, the local animals are quickly depleted. One way to compensate for this is for the men to leave their families and gardens and go out on long-distance hunts. Camping in the forest, with minimal food, they hunt from dawn to dusk for up to a week. Trekking, however, offers an alternative that keeps family members together and allows long-term exploitation of other forest areas. My studies show that on treks, hunting yields are double those near the garden location. Consumption of wild foods increases from 10 percent to almost 70 percent. (The diet still includes some crops, retrieved from the gardens during the early and late stages of the trek.)

While the group is out trekking for weeks or months, the young plantains in the gardens are maturing. When the wild foods become harder to obtain, the trekkers begin their return. They may even say that they get tired of wild foods and that their minds turn again to plantains. The truth is that they must go back. They cannot subsist year-round as hunter-gatherers because the domesticated crops have allowed their average

village populations to grow to sixty or seventy. Wild foods are too dispersed to feed so large a group, even for one or two nights. But neither can the Yanomami be full-time farmers, because adequate protein is not provided at the garden sites.

Apart from fulfilling nutritional needs, there are other advantages to trekking. As a village grows larger, quarrels are more likely to erupt in the community. For example, even a large game animal does not yield enough meat for all the families. Meat is the only item in Yanomami culture that is shared village-wide. To be slighted in the distribution causes very intense feelings. When such tensions reach a peak, the village can split, with each faction going on its own trek in a different direction. This separation allows for a cooling off of emotions.

Splitting up also makes for a better return on foraging. While today fifty or sixty Yanomami may trek together, most likely in the past, when they were full-time hunters and gatherers, they would have had to restrict their group size to a maximum of twenty or twenty-five. In a smaller group, the killing of a large animal will provide each family with a larger and more choice piece than would be possible if the entire community were living together. The increased supply is

especially welcome because the Yanomami normally get to eat meat only twice a week and usually in very small portions.

When a large village splits up on the trek because of internal friction or because the group is simply too large to travel together, one group of families may begin new gardens at a distant campsite. On subsequent treks, the gardens will be expanded, and when they begin to produce crops, the families move there, eventually constructing a new communal shelter. In this way a village splits permanently, dealing peacefully with problems of disharmony and an inadequate supply of food, especially meat. Otherwise these problems can lead to a violent fission.

Trekking can also have a downside. When a community returns to its gardens after an extended stay in the forest, it sometimes finds that other Yanomami, also on trek, have made their way to the untended gardens and eaten the newly matured crops. This results in a severe food crisis for the returnees, and on occasion, hostilities develop between villages. These may take the form of a chest-pounding match (opponents take turns slugging each other in the chest), a club fight, or even a raid. In the case of a raid, trekking also has a role to play. When raiders return home after attacking

This woman sets out on a trek with all her household possessions.

A Reputation for War

R. Brian Ferguson

Ever since they were dubbed "the fierce people" by anthropologist Napoleon Chagnon in the 1960s, the Yanomami have typified primitive belligerence for hundreds of thousands of college students. The groups Chagnon lived with on the upper Orinoco River seemed endlessly embroiled in fights, duels, and treacherous raids, as the men competed over women and status or sought to avenge previous killings. The vivid descriptions of Yanomami character and warfare helped fuel a debate over whether humans were inevitably propelled toward violence. The debate was largely precipitated by Robert Ardrey's popular book *African Genesis* (1961), which argues that humans had a genetic heritage as "killer apes." Many academics countered that, far from being instinctive, warfare would have played a minor role throughout most of the human evolutionary career. They tied the advent of warfare to the agricultural revolution, with its sedentary communities and stores of food, and the subsequent rise of centralized states. Human nature, they declared, was almost by definition plastic, shaped by culture, and humans could be educated to solve their conflicts in other ways. Against the background of the Vietnam War, this was a more optimistic message.

Enter the Yanomami, a people apparently isolated from outside influences until recent times. They were proclaimed by some to be the living embodiment of a vio-

Kenneth Good

An adulterous affair caused two men to fight each other with clubs.

lent evolutionary heritage. Others, rejecting this grim interpretation, sought an adaptive explanation for Yanomami behavior. They proposed that in the tropical Amazonian forest, which lacked rich concentrations of resources, warfare and hostility served to break up groups into sustainable size and then space them suitably across the land-

scape. In this view, although warfare had its costs, it contributed to the Yanomami's ability to survive within the limitations of their ecosystem.

Both of these interpretations took for granted that the Yanomami way of life was pristine. But my historical studies, comparing the experiences of many different

another village, they and the rest of their community often leave on a trek to avoid becoming sitting ducks in a revenge raid.

More than 95 percent of the Yanomami still live in their traditional deep-woods environment. But a few communities that have settled along rivers have adopted new ways of making a living, made possible by access to manufactured goods from traders or from a Western settlement. These Yanomami spend less effort on inland hunting. Instead, fishing takes on greater importance, the men taking to the rivers in canoes. They use manufactured hooks and lines, often fishing at night with lights acquired through trade or labor. Once they acquire or learn to make dugout canoes, they can fish over a greater range without moving the communal shelter or trekking. Watercraft are also used to add to the

number of areas where gardens can be cleared, maintained, and harvested. They often use areas across the river from the settlement for gardening and hunting.

Yanomami river settlers grow larger gardens, aided in part by the greater availability of steel axes and machetes for forest clearing. They also learn from outsiders how to grow and process other foods besides plantains. Most common are cassava bread and manioc meal, both of which can be stored for use when plantains are not abundant. As a result, these communities engage in fewer treks; some have discontinued the practice altogether.

While the river settlements may have benefited from manufactured goods, Yanomami communities along the Venezuelan-Brazilian border have been dev-

astated by outside contacts. A Brazilian policy of opening this area to settlers, cattle ranchers, loggers, and gold miners has resulted in the poisoning of rivers and streams with byproducts of gold processing and the stripping of thousands of acres of forest for logging and pastures. An international outcry has provoked some government effort to halt this activity, but control of these very remote areas has been spotty at best. As a result, the Yanomami who live there have been deprived of the forest they use to feed themselves.

In 1993, the conflict of interests resulted in tragedy. With their large stores of steel tools, clothing, medicines, shotguns, and shells, Brazilian gold-mining camps in Yanomami territory had become a major attraction to nearby vil-

Yanomami groups, have led me to reject that view. I have found that these Amazonians have been affected by the presence of European Americans for up to 350 years, and that Yanomami warfare can only be understood in this light.

Outside influences began in the 1630s, when Portuguese, Spanish, and Dutch colonists, or their indigenous allies, came raiding for slaves. The ensuing violence wiped out the more complex societies that had existed in the Yanomami region—densely settled chiefdoms of river traders—and restricted the Yanomami to highland sanctuaries. Both peaceable and violent contacts between Yanomami and outsiders occurred from the mid-eighteenth century until 1950, when the first Protestant mission settled in alongside a Yanomami village, initiating extensive interactions that still continue.

When the political history of Yanomami living in various parts of their territory is reconstructed, a connection emerges between their wars (with one another or with neighboring peoples) and significant changes in the European American presence. The common thread in their fighting appears to be access to, and control over, sources of Western trade goods. Like other Amazonian groups, the Yanomami have rapidly come to regard steel tools, aluminum pots, cloth, and other manufactured items as necessities. Yanomami able to obtain these goods close to the source want them not only for their own use but also to trade with groups farther away. In exchange, other Yanomami provide local products, labor, wives, and political support. Friction arises because the interests involved in these exchange relationships are

so vital and the inequalities are so pronounced. This friction can lead to raiding, directed at protecting or improving positions within the radiating trade networks.

In the first decade in this century, for example, the frenzied rubber-tapping boom in Amazonia led to a surge in Western trade goods passing along the Uraricoera and other rivers near Brazilian Yanomami territory. In a series of raids, ambushes, and at least one pitched battle, some local Yanomami groups carved out a niche in the trade system. They then gave up raiding, but soon were pressed from behind by the "wild" Yanomami in the mountains.

For some Yanomami, including those living around the mission posts of the upper Orinoco River, contact with resident outsiders has led to a much more sedentary way of life. Over time, hunting depleted local game supplies and was replaced by fishing, more intensive cultivation, and the consumption of mission foods. Having lost their mobile way of life, these groups are unable to follow the traditional option of moving away when frictions arise. And with little hunting, they lose the custom of sharing meat, which as Kenneth Good has observed, is a source of solidarity. Worst of all, their exposure to outsiders brings them new diseases, with epidemics tearing great holes in the social fabric. For some Yanomami, such as those encountered by Chagnon, long and strong contact with the outside world created so much disruption that, for a time, violence became almost normal in interpersonal relations.

The Yanomami case shows the extraordinary reach and transforming effects a

centrally governed society, or state, may have, extending way beyond its last outpost. The impact of disease, trade goods, migrations, and political restructurings can spread far in advance of face-to-face contact, and when the state's advance agents to arrive, they commonly bring even more destruction with them. Because they may possess firearms or dispense coveted trade goods, even contemporary missionaries and anthropologists can become important players in these conflicts and the focus of violent competition. That is what happened on the upper Orinoco.

The changing economic and political conditions in a remote "tribal zone" can lead to bloodshed, sometimes creating warfare in regions where little or none existed in the past. For centuries, Westerners have looked upon such carnage and used it to justify the obliteration of indigenous cultures in the name of civilization. What has not been acknowledged is that the "savage" behavior is itself often a result of foreign intrusion; that local conflicts are firmly connected to global processes. The Yanomami have taught us to proceed with extreme caution before assuming warfare in indigenous groups is pristine and isolated. Anthropologists can lead the way in applying this important lesson to so-called ethnic or tribal warfare in Africa and Europe.

R. Brian Ferguson, an associate professor of anthropology at the Newark campus of Rutgers University, is the author of Yanomami Warfare: A Political History *(Santa Fe: SAR Press, 1995).*

lagers, particularly the young men. The miners found the Yanomami's persistent requests for goods a great irritant and even threatened to respond with violence. The friction came to a head when a group of miners, annoyed by the requests, as well as by a demand that they return a confiscated shotgun, decided to kill the young men. Encountering them on the trail, they shot several of them execution-style. After a series of retaliatory raids by the Yanomami, the miners raided the village, killing about twelve.

Those shot included men, women, and children, some of whom were hacked, dismembered, and decapitated with machetes after being gravely wounded.

Perhaps it is unrealistic to hope the Yanomami will be allowed to continue living by their traditional culture. But more is at stake than whether they will be absorbed culturally by the surrounding societies. Their very physical survival is in jeopardy. As national governments open up the tropical forests to development, the Yanomami will be pushed off

the land. Already their rivers and streams are being polluted, while the animals they hunt for critical protein are being driven away by machinery used in lumbering and mining. Intensified by outside contact, malaria and respiratory diseases are also taking a toll. If these trends continue without restrictions, the Yanomami will die out. Their destiny is ultimately in the hands of those who have come to control the lands where the Yanomami have trekked for so many generations.

Mystique of the Masai

*Pastoral as well as warlike, they have persisted in
maintaining their unique way of life*

Ettagale Blauer

*Ettagale Blauer is a New York-based
writer who has studied the Masai culture extensively in numerous trips to Africa and who specializes in writing
about Africa and jewelry.*

The noble bearing, self-assurance, and
great beauty of the Masai of East Africa
have been remarked upon from the time
the first Europeans encountered them on
the plains of what are now Kenya and
Tanzania. (The word 'Masai' derives
from their spoken language, Maa.) Historically, the Masai have lived among
the wild animals on the rolling plains of
the Rift Valley, one of the most beautiful
parts of Africa. Here, the last great herds
still roam freely across the plains in
their semiannual migrations.

Although the appearance of people
usually marks the decline of the game,
it is precisely the presence of the Masai
that has guaranteed the existence of
these vast herds. Elsewhere in Kenya
and Tanzania, and certainly throughout
the rest of Africa, the herds that once
roamed the lands have been decimated.
But the Masai are not hunters, whom
they call *iltorrobo*—poor men—because
they don't have cattle. The Masai do not
crave animal trophies, they do not value
rhinoceros horns for aphrodisiacs, meat
is not part of their usual diet, and they

don't farm the land, believing it to be a
sacrilege to break the earth. Traditionally, where Masai live, the game is un-
molested.

In contrast to their peaceful and harmonious relationship to the wildlife,
however, the Masai are warlike in relationship to the neighboring tribes, conducting cattle raids where they take
women as well as cattle for their prizes,
and they have been fiercely independent
in resisting the attempts of colonial governments to change or subdue them.
Although less numerous than the neighboring Kikuyu, the Masai have a strong
feeling of being "chosen" people, and
have been stubborn in maintaining their
tribal identity.

However, that traditional tribal way
of life is threatened by the exploding
populations of Kenya and Tanzania (41
million people), who covet the vast open
spaces of Masai Mara, Masai Amboseli,
and the Serengeti Plain. Today, more
than half of the Masai live in Kenya,
with a style of life that requires extensive territory for cattle herds to roam in
search of water and pastureland, and the
freedom to hold ceremonies that mark
the passage from one stage of life to the
next. The Masai's need for land for their
huge herds of cattle is not appreciated
by people who value the land more for

agriculture than for pasturage and for
herds of wild animals.

The Masai live in countries that are
attractive to tourists and whose leaders
have embraced the values and life-style
of the Western world. These two facts
make it increasingly difficult for the
Masai to live according to traditional
patterns. The pressure to change in
Kenya comes in part from their proximity to urban centers, especially the capital city of Nairobi, whose name is a
Masai word meaning cool water.

Still, many Masai live in traditional
homes and dress in wraps of bright cloth
or leather, decorated with beaded jewelry, their cattle nearby. But the essence
of the Masai culture—the creation of
age-sets whose roles in life are clearly
delineated—is under constant attack. In
both Kenya and Tazania, the governments continually try to "civilize" the
Masai, to stop cattle raiding, and especially to put an end to the *morani*—the
warriors—who are seen as the most disruptive of the age-sets.

TRADITIONAL LIFE

Masai legends trace the culture back
some 300 years, and are recited according to age-groups, allowing fifteen years
for each group. But anthropologists be-

lieve they arrived in the region some 1,000 years ago, having migrated from southern Ethiopia. As a racial group, they are considered a Nilo-Hamitic mix. Although deep brown in color, their features are not negroid. (Their extensive use of ochre may give their skin the look of American Indians but that is purely cosmetic.)

Traditional Masai people are governed by one guiding principle: that all the cattle on earth are theirs, that they were put there for them by *Ngai*, who is the god of both heaven and earth, existing also in the rains which bring the precious grass to feed the cattle. Any cattle they do not presently own are only temporarily out of their care, and must be recaptured. The Masai do not steal material objects; theft for them is a separate matter from raiding cattle, which is seen as the *return* of cattle to their rightful owners. From this basic belief, an entire culture has grown. The grass that feeds the cattle and the ground on which it grows are sacred; to the Masai, it is sacrilege to break the ground for any reason, whether to grow food or to dig for water, or even to bury the dead.

Cattle provide their sole sustenance: milk and blood to drink, and the meat feast when permitted. Meat eating is restricted to ceremonial occasions, or when it is needed for gaining strength, such as when a woman gives birth or someone is recovering from an illness. When they do eat meat at a ceremony they consume their own oxen, which are sacrificed for a particular reason and in the approved way. Hunting and killing for meat are not Masai activities. It is this total dependence on their cattle, and their disdain for the meat of game animals, that permits them to coexist with the game, and which, in turn, has kept intact the great herds of the Masai Mara and the Serengeti Plain. Their extraordinary diet of milk, blood, and occasionally, meat, keeps them sleek and fit, and Westerners have often noted their physical condition with admiration.

In 1925 Norman Leys wrote, "Physically they are among the handsomest of mankind, with slender bones, narrow hips and shoulders and most beautifully rounded muscles and limbs." That same description holds today. The Masai live

A map of Masai Land. The Masai's traditional territory exists within the two countries of Kenya and Tanzania.

EMIKO OZAKI/THE WORLD & I

on about 1,300 calories a day, as opposed to our consumption of nearly 3,000. They are invariably lean.

Traditional nomadic life of the Masai, however, was ferocious and warlike in relation to other tribes. The warriors *(morani)* built *manyattas,* a type of shelter, throughout the lands and used each for a few months at a time, then moved to another area when the grazing was used up. As the seasons changed, they would return to those manyattas. They often went out raiding cattle from neighboring tribes whom they terrorized with their great ferocity.

A large part of that aggressiveness is now attributed to drugs; the morani worked themselves into a frenzy as they prepared for a raid, using the leaves and barks of certain trees known to create such moods. A soup was made of fat, water, and the bark of two trees, *il kitosloswa* and *il kiluretti*. From the description, these seem to act as hallucino-

gens. As early as the 1840s, Europeans understood that the morani's extremely aggressive behavior derived from drug use. Drugs were used for endurance and for strength throughout warriorhood. During a meat feast, which could last a month, they took stimulants throughout, raising them to a virtual frenzy. This, combined with the natural excitement attendant to crowd behavior, made them formidable foes.

Having gained this supernatural energy and courage, they were ready to go cattle raiding among other tribes. To capture the cattle, the men of the other tribe had to be killed. Women were never touched in battle, but were taken to Masailand to become Masai wives. The rate of intermarriage was great during these years. Today, intermarriage is less frequent and the result mostly of chance meetings with other people. It is likely that intermarriage has actually prolonged the life of the Masai as a people; many observers from the early 1900s remarked upon the high rate of syphilis among the Masai, attributable to their habit of taking multiple sexual partners. Their birthrate is notably lower than the explosive population growth of the other peoples of Kenya and Tanzania. Still, they have increased from about 25,000 people at the turn of the century to the estimated 300,000–400,000 they are said to number today.

While the ceaseless cycle of their nomadic life has been sharply curtailed, many still cross the border between the two countries as they have for hundreds of years, leading their cattle to water and grazing lands according to the demands of the wet and dry seasons. They are in tune with the animals that migrate from the Serengeti Plain in Tanzania to Masai Mara in Kenya, and back again.

MALE AGE-SETS

The life of a traditional Masai male follows a well-ordered progression through a series of life stages.

Masai children enjoy their early years as coddled and adored love objects. They are raised communally, with great affection. Children are a great blessing in Africa. Among the Masai, with the lack of emphasis on paternity, and with a woman's prestige tied to her children, natural love for children is enhanced by their desirability in the society. Children are also desired because they bring additional cattle to a family, either as bride-price in the case of girls or by raiding in the case of boys.

During their early years, children play and imitate the actions of the elders, a natural school in which they learn the rituals and daily life practices of their people. Learning how to be a Masai is the lifework of every one in the community. Infant mortality in Africa remains high; catastrophic diseases introduced by Europeans, such as smallpox, nearly wiped them out. That memory is alive in their oral traditions; having children is a protection against the loss of the entire culture, which they know from experience could easily happen. Africans believe that you must live to see your face reflected in that of a child; given the high infant mortality rate, the only way to protect that human chain is by having as many children as possible.

For boys, each stage of life embraces an age-group created at an elaborate ceremony, the highlight of their lives being the elevation to moran. Once initiated, they learn their age-group's specific duties and privileges. Males pass through four stages: childhood, boyhood, warriorhood, and elderhood. Warriors, divided into junior and senior, form one generation, or age-set.

Four major ceremonies mark the passage from one group to another: boys who are going to be circumcised participate in the *Alamal Lenkapaata* ceremony, preparation for circumcision; *Emorata* is followed by initiation into warriorhood—status of moran; the passage from warrior to elderhood is marked by the *Eunoto* ceremony; and total elderhood is confirmed by the *Olngesherr.* All ceremonies have in common ritual head shaving, continual blessings, slaughter of an animal, ceremonial painting of face or body, singing, dancing, and feasting. *Laibons*—spiritual advisers—must be present at all ceremonies, and the entire tribe devotes itself to these preparations.

Circumcision is a rite of passage and more for teenage boys. It determines the role the boy will play throughout his life, as leader or follower. How he conducts himself during circumcision is keenly observed by all; a boy who cries out during the painful operation is branded a coward and shunned for a long time; his mother is disgraced. A boy who is brave, and who had led an exemplary life, becomes the leader of his age-group.

It takes months of work to prepare for these ceremonies so the exact date of such an event is rarely known until the last minute. Westerners, with contacts into the Masai community, often stay ready for weeks, hoping to be on hand when such a ceremony is about to take place. Each such ceremony may well be the last, it is thought.

Before they can be circumcised, boys must prove themselves ready. They tend the cattle—the Masai's only wealth—and guard them from predators whose tracks they learn to recognize. They know their cattle individually, the way we know people. Each animal has a name and is treated as a personality. When they feel they are ready, the boys approach the junior elders and ask them to open a new circumcision period. If this is approved, they begin a series of rituals, among them the Alamal Lenkapaata, the last step before the formal initiation. The boys must have a liabon, a leader with the power to predict the future, to guide them in their decisions. He creates a name for this new generation. The boys decorate themselves with chalky paint, and spend the night out in the open. The elders sing and celebrate and dance through the night to honor the boys.

An Alamal Lenkapaata held in 1983 was probably the most recent to mark the opening of a new age-set. Ceremonies were held in Ewaso Ngiro, in the Rift Valley. As boys joined into groups and danced, they raised a cloud of dust around themselves. All day long, groups would form and dance, then break apart and later start again.

Under a tree, elders from many areas gathered together and their discussion was very intense. John Galaty, professor of anthropology from McGill University in Montreal, who has studied the Masai extensively, flew in specifically to attend this ceremony. He is fluent in Masai and translated the elders' talk. "We are lucky," they said, "to be able to have this ceremony. The government does not want us to have it. We have to be very careful. The young men have to be warned that there should be no cattle raiding." And there wasn't any.

An ox was slaughtered, for meat eating is a vital element of this ceremony. The boys who were taking part cut off hunks of meat which they cooked over an open fire. Though there was a hut set aside for them, the boys spent little time sleeping. The next day, all the elders gathered to receive gifts of sugar and salt from John Keen, a member of Kenya's parliament, and himself a Masai. (Kenya has many Masai in government, including the Minister of Finance, George Saitoti.) The dancing, the meat eating, all the elements of the ceremony continued for several days. If this had been a wealthy group, they might have kept up the celebration for as long as a month.

Once this ceremony is concluded, the boys are allowed to hold councils and to discuss important matters. They choose one from their own group to be their representative. The Alamal Lenkapaata ceremony includes every boy of suitable age, preparing him for circumcision and then warriorhood. The circumcisions will take place over the next few years, beginning with the older boys in this group. The age difference may be considerable in any age-group since these ceremonies are held infrequently; once a circumcision period ends, though, it may not be opened again for many years.

THE MORAN

The Masai who exemplifies his tribe is the moran. This is the time of life that expresses the essence of the Masai—bravery, willingness to defend their people and their cattle against all threats, confidence to go out on cattle raids to increase their own herds, and ability to stand up to threats even from Europeans, whose superior weapons subdued the Masai but never subjugated them. The Masai moran is the essence of that almost mythical being, the noble savage, a description invented by Europeans but here actually lived out. With his spear, his elaborately braided and reddened hair, his bountiful beaded jewelry, his beautiful body and proud bearing, the moran is the symbol of everything that is attractive about the Masai. When a young man becomes a moran, his entire culture looks upon him with reverence.

The life a moran enjoys as his birthright is centered on cattle raiding, enhancing his appearance, and sex. The need to perform actual work, such as building fences, rescuing a cow that has gone astray, and standing ready to defend their homeland—Masailand—is only occasionally required. Much of his time is devoted to the glorification of his appearance. His body is a living showcase of Masai art.

From the moment a boy undergoes the circumcision ceremony, he looks ahead to the time when he will be a moran. He grows his hair long so it can be braided into myriad tiny plaits, thickened with ochre and fat. The age-mates spend hours at this, the whole outdoors being their salon. As they work, they chat, always building the bonds between them. Their beaded jewelry is made by their girlfriends. Their bare legs are ever-changing canvases on which they trace patterns, using white chalk and ochre. Though nearly naked, they are a medley of patterns and colors.

After being circumcised, the young men "float" in society for up to two years, traveling in loose groups and living in temporary shelters called *inkangitie*. After that time they can build a manyatta. Before fully becoming a moran, however, they must enter a "holy house" at a special ceremony. Only a young man who has not slept with a circumcised woman can enter the holy house. The fear of violating this taboo is very strong, and young men who do not enter the house are beaten by their parents and carry the disrespect of the tribe all their lives.

The dancing of the morani celebrates everything that they consider beautiful and strong: morani dance competitively by jumping straight into the air, knees straight, over and over again, each leap trying to go higher than the last, as they sing and chant and encourage each other. The morani also dance with their young girlfriends. Each couple performs sinuous motions repeatedly, then breaks off and another couple takes their place. A hypnotic rhythm develops as they follow the chanting and hand clapping of their mates.

Although they are now forbidden by the governments of Kenya and Tanzania to kill a lion—a traditional test of manhood—or to go cattle raiding, they retain all the trappings of a warrior, without the possibility of practicing their skill. They occasionally manage a cattle raid, but even without it, they still live with pride and dignity. Masai remain morani for about fifteen years, building up unusually strong relationships among their age-mates with whom they live during that time. Hundreds of boys may become morani at one time.

Traditionally, every fifteen years saw the advent of a new generation of warriors. Now, both colonial governments and independent black-ruled governments have tampered with this social process, and have been successful in reducing the time men spend as warriors. By forcing this change, the governments hope to mold the Masai male into a more tractable citizen, especially by forbidding such disruptive activities as lion killing and cattle raiding. But tinkering with the Masai system can have unforeseen and undesirable consequences. It takes a certain number of years before a moran is ready to take on the duties of that age-group. They need time to build up herds of cattle to be used for bride-price and to learn to perform the decision-making tasks expected. This change also leaves the younger boys without warriors to keep them in check, and to guide them through the years leading up to the circumcision ceremony.

More significantly, since 1978 it has been illegal to build a manyatta, and warriors from that time have been left with no place to live. Their mothers cannot live with them, they cannot tend their cattle or increase their herds, they have no wives or jobs. Since, once they become warriors, they are not allowed to enter another person's house to eat, they are forced to steal other peoples' cattle and live off the land.

Circumcision exists for women as well as for men. From the age of nine until puberty, young girls live with the morani as sexual partners; it is an accepted part of Masai life that girls do not reach puberty as virgins. It is because of this practice that syphilis causes the most serious problems for the Masai. The girls, unfamiliar with their bodies, contract the disease and leave it untreated until sterility results. This sexual activity changes dramatically when a girl reaches puberty. At that time, she is circumcised and forbidden to stay with the warriors. This is to prevent her from becoming pregnant before she is married. As soon as she recovers from the circumcision, or clitoridectomy, an operation that destroys her ability to experience orgasm, she is considered ready for marriage. Circumcision is seen as a means of equalizing men and women. By removing any vestige of the appearance of the organs of the opposite sex, it purifies the gender. Although female circumcision has long been banned by the Kenyan government, few girls manage to escape the operation.

While the entire tribe devotes itself to the rituals that perpetuate the male age-set system, girls travel individually through life in their roles as lovers, wives, and child bearers, in all instances subservient to the boys and men. They have no comparable age-set system and hence do not develop the intensely felt friendships of the men who move through life together in groups, and who, during the period of senior warriorhood live together, away from their families.

It is during this period that the mothers move away from their homes. They build manyattas in which they live with their sons who have achieved the status of senior morani, along with their sons' girlfriends, and away from their own small children. The husbands, other wives, and the other women of the tribe, take care of these children.

The male-female relationship is dictated according to the male age-sets. When a newly circumcised girl marries, she joins the household of her husband's family, and likely will be one among several of his wives. Her role is to milk the cows, to build the house, and to bear children, especially male children. Only through childbirth can she achieve high status; all men, on the other hand, achieve status simply by graduating from one age-set to the next.

A childless Masai woman is virtually without a role in her society. One of the rarest ceremonies among the Masai is a blessing for women who have not given birth and for women who want more children. While the women play a peripheral role in the men's ceremonies, the men are vital to the women's, for it is a man who blesses the women. To prepare for the ritual, the women brew great quantities of beer and offer beer and lambs to the men who are to bless them.

In their preparation for this ceremony, and in conducting matters that pertain to their lives, the women talk things out democratically, as do the men. They gather in the fields and each woman presents her views. Not until all who want to speak have done so does the group move toward a consensus. As with the men, a good speaker is highly valued and her views are listened to attentively. But these sessions are restricted to women's issues; the men have the final say over all matters relating to the tribe. Boys may gather in councils as soon as they have completed the Alamal Lenkapaata; girls don't have similar opportunities. They follow their lovers, the morani, devotedly, yet as soon as they reach the age when they can marry, they are wrenched out of this love relationship and given in marriage to much older men, men who have cattle for bride-price.

Because morani do not marry until they are elevated to elderhood, girls must accept husbands who are easily twice their age. But just as the husband has more than one wife, she will have lovers, who are permitted as long as they are members of her husband's circumcision group, not the age group for whom she was a girlfriend. This is often the cause of tension among the Masai. All the children she bears are considered to be her husband's even though they may not be his biologically. While incest taboos are clearly observed and various other taboos also pertain, multiple partners are expected. Polygamy in Masailand (and anywhere it prevails) dictates that some men will not marry at all. These men are likely to be those without cattle, men who cannot bring bride-price. For the less traditional, the payment of bride-price is sometimes made in cash, rather than in cattle, and to earn money, men go to the cities to seek work. Masai tend to find jobs that permit them to be outside and free; for this reason, many of the night watchmen in the capital city of Nairobi are Masai. They sit around fires at night, chatting, in an urban version of their life in the countryside. . . .

RAIDING, THEFT, AND THE LAW

Though now subject to national laws, the Masai do not turn to official bodies or courts for redress. They settle their own disputes democratically, each man giving his opinion until the matter at hand is settled. Men decide all matters for the tribe (women do not take part in these discussions), and they operate virtually without chiefs. The overriding concern is to be fair in the resolution of problems because kinship ties the Masai together in every aspect of their lives. Once a decision is made, punishment is always levied in the form of a fine. The Masai have no jails, nor do they inflict physical punishment. For a people who value cattle as much as they do, there is no greater sacrifice than to give up some of their animals.

The introduction of schools is another encroachment upon traditional life which was opposed by the Masai. While most African societies resisted sending their children to school, the Masai reacted with particular intensity. They compared school to death or enslavement; if children did go to school, they would be lost to the Masai community. They would forget how to survive on the land, how to identify animals by their tracks, and how to protect the cattle. All of these things are learned by example and by experience.

David Read is a white Kenyan, fluent in Masai who said that, as a boy: "I may not have been able to read or write, but I knew how to live in the bush. I could hunt my dinner if I had to."

The first school in their territory was opened in 1919 at Narok but few children attended. The Masai scorned the other tribes, such as the Kikuyu, who later embraced Western culture and soon filled the offices of the government's bureaucracies. The distance between the Masai and the other tribes became even greater. The Masai were seen as a painful reminder of the primitivism that Europeans as well as Africans had worked so hard to erase. Today, however, many Masai families will keep one son at home to maintain traditional life, and send another one to school. In this way, they experience the benefits of literacy, opportunities for employment, money, connections to the government, and new knowledge, especially veterinary practices, while keeping their traditions intact. Masai who go to school tend to succeed, many of them graduating from college with science degrees.

Some take up the study of animal diseases, and bring this knowledge back to help their communities improve the health of their cattle. The entire Masai herd was once nearly wiped out during the rinderpest epidemic in the late nineteenth century. Today, the cattle are threatened by tsetse flies. But where the Masai were able to rebuild their herds in the past, today, they would face tremendous pressure to give up cattle raising entirely.

LIVING CONDITIONS

While the Masai are admired for their great beauty, their living conditions are breeding grounds for disease. Since they keep their small livestock (sheep and goats) in the huts where they live, they are continually exposed to the animals' excrement. The cattle are just outside, in an open enclosure, and their excrement is added to the mix. Flies abound wherever cattle are kept, but with the animals living right next to the huts, they are ever-present. Like many tribal groups living in relative isolation, the Masai are highly vulnerable to diseases brought in by others. In the 1890s, when the rinderpest hit their cattle, the Masai were attacked by smallpox which, coupled with drought, reduced their numbers almost to the vanishing point.

For the most part, the Masai rely on the remedies of their traditional medicine and are renowned for their extensive knowledge and use of natural plants to treat illnesses and diseases of both people and cattle. Since they live in an area that had hardly any permanent sources of water, the Masai have learned to live without washing. They are said to have one bath at birth, another at marriage. Flies are pervasive; there is scarcely a picture of a Masai taken in their home environment that does not show flies alit on them.

Their rounded huts, looking like mushrooms growing from the ground, are built by the women. On a frame of wooden twigs, they begin to plaster mud and cow dung. Layers and layers of this are added until the roof reaches the desired thickness. Each day, cracks and holes are repaired, especially after the rains, using the readily available dung. Within the homes, they use animal hides. Everything they need can be made from the materials at hand. There are a few items such as sugar, tea, and cloth that they buy from the *dukas*, or Indian shops, in Narok, Kajiado, and other nearby towns, but money is readily obtained by selling beaded jewelry, or simply one's own image. Long ago, the Masai discovered their photogenic qualities. If they cannot survive as warriors by raiding, they will survive as icons of warriors, permitting tourists to take their pictures for a fee, and that fee is determined by hard bargaining. One does not simply take a picture of a Masai without payment; that is theft.

Their nomadic patterns have been greatly reduced; now they move only the cattle as the seasons change. During the dry season, the Masai stay on the higher parts of the escarpment and use the pastures there which they call *osukupo*. This offers a richer savannah with more trees. When the rains come, they move down to the pastures of the Rift Valley to the plains called *okpurkel*.

Their kraals are built a few miles from the water supply. The cattle drink on one day only, then are grazed the next, so they can conserve the grazing by using a larger area than they would be able to if they watered the cattle every day. But their great love of cattle has inevitably brought them to the point of overstocking. As the cattle trample their way to and from the waterhole, they destroy all vegetation near it, and the soil washes away. Scientists studying Masai land use have concluded that with the change from a totally nomadic way of life, the natural environmental resistance of this system was destroyed; there is no self-regulating mechanism left. Some Masai have permitted wheat farming on their land for the exploding Kenyan population, taking away the marginal lands that traditionally provided further grazing for their cattle.

PRESSURE TO CHANGE

In June 1901, Sir Charles Eliot, colonial governor of Kenya, said, "I regard the Masai as the most important and dangerous of the tribes with whom we have to deal in East Africa and I think it will be long necessary to maintain an adequate military force in the districts which they inhabit."

The traditional Masai way of life has been under attack ever since. The colonial British governments of Kenya and Tanzania (then Tanganyika) outlawed Masai cattle raiding and tried to stifle the initiation ceremony; the black governments that took over upon independence in the 1960s continued the process. The Masai resisted these edicts, ignored them, and did their best to circumvent them throughout the century. In some areas, they gave in entirely—cattle raiding, the principal activity of the morani—rarely occurs, but their ceremonies, the vital processes by which a boy becomes a moran and a moran becomes an elder, remain intact, although they have been banned over and over again. Stopping these ceremonies is more difficult than just proclaiming them to be over, as the Kenyan government did in 1985.

Some laws restrict the very essence of a Masai's readiness to assume the position of moran. Hunting was banned entirely in Kenya and nearly so in Tanzania (except for expensive permits issued to tourists, and restricted to designated hunting blocks), making it illegal for a moran to kill a lion to demonstrate his bravery and hunting skills. Although the Masai ignore the government whenever possible, at times such as this, conflict is unavoidable. Lions are killed occasionally, but stealthily; some modern Masai boys say, "Who needs to kill a lion? It doesn't prove anything."

The Kenyan governments requirement that Masai children go to school has also affected the traditional roles of girls and women, who traditionally married at age twelve or thirteen and left school. Now the government will send fathers and husbands to jail for taking these girls out of school. There was a case in Kenya in 1986 of a girl who wrote to the government protesting the fact that her father had removed her from school to prepare for marriage. Her mother carried the letter to the appropriate government officials, the father was tried, and the girl was allowed to return to school.

Sometimes there is cooperation between governmental policy and traditional life-style. Ceremonies are scheduled to take place in school holidays, and while government policies continue to erode traditional customs, the educated and traditional groups within the Masai community try to support each other.

TRADITION IN THE FACE OF CHANGE

Although the Masai in both countries are descended from the same people, national policies have pushed the Kenyan Masai further away from their traditions. The Tanzanian Masai, for example, still dress occasionally in animal skins, decorated with beading. The Kenyan Masai dress almost entirely in cloth, reserving skins for ceremonial occasions.

In 1977, Kenya and Tanzania closed their common border, greatly isolating the Tanzanian Masai from Western contact. Though the border has been reopened, the impact on the Masai is clear. The Kenyan Masai became one of the sights of the tourist route while the Tanzanian Masai were kept from such interaction. This has further accelerated change among the Kenyan Masai. Tepilit Ole Saitoti sees a real difference in character between the Masai of Kenya and Tanzania. "Temperamentally" he says, "the Tanzanian Masai tend to be calmer and slower than those in Kenya."

Tribal people throughout Africa are in a constant state of change, some totally urbanized, their traditions nearly forgotten; others are caught in the middle, part of the tribe living traditionally, some moving to the city and adopting Western ways. The Masai have retained their culture, their unique and distinctive way of life, longer than virtually all the other tribes of East Africa, and they have done so while living in the very middle of the tourist traffic. Rather than disappear into the bush, the Masai use their attractiveness and mystique to their own benefit. Masai Mara and Amboseli, two reserves set aside for them, are run by them for their own profit.

Few tribes in Africa still put such a clear cultural stamp on an area; few have so successfully resisted enormous efforts to change them, to modernize and "civilize" them, to make them fit into the larger society. We leave it to Tepilit Ole Saitoti to predict the future of his own people: "Through their long and difficult history, the Masai have fought to maintain their traditional way of life. Today, however, they can no longer resist the pressures of the modern world. The survival of Masai culture has ceased to be a question; in truth, it is rapidly disappearing."

Bibliography

Bleeker, Sonia, *The Masai, Herders of East Africa,* 1963

Fedders, Andrew, *Peoples and Cultures of Kenya,* TransAfrica Books, Nairobi, 1979.

Fisher, Angela, *Africa Adorned,* Harry N. Abrams Inc., New York, 1984.

Kinde, S. H., *Last of the Masai,* London, 1901.

Kipkorir, B., *Kenya's People, People of the Rift Valley,* Evans Bros. Ltd., London, 1978

Lamb, David, *The Africans,* Vintage Books, New York, 1984.

Moravia, Alberto, *Which Tribe Do You Belong To?,* Farrar, Straus & Giroux, Inc., New York, 1974.

Ole Saitoti, Tepilit, *Masai,* Harry N. Abrams, Inc., New York, 1980.

Ricciardi, Mirella, *Vanishing Africa,* Holt, Rinehard & Winston, 1971.

Sankan, S. S., *The Masai,* Kenya Literature Bureau, Nairobi, 1971.

Thomson, Joseph, *Through Masai Land,* Sampson Low, Marstan & Co., London, 1885.

Tignor, Robert, *The Colonial Transformation of Kenya, The Kamba, Kikuyu and Masai from 1900 to 1939,* Princeton, NJ, 1976.

Too Many Bananas, Not Enough Pineapples, and No Watermelon at All: Three Object Lessons in Living with Reciprocity

David Counts

McMaster University

NO WATERMELON AT ALL

The woman came all the way through the village, walking between the two rows of houses facing each other between the beach and the bush, to the very last house standing on a little spit of land at the mouth of the Kaini River. She was carrying a watermelon on her head, and the house she came to was the government "rest house," maintained by the villagers for the occasional use of visiting officials. Though my wife and I were graduate students, not officials, and had asked for permission to stay in the village for the coming year, we were living in the rest house while the debate went on about where a house would be built for us. When the woman offered to sell us the watermelon for two shillings, we happily agreed, and the kids were delighted at the prospect of watermelon after yet another meal of rice and bully beef. The money changed hands and the seller left to return to her vil-

lage, a couple of miles along the coast to the east.

It seemed only seconds later that the woman was back, reluctantly accompanying Kolia, the man who had already made it clear to us that he was the leader of the village. Kolia had no English, and at that time, three or four days into our first stay in Kandoka Village on the island of New Britain in Papua New Guinea, we had very little Tok Pisin. Language difficulties notwithstanding, Kolia managed to make his message clear: The woman had been outrageously wrong to sell us the watermelon for two shillings and we were to return it to her and reclaim our money immediately. When we tried to explain that we thought the price to be fair and were happy with the bargain, Kolia explained again and finally made it clear that we had missed the point. The problem wasn't that we had paid too much; it was that we had paid at all. Here he was, a leader, responsible for us while we were living in his village, and we had shamed him. How would it look if he let guests in his village *buy* food? If we wanted watermelons, or bananas, or

anything else, all that was necessary was to let him know. He told us that it would be all right for us to give little gifts to people who brought food to us (and they surely would), but *no one* was to sell food to us. If anyone were to try—like this woman from Lauvore—then we should refuse. There would be plenty of watermelons without us buying them.

The woman left with her watermelon, disgruntled, and we were left with our two shillings. But we had learned the first lesson of many about living in Kandoka. We didn't pay money for food again that whole year, and we did get lots of food brought to us . . . but we never got another watermelon. That one was the last of the season.

LESSON 1: *In a society where food is shared or gifted as part of social life, you may not buy it with money.*

TOO MANY BANANAS

In the couple of months that followed the watermelon incident, we managed to become at least marginally competent in

From *The Humbled Anthropologist: Tales from the Pacific* by David Counts, 1990, pp. 18-24. Published by Wadsworth Publishing Company. © 1990 by David Counts. Reprinted by permission.

Tok Pisin, to negotiate the construction of a house on what we hoped was neutral ground, and to settle into the routine of our fieldwork. As our village leader had predicted, plenty of food was brought to us. Indeed, seldom did a day pass without something coming in— some sweet potatoes, a few taro, a papaya, the occasional pineapple, or some bananas—lots of bananas.

We had learned our lesson about the money, though, so we never even offered to buy the things that were brought, but instead made gifts, usually of tobacco to the adults or chewing gum to the children. Nor were we so gauche as to haggle with a giver over how much of a return gift was appropriate, though the two of us sometimes conferred as to whether what had been brought was a "two-stick" or a "three-stick" stalk, bundle, or whatever. A "stick" of tobacco was a single large leaf, soaked in rum and then twisted into a ropelike form. This, wrapped in half a sheet of newsprint (torn for use as cigarette paper), sold in the local trade stores for a shilling. Nearly all of the adults in the village smoked a great deal, and they seldom had much cash, so our stocks of twist tobacco and stacks of the Sydney *Morning Herald* (all, unfortunately, the same day's issue) were seen as a real boon to those who preferred "stick" to the locally grown product.

We had established a pattern with respect to the gifts of food. When a donor appeared at our veranda we would offer our thanks and talk with them for a few minutes (usually about our children, who seemed to hold a real fascination for the villagers and for whom most of the gifts were intended) and then we would inquire whether they could use some tobacco. It was almost never refused, though occasionally a small bottle of kerosene, a box of matches, some laundry soap, a cup of rice, or a tin of meat would be requested instead of (or even in addition to) the tobacco. Everyone, even Kolia, seemed to think this arrangement had worked out well.

Now, what must be kept in mind is that while we were following their rules—or seemed to be—we were *really still buying food*. In fact we kept a running account of what came in and what

we "paid" for it. Tobacco as currency got a little complicated, but since the exchange rate was one stick to one shilling, it was not too much trouble as long as everyone was happy, and meanwhile we could account for the expenditure of "informant fees" and "household expenses." Another thing to keep in mind is that not only did we continue to think in terms of our buying the food that was brought, we thought of them as *selling it*. While it was true they never quoted us a price, they also never asked us if we needed or wanted whatever they had brought. It seemed clear to us that when an adult needed a stick of tobacco, or a child wanted some chewing gum (we had enormous quantities of small packets of Wrigley's for just such eventualities) they would find something surplus to their own needs and bring it along to our "store" and get what they wanted.

By late November 1966, just before the rainy season set in, the bananas were coming into flush, and whereas earlier we had received banana gifts by the "hand" (six or eight bananas in a cluster cut from the stalk), donors now began to bring bananas, "for the children," by the *stalk!* The Kaliai among whom we were living are not exactly specialists in banana cultivation— they only recognize about thirty varieties, while some of their neighbors have more than twice that many—but the kinds they produce differ considerably from each other in size, shape, and taste, so we were not dismayed when we had more than one stalk hanging on our veranda. The stalks ripen a bit at the time, and having some variety was nice. Still, by the time our accumulation had reached *four* complete stalks, the delights of variety had begun to pale a bit. The fruits were ripening progressively and it was clear that even if we and the kids ate nothing but bananas for the next week, some would still fall from the stalk onto the floor in a state of gross overripeness. This was the situation as, late one afternoon, a woman came bringing yet another stalk of bananas up the steps of the house.

Several factors determined our reaction to her approach: one was that there was literally no way we could possibly use the bananas. We hadn't quite reached the point of being crowded off

our veranda by the stalks of fruit, but it was close. Another factor was that we were tired of playing the gift game. We had acquiesced in playing it—no one was permitted to sell us anything, and in turn we only gave things away, refusing under any circumstances to sell tobacco (or anything else) for money. But there had to be a limit. From our perspective what was at issue was that the woman wanted something and she had come to trade for it. Further, what she had brought to trade was something we neither wanted nor could use, and it should have been obvious to her. So we decided to bite the bullet.

The woman, Rogi, climbed the stairs to the veranda, took the stalk from where it was balanced on top of her head, and laid it on the floor with the words, "Here are some bananas for the children." Dorothy and I sat near her on the floor and thanked her for her thought but explained, "You know, we really have too many bananas—we can't use these; maybe you ought to give them to someone else. . . ." The woman looked mystified, then brightened and explained that she didn't want anything for them, she wasn't short of tobacco or anything. They were just a gift for the kids. Then she just sat there, and we sat there, and the bananas sat there, and we tried again. "Look," I said, pointing up to them and counting, "we've got four stalks already hanging here on the veranda—there are too many for us to eat now. Some are rotting already. Even if we eat only bananas, we can't keep up with what's here!"

Rogi's only response was to insist that these were a gift, and that she didn't want anything for them, so we tried yet another tack: "Don't *your* children like bananas?" When she admitted that they did, and that she had none at her house, we suggested that she should take them there. Finally, still puzzled, but convinced we weren't going to keep the bananas, she replaced them on her head, went down the stairs, and made her way back through the village toward her house.

As before, it seemed only moments before Kolia was making his way up the stairs, but this time he hadn't brought the woman in tow. "What was wrong with those bananas? Were they no good?" he demanded. We explained that there was nothing wrong with the bananas at all, but that we simply couldn't use them and it seemed foolish to take them when we had so many and Rogi's own children had none. We obviously didn't make ourselves clear because Kolia then took up the same refrain that Rogi had—he insisted that we shouldn't be worried about taking the bananas, because they were a gift for the children and Rogi hadn't wanted anything for them. There was no reason, he added, to send her away with them—she would be ashamed. I'm afraid we must have seemed as if we were hard of hearing or thought he was, for our only response was to repeat our reasons. We went through it again—there they hung, one, two, three, *four* stalks of bananas, rapidly ripening and already far beyond our capacity to eat—we just weren't ready to accept any more and let them rot (and, we added to ourselves, pay for them with tobacco, to boot).

Kolia finally realized that we were neither hard of hearing nor intentionally offensive, but merely ignorant. He stared at us for a few minutes, thinking, and then asked: "Don't you frequently have visitors during the day and evening?" We nodded. Then he asked, "Don't you usually offer them cigarettes and coffee or milo?" Again, we nodded. "Did it ever occur to you to suppose," he said, "that your visitors might be hungry?" It was at this point in the conversation, as we recall, that we began to see the depth of the pit we had dug for ourselves. We nodded, hesitantly. His last words to us before he went down the stairs and stalked away were just what we were by that time afraid they might be. "When your guests are hungry, *feed them bananas!*"

LESSON 2: Never refuse a gift, and never fail to return a gift. If you cannot use it, you can always give it away to someone else—there is no such thing as too much—there are never too many bananas.

NOT ENOUGH PINEAPPLES

During the fifteen years between that first visit in 1966 and our residence

there in 1981 we had returned to live in Kandoka village twice during the 1970s, and though there were a great many changes in the village, and indeed for all of Papua New Guinea during that time, we continued to live according to the lessons of reciprocity learned during those first months in the field. We bought no food for money and refused no gifts, but shared our surplus. As our family grew, we continued to be accompanied by our younger children. Our place in the village came to be something like that of educated Kaliai who worked far away in New Guinea. Our friends expected us to come "home" when we had leave, but knew that our work kept us away for long periods of time. They also credited us with knowing much more about the rules of their way of life than was our due. And we sometimes shared the delusion that we understood life in the village, but even fifteen years was not long enough to relieve the need for lessons in learning to live within the rules of gift exchange.

In the last paragraph I used the word *friends* to describe the villagers intentionally, but of course they were not all our friends. Over the years some really had become friends, others were acquaintances, others remained consultants or informants to whom we turned when we needed information. Still others, unfortunately, we did not like at all. We tried never to make an issue of these distinctions, of course, and to be even-handed and generous to all, as they were to us. Although we almost never actually refused requests that were made of us, over the long term our reciprocity in the village was balanced. More was given to those who helped us the most, while we gave assistance or donations of small items even to those who were not close or helpful.

One elderly woman in particular was a trial for us. Sara was the eldest of a group of siblings and her younger brother and sister were both generous, informative, and delightful persons. Her younger sister, Makila, was a particularly close friend and consultant, and in deference to that friendship we felt awkward in dealing with the elder sister.

Sara was neither a friend nor an informant, but she had been, since she re-

turned to live in the village at the time of our second trip in 1971, a constant (if minor) drain on our resources. She never asked for much at a time. A bar of soap, a box of matches, a bottle of kerosene, a cup of rice, some onions, a stick or two of tobacco, or some other small item was usually all that was at issue, but whenever she came around it was always to ask for something—or to let us know that when we left, we should give her some of the furnishings from the house. Too, unlike almost everyone else in the village, when she came, she was always empty-handed. We ate no taro from her gardens, and the kids chewed none of her sugarcane. In short, she was, as far as we could tell, a really grasping, selfish old woman—and we were not the only victims of her greed.

Having long before learned the lesson of the bananas, one day we had a stalk that was ripening so fast we couldn't keep up with it, so I pulled a few for our own use (we only had one stalk at the time) and walked down through the village to Ben's house, where his five children were playing. I sat down on his steps to talk, telling him that I intended to give the fruit to his kids. They never got them. Sara saw us from across the open plaza of the village and came rushing over, shouting, "My bananas!" Then she grabbed the stalk and went off gorging herself with them. Ben and I just looked at each other.

Finally it got to the point where it seemed to us that we had to do something. Ten years of being used was long enough. So there came the afternoon when Sara showed up to get some tobacco—again. But this time, when we gave her the two sticks she had demanded, we confronted her.

First, we noted the many times she had come to get things. We didn't mind sharing things, we explained. After all, we had plenty of tobacco and soap and rice and such, and most of it was there so that we could help our friends as they helped us, with folktales, information, or even gifts of food. The problem was that she kept coming to get things, but never came to talk, or to tell stories, or to bring some little something that the kids might like. Sara didn't argue—she agreed. "Look," we suggested, "it doesn't have to be much, and we don't mind giving you things—but you can help us. The kids like pineapples, and we don't have any—the next time you need something, bring something—like maybe a pineapple." Obviously somewhat embarrassed, she took her tobacco and left, saying that she would bring something soon. We were really pleased with ourselves. It had been a very difficult thing to do, but it was done, and we were convinced that either she would start bringing things or not come. It was as if a burden had lifted from our shoulders.

It worked. Only a couple of days passed before Sara was back, bringing her bottle to get it filled with kerosene. But this time, she came carrying the biggest, most beautiful pineapple we had seen the entire time we had been there. We had a friendly talk, filled her kerosene container, and hung the pineapple up on the veranda to ripen just a little

further. A few days later we cut and ate it, and whether the satisfaction it gave came from the fruit or from its source would be hard to say, but it was delicious. That, we assumed, was the end of that irritant.

We were wrong, of course. The next afternoon, Mary, one of our best friends for years (and no relation to Sara), dropped by for a visit. As we talked, her eyes scanned the veranda. Finally she asked whether we hadn't had a pineapple there yesterday. We said we had, but that we had already eaten it. She commented that it had been a really nice-looking one, and we told her that it had been the best we had eaten in months. Then, after a pause, she asked, "Who brought it to you?" We smiled as we said, "Sara!" because Mary would appreciate our coup—she had commented many times in the past on the fact that Sara only *got* from us and never gave.

She was silent for a moment, and then she said, "Well, I'm glad you enjoyed it—my father was waiting until it was fully ripe to harvest it for you, but when it went missing I though maybe it was the one you had here. I'm glad to see you got it. I thought maybe a thief had eaten it in the bush."

LESSON 3: *Where reciprocity is the rule and gifts are the idiom, you cannot demand a gift, just as you cannot refuse a request.*

It says a great deal about the kindness and patience of the Kaliai people that they have been willing to be our hosts for all these years despite our blunders and lack of good manners. They have taught us a lot, and these three lessons are certainly not the least important things we learned.

From Shells to Money

Ceremonial Exchange among the Simbu of Papua New Guinea

High in the mountains of New Guinea, a transformation is taking place as money becomes increasingly important for the formerly secluded Simbu tribespeople

Karl F. Rambo

Karl F. Rambo is currently conducting research in the Papua New Guinea highlands on the economic consequences of rural migration.

While conducting fieldwork among the Simbu in 1985 and 1986, I occasionally encountered people in the small roadside markets selling crescents of large, old pearl shells, to be worn about the neck. Although the price for these was generally only about U.S. $5, the once highly prized shells drew few interested purchasers. In my discussions with the sellers, they invariably mentioned how —in the past—one such shell would form a substantial portion of the bride-price given by the groom's family to the bride's family in the ceremonial gift given at a marriage. Now money equal to thousands of dollars, collected from many people and displayed on tall bamboo poles, is the valuable supplementing traditional items such as pork. Gifts of purchased cartons of beer, stacked and displayed at the ceremonies, are now much more frequent than the once-common ceremonial gifts of colorful bird of paradise plumes.

This adoption of cash into the ceremonial system has affected the course of economic change and development in the New Guinea highlands in an unusual way. Although the Simbu people now eagerly desire money, what motivates their actions is more than a desire for material goods.

Until relatively recently, these people were remote from any of the effects of the market economies that link together much of the rest of the world. Prior to contact with the outside world, the Simbu relied almost solely on the products they themselves produced. At that time the New Guinea highlands lay at the end of multistaged trading systems that extended hundreds of kilometers to the coasts, the source of a most precious traditional valuable—seashells. The source of the shells was so remote that some highlanders believed they grew on trees. Prior to the arrival of Australian colonialists, small quantities of shells passed through many hands on their way to the highlands. There, they became one of the most important items needed for the ceremonial gift exchanges.

These ceremonial exchanges were, and continue to be, essential for establishing and maintaining social relationships between the individual members of the small tribes of the region. Today however, this area no longer remains as isolated from the rest of the world as in the past. Money, and goods purchased with money, has for the most part replaced shells and many other traditional goods previously used in these exchanges. The advent of money in the Papua New Guinea highlands and its in-corporation into the ceremonial exchange system have resulted in the amalgamation of elements of two sometimes conflicting economic value systems.

The recent changes in the highlands of Papua New Guinea are of particular interest to anthropologists and other social scientists in that these changes are recent and well documented. People who were for all intents completely isolated from the industrialized and industrializing world become involved in a worldwide economy when they produce goods or sell their labor in a money-linked market. The last three centuries are replete with examples of incorporation of cultures into such a worldwide economy. In many ways, each case recapitulates the earlier adoption of money by peoples who now rely almost exclusively on a monied, market economy. Money has facilitated the incorporation of many far-flung peoples by providing a medium of exchange that translates the value of many material things and services into a common system. Often, however, with the development of a money economy come greatly increased economic stratification and a loss of economic independence. But because the Simbu have maintained their interest in ceremonial exchanges, they have ameliorated some of the negative effects associated with involvement in the cash-oriented market economy.

This article originally appeared in *The World & I,* May 1989, pp. 645-653. Reprinted by permission of *The World & I,* a publication of The Washington Times Corporation. © 1989.

KARL RAMBO

In preparation for a final marriage ceremony, long bamboo poles, covered in money, are placed in the ground. In the wedding ceremony the groom's relatives give money, pigs, and store-bought goods to the bride's relatives.

But before one can understand this interesting economic transformation, one should know something about the environment, culture, and history of the Simbu. The interaction of these elements with the introduced cash economy has resulted in a melding of the old with the new to produce a monied economy unlike those commonly found in the industrialized world.

Ceremonial Exchange in Traditional Simbu Society

Lying at the heart of the central highlands of the now independent country of Papua New Guinea, Simbu is the most densely populated province in the country, with more than 180,000 people living in an area slightly larger than the state of Delaware. The majority ethnic group, named the Simbu (or Chimbu) by the first Australian patrol that entered the area, live along the slopes of the

mountains bordering the Wahgi River, which runs past some of the highest mountains in the country. In 1933, Australian gold miners and colonial government patrol officers were the first representatives of the outside, Europeanized world to enter the New Guinea mountain valleys the Simbu inhabited. Although little gold was discovered in the area, thousands of tribespeople were found in a locale previously thought to be too rugged for human habitation.

The mountainous, high-altitude terrain that isolated the Simbu and other highland peoples is also responsible for an environment unlike those of the hot coastal and lowland areas with their infertile soils. The climate of this area is temperate, with cool evenings and warm days. Drought conditions are rare. A year-round springlike climate and a lack of many of the tropical diseases found elsewhere in New Guinea contribute to a relatively densely settled population. In most of the northern areas of the

province, population densities exceed 150 people per square kilometer.

"Simbu" is the word in the local language first heard by the initial Australian patrol. It is an expression of astonishment called out by the local people when they saw their first white men. Initially, the Simbu people thought the explorers were the reincarnated spirits of their dead relatives. The physical appearance of the early patrol members, as well as their control of a vast quantity of wealth in the form of shells, made them seem otherworldly.

The Simbu like many other cultural groups in the central highlands, are not traditionally a single political group but rather are divided into many tribal units of twenty-five hundred to five thousand people, each identified with discrete territories. The membership of each tribe is further subdivided into patrilineal clans and subclans. Although parliamentary democracy has been practiced for some time, tribal identification and loyalty remain very strong. Today, as in precontact times, warfare breaks out between neighboring tribes. Members of any single clan must find marriage partners outside their own clan. Through marriage, clan members are linked by kinship to members of other clans in their own tribe as well as to people in clans in other tribes. These political, economic, and social links between people are created and maintained through a complex web of ceremonial exchanges of valuables. All important events are marked by the giving of prestations (valuables). The kind of valuables given in these ceremonies has changed over the years with the introduction of money and items purchased with money. Although the Simbu are connected to the rest of the world through the market economy of which they are now a part, the introduction of money and markets has not meant the total abandonment of previously existing economic practices. It is important to look at the nature and form of these ceremonial exchanges be-

fore discussing the changes brought through the introduction of money.

For the Simbu, the bestowing of goods that accompanies ceremonies helps to create social obligations and reciprocal relations with other people and with other clans and tribes. The ceremonies are held in conjunction with a number of events such as marriages, funerals, and the seasonal harvest of particular fruits and vegetables. These events are held regularly. The largest of such events, called *bugla ingu* in the local language, is held once every seven to ten years. In the bugla ingu, entire clans and tribes organize to hold a series of gift prestations culminating in an enormous pig kill, in which thousands of pigs are killed, cooked, and given away to visiting friends and relatives. For the Simbu, maintaining good social relationships with others, both within the outside the patrilineal clans, is inseparable from such gift exchanges. The amounts given in many such ceremonies require the cooperation of many people.

It is useful to contrast the type of economic transactions that take place in Simbu ceremonial exchange with the types of transaction most familiar to Westerners—barter and trade. Barter and trade consist of discrete economic transactions completed with the giving and receiving of goods, services, or money. Social relationships are often independent of such transactions and, once the deal is completed, there are few continuing social obligations between the parties involved. In addition, forces other than social relationships between the transactors (i.e., supply and demand) regulate the amount of goods or services changing hands.

In ceremonial exchanges such as those in Simbu, however, the exchange is not independent of the social relationship between transactors. Each individual demonstrates his prosperity and ability to produce and shows his willingness and ability to maintain social obligations with each item he gives to an exchange partner. Although there is

KARL RAMBO
A Simbu man rests from his work in a newly planted sweet potato garden. The slopes on mountain gardens can be as steep as 45 degrees.

a general expectation that the recipient will reciprocate with a return presentation at an unspecified future date (and therefore continue the relationship), the purpose of participating in such exchanges is not to maximize a material return from the original gift. In fact, the opposite is closer to reality. Great prestige is gained by giving valuables to an exchange partner. The partner, to maintain the relationship, must return to the original giver at least as much as originally received plus, if he wishes to garner prestige, slightly more. This amount, over and above the original gift, then becomes debt that must be repaid. Added to this will be any additional goods that become debts incurred by the exchange partner. The competitive nature of these exchanges is acknowledged by the men involved.

In addition to the absence of separation between the giving of the ceremonial prestation and the social relationship between the participants, there is an attempt not to maximize one's economic holdings but to maximize prestige in the community by participating often and generously in the many prestations. Not only is prestige gained, but social ties are maintained with a network of individuals, many of them the affinal relatives (inlaws) acquired at marriage. Although men are the transactors in these situations, the women are the central links to many of the social/exchange relationships, for it is with the wives' male kin that many of the transactions are arranged.

Each marriage establishes a new exchange relationship between the groom and his close relatives and the bride's father, brothers, and close kin. Gifts must be made to the bride's family at marriage, and this is followed by a lifetime of exchanges at the birth of children, the death of children or the wife, at various points in the wife's children's lives, and at any vegetable exchange (*mogena biri*) or bugla ingu where the wife's group (clan or subclan) is invited. In addition to the relationships with wives' relatives, similar relationships exist with the men's mothers' male kin, their sisters' husbands, and their daughters' husbands. The valuables given in these ceremonies are expected to be returned in the future. An immediate exact equivalent is not expected, but eventually food or goods deemed at least similar in value should be repaid.

The relationships between these men are multi-functional. Ceremonial exchanges serve to distribute certain scarce resources that are not available in a territory—giving forest products and fruits that grow only at lower altitudes, for instance, to people who otherwise would not have access to these things. Mutual aid in work is sometimes extended between exchange partners.

Very important is the support given to men in other tribes in times of war. This is particularly true when there are many such interpersonal relationships between men of two groups. Without the support of others beyond one's clan and tribe, there is danger that if hostilities arise one would not have enough allies to prevent being chased off one's land. If the relationships to men outside one's clan and tribe are not maintained with frequent contributions to ceremonial exchanges, one faces the possibility of not having adequate allies in time of conflict. In fact, long delays in returning goods can add to hostility over other issues, such as marriage disputes and conflicting land claims, turning previous allies into warring enemies.

Although the ceremonial exchange of items is between individuals, individuals are representatives of their clans and subclans. Often the individual prestations are organized and combined so that the men of one clan give goods to their ceremonial exchange partners in another clan in one large display. For example, at a mogena biri, the valuables

KARL RAMBO

Coffee cherries, the berries containing coffee beans, are hand-picked when ripe. Coffee is the major cash crop that finances ceremonial gift presentations. This man's shirt reflects the influence of Christian missions in Simbu.

Movement Toward a Cash Economy

The initial Western contact with the Simbu was quickly followed by the establishment of a patrol post with a single Australian government officer in residence, and several Catholic and Lutheran missions. Although before the Second World War the changes they brought about were not extreme for most Simbu people, these Westerners did introduce a large quantity of high-quality pearl shell that was flown into the area from the coasts and traded for food and services.

Large-scale economic change did not occur until after the war, when men began to be sent to the coasts to work as laborers on plantations. After finishing their labor contracts, usually after two years, the men returned to their Simbu homes carrying imported manufactured goods such as cloth, metal tools, and cooking pots. These items were valued for their novelty as well as their usefulness.

Opportunities to acquire these sought-after imported goods were limited during this early period because the Simbu lacked the means to earn enough locally for their purchase. This problem was greatly alleviated when, in the late 1950s, coffee was introduced as a cash crop into the Simbu area. Coffee growing was particularly suited to the social and ecological situation in Simbu, and it was quickly adopted by the local people. The cool, temperate conditions were perfect for growing high-quality *arabica* coffee varieties. The poor road network had hampered development by placing delays and weight restrictions on export crops. Dried coffee beans, being durable and of high value for their weight, were perfect for such a situation. In addition, coffee requires relatively little year-round labor and does well as a subsidiary crop to subsistence food crops.

Coffee is still today by far the most important cash crop for the Simbu and the source of most of their money. Other sources of monetary income include growing cardamom, selling vegetables at small markets, and receiving occasional remittances from employed rela-

KARL RAMBO

An unmarried woman, dressed to participate in a dance competition at an Independence Day celebration, surrounded by spectators in modern dress.

are placed in a huge pile, twenty to forty feet in diameter, and the recipients, decorated in traditional finery of bird-plume headdresses, dance around the pile chanting, beating drums, and brandishing spears. Speeches are made relating past exchanges and the close relationships between members of each group, and then the entire pile is disassembled and each parcel given to the proper recipient.

Before contact with the colonial government, most of the items used in ceremonial exchanges were of local origin. Although shells, feathers, stone ax blades, and salt were often imported over long distances, pigs and other locally produced foods predominated in prestations. Each tribe was politically,

and in large measure economically, self-contained. Money was unknown in the area. Although in some other non-Western societies shells were used in much the same way we use money, nothing served as such a universal medium of exchange for the precontact Simbu. Pigs, one of the few domesticated animals, were raised on the same sweet potatoes that made up more than 85 percent of the Simbu people's diet, and pork was the most important item given in the ceremonial exchanges. It was rarely eaten on other occasions. Prior to the arrival of Christian missions, ceremonial sacrifice of pigs not only provided meat to be given to one's exchange partners but also served to appease the ancestral spirits.

tives. Average annual household income today approximates U.S. $250 per year.

Although their income is low by American standards, many of the Simbu's basic subsistence needs are satisfied without resorting to the marketplace. Most of the food consumed is produced in family gardens, and many other material needs, like housing and firewood, are obtained with little or no cash expenditure. Much of the money that does pass through the hands of the average Simbu is not spent directly on consumer goods but is channeled first through the now monetized ceremonial gifts.

Because it now requires cash to properly participate in many ceremonial exchange obligations, a man who wishes to obtain a modicum of prestige must have some source of money income. Those who do not contribute to prestations soon become known as insignificant "rubbish" men. The emphasis is, therefore, not on earning cash so as to acquire material goods for oneself, but rather to earn the money necessary to contribute cash to marriage, bride-price, or death compensations, or to buy cartons of beer to present to one's exchange partners at ceremonies. If too much of an individual's income is spent on himself without adequate compensation's being paid to supporters, he gains a reputation as being stingy. In addition to gaining a bad reputation, such an individual may have difficulty obtaining financial and other types of help when needed.

Although the monetization of ceremonial exchanges now encourages participation in activities with cash rewards, for the most part it discourages the accumulation of capital by individuals for reinvestment into money-making ventures. Small business ventures, such as stores, cattle projects, or commercial trucks, are generally begun with financial help and labor donated by kin and other associates. This help is given like a ceremonial prestation and is treated as such. Great pressure is then put on the leader of a venture to pay back these investments.

Often the response of the owner of a small venture such as a rural trade store is to slowly deplete the stock of the store by giving away store goods or cash receipts to his exchange partners. Since prestige is gained by reimbursing the network of investors, the organizer gains status and maintains a network of content exchange partners even though the business venture fails. Since the Simbu are rarely dependent on money-producing ventures for basic necessities such as food, the economic failure of such enterprises does not have serious consequences for the organizer. In fact, since success in the community depends on maintaining ceremonial exchange relations with other people, the economic failure of a business through its dismantlement and distribution of its assets often has a positive result.

In addition to leveling individual wealth by discouraging accumulation, channeling cash into prestations distributes wealth to a wide circle of people. Thousands of dollars often change hands at such events as weddings or funerals (when death compensation payments, a form of "blood money," are given to a dead person's relatives by the relatives of the person accused of causing the death). After the money is removed from the bamboo poles on which it is displayed, it is distributed widely by the initial receiver, with many individuals receiving only small amounts. So although theoretically as much money is received from the ceremonial exchanges as is put into them, the funds received are often in smaller (but more frequent) amounts. These smaller amounts of money are more prone to be spent quickly on items such as canned fish and bottled beer.

To be sure, there are a few Simbu men who have managed to become quite wealthy. By being politically savvy and practicing good management, these people have been able to satisfy the demands of their local supporters and exchange partners and succeed in business. In other areas of the Papua New Guinea highlands, where lower population densities allow for greater availability of land and therefore greater individual economic opportunity, other social scientists have reported on a number of such wealthy men. But even in these areas, such people are only a tiny fraction of the population.

So although the pearl shells sold in the markets no longer have the value they once did, and money has become predominant in the Simbu economy, indigenous institutions such as ceremonial gift exchange are maintained. Shells and other imported valuables of the past have been supplanted by another import—cash. But in many ways the economic strategy of maximizing social relationships rather than individual wealth remains intact.

As long as this remains the case, the opportunities for many individuals to achieve long-term capitalistic success, to develop businesses by turning profits back into the businesses rather than toward ceremonial exchanges, remain remote. But the importance of tribal social ties, and the ceremonial prestations that maintain those ties, serves to ameliorate many of the negative side effects of incorporation into the world money-based economy.

Additional Reading

Paula Brown, *The Chimbu: A Study of Change in the New Guinea Highlands,* Schenkman Press, Cambridge, Mass., 1972.

————, *Highland Peoples of New Guinea,* Cambridge University Press, U.K., 1978.

Bob Connolly and Robin Anderson, *First Contact,* Viking Penguin Inc., New York, 1987.

Ben R. Finney, *Big-Men and Business: Entrepreneurship and Economic Growth in the New Guinea Highlands,* University of Hawaii Press, Honolulu, 1973.

————, *Business Development in the Highlands of New Guinea,* East-West Center, Honolulu, 1987.

Allen Johnson, "In Search of the Affluent Society," *Human Nature* 1(9), 1978.

Andrew Strathern, ed., *Inequality in New Guinea Highlands Societies,* Cambridge University Press, 1982.

HUE & CRY

CONTINENTAL DIVIDES

*Had the early peoples of Africa and Australia inhabited a landscape more like
Eurasia, their descendants might rule a superpower today*

BY JARED DIAMOND

IN JULY 1972 I WAS WALKING ALONG A beach on the tropical island of New Guinea, where as a biologist I study bird evolution. I had heard about a charismatic local politician named Yali, who was touring the district then. By chance, Yali was walking in the same direction as I was on that day, and he overtook me. We walked together for an hour, talking the entire time.

Yali radiated charisma and energy. His eyes flashed in a mesmerizing way. Our conversation began with a subject then on every New Guinean's mind, the rapid pace of political developments. Papua New Guinea, as Yali's nation is now called, was at that time still an Australian-administered trust territory of the United Nations, but independence was in the air. After a while, Yali turned the conversation and began to quiz me about my work. He had never been outside New Guinea and had not been educated beyond high school, but his curiosity was insatiable. I explained to him how different groups of birds had colonized New Guinea over the course of millions of years. Yali then asked how the ancestors of his own people had reached New Guinea over the past tens of thousands of years, and how white Europeans had

colonized New Guinea within the past two hundred years.

The conversation remained friendly, even though the tension between the two societies that Yali and I represented was familiar to both of us. Two centuries ago all New Guineans still used stone tools similar to the ones superseded in Europe by metal tools thousands of years ago, and they dwelt in villages not organized under any centralized political authority. Whites had arrived and imposed centralized government. Whites had also brought material goods whose value New Guineans instantly recognized, ranging from steel axes, matches and medicines to clothing, soft drinks and umbrellas. In New Guinea all such goods were referred to collectively as "cargo."

Many of the white colonialists openly despised the New Guineans as "primitive." Even the least able of New Guinea's white "masters," as they were still called in 1972, enjoyed a far higher standard of living than New Guineans did, higher even than that of charismatic politicians such as Yali. All those things must have been on Yali's mind when, with yet another penetrating glance of his flashing eyes, he asked me: "Why is it that you white people developed so

much cargo and brought it to New Guinea, but we black people had little cargo of our own?"

Yali's question exemplifies a much larger set of contrasts. Peoples of Eurasian origin, especially those still living in Europe and eastern Asia, plus those transplanted to North America, dominate the modern world in wealth and power. Other peoples, including most Africans, have thrown off European colonial domination, but they remain far behind in wealth and power. Still other peoples, such as the aboriginal inhabitants of Australia, the Americas and southernmost Africa, have been decimated, subjugated and, in some cases, even exterminated by European colonialists.

Why did wealth and power become distributed as it did, rather than in some other way? For instance, why weren't Native Americans, Africans and Aboriginal Australians the ones who decimated, subjugated or exterminated Europeans and Asians?

THE *PROXIMATE* REASONS ARE CLEAR enough. As of the year 1500, when Europe's worldwide colonial expansion was just beginning, peo-

From *The Sciences,* March/April 1997, pp. 32-37. Adapted from *Guns, Germs, and Steel: The Fates of Human Societies* by Jared Diamond. © 1997 by Jared Diamond. Reprinted by permission of W. W. Norton & Company, Inc.

ples from different continents already differed greatly in technology and political organization. Empires with steel weapons could conquer or exterminate tribes with weapons of stone and wood. All such differences had developed since the end of the last Ice Age, around 11,000 B.C., when all peoples on all continents were still hunter-gatherers. But while Aboriginal Australians and many Native Americans remained hunter-gatherers, most of Eurasia and much of the Americas and sub-Saharan Africa gradually developed agriculture, herding, metallurgy and complex political organization. Parts of Eurasia, and one area of the Americas, independently developed writing as well. Each of those new developments appeared earlier in Eurasia than elsewhere.

Why did human development proceed at such different rates on different continents? Professional historians still disagree about the solution; most are no longer even asking the question. Early European explorers assumed that the wide differences among the world's peoples arose from differences in innate ability. Later the explanations were recast in terms of Darwinian natural selection, evolutionary descent and genetics. Even today, when segments of Western society publicly repudiate racism, many (perhaps most!) Westerners still accept racist explanations privately or subconsciously. In Japan and many other countries, such explanations are still advanced publicly and without apology.

The objection to such racist explanations is not just that they are loathsome, but that they are also wrong. Peoples who until recently were technologically primitive—such as Aboriginal Australians and New Guineans—routinely master industrial technologies when given opportunities to do so. And despite enormous efforts, no cognitive psychologist has convincingly established the postulated genetic deficiency in I.Q. of non-white peoples.

peoples not because of biological differences among peoples, but because of differences among peoples' environments. The hypothesis that environmental geography and biogeography influenced societal development is an old idea. Nowadays, though, that view is not held in esteem by historians; it is considered wrong or simplistic, or it is caricatured as environmental determinism and dismissed, or else the entire enterprise of trying to understand worldwide differences is avoided as too difficult. The result is an enormous intellectual gap (since the broadest pattern of history remains unexplained) and a much more serious moral one. Without some convincing, detailed, agreed-upon explanation for the broad pattern of history, most people will continue to suspect that the racist biological explanation is correct after all.

The time is now ripe for a fresh look at those questions, because of new information from scientific disciplines seemingly remote from human history. Those disciplines include especially genetics, molecular biology and biogeography, as applied to crops and their wild ancestors; the same disciplines plus behavioral ecology, as applied to domestic animals and their wild ancestors; the molecular biology of human disease microorganisms and related animal pathogens; the epidemiology of human diseases; human genetics; linguistics; archaeological studies on all continents and major islands; and studies of the histories of technology, writing and political organization.

As a result of advances in those and other fields, it has become conceivable that history might one day be established as a science on a par with recognized historical sciences such as evolutionary biology, geology and climatology—disciplines in which controlled experiments are usually impracticable and progress relies on deriving broad patterns from the unplanned "natural experiments" that the world happens to provide.

lands, 500 miles east of New Zealand, centuries of independence came to a brutal end for the Moriori people in December 1835. On November 19 of that year, a ship carrying 500 Maori armed with guns, clubs and axes had arrived from the North Island of New Zealand, followed on December 5 by a shipload of 400 more Maori. Bands of Maori began to walk through Moriori settlements, announcing that the Moriori were now their slaves and killing Moriori who objected. The Moriori (who outnumbered the Maori by two to one) had a tradition of resolving disputes peacefully, and so they decided in a council meeting not to fight back but to offer peace, friendship and a division of resources.

Before they could deliver their offer, however, the Maori attacked en masse. Within days they killed hundreds of Moriori, cooked and ate many of the bodies and enslaved all the others, killing most of them as well over the next few years, as it suited their whim. In the words of a Maori conqueror, "We took possession . . . in accordance with our customs and we caught all the people. Not one escaped. Some ran away from us, these we killed, and others we killed—but what of that? It was in accordance with our custom."

The tragedy of the Moriori is similar to many other such tragedies in both the modern and ancient worlds, in which numerous ill-equipped people face a few well-equipped opponents. What makes the Moriori-Maori collision grimly illuminating is that both groups had diverged from a common origin less than a millennium earlier. The modern Maori are descendants of Polynesian farmers who colonized New Zealand around 1000 A.D. Soon thereafter a group of those Maori in turn colonized the Chatham Islands and became the Moriori. In the centuries after the two groups separated, they evolved in opposite directions. Maori tropical crops could not grow in the Chathams' cold climate, and the colonists had no alternative except to revert to being hunter-gatherers. Without crop surpluses to store or redistribute, they could not support and feed nonhunting craft specialists, armies, bureaucrats and chiefs. In addition, the

MY OWN RESEARCH AND READING have led me to a different explanation: that history followed different courses for different

FOR A CRUCIBLE OF SUCH NATURAL experiments, one need look no farther than Yali's home territory, the South Pacific. On the Chatham Is-

Chathams are relatively small and remote islands, capable of supporting a total population of only about 2,000 hunter-gatherers. With no other accessible islands to colonize, all Moriori had no option but to remain in the Chathams and learn to get along with one another. The result was a small, unwarlike population with simple technology and weapons and without strong leadership or organization.

In contrast, the northern and warmer part of New Zealand, by far the largest island group in Polynesia, was suitable for Polynesian agriculture. Those Maori who remained in New Zealand increased in numbers until there were more than 100,000 of them. They developed locally dense populations chronically engaged in ferocious wars with neighboring populations. With the crop surpluses that they could grow and store, they fed craft specialists, chiefs and part-time soldiers. They needed and developed varied tools for growing their crops, fighting and making art. They erected elaborate ceremonial buildings and prodigious numbers of forts. And so, of course, it was the Maori who slaughtered the Moriori, not vice versa, when the two groups finally came into contact again after 500 years of separation.

As an example of how environment affects society, the Maori-Moriori collision is a small test within a medium-size test. Scattered over the Pacific Ocean beyond New Guinea and Melanesia are thousands of islands differing greatly in area, isolation, elevation, climate, productivity and geological and biological resources. For most of human history those islands lay impossibly far beyond the reach of watercraft. Around 1200 B.C., however, a group of farming, fishing and seafaring people from the Bismarck Archipelago north of New Guinea finally reached some of those islands. In the following centuries their descendants colonized virtually every habitable scrap of land in the Pacific. The process was mostly complete by 500 A.D., and the last few islands were settled around or soon after 1000 A.D.

In their subsistence modes, Polynesians ranged from the hunter-gatherers of the Chathams, through slash-and-burn farmers, to practitioners of intensive food production living at some of the highest population densities of any human societies. In social organization, Polynesian societies ranged from fairly egalitarian village societies to some of the most stratified societies in the world, with many hierarchically ranked lineages, and with chief and commoner classes whose members married within their own class. In political organization, Polynesian islands ranged from landscapes divided into independent tribal or village units, up to multi-island proto-empires that maintained standing military establishments devoted to wars of conquest and inter-island invasions. Finally, Polynesian material culture ranged from production of no more than personal utensils to the construction of monumental stone architecture.

All those differences among Polynesian societies developed within a relatively short time and over a modest fraction of the earth's surface, as environmentally related variations on a single ancestral society. The categories of cultural differences within Polynesia are essentially the same as the categories that developed in the rest of the world. Of course, the range of variation throughout the world, in environments as well as in human societies, is much greater than the variation within Polynesia alone. But with allowances for scale (continents instead of islands; millennia instead of centuries) the history of humanity since the most recent Ice Age represents the same basic experiment.

Suppose some enterprising archaeologist were to invent a time machine and embark on a world tour, circa 11,000 B.C. Strictly on the basis of the state of the world at that time, could the archaeologist predict the state of the world today?

If a head start counts for anything, Africa would appear to have had an enormous advantage: at least five million more years of separate proto-human existence than on any other continent. Furthermore, human genetic diversity is highest in Africa; perhaps more diverse people would collectively generate more diverse inventions.

The development of human societies, however, is not a footrace. What, really, does a "head start" mean? If it means the time required to populate a continent after the arrival of the first few pioneering colonists, that time is relatively brief: for example, less than 1,000 years to fill up the entire New World. Granted, adapting to some extreme environments did take time: for instance, 9,000 years were needed to occupy the High Arctic after the rest of North America was inhabited. But people would have explored and adapted to most other areas quickly, once modern human inventiveness had developed.

WHAT COULD ONE predict from the state of the world in 11,000 B.C. about the state of the world today?

The archaeologist might therefore conclude that Africa's apparently enormous head start would be overtaken by the earliest Americans within at most a millennium. Thereafter, the Americas' larger land area (50 percent greater than that of Africa) and much greater environmental diversity would give the advantage to Native Americans over Africans.

Examining Eurasia, the archaeologist might reason as follows: Eurasia is the world's largest continent. It has been occupied for longer than any other continent except Africa. Africa's long occupation by primitive proto-humans might count for little anyway, since fully modern humans could recapitulate those slow early developments so quickly. The archaeologist might look at the Upper Paleolithic flowering of southwestern Europe between 20,000 and 12,000 years ago, with all those famous artworks and complex tools, and wonder whether Eurasia was already getting a head start then, at least locally.

FINALLY THE ARCHAEOLOGIST WOULD turn to Australia–New Guinea. At first glance the region would seem to have several strikes against it. It is small and isolated; a large fraction of it is covered by desert capable of supporting few people; and it was occupied later than Africa and Eurasia were. All that might lead one to predict slow development in Australia–New Guinea.

But remember that Australians and New Guineans had by far the earliest watercraft in the world. They were creating cave paintings apparently at least as early as the Cro-Magnons in Europe. Jonathan Kingdon of Oxford University and Tim F. Flannery of the Australian Museum in Sydney have noted that the colonization of Australia–New Guinea from the islands of the Asian continental shelf required people to learn to deal with the new environments they encountered on the islands of central Indonesia—a maze of coastlines offering the richest marine resources, coral reefs and mangroves in the world. As the colonists crossed the straits separating each Indonesian island from the next one to the east, they adapted anew, filled up that next island, and went on to colonize the next island again—an unprecedented golden age of successive human population explosions that might have triggered the evolution of modern human behavior and continued to propel human development there long afterwards.

Thus an observer transported back in time to 11,000 B.C. would have had trouble saying on which continent human societies would develop most quickly. A strong case could have been made for any of them. With hindsight, of course, we all know the answer is Eurasia. But the reasons for the more rapid development of Eurasian societies were not at all the straightforward ones my imaginary archaeologist of 11,000 B.C. might have guessed.

How, then, shall historians answer Yali? Why did Eurasians, overall, develop so much "cargo"? I would maintain that if the populations of Aboriginal Australia and Eurasia could have been interchanged during the Late Pleistocene, the original Aboriginal Australians would be the ones occupying most of the Americas and Australia, as well as Eurasia, whereas the original Aboriginal Eurasians would be the ones reduced to downtrodden population fragments in Australia.

ONE MIGHT AT FIRST BE INCLINED to dismiss such an assertion as meaningless, because the experiment is imaginary and my claim about its outcome cannot be verified. But historians can evaluate related hypotheses through retrospective tests. For example, one can examine what took place when European farmers were transplanted to Greenland or the U.S. Great Plains, and when farmers coming ultimately from China emigrated to the Chatham Islands, the rain forests of Borneo or the volcanic soils of Java or Hawaii. Those tests confirm that the same ancestral people either ended up extinct, or returned to living as hunter-gatherers, or went on to build complex states, depending on their environments.

Four sets of differences among the continents appear to me to be the most important ones. The first set comprises continental differences in the wild plant and animal species available as starting materials for domestication. The reason is that food production was critical for the accumulation of food surpluses that could feed non-food-producing specialists, and for the buildup of large populations who could enjoy a military advantage through mere numbers even before they had developed any technological or political advantage. For both those reasons, all developments of economically complex, socially stratified, politically centralized societies beyond the level of small nascent chiefdoms were based on food production.

The number of wild candidate species for domestication varied greatly among the continents, not only because of differences in continental areas, but also (in the case of large mammals) because of differences in Late Pleistocene extinctions. Those extinctions, in which human beings almost certainly played a large role, were much more severe in Australia and the Americas than they were in Eurasia or Africa. As a result, Africa ended up biologically poorer than the much larger land mass of Eurasia, and the Americas and Australia ended up poorer still.

IN THE CASE OF TECHNOLOGICAL INNOVATIONS and political institutions, most societies acquire much more from other societies than they invent themselves. Thus diffusion and migration within a continent make an important contribution to the development of that continent's societies, which tend in the long run to share each other's developments insofar as environments permit.

Hence factors that affect rates of diffusion and migration constitute a second important set of differences among the continents. Human population movements were most rapid within Eurasia, because of the continent's east-west major axis and its relatively modest ecological and geographic barriers. The reasoning is straightforward when it comes to the movement of crops and livestock, since they depend strongly on climate and hence on latitude. But similar reasoning also applies to the diffusion of technological innovations, insofar as they are best suited without modification to specific environments. Diffusion was slower in Africa and especially in the Americas, because on those continents the major axes run north-south and the resulting geographic and ecological barriers are relatively strong.

A third, related set of factors affects diffusion between continents. Simply put, some continents are more isolated than others. In the past 6,000 years diffusion has been easiest from Eurasia to sub-Saharan Africa, contributing most of Africa's species of livestock. But interhemispheric diffusion made no contribution to Native America's complex societies, isolated from Eurasia at low latitudes by broad oceans and at high latitudes by geography and climate. To Aboriginal Australia, isolated from Eurasia by water, Eurasia's sole proven contribution was the dingo.

The fourth and last set of factors is simply related to size: the differences among the continents in area or total population. A larger area or a greater population presumably gave rise to more potential inventors, more competing societies, more innovations available to adopt—and more pressure to adopt and retain innovations, because societies failing to do so tend to be eliminated by the competition. That fate befell African pygmies and many other hunter-gatherer populations displaced by farmers. Conversely, it also befell the stubborn, hopelessly conservative Greenland Norse farmers, replaced by Inuit (Eskimo) hunter-gatherers whose subsistence methods and technology were far superior to those of the Norse under Greenland conditions. Among the world's land masses, area and the number of competing societies were greatest for Eurasia, lower for the Americas and Africa, and much lower for Australia.

THOSE FOUR SETS OF FACTORS CONstitute huge environmental differences among the continents, ones that can be quantified objectively and that are not subject to dispute. As such, they provide a basis for long-term interregional comparisons of human societies—and thus, in my view, at least a foothold for converting the study of human history into something like a science. At present, of course, history is considered one of the humanities or, at best, the least scientific of the social sciences. There is a sense that it is nothing but a mass of details, "just one damn fact after another."

That impression is false. Broad historical patterns really do exist, and the search for their explanation is as productive as it is fascinating. One cannot deny that it is more difficult to extract general principles from studying history than from studying planetary orbits. Nevertheless, successful methodologies for analyzing historical problems have been worked out in several fields. As a result, the histories of dinosaurs, nebulas and glaciers are generally acknowledged to belong to fields of science rather than to the humanities.

Introspection gives students of history far more insight into the ways of other people than into the ways of, say, the dinosaurs. I am thus optimistic that historical studies of human societies can be pursued as scientifically as studies of dinosaurs can—and with profit to our own society today, by teaching us what shaped the modern world and what might shape our future.

JARED DIAMOND is a professor of physiology at the UCLA School of Medicine in California. He is the author of The Third Chimpanzee *(HarperCollins, 1992), and* Why Is Sex Fun? The Evolution of Human Sexuality *(BasicBooks, 1997).*

Other Families, Other Ways

Since most people in small-scale societies of the past spent their whole lives within a local area, it is understandable that their primary interactions—economic, religious, and otherwise—were with their relatives. It also makes sense that through marriage customs, they strengthened those kinship relationships that clearly defined their mutual rights and obligations. Indeed, the resulting family structure may be surprisingly flexible and adaptive, as witnessed in the essay "When Brothers Share a Wife," by Melvyn Goldstein, and in Serena Nanda's presentation, "Arranging a Marriage in India." Even when urban American youth pull away from unstable and abusive families in search of the security offered by a street gang, Mark Fleisher ("On the Streets of America") shows how they are really just substituting one kind of family for another.

For these reasons, anthropologists have looked upon family and kinship as the key mechanisms for transmitting culture from one generation to the next. Social changes may have been slow to take place throughout the world, but as social horizons have widened, family relationships and community alliances are increasingly based upon new principles. Kinship networks have diminished in size and strength as people have increasingly become involved with others as coworkers in a market economy. Our associations depend more and more upon factors such as personal aptitudes, educational backgrounds, and job opportunities. Yet the family is still there. It is smaller, but it still functions in its age-old nurturing and protective role, even under conditions where there is little affection (see "Who Needs Love! In Japan, Many Couples Don't"

by Nicholas Kristof) or under conditions of extreme poverty and a high infant mortality rate (see "Death without Weeping" by Nancy Scheper-Hughes). Beyond the immediate family, the situation is in a state of flux. Certain ethnic groups, especially those in poverty, still have a need for the broader network and in some ways seem to be reformulating those ties.

Where the changes described in this section will lead us and which ones will ultimately prevail, we do not know. One thing is certain: anthropologists will be there to document the trends, for the discipline of anthropology has had to change as well. One important feature of the essays in this section is the growing interest of anthropologists in the study of complex societies where old theoretical perspectives are increasingly inadequate.

Current trends, however, do not necessarily mean the eclipse of the kinship unit. The large family network is still the best guarantee of individual survival and well-being in an urban setting.

Looking Ahead: Challenge Questions

Why do you think "fraternal polyandry" is socially acceptable in Tibet but not in our society?

How does an urban street gang function as a family?

How do differences in child care relate to economic circumstances?

What are the pros and cons of arranged marriages versus freedom of choice?

When Brothers Share a Wife

Among Tibetans, the good life relegates many women to spinsterhood

Melvyn C. Goldstein

Melvyn C. Goldstein, now a professor of anthropology at Case Western Reserve University in Cleveland, has been interested in the Tibetan practice of fraternal polyandry (several brothers marrying one wife) since he was a graduate student in the 1960s.

Eager to reach home, Dorje drives his yaks hard over the 17,000-foot mountain pass, stopping only once to rest. He and his two older brothers, Pema and Sonam, are jointly marrying a woman from the next village in a few weeks, and he has to help with the preparations.

Dorje, Pema, and Sonam are Tibetans living in Limi, a 200-square-mile area in the northwest corner of Nepal, across the border from Tibet. The form of marriage they are about to enter—fraternal polyandry in anthropological parlance—is one of the world's rarest forms of marriage but is not uncommon in Tibetan society, where it has been practiced from time immemorial. For many Tibetan social strata, it traditionally represented the ideal form of marriage and family.

The mechanics of fraternal polyandry are simple. Two, three, four, or more brothers jointly take a wife, who leaves her home to come and live with them.

Traditionally, marriage was arranged by parents, with children, particularly females, having little or no say. This is changing somewhat nowadays, but it is still unusual for children to marry without their parents' consent. Marriage ceremonies vary by income and region and range from all the brothers sitting together as grooms to only the eldest one formally doing so. The age of the brothers plays an important role in determining this: very young brothers almost never participate in actual marriage ceremonies, although they typically join the marriage when they reach their midteens.

The eldest brother is normally dominant in terms of authority, that is, in managing the household, but all the brothers share the work and participate as sexual partners. Tibetan males and females do not find the sexual aspect of sharing a spouse the least bit unusual, repulsive, or scandalous, and the norm is for the wife to treat all the brothers the same.

Offspring are treated similarly. There is no attempt to link children biologically to particular brothers, and a brother shows no favoritism toward his child even if he knows he is the real father because, for example, his other brothers were away at the time the wife became pregnant. The children, in turn, consider all of the brothers as their fathers and treat them equally, even if they also know who is their real father. In some regions children use the term "father" for the eldest brother and "father's brother" for the others, while in other areas they call all the brothers by one term, modifying this by the use of "elder" and "younger."

Unlike our own society, where monogamy is the only form of marriage permitted, Tibetan society allows a variety of marriage types, including monogamy, fraternal polyandry, and polygyny. Fraternal polyandry and monogamy are the most common forms of marriage, while polygyny typically occurs in cases where the first wife is barren. The widespread practice of fraternal polyandry, therefore, is not the outcome of a law requiring brothers to marry jointly. There is choice, and in fact, divorce traditionally was relatively simple in Tibetan society. If a brother in a polyandrous marriage became dissatisfied and wanted to separate, he simply left the main house and set up his own household. In such cases, all the children stayed in the main household with the remaining brother(s), even if the departing brother was known to be the real father of one or more of the children.

The Tibetans' own explanation for choosing fraternal polyandry is materialistic. For example, when I asked Dorje why he decided to marry with his two brothers rather than take his own wife, he thought for a moment, then said it prevented the division of his family's farm (and animals) and thus facilitated all of them achieving a higher standard of living. And when I later asked Dorje's bride whether it wasn't difficult for her to cope with three brothers as husbands, she laughed and echoed the rationale of avoiding fragmentation of the family and land, adding that she expected to be better off economically, since she would have three husbands working for her and her children.

Exotic as it may seem to Westerners, Tibetan fraternal polyandry is thus in many ways analogous to the way primogeniture functioned in nineteenth-century England. Primogeniture dictated that the eldest son inherited the family estate, while younger sons had to leave home and seek their own employment— for example, in the military or the clergy. Primogeniture maintained family estates intact over generations by permitting only one heir per generation. Fraternal polyandry also accomplishes this but does so by keeping all the brothers together with just one wife so that there is only one *set* of heirs per generation.

While Tibetans believe that in this way fraternal polyandry reduces the risk of family fission, monogamous marriages among brothers need not necessarily precipitate the division of the family estate: brothers could continue to live together, and the family land could continue to be worked jointly. When I asked Tibetans about this, however, they invariably responded that such joint families are unstable because each wife is primarily oriented to her own children and interested in their success and well-being over that of the children of the other wives. For example, if the youngest brother's wife had three sons while the eldest brother's wife had only one daughter, the wife of the youngest brother might begin to demand more resources

Family Planning in Tibet

An economic rationale for fraternal polyandry is outlined in the diagram below, which emphasizes only the male offspring in each generation. If every wife is assumed to bear three sons, a family splitting up into monogamous households would rapidly multiply and fragment the family land. In this case, a rule of inheritance, such as primogeniture, could retain the family land intact, but only at the cost of creating many landless male offspring. In contrast, the family practicing fraternal polyandry maintains a steady ratio of persons to land.

Joe LeMonnier

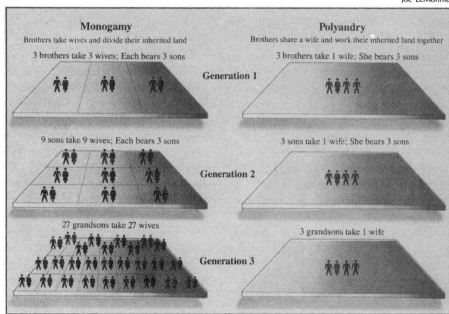

for her children since, as males, they represent the future of the family. Thus, the children from different wives in the same generation are competing sets of heirs, and this makes such families inherently unstable. Tibetans perceive that conflict will spread from the wives to their husbands and consider this likely to cause family fission. Consequently, it is almost never done.

Although Tibetans see an economic advantage to fraternal polyandry, they do not value the sharing of a wife as an end in itself. On the contrary, they articulate a number of problems inherent in the practice. For example, because authority is customarily exercised by the eldest brother, his younger male siblings have to subordinate themselves with little hope of changing their status within the family. When these younger brothers are aggressive and individualistic, tensions and difficulties often occur despite there being only one set of heirs.

In addition, tension and conflict may arise in polyandrous families because of sexual favoritism. The bride normally sleeps with the eldest brother, and the two have the responsibility to see to it

that the other males have opportunities for sexual access. Since the Tibetan subsistence economy requires males to travel a lot, the temporary absence of one or more brothers facilitates this, but there are also other rotation practices. The cultural ideal unambiguously calls for the wife to show equal affection and sexuality to each of the brothers (and vice versa), but deviations from this ideal occur, especially when there is a sizable difference in age between the partners in the marriage.

Dorje's family represents just such a potential situation. He is fifteen years old and his two older brothers are twenty-five and twenty-two years old. The new bride is twenty-three years old, eight years Dorje's senior. Sometimes such a bride finds the youngest husband immature and adolescent and does not treat him with equal affection; alternatively, she may find his youth attractive and lavish special attention on him. Apart from that consideration, when a younger male like Dorje grows up, he may consider his wife "ancient" and prefer the company of a woman his own age or younger. Consequently, although men and women do not find the idea of sharing a bride or bridegroom repulsive, individual likes and dislikes can cause familial discord.

Two reasons have commonly been offered for the perpetuation of fraternal polyandry in Tibet: that Tibetans practice female infanticide and therefore have to marry polyandrously, owing to a shortage of females; and that Tibet, lying at extremely high altitudes, is so barren and bleak that Tibetans would starve without resort to this mechanism. A Jesuit who lived in Tibet during the eighteenth century articulated this second view: "One reason for this most odious custom is the sterility of the soil, and the small amount of land that can be cultivated owing to the lack of water. The crops may suffice if the brothers all live together, but if they form separate families they would be reduced to beggary."

Both explanations are wrong, however. Not only has there never been institutionalized female infanticide in Tibet, but Tibetan society gives females considerable rights, including inheriting the family estate in the absence of brothers. In such cases, the woman takes a bridegroom who comes to live in her family and adopts her family's name and identity. Moreover, there is no demographic evidence of a shortage of females. In Limi, for example, there were (in 1974) sixty females and fifty-three males in the fifteen- to thirty-five-year age category, and many adult females were unmarried.

The second reason is also incorrect. The climate in Tibet is extremely harsh, and ecological factors do play a major role perpetuating polyandry, but polyandry is not a means of preventing starvation. It is characteristic, not of the poorest segments of the society, but rather of the peasant landowning families.

In the old society, the landless poor could not realistically aspire to prosperity, but they did not fear starvation. There was a persistent labor shortage throughout Tibet, and very poor families with little or no land and few animals could subsist through agricultural labor, tenant farming, craft occupations such as carpentry, or by working as servants. Although the per person family income could increase somewhat if brothers married polyandrously and pooled their wages, in the absence of inheritable land, the advantage of fraternal polyandry was not generally sufficient to prevent them from setting up their own households. A more skilled or energetic younger brother could do as well or better alone, since he would completely control his income and would not have to share it with his siblings. Consequently, while there was and is some polyandry among the poor, it is much less frequent and more prone to result in divorce and family fission.

An alternative reason for the persistence of fraternal polyandry is that it reduces population growth (and thereby reduces the pressure on resources) by relegating some females to lifetime spinsterhood. Fraternal polyandrous marriages in Limi (in 1974) averaged 2.35 men per woman, and not surprisingly, 31 percent of the females of child-bearing age (twenty to forty-nine) were unmarried. These spinsters either continued to live at home, set up their own households, or worked as servants for other families. They could also become Buddhist nuns. Being unmarried is not synonymous with exclusion from the reproductive pool. Discreet extramarital relationships are tolerated, and actually half of the adult unmarried women in Limi had one or more children. They raised these children as single mothers, working for wages or weaving cloth and blankets for sale. As a group, however, the unmarried woman had far fewer offspring than the married women, averaging only 0.7 children per woman, compared with 3.3 for married women, whether polyandrous, monogamous, or polygynous. While polyandry helps regulate population, this function of polyandry is not consciously perceived by Tibetans and is not the reason they consistently choose it.

If neither a shortage of females nor the fear of starvation perpetuates fraternal polyandry, what motivates brothers, particularly younger brothers, to opt for this system of marriage? From the perspective of the younger brother in a landholding family, the main incentive is the attainment or maintenance of the good life. With polyandry, he can expect a more secure and higher standard of living, with access not only to this family's land and animals but also to its inherited collection of clothes, jewelry, rugs, saddles, and horses. In addition, he will experience less work pressure and much greater security because all responsibility does not fall on one "father." For Tibetan brothers, the question is whether to trade off the greater personal freedom inherent in monogamy for the real or potential economic security, affluence, and social prestige associated with life in a larger, labor-rich polyandrous family.

A brother thinking of separating from his polyandrous marriage and taking his own wife would face various disadvantages. Although in the majority of Tibetan regions all brothers theoretically have rights to their family's estate, in reality Tibetans are reluctant to divide their land into small fragments. Generally, a younger brother who insists on leaving the family will receive only a small plot of land, if that. Because of its power and wealth, the rest of the family usually can block any attempt of the younger brother to increase his share of land through litigation. Moreover, a younger brother may not even get a house and cannot expect to receive much above the minimum in terms of movable possessions, such as furniture, pots, and pans. Thus, a brother contemplating going it on his own must plan on achieving economic security and the good life not through inheritance but through his own work.

The obvious solution for younger brothers—creating new fields from virgin land—is generally not a feasible option. Most Tibetan populations live at high altitudes (above 12,000 feet), where arable land is extremely scarce. For example, in Dorje's village, agriculture ranges only from about 12,900 feet, the lowest point in the area, to 13,300 feet. Above that altitude, early frost and snow destroy the staple barley crop. Furthermore, because of the low rainfall caused by the Himalayan rain shadow, many areas in Tibet and northern Nepal that are within the appropriate altitude range for agriculture have no reliable sources of irrigation. In the end, although there is plenty of unused land in such areas, most of it is either too high or too arid.

Even where unused land capable of being farmed exists, clearing the land and building the substantial terraces necessary for irrigation constitute a great undertaking. Each plot has to be completely dug out to a depth of two to two and half feet so that the large rocks and boulders can be removed. At best, a man might be able to bring a few new fields under cultivation in the first years after separating from his brothers, but he could not expect to acquire substantial amounts of arable land this way.

In addition, because of the limited farmland, the Tibetan subsistence economy characteristically includes a strong emphasis on animal husbandry. Tibetan farmers regularly maintain cattle, yaks, goats, and sheep, grazing them in the areas too high for agriculture. These herds produce wool, milk, cheese, butter, meat, and skins. To obtain these resources, however, shepherds must accompany the animals on a daily basis. When first setting up a monogamous household, a younger brother like Dorje would find it difficult to both farm and manage animals.

In traditional Tibetan society, there was an even more critical factor that operated to perpetuate fraternal polyandry—a form of hereditary servitude somewhat analogous to serfdom in Europe. Peasants were tied to large estates held by aristocrats, monasteries, and the Lhasa government. They were allowed the use of some farmland to produce their own subsistence but were required to provide taxes in kind and corvée (free labor) to their lords. The corvée was a substantial hardship, since a peasant household was in many cases required to furnish the lord with one laborer daily for most of the year and more on specific occasions such as the harvest. This enforced labor, along with the lack of new land and ecological pressure to pursue both agriculture and animal husbandry, made polyandrous families particularly beneficial. The polyandrous family allowed an internal division of adult labor, maximizing economic advantage. For example, while the wife worked the family fields, one brother could perform the lord's corvée, another could look after the animals, and a third could engage in trade.

Although social scientists often discount other people's explanations of why they do things, in the case of Tibetan fraternal polyandry, such explanations are very close to the truth. The custom, however, is very sensitive to changes in its political and economic milieu and, not surprisingly, is in decline in most Tibetan areas. Made less important by the elimination of the traditional serf-based economy, it is disparaged by the dominant non-Tibetan leaders of India, China, and Nepal. New opportunities for economic and social mobility in these countries, such as the tourist trade and government employment, are also eroding the rationale for polyandry, and so it may vanish within the next generation.

Children at Risk

On the Streets of America

Kids have only a slight chance of getting off the street when most of the people they know are criminals, gang members, and drug addicts.

Story by Mark S. Fleisher

Riddled by pellets from a 12 gauge shotgun, a broken street light fixture lies atop debris at the side of the street. "About seven last night, a guy fixed it and put in a new light," says Rick (pseudonyms are used), a member of a youth gang known as the Fairview Hawks. "And now look at it." He points to the thick shards of glass next to the light pole where the lamp once illuminated a segment of Fairview, a narrow, north-south street traversing rolling hills in a residential area of a midwestern city.

A working-class neighborhood, the Fairview district consists of small wood-frame houses nestled under the branches of old trees. Although less than ten min-

utes from major freeways to the east and the downtown businesses to the west, this area has virtually no condominiums, strip malls, movie theaters, or restaurants—no white-collar families that support urban growth. Except for the police, utility workers, and letter carriers, few outsiders cruise up and down Fairview. In part that's because the Fairview Hawks loom over the physical and social landscape. The gang consists of some seventy blacks, whites, and Latinos, about three-fourths of them male, ranging in age from the early teens to early twenties.

Fairview Hawks control an area of about ten square blocks between 57th and 61st streets, which run east-west. "The corner of 60th and Fairview is ours!" asserts G-Love, who by virtue of her age (nineteen) and her status as a founding member has assumed the informal role of one of the gang's leaders. Like gangs, or "sets," in other urban and rural areas, Fairview Hawks demark their territory with graffiti and protect it

with violence. Spray paint on houses, garages, sidewalks, and driveways all around the neighborhood are signs of ownership: "FH" for Fairview Hawks and a dollar sign, which indicates a love of money. Green is the Fairview Hawks' color. "I love money, and money's green," says G-Love.

Even though they are engaged in unlawful activities and have been called a gang by outsiders, the Fairview Hawks don't think of themselves that way. "We're a family," says seventeen-year-old Poodle (sometimes known as Poodle Bitch, because of her occasionally irascible temperament). "We ain't no gang," asserts fifteen-year-old Renée. "A clique, that's what we are. I call us a cliquilation." She smiles, proud of her linguistic creativity.

And certainly the Fairview Hawks are not an example of a drug gang, a group of street criminals (most often adults with criminal histories) whose main enterprise is to sell drugs and who use violence to protect or expand their drug-selling territory. Instead, this type

Anthropologist **Mark S. Fleisher** studied the culture and language of the Hesquiat Indians of British Columbia and the Clallam Indians of Washington State before changing his focus to street criminals and youth gangs. An associate professor of criminal justice sciences at Illinois State University, Fleisher is the author of *Warehousing Violence* (Sage Publications, 1989) and *Beggars and Thieves: Lives of Urban Street Criminals* (University of Wisconsin Press, 1995).

of gang fills the social needs of its members, whose early family lives left them alienated, emotionally unstable, and without educational aspirations.

The Fairview Hawks formed a few years ago, partly to counter harassment from North, a gang from the city's north side. G-Love says she and Fat Sal, TJ, Buck, Sweet Pea, and Frosty were sitting on her front porch and decided to transform themselves from a bunch of neighborhood kids into a clique with a color and graffiti. Others soon joined. About twenty members get together every day; Caramel, eighteen, calls this the "everyday group." But on weekend nights and at times when Fairview Hawks experience trouble from other gangs, the group expands quickly.

Many Fairview Hawks started out as members of other city gangs. "Everyone's chillin" with their own set, but they're down with Fairview," says Caramel, who—along with G-Love, Afro, Brawn, and Vinny—held membership in various Crip sets. Others, including Ann, Chucky D, Jenny, Lucky, and Green Bean (he's tall, thin and wears green clothing) were Latin Counts. Most gangs in the city categorize themselves as Crips or Bloods, using gang names that originated in Los Angeles about 1970 and spread around America. The names are often used by youngsters who have no knowledge of, or social affiliation with, the Los Angeles originals. The two types of gangs are customarily archenemies, but Fairview Hawks who identify themselves as Crips or Bloods get along well, by virtue of sharing a neighborhood and growing up together (many of them are brothers, sisters, or cousins).

Nearly all the gang members are school age, but they don't attend school. Most have been arrested a number of times for truancy, violent crimes, or drug dealing while others have been suspended for carrying weapons in school and for recurrent misbehavior. G-Love and Sweet Pea say that when they started elementary school, they didn't get along with anyone there, hated the teachers, didn't want to listen to orders, and ran away to the street. By the eleventh grade, both had dropped out and preferred the company of youngsters on

the street to those in the playground. "Kids on the street were like me," notes G-Love.

Daily life for street kids is simple, often boring, and relatively free from the stresses that affect mainstream adolescents.

Daily life for these street kids is simple, often boring, and relatively free from the stresses that affect mainstream adolescents. When school kids are running around the neighborhood on early morning paper routes, waiting for the school bus, attending algebra and chemistry class, doing homework, practicing team sports, heading off to part-time jobs, and worrying about scores on college entrance exams and picking a college, Fairview Hawks are asleep, numbing themselves with drugs, or just hanging out.

The gang has four "chill spots," or houses where the kids are permitted to hang out. G-Love's mother's house is the biggest, most popular spot. Up the street, kids chill at Tonya's and rely on her for support. "Tonya—she's a mom, she's got kids and everything—is like the mom of the family," says Caramel. "She's close to Dan, TJ, Chucky D, and Kirk. She is the one that all the boys write and call from prison. If any of us go to jail, we always call Tonya's house." Caramel laughs.

The day begins sometime between one and three in the afternoon. Sleeping all morning and most of the afternoon is a regular practice because these teenagers don't go to sleep until three or four A.M. They don't have to awaken early because they've all quit school and only a few have jobs. And those who do get jobs usually quit within weeks. Between four and six in the afternoon, the everyday group starts to congregate around G-Love's front porch; a few go inside to watch TV or play video games.

Before long, someone walks a few blocks to a gas station convenience store on 61st and buys some forty-ounce bot-

tles of malt liquor or beer. Then someone rolls a joint (marijuana cigarette) or prepares a blunt (a hollowed-out, blunt-tipped cigar filled with marijuana). Or someone lights up what they call a "dank stick"—a cigarette dipped in formaldehyde that's been cut, or thinned, with nail polish remover or even wood alcohol or brake fluid. Smokers of dank become high instantly: legs weaken and bodies sag lifelessly. Sweet Pea says, "It makes you not think about none of your problems at all."

The kids chat and gossip and listen to music. On some weekend evenings, they may move into someone's house and dance to rap music. Boys may toss a football up and down Fairview in front of G-Love's house or play basketball at a public park a few blocks away. Less often, gang members go swimming in a public pool, attend a movie, or go wading in a large public fountain that's a few miles away. Favorite pastimes are dominoes and craps—they love to gamble.

G-Love says they usually don't go looking for trouble unless they're really "messed up" (drunk and/or high on drugs) and have a car. Nevertheless, violence is a fact of life and includes drive-by and walk-by shootings. Although they weren't the intended victims, Caramel and G-Love were injured during a walk-by shooting one August evening. They were sitting in G-Love's car, just around the block from her mother's house, when a North gunman fired an SKS assault rifle at them for "two or three minutes," according to Caramel. A number of Fairview boys at the scene were unhurt, but G-Love was hit in the face and back by fragments of shattered glass or metal, and Caramel was hit in the foot by a bullet and received other wounds. G-Love managed to drive the car away from the scene. Shootings like this one are an "ongoing process," explains Caramel. "They'd shoot at our friends, so we'd get mad and retaliate back on them, then they'd get mad and retaliate back on us."

I watched one afternoon as gang members prepared for battle, having spotted several members of North a few blocks west of Fairview and 60th. Hostile words and threats were exchanged, and boys emerged from houses along Fairview and dashed toward a high spot on the hill next to G-Love's, a vantage point from which to fire down on enemy gang members driving below. Weapons appeared from hiding spots: shotguns, high-powered rifles, an assault weapon, a semiautomatic weapon, and powerful handguns. "It's some funny shit, man," declared a young warrior. "I'm gonna jump right out in the middle of the street. It's the Fourth of July!" Another exclaimed, "I'm ready to rock 'n' roll. I'm ready to ride." They darted back and forth along the ridge, seemingly oblivious of their own exposure to danger.

According to several Fairview Hawks, quite a few of the gang members have been wounded or killed by firearms during the year. A twenty-five-year-old man was shot in the chest four to six times by unknown killers. A twenty-three-year old was murdered by North gang members, two years to the day after his brother was killed by Bloods. A sixteen-year-old was shot accidentally, and his

---

The street can be dangerous, but most of these teen-agers were first exposed to violence at home.

---

fifteen-year-old brother was shot by a rival; both survived. A seventeen-year-old boy was shot in the head by a rival and now sits permanently in a wheelchair. A fourteen-year-old boy was accidentally shot in the head by his best friend as they handled a .45 caliber handgun. A thirteen-year-old girl survived being shot in the chest with a .38 handgun by North. A sixteen-year-old was shot in the arm with a 12 gauge shotgun at close range in a drive-by shooting on Fairview. Two seventeen-year-old boys survived being shot at by rivals. Gang-related tragedy hits the families of these kids, too.

"Violence doesn't scare me. I'm used to it. It's normal," says Poodle in a matter-of-fact voice. "I seen shootings and drive-bys." Fist fights don't frighten her

either. Indeed, she was arrested for assault after punching her mother in the face during a court hearing. ("We used to get into fist fights at home, too.") But Caramel says, "My biggest fear is watching all my friends die. I don't want to fear dying. I don't want to die violently. It'll all get better someday. I wish it would all stop."

Life in the Fairview district can be dangerous, but most of these teen-agers were first exposed to violence at home. In years of research in prisons and jails and on street corners in Seattle and other cities, I have interviewed and hung out with hundreds of gang members and adult street criminals, ranging in age from the late preteens to nearly seventy. The families they were born into usually offered only fragile and undependable social ties, with children bound only weakly to their parents or other adults who helped raise them (stepparents, aunts, uncles, cousins, grandparents).

Most commonly, the parents are alcoholics, and many use other drugs as well, such as marijuana, heroin, and cocaine. Many fathers are criminals, often drug dealers. Mothers, and sometimes grandmothers, engage in criminal activities with their husbands, brothers, sons, and nephews. Even women who do not participate in crime are active consumers of the money and goods obtained illegally. Parents fight with each other and beat their sons and daughters. In many cases, men sexually molest their sons, daughters, or stepchildren. Mothers of these children are passive bystanders who pretend not to know—fearful, they say, that they might be beaten themselves or have their supply of drugs cut off.

As the children mature, the neglect and the emotional and physical abuse heaped on them persist. Eventually they pull away, abandon their homes, and embrace street life with a calamitous zest. Enjoying the freedom of living by their own rules, they set off on a life of drug and alcohol addiction, personal irresponsibility, an inability to form meaningful social attachments, an incapacity to sort important aspects of their lives from unimportant ones, impulsive behavior, aggression to relieve stress, and no sense of lifelong priorities. Many of these damaged adolescents feel as if

the course of their lives is outside their control. When confronted with the facts about their drug and alcohol use, dim future, violent behavior, and lack of education, they often respond, "It's just who I am."

Fairview Hawks, like young gang members I've studied in many other cities, usually are the products of particularly destructive family experiences. Institutionalization is also common in their backgrounds. Caramel recounts a series of seven placements in residential treatment programs, hospitals, and juvenile detention facilities, from when she was age ten to seventeen, including nearly a year in a state hospital at age thirteen. She says they told her she had "an anger problem and a chemical imbalance." During her last commitment to a treatment facility, Caramel met G-Love, who also was a patient.

G-Love says she smoked her first joint when she was eight, and by age twelve she drank and smoked "bud" (marijuana) every day, gambled, enjoyed an occasional street fight, and stole cars. After a car theft when she was twelve years old, G-Love was remanded by a juvenile court judge to a thirty-day psychiatric evaluation. But she rebelled, and a month turned into four years in custody. "I hated the matrons," she says with a scowl, and "I fought them, jumped them, beat them whenever I could, and I ran away. But they kept bringing me back." G-Love adjusted slowly and learned to live with counseling, planned recreation, good food, and a clean bed.

These kids are unlikely to get help unless they are convicted of a felony and sentenced to prison. And ironically, prison isn't the worst thing that can happen to them. In fact, it is a way of insuring that they will stay alive, get treatment for addictions to alcohol and other drugs, receive a moderate level of education, and obtain medical and psychological or psychiatric care. Most prisons, despite exaggerated stereotypes, are cleaner and safer than inner-city neighborhoods. In prison, there are no drive-by shootings.

Whether so-called rehabilitation programs can be considered successful depends on who is evaluating the programs. Educated people, among them those whose incomes depend on the existence of such programs, often claim that education and job training will stop crime and offer street criminals lawful opportunities. My years of street ethnography show a different picture: Persistent criminals, as well as gang members, are living a life style they have chosen. They don't fear the criminal justice system, and in the end, most reject attempts to force them into a way of life they neither want nor understand. Sitting in classrooms studying, commuting to and from work, spending forty or more hours a week behind a desk, and paying taxes aren't attractive alternatives to the street criminals and gang members I've known.

Fairview Hawks and kids like them usually are raised by parents for whom school has no meaning. School is just a place to hang out with fellow gang members. And a close look at household life shows that the parents of gang members often discourage children's school attendance, because the school day and homework take time away from selling drugs or stolen property, thus reducing household income and the amount of cash that mom or dad can spend on drugs and alcohol. And even if the children are educated, who will hire them?

Some gang members and adult street criminals do find a way to get off the street and into a lawful life style. Grassroots organizations that reach people on street corners and in gang neighborhoods are a more effective intervention tool than expensive, bureaucracy-laden government programs. The Fairview Hawks are more likely to get help from people who aren't afraid of going into the inner city, having once lived on the street themselves.

Flaco, in his mid-forties, used to work for a neighborhood organization and is now setting up his own project. He is the first bilingual Latino to become a certified drug and alcohol counselor in the state. He even received a certificate of recognition from the Points of Light Foundation inspired by President Bush. But for many years, his life consisted of drugs, crime, gangs, and prison.

Born in Nogales, Mexico, and raised in Tucson, Arizona, Flaco lived until the age of nine with his mother and stepfather. Then his mother was hospitalized and his stepfather was unable to care adequately for Flaco and his six brothers. His mother's relatives offered to care for the children, but they only wanted Flaco's brothers. He was left on his own. "I remember the conversation where my brothers were chosen, but no one wanted me. 'OK,' I thought, 'if no one wants me, I don't want nobody.'"

Flaco soon began sniffing glue and gas fumes; by age ten, he was regularly smoking weed; by age twelve or thirteen, he was a member of a gang in south Tucson. He shot (injected) heroin for the first time at age fifteen. For the next two decades, his life was dominated by heroin. "If God made anything better than heroin," says Flaco, "he kept it for himself."

At age twenty, Flaco was imprisoned in the maximum security unit at the Arizona State Prison for selling heroin, among other charges, and within a year, he became associated with one of America's most infamous prison gangs, known for its violence and drug distribution inside prison walls. For nearly fourteen years, Flaco lived by the sword and the syringe. "I felt closer to the guys in prison than to my own family. Sometimes I forgot I had a family. I never got a visit, and I lost all contact with the world."

On September 1, 1985, Flaco was released. At age thirty-three, he didn't know how to live on the outside. "My [criminal] behavior and attitude kept me alive all along, and now they expected me to get rid of all that. I didn't know if I could make it." Flaco decided to stay drug free for twelve months, just to see what the world looked like. He has managed to stay drug free ever since.

Unfortunately, kinds have only a slight chance of getting off the street when the majority of the people they know—including their own brothers, sisters, cousins, mothers, and fathers—are active criminals, gang members, and drug addicts. Supportive, intimate ties are op-

tional on the street, where relationships exist in the moment and people are responsible only for themselves. As a field researcher studying adult street criminals and young gang members, I found that reciprocity and frequent contact were vital to sustain open relationships. But I learned to limit my natural urge to get personally involved. "I am a street ethnographer," I told myself, "an observer, not a cop, social worker, or surrogate father."

But watching adults destroy their lives with drugs and alcohol and criminal behavior was easier to endure than watching adolescents do the same things. Adults, I told myself, have control over their own lives. If a thirty-five-year-old street criminal chooses to shoot heroin, that is entirely his decision. But I watched teen-agers pollute themselves with alcohol, marijuana, and dank, and no adults seemed to care about this drug abuse. Every day I spent with the Fairview Hawks brought me disturbing dreams. I knew that many of these youngsters had committed serious crimes, but many of them had not, yet all were trying to survive as best they could, alone on the street, without community members rescuing them.

One thing I learned from studying Fairview Hawks is this: These youngsters would probably not be alcoholics, drug addicts, gang members, and convicted felons if their parents or other adults truly cared about them. And this is the most painful thing I have learned on the streets.

Books to Read

Beggers and Thieves: Lives of Urban Street Criminals, *by Mark S. Fleisher (University of Wisconsin Press, 1995)*

The American Street Gang: Its Nature, Prevalence, and Control, *by Malcolm W. Klein (Oxford University Press, 1995)*

Death Without Weeping

Has poverty ravaged mother love in the shantytowns of Brazil?

Nancy Scheper-Hughes

Nancy Scheper-Hughes is a professor in the Department of Anthropology at the University of California, Berkeley. She has written Death Without Weeping: Violence of Everyday Life in Brazil *(1992).*

I have seen death without weeping,
The destiny of the Northeast is death,
Cattle they kill,
To the people they do something worse
—Anonymous Brazilian singer (1965)

"Why do the church bells ring so often?" I asked Nailza de Arruda soon after I moved into a corner of her tiny mud-walled hut near the top of the shantytown called the Alto do Cruzeiro (Crucifix Hill). I was then a Peace Corps volunteer and community development/health worker. It was the dry and blazing hot summer of 1965, the months following the military coup in Brazil, and save for the rusty, clanging bells of N. S. das Dores Church, an eerie quiet had settled over the market town that I call Bom Jesus da Mata. Beneath the quiet, however, there was chaos and panic. "It's nothing," replied Nailza, "just another little angel gone to heaven."

Nailza had sent more than her share of little angels to heaven, and sometimes at night I could hear her engaged in a muffled but passionate discourse with one of them, two-year-old Joana. Joana's photograph, taken as she lay propped up in her tiny cardboard coffin, her eyes open, hung on a wall next to one of Nailza and Ze Antonio taken on the day they eloped.

Nailza could barely remember the other infants and babies who came and went in close succession. Most had died unnamed and were hastily baptized in their coffins. Few lived more than a month or two. Only Joana, properly baptized in church at the close of her first year and placed under the protection of a powerful saint, Joan of Arc, had been expected to live. And Nailza had dangerously allowed herself to love the little girl.

In addressing the dead child, Nailza's voice would range from tearful imploring to angry recrimination: "Why did you leave me? Was your patron saint so greedy that she could not allow me one child on this earth?" Ze Antonio advised me to ignore Nailza's odd behavior, which he understood as a kind of madness that, like the birth and death of children, came and went. Indeed, the premature birth of a stillborn son some months later "cured" Nailza of her "inappropriate" grief, and the day came when she removed Joana's photo and carefully packed it away.

More than fifteen years elapsed before I returned to the Alto do Cruzeiro, and it was anthropology that provided the vehicle of my return. Since 1982 I have returned several times in order to pursue a problem that first attracted my attention in the 1960s. My involvement with the people of the Alto do Cruzeiro now spans a quarter of a century and three generations of parenting in a community where mothers and daughters are often simultaneously pregnant.

The Alto do Cruzeiro is one of three shantytowns surrounding the large market town of Bom Jesus in the sugar plantation zone of Pernambuco in Northeast Brazil, one of the many zones of neglect that have emerged in the shadow of the now tarnished economic miracle of Brazil. For the women and children of the Alto do Cruzeiro the only miracle is that some of them have managed to stay alive at all.

The Northeast is a region of vast proportions (approximately twice the size of Texas) and of equally vast social and developmental problems. The nine states that make up the region are the poorest in the country and are representative of the Third World within a dynamic and rapidly industrializing nation. Despite waves of migrations from the interior to the teeming shantytowns of coastal cities, the majority still live in rural areas on farms and ranches, sugar plantations and mills.

Life expectancy in the Northeast is only forty years, largely because of the appallingly high rate of infant and child mortality. Approximately one million children in Brazil under the age of five die each year. The children of the Northeast, especially those born in shantytowns on the periphery of urban life, are at a very high risk of death. In these areas, children are born without the traditional protection of breast-feeding, subsistence gardens, stable marriages, and multiple adult caretakers that exists in the interior. In the hillside shantytowns that spring up around cities or, in this case, interior market towns, marriages are brittle, single parenting is the norm, and women are frequently forced into the shadow economy of domestic

From *Natural History*, October 1989, pp. 8, 10, 12, 14, 16. © 1989 by Nancy Scheper-Hughes. Reprinted by permission.

work in the homes of the rich or into unprotected and oftentimes "scab" wage labor on the surrounding sugar plantations, where they clear land for planting and weed for a pittance, sometimes less than a dollar a day. The women of the Alto may not bring their babies with them into the homes of the wealthy, where the often-sick infants are considered sources of contamination, and they cannot carry the little ones to the riverbanks where they wash clothes because the river is heavily infested with schistosomes and other deadly parasites. Nor can they carry their young children to the plantations, which are often several miles away. At wages of a dollar a day, the women of the Alto cannot hire baby sitters. Older children who are not in school will sometimes serve as somewhat indifferent caretakers. But any child not in school is also expected to find wage work. In most cases, babies are simply left at home alone, the door securely fastened. And so many also die alone and unattended.

Bom Jesus da Mata, centrally located in the plantation zone of Pernambuco, is within commuting distance of several sugar plantations and mills. Consequently, Bom Jesus has been a magnet for rural workers forced off their small subsistence plots by large landowners wanting to use every available piece of land for sugar cultivation. Initially, the rural migrants to Bom Jesus were squatters who were given tacit approval by the mayor to put up temporary straw huts on each of the three hills overlooking the town. The Alto do Cruzeiro is the oldest, the largest, and the poorest of the shantytowns. Over the past three decades many of the original migrants have become permanent residents, and the primitive and temporary straw huts have been replaced by small homes (usually of two rooms) made of wattle and daub, sometimes covered with plaster. The more affluent residents use bricks and tiles. In most Alto homes, dangerous kerosene lamps have been replaced by light bulbs. The once tattered rural garb, often fashioned from used sugar sacking, has likewise been replaced by store-brought clothes, often castoffs from a wealthy *patrão* (boss). The trappings are modern, but the hun-

ger, sickness, and death that they conceal are traditional, deeply rooted in a history of feudalism, exploitation, and institutionalized dependency.

My research agenda never wavered. The questions I addressed first crystalized during a veritable "die-off" of Alto babies during a severe drought in 1965. The food and water shortages and the political and economic chaos occasioned by the military coup were reflected in the handwritten entries of births and deaths in the dusty, yellowed pages of the ledger books kept at the public registry office in Bom Jesus. More than 350 babies died in the Alto during 1965 alone—this from a shantytown population of little more than 5,000. But that wasn't what surprised me. There were reasons enough for the deaths in the miserable conditions of shantytown life. What puzzled me was the seeming indifference of Alto women to the death of their infants, and their willingness to attribute to their own tiny offspring an aversion to life that made their death seem wholly natural, indeed all but anticipated.

Although I found that it was possible, and hardly difficult, to rescue infants and toddlers from death by diarrhea and dehydration with a simple sugar, salt, and water solution (even bottled Coca-Cola worked fine), it was more difficult to enlist a mother herself in the rescue of a child she perceived as ill-fated for life or better off dead, or to convince her to take back into her threatened and besieged home a baby she had already come to think of as an angel rather than as a son or daughter.

I learned that the high expectancy of death, and the ability to face child death with stoicism and equanimity, produced patterns of nurturing that differentiated between those infants thought of as thrivers and survivors and those thought of as born already "wanting to die." The survivors were nurtured, while stigmatized, doomed infants were left to die, as mothers say, *a mingua,* "of neglect." Mothers stepped back and allowed nature to take its course. This pattern, which I call mortal selective neglect, is called passive infanticide by anthropologist Marvin Harris. The Alto situation, although culturally specific in the form

that it takes, is not unique to Third World shantytown communities and may have its correlates in our own impoverished urban communities in some cases of "failure to thrive" infants.

I use as an example the story of Zezinho, the thirteen-month-old toddler of one of my neighbors, Lourdes. I became involved with Zezinho when I was called in to help Lourdes in the delivery of another child, this one a fair and robust little tyke with a lusty cry. I noted that while Lourdes showed great interest in the newborn, she totally ignored Zezinho who, wasted and severely malnourished, was curled up in a fetal position on a piece of urine- and feces-soaked cardboard placed under his mother's hammock. Eyes open and vacant, mouth slack, the little boy seemed doomed.

When I carried Zezinho up to the community day-care center at the top of the hill, the Alto women who took turns caring for one another's children (in order to free themselves for part-time work in the cane fields or washing clothes) laughed at my efforts to save Ze, agreeing with Lourdes that here was a baby without a ghost of a chance. Leave him alone, they cautioned. It makes no sense to fight with death. But I did do battle with Ze, and after several weeks of force-feeding (malnourished babies lose their interest in food), Ze began to succumb to my ministrations. He acquired some flesh across his taut chest bones, learned to sit up, and even tried to smile. When he seemed well enough, I returned him to Lourdes in her miserable scrap-material lean-to, but not without guilt about what I had done. I wondered whether returning Ze was at all fair to Lourdes and to his little brother. But I was busy and washed my hands of the matter. And Lourdes did seem more interested in Ze now that he was looking more human.

When I returned in 1982, there was Lourdes among the women who formed my sample of Alto mothers—still struggling to put together some semblance of life for a now grown Ze and her five other surviving children. Much was made of my reunion with Ze in 1982, and everyone enjoyed retelling the story of Ze's rescue and of how his mother had given him up for dead. Ze would laugh the loudest when told how I had had to force-feed him like a fiesta turkey. There was no hint of guilt on the part of Lourdes and no resentment on the part of Ze. In fact, when questioned in private as to who was the best friend he ever had in life, Ze took a long drag on his cigarette and answered without a trace of irony, "Why my mother, of course." "But of course," I replied.

Part of learning how to mother in the Alto do Cruzeiro is learning when to let go of a child who shows that it "wants" to die or that it has no "knack" or no "taste" for life. Another part is learning when it is safe to let oneself love a child. Frequent child death remains a powerful shaper of maternal thinking and practice. In the absence of firm expectation that a child will survive, mother love as we conceptualize it (whether in popular terms or in the psychobiological notion of maternal bonding) is attenuated and delayed with consequences for infant survival. In an environment already precarious to young life, the emotional detachment of mothers toward some of their babies contributes even further to the spiral of high mortality—high fertility in a kind of macabre lock-step dance of death.

The average woman of the Alto experiences 9.5 pregnancies, 3.5 child deaths, and 1.5 stillbirths. Seventy percent of all child deaths in the Alto occur in the first six months of life, and 82 percent by the end of the first year. Of all deaths in the community each year, about 45 percent are of children under the age of five.

Women of the Alto distinguish between child deaths understood as natural (caused by diarrhea and communicable diseases) and those resulting from sorcery, the evil eye, or other magical or supernatural afflictions. They also recognize a large category of infant deaths seen as fated and inevitable. These hopeless cases are classified by mothers under the folk terminology "child sickness" or "child attack." Women say that there are at least fourteen different types of hopeless child sickness, but most can be subsumed under two categories—chronic and acute. The chronic cases refer to infants who are born small and wasted.

They are deathly pale, mothers say, as well as weak and passive. They demonstrate no vital force, no liveliness. They do not suck vigorously; they hardly cry. Such babies can be this way at birth or they can be born sound but soon show no resistance, no "fight" against the common crises of infancy: diarrhea, respiratory infections, tropical fevers.

The acute cases are those doomed infants who die suddenly and violently. They are taken by stealth overnight, often following convulsions that bring on head banging, shaking, grimacing, and shrieking. Women say it is horrible to look at such a baby. If the infant begins to foam at the mouth or gnash its teeth or go rigid with its eyes turned back inside its head, there is absolutely no hope. The infant is "put aside"—left alone—often on the floor in a back room, and allowed to die. These symptoms (which accompany high fevers, dehydration, third-stage malnutrition, and encephalitis) are equated by Alto women with madness, epilepsy, and worst of all, rabies, which is greatly feared and highly stigmatized.

Most of the infants presented to me as suffering from chronic child sickness were tiny, wasted famine victims, while those labeled as victims of acute child attack seemed to be infants suffering from the deliriums of high fever or the convulsions that can accompany electrolyte imbalance in dehydrated babies.

Local midwives and traditional healers, praying women, as they are called, advise Alto women on when to allow a baby to die. One midwife explained: "If I can see that a baby was born unfortuitously, I tell the mother that she need not wash the infant or give it a cleansing tea. I tell her just to dust the infant with baby powder and wait for it to die." Allowing nature to take its course is not seen as sinful by these often very devout Catholic women. Rather, it is understood as cooperating with God's plan.

Often I have been asked how consciously women of the Alto behave in this regard. I would have to say that consciousness is always shifting between allowed and disallowed levels of awareness. For example, I was awakened early one morning in 1987 by two neighborhood children who had been sent to

fetch me to a hastily organized wake for a two-month-old infant whose mother I had unsuccessfully urged to breast-feed. The infant was being sustained on sugar water, which the mother referred to as *soro* (serum), using a medical term for the infant's starvation regime in light of his chronic diarrhea. I had cautioned the mother that an infant could not live on *soro* forever.

The two girls urged me to console the young mother by telling her that it was "too bad" that her infant was so weak that Jesus had to take him. They were coaching me in proper Alto etiquette. I agreed, of course, but asked, "And what do *you* think?" Xoxa, the eleven-year-old, looked down at her dusty flip-flops and blurted out, "Oh, Dona Nanci, that baby never got enough to eat, but you must never say that!" And so the death of hungry babies remains one of the best kept secrets of life in Bom Jesus da Mata.

Most victims are waked quickly and with a minimum of ceremony. No tears are shed, and the neighborhood children form a tiny procession, carrying the baby to the town graveyard where it will join a multitude of others. Although a few fresh flowers may be scattered over the tiny grave, no stone or wooden cross will mark the place, and the same spot will be reused within a few months' time. The mother will never visit the grave, which soon becomes an anonymous one.

What, then, can be said of these women? What emotions, what sentiments motivate them? How are they able to do what, in fact, must be done? What does mother love mean in this inhospitable context? Are grief, mourning, and melancholia present, although deeply repressed? If so, where shall we look for them? And if not, how are we to understand the moral visions and moral sensibilities that guide their actions?

I have been criticized more than once for presenting an unflattering portrait of poor Brazilian women, women who are, after all, themselves the victims of severe social and institutional neglect. I have described these women as allowing some of their children to die, as if this were an unnatural and inhuman act rather than, as I would assert, the way any one of us might act, reasonably and rationally, under similarly desperate conditions. Perhaps I have not emphasized enough the real pathogens in this environment of high risk: poverty, deprivation, sexism, chronic hunger, and economic exploitation. If mother love is, as many psychologists and some feminists believe, a seemingly natural and universal maternal script, what does it mean to women for whom scarcity, loss, sickness, and deprivation have made that love frantic and robbed them of their grief, seeming to turn their hearts to stone?

Throughout much of human history—as in a great deal of the impoverished Third World today—women have had to give birth and to nurture children under ecological conditions and social arrangements hostile to child survival, as well as to their own well-being. Under circumstances of high childhood mortality, patterns of selective neglect and passive infanticide may be seen as active survival strategies.

They also seem to be fairly common practices historically and across cultures. In societies characterized by high childhood mortality and by a correspondingly high (replacement) fertility, cultural practices of infant and child care tend to be organized primarily around survival goals. But what this means is a pragmatic recognition that not all of one's children can be expected to live. The nervousness about child survival in areas of northeast Brazil, northern India, or Bangladesh, where a 30 percent or 40 percent mortality rate in the first years of life is common, can lead to forms of delayed attachment and a casual or benign neglect that serves to weed out the worst bets so as to enhance the life chances of healthier siblings, including those yet to be born. Practices similar to those that I am describing have been recorded for parts of Africa, India, and Central America.

Life in the Alto do Cruzeiro resembles nothing so much as a battlefield or an emergency room in an overcrowded inner-city public hospital. Consequently, mortality is guided by a kind of "lifeboat ethics," the morality of triage. The seemingly studied indifference toward the suffering of some of their infants, conveyed in such sayings as "little crit-

ters have no feelings," is understandable in light of these women's obligation to carry on with their reproductive and nurturing lives.

In their slowness to anthropomorphize and personalize their infants, everything is mobilized so as to prevent maternal overattachment and, therefore, grief at death. The bereaved mother is told not to cry, that her tears will dampen the wings of her little angel so that she cannot fly up to her heavenly home. Grief at the death of an angel is not only inappropriate, it is a symptom of madness and of a profound lack of faith.

Infant death becomes routine in an environment in which death is anticipated and bets are hedged. While the routinization of death in the context of shantytown life is not hard to understand, and quite possible to empathize with, its routinization in the formal institutions of public life in Bom Jeses is not as easy to accept uncritically. Here the social production of indifference takes on a different, even a malevolent, cast.

In a society where triplicates of every form are required for the most banal events (registering a car, for example), the registration of infant and child death is informal, incomplete, and rapid. It requires no documentation, takes less than five minutes, and demands no witnesses other than office clerks. No questions are asked concerning the circumstances of the death, and the cause of death is left blank, unquestioned and unexamined. A neighbor, grandmother, older sibling, or common-law husband may register the death. Since most infants die at home, there is no question of a medical record.

From the registry office, the parent proceeds to the town hall, where the mayor will give him or her a voucher for a free baby coffin. The full-time municipal coffinmaker cannot tell you exactly how many baby coffins are dispatched each week. It varies, he says, with the seasons. There are more needed during the drought months and during the big festivals of Carnaval and Christmas and São Joao's Day because people are to busy, he supposes, to take their babies to the clinic. Record keeping is sloppy.

Similarly, there is a failure on the part of city-employed doctors working at two free clinics to recognize the malnutrition

of babies who are weighed, measured, and immunized without comment and as if they were not, in fact, anemic, stunted, fussy, and irritated starvation babies. At best the mothers are told to pick up free vitamins or a health "tonic" at the municipal chambers. At worst, clinic personnel will give tranquilizers and sleeping pills to quiet the hungry cries of "sick-to-death" Alto babies.

The church, too, contributes to the routinization of, and indifference toward, child death. Traditionally, the local Catholic church taught patience and resignation to domestic tragedies that were said to reveal the imponderable workings of God's will. If an infant died suddenly, it was because a particular saint had claimed the child. The infant would be an angel in the service of his or her heavenly patron. It would be wrong, a sign of a lack of faith, to weep for a child with such good fortune. The infant funeral was, in the past, an event celebrated with joy. Today, however, under the new regime of "liberation theology," the bells of N. S. das Dores parish church no longer peal for the death of Alto babies, and no priest accompanies the procession of angels to the cemetery where their bodies are disposed of casually and without ceremony. Children bury children in Bom Jesus da Mata. In this most Catholic of communities, the coffin is handed to the disabled and irritable municipal gravedigger, who often chides the children for one reason or another. It may be that the coffin is larger than expected and the gravedigger can find no appropriate space. The children do not wait for the gravedigger to complete his task. No prayers are recited and no sign of the cross made as the tiny coffin goes into its shallow grave.

When I asked the local priest, Padre Marcos, about the lack of church ceremony surrounding infant and childhood death today in Bom Jesus, he replied; "In the old days, child death was richly celebrated. But those were the baroque customs of a conservative church that wallowed in death and misery. The new church is a church of hope and joy. We no longer celebrate the death of child angels. We try to tell mothers that Jesus doesn't want all the dead babies they send him." Similarly, the new church has changed its baptismal customs, now often refusing to baptize dying babies brought to the back door of a church or rectory. The mothers are scolded by the church attendants and told to go home and take care of their sick babies. Baptism, they are told, is for the living; it is not to be confused with the sacrament of extreme unction, which is the anointing of the dying. And so it appears to the women of the Alto that even the church has turned away from them, denying the traditional comfort of folk Catholicism.

The contemporary Catholic church is caught in the clutches of a double bind. The new theology of liberation imagines a kingdom of God on earth based on justice and equality, a world without hunger, sickness, or childhood mortality. At the same time, the church has not changed its official position on sexuality and reproduction, including its sanctions against birth control, abortion, and sterilization. The padre of Bom Jesus da Mata recognizes this contradiction intuitively, although he shies away from discussions on the topic, saying that he prefers to leave questions of family planning to the discretion and the "good consciences" of his impoverished parishioners. But this, of course, sidesteps the extent to which those good consciences have been shaped by traditional church teachings in Bom Jesus, especially by his recent predecessors. Hence, we can begin to see that the seeming indifference of Alto mothers toward the death of some of their infants is but a pale reflection of the official indifference of church and state to the plight of poor women and children.

Nonetheless, the women of Bom Jesus are survivors. One woman, Biu, told me her life history, returning again and again to the themes of child death, her first husband's suicide, abandonment by her father and later by her second husband, and all the other losses and disappointments she had suffered in her long forty-five years. She concluded with great force, reflecting on the days of Carnaval '88 that were fast approaching:

No, Dona Nanci, I won't cry, and I won't waste my life thinking about it from morning to night. . . . Can I argue with God for the state that I'm in? No! And so I'll dance and I'll jump and I'll play Carnaval! And yes, I'll laugh and people will wonder at a *pobre* like me who can have such a good time.

And no one did blame Biu for dancing in the streets during the four days of Carnaval—not even on Ash Wednesday, the day following Carnaval '88 when we all assembled hurriedly to assist in the burial of Mercea, Biu's beloved *casula*, her last-born daughter who had died at home of pneumonia during the festivities. The rest of the family barely had time to change out of their costumes. Severino, the child's uncle and godfather, sprinkled holy water over the little angel while he prayed: "Mercea, I don't know whether you were called, taken, or thrown out of this world. But look down at us from your heavenly home with tenderness, with pity, and with mercy." So be it.

Arranging a Marriage in India

Serena Nanda

John Jay College of Criminal Justice

Sister and doctor brother-in-law invite correspondence from North Indian professionals only, for a beautiful, talented, sophisticated, intelligent sister, 5′3″, slim, M.A. in textile design, father a senior civil officer. Would prefer immigrant doctors, between 26–29 years. Reply with full details and returnable photo.

A well-settled uncle invites matrimonial correspondence from slim, fair, educated South Indian girl, for his nephew, 25 years, smart, M.B.A., green card holder, 5′6″. Full particulars with returnable photo appreciated.

Matrimonial Advertisements,
India Abroad

In India, almost all marriages are arranged. Even among the educated middle classes in modern, urban India, marriage is as much a concern of the families as it is of the individuals. So customary is the practice of arranged marriage that there is a special name for a marriage which is not arranged: It is called a "love match."

On my first field trip to India, I met many young men and women whose parents were in the process of "getting them married." In many cases, the bride and groom would not meet each other before the marriage. At most they might meet for a brief conversation, and this meeting would take place only after their parents had decided that the match was suitable. Parents do not compel their children to marry a person who either marriage partner finds objectionable. But only after one match is refused will another be sought.

As a young American woman in India for the first time, I found this custom of arranged marriage oppressive. How could any intelligent young person agree to such a marriage without great reluctance? It was contrary to everything I believed about the importance of romantic love as the only basis of a happy marriage. It also clashed with my strongly held notions that the choice of such an intimate and permanent relationship could be made only by the individuals involved. Had anyone tried to arrange my marriage, I would have been defiant and rebellious!

At the first opportunity, I began, with more curiosity than tact, to question the young people I met on how they felt about this practice. Sita, one of my young informants, was a college graduate with a degree in political science. She had been waiting for over a year while her parents were arranging a match for her. I found it difficult to accept the docile manner in which this well-educated young woman awaited the outcome of a process that would result in her spending the rest of her life with a man she hardly knew, a virtual stranger, picked out by her parents.

"How can you go along with this?" I asked her, in frustration and distress. "Don't you care who you marry?"

"Of course I care," she answered. "This is why I must let my parents choose a boy for me. My marriage is too important to be arranged by such an inexperienced person as myself. In such matters, it is better to have my parents' guidance."

I had learned that young men and women in India do not date and have very little social life involving members of the opposite sex. Although I could not disagree with Sita's reasoning, I continued to pursue the subject.

"But how can you marry the first man you have ever met? Not only have you missed the fun of meeting a lot of different people, but you have not given yourself the chance to know who is the right man for you."

"Meeting with a lot of different people doesn't sound like any fun at all," Sita answered. "One hears that in America the girls are spending all their time worrying about whether they will meet a man and get married. Here we have the chance to enjoy our life and let our parents do this work and worrying for us."

She had me there. The high anxiety of the competition to "be popular" with the opposite sex certainly was the most prominent feature of life as an American teenager in the late fifties. The endless worrying about the rules that governed our behavior and about our popularity ratings sapped both our self-esteem and our enjoyment of adolescence. I reflected that absence of this competition in India most certainly may have contributed to the self-confidence and natural charm of so many of the young women I met.

And yet, the idea of marrying a perfect stranger, whom one did not know and did not "love," so offended my American ideas of individualism and romanticism, that I persisted with my objections.

"I still can't imagine it," I said. "How can you agree to marry a man you hardly know?"

"But of course he will be known. My parents would never arrange a marriage for me

From *The Naked Anthropologist*, edited by Philip R. Devita, 1992, pp. 34-45. Published by Wadsworth Publishing Company.

without knowing all about the boy's family background. Naturally we will not rely only on what the family tells us. We will check the particulars out ourselves. No one will want their daughter to marry into a family that is not good. All these things we will know beforehand."

Impatiently, I responded, "Sita, I don't mean know the family, I mean, know the man. How can you marry someone you don't know personally and don't love? How can you think of spending your life with someone you may not even like?"

"If he is a good man, why should I not like him?" she said. "With you people, you know the boy so well before you marry, where will be the fun to get married? There will be no mystery and no romance. Here we have the whole of our married life to get to know and love our husband. "This way is better, is it not?"

Her response made further sense, and I began to have second thoughts on the matter. Indeed, during months of meeting many intelligent young Indian people, both male and female, who had the same ideas as Sita, I saw arranged marriages in a different light. I also saw the importance of the family in Indian life and realized that a couple who took their marriage into their own hands was taking a big risk, particularly if their families were irreconcilably opposed to the match. In a country where every important resource in life—a job, a house, a social circle—is gained through family connections, it seemed foolhardy to cut oneself off from a supportive social network and depend solely on one person for happiness and success.

Six years later I returned to India to again do fieldwork, this time among the middle class in Bombay, a modern, sophisticated city. From the experience of my earlier visit, I decided to include a study of arranged marriages in my project. By this time I had met many Indian couples whose marriages had been arranged and who seemed very happy. Particularly in contrast to the fate of many of my married friends in the United States who were already in the process of divorce, the positive aspects of arranged marriages appeared to me to outweigh the negatives. In fact, I thought I might even participate in arranging a marriage myself. I had been fairly successful in the United States in "fixing up" many of my friends, and I was confident that my matchmaking skills could be easily applied to this new situation, once I learned the basic rules. "After all," I thought, "how complicated can it be? People want pretty much the same things in a marriage whether it is in India or America."

An opportunity presented itself almost immediately. A friend from my previous Indian trip was in the process of arranging for the marriage of her eldest son. In India there is a perceived shortage of "good boys," and since my friend's family was eminently respectable and the boy himself personable,

well educated, and nice looking, I was sure that by the end of my year's fieldwork, we would have found a match.

The basic rule seems to be that a family's reputation is most important. It is understood that matches would be arranged only within the same caste and general social class, although some crossing of subcastes is permissible if the class positions of the bride's and groom's families are similar. Although dowry is now prohibited by law in India, extensive gift exchanges took place with every marriage. Even when the boy's family do not "make demands," every girl's family nevertheless feels the obligation to give the traditional gifts, to the girl, to the boy, and to the boy's family. Particularly when the couple would be living in the joint family—that is, with the boy's parents and his married brothers and their families, as well as with unmarried siblings—which is still very common even among the urban, upper-middle class in India, the girls' parents are anxious to establish smooth relations between their family and that of the boy. Offering the proper gifts, even when not called "dowry," is often an important factor in influencing the relationship between the bride's and groom's families and perhaps, also, the treatment of the bride in her new home.

In a society where divorce is still a scandal and where, in fact, the divorce rate is exceedingly low, an arranged marriage is the beginning of a lifetime relationship not just between the bride and groom but between their families as well. Thus, while a girl's looks are important, her character is even more so, for she is being judged as a prospective daughter-in-law as much as a prospective bride. Where she would be living in a joint family, as was the case with my friend, the girls's ability to get along harmoniously in a family is perhaps the single most important quality in assessing her suitability.

My friend is a highly esteemed wife, mother, and daughter-in-law. She is religious, soft-spoken, modest, and deferential. She rarely gossips and never quarrels, two qualities highly desirable in a woman. A family that has the reputation for gossip and conflict among its womenfolk will not find it easy to get good wives for their sons. Parents will not want to send their daughter to a house in which there is conflict.

My friend's family were originally from North India. They had lived in Bombay, where her husband owned a business, for forty years. The family had delayed in seeking a match for their eldest son because he had been an Air Force pilot for several years, stationed in such remote places that it had seemed fruitless to try to find a girl who would be willing to accompany him. In their social class, a military career, despite its economic security, has little prestige and is considered a drawback in finding a suitable bride. Many families would not allow their daughters to marry a man in an occupation

so potentially dangerous and which requires so much moving around.

The son had recently left the military and joined his father's business. Since he was a college graduate, modern, and well traveled, from such a good family, and, I thought, quite handsome, it seemed to me that he, or rather his family, was in a position to pick and choose. I said as much to my friend.

While she agreed that there were many advantages on their side, she also said, "We must keep in mind that my son is both short and dark; these are drawbacks in finding the right match." While the boy's height had not escaped my notice, "dark" seemed to me inaccurate; I would have called him "wheat" colored perhaps, and in any case, I did not realize that color would be a consideration. I discovered, however, that while a boy's skin color is a less important consideration than a girl's, it is still a factor.

An important source of contacts in trying to arrange her son's marriage was my friend's social club in Bombay. Many of the women had daughters of the right age, and some had already expressed an interest in my friend's son. I was most enthusiastic about the possibilities of one particular family who had five daughters, all of whom were pretty, demure, and well educated. Their mother had told my friend, "You can have your pick for your son, whichever one of my daughters appeals to you most."

I saw a match in sight. "Surely," I said to my friend, "we will find one there. Let's go visit and make our choice." But my friend held back; she did not seem to share my enthusiasm, for reasons I could not then fathom.

When I kept pressing for an explanation of her reluctance, she admitted, "See, Serena, here is the problem. The family has so many daughters, how will they be able to provide nicely for any of them? We are not making any demands, but still, with so many daughters to marry off, one wonders whether she will even be able to make a proper wedding. Since this is our eldest son, it's best if we marry him to a girl who is the only daughter, then the wedding will truly be a gala affair." I argued that surely the quality of the girls themselves made up for any deficiency in the elaborateness of the wedding. My friend admitted this point but still seemed reluctant to proceed.

"Is there something else," I asked her, "some factor I have missed?" "Well," she finally said, "there is one other thing. They have one daughter already married and living in Bombay. The mother is always complaining to me that the girl's in-laws don't let her visit her own family often enough. So it makes me wonder, will she be that kind of mother who always wants her daughter at her own home? This will prevent the girl from adjusting to our house. It is not a good thing." And so, this family of five daughters was dropped as a possibility.

Somewhat disappointed, I nevertheless respected my friend's reasoning and geared up for the next prospect. This was also the daughter of a woman in my friend's social club. There was clear interest in this family and I could see why. The family's reputation was excellent; in fact, they came from a sub-caste slightly higher than my friend's own. The girl, who was an only daughter, was pretty and well educated and had a brother studying in the United States. Yet, after expressing an interest to me in this family, all talk of them suddenly died down and the search began elsewhere.

"What happened to that girl as a prospect?" I asked one day. "You never mention her any more. She is so pretty and so educated, what did you find wrong?"

"She is too educated. We've decided against it. My husband's father saw the girl on the bus the other day and thought her forward. A girl who 'roams about' the city by herself is not the girl for our family." My disappointment this time was even greater, as I thought the son would have liked the girl very much. But then I thought, my friend is right, a girl who is going to live in a joint family cannot be too independent or she will make life miserable for everyone. I also learned that if the family of the girl has even a slightly higher social status than the family of the boy, the bride may think herself too good for them, and this too will cause problems. Later my friend admitted to

me that this had been an important factor in her decision not to pursue the match.

The next candidate was the daughter of a client of my friend's husband. When the client learned that the family was looking for a match for their son, he said, "Look no further, we have a daughter." This man then invited my friends to dinner to see the girl. He had already seen their son at the office and decided that "he liked the boy." We all went together for tea, rather than dinner—it was less of a commitment—and while we were there, the girl's mother showed us around the house. The girl was studying for her exams and was briefly introduced to us.

After we left, I was anxious to hear my friend's opinion. While her husband liked the family very much and was impressed with his client's business accomplishments and reputation, the wife didn't like the girl's looks. "She is short, no doubt, which is an important plus point, but she is also fat and wears glasses." My friend obviously thought she could do better for her son and asked her husband to make his excuses to his client by saying that they had decided to postpone the boy's marriage indefinitely.

By this time almost six months had passed and I was becoming impatient. What I had thought would be an easy matter to arrange was turning out to be quite complicated. I began to believe that between my friend's desire for a girl who was modest enough to fit into her joint family, yet attrac-

tive and educated enough to be an acceptable partner for her son, she would not find anyone suitable. My friend laughed at my impatience: "Don't be so much in a hurry," she said. "You Americans want everything done so quickly. You get married quickly and then just as quickly get divorced. Here we take marriage more seriously. We must take all the factors into account. It is not enough for us to learn by our mistakes. This is too serious a business. If a mistake is made we have not only ruined the life of our son or daughter, but we have spoiled the reputation of our family as well. And that will make it much harder for their brothers and sisters to get married. So we must be very careful."

What she said was true and I promised myself to be more patient, though it was not easy. I had really hoped and expected that the match would be made before my year in India was up. But it was not to be. When I left India my friend seemed no further along in finding a suitable match for her son than when I had arrived.

Two years later, I returned to India and still my friend had not found a girl for her son. By this time, he was close to thirty, and I think she was a little worried. Since she knew I had friends all over India, and I was going to be there for a year, she asked me to "help her in this work" and keep an eye out for someone suitable. I was flattered that my judgment was respected, but knowing now how complicated the process was, I had lost my earlier confidence as a matchmaker. Nevertheless, I promised that I would try.

It was almost at the end of my year's stay in India that I met a family with a marriageable daughter whom I felt might be a good possibility for my friend's son. The girl's father was related to a good friend of mine and by coincidence came from the same village as my friend's husband. This new family had a successful business in a medium-sized city in central India and were from the same subcaste as my friend. The daughter was pretty and chic; in fact, she had studied fashion design in college. Her parents would not allow her to go off by herself to any of the major cities in India where she could make a career, but they had compromised with her wish to work by allowing her to run a small dress-making boutique from their home. In spite of her desire to have a career, the daughter was both modest and home-loving and had had a traditional, sheltered upbringing. She had only one other sister, already married, and a brother who was in his father's business.

I mentioned the possibility of a match with my friend's son. The girl's parents were most interested. Although their daughter was not eager to marry just yet, the idea of living in Bombay—a sophisticated, extremely fashion-conscious city where she could continue her education in clothing design—was a great inducement. I gave the girl's father my friend's address and suggested that when

Even today, almost all marriages in India are arranged. It is believed that parents are much more effective at deciding whom their daughters should marry.

they went to Bombay on some business or whatever, they look up the boy's family.

Returning to Bombay on my way to New York, I told my friend of this newly discovered possibility. She seemed to feel there was potential but, in spite of my urging, would not make any moves herself. She rather preferred to wait for the girl's family to call upon them. I hoped something would come of this introduction, though by now I had learned to rein in my optimism.

A year later I received a letter from my friend. The family had indeed come to visit Bombay, and their daughter and my friend's daughter, who were near in age, had become very good friends. During that year, the two girls had frequently visited each other. I thought things looked promising.

Last week I received an invitation to a wedding: My friend's son and the girl were getting married. Since I had found the match, my presence was particularly requested at the wedding. I was thrilled. Success at last! As I prepared to leave for India, I began thinking, "Now, my friend's younger son, who do I know who has a nice girl for him . . . ?"

Appendix

Further Reflections on Arranged Marriage . . .

This essay was written from the point of view of a family seeking a daughter-in-law. Arranged marriage looks somewhat different from the point of view of the bride and her family. Arranged marriage continues to be preferred, even among the more educated, Westernized sections of the Indian population. Many young women from these families still go along, more or less willingly, with the practice, and also with the specific choices of their families. Young women do get excited about the prospects of their marriage, but there is also ambivalence and increasing uncertainty, as the bride contemplates leaving the comfort and familiarity of her own home, where as a "temporary guest" she had often been indulged, to live among strangers. Even in the best situation she will now come under the close scrutiny of her husband's family. How she dresses, how she behaves, how she gets along with others, where she goes, how she spends her time, her domestic abilities—all of this and much more—will be observed and commented on by a whole new set of relations. Her interaction with her family of birth will be monitored and curtailed con-siderably. Not only will she leave their home, but with increasing geographic mobility, she may also live very far from them, perhaps even on another continent. Too much expression of her fondness for her own family, or her desire to visit them, may be interpreted as an inability to adjust to her new family, and may become a source of conflict. In an arranged marriage the burden of adjustment is clearly heavier for a woman than for a man. And that is in the best of situations.

In less happy circumstances, the bride may be a target of resentment and hostility from her husband's family, particularly her mother-in-law or her husband's unmarried sisters, for whom she is now a source of competition for the affection, loyalty, and economic resources of their son or brother. If she is psychologically, or even physically abused, her options are limited, as returning to her parents' home, or divorce, are still very stigmatized. For most Indians, marriage and motherhood are still considered the only suitable roles for a woman, even for those who have careers, and few women can comfortably contemplate remaining unmarried. Most families still consider "marrying off" their daughters as a compelling religious duty and social necessity. This increases a bride's sense of obligation to make the marriage a success, at whatever cost to her own personal happiness.

The vulnerability of a new bride may also be intensified by the issue of dowry, which although illegal, has become a more pressing issue in the consumer conscious society of contemporary urban India. In many cases, where a groom's family is not satisfied with the amount of dowry a bride brings to her marriage, the young bride will be constantly harassed to get her parents to give more. In extreme cases, the bride may even be murdered, and the murder disguised as an accident or suicide. This also offers the husband's family an opportunity to arrange another match for him, thus bringing in another dowry. This phenomena, called dowry death, calls attention not just to the "evils of dowry" but also to larger issues of the powerlessness of women as well.

Serena Nanda
March 1998

Who Needs Love! In Japan, Many Couples Don't

Nicholas D. Kristof

OMIYA, Japan—Yuri Uemura sat on the straw tatami mat of her living room and chatted cheerfully about her 40-year marriage to a man whom, she mused, she never particularly liked.

"There was never any love between me and my husband," she said blithely, recalling how he used to beat her. "But, well, we survived."

A 72-year-old midwife, her face as weathered as an old baseball and etched with a thousand seams, Mrs. Uemura said that her husband had never told her that he liked her, never complimented her on a meal, never told her "thank you," never held her hand, never given her a present, never shown her affection in any way. He never calls her by her name, but summons her with the equivalent of a grunt or a "Hey, you."

"Even with animals, the males cooperate to bring the females some food," Mrs. Uemura said sadly, noting the contrast to her own marriage. "When I see that, it brings tears to my eyes."

In short, the Uemuras have a marriage that is as durable as it is unhappy, one couple's tribute to the Japanese sanctity of family.

The divorce rate in Japan is at a record high but still less than half that of the United States, and Japan arguably has one of the strongest family structures in the industrialized world. As the United States and Europe fret about the disintegration of the traditional family, most Japanese families remain as solid as the small red table on which Mrs. Uemura rested her tea.

A study published last year by the Population Council, an international nonprofit group based in New York, suggested that the traditional two-parent household is on the wane not only in America but throughout most of the world. There was one prominent exception: Japan.

In Japan, for example, only 1.1 percent of births are to unwed mothers—virtually unchanged from 25 years ago. In the United States, the figure is 30.1 percent and rising rapidly.

Yet if one comes to a little Japanese town like Omiya to learn the secrets of the Japanese family, the people are not as happy as the statistics.

"I haven't lived for myself," Mrs. Uemura said, with a touch of melancholy, "but for my kids, and for my family, and for society."

Mrs. Uemura's marriage does not seem exceptional in Japan, whether in the big cities or here in Omiya. The people of Omiya, a community of 5,700 nestled in the rain-drenched hills of the Kii Peninsula in Mie Prefecture, nearly 200 miles southwest of Tokyo, have spoken periodically to a reporter about various aspects of their daily lives. On this visit they talked about their families.

Survival Secrets

Often, the Couples Expect Little

Osamu Torida furrowed his brow and looked perplexed when he was asked if he loved his wife of 33 years.

"Yeah, so-so, I guess," said Mr. Torida, a cattle farmer. "She's like air or water. You couldn't live without it, but most of the time, you're not conscious of its existence."

The secret to the survival of the marriage, Mr. Torida acknowledged, was not mutual passion.

"Sure, we had fights about our work," he explained as he stood beside his barn. "But we were preoccupied by work and our debts, so we had no time to fool around."

That is a common theme in Omiya. It does not seem that Japanese families survive because husbands and wives love each other more than American couples, but rather because they perhaps love each other less.

"I think love marriages are more fragile than arranged marriages," said Tomika Kusukawa, 49, who married her high-school sweetheart and now runs a car repair shop with him. "In love marriages, when something happens or if the couple falls out of love, they split up."

If there is a secret to the strength of the Japanese family it consists of three ingredients: low expectations, patience, and shame.

The advantage of marriages based on low expectations is that they have built in shock absorbers. If the couple discover that they have nothing in common, that they do not even like each other, then that is not so much a reason for divorce as it is par for the course.

Even the discovery that one's spouse is having an affair is often not as traumatic in a Japanese marriage as it is in the West. A little sexual infidelity on the part of a man (though not on the part of his wife) was traditionally tolerated, so long as he did not become so besotted as to pay his mistress more than he could afford.

Tsuzuya Fukuyama, who runs a convenience store and will mark her 50th wedding anniversary this year, toasted her hands on an electric heater in the front of the store and declared that a woman would be wrong to get angry if her husband had an affair.

"It's never just one side that's at fault," Mrs. Fukuyama said sternly. "Maybe the husband had an affair because his wife wasn't so hot herself. So she should look at her own faults."

Mrs. Fukuyama's daughter came to her a few years ago, suspecting that her husband was having an affair and asking what to do.

"I told her, 'Once you left this house, you can only come back if you divorce; if you're not prepared to get a divorce, then you'd better be patient,' " Mrs. Fukuyama recalled. "And so she was patient. And then she got pregnant and had a kid, and now they're close again."

The word that Mrs. Fukuyama used for patience is "gaman," a term that comes up whenever marriage is discussed in Japan. It means toughing it out, enduring hardship, and many Japanese regard gaman with pride as a national trait.

Many people complain that younger folks divorce because they do not have enough gaman, and the frequency with

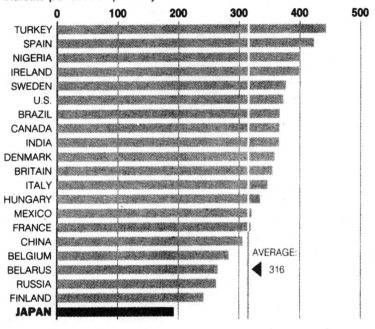

GETTING ALONG

Matchmaker, Matchmaker

How countries compare on an index of compatibility of spouses, based on answers to questions about politics, sex, social issues, religion and ethics, from a survey by the Dentsu Research Institute and Leisure Development Center in Japan. A score of 500 would indicate perfect compatibility.

TURKEY
SPAIN
NIGERIA
IRELAND
SWEDEN
U.S.
BRAZIL
CANADA
INDIA
DENMARK
BRITAIN
ITALY
HUNGARY
MEXICO
FRANCE
CHINA
BELGIUM
BELARUS
RUSSIA
FINLAND
JAPAN

AVERAGE: ◄ 316

New York Times

which the term is used suggests a rather bleak understanding of marriage.

"I didn't know my husband very well when we married, and afterward we used to get into bitter fights," said Yoshiko Hirowaki, 56, a store owner. "But then we had children, and I got very busy with the kids and with this shop. Time passed."

Now Mrs. Hirowaki has been married 34 years, and she complains about young people who do not stick to their vows.

"In the old days, wives had more gaman," she said. "Now kids just don't have enough gaman."

The durability of the Japanese family is particularly wondrous because couples are, by international standards, exceptionally incompatible.

One survey asked married men and their wives in 37 countries how they felt about politics, sex, religion, ethics and social issues. Japanese couples ranked

dead last in compatibility of views, by a huge margin. Indeed, another survey found that if they were doing it over again, only about one-third of Japanese would marry the same person.

Incompatibility might not matter so much, however, because Japanese husbands and wives spend very little time talking to each other.

"I kind of feel there's nothing new to say to her," said Masayuki Ogita, an egg farmer, explaining his reticence.

In a small town like Omiya, couples usually have dinner together, but in Japanese cities there are many "7-11 husbands," so called because they leave at 7 A.M. and return after 11 P.M.

Masahiko Kondo now lives in Omiya, working in the chamber of commerce, but he used to be a salesman in several big cities. He would leave work each morning at 7, and about four nights a week would go out for after-work drinking or mah-jongg sessions with buddies.

"I only saw my baby on Saturdays or Sundays," said Mr. Kondo, a lanky good-natured man of 37. "But in fact, I really enjoyed that life. It didn't bother me that I never spent time with my kid on weekdays."

Mr. Kondo's wife, Keiko, had her own life, spent with her child and the wives of other workaholic husbands.

"We had birthday parties, but they were with the kids and the mothers," she remembers. "No fathers ever came."

A national survey found that 30 percent of fathers spend less than 15 minutes a day on weekdays talking with or playing with their children. Among eighth graders, 51 percent reported that they never spoke with their fathers on weekdays.

As a result, the figures in Japan for single-parent households can be deceptive. The father is often more a theoretical presence than a homework-helping reality.

Still, younger people sometimes want to see the spouses in daylight, and a result is a gradual change in focus of lives from work to family. Two decades ago, nearly half of young people said in surveys that they wanted their fathers to put priority on work rather than family. Now only one-quarter say that.

Social Pressures

Shame Is Keeping Bonds in Place

For those who find themselves desperately unhappy, one source of pressure to keep plugging is shame.

"If you divorce, you lose face in society," said Tatsumi Kinoshita, a tea farmer. "People say, 'His wife escaped.' So folks remain married because they hate to be gossiped about."

Shame is a powerful social sanction in Japan, and it is not just a matter of gossip. Traditionally, many companies were reluctant to promote employees who had divorced or who had major problems at home.

"If you divorce, it weakens your position at work," said Akihiko Kanda, 27, who works in a local government office. "Your bosses won't give you such good ratings, and it'll always be a negative factor."

The idea, Mr. Kanda noted, is that if an employee cannot manage his own life properly, he should not be entrusted with important corporate matters.

Financial sanctions are also a major disincentive for divorce. The mother gets the children in three-quarters of divorces, but most mothers in Japan do not have careers and have few financial resources. Fathers pay child support in only 15 percent of all divorces with children, partly because women often hesitate to go to court to demand payments and partly because men often fail to pay even when the court orders it.

"The main reason for lack of divorce is that women can't support themselves," said Mizuko Kanda, a 51-year-old housewife. "My friends complain about their husbands and say that they'd divorce if they could, but they can't afford to."

The result of these social and economic pressures is clear.

Even in Japan, there are about 24 divorces for every 100 marriages, but that compares with 32 in France, and 42 in England, and 55 in the United States.

The Outlook

Change Creeps In, Imperiling Family

But society is changing in Japan, and it is an open question whether these changes will undermine the traditional family as they have elsewhere around the globe.

The nuclear family has already largely replaced the extended family in Japan, and shame is eroding as a sanction. Haruko Okumura, for example, runs a kindergarten and speaks openly about her divorce.

"My Mom was uneasy about it, but I never had an inferiority complex about being divorced," said Mrs. Okumura, as dozens of children played in the next room. "And people accepted me easily."

Mrs. Okumura sees evidence of the changes in family patterns every day: fathers are playing more of a role in the kindergarten. At Christmas parties and sports contests, fathers have started to show up along with mothers. And Mrs. Okumura believes that divorce is on the upswing.

"If there's a weakening of the economic and social pressures to stay married," she said, "surely divorce rates will soar."

Already divorce rates are rising, approximately doubling over the last 25 years. But couples are very reluctant to divorce when they have children, and so single-parent households account for exactly the same proportion today as in 1965.

Shinsuke Kawaguchi, a young tea farmer, is one of the men for whom life is changing. Americans are not likely to be impressed by Mr. Kawaguchi's openmindedness, but he is.

"I take good care of my wife," he said. "I may not say 'I love you,' but I do hold her hand. And I might say, after she makes dinner, 'This tastes good.'"

"Of course," Mr. Kawaguchi quickly added, "I wouldn't say that unless I'd just done something really bad."

Even Mrs. Uemura, the elderly woman whose husband used to beat her, said that her husband was treating her better.

"The other day, he tried to pour me a cup of tea," Mrs. Uemura recalled excitedly. "It was a big change. I told all my friends."

Gender and Status

The feminist movement in the United States has had a significant impact upon the development of anthropology. Feminists have rightly charged that anthropologists have tended to gloss over the lives of women in studies of society and culture. In part this is because, until recent times, most anthropologists have been men. The result has been an undue emphasis upon male activities as well as male perspectives in descriptions of particular societies.

These charges, however, have proven to be a firm corrective. In the last few years, anthropologists have begun to study women and, more particularly, the sexual division of labor and its relation to biology as well as to social and political status. In addition, these changes in emphasis have been accompanied by an increase in the number of women in the field.

Feminist anthropologists have begun to attack critically many of the established anthropological beliefs. They have shown, for example, that field studies of nonhuman primates, which were often used to demonstrate the evolutionary basis of male dominance, distorted the actual evolutionary record by focusing primarily on baboons. (Male baboons are especially dominant and aggressive.) Other, less-quoted primate studies show how dominance and aggression are highly situational phenomena, sensitive to ecological variation. Feminist anthropologists have also shown that the subsistence contribution of women has likewise been ignored by anthropologists. A classic case is that of the !Kung, a hunting and gathering people in southern Africa, where women provide the bulk of the foodstuffs, including most of the available protein, and who, not coincidentally, enjoy a more egalitarian relationship than usual with men. Even when the issue is premarital virginity for women, Alice Schlegel, in "Status, Property, and the Value on Virginity," shows that the concern for biological paternity may have more to do with maintaining or enhancing a family's social status than with male domination per se.

The most common occurrence, at least in recent history, has been male domination over women. Recent studies have concerned themselves with why there has been such gender inequality. Although the subordination of women is widespread, Ernestine Friedl, in "Society and Sex Roles," explains that the sex that controls the valued goods of exchange in a society is the dominant one. Thus, since this control is a matter of cultural variation, male authority is not biologically predetermined. Indeed, women have played visibly prominent roles in many cultures, as addressed by Leslie Marmon Silko in "Yellow Woman and a Beauty of the Spirit." Even so, sexual equality is still far from being a reality in many parts of the world. And, as we see in "The Initiation of a Maasai Warrior" and in "Bundu Trap," gender relationships are deeply embedded in social experience.

Looking Ahead: Challenge Questions

What is it about foraging societies that encourages an egalitarian relationship between the sexes? Why are the Eskimo an exception?

What kinds of shifts in the social relations of production are necessary for women to achieve equality with men?

What was meant by "beauty" in the old-time Pueblo culture? How and why is diversity valued in Pueblo culture?

What are bridewealth and dowry, and under what circumstances do they occur? How does female circumcision differ from male circumcision in terms of its social functions?

What kinds of personal dilemmas do women face in a changing society?

UNIT 5

Society and Sex Roles

Ernestine Friedl

Ernestine Friedl is a professor of anthropology at Duke University; a former president of the American Anthropological Association, a fellow of the American Academy of Arts and Sciences, and an advisory editor to Human Nature. *She received her Ph.D. from Columbia University in 1950. Until recently, Friedl was a firm believer in the relative equality of women in the field of anthropology and had little interest in the anthropological study of women. None of her field work among the Pomo and Chippewa Indians of North America, or in rural and urban Greece was concerned with women's issues.*

In the early 1970s, while serving on the American Anthropological Association Committee on the Status of Women, Friedl became convinced that women were discriminated against as much in anthropology as in the other academic disciplines. Since that time, she has devoted her efforts to the cross-cultural study of sex roles and has written one book on the topic, Women and Men: An Anthropologist's View *Friedl now accounts for her own success in part by the fact that she attended an all-women's college and taught for many years at the City University of New York, a university system that included a women's college.*

"Women must respond quickly to the demands of their husbands," says anthropologist Napoleon Chagnon describing the horticultural Yanomano Indians of Venezuela. When a man returns from a hunting trip, "the woman, no matter what she is doing, hurries home and quietly but rapidly prepares a meal for her husband. Should the wife be slow in doing this, the husband is within his rights to beat her. Most reprimands . . . take the form of blows with the hand or with a piece of firewood. . . . Some of them chop their wives with the sharp edge of a machete or axe, or shoot them with a barbed arrow in some nonvital area, such as the buttocks or leg."

Among the Semai agriculturalists of central Malaya, when one person refuses the request of another, the offended party suffers *punan,* a mixture of emotional pain and frustration. "Enduring *punan* is commonest when a girl has refused the victim her sexual favors," reports Robert Dentan. "The jilted man's 'heart becomes sad.' He loses his energy and his appetite. Much of the time he sleeps, dreaming of his lost love. In this state, he is in fact very likely to injure himself 'accidentally.' " The Semai are afraid of violence; a man would never strike a woman.

The social relationship between men and women has emerged as one of the principal disputes occupying the attention of scholars and the public in recent years. Although the discord is sharpest in the United States, the controversy has spread throughout the world. Numerous national and international conferences, including one in Mexico sponsored by the United Nations, have drawn together delegates from all walks of life to discuss such questions as the social and political rights of each sex, and even the basic nature of males and females.

Whatever their position, partisans often invoke examples from other cultures to support their ideas about the proper role of each sex. Because women are clearly subservient to men in many societies, like the Yanomamo, some experts conclude that the natural pattern is for men to dominate. But among the Semai no one has the right to command others, and in West Africa women are often chiefs. The place of women in these societies supports the argument of those who believe that sex roles are not fixed, that if there is a natural order, it allows for many different arrangements.

The argument will never be settled as long as the opposing sides toss examples from the world's cultures at each other like intellectual stones. But the effect of biological differences on male and female behavior can be clarified by looking at known examples of the earliest forms of human society and examining the relationship between technology, social organization, environment, and sex roles. The problem is to determine the conditions in which different degrees of male dominance are found, to try to discover the social and cultural arrangements that give rise to equality or inequality between the sexes, and to attempt to apply this knowledge to our understanding of the changes taking place in modern industrial society.

As Western history and the anthropological record have told us, equality between the sexes is rare; in most known societies females are subordinate. Male dominance is so widespread that it is virtually a human universal; societies in which women are consistently dominant do not exist and have never existed.

Evidence of a society in which women control all strategic resources like food and water, and in which women's activities are the most prestigious has never been found. The Iroquois of North America and the Lovedu of Africa came closest. Among the Iroquois, women raised food, controlled its distribution, and helped to choose male political leaders. Lovedu women ruled as queens, exchanged valuable cattle, led ceremonies, and controlled their own sex lives. But among both the Iroquois and the Lovedu, men owned the land and held other positions of power and prestige. Women were equal to men; they did not have ultimate authority over them. Neither culture was a true matriarchy.

Patriarchies are prevalent, and they appear to be strongest in societies in which men control significant goods that are exchanged with people outside the family. Regardless of who produces food, the person who gives it to others creates the obligations and alliances that are at the center of all political relations. The greater the male monopoly on the distribution of scarce items, the stronger their control of women seems to be. This is most obvious in relatively simple hunter-gatherer societies.

Hunter-gatherers, or foragers, subsist on wild plants, small land animals, and small river or sea creatures gathered by hand; large land animals and sea mammals hunted with spears, bows and arrows, and blow guns; and fish caught with hooks and nets. The 300,000 hunter-gatherers alive in the world today include the Eskimos, the Australian aborigines, and the Pygmies of Central Africa.

Foraging has endured for two million years and was replaced by farming and animal husbandry only 10,000 years ago; it covers more than 99 percent of human history. Our foraging ancestry is not far behind us and provides a clue to our understanding of the human condition.

Hunter-gatherers are people whose ways of life are technologically simple and socially and politically egalitarian. They live in small groups of 50 to 200 and have neither kings, nor priests, nor social classes. These conditions permit anthropologists to observe the essential bases for inequalities between the sexes without the distortions induced by the complexities of contemporary industrial society.

The source of male power among hunter-gatherers lies in their control of a scarce, hard to acquire, but necessary nutrient—animal protein. When men in a hunter-gatherer society return to camp with game, they divide the meat in some customary way. Among the !Kung San of Africa, certain parts of the animal are given to the owner of the arrow that killed the beast, to the first hunter to sight the game, to the one who threw the first spear and to all men in the hunting party. After the meat has been divided, each hunter distributes his share to his blood relatives and his in-laws, who in turn share it with others. If an animal is large enough, every member of the band will receive some meat.

Vegetable foods, in contrast, are not distributed beyond the immediate household. Women give food to their children, to their husbands, to other members of the household, and rarely, to the occasional visitor. No one outside the family regularly eats any of the wild fruit and vegetables that are gathered by the women.

The meat distributed by the men is a public gift. Its source is widely known, and the donor expects a reciprocal gift when other men return from a successful hunt. He gains honor as a supplier of a scarce item and simultaneously obligates others to him.

These obligations constitute a form of power or control over others, both men and women. The opinions of hunters play an important part in decisions to move the village; good hunters attract the most desirable women; people in other groups join camps with good hunters; and hunters, because they already participate in an internal system of exchange, control exchange with other groups for flint, salt, and steel axes. The male monopoly on hunting unites men in a system of exchange and gives them power; gathering vegetable food does not give women equal power even among foragers who live in the tropics, where the food collected by women provides more than half the hunter-gatherer diet.

If dominance arises from a monopoly on big-game hunting, why has the male monopoly remained unchallenged? Some women are strong enough to participate in the hunt and their endurance is certainly equal to that of men. Dobe San women of the Kalahari Desert in Africa walk an average of 10 miles a day carrying from 15 to 33 pounds of food plus a baby.

Women do not hunt, I believe, because of four interrelated factors: variability in the supply of game; the different skills required for hunting and gathering; the incompatibility between carrying burdens and hunting; and the small size of semi-nomadic foraging populations.

Because the meat supply is unstable, foragers must make frequent expeditions to provide the band with gathered food. Environmental factors such as seasonal and annual variation in rainfall often affect the size of the wildlife population. Hunters cannot always find game, and when they do encounter animals, they are not always successful in killing their prey. In northern latitudes, where meat is the primary food, periods of starvation are known in every generation. The irregularity of the game supply leads hunter-gatherers in areas where plant foods are available to depend on these predictable foods a good part of the time. Someone must gather the fruits, nuts, and roots and carry them back to camp to feed unsuccessful hunters, children, the elderly, and anyone who might not have gone foraging that day.

Foraging falls to the women because hunting and gathering cannot be combined on the same expedition. Although gatherers sometimes notice signs of game as they work, the skills required to track game are not the same as those required to find edible roots or plants. Hunters scan the horizon and the land for traces of large game; gatherers keep their eyes to the ground, studying the distribution of plants and the texture of the soil for hidden roots and animal holes. Even if a woman who was collecting plants came across the track of an antelope, she could not follow it; it is impossible to carry a load and hunt at the same time. Running with a heavy load is difficult, and should the animal be sighted, the hunter would be off balance and could neither shoot an arrow nor throw a spear accurately.

In the maritime Inuit (Eskimo) societies, inequality between the sexes is matched by the ability to supply food for the group. The men hunt for meat and control the economy. Women perform all the other duties that support life in the community, and are virtually treated as objects. (Photo credit: American Museum of Natural History—Dr. F. Rainey)

Pregnancy and child care would also present difficulties for a hunter. An unborn child affects a woman's body balance, as does a child in her arms, on her back, or slung at her side. Until they are two years old, many hunter-gatherer children are carried at all times, and until they are four, they are carried some of the time.

An observer might wonder why young women do not hunt until they become pregnant, or why mature women and men do not hunt and gather on alternate days, with some women staying in camp to act as wet nurses for the young. Apart from the effects hunting might have on a mother's milk production, there are two reasons. First, young girls begin to bear children as soon as they are physically mature and strong enough to hunt, and second, hunter-gatherer bands are so small that there

are unlikely to be enough lactating women to serve as wet nurses. No hunter-gatherer group could afford to maintain a specialized female hunting force.

Because game is not always available, because hunting and gathering are specialized skills, because women carrying heavy loads cannot hunt, and because women in hunter-gatherer societies are usually either pregnant of caring for young children, for most of the last two million years of human history men have hunted and women have gathered.

If male dominance depends on controlling the supply of meat, then the degree of male dominance in a society should vary with the amount of meat available and the amount supplied by the men. Some regions, like the East African grasslands and the North American woodlands, abounded with species of large mammals; other zones, like tropi-

cal forests and semi-deserts, are thinly populated with prey. Many elements effect the supply of game, but theoretically, the less meat provided exclusively by the men, the more egalitarian the society.

All known hunter-gatherer societies fit into four basic types; those in which men and women work together in communal hunts and as teams gathering edible plants, as did the Washo Indians of North America; those in which men and women each collect their own plant foods although the men supply some meat to the group, as do the Hadza of Tanzania; those in which male hunters and female gatherers work apart but return to camp each evening to share their acquisitions, as do the Tiwi of North Australia; and those in which the men provide all the food by hunting large game, as do the Eskimo. In each case the extent of male dominance increases directly with the proportion of meat supplied by individual men and small hunting parties.

Among the most egalitarian of hunter-gatherer societies are the Washo Indians, who inhabited the valleys of the Sierra Nevada in what is now southern California and Nevada. In the spring they moved north to Lake Tahoe for the large fish runs of sucker and native trout. Everyone—men, women, and children—participated in the fishing. Women spent the summer gathering edible berries and seeds while the men continued to fish. In the fall some men hunted deer but the most important source of animal protein was the jack rabbit, which was captured in communal hunts. Men and women together drove the rabbits into nets tied end to end. To provide food for the winter, husbands and wives worked as teams in the late fall to collect pine nuts.

Since everyone participated in most food-gathering activities, there were no individual distributions of food and relatively little difference in male and female rights. Men and women were not segregated from each other in daily activities; both were free to take lovers after marriage; both had the right to separate whenever they chose; menstruating women were not isolated from the rest of the group; and one of the two major Washo rituals celebrated hunting while the other celebrated gathering. Men were accorded more prestige if they had killed a deer, and men directed decisions about the seasonal movement of the group. But if no male leader stepped forward, women were permitted to lead. The distinctive feature of groups such as the Washo is the relative equality of the sexes.

The sexes are also relatively equal among the Hadza of Tanzania but this near-equality arises because men and women tend to work alone to feed themselves. They exchange little food. The Hadza lead a leisurely life in the seemingly barren environment of the East African Rift Gorge that is, in fact, rich in edible berries, roots, and small game. As a result of this abundance, from the time they are 10 years old, Hadza men and women gather much of their own food.

Women take their young children with them into the bush, eating as they forage, and collect only enough food for a light family meal in the evening. The men eat berries and roots as they hunt for small game, and should they bring down a rabbit or a hyrax, they eat the meat on the spot. Meat is carried back to the camp and shared with the rest of the group only on those rare occasions when a poisoned arrow brings down a large animal—an impala, a zebra, an eland, or a giraffe.

Because Hadza men distribute little meat, their status is only slightly higher than that of the women. People flock to the camp of a good hunter and the camp might take on his name because of his popularity, but he is in no sense a leader of the group. A Hadza man and a woman have an equal right to divorce and each can repudiate a marriage simply by living apart for a few weeks. Couples tend to live in the same camp as the wife's mother but they sometimes make long visits to the camp of the husband's mother. Although a man may take more than one wife, most Hadza males cannot afford to indulge in this luxury. In order to maintain a marriage, a man must supply both his wife and his mother-in-law with some meat and trade goods, such as beads and cloth, and the Hadza economy gives few men the wealth to provide for more than one wife and mother-in-law. Washo equality is based on cooperation; Hadza equality is based on independence.

In contrast to both these groups, among the Tiwi of Melville and Bathurst Islands off the northern coast of Australia, male hunters dominate female gatherers. The Tiwi are representative of the most common form of foraging society, in which the men supply large quantities of meat, although less than half the food consumed by the group. Each morning Tiwi women, most with babies on their backs, scatter in different directions in search of vegetables, grubs, worms, and small game such as bandicoots, lizards, and opossums. To track the game, they use hunting dogs. On most days women return to camp with some meat and with baskets full of *korka,* the nut of a native palm, which is soaked and mashed to make a por-

ridge-like dish. The Tiwi men do not hunt small game and do not hunt every day, but when they do they often return with kangaroo, large lizards, fish, and game birds.

The porridge is cooked separately by each household and rarely shared outside the family, but the meat is prepared by a volunteer cook, who can be male or female. After the cook takes one of the parts of the animal traditionally reserved for him or her, the animal's "boss," the one who caught it, distributes the rest to all near kin and then to all others residing with the band. Although the small game supplied by the women is distributed in the same way as the big game supplied by the men, Tiwi men are dominant because the game they kill provides most of the meat.

The power of the Tiwi men is clearest in their betrothal practices. Among the Tiwi, a woman must always be married. To ensure this, female infants are betrothed at birth and widows are remarried at the gravesides of their late husbands. Men form alliances by exchanging daughters, sisters, and mothers in marriage and some collect as many as 25 wives. Tiwi men value the quantity and quality of the food many wives can collect and the many children they can produce.

The dominance of the men is offset somewhat by the influence of adult women in selecting their next husbands. Many women are active strategists in the political careers of their male relatives, but to the exasperation of some sons attempting to promote their own futures, widowed mothers sometimes insist on selecting their own partners. Women also influence the marriages of their daughters and granddaughters, especially when the selected husband dies before the bestowed child moves to his camp.

Among the Eskimos, representative of the rarest type of forager society, inequality between the sexes is matched by inequality in supplying the group with food. Inland Eskimo men hunt caribou throughout the year to provision the entire society, and maritime Eskimo men depend on whaling, fishing, and some hunting to feed their extended families. The women process the carcasses, cut and sew skins to make clothing, cook, and care for the young; but they collect no food of their own and depend on the men to supply all the raw materials for their work. Since men provide all the meat, they also control the trade in hides, whale oil, seal oil, and other items that move between the maritime and inland Eskimos.

Eskimo women are treated almost exclusively as objects to be used, abused, and traded by men. After puberty all Eskimo girls are fair game for any interested male. A man shows his intentions by grabbing the belt of a women and if she protests, he cuts off her trousers and forces himself upon her. These encounters are considered unimportant by the rest of the group. Men offer their wives' sexual services to establish alliances with trading partners and members of hunting and whaling parties.

Despite the consistent pattern of some degree of male dominance among foragers, most of these societies are egalitarian compared with agricultural and industrial societies. No forager has any significant opportunity for political leadership. Foragers, as a rule, do not like to give or take orders, and assume leadership only with reluctance. Shamans (those who are thought to be possessed by spirits) may be either male or female. Public rituals conducted by women in order to celebrate the first menstruation of girls are common, and the symbolism in these rituals is similar to that in the ceremonies that follow a boy's first kill.

In any society, status goes to those who control the distribution of valued goods and services outside the family. Equality arises when both sexes work side by side in food production, as do the Washo, and the products are simply distributed among the workers. In such circumstances, no person or sex has greater access to valued items than do others. But when women make no contribution to the food supply, as in the case of the Eskimo, they are completely subordinate.

When we attempt to apply these generalizations to contemporary industrial society, we can predict that as long as women spend their discretionary income from jobs on domestic needs, they will gain little social recognition and power. To be an effective source of power, money must be exchanged in ways that require returns and create obligations. In other words, it must be invested.

Jobs that do not give women control over valued resources will do little to advance their general status. Only as managers, executives, and professionals are women in a position to trade goods and services, to do others favors, and therefore to obligate others to them. Only as controllers of valued resources can women achieve prestige, power, and equality.

Within the household, women who bring in income from jobs are able to function on a more nearly equal basis with their husbands. Women who contribute services to their husbands and children without pay, as do some middle-class Western housewives, are especially vulnerable to dominance. Like Eskimo women, as long as their services are limited to domestic distribution they have little power relative to their husbands and none with respect to the outside world.

As for the limits imposed on women by their procreative functions in hunter-gatherer societies, child-bearing and child care are organized around work as much as work is organized around reproduction. Some foraging groups space their children three to four years apart and have an average of only four to six children, far fewer than many women in other cultures. Hunter-gatherers nurse their infants for extended periods, sometimes for as long as four years. This custom suppresses ovulation and limits the size of their families. Sometimes, although rarely, they practice infanticide. By limiting reproduction, a woman who is gathering food has only one child to carry.

Different societies can and do adjust the frequency of birth and the care of children to accommodate whatever productive activities women customarily engage in. In horticultural societies, where women work long hours in gardens that may be far from home, infants get food to supplement their mothers' milk, older children take care of younger children, and pregnancies are widely spaced. Throughout the world, if a society requires a woman's labor, it finds ways to care for her children.

In the United States, as in some other industrial societies, the accelerated entry of women with preschool children into the labor force has resulted in the development of a variety of child-care arrangements. Individual women have called on friends, relatives, and neighbors. Public and private child-care centers are growing. We should realize that the declining birth rate, the increasing acceptance of childless or single-child families, and a de-emphasis on motherhood are adaptations to a sexual division of labor reminiscent of the system of production found in hunter-gatherer societies.

In many countries where women no longer devote most of their productive years to childbearing, they are beginning to demand a change in the social relationship of the sexes. As women gain access to positions that control the exchange of resources, male dominance may become archaic, and industrial societies may one day become an egalitarian as the Washo.

References

Friedl, Ernestine, *Women and Men: An Anthropologist's View,* Holt, Rinehart and Winston, 1975.

Martin, M. Kay, and Barbara Voorhies, eds., *Female of the Species,* Columbia University Press, 1977.

Murphy, Yolanda, and Robert Murphy, *Women of the Forest,* Columbia University Press, 1974.

Reiter, Rayna, ed., *Toward an Anthropology of Women,* Monthly Review Press, 1975.

Rosaldo, M. Z., and Louise Lamphere, eds., *Women, Culture, and Society,* Stanford University Press, 1974.

Schlegel, Alice, ed., *Sexual Stratification; A Cross-Cultural View,* Columbia University Press, 1977.

Strathern, Marilyn, *Women in Between: Female Roles in a Male World,* Academic Press, 1972.

Yellow Woman and a Beauty of the Spirit

For a Laguna Pueblo Child Who Looked 'Different,' There Was Comfort in the Old Ways—A World in Which Faces and Bodies Could Not Be Separated From Hearts and Souls

Leslie Marmon Silko

Leslie Marmon Silko's most recent book is "Almanac of the Dead," published by Simon & Schuster. She lives in Tucson, Ariz.

From the time I was a small child, I was aware that I was different. I looked different from my playmates. My two sisters looked different too. We didn't look quite like the other Laguna Pueblo children, but we didn't look quite white either. In the 1880s, my great grandfather had followed his older brother west from Ohio to the New Mexico territory to survey the land for the U.S. government. The two Marmon brothers came to the Laguna Pueblo Reservation because they had an Ohio cousin who already lived there. The Ohio cousin was involved in sending Indian children thousands of miles away from their families to the War Department's big Indian boarding school in Carlisle, Pa. Both brothers married "full blood" Laguna Pueblo women. My great-grandfather had first married my great-grandmother's older sister, but she died in childbirth and left two small children. My great-grandmother was 15 or 20 years younger than my great-grandfa-

ther. She had attended Carlisle Indian School and spoke and wrote English beautifully.

I called her Grandma A'mooh because that's what I heard her say whenever she saw me. "A'mooh" means "granddaughter" in the Laguna language. I remember this word because her love and her acceptance of me as a small child were so important. I had sensed immediately that something about my appearance was not acceptable to some people, white and Indian. But I did not see any signs of that strain or anxiety in the face of my beloved Grandma A'mooh.

Younger people, people my parents' age, seemed to look at the world in a more "modern" way. The "modern" way included racism. My physical appearance seemed not to matter to the old-time people. They looked at the world very differently; a person's appearance and possessions did not matter nearly as much as a person's behavior. For them, a person's value lies in how that person interacts with other people, how that person behaves toward the animals and the Earth. That is what matters most to

the old-time people. The Pueblo people believed this long before the Puritans arrived with their notions of sin and damnation, and racism. The old-time beliefs persist today; thus I will refer to the old-time people in the present tense as well as the past. Many worlds may coexist here.

I spent a great deal of time with my great-grandmother. Her house was next to our house, and I used to wake up at dawn, hours before my parents or younger sisters, and I'd go wait on the porch swing or on the back steps by her kitchen door. She got up at dawn, but she was more than 80 years old so she needed a little while to get dressed and to get the fire going in the cookstove. I had been carefully instructed by my parents not to bother her and to behave, and to try to help her any way I could. I always loved the early mornings when the air was so cool with a hint of rain smell in the breeze. In the dry New Mexico air, the least hint of dampness smells sweet.

My great-grandmother's yard was planted with lilac bushes and iris; there were four o'clocks, cosmos, morning glories and hollyhocks and old-fashioned rose bushes that I helped her water. If the garden hose got stuck on one of the big rocks that lined the path in the yard, I ran and pulled it free. That's what I came to do early every morning: to help Grandma water the plants before the heat of the day arrived.

Grandma A'mooh would tell about the old days, family stories about relatives who had been killed by Apache raiders who stole the sheep our relatives had been herding near Swahnee. Sometimes she read the Bible stories that we kids liked because of the illustrations of Jonah in the mouth of a whale and Daniel surrounded by lions. Grandma A'mooh would send me home when she took her nap, but when the sun got low and the afternoon began to cool off, I would be back on the porch swing, waiting for her to come out to water the plants and to haul in firewood for the evening. When Grandma was 85, she still chopped her own kindling. She used to let me carry in the coal bucket for her, but she would not allow me to use the ax. I carried armloads of kindling too, and I learned to be proud of my strength.

I was allowed to listen quietly when Aunt Susie or Aunt Alice came to visit Grandma. When I got old enough to cross the road alone, I went and visited them almost daily. They were vigorous women who valued books and writing. They were usually busy chopping wood or cooking but never hesitated to take time to answer my questions. Best of all they told me the "hummah-hah" stories, about an earlier time when animals and humans shared a common language. In the old days, the Pueblo people had educated their children in this manner; adults took time out to talk to and teach young people. Everyone was a teacher, and every activity had the potential to teach the child.

But as soon as I started kindergarten at the Bureau of Indian Affairs day school, I began to learn more about the difference between the Laguna Pueblo world and the outside world. It was at school that I learned just how different I looked from my classmates. Sometimes tourists driving past on Route 66 would stop by Laguna Day School at recess time to take photographs of us kids. One day, when I was in the first grade, we all crowded around the smiling white tourists who peered at our faces. We all wanted to be in the picture because afterward the tourists sometimes gave us each a penny. Just as we were all posed and ready to have our picture taken, the tourist man looked at me. "Not you," he said and motioned for me to step away from my classmates. I felt so embarrassed that I wanted to disappear. My classmates were puzzled by the tourists' behavior, but I knew the tourists didn't want me in their snapshot because I looked different, because I was part white.

In the view of the old-time people, we are all sisters and brothers because the Mother Creator made all of us—all colors and all sizes. We are sisters and brothers, clanspeople of all the living beings around us. The plants, the birds, fish, clouds, water, even the clay—they all are related to us. The old-time people believe that all things, even rocks and water, have spirit and being. They understood that all things only want to continue being as they are. Thus the old folks used to tell us kids not to disturb the earth unnecessarily. All things as they were created exist already in harmony with one another as long as we do not disturb them.

As the old story tells us, Tse'its'i'nako, Thought Woman, the Spider, thought of her three sisters, and as she thought of them, they came into being. Together with Thought Women, they thought of the sun and the stars and the moon. The Mother Creators imagined the earth and the oceans, the animals and the people, and the Kat'sina spirits that reside in the mountains. The Mother Creators imagined all the plants that flower and the trees that bear fruit. As Thought Woman and her sisters thought of it, the whole universe came into being. In this universe, there is no absolute good or absolute bad; there are only balances and harmonies that ebb and flow. Some years the desert receives abundant rain, other years there is too little rain, and sometimes there is so much rain that floods cause destruction. But rain itself is neither innocent or guilty. The rain is simply itself.

My great-grandmother was dark and handsome. Her expression in photographs is one of confidence and strength. I do not know if white people then or now would consider her beautiful. I do not know if the old-time Laguna Pueblo people considered her beautiful or if the old-time people even thought in those terms. To the Pueblo way of thinking, the act of comparing one living being with another was silly, because each being or thing is unique and therefore incomparably valuable because it is the only one of its kind. The old-time people thought it was crazy to attach such importance to a person's appearance. I understood very early that there were two distinct ways of interpreting the world. There was the white people's way, and there was the Laguna way. In the Laguna way, it was bad manners to make comparisons that might hurt another person's feelings.

In everyday Pueblo life, not much attention was paid to one's physical appearance or clothing. Ceremonial clothing was quite elaborate but was used only for the sacred dances. The traditional Pueblo societies were communal and strictly egalitarian, which means that no matter how well or how poorly one might have dressed, there was no "social ladder" to fall from. All food and other resources were strictly shared so that no one person or group had more than another. I mention social status because it seems to me that most of the definitions of beauty in contemporary Western culture are really codes for determining social status. People no longer hide their face-lifts, and they discuss their liposuctions because the point of the procedures isn't just cosmetic, it is social. It says to the world, "I have enough spare cash that I can afford surgery for cosmetic purposes."

In the old-time Pueblo world, beauty was manifested in behavior and in one's relationships with other living beings. Beauty was as much a feeling of harmony as it was a visual, aural or sensual effect. The whole person had to be beautiful, not just the face or the body; faces and bodies could not be separated from hearts and souls. Health was foremost in achieving this sense of well-being and harmony; in the old-time Pueblo world, a person who did not look healthy inspired feelings of worry and anxiety, not feelings of well-being. A healthy person, of course, is in harmony with the world around her; she is at peace with herself too. Thus an unhappy person or spiteful person would not be considered beautiful.

In the old days, strong, sturdy women were most admired. One of my most vivid preschool memories is of the crew of Laguna women, in their 40s and 50s, who came to cover our house with adobe plaster. They handled the ladders with great ease, and while two women ground the adobe mud on stones and added straw, another woman loaded the hod with mud and passed it up to the two women on ladders, who were smoothing the plaster on the wall with their hands. Since women owned the houses, they did the plastering. At Laguna, men did the basket-making and the weaving of fine textiles; men helped a great deal with the child-care too. Because the Creator is female, there is no stigma on being female; gender is not used to control behavior. No job was a "man's job" or a "woman's job"; the most able person did the work.

My Grandma Lily had been a Ford Model A mechanic when she was a teenager. I remember when I was young, she was always fixing broken lamps and appliances. She was small and wiry, but she could lift her weight in rolled roofing or boxes of nails. When she was 75, she was still repairing washing machines in my uncle's coin-operated laundry.

The old-time people paid no attention to birthdays. When a person was ready to do something, she did it. When she no longer was able, she stopped. Thus the traditional Pueblo people did not worry about aging or about looking old because there were no social boundaries drawn by the passage of years. It was not remarkable for young men to marry women as old as their mothers. I never heard anyone talk about "women's work" until after I left Laguna for college. Work was there to be done by any able-bodied person who wanted to do it. At the same time, in the old-time Pueblo world, identity was acknowledged to be always in a flux; in the old stories, one

minute Spider Woman is a little spider under a yucca plant, and the next instant she is a spritely grandmother walking down the road.

When I was growing up, there was a young man from a nearby village who wore nail polish and women's blouses and permed his hair. People paid little attention to his appearance; he was always part of a group of other young men from his village. No one ever made fun of him. Pueblo communities were, and still are, very interdependent, but they also have to be tolerant of individual eccentricities because survival of the group means everyone has to cooperate.

In the old Pueblo world, differences were celebrated as signs of the Mother Creators' grace. Persons born with exceptional physical or sexual differences were highly respected and honored because their physical differences gave them special positions as mediators between this world and the spirit world. The great Navajo medicine man of the 1920s, the Crawler, had a hunchback and could not walk upright, but he was able to heal even the most difficult cases. Before the arrival of Christian missionaries, a man could dress as a woman and work with the women and even marry a man without any fanfare. Likewise, a woman was free to dress like a man, to hunt and go to war with the men and to marry a woman. In the old Pueblo world view, we are all a mixture of male and female, and this sexual identity is changing constantly. Sexual inhibition did not begin until the Christian missionaries arrived. For the old-time people, marriage was about teamwork and social relationships, not about sexual excitement. In the days before the Puritans came, marriage did not mean an end to sex with people other than your spouse. Women were just at likely as men to have a "si'ash," or lover.

New life was so precious that pregnancy was always appropriate, and pregnancy before marriage was celebrated as a good sign. Since the children belonged to the mother and her clan, and women owned and bequeathed the houses and farmland, the exact determination of paternity wasn't critical. Although fertility was prized, infertility was no problem because mothers with unplanned preg-

nancies gave their babies to childless couples within the clan in open adoption arrangements. Children called their mother's sisters "mother" as well, and a child became attached to a number of parent figures.

In the sacred kiva ceremonies, men mask and dress as women to pay homage and to be possessed by the female energies of the spirit beings. Because differences in physical appearance were so highly valued, surgery to change one's face and body to resemble a model's face and body would be unimaginable. To be different, to be unique was blessed and was best of all.

The traditional clothing of Pueblo women emphasized a woman's sturdiness. Buckskin leggings wrapped around the legs protected her from scratches and injuries while she worked. The more layers of buckskin, the better. All those layers gave her legs the appearance of strength, like sturdy tree trunks. To demonstrate sisterhood and brotherhood with the plants and animals, the old-time people make masks and costumes that transform the human figures of the dancers into the animal beings they portray. Dancers paint their exposed skin; their postures and motions are adapted from their observations. But the motions are stylized. The observer sees not an actual eagle or actual deer dancing, but witnesses a human being, a dancer, gradually changing into a woman/buffalo or a man/deer. Every impulse is to reaffirm the urgent relationships that human beings have with the plant and animal world.

In the high desert plateau country, all vegetation, even weeds and thorns, becomes special, and all life is precious and beautiful because without the plants, the insects and the animals, human beings living here cannot survive. Perhaps human beings long ago noticed the devastating impact human activity can have on the plants and animals; maybe this is why tribal cultures devised the stories about humans and animals intermarrying, and the clans that bind humans to animals and plants through a whole complex of duties.

We children were always warned not to harm frogs or toads, the beloved children of the rain clouds, because terrible floods would occur. I remember in the summer the old folks used to stick big bolls of cotton on the outside of their screen doors as bait to keep the flies from going in the house when the door was opened. The old folks staunchly resisted the killing of flies because once, long, long ago, when human beings were in a great deal of trouble, green bottle fly carried the desperate messages of human beings to the Mother Creator in the Fourth World below this one. Human beings had outraged the Mother Creator by neglecting the Mother Corn altar while they dabbled with sorcery and magic. The Mother Creator disappeared, and with her disappeared the rain clouds, and the plants and the animals too. The people began to starve, and they had no way of reaching the Mother Creator down below. The green bottle fly took the message to the Mother Creator, and the people were saved. To show their gratitude, the old folks refused to kill any flies.

The old stories demonstrate the interrelationships that the Pueblo people have maintained with their plant and animal clanspeople. Kochininako, Yellow Woman, represents all women in the old stories. Her deeds span the spectrum of human behavior and are mostly heroic acts, though in at least one story, she chooses to join the secret Destroyer Clan, which worships destruction and death. Because Laguna Pueblo cosmology features a female creator, the status of women is equal with the status of men, and women appear as often as men in the old stories as hero figures. Yellow Woman is my favorite because she dares to cross traditional boundaries of ordinary behavior during times of crisis in order to save the Pueblo; her power lies in her courage and in her uninhibited sexuality, which the old-time Pueblo stories celebrate again and again because fertility was so highly valued.

The old stories always say that Yellow Woman was beautiful, but remember that the old-time people were not so much thinking about physical appearances. In each story, the beauty that Yellow Woman possesses is the beauty of her passion, her daring and her sheer strength to act when catastrophe is imminent.

In one story, the people are suffering during a great drought and accompanying famine. Each day, Kochininako has to walk farther and farther from the village to find fresh water for her husband and children. One day she travels far, far to the east, to the plains, and she finally locates a freshwater spring. But when she reaches the pool, the water is churning violently as if something large had just gotten out of the pool. Kochininako does not want to see what huge creature had been at the pool, but just as she fills her water jar and turns to hurry away, a strong, sexy man in buffalo skin leggings appears by the pool. Little drops of water glisten on his chest. She cannot help but look at him because he is so strong and so good to look at. Able to transform himself from human to buffalo in the wink of an eye, Buffalo Man gallops away with her on his back. Kochininako falls in love with Buffalo Man, and because of this liaison, the Buffalo People agree to give their bodies to the hunters to feed the starving Pueblo. Thus Kochininako's fearless sensuality results in the salvation of the people of her village, who are saved by the meat the Buffalo people "give" to them.

My father taught me and my sisters to shoot .22 rifles when we were 7; I went hunting with my father when I was 8, and I killed my first mule deer buck when I was 13. The Kochininako stories were always my favorite because Yellow Woman had so many adventures. In one story, as she hunts rabbits to feed her family, a giant monster pursues her, but she has the courage and presence of mind to outwit it.

In another story, Kochininako has a fling with Whirlwind Man and returns to her husband 10 months later with twin baby boys. The twin boys grow up to be great heroes of the people. Once again, Kochininako's vibrant sexuality benefits her people.

The stories about Kochininako made me aware that sometimes an individual must act despite disapproval, or concern for "appearances" or "what others may say." From Yellow Woman's adventures, I learned to be comfortable with my differences. I even imagined that Yellow Woman had yellow skin, brown hair and green eyes like mine, although her name does not refer to her color, but rather to the ritual color of the East.

There have been many other moments like the one with the camera-toting tourist in the schoolyard. But the old-time people always say, remember the stories, the stories will help you be strong. So all these years I have depended on Kochininako and the stories of her adventures.

Kochininako is beautiful because she has the courage to act in times of great peril, and her triumph is achieved by her sensuality, not through violence and destruction. For these qualities of the spirit, Yellow Woman and all women are beautiful.

Status, Property, and the Value on Virginity

Alice Schlegel

One way to assess a woman's autonomy is to ask whether she controls her own sexuality. Thus, the prohibition on premarital sex for females is often considered a measure of men's control over women's lives. There are certain difficulties with this assumption, however. First, the way a people feels about premarital sex is not necessarily consonant with its attitude toward extramarital sex, as many people allow premarital freedom but condemn adultery, while others, such as the South African Lovedu (Sacks 1979), insist on premarital virginity but turn a blind eye to discreet extramarital affairs.

Second, this assumption fails to recognize that in most societies, the value placed on virginity applies to adolescent girls, not to adult women. With few exceptions worldwide, girls are still physically adolescent when they marry, generally within three or four years after puberty. More important, young people are generally not social adults until they marry, so that the premarital female is socially an adolescent girl. Some societies, such as our own and that of 17th-century England (Stone 1977), for

example, are exceptions to this, having a stage that I call "youth" intervening between adolescence and full adulthood. However, in most parts of the world the bride is a teenage girl who in most aspects of her life is still very much under the authority of her parents.

If virginity is not, then, a very good measure of female subordination, we must look for other aspects of girls' and young women's lives that are associated with the proscription of premarital sex. One common notion is that virginity is valued when men have to "pay" for wives by transferring goods in the form of bridewealth to the women's families. This notion is based on the assumption that there is some innate preference for virgins which can be activated when men have the upper hand, so to speak, because they are paying for the bride. It must be noted, of course, that there is no universal preference for virgin brides. Such an assumption projects onto other cultures the attitudes that have developed historically in our own. Moreover, the belief that when men give bridewealth they pay for virgin brides is shaken when we read in Goody (1973:25)

that dowry-giving societies, in which the bride's family pays, are generally intolerant of premarital sex for girls. Here the family pays to give, not to receive, a virgin bride.

There is a connection between marriage transactions—the movement of goods or services at the time of a marriage—and the value on virginity, but it is not obvious what that connection is. In this paper, I argue that the virginity of daughters protects the interests of brides' families when they use marital alliances to maintain or enhance their social status. To illuminate this issue, it is necessary to understand the varying effects that marriage transactions have on the transmission or retention of property and on the social debts thus incurred.

MARRIAGE TRANSACTIONS

The form of marriage transaction that has received the most attention in the anthropological literature is *bridewealth*, goods given by the groom, usually with the assistance of his kin, to the family of the bride. Bridewealth generally does not remain with the family that receives it: it or its equivalent is used to obtain wives for brothers of the bride or an additional wife for her father. Thus, goods and women circulate and countercirculate. In the large majority of bridewealth-giving societies, which are patrilocal, households end up with as many women as they have produced, by replacing daughters with daughters-in-law and sisters with wives.

Women exchange is also a form of replacement, the exchange being direct rather than mediated by a transfer of property. Women exchange and bridewealth are most frequently found where women have economic value through their large contribution to subsistence (cf. Schlegel and Barry 1986). In each case the result is a kind of social homeostasis, both among the families through which women and goods circulate and within the household that sooner or later gains a woman to replace each one it has lost.

Brideservice is often considered to be analogous to bridewealth, with payment in labor rather than goods. They differ significantly, however, in that the benefit of brideservice goes directly to the bride's household and is not circulated as are bridewealth goods. Thus, families with many daughters receive much free labor, while families with few get little.

While *gift exchange,* in which relatively equal amounts are exchanged between the families of the bride and groom, can occur at all levels of social complexity, it is often found in societies with important status differences in rank or wealth; it occurs most often in Asia, native North America, and the Pacific. Since residence is predominantly patrilocal in gift-exchanging societies, the bride-receiving household is socially, although not economically, in debt to the bride-giving one. The exchange of equivalent goods is a way of ensuring that the intermarrying families are of the same social status, as indicated by the wealth that they own or can call up from among their kin and dependents.

Status is a major consideration in dowry-giving societies. The bride's dowry is sometimes matched against the groom's settlement, thus ensuring equivalence, a usual practice among European land-owning peasants or elites. Dowry can also be used to "buy" a high status son-in-law, a common practice in South Asia and one also known in Europe. Dowry or a bride's anticipated inheritance can be used to attract a poor but presentable groom, a client son-in-law whose allegiance will be primarily to the house into which he has married and on which he is dependent. This strategy seems to have been practiced by mercantile families in Europe and Latin America. Dowry was associated historically with the property-owning classes of the Old High Culture areas such as the Mediterranean (ancient Mesopotamia, Greece, and Rome) and Asia (India, China, and Japan), and was the common form throughout Europe until recently.

The final form of marriage transaction to be examined here is *indirect dowry,* which contains some features of both bridewealth, in that goods are given by the groom's family, and dowry, in that the goods end up with the new conjugal couple. Sometimes the groom's kin give goods directly to the bride, but more often they give goods to her father, who then gives goods to the new couple. The latter form has frequently been confused with bridewealth, as in the Islamic *mahr.* Indirect dowry tends to be found both on the fringes of and within the Old High Culture areas, such as Egypt, where it has been introduced along with conversion to Islam, replacing the simple dowry of earlier times. In its classic form, indirect dowry appears to be a way of establishing the properly rights of the conjugal couples that make up larger households, in anticipation of eventual fission. In addition, it allows for status negotiation without either family being put in the other's economic or social debt.

There are variations within these major types, and there are additional features (such as the European dower) that are secondary and limited in distribution. In complex societies, the form of transaction may vary according to region or class. In prerevolutionary China, for example, the landed or mercantile elite gave dowry while the landless peasantry gave indirect dowry. In modern China, marriage transactions have disappeared from urban areas, whereas bridewealth has replaced indirect dowry among peasants (Fang 1990).

WHY VALUE VIRGINITY?

Since the burden of controlling a girl's sexuality through socialization or surveillance falls upon her family, it is instructive to consider what benefits are to be derived from preserving the virginity of daughters and sisters. Goody (1976) sees restrictiveness as a way of avoiding inappropriate marriages: by controlling a girl's sexuality, her family can better control her marriage choice, for the loss of virginity may "diminish a girl's honour and reduce her marriage chances" (Goody 1976:14). However, this presupposes that preserving virginity has some inherent value, whereas that value is precisely what needs to be explained.

I argue that virginity is valued in those societies in which young men may seek to better their chances in life by allying themselves through marriage to a wealthy or powerful family. In preserving a daughter's virginity, a family is protecting her from seduction, impregnation, and paternity claims on her child. This is most critical when certain kinds of property transactions are involved. In societies in which dowry is given (or daughters inherit), it would be attractive to seduce a dowered daughter (or heiress), demanding her as wife along with her property. Her parents would be reluctant to refuse, since the well-being of their grandchildren would depend upon their inheritance from both of their parents, and another man would be unlikely to marry the mother if it meant that he had not only to support her children but also to make them his heirs. (The widow with children would be a different matter, since these children would have received property through their father and would make no claims on their stepfather beyond support, for which their labor would provide compensation.)

To illustrate that upward mobility through marriage with a dowered daughter or heiress is known in dowry-giving societies, let us consider a common theme of European fairy tales. A poor but honest young man goes through trials to win the hand of the princess, who inherits her father's kingdom. Or, he wins her heart, and through the good offices of a fairy godmother or other spirit helper, they evade her wrathful father and are eventually reconciled with him. This more or less legitimate means to upward mobility is not so different from the illegitimate one, by which he wins the girl through seduction.

This line of reasoning was familiar to the seventeenth- and eighteenth-century English, as Trumbach tells it:

> Stealing a son ... was not the great crime. It was, rather, the theft of a daughter that was the real nightmare. For a woman's property became her husband's and she took his social standing. ... To steal an heiress was therefore the quickest way to make a man's fortune—this was the common doctrine of the stage before 1710— and it had a special appeal to younger sons. (1978:101–102)

As the table shows, the value on virginity is statistically associated with the type of economic exchange linked to the marriage transaction.

All of the dowry-giving societies in the sample value virginity except the Haitians. Nevertheless, as Herskovits, writing about Haiti, points out: "Even though pre-marital relations are commonplace, ... the pregnancy of an unmarried girl is regarded as both reprehensible and unfortunate, and she is severely beaten for it by her family" (1971:111). Their fear of her seduction is well founded, for if they disapprove of a suitor and reject him, the young man "uses all persuasion to give her a child and, this achieved, abandons her to show his contempt for the family that has formally refused to accept him as a son-in-law" (Herskovits 1971:110). To avoid childbearing, women and girls resort to magical means of contraception and the more effective abortion.

The majority of societies that exchange gifts and give indirect dowry also expect brides to be virgins. This is particularly true in the case of gift exchange, in which a bride's family gives quantities of property along with her,

receiving a more or less equivalent amount from the family of the groom. As noted earlier, gift exchange is a way of ensuring that the two families are of equal wealth or of equal social power. Impregnating a girl would give a boy and his family a claim on that girl and an alliance with her family, even though they would have to come up with something themselves for the exchange (not necessarily equivalent to what a more appropriate suitor would give; see the case of the Omaha, discussed below). As in dowry-giving societies, an emphasis on virginity discourages a man who is tempted to jump the status barrier by claiming fatherhood of a woman's child. The sample does, however, include three exceptions to the general requirement of virginity in gift-exchanging societies, and it is instructive to examine these deviant cases.

Malinowski (1932) has discussed at some length the sexual freedom of girls in the Trobriand Islands in Melanesia. However, we must recall that the Trobriand Islanders do not, at least ideologically, associate sexual intercourse with pregnancy. Weiner (1976:122) relates two cases in which pregnancy was attributed to magic, and her informants maintained that women could conceive without male assistance. No boy, then, can make a claim on a girl simply because he has been sleeping with her and she has become pregnant. Fatherhood can only be attained after marriage, when it is socially defined.

Among the Omaha Indians of the Great Plains, virginity was not considered important for most girls (as coded in Broude and Greene [1980]), but according to Fletcher and LaFlesche (1911), virgins were held in greater esteem than those who had lost their virginity. It was a special privilege to marry a girl who had been tattooed with the "mark of honor," which was given to a virgin of a prominent family on the occasion of her father's or another close relative's initiation into one of the ceremonial societies. Only the marriages in prominent families involved significant gift exchange. In ordinary marriages, the young husband was expected to work a year or two for his father-in-law, making brideservice a more common feature

than gift exchange. Thus, it was in the important marriages, accompanied by the exchange of goods of much value, that the bride was expected to be a virgin. Omaha elite families faced the danger that a daughter might be seduced by a youth who would persuade her to elope. As long as his family recognized the marriage and brought some gifts to the bride's father, the marriage was legitimate in the eyes of the community. Maintaining the virginity of high-status girls protected their families from unwanted alliances.

In the Polynesian islands of Samoa, similarly, girls from untitled families had sexual freedom (as coded in Broude and Greene [1980]) but the daughters of titled chiefs did not. Samoa had an ambilineal descent system, in that children could be affiliated either to the mother's or the father's group. If the mother's rank was higher than the father's, the children's status would be elevated above their father's. High-status families would wish to guard their daughters against potential social climbers, who might be tempted to improve their children's position in life by seducing and marrying socially superior girls. It appears that only the arranged marriages, generally of high-status people, involved much gift exchange. Most marriages were of the "elopement" type and were much less expensive than the arranged ones (Shore 1981). Thus, as in the case of the Omaha, intracultural comparison demonstrates a correlation between the type of marriage transaction and the value on virginity.

It is clear that when no property accompanies the marriage, virginity is of little interest. If the groom gives goods or labor, the picture is mixed, but fewer societies are restrictive than permissive. In societies in which the bride's side gives considerable property, as with gift exchange, dowry, and, in many cases, indirect dowry, virginity is most likely to be valued. Thus, there is an association between the giving of property, particularly from the bride's side, and control of the girl's sexuality. I have interpreted this as a means by which the families of girls prevent their being seduced by ineligible boys, resulting in alliances that could be an embarrassment.

Correlations of value on virginity with type of marriage transaction[1]

Virginity valued	Marriage transaction					
	None	Bride-wealth[2]	Bride-service	Gift exchange	Dowry and Indirect dowry	Total
Yes	3	16	6	9	18	52
No	26	27	10	3	7	73

N = 125; Chi-square = 27. 13; p <.0001

[1]Information on attitudes toward premarital sex for females comes primarily from the code "Attitude Toward Premarital Sex (Female)" in Broude and Greene (1980), which is based on the Standard Sample of 186 preindustrial societies. I have altered the code established by Broude and Greene for four societies based on the ethnographic literature. The second source is a body of data collected by Herbert Barry and me on adolescent socialization in Standard Sample societies not coded by Broude and Greene.
[2]Includes token bridewealth.

This is particularly the case when status negotiation is a prominent feature of marital alliances, in those societies in which families use the marriages of their daughters to maintain or enhance their social position. Such considerations are likely to be found only in rank or class societies.

VIRGINITY AND FATHERHOOD

The question of the value on virginity revolves around two issues: whether premarital sexual intercourse leads to pregnancy, and whether biological fatherhood alone gives a man a claim on a child and its mother. There should be less concern over virginity when sexual intercourse is not likely to lead to pregnancy than when it is. Safe, socially condoned abortion is a reliable way of preventing unwanted births, and virginity is not such an issue if abortion is freely available, as it has been in Southeast Asia since at least the sixteenth century. Even there, however, the elite have secluded their daughters, possibly in imitation of the Hindu, Buddhist, or Moslem aristocrats whom they have emulated in other ways (cf. Reid 1988:163).

Although abortive techniques are widely known and practiced, even where proscribed (Devereux 1976), there is little evidence to indicate the extent to which illicit abortions are available to unmarried girls. Desperate girls, with the help of their mothers, surely must resort to them, as anecdotal information indicates; but whether or not they are successful, and whether or not the girls can keep them secret, are open to question. Illicit abortion is a last-ditch measure for preventing unwanted births and must take a distant second place to the maintenance of virginity.

Impregnating a girl does not automatically give a boy or man a claim to her child or to her. In the Trobriand Islands, as we have seen, biological fatherhood alone is simply not recognized. In other places, it may be recognized without giving the impregnator a paternity claim. Such a claim may have to be paid for either directly or indirectly through bridewealth and marriage to the mother; if it is not, the child is absorbed into the mother's kin group. This practice appears to be more common in Africa than in other regions, although the question requires a study in its own right. I suggest that the acceptance of illegitimate children is greater when children are a distinct economic asset.

They are likely to be so in underpopulated areas, such as are found throughout much of Africa (Kopytoff 1987). In such places, the availability of labor rather than of land is the major constraint on the economic success and expansion of the productive unit, the family and the kin group, and illegitimate origins do not detract from the potential labor value of a child. A similar explanation may hold for some European peasantries.

Where land is in short supply in preindustrial societies and family resources consist of private property, heirship is a central concern. A bastard is less likely to be welcomed, since it is totally dependent on the mother's family and does not draw in resources from the father. Bastards may be better received when the father is of much higher status than the mother—when he is, for example, a king or the noble impregnator of a peasant girl. In such cases, so long as paternity is acknowledged, the child provides a left-handed link to wealth and power, one that otherwise would be beyond the reach of the mother's family.

If children are not an unqualified asset to the mother's family, the rules of social life are likely to include the prescription that fathers take responsibility for their children, thus bringing biological and social fatherhood closer together. The responsibility for one's child can be restated as the right to that child, and biological fatherhood becomes a claim on social fatherhood. When the status of the mother is equal to or lower than that of the impregnator, it is to her advantage to use the rule of responsibility to press for marriage or at least support, so long as the impregnator is willing (or is unable to escape). Turning this on its head, when the mother is of greater wealth or higher status, particularly when her status or property will be inherited by her child, it is to the advantage of the impregnator to use the rule of responsibility to press *his* claim on the child and its mother. It is in precisely such situations, I propose, that virginity is valued, as it is the surest way of preventing such claims.

This is not to deny that virginity may acquire secondary meanings. In its extreme form, a value on virginity can lead to a value on chastity so great that widows are discouraged from remarriage. Such was the case in India for the higher castes (Ullrich 1977), throughout pre-revolutionary China (Chiao 1971), and in early Christian Europe (Verdon 1988). In such places celibacy comes to be seen as a spiritually higher state than married sexuality. In this form, the ideal of virginity has been incorporated into some religions and has been diffused along with conversion.

While the eighteenth-century English, living at a time of expanding wealth and social mobility, were aware of the social advantage of seducing an heiress and spoke freely about it, it is improbable that most peoples would give this as the reason for keeping their daughters virginal. In Eurasia, at any rate, one is much more likely to get explanations involving purity and the shame that follows its loss. We weave significance around the hard facts of existence, and virginity, a practical concern, can be a sign of spiritual purity when the invasion of the body implies the invasion of the spirit or when the seduction of female kin comes to symbolize the violability of the lineage.

The idealization of virginity is most common in Eurasia, and it is found in some other areas, such as Polynesia or native North America, where certain categories of girls are expected to be virginal. It is noteworthy that belief in the purity or spiritual power of virginity, chastity, and celibacy developed in those regions where dowry or gift-exchange was the established form or the form practiced by the elite and aspired to by those who would imitate them. Ideology does not arise *de novo* but is grounded in existential concerns and issues. I suggest that the ideology of virginity has its source in pragmatic concerns about status maintenance and improvement.

As a practical matter, ensuring that daughters and sisters remain virginal puts a heavy burden of surveillance on parents and brothers. The effort required is worthwhile when the stakes are high, as when considerable property and status are involved, or the secondary meanings of virginity are such that the purity of the girl and thus the honor of her family are at issue. In many parts of the Mediterranean world, control over female sexuality is a lived metaphor for control over social relations. The transgressing girl is defying her male kin and giving away what only they have the right to bestow (cf. Schneider 1971).

Elsewhere, particularly among poorer people in societies that value virginity, the daughter's choice of husband is of minor consequence. Thus, there is no point in restricting her. Even when virginity is generally accorded a high value, it may be an ideal to which only a minority aspire. Recognizing this makes it easier to reconcile the seeming contradiction between the high value placed on virginity and the high rate of bastardy at various times and places throughout European history.

IMPLICATIONS OF THE PROPOSITION

Regarding a value on virginity is a way of forestalling male social climbing through seduction causes us to take a fresh look at the interest, in some places, in seducing virgins and the self-congratulation or acclaim by peers that accompanies the successful boy or man in this pursuit. It has nothing to do with sexual pleasure, for the experienced girl or woman is a more satisfying sexual partner than the virgin. What, then, is the point?

First, of course, is the thrill of the forbidden. However, seducing a virgin can be as much of a coup in sexually permissive societies like Samoa as it is in the restrictive ones. In a discussion of adolescent sexuality in the Trobriand Islands, Weiner (1988:71) has pointed out that attracting lovers is not a frivolous pastime but rather "the first step toward entering the adult world of strategies, where the line between influencing others while not allowing others to gain control of oneself must be carefully learned." If the game of seduction is serious business, then how much more is this true when seduction can lead to status improvement. We can understand the Cinderella story and its variants as a tale of upward mobility for women through sexual attraction—but what about upwardly mobile men?

Winning the heart of a high-status woman as a path to a better life may be a male fantasy in all societies that are divided by rank or class, or at least those in which men will not be killed or severely punished for the attempt. Boys and youths have nothing to lose and much to gain if they can make a paternity claim on the child of a high-status girl. In such a setting, where only a few can succeed, all boys will be tempted to refine their skills with virgins of their own rank while hoping for their big chance with a *taupou* (the Samoan "village princess") or her equivalent.

It is well recognized that women use their sexual attractiveness to try to improve their position through a socially advantageous marriage or liaison, when such possibilities are open to them. (The seclusion of girls not only protects daughters against seduction but also protects sons against inconvenient romantic attachments, thus reinforcing parental control over the marriages of children of both sexes.) It should not surprise us that men and boys do the same if the opportunity arises. When sexual success can be translated into social success, it is predictable that men and boys will make themselves attractive to women and that sexual exploits will become a major topic of discussion, teasing, and boasting. In such cases, male competitiveness is channeled into overt sexual competition. The man who seduces a dowered virgin has his fortune made.

CONCLUSION

The trend in the modern world follows the pattern established for the preindustrial societies in the sample. With readily available contraception and abortion, extramarital sexual relations do not have to result in pregnancy or illegitimate birth. Even if a paternity claim is pressed, there is no obligation in our individual-centered society to honor it, as economic opportunities for women as well as welfare payments by the state make it possible to support a child without a husband.

Equally important, the dowry has lapsed in most European and European-derived cultures. Parental investment in daughters is increasingly in the form of education, not dowry. Furthermore, the daughter's choice of a husband does not have the significance for the family today that it did in earlier times. For most people in the industrial world, there is little in the way of a family estate to preserve. Even among the rich, a rebellious daughter and her husband can be cut out of the will, since in modern societies the disposal of assets is up to the individual with legal ownership of them. Thus, a daughter's choice of a husband is not critical to the well-being of the family and the maintenance of its assets.

Most commentators on the "sexual revolution" point to the availability of new contraception and abortion technology as the deciding factor in the changing of our sexual habits. But contraception and abortion have a long history in civilization; techniques to reduce fertility have been known and used in Europe and elsewhere for centuries, albeit clandestinely. Technology alone, without significant changes in social relations, is not enough to alter such deep-seated cultural values as the value on virginity. As marriage transactions disappear and social status is gained more through achievement than through the family into which one is born or marries, parental control over marriage declines and disappears. The choice of a son-in-law is no longer a central concern, and the virginity of daughters loses its salience.

Bundu Trap

I still remember the stories my sister told me about girls whose parents fooled them to get them into the hands of Mami Sowe.

Memuna M. Sillah

In West Africa, initiation of girls into a secret society of women centers on circumcision, and preparations may take months. Planning is handled exclusively by women within the family because it is considered inappropriate to discuss the subject with men. Several families may have their children initiated together to reduce costs and for solidarity and comfort. The girls usually leave home to stay in a hut, called a Bundu bush in Sierra Leone, with other girls their age for months—and sometimes years—while they receive instructions and training in wifely and motherly duties that have been prescribed by the community and handed down to generations of women before them.

The most important decision for a mother is the choice of a circumciser—called a sowe *in Sierra Leone—usually an old, experienced "professional" who has studied under a superior for years. The community sees her as endowed with special powers to perform the surgery. The instrument of the profession is a small penknife or a blade, considered a sacred object given by the gods especially for the circumcision.*

Although a girl may be given only a few weeks' or days' notice of the ceremony, she grows up knowing that she will someday be initiated into society. Envying the fuss made over older sisters and female cousins during their initiation period, she longs for the deferential treatment they receive on returning home:

Parental supervision then is lax, and new and permissive wardrobes—in essence, advertisements to potential husbands—are usually provided.

While a few girls have gone so far as to run away from home in protest of the operation, most abandon their initial resistance after being told of the elaborate gifts they will receive from relatives. Nonetheless, the weeks before the ceremony are charged with apprehension. The story that follows is based on my own childhood experiences in Sierra Leone and, to a lesser extent, on those of girls I knew.

For all my eight years, I've been conditioned to fear the Bundu[1] bush; by Mother, my aunties, my older sister, Fanta, and many more. I've heard horror stories of young girls being circumcised without their parents' consent because they unwittingly strayed into a Bundu bush. And simply hearing the name of a certain Mami Sowe after sunset keeps me awake half the night.

Almost every circumcised girl in Freetown has a story to tell about how she was lured into the Bundu bush. Most of the younger girls know that the bush is only a tent built with straw mats, not the thick, faraway bushes where Bundu activities used to take place. Still, few walk in voluntarily—except, of course, girls in the small villages, who look forward to circumcision with great expectation and joy.

Mother says they must get married as early as possible because that's all they have to look forward to.

Suddenly, Mother wants me to go to the bush. She has fixed food for Fanta and my three cousins who were circumcised four weeks ago and wants me to take it over. Now she's changing the entire story.

"Nobody will touch you. They don't want little girls like you."

"But they've caught little girls before. Remember the story you told me about the girl who was there three weeks before her parents knew where she was?"

"OK," she says, smiling. "You don't have to go inside. You can stand outside and call out Granny's name. She'll send to get you."

"What if someone pushes me inside?"

"Nobody will do that when you're carrying a tray of food on your head. Go wash your feet and get dressed before the food gets cold."

"Maybe this is just a plot to get me to Mami Sowe like they did to Fanta." My mother shrugs me off and leaves the kitchen. I want to see how my sister and cousins look in the Bundu wraps my mother bought them and in the necklaces of cloves and spices they'll be wearing as jewelry. But I still remember the stories Fanta's been telling me about

1. Circumcision; secret society of circumcised women.

girls whose parents fool them to get them into the hands of Mami Sowe. Like the one about one girl who was asked to deliver some expensive gold jewelry into her auntie's hands. The girl waited at the appointed place for about thirty minutes before her auntie appeared with two other women. Fanta said that had this girl frequented Bundu bushes before, she would have recognized the women as Mami Sowe's assistants. Minutes later one of the women forced a large piece of cloth into the girl's mouth. By the time the girl was able to breathe through her mouth again, she was bleeding profusely. Fanta never told me where the bleeding came from, although my brother Amadu said they broke the girl's teeth when they forced the cloth into her mouth.

My mother returns to the kitchen, holding a tray and kitchen towel. She busies herself packing two large bowls into the tray. I help her wipe excess oil off the covers and try some last-ditch delaying tactics.

"I don't know where the bush is or how to get there," I say.

My mother smiles softly. "They're expecting you. Now, change your clothes before the food gets cold."

"Why shouldn't Amadu take the food? He's the older one."

"Go get dressed before I get angry." She is shouting now as she goes down the kitchen steps. I follow her into the house. She pushes me into her bedroom and points to a dress lying on the bed. "Put that on before you come out." She gives the orders as she pulls a red-and-white checkered towel from the basket on the floor. I am getting nervous, but I don't want her to notice. I figure if it is decided I should be circumcised this summer, Mother will figure out a way to get me out of the house, will or woe. But I am not going to make it easy for her.

I feign a struggle, pulling the dress down over my face. She ignores me. I try conversation.

"How have they been, Fanta and Mbalia and Yanati and Seray? How have they been since they've been at the bush?"

"They look very nice in the cotton material I bought them, and they've all put on weight."

"What do they eat there?" I ask with great interest.

"Every kind of food you can think of. Last Friday, Mbalia asked for *sattie*,[2] and Auntie Mbalia prepared it for them in the morning. Then Auntie Seray prepared couscous and salads for Yanati in the afternoon, and Auntie Fanta roasted a whole duck for dinner. It's been like that every day."

This is my favorite part of the entire Bundu process—the eating and drinking to the heart's content. The thought actually calms me down a little as I begin to imagine cassava leaves, potato leaves, *obiata*,[3] jollof rice,[4] plantains, okra, and *foofo*,[5] all lined up in front of my diet-conscious sister and cousins.

"What did you cook?" I ask, following my mother back to the kitchen.

She replies, "Yanati said she wanted to eat some fried fish with plantains before the ceremony tonight. So that's . . ."

"What ceremony?" I ask jumpily, wondering if it has anything to do with me.

"We're going to do a small ceremony tonight, so the girls will be able to come outside and walk around the yard. Maybe in a few weeks they can go out into the streets."

"I'll just leave the tray at Granny's house, and somebody else will take it to the bush."

As the women work, they sing. They move their heads and wave the knives in their hands to the rhythm of the song.

"You have nothing to worry about. Granny is there. She won't let them touch you," Mother says as she spreads the towel over the food and places the tray on my head.

I grab the sides of the heavy tray with both hands and bite my lower lip as I make my way out toward the gate.

"Keep both hands on the tray," Mother shouts as I leave the confines of her gate.

Before I reach the empty lot next to Granny's house, I hear the sound of women singing and clapping. The women sit in clusters of five to seven—one group is peeling onions, another is skinning fowls, another pounding flour

in large mortars, another cutting meat. As the women work, they sing, moving their heads or waving the knives in their hands to the rhythm of the song. I try to weave my way through the enormous pots and bowls, the white powder from the mortars, the obese legs sprawled between one bowl and another. Auntie Ole, Haja[6] Khadi, Auntie Memuna, Haja Fatmata, Miss Conteh, Haja Alari. I call out those names I remember and smile broadly to the others.

It doesn't seem as bad as I had imagined. I feel as though I could leave the food with one of these aunties or hajas and return home safely, but I move on, even quickening my now light steps until suddenly I see it. Spiked stalks of dried bamboo leaves protrude from the roof of a dark hut standing ahead of me on the farthest end of the yard. Its fragile walls of straw mats are square in shape, and from where I am standing, I can see no doors. Just as I begin to imagine being locked up inside with Mami Sowe, with no way of escape, I see a woman sitting by what finally is beginning to look like a doorway to the bush. She is cutting cloth—the same cloth my mother said she bought for Fanta and the others. I remember mother saying they looked good in it, so why is it only being cut now? I don't have time to answer my own question. The woman's voice cuts its way through my thoughts like a butcher's knife on brisket.

"Send her over here."

My blood stops cold, my legs weaken under me, and my head begins to spin. Voices murmur around me. Ear-piercing clanks cause my head to feel as though every piece of flesh is suddenly scalpeled from the inside. A wet piece of cloth passes through my mouth. I feel the soaked sponge of red fluid on my face and neck—and then a soft voice.

"Your mother is not going to be pleased."

Other voices intervene. "You were not paying attention. What happened to you?"

---

2. Rice porridge.
3. Sisal leaves cooked in West African sauce.
4. Senegal-style red rice.
5. Cooked cassava dough.
6. Title of honor for a woman who has been on a pilgrimage to Mecca.

"Leave her alone, she was just afraid, coming to a Bundu bush."

"You mean she is still not . . . ?"

"Oh yes, don't you know her? She's Siminie, Mariatu's daughter."

"Take her in to Granny Yamakoro. She's inside."

"Wait, let her rest a little out here first."

"No, let her go inside and rest."

"Let her take the empty bowls with her."

"No, let her go for now."

"Where's the food?" I gasp when I manage to remove the palm-oil-soaked towel from my face. Just as I am asking the question, I see Mother's bowls, bottoms up on the floor, mud-red pieces of fish and plantain on the ground.

Inside the Bundu bush is the smell of burned, perfumed palm oil and the sound of the women's Mandingo songs.

The voices continue: "Let her go wash her face."

"Someone give her some soap."

"No, just water will do."

The setting inside the Bundu bush is similar to the one outside, except for the strong smell of burned, perfumed palm oil and the vivacious claps accompanying the Mandingo[7] songs. About a dozen more aunties sit on the mud floor, which is covered with straw mats similar to those used to panel the windowless bush. Granny is sitting on her special wide bench, the only seat that can contain all of her behind. As soon as she sees me, she motions for me to enter. Still mute from the food accident, I enter like one drugged. Granny places my skinny body between her thick legs. The warmth relaxes me a little, and my eyes begin to search for Fanta and my cousins.

They're all sitting on the floor, with straightened backs and stretched-out legs, like Barbie dolls. The tallest of the four, Fanta, sits at the far end of the room. Mbalia is sitting next to her, then Seray; Yanati, the shortest, is at the other extreme end. They're all topless to their waists, which are wrapped in the black-and-blue cotton cloth Mother had bought. Their heads are tied with the same cloth. Between the head-tie and the waist wrap, their bare breasts—full and firm, garnished with palm oil and dried, beaded cloves—jump up and down as the girls clap their hands. The girls' breasts carry the same vigorous rhythm of the dancing heads of the women sitting opposite them. While the aunties seem to be enjoying the songs, the girls look as though they would be happy to leave any time.

I notice my cousins have all put on weight. Fanta's face looks sour, the way it does when she's eating tamarinds. I'm dying to ask her why, in all her seventeen years, she did not suspect anything when Auntie Iye came to take her shopping. But I dare not leave the security of Granny's legs.

Standing in front of the Bundu girls is a short, fleshy woman with extremely tiny eyes and sharp, almost loony eye-blinks, leading the song with a long, thin stick that she waves over their heads. She is dressed in ordinary, even dirty-looking, clothes, but something about her holds me hostage. Maybe it is her baritone voice, which supports the song when the other women forget a line, or the looks she throws out when the girls mispronounce an old Mandingo word. Or, maybe it is her grandly gesticulating manner and the flabby piece of extra flesh waving under her arm, or the way she uses the stick to control the song and at the same time separate Fanta's tightly set legs or straighten Yanati's slouch. As soon as the song ends, the woman with the stick starts another, pausing slightly to look over to where Granny is sitting. When Granny smiles and nods her head, the woman continues with added confidence, then gives the silent girls on the mat a strong look. Seray slouches and lowers her head on her chest. The woman gives her three quick taps on the shoulder, and her back straightens again. Fanta frowns, and Auntie Mbalia admonishes her with a tight wink. Yanati and Mbalia mouth the words, anxiety crowding their faces. Sensing the impending judgment, the mothers and aunties quickly double their enthusiasm and, adding to Granny's frail voice, carry off the song. The girls begin to clap again, their breasts following en-ergetically. I can actually feel the relief I see on their faces. Yanata and Mbalia smile at each other.

I find myself thinking that I will get Granny to teach me all the Bundu songs before my time comes, because I wouldn't want to offend this peculiar woman. I'm thinking I'll ask Fanta to teach me all she has learned when she returns home. That way. . . . "Come this way with me, Siminie."

A large hand grabs mine, axing my thoughts at the same time. I turn around to see the face of one of three women in the bush I do not recognize. Something about her face cuts a vein in my heart. I try to climb onto Granny's chest, clutching at her.

"Don't let her take me away, Granny."

Granny peels my fingers off her clothes.

"You're going to choke me."

My aunties and cousins, meanwhile, are rolling over one another with laughter. Only Fanta looks worried. The woman with the stick allows a smile to escape.

"What are you afraid of?" she asks aggressively, feigning a confrontation.

"She's lucky we've waited this long. At her age, I had already forgotten what Bundu was like," Auntie Mbalia says.

"Don't listen to them," Granny says, putting her arms around me. "I am your father's mother. While I'm alive, I'm the only person who can give consent for you to be brought into this Bundu society."

"Oh, but I'm your father's sister. I can do it too," Auntie Mbalia insists.

"No, you cannot. Granny is older than you. She won't let you," I scream from the safety of Granny's lap. Everybody laughs again.

I notice that the girls on the mat are beginning to lose their straight backs and Barbie legs. Fanta is resting on the palms of both hands behind her back, Yanati is slouching, Seray has one hand on Yanati's shoulder; only Mbalia maintains a straight back. Even the woman with the thin rod now seems more interested in me than in her pupils.

---

7. A minority tribe of Sierra Leone.

"The little girl understands things well," she says, nodding to Auntie Mbalia.

"Oh, but if her granny is not around, I will be the one in charge. I hope she knows that."

Then turning to me, Auntie Mbalia adds, "Just pray for your granny to be alive until you finish school."

Granny puts her arms around me. I know that I have been saved so far only because she, like my mother, believes in education.

Even though Auntie Mbalia loves to tease me, I know she is serious about having me circumcised as soon as possible. Her own three daughters were all circumcised only a few days after birth. Auntie Mbalia believes in doing things "the way our people did." I know I have been saved so far only because Granny, like my mother, believes in education. Granny single-handedly put her two sons through school after her husband died, when my father, the elder, was only six years old. She has not regretted the sacrifice; her children provide adequately for her today.

"I'm not dying yet. I won't die until I've seen all my granddaughters circumcised," Granny says defensively.

"Amin,[8] Amin, Amin," the women chorus, including Auntie Mbalia. The woman with the stick sets herself down on the floor.

"That's the dream of every grandmother. Allah will answer your prayers." She is almost whispering now, her face changing into the same serious mold it had when she scrutinized her pupils. She settles the rod on the ground beside her, pulls her clothes together and tucks them between her legs. "That was my grandmother's biggest dream," she begins. "She was a *sowe* herself in my village, and she taught me everything I know today. I used to go with her to the bushes to pick the leaves she used. We would wake up early in the morning, be-

fore even the fowls began to crow, to set off for the bushes. Even though I was only about six or seven years old, she only had to say my name once, and I was jumping out of the mat. I used to sleep on the ground beside her. There would be nobody on the paths from the moment we left the hut until we returned from the depth of the bushes. My grandmother liked it that way—she tried to avoid bad spirits who might spoil the power of the leaves. She knew the strength of every leaf in the bush, the old woman. All her life as a *sowe*, almost forty years, she never once lost a child in operation. Not a single one."

The women punctuate the story with impressive *Alhamdudilais*.[9]

"And remember, with us Temne[10] people, we put our children through society at a very early age, sometimes as young as five years, for both girls and boys. You know the sooner we were prepared for marriage, the better it was for our parents. . . ."

"But in Freetown, most Temne girls who go to school don't go through society until after they finish school," Fanta argues. I had almost forgotten what Fanta's voice sounded like. It is the first time I've heard any of the girls speak since I entered the bush.

I don't know how the thin stick got from the floor to the air. I just see it there, flying about.

"Did I ask any of my girls a question?" The woman with the stick is talking to the bamboo ceiling. She turns to the other women and asks, "People, did I give Fanta permission to talk? Is Fanta allowed to talk when society women are talking? Fanta who is still not healed, Fanta who still has more than half the trials of society to pass through—can she talk when the rest of us are talking? Women, please tell me."

I notice Auntie Fanta vehemently loosening a small knot at the edge of her clothes. Hiding behind her namesake, she unfolds a small stack of bills and retrieves two notes, which she folds up into an even smaller stack. She ties her wrap again and stands up.

"Mami Sowe, you did not throw any words at Fanta, and Fanta should not have the mind to talk before she's asked to do so. But she's only been here three

weeks. Let us please forgive her. In time, she'll learn the ways of a woman. That's the reason. . . ." I do not hear the rest of Auntie Fanta's words. The name Mami Sowe has just taken effect on me.

"Is she Mami Sowe?" I ask in Granny's ears.

Granny does not answer.

Auntie Fanta tries to press the folded notes into the woman's hand.

"Let this pay the fine."

"But did I ask for a fine yet? You Fantas are all alike. You think I'm cheap? Don't you know that if there's a fine, I should tell you what the fine should be? This is the problem with Bundu in towns. There is no respect for the *sowe*. Get away from me." She pushes Auntie Fanta with her elbow.

The women are laughing, and I suddenly find them all very strange. I am actually standing in Mami Sowe's presence, and I did not know it, just as Fanta did not suspect the shopping expedition with Auntie Iye would end up in the Bundu bush. Me, finally in the hands of Mami Sowe. Even as the women laugh, they're nodding their heads in agreement with Mami Sowe. They all agree with everything she says.

Auntie Fanta stands up and playfully pulls at the extra flesh under Mami Sowe's armpit.

"What do you expect? We're in Freetown; this is British Bundu."

Mami Sowe points a hand at Auntie Fanta. "Then maybe you should have taken your children to the British so they can circumcise them."

"Oh, they can do that in hospitals nowadays, you know, and you don't even have to go through all the expenses. You do it quietly there, everything is faster, and you bring them home sooner."

This is the first time I'm hearing this. There's Bundu in the hospitals too? First there was injection, now there's circumcision. I must remember that next time mother asks me to accompany her to visit some relative at the hospital. But I'm not the only person who is shocked.

---

8. "Amen."
9. "Thanks be to God."
10. A majority tribe in Sierra Leone.

Mami Sowe's mouth is agape. She recovers soon enough and takes on Auntie Fanta.

"Can the hospitals perform the different ceremonies? Can they teach your daughters to fetch water from a well, to cook, to know when to talk, to know how to address elders? Can the hospitals prepare them for marriage? Can the hospitals find them husbands? Only a fool like you will put your daughters through all that pain without teaching them anything. Just move out of my way."

Everybody laughs again. One of the laughs from the mat is so loud that it startles Mami Sowe. She turns around and addresses the girls in a commanding tone. "Who laughed like that?" The girls on the mat look at one another and maintain a cold silence. "I want to know the person who laughed so loud just now. I want her to sell me some raw fish."[11]

The silence is beginning to freeze.

"If you all think you will leave my bush without good manners, then my name is not Mami Sowe."

Mami Sowe's countenance has taken an even sterner look than the one it had when I first walked into the bush. She now looks like what I'd always imagined her to be—a heartless, merciless inflicter of pain on little girls. She pans the faces of her pupils from one end of the room to another. Auntie Mbalia cuts through the silence.

"You have to learn to adjust your behavior in this bush. Whatever loose ways you have acquired during your lifetime, this is the place where you offload them and leave them on these mats."

Auntie Seray adjusts her head-tie to deliver her portion of the speech: "You must listen to instructions and learn to comport yourselves well in this bush. This is the beginning of your adult life, your life as a woman, a respectable woman in society. The skills you learn here will be with you for the rest of your lives. If you cannot own up to your responsibilities here, where else will you be able to do that?"

Mami Sowe is now looking so pleased, I almost think the speeches were meant to please her and were not for the girls.

Auntie Seray moves closely to her namesake and, rubbing her legs, whispers a few words into her ear.

Seray adjusts herself on the mat.

"OK, I was the one who laughed," she says. Then, as if angered by her own confession, she tosses her chin up and adds, "What's wrong with laughing, anyway?"

Seray barely finishes her sentence before her mother in some magical way gets the stick from Granny's hands and starts hitting Seray incessantly on the head.

"What's wrong with this child? She should have been circumcised long before this."

I wriggle my small body between Granny's legs to hide my presence, lest they decide to have me circumcised before I become like Seray.

I know one day I will be circumcised. But I also know that when the time comes, I will not surrender without a fight.

Granny is crying and swaying her behind from side to side, unable to get up from her bench, and wanting everyone to see her distress. "All these witches walking around this bush ever since these children were brought here, trying to destroy my grandchildren, trying to distract them from the lessons they should be learning." Then wiping her tears, she says decisively, "Tomorrow, first thing in the morning, I am sending for Pa Morlia[12] to drive out the bad spirits. I will put an end to this, or my name is not Yamakoro."

The attention of everyone now turns to calming down Granny. They remind her of her high blood pressure, ask her to look to God, assure her that Seray will change, show her examples of wild girls who changed and ended up getting good husbands. Mami Sowe is rubbing Granny's back; a soft look now blankets her face.

The conciliatory mood in the room is interrupted by the entrance of one of the women who were cutting meat outside. She walks over and kneels down beside Mami Sowe, then whispers something in her ears. Mami Sowe in turn whispers into Granny's ear, and

Granny straightens up, then makes a hand movement I do not understand to Auntie Mbalia. The latter looks at me, then at Auntie Fanta, then back at me.

"Granny, can I go to the bathroom?" I ask quietly.

"Not yet," she answers, then points to the meat-cutting woman. "Go with Auntie Zainab. She will take you home," she says, and she continues whispering with Mami Sowe.

Confused, I try to remember how I arrived here. I had told mother I didn't know how to get to the Bundu bush, but that was only an excuse not to come. In fact, I had located the bush the very first week my sister and cousins started their confinement here, and I'd increased considerably my reasons for passing by Granny's house during every errand I ran. While I usually give all Bundu bushes a wide berth, it has been difficult to distance myself from this one holding Fanta and my cousins within. Sometimes, while standing in front of it, I was petrified and mesmerized at the same time. All the women in my family are Bundu women. I know that one day, with or without my consent, I will be circumcised. But I also know that when the time comes, I will not give in without a fight.

My mother is sitting on the kitchen steps, her face in her hands. As soon as she sees me, she stands up.

"If you didn't want to take the food for me, you should have said so."

I do not believe my mother is talking like that. I cannot contest her now so I just let her talk while I catch my breath.

"All that food I spent the whole day preparing; for you to go and throw it all away like that, in the blink of an eye."

"I was afraid," I manage to add through breaths. "I thought. . . ."

"I don't want to know what you thought. I warned you to keep your hands on the tray. I don't know why you think you can keep a tray on your head without your hands on it."

"I was holding it. I held it all the way to Granny's house."

"And what were you standing in the bush for? What business did you have

---

11. "She sounds like a fishwife."
12. A shaman who will cast out "bad spirits."

there when they wanted to start the ceremonies?"

"Granny wanted a strange woman to take me away," I reply.

"You were standing there like a dead body. She was going to bring you home."

"I know my way home," I answer defensively.

"You know your way home, and you couldn't keep a tray of food on your head."

"I told you I was afraid they were going to catch me."

The way Mother is looking at me, I know that if a garbage truck for children came along at this moment, she would happily throw me in.

"They should have just circumcised you then so you could stay there. Maybe they'll find you a husband after that. You're no use to me."

I know my mother is just upset, so I don't say anything. I go inside the house and change my clothes, happy I came back—at least for now.

Born in Sierra Leone, Memuna M. Sillah grew up "in the midst of quiet, yet constant, revolts, especially by teenage girls, against the unnecessary pain caused by genital mutilation." Sillah came to the United States eight years ago, after living in London, Paris, and Kingston, Jamaica. Now a graduate student in sociology at City College of the City University of New York (CUNY), she has been actively concerned with the problem of female genital mutilation since 1993, when she chose the topic for a term paper in Asha Samad's course on violations of women's rights. "I then learned," Sillah writes, "how widespread the practice is in Africa and other parts of the world— and the drastic forms it can take. This knowledge awakened my old teenage passions against the practice." Sillah is now at work on a novel about immigrant African women in the United States.

Afterword

Asha Samad

Worldwide, some 80 to 100 million women have undergone an operation first recorded in Egypt more than 4,000 years ago. Since then, "female circumcision" in various forms has been customary in many African and in some Asian, Middle Eastern, and indigenous Central and South American cultures. Very different from male circumcision (the removal of the foreskin of the penis), female circumcision can involve the partial or total removal of the clitoris and/or "infibulation," surgical modification and suturing together of the labia. In some areas (Chad, Somalia, Sudan), "decircumcisions" are necessary to open infibulations before marriage and childbirth. While many associate female circumcision with Muslim tradition, it predates Judaism, Christianity, and Islam. It has also been practiced by Jewish communities and Christians living in regions where circumcision is customary.

Condemned by African women's groups and the World Health Organization as abusive and often dangerous, female circumcision persists even where modern African governments seek to limit or prohibit it. While most women survive these mutilating operations, they may suffer immediate and lasting physical effects. Hemorrhaging, infection, and infertility are among the serious complications. The inability to pass urine normally, pain during sexual intercourse, and excessively difficult deliveries are common results. Although harder to measure, emotional and psychological effects may also ensue.

All groups circumcising females also circumcise males. Such groups regard the rite as an essential part of a child's socialization. The operation is done at different ages in different societies—ranging from a few days after birth until puberty. However, among some ethnic groups it is done just prior to marriage, or, as in Rivers state, Nigeria, in the seventh month of the woman's first pregnancy. The rite can symbolize the stability of the group as expressed in the faithfulness of its females— the passers-on of its customs and the maintainers of its families. The custom also reinforces respect and authority. The day of circumcision thus involves not only pain but also recognition for having become a full adult and a marriageable member of society.

Other obvious functions of female circumcision include control of female sexuality and marital chastity. In patrilineal societies, authority over the bride is transferred at marriage to the spouse's patriline. The bride's moral and economic value to her patriline and to her spouse is dependent upon her unquestioned virginity as demonstrated by the intact infibulation.

Many groups feel that attempts to prevent them from practicing circumcision represent an attack on their cultural integrity by "colonial," Western interests and westernized African governments. (The Masai, for instance, are loath to change customs at the behest of a government that has moved them out of their traditional lands.) They may fear that loss of a cohesive tradition, with nothing to replace it, will result in daughters who are as "loose" as uncircumcised African and Western women are perceived to be. More generally, they believe that an uncircumcised daughter may become centered on herself, rather than family, home, and group.

Some westernized Africans now debate the value of female circumcision. But fear that uncircumcised daughters will not be acceptable as brides in their communities spurs many to perpetuate the custom. Some parents may seek modified forms of the operation for their daughters and may have the procedure performed in private clinics or at home under anesthesia and in antiseptic conditions.

Some—usually Western-educated African women, often of independent means, or those living in the immigrant and refugee communities of Europe and North America—have fully rejected the procedure and are educating women about its deleterious effects and organizing to end the custom. At the same time, other women protest what they consider outside interference in the most intimate aspects of their culture. They ask why Western women—whose own culture often leads them to radically alter their appearance, even through surgery—are so intolerant of the practices of others.

What African women on both sides of the issue resent most is being looked upon by the rest of the world as self-mutilating primitives. Even opponents of circumcision feel that women from the ethnic groups practicing this ancient custom should be the ones leading the fight to eradicate it.

The Initiation of a Maasai Warrior

Tepilit Ole Saitoti

"Tepilit, circumcision means a sharp knife cutting into the skin of the most sensitive part of your body. You must not budge; don't move a muscle or even blink. You can face only one direction until the operation is completed. The slightest movement on your part will mean you are a coward, incompetent and unworthy to be a Maasai man. Ours has always been a proud family, and we would like to keep it that way. We will not tolerate unnecessary embarrassment, so you had better be ready. If you are not, tell us now so that we will not proceed. Imagine yourself alone remaining uncircumcised like the water youth [white people]. I hear they are not circumcised. Such a thing is not known in Maasailand; therefore, circumcision will have to take place even if it means holding you down until it is completed."

My father continued to speak and every one of us kept quiet. "The pain you will feel is symbolic. There is a deeper meaning in all this. Circumcision means a break between childhood and adulthood. For the first time in your life, you are regarded as a grown-up, a complete man or woman. You will be expected to give and not just to receive. To protect the family always, not just to be protected yourself. And your wise judgment will for the first time be taken into consideration. No family affairs will be discussed without your being consulted. If you are ready for all these

responsibilities, tell us now. Coming into manhood is not simply a matter of growth and maturity. It is a heavy load on your shoulders and especially a burden on the mind. Too much of this—I am done. I have said all I wanted to say. Fellows, if you have anything to add, go ahead and tell your brother, because I am through. I have spoken."

After a prolonged silence, one of my half-brothers said awkwardly, "Face it, man . . . it's painful. I won't lie about it, but it is not the end. We all went through it, after all. Only blood will flow, not milk." There was laughter and my father left.

My brother Lellia said, "Men, there are many things we must acquire and preparations we must make before the ceremony, and we will need the cooperation and help of all of you. Ostrich feathers for the crown and wax for the arrows must be collected."

"Are you *orkirekenyi?*" one of my brothers asked. I quickly replied no, and there was laughter. *Orkirekenyi* is a person who has transgressed sexually. For you must not have sexual intercourse with any circumcised woman before you yourself are circumcised. You must wait until you are circumcised. If you have not waited, you will be fined. Your father, mother, and the circumciser will take a cow from you as punishment.

Just before we departed, one of my closest friends said, "If you kick the

knife, you will be in trouble." There was laughter. "By the way, if you have decided to kick the circumciser, do it well. Silence him once and for all." "Do it the way you kick a football in school." "That will fix him," another added, and we all laughed our heads off again as we departed.

The following month was a month of preparation. I and others collected wax, ostrich feathers, honey to be made into honey beer for the elders to drink on the day of circumcision, and all the other required articles.

Three days before the ceremony my head was shaved and I discarded all my belongings, such as my necklaces, garments, spear, and sword. I even had to shave my pubic hair. Circumcision in many ways is similar to Christian baptism. You must put all the sins you have committed during childhood behind and embark as a new person with a different outlook on a new life.

The circumciser came the following day and handed the ritual knives to me. He left drinking a calabash of beer. I stared at the knives uneasily. It was hard to accept that he was going to use them on my organ. I was to sharpen them and protect them from people of ill will who might try to blunt them, thus rendering them inefficient during the ritual and thereby bringing shame on our family. The knives threw a chill down my spine; I was not sure I was sharpening them properly, so I took them to my closest brother for him to check out, and he assured me that the knives were all right. I hid them well and waited.

Tension started building between me and my relatives, most of whom worried that I wouldn't make it through the ceremony valiantly. Some even snarled at me, which was their way of encouraging me. Others threw insults and abusive words my way. My sister Loiyan in particular was more troubled by the whole affair than anyone in the whole family. She had to assume my mother's role during the circumcision. Were I to fail my initiation, she would have to face the consequences. She would be spat upon and even beaten for representing the mother of an unworthy son. The same fate would befall my father, but he seemed unconcerned. He had this weird belief that because I was not particularly handsome, I must be brave. He kept saying, "God is not so bad as to have made him ugly and a coward at the same time."

Failure to be brave during circumcision would have other unfortunate consequences: the herd of cattle belonging to the family still in the compound would be beaten until they stampeded; the slaughtered oxen and honey beer prepared during the month before the ritual would go to waste; the initiate's food would be spat upon and he would have to eat it or else get a severe beating. Everyone would call him Olkasiodoi, the knife kicker.

Kicking the knife of the circumciser would not help you anyway. If you struggle and try to get away during the ritual, you will be held down until the operation is completed. Such failure of nerve would haunt you in the future. For example, no one will choose a person who kicked the knife for a position of leadership. However, there have been instances in which a person who failed to go through circumcision successfully became very brave afterwards because he was filled with anger over the incident; no one dares to scold him or remind him of it. His agemates, particularly the warriors, will act as if nothing had happened.

During the circumcision of a woman, on the other hand, she is allowed to cry as long as she does not hinder the operation. It is common to see a woman crying and kicking during circumcision. Warriors are usually summoned to help hold her down.

For women, circumcision means an end to the company of Maasai warriors. After they recuperate, they soon get married, and often to men twice their age.

The closer it came to the hour of truth, the more I was hated, particularly by those closest to me. I was deeply troubled by the withdrawal of all the support I needed. My annoyance turned into anger and resolve. I decided not to budge or blink, even if I were to see my intestines flowing before me. My resolve was hardened when newly circumcised warriors came to sing for me. Their songs were utterly insulting, intended to annoy me further. They tucked their wax arrows under my crotch and rubbed them on my nose. They repeatedly called me names.

By the end of the singing, I was fuming. Crying would have meant I was a coward. After midnight they left me alone and I went into the house and tried to sleep but could not. I was exhausted and numb but remained awake all night.

At dawn I was summoned once again by the newly circumcised warriors. They piled more and more insults on me. They sang their weird songs with even more vigor and excitement than before. The songs praised warriorhood and encouraged one to achieve it at all costs. The songs continued until the sun shone on the cattle horns clearly. I was summoned to the main cattle gate, in my hand a ritual cowhide from a cow that had been properly slaughtered during my naming ceremony. I went past Loiyan, who was milking a cow, and she muttered something. She was shaking all over. There was so much tension that people could hardly breathe.

I laid the hide down and a boy was ordered to pour ice-cold water, known as engare entolu (ax water), over my head. It dripped all over my naked body and I shook furiously. In a matter of seconds I was summoned to sit down. A large crowd of boys and men formed a semicircle in front of me; women are not allowed to watch male circumcision and vice-versa. That was the last thing I saw clearly. As soon as I sat down, the circumciser appeared, his knives at the ready. He spread my legs and said, "One cut," a pronouncement necessary to prevent an initiate from claiming that he had been taken by surprise. He splashed a white liquid, a ceremonial paint called enturoto, across my face. Almost immediately I felt a spark of pain under my belly as the knife cut through my penis' foreskin. I happened to choose to look in the direction of the operation. I continued to observe the circumciser's fingers working mechanically. The pain became numbness and my lower body felt heavy, as if I were weighed down by a heavy burden. After fifteen minutes or so, a man who had been supporting from behind pointed at something, as if to assist the circumciser. I came to learn later that the circumciser's eyesight had been failing him and that my brothers had been mad at him because the operation had taken longer than was usually necessary. All the same, I remained pinned down until the operation was over. I heard a call for milk to wash the knives, which signaled the end, and soon the ceremony was over.

With words of praise, I was told to wake up, but I remained seated. I waited for the customary presents in appreciation of my bravery. My father gave me a cow and so did my brother Lillia. The man who had supported my back and my brother-in-law gave me a heifer. In all I had eight animals given to me. I was carried inside the house to my own bed to recuperate as activities intensified to celebrate my bravery.

I laid on my own bed and bled profusely. The blood must be retained within the bed, for according to Maasai tradition, it must not spill to the ground. I was drenched in my own blood. I stopped bleeding after about half an hour but soon was in intolerable pain. I was supposed to squeeze my organ and force blood to flow out of the wound, but no one had told me, so the blood coagulated and caused unbearable pain. The circumciser was brought to my aid and showed me what to do, and soon the pain subsided.

The following morning, I was escorted by a small boy to a nearby valley to walk and relax, allowing my wound to drain. This was common for everyone who had been circumcised, as well as for women who had just given birth. Having lost a lot of blood, I was extremely weak. I walked very slowly, but in spite of my caution I fainted. I tried to hang on to bushes and shrubs, but I fell, irritating my wound. I came out of unconsciousness quickly, and the boy who was escorting me never realized what had happened. I was so scared that I told him to lead me back home. I could have died without there being anyone around who could have helped me. From that day on, I was selective of my company while I was feeble.

In two weeks I was able to walk and was taken to join other newly circumcised boys far away from our settlement. By tradition Maasai initiates are required to decorate their headdresses with all kinds of colorful birds they have killed. On our way to the settlement, we hunted birds and teased girls by shooting them with our wax blunt arrows. We danced and ate and were well treated wherever we went. We were protected from the cold and rain during the healing period. We were not allowed to touch food, as we were regarded as unclean, so whenever we ate we had to use specially prepared sticks instead. We remained in this pampered state until our wounds healed and our headdresses were removed. Our heads were shaved, we discarded our black cloaks and bird headdresses and embarked as newly shaven warriors, Irkeleani.

As long as I live I will never forget the day my head was shaved and I emerged a man, a Maasai warrior. I felt a sense of control over my destiny so great that no words can accurately describe it. I now stood with confidence, pride, and happiness of being, for all around me I was desired and loved by beautiful, sensuous Maasai maidens. I could now interact with women and even have sex with them, which I had not been allowed before. I was now regarded as a responsible person.

In the old days, warriors were like gods, and women and men wanted only to be the parent of a warrior. Everything else would be taken care of as a result. When a poor family had a warrior, they

ceased to be poor. The warrior would go on raids and bring cattle back. The warrior would defend the family against all odds. When a society respects the individual and displays confidence in him the way the Maasai do their warriors, the individual can grow to his fullest potential. Whenever there was a task requiring physical strength or bravery, the Maasai would call upon their warriors. They hardly ever fall short of what is demanded of them and so are characterized by pride, confidence, and an extreme sense of freedom. But there is an old saying in Maasai: "You are never a free man until your father dies." In other words, your father is paramount while he is alive and you are obligated to respect him. My father took advantage of this principle and held a tight grip on all his warriors, including myself. He always wanted to know where we all were at any given time. We fought against his restrictions, but without success. I, being the youngest of my father's five warriors, tried even harder to get loose repeatedly, but each time I was punished severely.

Roaming the plains with other warriors in pursuit of girls and adventure was a warrior's pastime. We would wander from one settlement to another, singing, wrestling, hunting, and just playing. Often I was ready to risk my father's punishment for this wonderful freedom.

One clear day my father sent me to take sick children and one of his wives to the dispensary in the Korongoro Highlands. We rode in the L. S. B. Leakey lorry. We ascended the highlands and were soon attended to in the local hospital. Near the conservation offices I met several acquaintances, and one of them told me of an unusual circumcision that was about to take place in a day or two. All the local warriors and girls were preparing to attend it.

The highlands were a lush green from the seasonal rains and the sky was a purple-blue with no clouds in sight. The land was overflowing with milk, and the warriors felt and looked their best, as they always did when there was plenty to eat and drink. Everyone was at ease. The demands the community usually made on warriors during the dry season when water was scarce and wells

had to be dug were now not necessary. Herds and flocks were entrusted to youths to look after. The warriors had all the time for themselves. But my father was so strict that even at times like these he still insisted on overworking us in one way or another. He believed that by keeping us busy, he would keep us out of trouble.

When I heard about the impending ceremony, I decided to remain behind in the Korongoro Highlands and attend it now that the children had been treated. I knew very well that I would have to make up a story for my father upon my return, but I would worry about that later. I had left my spear at home when I boarded the bus, thinking that I would be coming back that very day. I felt lighter but now regretted having left it behind; I was so used to carrying it wherever I went. In gales of laughter resulting from our continuous teasing of each other, we made our way toward a distant kraal. We walked at a leisurely pace and reveled in the breeze. As usual we talked about the women we desired, among other things.

The following day we were joined by a long line of colorfully dressed girls and warriors from the kraal and the neighborhood where we had spent the night, and we left the highland and headed to Ingorienito to the rolling hills on the lower slopes to attend the circumcision ceremony. From there one could see Oldopai Gorge, where my parents lived, and the Inaapi hills in the middle of the Serengeti Plain.

Three girls and a boy were to be initiated on the same day, an unusual occasion. Four oxen were to be slaughtered, and many people would therefore attend. As we descended, we saw the kraal where the ceremony would take place. All those people dressed in red seemed from a distance like flamingos standing in a lake. We could see lines of other guests heading to the settlements. Warriors made gallant cries of happiness known as *enkiseer.* Our line of warriors and girls responded to their cries even more gallantly.

In serpentine fashion, we entered the gates of the settlement. Holding spears in our left hands, we warriors walked proudly, taking small steps, swaying like palm trees, impressing our girls, who walked parallel to us in another line, and of course the spectators, who gazed at us approvingly.

We stopped in the center of the kraal and waited to be greeted. Women and children welcomed us. We put our hands on the children's heads, which is how children are commonly saluted. After the greetings were completed, we started dancing.

Our singing echoed off the kraal fence and nearby trees. Another line of warriors came up the hill and entered the compound, also singing and moving slowly toward us. Our singing grew in intensity. Both lines of warriors moved parallel to each other, and our feet pounded the ground with style. We stamped vigorously, as if to tell the next line and the spectators that we were the best.

The singing continued until the hot sun was overhead. We recessed and ate food already prepared for us by other warriors. Roasted meat was for those who were to eat meat, and milk for the others. By our tradition, meat and milk must not be consumed at the same time, for this would be a betrayal of the animal. It was regarded as cruel to consume a product of the animal that could be obtained while it was alive, such as milk, and meat, which was only available after the animal had been killed.

After eating we resumed singing, and I spotted a tall, beautiful *esiankiki* (young maiden) of Masiaya whose family was one of the largest and richest in our area. She stood very erect and seemed taller than the rest.

One of her breasts could be seen just above her dress, which was knotted at the shoulder. While I was supposed to dance generally to please all the spectators, I took it upon myself to please her especially. I stared at and flirted with her, and she and I danced in unison at times. We complemented each other very well.

During a break, I introduced myself to the *esiankiki* and told her I would like to see her after the dance. "Won't you need a warrior to escort you home later when the evening threatens?" I said. She replied, "Perhaps, but the evening is still far away."

I waited patiently. When the dance ended, I saw her departing with a group of other women her age. She gave me a sidelong glance, and I took that to mean come later and not now. With so many others around, I would not have been able to confer with her as I would have liked anyway.

With another warrior, I wandered around the kraal killing time until the herds returned from pasture. Before the sun dropped out of sight, we departed. As the kraal of the *esiankiki* was in the lowlands, a place called Enkoloa, we descended leisurely, our spears resting on our shoulders.

We arrived at the woman's kraal and found that cows were now being milked. One could hear the women trying to appease the cows by singing to them. Singing calms cows down, making it easier to milk them. There were no warriors in the whole kraal except for the two of us. Girls went around into warriors' houses as usual and collected milk for us. I was so eager to go and meet my *esiankiki* that I could hardly wait for nightfall. The warriors' girls were trying hard to be sociable, but my mind was not with them. I found them to be childish, loud, bothersome, and boring.

As the only warriors present, we had to keep them company and sing for them, at least for a while, as required by custom. I told the other warrior to sing while I tried to figure out how to approach my *esiankiki*. Still a novice warrior, I was not experienced with women and was in fact still afraid of them. I could flirt from a distance, of course. But sitting down with a woman and trying to seduce her was another matter. I had already tried twice to approach women soon after my circumcision and had failed. I got as far as the door of one woman's house and felt my heart beating like a Congolese drum; breathing became difficult and I had to turn back. Another time I managed to get in the house and succeeded in sitting on the bed, but then I started trembling until the whole bed was shaking, and conversation became difficult. I left the house and the woman, amazed and speechless, and never went back to her again.

Tonight I promised myself I would be brave and would not make any silly, ridiculous moves. "I must be mature and not afraid," I kept reminding myself, as I remembered an incident involving one of my relatives when he was still very young and, like me, afraid of women. He went to a woman's house and sat on a stool for a whole hour; he was afraid to awaken her, as his heart was pounding and he was having difficulty breathing.

When he finally calmed down, he woke her up, and their conversation went something like this:

"Woman, wake up."

"Why should I?"

"To light the fire."

"For what?"

"So you can see me."

"I already know who you are. Why don't *you* light the fire, as you're nearer to it than me?"

"It's your house and it's only proper that you light it yourself."

"I don't feel like it."

"At least wake up so we can talk, as I have something to tell you."

"Say it."

"I need you."

"I do not need one-eyed types like yourself."

"One-eyed people are people too."

"That might be so, but they are not to my taste."

They continued talking for quite some time, and the more they spoke, the braver he became. He did not sleep with her that night, but later on he persisted until he won her over. I doubted whether I was as strong-willed as he, but the fact that he had met with success encouraged me. I told my warrior friend where to find me should he need me, and then I departed.

When I entered the house of my *esiankiki*, I called for the woman of the house, and as luck would have it, my lady responded. She was waiting for me. I felt better, and I proceeded to talk to her like a professional. After much talking back and forth, I joined her in bed.

The night was calm, tender, and loving, like most nights after initiation ceremonies as big as this one. There must have been a lot of courting and lovemaking.

Maasai women can be very hard to deal with sometimes. They can simply reject a man outright and refuse to change their minds. Some play hard to get, but in reality are testing the man to see whether he is worth their while. Once a friend of mine while still young was powerfully attracted to a woman nearly his mother's age. He put a bold move on her. At first the woman could not believe his intention, or rather was amazed by his courage. The name of the warrior was Ngengeiya, or Drizzle.

"Drizzle, what do you want?"

The warrior stared her right in the eye and said, "You."

"For what?"

"To make love to you."

"I am your mother's age."

"The choice was either her or you."

This remark took the woman by surprise. She had underestimated the saying "There is no such thing as a young warrior." When you are a warrior, you are expected to perform bravely in any situation. Your age and size are immaterial.

"You mean you could really love me like a grown-up man?"

"Try me, woman."

He moved in on her. Soon the woman started moaning with excitement, calling out his name. "Honey Drizzle, Honey Drizzle, you *are* a man." In a breathy, stammering voice, she said, "A real man."

Her attractiveness made Honey Drizzle ignore her relative old age. The Maasai believe that if an older and a younger person have intercourse, it is the older person who stands to gain. For instance, it is believed that an older woman having an affair with a young man starts to appear younger and healthier, while the young man grows older and unhealthy.

The following day when the initiation rites had ended, I decided to return home. I had offended my father by staying away from home without his consent, so I prepared myself for whatever punishment he might inflict on me. I walked home alone.

Religion, Belief, and Ritual

The anthropological interest in religion, belief, and ritual is not concerned with the scientific validity of such phenomena but rather the way in which people relate various concepts of the supernatural to their everyday lives. With this practical perspective, some anthropologists have found that traditional spiritual healing is just as helpful in the treatment of illness as modern medicine (see "A Different Drummer" as an example), that voodoo is a form of social control (as in "The Secrets of Haiti's Living Dead"), and that the ritual and spiritual preparation for playing the game of baseball can be just as important as spring training ("Baseball Magic").

Every society is composed of feeling, thinking, and acting human beings who at one time or another are either conforming to or altering the social order into which they were born. Religion is an ideological framework that gives special legitimacy and validity to human experience within any given sociocultural system. In this way, monogamy as a marriage form, or monarchy as a political form, ceases to be simply one of many alternative ways in which a society can be organized, but becomes, for the believer, the only legitimate way. Religion renders certain human values and activities as sacred and inviolable. It is this mythic function that helps to explain the strong ideological attachments that some people have regardless of the scientific merits of their points of view.

While under some conditions religion may in fact be "the opiate of the masses," under other conditions such a belief system may be a rallying point for social and economic protest. A contemporary example of the former might be the "Moonies" (members of the Unification Church founded by Sun Myung Moon), while a good example of the latter is the role of the black church in the American civil rights movement, along with the prominence of such religious figures as Martin Luther King Jr. and Jesse Jackson. A word of caution must be set forth concerning attempts to understand belief systems of other cultures. At times the prevailing attitude seems to be, "What I believe in is religion, and what you believe in is superstition." While anthropologists generally do not subscribe to this view, some tend to explain behavior that seems, on the surface, to be incomprehensible and impractical as some form of religious ritual. The articles in this unit should serve as a strong warning concerning the pitfalls of that approach.

"Psychotherapy in Africa" shows how important traditional belief systems, combined with community involvement, can be to the physical and psychological well-being of the individual. This perspective is so important that the treatment of illness is hindered without it. "The Mbuti Pygmies: Change and Adaptation" describes ritual that is subtle, informal, and yet absolutely necessary for social harmony and stability. "Real Men Don't Eat Deer" shows the importance of food taboos in maintaining tribal identity.

Mystical beliefs and ritual are not absent from the modern world. "Rituals of Death" draws striking parallels between capital punishment in the United States and human sacrifice among the Aztecs of Mexico. "The Tnevnoc Cult" shows that socialization practices that would be considered extreme in one context might be thought of as acceptable and appropriate in another setting. "Body Ritual among the Nacirema" reveals that even our daily routines have mystic overtones. Finally, "Baseball Magic" examines the need for ritual and taboo in the "great American pastime."

In summary, the writings in this unit show religion, belief, and ritual in relationship to practical human affairs.

Looking Ahead: Challenge Questions

How can modern medicine be combined with traditional healing to take advantage of the best aspects of both?

In what respects do perceptions of disease affect treatment and recovery?

How does ritual contribute to a sense of personal security, individual responsibility, and social equality?

How do food taboos contribute to tribal identity?

How has voodoo become such an important form of social control in rural Haiti?

In what ways can capital punishment be seen as a ritual with social functions?

In what ways are magic rituals practical and rational?

How do rituals and taboos get established in the first place?

How important are ritual and taboo in our modern industrial society?

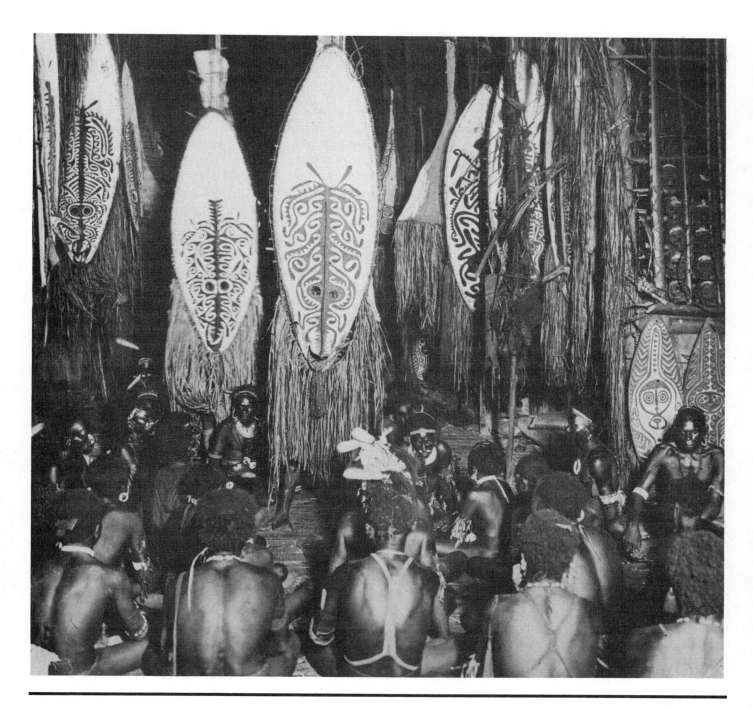

Human Nature

A Different Drummer

By Michael Harner

While on an anthropological expedition to the Peruvian Amazon for the American Museum of Natural History in 1960–61, I lived for the better part of a year in a village of Conibo Indians on a remote lake near the lower Río Tamaya. After I had spent months in a relatively futile effort to learn about their spiritual beliefs, the Conibo finally advised me that there was only one way to learn, and that was to take *ayahuasca,* the consciousness-changing brew their shamans used to reach the hidden worlds of the spirits. *Ayahuasca* is a boiled mixture that contains a particular species of *Banisteriopsis* vine, along with one or more other components, such as *Psychotria* leaves or the leaves of another species of *Banisteriopsis.*

At the time I first took the brew, I was unacquainted with psychedelics. Timothy Leary was only just having his first psychedelic experience, and knowledge of LSD was not yet a part of American culture. I also believed myself to be an atheist. I was simply taking the *ayahuasca* potion in the interests of anthropology because participant observation is one of the cornerstones of serious research.

The Conibo were right, for when I finally drank the potion one night, the results astonished me. Not only did I enter amazingly real, unknown worlds, but in later describing them to a Conibo shaman, I discovered he was already familiar with them, even volunteering details

I had not yet had a chance to tell him. I realized anthropology had underestimated the seriousness of shamanic knowledge and that I had entered a reality far deeper than human culture.

The same shaman encouraged me to continue to work with *ayahuasca* so that I could become initiated into full-fledged shamanic practice. As we worked night after night in an altered state of consciousness, I learned much more about the nonordinary worlds of the shaman, especially that in them one can find and merge with compassionate spiritual powers to help heal the sick and suffering of our ordinary world. I also learned techniques of shamanic divination, methods of obtaining spiritual answers to difficult questions.

Following this experience, I received similar initiations into Amazonian shamanism from the Untsuri Shuar (Jívaro) people of eastern Ecuador, with whom I had previously lived for a year as an ethnographer. I also started to search the cross-cultural literature, expecting to find evidence of the use of indigenous psychedelics in shamanism worldwide. I eventually concluded, however, that the Amazonians' use of psychedelics was a minority practice. The much more common method to enter the shaman's altered state of consciousness was monotonous percussive sound, achieved especially through drumming.

With experimentation, I learned what the shamans already knew: monotonous

drumming, in a frequency of four to seven beats per second, was another valid doorway to the other reality. This "sonic driving" is in approximately the same frequency range as the brain's own theta waves, and its effectiveness is probably partly due to its stimulation of the brain in that range. Compared with drugs, such drumming was also safe, and its effects were short term.

My research among the Inuit of the Canadian Arctic and the peoples of the Northwest Coast of North America reinforced my conclusion that most of the world's shamans use drums or other percussion instruments as "horses" or "canoes" that transport them into the hidden reality of the spirits. Among the Sami (Lapps) of northern Scandinavia, who retained shamanism longer than any other culture in Europe, a few households still have what they call the magic drum. Doing research in the Soviet Union, I learned that the truly professional Siberian shamans generally employed only the drum, even when the psychedelic mushroom *Amanita muscaria* was locally available and was being used by others.

With the shaman's drum, I was able to continue my practice of shamanism in the United States. I lectured on the subject, in and outside of my university teaching, and inevitably, others asked me to introduce them to the practice of shamanism. Thus I began to teach shamanic healing and divination work, first to one or two people at a time, and then, by the mid-1970s, in workshops for groups of students at New Age learning centers such as California's Esalen Institute.

Continuing cross-cultural research, fieldwork, and personal experimentation led me to the fundamental principles of shamanic practice, which I found to be basically the same among indigenous peoples, whether in Siberia, Australia, southern Africa, or North and South America. This "core shamanism," as I call it, is what I taught. Instead of imitating the practices of some ethnic group, my students were able to build on these bare bones of practical shamanic knowledge to fit their own culture. With this basis, the spirits became their teachers—the classic way for shamans to acquire most of their knowledge.

Shamans probably played an important role in European societies from at least the Upper Paleolithic, but this heritage was virtually destroyed in the Middle Ages and early Renaissance by the Church and the Inquisition. Such persecution was common in most of the major civilizations, East and West, because the shamans' ongoing journeys to the gods tended to undermine the authority of state religions. With this in mind, I gave up my university career in 1987 and founded the Foundation for Shamanic Studies, whose purpose is to help Westerners recover this lost shamanic heritage and to help indigenous peoples revive and preserve their own shamanic practices.

I first entered the spirit worlds of the shamans in pursuit of anthropological research. I came away with a new mission— restoring shamanism to the Western world.

Recently, for example, a team from the foundation traveled to the central Asian republic of Tuva (part of the Russian Federation) at the invitation of its president, to help revive shamanism, which had been outlawed there—with the death penalty for practitioners— during the period of Communist domination. In cooperation with the remaining Tuvan shamans, the team performed numerous public healings, demonstrating that shamanism and shamanic healing were valued in America and compatible with modern life. At the conclusion of our visit, the president announced that thereafter shamanism would be respected on a par with Buddhism and Christianity.

In the United States, Europe, and elsewhere, more and more people are learning the practice of shamanism, including health care professionals seeking a more holistic approach. Shamanism has always been done in conjunction with the application of plant remedies, bone setting, and other healing practices. It is not an "alternative" method but a complementary one that looks after the spiritual side of healing.

Much has happened since the shamans introduced me to hidden spirit worlds thirty-six years ago. For me, entering these worlds has transformed my understanding of reality and added great meaning to existence. To the question you often hear today, "Is this all there is?" I can answer with assurance, "No, there is far more than one can even imagine."

Psychotherapy in Africa

Thomas Adeoye Lambo

Thomas Adeoye Lambo is deputy director-general of the World Health Organization in Geneva and an advisory editor of Human Nature. *He was born in Abeokuta, Nigeria, in 1923 and lived there until he finished secondary school. He studied medicine at the University of Birmingham in England, later specializing in psychiatry. Lambo first received international acclaim in 1954 when he published reports on the neuropsychiatric problems of Nigeria's Yoruba tribe and on the establishment of the Aro village hospital. Lambo served as medical director of Aro until 1962, when he was appointed to the first Chair of Psychiatry at Nigeria's Ibadan University; in 1968 he became vice-chancellor of the University. Lambo's psychiatric research and approach to therapy have consistently blended biology, culture, and social psychology.*

Some years ago, a Nigerian patient came to see me in a state of extreme anxiety. He had been educated at Cambridge University and was, to all intents and purposes, thoroughly "Westernized." He had recently been promoted to a top-level position in the administrative service, bypassing many of his able peers. A few weeks after his promotion, however, he had had an unusual accident from which he barely escaped with his life. He suddenly became terrified that his colleagues had formed a conspiracy and were trying to kill him.

His paranoia resisted the usual methods of Western psychiatry, and he had to be sedated to relieve his anxiety. But one day he came to see me, obviously feeling much better. A few nights before, he said, his grandfather had appeared to him in a dream and had assured him of a long and healthy life. He had been promised relief from fear and anxiety if he would sacrifice a goat. My patient bought a goat the following day, carried out all the detailed instructions of his grandfather, and quickly recovered. The young man does not like to discuss this experience because he feels it conflicts with his educational background, but occasionally, in confidence, he says: "There is something in these native things, you know."

To the Western eye, such lingering beliefs in ritual and magic seem antiquated and possibly harmful—obstacles in the path of modern medicine. But the fact is that African cultures have developed indigenous forms of psychotherapy that are highly effective because they are woven into the social fabric. Although Western therapeutic methods are being adopted by many African therapists, few Africans are simply substituting new methods for traditional modes of treatment. Instead, they have attempted to combine the two for maximum effectiveness.

The character and effectiveness of medicine for the mind and the body always and everywhere depend on the culture in which the medicine is practiced. In the West, healing is often considered to be a private matter between patient and therapist. In Africa, healing is an integral part of society and religion, a matter in which the whole community is involved. To understand African psychotherapy one must understand African thought and its social roots.

It seems impossible to speak of a single African viewpoint because the continent contains a broad range of cultures. The Ga, the Masai, and the Kikuyu, for example, are as different in their specific ceremonies and customs as are the Bantus and the Belgians. Yet in sub-Saharan black Africa the different cultures do share a consciousness of the world. They have in common a characteristic perception of life and death that makes it possible to describe their overriding philosophy. (In the United States, Southern Baptists and Episcopalians are far apart in many of their rituals and beliefs, yet one could legitimately say that both share a Christian concept of life.)

The basis of most African value systems is the concept of the unity of life and time. Phenomena that are regarded as opposites in the West exist on a single continuum in Africa. African thought draws no sharp distinction between animate and inanimate, natural and supernatural, material and mental, conscious and unconscious. All things exist in dynamic correspondence, whether they are visible or not. Past, present, and future blend in harmony; the world does not change between one's dreams and the daylight.

Essential to this view of the world is the belief that there is continuous communion between the dead and the living. Most African cultures share the idea that the strength and influence of every clan is anchored by the spirits of its deceased heroes. These heroes are omnipotent and indestructible, and their importance is comparable to that of the Catholic saints. But to Africans, spirits and deities are ever present in human affairs; they are the guardians of the established social order.

The common element in rituals throughout the continent—ancestor cults, deity cults, funeral rites, agricultural rites—is the unity of the people with the world of spirits, the mystical and emotional bond between the natural and supernatural worlds.

Because of the African belief in deities and ancestral spirits, many Westerners think that African thought is more concerned with the supernatural causes of events than with their natural causes. On one level this is true. Africans attribute nearly all forms of illness and disease, as well as personal and communal catastrophes, accidents, and deaths to the magical machinations of their enemies and to the intervention of gods and ghosts. As a result there is a deep faith in the power of symbols to produce the effects that are desired. If a man finds a hair, or a piece of material, or a bit of a fingernail belonging to his enemy, he believes he has only to use the object ritualistically in order to bring about the enemy's injury or death.

As my educated Nigerian patient revealed by sacrificing a goat, the belief in the power of the supernatural is not confined to uneducated Africans. In a survey of African students in British universities conducted some years ago, I found that the majority of them firmly believed that their emotional problems

had their origin in, or could at least be influenced by, charms and diabolical activities of other African students or of people who were still in Africa. I recently interviewed the student officers at the Nigeria House in London and found no change in attitude.

The belief in the power of symbols and magic is inculcated at an early age. I surveyed 1,300 elementary-school children over a four-year period and found that 85 percent used native medicine of some sort—incantations, charms, magic —to help them pass exams, to be liked by teachers, or to ward off the evil effects of other student "medicines." More than half of these children came from Westernized homes, yet they held firmly to the power of magic ritual.

Although most Africans believe in supernatural forces and seem to deny natural causality, their belief system is internally consistent. In the Western world, reality rests on the human ability to master things, to conquer objects, to subordinate the outer world to human will. In the African world, reality is found in the soul, in a religious acquiescence to life, not in its mastery. Reality rests on the relations between one human being and another, and between all people and spirits.

The practice of medicine in Africa is consistent with African philosophy. Across the African continent, sick people go to acknowledged diviners and healers—they are often called witch doctors in the West—in order to discover the nature of their illness. In almost every instance, the explanation involves a deity or an ancestral spirit. But this is only one aspect of the diagnosis, because the explanation given by the diviner is also grounded in natural phenomena. As anthropologist Robin Horton observes: "The diviner who diagnoses the intervention of a spiritual agency is also expected to give some acceptable account of what moved the agency in question to intervene. And this account very commonly involves reference to some event in the world of visible, tangible happenings. Thus if a diviner diagnoses the action of witchcraft influence or lethal medicine spirits, it is usual for him to add something about the human hatreds, jealousies, and

misdeeds that have brought such agencies into play. Or, if he diagnoses the wrath of an ancestor, it is usual for him to point to the human breach of kinship morality which has called down this wrath."

The causes of illness are not simply attributed to the unknown or dropped into the laps of the gods. Causes are always linked to the patient's immediate world of social events. As Victor Turner's study of the Ndembu people of central Africa revealed, diviners believe a patient "will not get better until all the tensions and aggressions in the group's interrelations have been brought to light and exposed to ritual treatment." In my work with the Yoruba culture, I too found that supernatural forces are regarded as the agents and consequences of human will. Sickness is the natural effect of some social mistake—breaching a taboo or breaking a kinship rule.

African concepts of health and illness, like those of life and death, are intertwined. Health is not regarded as an isolated phenomenon but reflects the integration of the community. It is not the mere absence of disease but a sign that a person is living in peace and harmony with his neighbors, that he is keeping the laws of the gods and the tribe. The practice of medicine is more than the administration of drugs and potions. It encompasses all activities—personal and communal—that are directed toward the promotion of human well-being. As S. R. Burstein wrote, to be healthy requires "averting the wrath of gods or spirits, making rain, purifying streams or habitations, improving sex potency or fecundity or the fertility of fields and crops —in short, it is bound up with the whole interpretation of life."

Native healers are called upon to treat a wide range of psychiatric disorders, from schizophrenia to neurotic syndromes. Their labels may not be the same, but they recognize the difference between an incapacitating psychosis and a temporary neurosis, and between a problem that can be cured (anxiety) and one that cannot (congenital retardation or idiocy). In many tribes a person is defined as mad when he talks nonsense, acts foolishly and irresponsibly, and is unable to look after himself.

It is often assumed that tribal societies are a psychological paradise and that mental illness is the offspring of modern civilization and its myriad stresses. The African scenes in Alex Haley's *Roots* tend to portray a Garden of Eden, full of healthy tribesmen. But all gardens have snakes. Small societies have their own peculiar and powerful sources of mental stress. Robin Horton notes that tribal societies have a limited number of roles to be filled, and that there are limited choices for individuals. As a result each tribe usually has a substantial number of social misfits. Traditional communities also have a built-in set of conflicting values: aggressive ambition versus a reluctance to rise above one's neighbor; ruthless individualism versus acceptance of one's place in the lineage system. Inconsistencies such as these, Horton believes, "are often as sharp as those so well known in modern industrial societies . . . One may even suspect that some of the young Africans currently rushing from the country to the towns are in fact escaping from a more oppressive to a less oppressive psychological environment."

Under typical tribal conditions, traditional methods are perfectly effective in the diagnosis and treatment of mental illness. The patient goes to the tribal diviner, who follows a complex procedure. First the diviner (who may be a man or a woman) determines the "immediate" cause of the illness—that is, whether it comes from physical devitalization or from spiritual possession. Next he or she diagnoses the "remote" cause of the ailment: Had the patient offended one of his ancestor spirits or gods? Had a taboo been violated? Was some human agent in the village using magic or invoking the help of evil spirits to take revenge for an offense?

The African diviner makes a diagnosis much as a Western psychoanalyst does: through the analysis of dreams, projective techniques, trances and hypnotic states (undergone by patient and healer alike), and the potent power of words. With these methods, the diviner defines the psychodynamics of the patient and gains insight into the complete life situation of the sick person.

One projective technique of diagnosis—which has much in common with the Rorschach test—occurs in *Ifa* divination, a procedure used by Yoruba healers. There are 256 *Odus* (incantations) that are poetically structured; each is a dramatic series of words that evoke the patient's emotions. Sometimes the power of the *Odus* lies in the way the words are used, the order in which they are arranged, or the starkness with which they express a deep feeling. The incantations are used to gain insight into the patient's problem. Their main therapeutic value, as in the case with the Rorschach ink blots, is to interpret omens, bring up unconscious motives, and make unknown desires and fears explicit.

Once the immediate and remote causes are established, the diagnosis is complete and the healer decides on the course of therapy. Usually this involves an expiatory sacrifice meant to restore the unity between man and deity. Everyone takes part in the treatment; the ritual involves the healer, the patient, his family, and the community at large. The group rituals—singing and dancing, confessions, trances, storytelling, and the like—that follow are powerful therapeutic measures for the patient. They release tensions and pressures and promote positive mental health by tying all individuals to the larger group. Group rituals are effective because they are the basis of African social life, an essential part of the lives of "healthy" Africans.

Some cultures, such as the N'jayei society of the Mende in Sierra Leone and the Yassi society of the Sherbro, have always had formal group therapy for their mentally ill. When one person falls ill, the whole tribe attends to his physical and spiritual needs.

Presiding over all forms of treatment is the healer, or *nganga*. My colleagues and I have studied and worked with these men and women for many years, and we are consistently impressed by their abilities. Many of those we observed are extraordinary individuals of great common sense, eloquence, boldness, and charisma. They are highly respected within their communities as people who through self-denial, dedication, and prolonged meditation and training have discovered the secrets of the healing art and its magic (a description of Western healers as well, one might say).

The traditional *nganga* has supreme self-confidence, which he or she transmits to the patient. By professing an ability to commune with supernatural beings—and therefore to control or influence them—the healer holds boundless power over members of the tribe. Africans regard the *nganga*'s mystical qualities and eccentricities fondly, and with awe. So strongly do people believe in the *nganga*'s ability to find out which ancestral spirit is responsible for the psychological distress of the patient, that pure suggestion alone can be very effective.

For centuries the tribal practice of communal psychotherapy served African society well. Little social stigma was attached to mental illness; even chronic psychotics were tolerated in their communities and were able to function at a minimal level. (Such tolerance is true of many rural cultures.) But as the British, Germans, French, Belgians, and Portuguese colonized many African countries, they brought a European concept of mental illness along with their religious, economic, and educational systems.

They built prisons with special sections set aside for "lunatics"—usually vagrant psychotics and criminals with demonstrable mental disorders—who were restricted with handcuffs and ankle shackles. The African healers had always drawn a distinction between mental illness and criminality, but the European colonizers did not.

In many African cultures today, the traditional beliefs in magic and religion are dying. Their remaining influence serves only to create anxiety and ambivalence among Africans who are living through a period of rapid social and economic change. With the disruption and disorganization of family units, we have begun to see clinical problems that once were rare: severe depression, obsessional neurosis, and emotional incapacity. Western medicine has come a long way from the shackle solution, but it is not the best kind of therapy for people under such stress. In spite of its high technological and material advancement, modern science does not satisfy the basic metaphysical and social needs of many people, no matter how sophisticated they are.

In 1954 my colleagues and I established a therapeutic program designed to wed the best practices of traditional and contemporary psychology. Our guiding premise was to make use of the therapeutic practices that already existed in the indigenous culture, and to recognize the power of the group in healing.

We began our experiment at Aro, a rural suburb of the ancient town of Abeokuta, in western Nigeria. Aro consists of four villages that lie in close proximity in the beautiful rolling countryside. The villages are home [to] Yoruba tribesmen and their relatives, most of whom are peasant farmers, fishermen, and craftsmen.

Near these four villages we built a day hospital that could accommodate up to 300 patients, and then we set up a village care system for their treatment. Our plan was to preserve the fundamental structure of African culture: closely knit groups, well-defined kin networks, an interlocking system of mutual obligations and traditional roles.

Patients came to the hospital every morning for treatment and spent their afternoons in occupational therapy, but they were not confined to the hospital. Patients lived in homes in the four villages or, if necessary, with hospital staff members who lived on hospital grounds—ambulance drivers, clerks, dispensary attendants, and gardeners. (This boarding-out procedure resembles a system that has been practiced for several hundred years in Gheel, a town in Belgium, where the mentally ill live in local households surrounding a central institution.)

We required the patients, who came from all over Nigeria, to arrive at the village hospital with at least one relative—a mother, sister, brother, or aunt—who would be able to cook for them, wash their clothes, take them to the hospital in the morning, and pick them up in the afternoon.

These relatives, along with the patients, took part in all the social activities of the villages: parties, plays, dances, storytelling. Family participation was successful from the beginning. We were able to learn about the family influences and stresses on the patient, and the family members learned how to adjust to the

sick relative and deal with his or her emotional needs.

The hospital staff was drawn from the four villages, which meant that the hospital employees were the "landlords" of most of the patients, in constant contact with them at home and at work. After a while, the distinction between the two therapeutic arenas blurred and the villages became extensions of the hospital wards.

Doctors, nurses, and superintendents visited the villages every day and set up "therapy" groups—often for dancing, storytelling, and other rituals—as well as occupational programs that taught patients traditional African crafts.

It is not enough to treat patients on a boarding-out or outpatient basis. If services are not offered to them outside of the hospital, an undue burden is placed on their families and neighbors. This increases the tension to which patients are exposed. As essential feature of our plan was to regard the villages as an extension of the hospital, subject to equally close supervision and control.

But we neither imposed the system on the local people nor asked them to give their time and involvement without giving them something in return. We were determined to inflict no hardships. The hospital staff took full responsibility for the administration of the villages and for the health of the local people. They held regular monthly meetings with the village elders and their councils to give the villagers a say in the system. The hospital also arranged loans to the villagers to expand, repair, or build new houses to take care of the patients; it paid for the installation of water pipes and latrines; it paid for a mosquito eradication squad; it offered jobs to many local people and paid the "landlords" a small stipend.

Although these economic benefits aided the community, no attempt was ever made to structure the villages in any way, or to tell the villagers what to do with the patients or how to treat them. As a result of economic benefits, hospital guidance, and a voice in their own management, village members supported the experiment.

In a study made after the program began, we learned that patients who were

boarded out under this system adapted more quickly and responded more readily to treatment than patients who lived in the hospital. Although the facilities available in the hospital were extensive—drug medication, group therapy sessions, modified insulin therapy, electro-convulsive shock treatments—we found that the most important therapeutic factor was the patient's social contacts, especially with people who were healthier than the patient. The village groups, unlike the hospital group, were unrehearsed, unexpected, and voluntary. Patients could choose their friends and activities; they were not thrown together arbitrarily and asked to "work things out." We believe that the boarded-out patients improved so quickly because of their daily contact with settled, tolerant, healthy people. They learned to function in society again without overwhelming anxiety.

One of the more effective and controversial methods we used was to collaborate with native healers. Just as New Yorkers have faith in their psychoanalysts, and pilgrims have faith in their priests, the Yoruba have faith in the *nganga;* and faith, as we are learning, is half the battle toward cure.

Our unorthodox alliance proved to be highly successful. The local diviners and religious leaders helped many of the patients recover, sometimes through a simple ceremony at a village shrine, sometimes in elaborate forms of ritual sacrifice, sometimes by interpreting the spiritual or magical causes of their dreams and illnesses.

At the beginning of the program patients were carefully selected for admission, but now patients of every sort are accepted: violent persons, catatonics, schizophrenics, and others whose symptoms make them socially unacceptable or emotionally withdrawn. The system is particularly effective with emotionally disturbed and psychotic children, who always come to the hospital with a great number of concerned relatives. Children who have minor neurotic disorders are kept out of the hospital entirely and treated exclusively and successfully in village homes.

The village care system was designed primarily for the acutely ill and for those whose illness was manageable, and the average stay for patients at Aro was, and is, about six months. But patients who were chronically ill and could not recover in a relatively short time posed a problem. For one thing, their relatives could not stay with them in the villages because of family and financial obligations in their home communities. We are working out solutions for such people on a trial-and-error basis. Some of the incapacitated psychotic patients now live on special farms; others live in Aro villages near the hospital and earn their keep while receiving regular supervision. The traditional healers keep watch over these individuals and maintain follow-up treatment.

We have found many economic, medical, and social advantages to our program. The cost has been low because we have concentrated on using human resources in the most effective and strategic manner. Medically and therapeutically, the program provides a positive environment for the treatment of character disorders, sociopathy, alcoholism, neuroses, and anxiety. Follow-up studies show that the program fosters a relatively quick recovery for these problems and that the recidivism rate and the need for aftercare are significantly reduced. The length of stay at Aro, and speed of recovery, is roughly one third of the average stay in other hospitals, especially for all forms of schizophrenia. Patients with neurotic disorders respond most rapidly. Because of its effectiveness, the Aro system has been extended to four states in Nigeria and to five countries in Africa, including Kenya, Ghana, and Zambia. At each new hospital the program is modified to fit local conditions.

Some observers of the Aro system argue that it can operate only in nonindustrial agrarian communities, like those in Africa and Asia, where families and villages are tightly knit. They say that countries marked by high alienation and individualism could not import such a program. Part of this argument is correct. The Aro approach to mental health rests on particularly African traditions, such as the *nganga,* and on the belief in the continuum of life and death, sickness and health, the natural and the supernatural.

But some lessons of the Aro plan have already found their way into Western psychotherapy. Many therapists recognize the need to place the sick person in a social context; a therapist cannot heal the patient without attending to his beliefs, family, work, and environment. Various forms of group therapy are being developed in an attempt to counteract the Western emphasis on curing the individual in isolation. Lately, family therapy has been expanded into a new procedure called network therapy in which the patient's entire network of relatives, coworkers, and friends become involved in the treatment.

Another lesson of Aro is less obvious than the benefits of group support. It is the understanding that treatment begins with a people's indigenous beliefs and their world view, which underlie psychological functioning and provide the basis for healing. Religious values that give meaning and coherence to life can be the healthiest route for many people. As Jung observed years ago, religious factors are inherent in the path toward healing, and the native therapies of Africa support his view.

A supernatural belief system, Western or Eastern, is not a sphere of arbitrary dreams but a sphere of laws that dictate the rules of kinship, the order of the universe, the route of happiness. The Westerner sees only part of the African belief system, such as the witch doctor, and wonders how wild fictions can take root in a reasonable mind. (His own fictions seem perfectly reasonable, of course.) But to the African, the religious-magical system is a great poem, allegorical of human experience, wise in its portrayal of the world and its creatures. There is more method, more reason, in such madness than in the insanity of most people today.

References

Burstein, S. R. "Public Health and Prevention of Disease in Primitive Communities." *The Advancement of Science,* Vol. 9, 1952, pp. 75–81.

Horton, Robin. "African Traditional Thought and Western Science." *Africa,* Vol. 37, 1967, pp. 50–71.

Horton, Robin. *The Traditional Background of Medical Practice in Nigeria.* Institute of Africa Studies, 1966.

Lambo, T. A. "A World View of Mental Health: Recent Developments and Future Trends." *American Journal of Orthopsychiatry,* Vol. 43, 1973, pp. 706–716.

Lambo, T. A. "Psychotherapy in Africa." *Psychotherapy and Psychosomatics,* Vol. 24, 1974, pp. 311–326.

The Mbuti Pygmies: Change and Adaptation

Colin M. Turnbull

THE EDUCATIONAL PROCESS

... In the first three years of life every Mbuti alive experiences almost total security. The infant is breast-fed for those three years, and is allowed almost every freedom. Regardless of gender, the infant learns to have absolute trust in both male and female parent. If anything, the father is just another kind of mother, for in the second year the father formally introduces the child to its first solid food. There used to be a beautiful ritual in which the mother presented the child to the father in the middle of the camp, where all important statements are made (anyone speaking from the middle of the camp must be listened to). The father took the child and held it to his breast, and the child would try to suckle, crying "*ema, ema,*" or "mother." The father would shake his head, and say "no, father ... *eba,*" but like a mother (the Mbuti said), then give the child its first solid food.

At three the child ventures out into the world on its own and enters the *bopi,* what we might call a playground, a tiny camp perhaps a hundred yards from the main camp, often on the edge of a stream. The *bopi* were indeed play-grounds, and often very noisy ones, full of fun and high spirits. But they were also rigorous training grounds for eventual economic responsibility. On entry to the *bopi,* for one thing, the child discovers the importance of age as a structural principle, and the relative unimportance of gender and biological kinship. The *bopi* is the private world of the children. Younger youths may occasionally venture in, but if adults or elders try, as they sometimes do when angry at having their afternoon snooze interrupted, they invariably get driven out, taunted, and ridiculed. Children, among the Mbuti, have rights, but they also learn that they have responsibilities. Before the hunt sets out each day it is the children, sometimes the younger youths, who light the hunting fire.

Ritual among the Mbuti is often so informal and apparently casual that it may pass unnoticed at first. Yet insofar as ritual involves symbolic acts that represent unspoken, perhaps even unthought, concepts or ideals, or invoke other states of being, alternative frames of mind and reference, then Mbuti life is full of ritual. The hunting fire is one of the more obvious of such rituals. Early in the morning children would take firebrands from the *bopi,* where they always lit their own fire with embers from their family hearths, and set off on the trail by which the hunt was to leave that day (the direction of each day's hunt was always settled by discussion the night before). Just a short distance from the camp they lit a fire at the base of a large tree, and covered it with special leaves that made it give off a column of dense smoke. Hunters leaving the camp, both men and women, and such youths and children as were going with them, had to pass by this fire. Some did so casually, without stopping or looking, but passing through the smoke. Others reached into the smoke with their hands as they passed, rubbing the smoke into their bodies. A few always stopped, for a moment, and let the smoke envelop them, only then almost dreamily moving off.

And indeed it *was* a form of intoxication, for the smoke invoked the spirit of the forest, and by passing through it the hunters sought to fill themselves with that spirit, not so much to make the hunt successful as to minimize the sacrilege of killing. Yet they, the hunters, could not light the fire themselves. After all, they were already contaminated by death. Even youths, who daily joined the hunt at the edges, catching any game that escaped the nets, by hand, if they could, were not pure enough to invoke the spirits of forestness. But young children were uncontaminated, as yet untainted by contact with the original sin of the Mbuti. It was their responsibility to light the fire, and if it was not lit then the hunt would not take place, or as the Mbuti put it, the hunt *could* not take place.

In this way even the children in Mbuti society, at the first of the four age levels that dominate Mbuti social structure, are given very real social responsibility and see themselves as a part of that structure, by virtue of their purity. After all, they have just been born from the source of all purity, the forest itself. By the same reasoning, the elders, who are about to return to that ultimate source of all being, through death, are at least closer to purity than the adults, who are daily contaminated by killing. Elders no longer go on the hunt. So, like the children, the elders have important sacred ritual responsibilities in the Mbuti division of labor by age.

In the *bopi* the children play, but they have no "games" in the strict sense of the word. Levi-Strauss has perceptively compared games with rituals, suggesting that whereas in a game the players start theoretically equal but end up unequal, in a ritual just the reverse takes place. All are equalized. Mbuti children could be seen every day playing in the *bopi*, but not once did I see a game, not one activity that smacked of any kind of competition, except perhaps that competition that it is necessary for us all to feel from time to time, competition with our own private and personal inadequacies. One such pastime (rather than game) was tree climbing. A dozen or so children would climb up a young sapling. Reaching the top, their weight brought the sapling bending down until it almost touched the ground. Then all the children leapt off together, shrieking as the young tree sprang upright again with a rush. Sometimes one child, male

or female, might stay on a little too long, either out of fear, or out of bravado, or from sheer carelessness or bad timing. Whatever the reason, it was a lesson most children only needed to be taught once, for the result was that you got flung upward with the tree, and were lucky to escape with no more than a few bruises and a very bad fright.

Other pastimes taught the children the rules of hunting and gathering. Frequently elders, who stayed in camp when the hunt went off, called the children into the main camp and enacted a mock hunt with them there. Stretching a discarded piece of net across the camp, they pretended to be animals, showing the children how to drive them into the nets. And, of course, the children played house, learning the patterns of cooperation that would be necessary for them later in life. They also learned the prime lesson of egality, other than for purposes of division of labor making no distinction between male and female, this nuclear family or that. All in the *bopi* were *apua'i* to each other, and so they would remain throughout their lives. At every age level—children, youth, adulthood, or old age—everyone of that level is *apua'i* to all the others. Only adults sometimes (but so rarely that I think it was only done as a kind of joke, or possibly insult) made the distinction that the Bira do, using *apua'i* for male and *amua'i* for female. Male or female, for the Mbuti, if you are the same age you are *apua'i*, and that means that you share everything equally, regardless of kinship or gender.

YOUTH AND POLITICS

Sometime before the age of puberty boys or girls, whenever they feel ready, move back into the main camp from the *bopi* and join the youths. This is when they must assume new responsibilities, which for the youths are primarily political. Already, in the *bopi*, the children become involved in disputes, and are sometimes instrumental in settling them by ridicule, for nothing hurts an adult more than being ridiculed by children.

The art of reason, however, is something they learn from the youths, and it is the youths who apply the art of reason to the settlement of disputes.

When puberty comes it separates them, for the first time in their experience, from each other as *apua'i*. Very plainly girls are different from boys. When a girl has her first menstrual period the whole camp celebrates with the wild *elima* festival, in which the girl, and some of her chosen girl friends, are the center of all attention, living together in a special *elima* house. Male youths sit outside the *elima* house and wait for the girls to come out, usually in the afternood, for the *elima* singing. They sing in antiphony, the girls leading, the boys responding. Boys come from neighboring territories all around, for this is a time of courtship. But there are always eligible youths within the camp as well, and the *elima* girl may well choose girls from other territories to come and join her, so there is more than enough excuse for every youth to carry on several flirtations, legitimate or illegitimate. I have known even first cousins to flirt with each other, but learned to be prudent enough not to pull out my kinship charts and point this out—well, not in public anyway.

The *elima* is more than a premarital festival, more than a joint initiation of youth into adulthood, and more than a rite of passage through puberty, though it is all those things. It is a public recognition of the opposition of male and female, and every *elima* is used to highlight the *potential* for conflict that lies in that opposition. As at other times of crisis, at puberty, a time of change and uncertainty, the Mbuti bring all the major forms of conflict out into the open. And the one that evidently most concerns them is the male/female opposition.

The adults begin to play a special form of "tug of war" that is clearly a ritual rather than a game. All the men are on one side, the women on the other. At first it looks like a game, but quickly it becomes clear that the objective is for *neither* side to win. As soon as the women begin to win, one of them will leave the end of the line and run around to join the men, assuming a deep male voice and in other ways ridiculing man-

1. EQUAL
   (direction of tug)
   sexes divided

2. men winning
   man transfers

3. women winning
   woman transfers

4. men winning
   man transfers

5. women winning
   woman transfers

until: EQUAL
   sexes reversed

△ = men
○ = women
△
⊘ } = man or woman who has changed sides

Tug of war. This is one of the Mbuti's many techniques of conflict resolution, involving role reversal and the principle of opposition without hostility.

hood. Then, as the men begin to win, a male will similarly join the women, making fun of womanhood as he does so. Each adult on changing sides attempts to outdo all the others in ridicul-ing the opposite sex. Finally, when nearly all have switched sides, and sexes, the ritual battle between the genders simply collapses into hysterical laughter, the contestants letting go of the rope, falling onto the ground, and rolling over with mirth. Neither side wins, both are equalized very nicely, and each learns the essential lesson, that there should be *no* contest. . . .

Real Men *Don't* Eat Deer

BY KATHARINE MILTON

KATHARINE MILTON, a physical anthropologist at the University of California at Berkeley, has been studying the dietary habits of indigenous groups in the Brazilian Amazon for 15 years. "I study any and all activities associated with food," Milton says, "from symbolic rituals to more pragmatic things, like how much protein is in this dead sloth."

THE POWERFUL BLAST OF A NEARBY shotgun brought me to my feet in a hurry. Though I'd been doing fieldwork with the Mat's for only a few weeks, all the hunting I'd observed had been carried out with blowguns or bows and arrows. I hadn't even seen a shotgun. Quickly, I looked out the doorway of my little hut, but there was nothing to be learned. During the day, an Amazonian village is generally a very dull place. Most adults scatter to hunt or work in the garden, and children leave to swim or play in the forest.

Walking in the direction of the shot, I spotted two young boys, and I asked them as best I could what had happened. They responded with animation, but my grasp of their language was so minimal that I couldn't understand much of what they said. I walked a little farther but, seeing nothing, decided to return to my hut, where I'd been sorting wild plants collected the day before. A little later several Mat's came by. One woman motioned for me to follow her. I did and

was led into a small field of sweet potatoes growing directly behind a row of thatch-roofed houses. Lying in the field, not 20 feet from the back of the nearest house, was a large and quite dead white-tailed deer.

After examining the deer, I waited around for someone to butcher the carcass and distribute the meat. Meat is the most highly valued food among forest peoples, and good hunters earn considerable respect and prestige. Yet no one came to cut up this deer; no one expressed the slightest interest in this large hide-covered bundle of chops and steaks. Finally I left, feeling puzzled. I returned an hour later but found the carcass lying just as I had left it. Now I was really confused. Why wasn't anyone cutting up the deer? Why would anyone shoot it if they weren't going to eat it?

One thing was clear. Since not a single Mat's ended up eating a bite of the deer, shooting it for food had not been the objective. Some villagers said the deer had been shot because it had ventured too close to the village and must have been a malevolent spirit. Others said the exact opposite: the deer should never have been shot because wild animals near the village were friendly spirits, possibly ancestors. Given the fact that the deer lay dead, I was inclined to believe the malevolent-spirit version of the story. Wasting costly shotgun shells on an animal one has no intention of

eating seems to be an extravagant act, unless there was some very compelling reason to do so.

But why weren't they eating the deer? No one would come out and say that deer were taboo to eat, although they did say that Mat's elders didn't eat deer. Yet no one of any age, old or young, appeared interested in eating it. Not wanting to waste the meat, I asked for help in cutting off a hind leg, which I later chopped up and cooked. After the meal, however, I felt ill. Deer were certainly not a taboo food to "my people," and logically I knew that deer meat is perfectly edible—but I must admit that eating something you know 165 people have refused does give you pause.

THE MAT'S ARE AN ISOLATED GROUP in a highly productive region of the Brazilian rain forest, south of the Amazon River and fairly close to the Peruvian border. During my three months as a visitor in their village, I learned that they had an incredibly long list of foods to avoid. They ate no insects of any type—a surprise, since every other indigenous group I'd worked with in Amazonia relished the nutritious large white larvae of palm beetles, as well as caterpillars, ants, and termites. Nor did they eat any anteater, armadillo, jaguar, snake, or stingray. I was particularly astonished when they told me they did not eat agouti, medium-size mammals that are eagerly hunted and eaten by all other indigenous groups of which I am aware.

Monkey flesh was another food they were pretty fussy about. Of the dozen or so local monkey species, only woolly monkeys and spider monkeys were eaten regularly. Indeed, so many woolly and spider monkeys were eaten during my study that I came to regard them as staple items of the Mat's diet. In addition, large land tortoises, which are generally a favored food among rain forest groups, could be eaten only by Mat's women and were totally avoided by men.

Why on earth would the Mat's avoid so many foods that other Amazonian groups relish? Before leaping to the conclusion that the Mat's are an irrational people, consider the diet of the average American. We do not sit down to a nice meal of horse, cat, or roasted larvae. Why not? These animals are highly nutritious and savored by many groups around the world. If someone was to ask you why Americans don't eat larvae or cats, your best response would probably be to mutter that these just weren't customary foods for us. And when I asked the Mat's why they didn't eat agouti or armadillo or insects, that is exactly what they said.

The more intriguing question is why Mat's, Americans, or any other society

---

You are what you eat, the saying goes. But what you don't eat says a lot too.

---

should have food taboos at all. Yet such taboos are universal. Two well-known examples are the Hindu prohibition against eating cow flesh and Muslim custom of avoiding swine. There are scores of less well known examples. Some Asians, for example, avoid eating chickens or their eggs, and many African herding peoples avoid eating fish.

Anthropologists have cooked up a smorgasbord of theories to account for the customs. In 1966 the British anthro-

pologist Mary Douglas wrote an influential book, *Purity and Danger,* about the symbolic functions of taboos. She argued that adherence to the dozens of dietary prohibitions in the Old Testament reinforced the cultural cohesion of the ancient Hebrews. The Old Testament, Douglas noticed, tabooed animals—such as pigs or catfish—that did not fit into specific categories. For example, pigs have cloven hooves like cows and goats, yet they do not chew the cud. Catfish are fish, but they do not have scales. Perhaps, Douglas reasoned, eating only foods that belonged to well-defined groups helped remind the Hebrews of their identity as a group of their own.

The prominent American anthropologist Marvin Harris has proposed a far more utilitarian view. He argues that there are usually sound economic or health reasons for prohibiting a particular food. The ban on killing cows in India, he thinks, can be explained in the following way: In India, where wood is scarce, cow dung is used to make cooking fires and walls for homes. Moreover, female cows provide milk, and male cattle pull plows or wagons. In other words, he argues that the products from cows—milk, labor, and dung—make them worth far more alive than dead.

The Douglas school might retort that beneficial effects of the taboo do not prove its cause. The taboo, they might argue, may well have originated for more symbolic reasons, and only later acquired a secondary material benefit. India is the hearth of old-world vegetarianism, and ahimsa—the practice of avoiding injuring living creatures—is one of the foundations of Hinduism and Buddhism. This concept debuted around the fifth and sixth centuries B.C. and thus predated the ritualized reverence for the cow.

It does, however, strengthen Harris's argument to note that the sacred cow concept appears to have emerged in India around 200 A.D.—just when the population had become very dense. All arable land was needed to grow food for humans, not cattle, and forests were rapidly being chopped into firewood. By the fourth century, the concept had spread so completely that killing a cow carried with it the death penalty. Gradually, throughout India, the cow became

a venerated icon, a symbol coming ultimately to stand for Mother India herself. Even today cow killing is banned in India's constitution.

How do these spiritual and materialist explanations transfer to the Amazon? Start by thinking tapir instead of cow. The tapir, a 300-pound relative of the horse, is the largest single packet of meat in the Amazonian rain forest. Tapirs lead a solitary, peaceful existence, wandering about eating fallen fruits and vegetation. Many peoples I have worked with in Amazonia consider tapir the best meat imaginable—the equivalent of jungle caviar. Yet American anthropologist Eric Ross, who worked in the Ecuadorian rain forest, discovered that the Achuara people prohibit eating tapir meat.

Ross proposed the following materialist explanation, in brief, for this puzzling behavior: Tapirs are big and fairly scarce in the tropical rain forest. Why be an expert hunter of something you rarely encounter? Thus, the materialist logic runs, the Achuara have a prohibition against eating tapir so hunters won't waste their time chasing after these rare and elusive beasts. This argument, however, ignores the fact that no one sets out to hunt tapirs per se. Why not kill and eat tapirs when you run across them, and kill and eat other things the rest of the time—as do most other forest-based indigenous peoples? There seems to be some other reason the Achuara avoid tapir meat.

Another anthropologist, David McDonald, argues that indigenous groups may be practicing food taboos as "a primitive environmental protection agency." He reasons that since different species of game animals tend to be sparsely distributed, they might easily be hunted to extinction. He came to this conclusion after examining the customs of 11 different Amazonian societies and noticing that each culture prohibited certain foods for subsets of the group—either by sex or age. These taboos, he argued, limited consumption of that prey animal, thus ensuring that no one species would be hunted to extinction. But though portions of this argument seem more or less reasonable, the hypothesis focuses only on dietary prohibitions affecting groups of different ages and sexes. It does not

161

address the question of why an entire culture, such as the Achuara, does not eat tapir. If no one ever eats it, what's the point? Who benefits except tapirs?

I BECAME INTERESTED IN THE FUNCTIONS of food taboos in the Amazon after spending time comparing dietary habits of different groups. By luck, I studied two groups that lived in the same region of the Brazilian state of Pará on tributaries of the Xingu River. These two groups, the Parakana and Arawete, spoke the same basic language (Tupi-Gurani), but they were also so hostile toward each other that to enter the hunting territory of your neighbor was to risk being killed on the spot.

I kept track of their diets, dutifully noting what they did—and did not—eat. Gradually, I began to see an interesting pattern. The favorite prey species of the Parakana, I noted, were land tortoises and tapirs. Yet they ate no monkeys of any kind nor did I note any consumption of large forest birds.

Imagine my surprise to find that their enemies to the north, the Arawete, did not eat tapir and focused much of their hunting on large forest birds. Indeed, the Arawete not only ate birds but even raised colorful baby macaws as mascots. Though at least one authority has reported that the Arawete eat monkeys, I noted no eating of monkey flesh by an Arawete during my stay. In fact, the only monkey killed, a howler monkey, was killed so that it could be used for fish bait.

Slightly farther to the north of the Arawete are the Arara, Carib speakers who migrated into this region from the north many centuries ago. Their most pre-

ferred, most hunted, and most eaten prey are monkeys—a dietary item scorned by the Parakana and eaten sparingly, if at all, by the Arawete.

It thus appeared to me that each group was tabooing the animal most preferred and desired by its despised neighbors. In other words, the food prohibitions shared by all members of a particular group appeared to serve as identification badges, a type of cultural boundary marker that identified and unified the group members. As I and many others have noted, the indigenous names of these forest groups generally translate into something such as "the people" or "the true people" or "the real people." The choice of this name implies that neighboring groups may be regarded as somehow different and in fact not quite human.

My friend Carlos Coimbra, Jr., a Brazilian anthropologist, noticed a similar pattern among the Zoro and Surui Indians, who, like the Arawete and Parakana, are neighbors and traditional enemies. The Surui, he says, abhor deer meat, which the Zoro relish.

Unfortunately, isolated neighboring indigenous groups that retain traditional food taboos are increasingly rare. Once contacted, groups often begin modeling their behavior after outsiders, who are happy to eat whatever game animal they can shoot. After observing taboo prey such as deer or tapir being eaten with impunity and gusto, traditional dietary customs are gradually abandoned. I believe, for example, that the Mat's traditionally did not eat deer. But the younger men, having seen outsiders eat deer, may have decided that the "trendy" thing to do was profess to me that they too ate deer—a practice of far less interest to older and

less impressionable members of the tribe. Yet when confronted with a dead deer, no one of any age, even the young men, could actually force themselves to break the taboo and eat its flesh.

How are these differences so strongly ingrained? As we know, all humans are members of a single species, *Homo sapiens,* and we all look basically the same. What distinguishes human groups are cultural practices—our customs and beliefs regarding the proper foods, the proper clothes, the proper adornments, the proper behavior. The "fashions" of behaviors and beliefs serve as badges of a common identity.

The food taboos I observed in Amazonia help the Parakana or the Arawete or the Mat's establish their own cultural identity, just as much as facial tattoos, lip and nose piercings, and other ritual practices do. In a world in which the support and comfort of your particular culture are all that distinguish you from the beasts of the forest and your "not quite human" neighbors, food taboos serve as a constant reminder of tribal identity and the behavior expected of "true" humans.

Moreover, since each hunting territory can support only a single group, fostering group identity is crucial to survival. Symbolic behavior helps erect a barrier that affirms group identity, thus strengthening group solidarity. But using symbols to establish group identity also underscores, perhaps unconsciously, how similar all humans are to one another. The "other," once we take a really good look, turns out to be remarkably similar to ourselves. So similar, in fact, that with a few alterations of dress and practice—and diet—the "them" could become us.

The Secrets of Haiti's Living Dead

A Harvard botanist investigates mystic potions, voodoo rites, and the making of zombies.

Gino Del Guercio

Gino Del Guercio is a national science writer for United Press International.

Five years ago, a man walked into l'Estère, a village in central Haiti, approached a peasant woman named Angelina Narcisse, and identified himself as her brother Clairvius. If he had not introduced himself using a boyhood nickname and mentioned facts only intimate family members knew, she would not have believed him. Because, eighteen years earlier, Angelina had stood in a small cemetery north of her village and watched as her brother Clairvius was buried.

The man told Angelina he remembered that night well. He knew when he was lowered into his grave, because he was fully conscious, although he could not speak or move. As the earth was thrown over his coffin, he felt as if he were floating over the grave. The scar on his right cheek, he said, was caused by a nail driven through his casket.

The night he was buried, he told Angelina, a voodoo priest raised him from the grave. He was beaten with a sisal whip and carried off to a sugar plantation in northern Haiti where, with other zombies, he was forced to work as a slave. Only with the death of the zombie master were they able to escape, and Narcisse eventually returned home.

Legend has it that zombies are the living dead, raised from their graves and animated by malevolent voodoo sorcer-

ers, usually for some evil purpose. Most Haitians believe in zombies, and Narcisse's claim is not unique. At about the time he reappeared, in 1980, two women turned up in other villages saying they were zombies. In the same year, in northern Haiti, the local peasants claimed to have found a group of zombies wandering aimlessly in the fields.

But Narcisse's case was different in one crucial respect; it was documented. His death had been recorded by doctors at the American-directed Schweitzer Hospital in Deschapelles. On April 30, 1962, hospital records show, Narcisse walked into the hospital's emergency room spitting up blood. He was feverish and full of aches. His doctors could not diagnose his illness, and his symptoms grew steadily worse. Three days after he entered the hospital, according to the records, he died. The attending physicians, an American among them, signed his death certificate. His body was placed in cold storage for twenty hours, and then he was buried. He said he remembered hearing his doctors pronounce him dead while his sister wept at his bedside.

At the Centre de Psychiatrie et Neurologie in Port-au-Prince, Dr. Lamarque Douyon, a Haitian-born, Canadian-trained psychiatrist, has been systematically investigating all reports of zombies since 1961. Though convinced zombies were real, he had been unable to find a scientific explanation for the phenomenon.

He did not believe zombies were people raised from the dead, but that did not make them any less interesting. He speculated that victims were only made to *look* dead, probably by means of a drug that dramatically slowed metabolism. The victim was buried, dug up within a few hours, and somehow reawakened.

The Narcisse case provided Douyon with evidence strong enough to warrant a request for assistance from colleagues in New York. Douyon wanted to find an ethnobotanist, a traditional-medicines expert, who could track down the zombie potion he was sure existed. Aware of the medical potential of a drug that could dramatically lower metabolism, a group organized by the late Dr. Nathan Kline—a New York psychiatrist and pioneer in the field of psychopharmacology—raised the funds necessary to send someone to investigate.

The search for that someone led to the Harvard Botanical Museum, one of the world's foremost institutes of ethnobiology. Its director, Richard Evans Schultes, Jeffrey professor of biology, had spent thirteen years in the tropics studying native medicines. Some of his best-known work is the investigation of curare, the substance used by the nomadic people of the Amazon to poison their darts. Refined into a powerful muscle relaxant called D-tubocurarine, it is now an essential component of the anesthesia used during almost all surgery.

Schultes would have been a natural for the Haitian investigation, but he was too busy. He recommended another Harvard ethnobotanist for the assignment, Wade Davis, a 28-year-old Canadian pursuing a doctorate in biology.

Davis grew up in the tall pine forests of British Columbia and entered Harvard in 1971, influenced by a Life magazine story on the student strike of 1969. Before Harvard, the only Americans he had known were draft dodgers, who seemed very exotic. "I used to fight forest fires with them," Davis says. "Like everybody else, I thought America was where it was at. And I wanted to go to Harvard because of that Life article. When I got there, I realized it wasn't quite what I had in mind."

Davis took a course from Schultes, and when he decided to go to South America to study plants, he approached his professor for guidance. "He was an extraordinary figure," Davis remembers. "He was a man who had done it all. He had lived alone for years in the Amazon." Schultes sent Davis to the rain forest with two letters of introduction and two pieces of advice: wear a pith helmet and try ayahuasca, a powerful hallucinogenic vine. During that expedition and others, Davis proved himself an "outstanding field man," says his mentor. Now, in early 1982, Schultes called him into his office and asked if he had plans for spring break.

"I always took to Schultes's assignments like a plant takes to water," says Davis, tall and blond, with inquisitive blue eyes. "Whatever Schultes told me to do, I did. His letters of introduction opened up a whole world." This time the world was Haiti.

Davis knew nothing about the Caribbean island—and nothing about African traditions, which serve as Haiti's cultural basis. He certainly did not believe in zombies. "I thought it was a lark," he says now.

Davis landed in Haiti a week after his conversation with Schultes, armed with a hypothesis about how the zombie drug—if it existed—might be made. Setting out to explore, he discovered a country materially impoverished, but rich in culture and mystery. He was impressed by the cohesion of Haitian so-

ciety; he found none of the crime, social disorder, and rampant drug and alcohol abuse so common in many of the other Caribbean islands. The cultural wealth and cohesion, he believes, spring from the country's turbulent history.

During the French occupation of the late eighteenth century, 370,000 African-born slaves were imported to Haiti between 1780 and 1790. In 1791, the black population launched one of the few successful slave revolts in history, forming secret societies and overcoming first the French plantation owners and then a detachment of troops from Napoleon's army, sent to quell the revolt. For the next hundred years Haiti was the only independent black republic in the Caribbean, populated by people who did not forget their African heritage. "You can almost argue that Haiti is more African than Africa," Davis says. "When the west coast of Africa was being disrupted by colonialism and the slave trade, Haiti was essentially left alone. The amalgam of beliefs in Haiti is unique, but it's very, very African."

Davis discovered that the vast majority of Haitian peasants practice voodoo, a sophisticated religion with African roots. Says Davis, "It was immediately obvious that the stereotypes of voodoo weren't true. Going around the countryside, I found clues to a whole complex social world." Vodounists believe they communicate directly with, indeed are often possessed by, the many spirits who populate the everyday world. Vodoun society is a system of education, law, and medicine; it embodies a code of ethics that regulates social behavior. In rural areas, secret vodoun societies, much like those found on the west coast of Africa, are as much or more in control of everyday life as the Haitian government.

Although most outsiders dismissed the zombie phenomenon as folklore, some early investigators, convinced of its reality, tried to find a scientific explanation. The few who sought a zombie drug failed. Nathan Kline, who helped finance Davis's expedition, had searched unsuccessfully, as had Lamarque Douyon, the Haitian psychiatrist. Zora Neale Hurston, an American black woman, may have come closest. An anthropological

pioneer, she went to Haiti in the Thirties, studied vodoun society, and wrote a book on the subject, *Tell My Horse*, first published in 1938. She knew about the secret societies and was convinced zombies were real, but if a power existed, she too failed to obtain it.

Davis obtained a sample in a few weeks.

He arrived in Haiti with the names of several contacts. A BBC reporter familiar with the Narcisse case had suggested he talk with Marcel Pierre. Pierre owned the Eagle Bar, a bordello in the city of Saint Marc. He was also a voodoo sorcerer and had supplied the BBC with a physiologically active powder of unknown ingredients. Davis found him willing to negotiate. He told Pierre he was a representative of "powerful but anonymous interests in New York," willing to pay generously for the priest's services, provided no questions were asked. Pierre agreed to be helpful for what Davis will only say was a "sizable sum." Davis spent a day watching Pierre gather the ingredients—including human bones—and grind them together with mortar and pestle. However, from his knowledge of poison, Davis knew immediately that nothing in the formula could produce the powerful effects of zombification.

Three weeks later, Davis went back to the Eagle Bar, where he found Pierre sitting with three associates. Davis challenged him. He called him a charlatan. Enraged, the priest gave him a second vial, claiming that this was the real poison. Davis pretended to pour the powder into his palm and rub it into his skin. "You're a dead man," Pierre told him, and he might have been, because this powder proved to be genuine. But, as the substance had not actually touched him, Davis was able to maintain his bravado, and Pierre was impressed. He agreed to make the poison and show Davis how it was done.

The powder, which Davis keeps in a small vial, looks like dry black dirt. It contains parts of toads, sea worms, lizards, tarantulas, and human bones. (To obtain the last ingredient, he and Pierre unearthed a child's grave on a nocturnal trip to the cemetery.) The poison is rubbed into the victim's skin. Within hours he begins to feel nauseated and has difficulty breathing. A pins-and-needles sensation afflicts his arms and legs, then progresses to the whole body. The subject becomes paralyzed; his lips turn blue for lack of oxygen. Quickly—sometimes within six hours—his metabolism is lowered to a level almost indistinguishable from death.

As Davis discovered, making the poison is an inexact science. Ingredients varied in the five samples he eventually acquired, although the active agents were always the same. And the poison came with no guarantee. Davis speculates that sometimes instead of merely paralyzing the victim, the compound kills him. Sometimes the victim suffocates in the coffin before he can be resurrected. But clearly the potion works well enough often enough to make zombies more than a figment of Haitian imagination.

Analysis of the powder produced another surprise. "When I went down to Haiti originally," says Davis, "my hypothesis was that the formula would contain *concombre zombi*, the 'zombie's cucumber,' which is a *Datura* plant. I thought somehow *Datura* was used in putting people down." *Datura* is a powerful psychoactive plant, found in West Africa as well as other tropical areas and used there in ritual as well as criminal activities. Davis had found *Datura* growing in Haiti. Its popular name suggested the plant was used in creating zombies.

But, says Davis, "there were a lot of problems with the *Datura* hypothesis. Partly it was a question of how the drug was administered. *Datura* would create a stupor in huge doses, but it just wouldn't produce the kind of immobility that was key. These people had to appear dead, and there aren't many drugs that will do that."

One of the ingredients Pierre included in the second formula was a dried fish, a species of puffer or blowfish, common to most parts of the world. It gets its name from its ability to fill itself with water and swell to several times its normal size when threatened by predators. Many of these fish contain a powerful poison known as tetrodotoxin. One of the most powerful nonprotein poisons known to man, tetrodotoxin turned up in every sample of zombie powder that Davis acquired.

Numerous well-documented accounts of puffer fish poisoning exist, but the most famous accounts come from the Orient, where *fugu* fish, a species of puffer, is considered a delicacy. In Japan, special chefs are licensed to prepare *fugu*. The chef removes enough poison to make the fish nonlethal, yet enough remains to create exhilarating physiological effects—tingles up and down the spine, mild prickling of the tongue and lips, euphoria. Several dozen Japanese die each year, having bitten off more than they should have.

"When I got hold of the formula and saw it was the *fugu* fish, that suddenly threw open the whole Japanese literature," says Davis. Case histories of *fugu* poisoning read like accounts of zombification. Victims remain conscious but unable to speak or move. A man who had "died" after eating *fugu* recovered seven days later in the morgue. Several summers ago, another Japanese poisoned by *fugu* revived after he was nailed into his coffin. "Almost all of Narcisse's symptoms correlated. Even strange things such as the fact that he said he was conscious and could hear himself pronounced dead. Stuff that I thought had to be magic, that seemed crazy. But, in fact, that is what people who get *fugu*-fish poisoning experience."

Davis was certain he had solved the mystery. But far from being the end of his investigation, identifying the poison

---

Richard Schultes

His students continue his tradition of pursuing botanical research in the likeliest of unlikely places.

Richard Evans Schultes, Jeffrey professor of biology emeritus, has two homes, and they could not be more different. The first is Cambridge, where he served as director of the Harvard Botanical Museum from 1970 until last year, when he became director emeritus. During his tenure he interested generations of students in the exotic botany of the Amazon rain forest. His impact on the field through his own research is worldwide. The scholarly ethnobotanist with steel-rimmed glasses, bald head, and white lab coat is as much a part of the Botanical Museum as the thousands of plant specimens and botanical texts on the museum shelves.

In his austere office is a picture of a crew-cut, younger man stripped to the waist, his arms decorated with tribal paint. This is Schultes's other persona. Starting in 1941, he spent thirteen years in the rain forests of South America, living with the Indians and studying the plants they use for medicinal and spiritual purposes.

Schultes is concerned that many of the people he has studied are giving up traditional ways. "The people of so-called primitive societies are becoming civilized and losing all their forefathers' knowledge of plant lore," he says. "We'll be losing the tremendous amounts of knowledge they've gained over thousands of years. We've interested in the practical aspects with the hope that new medicines and other things can be developed for our own civilization."

Schultes's exploits are legendary in the biology department. Once, while gathering South American plant specimens hundreds of miles from civilization, he contracted beri-beri. For forty days he fought creeping paralysis and overwhelming fatigue as he paddled back to a doctor. "It was an extraordinary feat of endurance," says disciple Wade Davis. "He is really one of the last nineteenth-century naturalists."

Hallucinogenic plants are one of Schultes's primary interests. As a Harvard undergraduate in the Thirties, he lived with Oklahoma's Kiowa Indians to observe their use of plants. He participated in their peyote ceremonies and wrote his thesis on the hallucinogenic cactus. He has also studied other hallucinogens, such as morning glory seeds, sacred mushrooms, and ayahuasca, a South American vision vine. Schultes's work has led to the development of anesthetics made from curare and alternative sources of natural rubber.

Schultes's main concern these days is the scientific potential of plants in the rapidly disappearing Amazon jungle. "If chemists are going to get material on 80,000 species and then analyze them, they'll never finish the job before the jungle is gone," he says. "The short cut is to find out what the [native] people have learned about the plant properties during many years of living in the very rich flora."

—G.D.G.

was, in fact, its starting point. "The drug alone didn't make zombies," he explains. "Japanese victims of puffer-fish poisoning don't become zombies, they become poison victims. All the drug could do was set someone up for a whole series of psychological pressures that would be rooted in the culture. I wanted to know why zombification was going on," he says.

He sought a cultural answer, an explanation rooted in the structure and beliefs of Haitian society. Was zombification simply a random criminal activity? He thought not. He had discovered that Clairvius Narcisse and "Ti Femme," a second victim he interviewed, were village pariahs. Ti Femme was regarded as a thief. Narcisse had abandoned his children and deprived his brother of land that was rightfully his. Equally suggestive, Narcisse claimed that his aggrieved brother had sold him to a *bokor,* a voodoo priest who dealt in black magic; he made cryptic reference to having been tried and found guilty by the "masters of the land."

Gathering poisons from various parts of the country, Davis had come into direct contact with the vodoun secret societies. Returning to the anthropological literature on Haiti and pursuing his contacts with informants, Davis came to understand the social matrix within which zombies were created.

Davis's investigations uncovered the importance of the secret societies. These groups trace their origins to the bands of escaped slaves that organized the revolt against the French in the late eighteenth century. Open to both men and women, the societies control specific territories of the country. Their meetings take place at night, and in many rural parts of Haiti the drums and wild celebrations that characterize the gatherings can be heard for miles.

Davis believes the secret societies are responsible for policing their communities, and the threat of zombification is one way they maintain order. Says Davis, "Zombification has a material basis, but it also has a societal logic." To the uninitiated, the practice may appear a random criminal activity, but in rural vodoun society, it is exactly the opposite—a sanction imposed by recognized authorities, a form of capital punishment. For rural Haitians, zombification is an even more severe punishment than death, because it deprives the subject of his most valued possessions: his free will and independence.

The vodounists believe that when a person dies, his spirit splits into several different parts. If a priest is powerful enough, the spiritual aspect that controls a person's character and individuality, known as *ti bon ange,* the "good little angel," can be captured and the corporeal aspect, deprived of its will, held as a slave.

From studying the medical literature on tetrodotoxin poisoning, Davis discovered that if a victim survives the first few hours of the poisoning, he is likely to recover fully from the ordeal. The subject simply revives spontaneously. But zombies remain without will, in a trance-like state, a condition vodounists attribute to the power of the priest. Davis thinks it possible that the psychological trauma of zombification may be augmented by *Datura* or some other drug; he thinks zombies may be fed a *Datura* paste that accentuates their disorientation. Still, he puts the material basis of zombification in perspective: "Tetrodotoxin and *Datura* are only templates on which cultural forces and beliefs may be amplified a thousand times."

Davis has not been able to discover how prevalent zombification is in Haiti. "How many zombies there are is not the question," he says. He compares it to capital punishment in the United States: "It doesn't really matter how many people are electrocuted, as long as it's a possibility." As a sanction in Haiti, the fear is not of zombies, it's of becoming one.

Davis attributes his success in solving the zombie mystery to his approach. He went to Haiti with an open mind and immersed himself in the culture. "My intuition unhindered by biases served me well," he says. "I didn't make any judgments." He combined this attitude with what he had learned earlier from his experiences in the Amazon. "Schultes's lesson is to go and live with the Indians as an Indian." Davis was able to participate in the vodoun society to a surprising degree, eventually even penetrating one of the Bizango societies and dancing in their nocturnal rituals. His appreciation of Haitian culture is apparent. "Everybody asks me how did a white person get this information? To ask the question means you don't understand Haitians—they don't judge you by the color of your skin."

As a result of the exotic nature of his discoveries, Davis has gained a certain notoriety. He plans to complete his dissertation soon, but he has already finished writing a popular account of his adventures. To be published in January by Simon and Schuster, it is called *The Serpent and the Rainbow,* after the serpent that vodounists believe created the earth and the rainbow spirit it married. Film rights have already been optioned; in October Davis went back to Haiti with a screenwriter. But Davis takes the notoriety in stride. "All this attention is funny," he says. "For years, not just me, but all Schultes's students have had extraordinary adventures in the line of work. The adventure is not the end point, it's just along the way of getting the data. At the Botanical Museum, Schultes created a world unto itself. We didn't think we were doing anything above the ordinary. I still don't think we do. And you know," he adds, "the Haiti episode does not begin to compare to what others have accomplished—particularly Schultes himself."

Rituals of Death

Capital Punishment and Human Sacrifice

**Elizabeth D. Purdum
and J. Anthony Paredes**

We were perplexed by the resurgence of enthusiasm for the death penalty in the United States. According to a 1986 *Gallup Report,* support for the death penalty in America has reached a near-record high in 50 years of polling, with 70 percent of Americans favoring execution of convicted murderers (Gallup, 1986). In a 1983 poll conducted in Florida, 72 percent of respondents were found to support the death penalty, compared with 45 percent in 1964 (Cambridge Survey Research, 1985). Still more perplexing is the finding that nearly half of those supporting the death penalty agree that "only the poor and unfortunate are likely to be executed" (Ellsworth and Ross, 1983:153). Equally startling is the revelation that although deterrence is often given as a primary justification for the death penalty, most people would continue to support it even if convinced that it had no greater deterrent effect than that of a life sentence (P. Harris, 1986). In addition, there is little if any evidence that capital punishment reduces the crime rate; there seems, rather, to be some historical evidence for a reverse correlation. Pickpocketing, a crime then punishable by hanging, was rampant among spectators at executions in England circa 1700 (Lofland, 1977). Bowers and Pierce (1980) argue, on the basis of increased murder rates in New York State in the month following executions, that capital punishment has a "brutalizing" effect and leads to more, not less, violence. Why, then, does capital punishment re-

ceive such widespread support in modern America?

Capital Punishment— Another "Riddle of Culture"

In theory, capital punishment should be no more a puzzle than any other seemingly bizarre, nonrational custom. Either human cultures are amendable to scientific explanation or they are not. And we anthropologists have not been timid about tackling everything from Arunta penile subincision to Hindu cow love as problems for scientific explication. As a first step in this task, we will compare capital punishment in Florida, the leader in the United States in death sentencing since Florida's 1972 capital punishment statute was affirmed by the U.S. Supreme Court in 1976, with certain forms of human sacrifice as practiced by the Aztecs of Mexico in the sixteenth century. This is not a capricious comparison. John Cooper (1976) pointedly seeks the "socio-religious origins of capital punishment" in ancient rites of, to use his term, "propitiatory death." But his study is narrowly constrained by canons of Western philosophy and history. By making a more exotic comparison, we hope to point the way to more nomothetic principles for understanding state-sanctioned homicide in complex societies. Albert Camus (1959) also perceived elements of religious ritual in French capital punishment, but argued that the practice continued

only because hidden from the view of the general public. Anticipating our comparisons here, anthropologist Colin Turnbull concludes in his article "Death by Decree" that the key to understanding capital punishment is to be found in its ritual element (1978). John Lofland (1977) has compared the dramaturgy of state executions circa 1700 in England with those of contemporary America, concluding that modern executions in their impersonal, unemotional, and private aspects appear humane, yet deny the reality of death and strip the condemned of any opportunity to die with dignity or courage.

It was the public media spectacle surrounding recent executions in Florida that triggered the thoughts leading to this paper. Detailed, minute-by-minute accounts of Florida's first post-1976 execution, widely reported press conferences with death row inmates, television images of the ambulance bearing the body of an executed criminal, news photos of mourners and revelers outside the prison on the night before an execution—all these served to transform a closely guarded, hidden expression of the ultimate power of the state into a very public ceremonial event. We were reminded of the pomp and circumstance for the masses accompanying the weird rites of Tenochtitlan that greeted sixteenth-century Spaniards. In such similarities, we thought, might lie the key to a dispassionate, anthropological understanding of capital punishment in modern America.

From *Facing the Death Penalty: Essays on a Cruel and Unusual Punishment,* edited by Michael Radelet, 1989, Chapter 10, pp. 139–155. © 1989 by Temple University Press. Reprinted by permission.

Before proceeding we must note that the Aztec state itself imposed capital punishment for a variety of crimes, ranging from murder to fornication to violations of the dress code for commoners. The available sources indicate, however, that among the Aztecs capital punishment was swift, rather unceremonious, and even brutish. It is the high drama of Aztec rituals of human sacrifice that shows the closest parallels with the bureaucratically regulated procedures for electrocution of the condemned at Starke, Florida, in the 1980s.

The Victims of Execution and Sacrifice

The death penalty is imposed on only a small percentage of Americans convicted of homicide—5 percent, according to a 1980 Georgia study (Baldus et al., 1983). Today there are 2,182 people on death row in the United States; 296 of these are in Florida (NAACP Legal Defense and Educational Fund, 1988). Since 1976, 18 persons have been executed in Florida. Prior to 1972, when the Supreme Court voided state death penalty statutes, it was clear that the death penalty was disproportionately applied to black men. Fifty-four percent of the 3,859 people executed in the United States between 1930 and 1967 were nonwhite. Among those executed for rape during the same period, 405 of 455 were black (U.S. Department of Justice, 1986). Nakell and Hardy's study of homicide cases in North Carolina from 1977 and 1978 revealed the effects of race of victim and race of defendant throughout the criminal justice process (1987). The relationship between race and execution consistently holds even when one controls for such factors as differential conviction rates and the relationship between the defendant and the victim (Radelet, 1981).

Recent studies (for example, Baldus et al., 1983a; Bowers and Pierce, 1980b; Gross and Mauro, 1984; Pasternoster, 1983; and Radelet, 1981) suggest that the defendant's race, since the reinstatement of the death penalty in 1976, is less important than it once was in predicting death sentences. These studies conclude that a more significant factor is the race of the victim: that is, people who kill whites are more likely to receive the death penalty than people who kill blacks.

Statistics aside, people familiar with death row inmates readily acknowledge that they are marginal members of society—economically, socially, and, even, in the case of Florida, geographically. Many come from backgrounds of extreme poverty and abuse. Michael Radelet and his colleagues (1983) report one common denominator among families who have members in prison: low socioeconomic status. Poverty makes it hard, if not impossible, for families to maintain ties with prisoners. Many inmates on death row have few family or social ties. Only about 15 of the 208 men on death row in Florida in 1983 had visitors each week; 60 others had visitors about once a month; and fewer than half received a visitor in any given year (Radelet et al., 1983). Many of Florida's inmates are from out of state. More than a few of Florida's death row inmates are also crazy, retarded, or both. For instance, Arthur Goode, who was convicted of murdering a nine-year-old boy, ate a half-gallon of butter pecan ice cream, his requested "last meal," then gave as his final statement his desire to marry a young boy. In the three weeks before his execution, Goode wrote letters to the governor and other prominent officials complaining of the lack of toilet paper to blow his nose (Radelet and Barnard, 1986). There is an inmate who believes that one of the people helping him with his court appeals is alternately a dead disc jockey or one of his own seven wives. Or, there is James Douglas Hill, a 26-year-old with an IQ of 66 and a serious speech impediment, who, having learned to read and write while in prison, sent to his mother this message:

> Hi mom me hour are you doing to day fine i hope i am doing ok for now But i miss you so varry varry much that i can cry But i am to Big to cry. . . . i miss you i miss you love James all way. By now. (Sherrill, 1984:555)

In 1987 James Douglas Hill was released on bail when substantial doubt about his guilt surfaced.

Detailed statistics on *whom* the Aztecs put to death in their rites of human sacrifice are not available, nor is the exact number of sacrificial victims. Nonetheless, the Aztecs of Central Mexico sacrificed humans on a scale unprecedented in any other society. Putting aside the question of whether the Aztecs were nutritionally motivated toward this human slaughter (Harner, 1977), annual estimates for central Mexico in the first decades of the sixteenth century vary from 20,000 (Cortes, as quoted by Fagan, 1984:230) to 250,000 sacrificed victims (Woodrow Borah, as quoted by Harner, 1977:119).

Most of the sacrificial victims were able-bodied male war captives from neighboring kingdoms, but the Aztecs reportedly also sacrificed large numbers of children—sold to the priests by the poor. The children's tears were believed to be particularly appealing to Tlaloc, the rain god. Women were also sometimes sacrificed, some of them presented as impersonations of certain female deities. Similarly, one of the most frequently recounted, and often highly romanticized, forms of Aztec human sacrifice was that in which a flawless young war captive was pampered and indulged for a year as the embodiment of a god, then killed with great ritual and sadness while the victim dutifully played his role in the deicidal drama. Most Aztec war captives enjoyed no such protracted special treatment. How god-impersonators were selected we do not know. Neither do we know how many war captives' lives were spared, if any, nor how many were doomed to a life of slavery.

Paralleling the numerous means of execution employed in the United States —electrocution, hanging, firing squad, deadly gas, lethal injection—the Aztecs sacrificed their victims with a variety of techniques. These included beheading, burning, and flights of arrows, but the most common method was to spread the victim on a large, elaborately carved stone, cut open his chest with an obsidian knife, then tear out his heart. We present here a brief, composite account of "ordinary" war captive sacrifice using the method of coronary excision.

Announcement of Death

According to Fray Diego Duran's account of the aftermath of a battle between the Aztecs and the Tepeacas, the Tepeacan captives were taken back to the Aztec capital, Tenochtitlan, with collars around their necks and their hands bound behind them. The captives "went along singing sadly, weeping and lamenting their fate," knowing they were to be sacrificed. Once they were in the capital, priests threw incense on them, offered them maize bread, and said:

> We welcome you
> To this city of Mexico Tenochtitlan
> . . . .
> Do you think that you have come to live;
> You have come to die.
> . . . .
> We salute you and comfort you with these words:
> You have not come because of weakness,
> But because of your manliness.
> You will die here but your fame will live forever.
>
> (Duran, 1964:101)

The announcement of a Florida death row inmate's impending death comes with the signing of a death warrant by the state governor, once all routine appeals and bids for clemency have failed. The criteria by which the decision is made to sign a warrant against a particular person at a particular time are not publicly known.

A death warrant is a single-page document in legal language, bordered in black. Each one bears the state seal and is officially witnessed by the secretary of state—not by some seemingly more likely authority such as the attorney general. Each death warrant is publicized by a news release issued shortly after the governor signs. Between 1972 and the end of 1988, Florida's three governors signed over two hundred death warrants. Once the warrant is signed in Tallahassee, the superintendent of Florida State Prison at Starke, 150 miles away, is immediately notified. Prison guards are sent to get the person named in the warrant from his or her cell. They bring the prisoner, who may have no forewarning of what is about to happen, to the assistant superintendent's office. There the superintendent or his designee reads the warrant aloud to the condemned. Following a string of "whereas's" tracing the history of the case, the warrant concludes:

> Now, therefore, I, [names governor], as Governor of the State of Florida and pursuant to the authority and responsibility vested by the Constitution and the laws of Florida do hereby issue this warrant directing the Superintendent of the Florida State Prison to cause the sentence of death to be executed upon [name person] on some day of the week beginning [for instance] Noon, Tuesday, the 29th day of October, 1989, and ending Noon, Tuesday, the 5th day of November, 1989, in accord with the provisions of the laws of the State of Florida.

The warrant is usually dated four weeks before the last day the warrant is in effect. Reportedly, warrants are never issued for executions to take place during the time the state supreme court is not in session or during the Christmas season. After the warrant is read, the prisoner is permitted to telephone a lawyer and a family member, if he or she has any.

Treatment After Announcement of Death

Aztec war captives were served "Divine Wine" (probably pulque) and paraded past images of the Aztec gods and past the emperor, Montezuma. They were given cloaks, loincloths, and sandals—sandals being a mark of nobility. Next, the prisoners were taken to the central marketplace, where they were given flowers and "shields of splendid featherwork" and forced to dance upon a platform. The condemned were also given tobacco to smoke, which, according to Duran, "comforted them greatly" (Duran, 1964:102).

The war captives were dispersed among the several wards of the city, and men were assigned to guard and maintain them with the charge:

> Take care that they do not escape Take care that they do not die! Behold, they are children of the Sun! Feed them well; let them be fat and desirable for the sacrifice. . . .
>
> (Duran, 1964:108)

Duran (1964) reports that captives were treated well and honored as if they were gods.

Many days passed during which craftsmen were instructed to carve a stone for the sacrificial altar. A few days later the altar was ready, and temple youths were given instructions about how the sacrifice was to be conducted. Guests were invited from neighboring states, and booths were decorated for spectators.

In Florida, the reading of the death warrant initiates a period officially designated as "death watch," marked by moving the person to a cell in "Q Wing," where he or she will be closer to the electric chair and isolated from other death row inmates. Most of the person's possessions are taken away, including photographs and tennis shoes, the only personally owned item of apparel that inmates are ordinarily allowed; the condemned is allowed to retain only those items listed in the "Execution Guidelines," a 39-page single-spaced document (Florida State Prison, 1983). The only books on the list are "religious tracts as distributed by Institution Chaplain, maximum possession ten (10)." Magazine and newspaper subscriptions may continue, but no new periodicals may be ordered. In a curious specific parallel with Aztec practice, there are no special restrictions on tobacco for prisoners on Q Wing. Three meals a day are fed to all "condemned inmates," and dietary restrictions for "medical reasons" continue to be observed. Indeed, meticulous, detailed instructions are given to prison personnel to ensure that the condemned person is kept in good health and not provided with any item that might be used to harm himself or attempt suicide. Moreover, under current procedures if a prisoner is determined to have become insane on death row, he or she is spared execution until restored to mental health (Radelet and Barnard, 1986).

Once death watch begins, social visits are "noncontact" and held in the "maximum security visiting park" any two days, Monday through Friday, 9 A.M. to 3 P.M. Other death row inmates are permitted "contact" social visits for six hours on Saturdays or Sundays. Legal visits for the condemned may continue to be the "contact" type during the death warrant, but only until one week before execution, when these visits, too, become noncontact. Media visits are scheduled through prison officials on Tuesday, Wednesday, and Thursday until Phase II of death watch begins, five days before the execution is scheduled to occur.

With Phase II of death watch, more property is taken from the prisoner. The condemned is allowed only a few so-called comfort items: "one TV located outside cell, 1 radio, 1 deck of cards, 1 Bible, 1 book, periodical, magazine or newspaper." Very specific day-by-day regulations and procedures now go into effect, beginning with "Execution Day—Minus Five (5)," when the "execution squad" is identified. Likewise, on Execution Day—Minus Four (4), testing of the electrical equipment to be used for execution begins. During Phase II the inmate is subjected to further limitations on visits, but during the 48 hours before the scheduled execution, the condemned may have an interview with a media representative of his or her choice. Execution Day—Minus Four (4) is a particularly busy day: the condemned reinventories his or her property and specifies in writing its disposition; specifies in writing his or her funeral arrangements; and is measured for a suit of clothing—the suit will be cheap—in which the condemned will, if he or she wants, be buried. On Day—Minus Three (3) there are "no activities," and Day—Minus Two (2) is devoted primarily to testing the equipment and "execution squad drill." On Execution Day—Minus One (1) the pace quickens, and it is on this day that the chef takes the person's order for the last meal.

Each time the prisoner is moved during Phase II of death watch, the entire prison is locked down and the condemned undergoes a complete body search upon being returned to his or her cell. A guard sits outside the condemned inmate's cell, as one always does during an active death warrant, but now the guard records every 15 minutes what the prisoner is doing.

Final Preparations for Death

On the day of an Aztec sacrifice, the visiting nobles were seated in their decorated booths and the prisoners were placed in a line before them and made to dance. The victims were smeared with plaster; white feathers were tied to their hair; their eyelids were blackened and their lips painted red. Priests who would perform the actual sacrifice stood in a long row according to their rank. Each priest was disguised as a god and carried a richly decorated sword and shield. The priests sat under a beautifully adorned arbor erected at the summit of a large, truncated pyramid. Chanters came forth and began to dance and sing.

In Florida, sometime around midnight on the night before an execution, the condemned is usually allowed a last one-hour contact visit. The person is permitted to see his own clergyman if he has one, but only the prison chaplain will be permitted to accompany the inmate to the place of execution. At 4:30 A.M. the prisoner is served his or her last meal, to be eaten on a paper plate with a spoon; if the prisoner has requested a steak, the chef has cut the meat into bite-sized pieces beforehand and arranged them to appear to be an intact steak. No later than 5:30 A.M., the official witnesses to the execution, 12 in number (one of whom may be designated by the condemned), must assemble at the main prison gate. At 5:50 A.M. the media witnesses, also 12 in number, are picked up at the "media onlooker area." Both types of witnesses will later be "escorted to the witness room of the execution chamber." At 6:00 A.M. an administrative assistant, three designated electricians, a physician, and a physician's assistant are assembled in the death chamber. The administrative assistant establishes telephone contact with the state governor's office. Meanwhile, the condemned inmate has his or her head and right calf shaved (to better conduct electricity), takes a shower under the supervision of a high-ranking prison official, and is dressed in his or her new burial clothes, omitting the suit jacket and shoes. Until recently, by informal custom the prison superintendent would then have a drink of whisky with the condemned in his cell, but public outcry was so great that the practice was discontinued. At 6:50 "conducting gel" is applied to the person's head and leg.

The superintendent reads the death warrant to the condemned a final time.

The Moment of Death

Each Aztec victim was taken singly to the sacrificial stone and tethered to it by a rope. In one form of sacrifice, in a mockery of self-defense, the victim was then given a sword edged with feathers rather than obsidian. The high priest rose and descended to the stone, walked around it twice and returned to his seat. Next, an old man disguised as an ocelot gave the captive four wooden balls and a drink of "Divine Wine" and instructed him to defend himself. Many victims tried to defend themselves against a series of ceremonially garbed priest-warriors, but others "unwilling to undergo such ceremony cast themselves upon the stone seeking a quick death" (Duran, 1964:112). Death was inevitable: as soon as the captive was wounded, four priests painted black, with long braided hair and garments resembling chasubles, spread-eagled the victim on the stone, each priest holding a limb. The high priest cut open the victim's chest with an obsidian knife, pulled out the victim's heart and offered the organ to the sun. The heart was deposited in a jar or placed on a brazier, and the next victim was brought forward.

The superintendent of Florida State Prison at Starke and two other prison officials escort the condemned inmate to the death chamber at 6:56 A.M. The person is strapped into the electric chair. At 7:00 A.M. the condemned is permitted to make a last statement. The governor directs the superintendent to proceed with the execution, traditionally concluding with the words "God save us all." The witnesses have been seated in their peculiarly carved, white high-backed chairs. The electrician places the sponge and cap on the inmate's head. The assistant superintendent engages the circuit breaker. The electrician activates the panel, the superintendent signals the executioner to throw the switch, and the "automatic cycle will begin." The actual executioner is an anonymous private citizen dressed in a black hood and robe who will be paid $150 for his services. Once the automatic cycle has run its course, the superintendent invites the doctor to conduct the examination. If all has gone well, the condemned is pronounced dead and the time recorded. A designated prison official proclaims, "The sentence of _____ has been carried out. Please exit to the rear at this time." By custom, someone in attendance waves a white cloth just outside the prison to signal the crowd assembled in a field across from it—reporters, death penalty opponents and proponents, and any others—that the deed is done. Official guidelines for the execution of more than one inmate on a single day exist, but we will dispense with those here.

After Death

Fray Bernardino de Sahagun (1951: 24) reports that after each Aztec captive had been slain, the body was taken gently away and rolled down the stairs of the sacrificial pyramid. At the bottom, the victim's head was cut off for display on a rack and the remainder of the corpse was taken to one of the special houses, *calpulli*, where "they divided [the bodies] up in order to eat them." Meanwhile, those who had taken part in the sacrifice entered a temple, removed their ritual garb, and were rewarded with fine clothes and a feast. The lords from the provinces who had been brought to observe were "shocked and bewildered."

As soon as a Florida inmate is pronounced dead in the electric chair, ambulance attendants are called into the chamber; they remove the inmate from the chair and take the body to a waiting ambulance, which transports the corpse to the medical examiner's office. There an autopsy is performed. Until recently, portions of the brain were removed for secret study by a University of Florida researcher investigating the relationship between "head trauma and violent behavior." This procedure was followed for 11 of the 13 men executed between 1979 and 1985, but was stopped in response to negative publicity. Once the autopsy is completed, the corpse is released to the funeral home for cremation or burial. If the deceased has made no arrangements for a private funeral, his

or her body is interred on the prison grounds. The executioner, meanwhile, is returned to his secret pick-up point and compensated. There is a "debriefing" at the prison of all the other participants in the execution save one.

The Native Explanations

What explanations are given by Aztecs and modern Americans for these decidedly gruesome acts? While we will probably never know what the Aztec man in the street thought of the sacrificial murders committed by his priests and nobles, official theology, if we may trust the sources, held that the gods had to be fed and placated to keep the crops growing, the sun high, and the universe in healthy order. Unfortunately for war captives, one of the gods' favorite foods was human hearts.

The explanations given by Americans for capital punishment generally are clothed in more pragmatic, secular terms. Most commonly, supporters of capital punishment invoke stimulus-response psychology and declare that such punishment will prevent others from committing heinous crimes. For instance, following the execution of an admitted child-murderer, Florida's governor declared that "he hoped the execution would be a warning to others who harbored the desire to mistreat children" (Sherrill, 1984:553). Other explanations emphasize the lower cost of execution as compared with long-term imprisonment, the need to provide families of murder victims with a sense of justice and mental repose, and what might be called the "social hygiene" approach: "[S]ome people just ought to be eliminated—we kill rattlesnakes, we don't keep them as pets," declared one Florida Supreme Court justice (*Tallahassee Democrat*, 15 Sept. 1985).

Despite the rationalistic cast of the most common public explanations for capital punishment, at least some of the explanations, or justifications, that surface into public view are unabashedly religious. The author of a letter to the Tallahassee Democrat (6 Feb. 1985) cited scripture to argue that earthly governments have the God-given right and

authority "to make and enforce laws, including the right to take human life." He urged his readers to submit " 'to every ordinance of man for the Lord's sake,' " for in so doing evildoers will be punished, those who do well will be praised, and " 'ye will put to silence the ignorance of foolish men' (I Peter 2:13–15)." We suspect that beneath more sophisticated explanations for capital punishment there is, if not an outright appeal to supernatural authority, the same deepseated set of nameless fears and anxieties that motivate humans everywhere to commit ceremonial acts that reassure and give substance to the Durkheimian view that "religion is society collectively worshipping itself."

Conclusion

The perceptive reader will have recognized the sometimes startling points of similarity between the conduct of some forms of Aztec human sacrifice and capital punishment in Florida. There are, of course, some profoundly important points of difference as well. We will not belabor the obvious here, but given the many commonalities in the organization, procedures, and even physical appurtenances between Aztec human sacrifice and Florida capital punishment, it is reasonable to propose that whatever psychosocial functions human sacrifice might have served in the Aztec empire, they are matched by similar functions for capital punishment in the United States. Just as Aztec ripping out of human hearts was couched in mystical terms of maintaining universal order and well-being of the state (putting aside the question of the utility of such practices as terror tactics with which to intimidate neighboring societies), we propose that capital punishment in the United States serves to assure many that society is not out of control after all, that the majesty of the Law reigns, and that God is indeed in his heaven. Precise, emic ("native") corroboration of our interpretation of capital punishment as the ultimate validator of law is provided by an automobile bumper sticker first seen in Tallahassee in 1987, shortly after the Florida legislature passed a controversial statute requiring automobile passengers to wear safety belts:

**I'LL BUCKLE UP—
WHEN BUNDY DOES
IT'S THE LAW**

"Bundy" is Theodore Bundy, Florida's most famous prisoner sentenced to be "buckled up" in the electric chair.

Sources as diverse as the populist *National Enquirer* (Mitteager, 1985) and the eminent legal scholar Lawrence Friedman (1973) instruct their readers that the crime rate is actually far lower today than 100 years ago. But through the mass media, the average American is subjected to a daily diet of fanatical terrorists, crazed rapists, revolting child molesters, and ghoulish murderers, to say nothing of dishonest politicians, unruly protestors, welfare and tax cheats, greedy gurus and philandering preachers, marauding street gangs, sexual perverts, and drug fiends, while all the time having to deal with the everyday personal irritations of a society in which, as Marvin Harris (1981) tells us, nothing works, mothers leave home, and gays come out of the closet. In an ironic twist on the anthropological debate (e.g., Isaac, 1983; Ortiz de Montellano, 1982; Price, 1978) over Harner's proposed materialist explanation of Aztec human sacrifice, we hypothesize that the current groundswell of support for capital punishment in the United States springs from the universal, ancient human impulse to do something in times of stress, even if it is only ritual. Bronislaw Malinowski observed that "there are no peoples however primitive without religion and magic" (1954:17); neither are there peoples so civilized that they are devoid of magic. All peoples turn to magic when knowledge, technology, and experience fail (Malinowski, 1954). In the face of all the evidence that capital punishment does no more to deter crime

than the bloody rituals of Tenochtitlan did to keep the sun in the sky, we must seek some broader, noninstrumental function that the death penalty serves. We propose, in short, that modern capital punishment is an institutionalized *magical* response to perceived disorder in American life and in the world at large, an attempted magical solution that has an especial appeal to the beleaguered, white, God-fearing men and women of the working class. And in certain aspiring politicians they find their sacrificial priests.

References

Baldus, David C.; Charles A. Pulaski, Jr.; and George Woodworth. 1983. "Comparative Review of Death Sentences: An Empirical Study of the Georgia Experience." *Journal of Criminal Law and Criminology* 74:661–753.

Bowers, William, J., and Glenn L. Pierce. 1980. "Deterrence or Brutalization: What Is the Effect of Executions?" *Crime and Delinquency* 26:453–84.

———. 1980. "Arbitrariness and Discrimination Under Post-*Furman* Capital Statutes." *Crime and Delinquency* 26:563–635.

Cambridge Survey Research. 1985. "An Analysis of Attitudes Toward Capital Punishment in Florida." Prepared for Amnesty International.

Camus, Albert, 1959. *Reflections on the Guillotine.* Michigan City, Ind.: Fridtjof-Karla.

Cooper, John W. 1976. "Propitiation as Social Maintenance: A Study of Capital Punishment Through the Sociology of Religion." M. A. thesis, Florida State University.

Duran, Fray Diego, 1964. *The Aztecs.* New York: Orion Press.

Ellsworth, Phoebe C., and Lee Ross. 1983. "Public Opinion and Capital Punishment: A Close Examination of the Views of Abolitionists and Retentionists." *Crime and Delinquency* 29: 116–69.

Fagan, Brian M. 1984. *The Aztecs.* New York: W. H. Freeman.

Florida State Prison. 1983. "Execution Guidelines During Active Death Warrant." Starke: Florida State Prison. Reprinted in part at pp. 235–40 of Amnesty International, *United States of America: The Death Penalty.* London: Amnesty International, 1987.

Friedman, Lawrence M. 1973. *A History of American Law.* New York: Simon and Schuster.

Gallup, George. 1986. "The Death Penalty." *Gallup Report* 244–45 (Jan.–Feb.) 10–16.

Gross, Samuel R., and Robert Mauro. 1984. "Patterns of Death: An Analysis of Racial Disparities in Capital Sentencing and Homicide Victimization." *Stanford Law Review* 37:27–153.

Harner, Michael. 1977. "The Ecological Basis for Aztec Sacrifice." *American Ethnologist* 4:117–35.

Harris, Marvin. 1981. *America Now: The Anthropology of a Changing Culture.* New York: Simon and Schuster.

Harris, Philip W. 1986. "Over-Simplification and Error in Public Opinion Surveys on Capital Punishment." *Justice Quarterly* 3:429–55.

Isaac, Barry L. 1983. "The Aztec 'Flowery War': A Geopolitical Explanation." *Journal of Anthropological Research* 39:415–32.

Lofland, John. 1977. "The Dramaturgy of State Executions." Pp. 275–325 in *State Executions Viewed Historically and Sociologically,* by Horace Bleackley. Montclair, N.J.: Patterson Smith.

Malinowski, Bronislaw. 1954. *Magic, Science and Religion and Other Essays.* Garden City, N.Y.: Doubleday.

Mitteager, James. 1985. "Think Crime Is Bad Now? It Was Much Worse 100 Years Ago." *National Enquirer,* 25 Nov., p. 25.

NAACP Legal Defense and Educational Fund. 1988. "Death Row, U.S.A." unpublished compilation, available from 99 Hudson St., New York, N.Y. 10013.

Nakell, Barry, and Kenneth A. Hardy. 1987 *The Arbitrariness of the Death Penalty.* Philadelphia: Temple University Press.

Ortiz de Montellano, Bernard R. 1982. "The Body Dangerous: Physiology and Social Stratification." *Reviews in Anthropology* 9:97–107.

Paternoster, Raymond. 1983. "Race of Victim and Location of Crime: The Decision to Seek the Death Penalty in South Carolina." *Journal of Criminal Law and Criminology* 74:754–85.

Price, Barbara J. 1978. "Demystification, Enriddlement and Aztec Cannibalism: A Materialist Rejoinder to Harner." *American Ethnologist* 5:98–115.

Radelet, Michael L. 1981. "Racial Characteristics and the Imposition of the Death Penalty." *American Sociological Review* 46:918–27.

Radelet, Michael L., and George W. Barnard. 1986. "Ethnics and the Psychiatric Determination of Competency to Be Executed." *Bulletin of the American Academy of Psychiatry and the Law* 14:37–53.

Radelet, Michael L.; Margaret Vandiver; and Felix M. Berardo. 1983. "Families, Prisons, and Men with Death Sentences: The Human Impact of Structured Uncertainty." *Journal of Family Issues* 4:593–612.

Sahagun, Fray Bernardino de. 1951. *General History of the Things of New Spain,* Santa Fe, N.M.: School of American Research and the University of Utah.

Sherrill, Robert. 1984. "In Florida, Insanity Is No Defense." *The Nation* 239:539, 552–56.

Turnbull, Colin. 1978. "Death by Decree." *Natural History* 87 (May):51–66.

U.S. Department of Justice. 1986. *Capital Punishment, 1984.* Washington, D.C.: U.S. Government Printing Office.

Body Ritual Among the Nacirema

Horace Miner

University of Michigan

The anthropologist has become so familiar with the diversity of ways in which different peoples behave in similar situations that he is not apt to be surprised by even the most exotic customs. In fact, if all of the logically possible combinations of behavior have not been found somewhere in the world, he is apt to suspect that they must be present in some yet undescribed tribe. This point has, in fact, been expressed with respect to clan organization by Murdock (1949: 71). In this light, the magical beliefs and practices of the Nacirema present such unusual aspects that it seems desirable to describe them as an example of the extremes to which human behavior can go.

Professor Linton first brought the ritual of the Nacirema to the attention of anthropologists twenty years ago (1936: 326), but the culture of this people is still very poorly understood. They are a North American group living in the territory between the Canadian Cree, the Yaqui and Tarahumare of Mexico, and the Carib and Arawak of the Antilles. Little is known of their origin, though tradition states that they came from the east. According to Nacirema mythology, their nation was originated by a culture hero, Notgnishaw, who is otherwise known for two great feats of strength—the throwing of a piece of wampum across the river Pa-To-Mac and the chopping down of a cherry tree in which the Spirit of Truth resided.

Nacirema culture is characterized by a highly developed market economy which has evolved in a rich natural habitat. While much of the people's time is devoted to economic pursuits, a large part of the fruits of these labors and a considerable portion of the day are spent in ritual activity. The focus of this activity is the human body, the appearance and health of which loom as a dominant concern in the ethos of the people. While such a concern is certainly not unusual, its ceremonial aspects and associated philosophy are unique.

The fundamental belief underlying the whole system appears to be that the human body is ugly and that its natural tendency is to debility and disease. Incarcerated in such a body, man's only hope is to avert these characteristics through the use of the powerful influences of ritual and ceremony. Every household has one or more shrines devoted to this purpose. The more powerful individuals in the society have several shrines in their houses and, in fact, the opulence of a house is often referred to in terms of the number of such ritual centers it possesses. Most houses are of wattle and daub construction, but the shrine rooms of the more wealthy are walled with stone. Poorer families imitate the rich by applying pottery plaques to their shrine walls.

While each family has at least one such shrine, the rituals associated with it are not family ceremonies but are private and secret. The rites are normally only discussed with children, and then only during the period when they are being initiated into these mysteries. I was able, however, to establish sufficient rapport with the natives to examine these shrines and to have the rituals described to me.

The focal point of the shrine is a box or chest which is built into the wall. In this chest are kept the many charms and magical potions without which no native believes he could live. These preparations are secured from a variety of specialized practitioners. The most powerful of these are the medicine men, whose assistance must be rewarded with substantial gifts. However, the medicine men do not provide the curative potions for their clients, but decide what the ingredients should be and then write them down in an ancient and secret language. This writing is understood only by the medicine men and by the herbalists who, for another gift, provide the required charm.

The charm is not disposed of after it has served its purpose, but is placed in the charm-box of the household shrine. As these magical materials are specific

From *American Anthropologist,* June 1956, pp. 503-507. © 1956 by the American Anthropological Association. Reprinted by permission. Not for further reproduction.

for certain ills, and the real or imagined maladies of the people are many, the charm-box is usually full to overflowing. The magical packets are so numerous that people forget what their purposes were and fear to use them again. While the natives are very vague on this point, we can only assume that the idea in retaining all the old magical materials is that their presence in the charm-box, before which the body rituals are conducted, will in some way protect the worshipper.

Beneath the charm-box is a small font. Each day every member of the family, in succession, enters the shrine room, bows his head before the charm-box, mingles different sorts of holy water in the font, and proceeds with a brief rite of ablution. The holy waters are secured from the Water Temple of the community, where the priests conduct elaborate ceremonies to make the liquid ritually pure.

In the hierarchy of magical practitioners, and below the medicine men in prestige, are specialists whose designation is best translated "holy-mouthmen." The Nacirema have an almost pathological horror and fascination with the mouth, the condition of which is believed to have a supernatural influence on all social relationships. Were it not for the rituals of the mouth, they believe that their teeth would fall out, their gums bleed, their jaws shrink, their friends desert them, and their lovers reject them. (They also believe that a strong relationship exists between oral and moral characteristics. For example, there is a ritual ablution of the mouth for children which is supposed to improve their moral fiber.)

The daily body ritual performed by everyone includes a mouth-rite. Despite the fact that these people are so punctilious about care of the mouth, this rite involves a practice which strikes the uninitiated stranger as revolting. It was reported to me that the ritual consists of inserting a small bundle of hog hairs into the mouth, along with certain magical powders, and then moving the bundle in a highly formalized series of gestures.

In addition to the private mouth-rite, the people seek out a holy-mouth-man once or twice a year. These practitioners have an impressive set of paraphernalia, consisting of a variety of augers, awls, probes, and prods. The use of these objects in the exorcism of the evils of the mouth involves almost unbelievable ritual torture of the client. The holy-mouth-man opens the client's mouth and, using the above mentioned tools, enlarges any holes which decay may have created in the teeth. Magical materials are put into these holes. If there are no naturally occurring holes in the teeth, large sections of one or more teeth are gouged out so that the supernatural substance can be applied. In the client's view, the purpose of these ministrations is to arrest decay and to draw friends. The extremely sacred and traditional character of the rite is evident in the fact that the natives return to the holy-mouth-men year after year, despite the fact that their teeth continue to decay.

It is to be hoped that, when a thorough study of the Nacirema is made, there will be a careful inquiry into the personality structure of these people. One has but to watch the gleam in the eye of a holy-mouth-man, as he jabs an awl into an exposed nerve, to suspect that a certain amount of sadism is involved. If this can be established, a very interesting pattern emerges, for most of the population shows definite masochistic tendencies. It was to these that Professor Linton referred in discussing a distinctive part of the daily body ritual which is performed only by men. This part of the rite involves scraping and lacerating the surface of the face with a sharp instrument. Special women's rites are performed only four times during each lunar month, but what they lack in frequency is made up in barbarity. As part of this ceremony, women bake their heads in small ovens for about an hour. The theoretically interesting point is that what seems to be a preponderantly masochistic people have developed sadistic specialists.

The medicine men have an imposing temple, or *latipso,* in every community of any size. The more elaborate ceremonies required to treat very sick patients can only be performed at this temple. These ceremonies involve not only the thaumaturge but a permanent group of vestal maidens who move sedately about the temple chambers in distinctive costume and headdress.

The *latipso* ceremonies are so harsh that it is phenomenal that a fair proportion of the really sick natives who enter the temple ever recover. Small children whose indoctrination is still incomplete have been known to resist attempts to take them to the temple because "that is where you go to die." Despite this fact, sick adults are not only willing but eager to undergo the protracted ritual purification, if they can afford to do so. No matter how ill the supplicant or how grave the emergency, the guardians of many temples will not admit a client if he cannot give a rich gift to the custodian. Even after one has gained admission and survived the ceremonies, the guardians will not permit the neophyte to leave until he makes still another gift.

The supplicant entering the temple is first stripped of all his or her clothes. In every-day life the Nacirema avoids exposure of his body and its natural functions. Bathing and excretory acts are performed only in the secrecy of the household shrine, where they are ritualized as part of the body-rites. Psychological shock results from the fact that body secrecy is suddenly lost upon entry into the *latipso*. A man, whose own wife has never seen him in an excretory act, suddenly finds himself naked and assisted by a vestal maiden while he performs his natural functions into a sacred vessel. This sort of ceremonial treatment is necessitated by the fact that the excreta are used by a diviner to ascertain the course and nature of the client's sickness. Female clients, on the other hand, find their naked bodies are subjected to the scrutiny, manipulation, and prodding of the medicine men.

Few supplicants in the temple are well enough to do anything but lie on their hard beds. The daily ceremonies, like the rites of the holy-mouth-men, involve discomfort and torture. With ritual precision, the vestals awaken their miserable charges each dawn and roll them about on their beds of pain while performing ablutions, in the formal movements of which the maidens are highly trained. At other times they insert magic wands in the supplicant's mouth or force him to eat substances which are supposed to be healing. From time to time the medicine men come to their clients and jab magically treated needles into their flesh. The fact that these temple ceremonies may not cure, and may even kill the neophyte, in no way decreases the people's faith in the medicine men.

There remains one other kind of practitioner, known as a "listener." This witch-doctor has the power to exorcise the devils that lodge in the heads of people who have been bewitched. The Nacirema believe that parents bewitch their own children. Mothers are particularly suspected of putting a curse on children while teaching them the secret body rituals. The counter-magic of the witch-doctor is unusual in its lack of ritual. The patient simply tells the "listener" all his troubles and fears, beginning with the earliest difficulties he can remember. The memory displayed by the Nacirema in these exorcism sessions is truly remarkable. It is not uncommon for the patient to bemoan the rejection he felt upon being weaned as a babe, and a few individuals even see their troubles going back to the traumatic effects of their own birth.

In conclusion, mention must be made of certain practices which have their base in native esthetics but which depend upon the pervasive aversion to the natural body and its functions. There are ritual fasts to make fat people thin and ceremonial feasts to make thin people fat. Still other rites are used to make women's breasts large if they are small, and smaller if they are large. General dissatisfaction with breast shape is symbolized in the fact that the ideal form is virtually outside the range of human variation. A few women afflicted with almost inhuman hypermammary development are so idolized that they make a handsome living by simply going from village to village and permitting the natives to stare at them for a fee.

Reference has already been made to the fact that excretory functions are ritualized, routinized, and relegated to secrecy. Natural reproductive functions are similarly distorted. Intercourse is taboo as a topic and scheduled as an act. Efforts are made to avoid pregnancy by the use of magical materials or by limiting intercourse to certain phases of the moon. Conception is actually very infrequent. When pregnant, women dress so as to hide their condition. Parturition takes place in secret, without friends or relatives to assist, and the majority of women do not nurse their infants.

Our review of the ritual life of the Nacirema has certainly shown them to be a magic-ridden people. It is hard to understand how they have managed to exist so long under the burdens which they have imposed upon themselves. But even such exotic customs as these take on real meaning when they are viewed with the insight provided by Malinowski when he wrote (1948:70):

> Looking from far and above, from our high places of safety in the developed civilization, it is easy to see all the crudity and irrelevance of magic. But without its power and guidance early man could not have mastered his practical difficulties as he has done, nor could man have advanced to the higher stages of civilization.

REFERENCES

Linton, Ralph. 1936. *The Study of Man.* New York, D. Appleton-Century Co.

Malinowski, Bronislaw. 1948. *Magic, Science, and Religion.* Glencoe, The Free Press.

Murdock, George P. 1949. *Social Structure.* New York, The Macmillan Co.

The Tnevnoc Cult*

David G. Bromley
Virginia Commonwealth University
Anson D. Shupe, Jr.
Indiana University/Purdue University

Accompanying the rapid growth of "new religions" in the 1970s has been escalating controversy centering on their methods of socializing new recruits. In this paper we examine the Tnevnoc Cult, a religious movement that flourished during the nineteenth century and was embroiled in a similar controversy. Many of the Tnevnocs' current socialization practices remain similar to those of the new religions although the Tnevnocs are not now regarded as controversial. By presenting a historical comparison between the Tnevnocs and new religions we demonstrate that the allegedly novel manipulative socialization practices of the new religions actually are remarkably similar to those employed by the Tnevnocs a century earlier. Further, we argue that the reaction of the anti-cult movement to the new religions also has historical parallels which suggest that it is the legitimacy accorded a group rather than its practices which shape public reactions and definitions.

The 1970s have witnessed a profusion of new religious movements ranging from the traditional Christian-based "Jesus Freaks" to groups of oriental origin such as the International Society for Krishna Consciousness (Hare Krishna), Guru Maharaj Ji's Divine Light Mission, and Sun Myung Moon's Unification Church. As these groups have grown in size and wealth there has been a parallel spread of alarm at the tactics by which they recruit and hold members. Allegations of deception, seduction, drugging, hypnosis and brainwashing have been leveled at these groups both by distraught parents of members and former members who have "escaped" or been deprogrammed and told their horror stories (Edwards, 1979; Thielmann, 1979; Mills, 1979). A number of behavioral scientists and other investigators have lent their support to these accusations and have attempted to formulate explanations for these swift and seemingly bizarre "conversions" (Conway and Siegelman, 1978; Patrick, 1976; Stoner and Parke, 1977).

It is the issue of manipulative "mind control" which has been the single most inflammatory allegation running through this popular literature. These accusations create the impression that these new religions have innovated or rediscovered techniques of indoctrination which transform otherwise normal individuals into followers who resemble robots or automatons in their slavish zeal, unquestioning obedience, and lack of individuality/free will. However, in the course of our own research (Shupe and Bromley, 1979; Shupe, Spielmann and Stigall, 1977), which has included an historical examination of the social context of these groups, we have discovered several past cases which are remarkably similar in many respects to these new religious groups.

This paper will attempt to demonstrate that what is currently termed the "cult menace" (particularly as it relates to recruitment, socialization and social organization) is not a novel development on the American religious scene. On the contrary, throughout our history the appearance of new religious movements has aroused very similar fears and accusations. Specifically, we shall examine the recruitment and indoctrination practices of the Tnevnoc Cult, a communal, sectarian group affiliated with a large and powerful international religious organization. Both the Tnevnocs and the larger parent body were targets of social repression in America during the nineteenth and early twentieth centuries. Since we are concerned primarily with recruitment and socialization in relation to contemporary charges of manipulation and mind control, we shall focus only on the parallels between the Tnevnocs and such contemporary groups as the Unification Church and Hare Krishna, not on the larger traditions or parent bodies of the groups of either era. The Tnevnocs no longer are as visible or as controversial as they once were due to a gradual trend toward accommodation both by the movement and by powerful

*This paper is the product of a joint effort. The order of authorship is random and does not imply any difference in the importance of contributions. The authors wish to thank Jeffrey Hadden, Theodore Long, Patrick McNamara and Horace Miner for their contributions to the development of this paper.

institutions within American society. However, as we document in the ethnographic composite which follows, many of the recruitment and socialization practices of even the accommodated twentieth century Tnevnocs are remarkably similar to those of the current "new religions." Because the Tnevnocs were rigidly segregated by sex and our data deal only with the female Tnevnoc component, we make no claim to generalize to the entire movement.

A Brief Ethnography of the Tnevnoc Cult

Like their modern-day counterparts in the current "cult explosion," such as the Unification Church and the Divine Light Mission, the Tnevnocs made a point of attempting to recruit members when they were still in their teenage and young adult years. This age cohort, Tnevnoc leaders recognized, was the least encumbered by domestic and occupational responsibilities, and its members were, not surprisingly, highly susceptible to idealistic, altruistic appeals. Much of this recruitment was openly conducted in schools and on campuses. On the basis of limited contacts with cult members, young girls were induced to commit themselves totally to the cult. If the cult succeeded in gaining control over them, it subjected them to such thorough indoctrination that they became totally dependent on the cult and in many cases lacked the will to free themselves from it.

Once a girl had been induced to join the cult she was immediately subjected to totalistic control. Like the Hare Krishna and the Children of God, members were forced to surrender all aspects of their former lives. Virtually all personal possessions were taken away, and individuals were prohibited from developing any outside involvements and commitments. Indeed, members were required to devote literally all of their time and energies to cult activities. The round of cult life was relentless and consuming. Members were routinely wakened at 4:30 A.M. to face an arduous day of menial labor interspersed with long hours of prayer, meditation, mindnumbing chanting, and compulsory religious ceremonies. Like Hare Krishna sect members who always carry prayer beads in cloth sacks attached to their wrists, Tnevnocs carried such beads which they used in their repetitive, monotonic chanting. Members gathered in candlelit, incense-filled rooms closed to outsiders for a variety of special rituals involving chanting and meditation. One particularly bizarre observance was a type of love/unity feast involving ritualistic cannibalism. Members consumed food which they were told symbolically represented parts of the dead founder's body.

The time not taken up with such rituals was devoted almost entirely to menial labor such as washing clothes, preparing food, and scrubbing floors. Indeed, only one hour of "free time" was allowed each day, but even during this brief period members were forbidden to be alone or in unsupervised groups, being required to remain together and monitored by cult leaders. All luxuries and even basic amenities were eliminated. For example, members slept each night on wooden planks with only thin straw mats as mattresses. They subsisted on a bland, spartan diet; food deprivation was even more severe than the meager diet implies, members being permitted to eat sweets only once a year and often being placed under considerable pressure to fast periodically. This combination of limited sleep, draining physical labor, and long hours of compulsory group rituals and worship, all supported by a meager subsistence-level diet, left members without sufficient time or energy to preserve even their own senses of individual identity.

All the members' former sources of emotional support also were severed upon joining the cult. During the first year members were forbidden to leave the communal (and often remote rural) setting in which their training took place and could receive no outside visitors beyond one family visitation. It thus became virtually impossible for parents and friends to maintain regular and frequent contact with members. For example, members were permitted to write only a minimal four letters per year. Further, just as do Unification Church leaders, Tnevnoc cult leaders deliberately disrupted family ties by creating a fictive kinship system in which they assumed parental roles intended to replace members' natural parents and siblings. Any other relationships which threatened cult control were also strictly forbidden. For example, sexual attachments of any kind were, without exception, tabooed. Lone Tnevnocs were never allowed in the presence of individuals of the opposite sex and they were forbidden to maintain close personal friendships with each other or even to touch physically. All loyalty had to be channeled to the cult, and its leaders, in authoritarian fashion, enforced those strictures. Leaders went so far as to assert that they were God's direct representatives on earth and therefore due absolute obedience by all members. This subservience was formalized in each member's written promise of absolute obedience for three years, after which time individuals often were led to make similar commitments for the remainder of their lives.

Perhaps most striking was the emergence of cult-induced personality changes. This began with the alteration of each individual's exterior appearance. Like the Hare Krishna, Tnevnoc cult members immediately upon joining had their hair cut off and were dispensed long flowing garments specifically designed to render members indistinguishable from one another. This concerted effort to wipe out any sense of individuality was carried to such extremes that members were never permitted to own or even to look into mirrors. The cult literally attempted to destroy the old individual, her identity, and her former life's associations by assigning a new cult name and designating the date of her entry into the group as the individual's "real" birthdate. Of course such identity changes were more difficult to monitor than behavioral conformity. One way cult leaders maintained close surveillance over the most private aspects of members' lives was to require members to reveal publicly and to record in diaries even the most minor infractions of elaborate cult rules, as well as improper thoughts and wishes.

This totalistic environment, with its rigid, all-encompassing code of behavior that individuals could not possibly follow without some minor infractions, engendered within members constant and inescapable feelings of inadequacy, self-doubt, anxiety and guilt. Cult leaders deliberately exacerbated these nagging feelings by instituting a series of humiliating, ego-destructive punishments for even the most trivial infractions of cult rules. For example, daydreaming or entertaining "improper" thoughts, however fleetingly, called down upon members ceremonies of public degradation. Members were forced to prostrate themselves in front of cult leaders and kiss their feet or, alternately, were denied food and reduced to crawling from member to member on their knees begging for the dregs of other member's meals. Such punishments became more severe as time went on, and members were expected to punish themselves regularly for these deviations. The cult went so far as to issue each member a ring to which were attached several lengths of chain with barbed points on the ends. Members were required to return alone to their beds at night at regular intervals and flagellate themselves with this cruel device as atonement for their infractions.

Not surprisingly, the grueling demands of cult membership and the ever-present feelings of guilt and anxiety created the potential for members to "give up" or defect. In addition to the docility created by the harsh conditions of the daily round of cult life, members were constantly pressured by cult leaders for greater personal sacrifice and evidence of complete commitment. Indeed, members competed with one another to express total selflessness and dedication. These constant exhortations and punishments designed to destroy any vestiges of individuality were reinforced by ceremonies intended to bind the individual inextricably to the group. One particularly ghoulish example was a macabre nuptial ceremony in which members were required to become the living brides of the dead cult leader. Overall these extreme and often bizarre tactics were extremely successful. Although on occasion individuals did manage to extricate themselves from the cult, most were permanently stripped of their individuality and autonomy and lived out their lives in subservient obedience.

Cults—Historical and Contemporary

Two important limitations of the preceding ethnographic composite of the Tnevnocs deserve mention. First, as no analogy is perfect, there are some differences between the Tnevnocs of the nineteenth century and the new religions of the present. For example, the Tnevnocs recruited children from families which were part of the larger international organization while most new religions recruit virtually all their members from families of other religious persuasions. Hence individual Tnevnoc members did not encounter the same hostility and resistance from their own families as did their latter day counterparts in the new religions. Too, in the Tnevnocs case much (but certainly not all) of the social repression was directed against the larger parent organization rather than specifically against the Tnevnocs themselves. Further, the Tnevnocs were organizationally more reclusive and did not arouse public antagonism by espousing programs for revolutionary social change, as have many of the new religions such as the Unification Church.

Second, the foregoing description of the Tnevnocs actually constitutes a caricature of the group insofar as it fails to convey the sense of majesty, purpose, personal fulfillment and belonging that Tnevnocs experienced individually and collectively. It also ignores the order, harmony, stability and integration of Tnevnoc communal organization. However, these same details also are missing from most contemporary accounts of new religious movements. It is precisely this lack of personal and organizational context and purpose which creates a sense that some of their practices are illegitimate and destructive (Bromley, Shupe and Ventimiglia, 1979).

What have been conveyed fairly accurately in our description of the Tnevnocs are some of the recruitment and socialization techniques by which both they and modern religious movements have sought to create and maintain deep commitment among their members. Certain types of groups historically have tried to harness all of their members' personal energies on a voluntary basis. These include not only the Tnevnocs but also elite military training

units, communes, monasteries and social movements seeking to effect radical social change (Kanter, 1972; Coser, 1974; Dornbusch, 1955). In order to gain control over all the members' time and energy such groups must develop high levels of commitment to them. In our research on the Unification Church and other new religious movements we have found that intense commitment can be generated and maintained to the extent that individuals' interest and group interests become *congruent*, that is, to the extent that individuals *wish to act as they are required* to act (Bromley and Shupe, 1979a, 1979b). This process involves totally immersing individuals in a set of activities which render them unavailable for other lines of action and constructing a symbolic system which provides a rationale and meaning for involvement in those activities. In a dynamic sense the process of building total commitment involves a *detachment* of individuals from former involvements and lifestyles, sources of emotional support and bases of personal identity, and *attachment* to new social roles, sources of affective support, and identity bases.

There is, in short, a simultaneous process of *desocialization* and *resocialization* (McHugh, 1966). The extensiveness and intensity of desocialization and resocialization depends in part on the selectivity groups can exercise in their recruitment activities (e.g., how readily they can attract individuals who already possess characteristics they require). However, since most newly formed groups and movements such as "new religions" have both low selectivity and high needs for member commitment, intense socialization practices usually are socially imperative.

Thus, if the practices of promoting total commitment in members are similar for various historical and contemporary religious groups, the different societal reactions to them cannot be explained solely in terms of those practices. Instead, societal response depends on the *degree of legitimacy*, defined in terms of the number and power of supporting groups, accorded a given religious body. The lower a group's legitimacy, the less resistance it can muster to counter social repression and the less control it has over its own public image. The major difference between the current societal reactions to the Tnevnocs and the Moonies, Hare Krishnas or Children of God, then, is that the Tnevnocs have now been accorded legitimacy, the persistence of at least some of the commitment maintenance practices described in this paper notwithstanding, while the latter groups have not.

Yet, as even a cursory review of American history reveals, virtually every major denomination and religious body was met initially with some degree of skepticism, ostracism or persecution. Indeed, the parallels with contemporary religious groups are striking. Much as the Unification Church, Hare Krishna, Children of God, and People's Temple are currently labeled "cults," the Tnevnocs once were perjoratively lumped together with groups such as the Mormons and Masons despite their enormous doctrinal and organizational diversity. The stereotypes and litany of charges leveled against contemporary "new religions" also are remarkably reminiscent of allegations against the earlier "new religions": political subversion, unconditional loyalty of members to authoritarian leaders, brutalizing of members, sexual indiscretions, and possession of mysterious, extraordinary powers (Sawatsky, 1978; Davis, 1960; Miller, 1979). And the atrocity stories told by apostates from earlier groups (Hopkins, 1830; Monk, 1836; Young, 1875) read much like the lurid tales told by former members of contemporary "new religions."

It is not our intent to argue that all of the accusations leveled against contemporary "new religions" are false. Groups with lofty ideals frequently assume airs of moral superiority and engage in duplicity and deception on the assumption that "the ends justify the means." But it also is true that groups which seek to initiate sweeping social change become the focus of hysterical reactions well out of proportion to the real threat they present. It is easy to be drawn into simplistic calls for repressing current religious "cults," either through anti-cult legislation or more vigilante-style actions such as "deprogramming," on the basis of caricatures like that presented here. Yet it should be kept in mind that contemporary scholars view the repression of religious movements during the nineteenth century as the result of undisguised xenophobic zeal and religious bigotry rather than as a legitimate response to any serious threat. It should also be kept in mind that all social movements encounter enormous pressure, both internal and external, to accommodate to the larger society. While it is premature to forecast the nature and degree of the accommodation of the latest group of "new religions," the past history of now established religious groups, the existing literature in the sociology of religious organizations (Weber, 1964; Niebuhr, 1929; Wilson, 1978) and already emerging trends within the new religions themselves (Bromley and Shupe, 1979a; Wallis, 1977) suggest that these groups may follow a parallel accommodationist course. One of the factors which would be most likely to impede this process would be prolonged, severe social repression. Thus not only does the current anti-cult movement constitute an abrogation of American religious pluralism, but ironically, it also may well have the effect of blocking the opportunity for these movements to follow the very course of accommodation which the anti-cultists profess to support.

References

Bromley, David G., Anson D. Shupe, Jr., and Joseph C. Ventimiglia. 1979. "The role of atrocities in the social construction of evil." Paper presented at the annual meeting of the *American Sociological Association.* Boston, August, 1979. *Forthcoming* in James T. Richardson (ed.), *Deprogramming Controversy: Sociological, Psychological, Legal and Historical Perspectives.* Transaction Press.

Bromley, David G. and Anson D. Shupe, Jr. 1979a. "Moonies" in America: Cult, Church and Crusade. Beverly Hills: Sage. 1979b. " 'Just a few years seem like a lifetime': a role theory approach to participation in religious movements." In Louis Kriesberg (ed.), *Research in Social Movements,* Conflict and Change. Greenwich: Jai Press.

Conway, Flo and Jim Siegelman. 1978. Snapping. New York: Free Press.

Coser, Lewis A. Greedy Institutions. 1974. New York: Free Press.

Davis, David. 1960. "Some themes of counter-subversion: an analysis of anti-Masonic, anti-Catholic, and anti-Mormon literature." *The Mississippi Valley Historical Review* 47:205–24.

Dornbusch, Sanford. 1955. "The military academy as an assimilating institution." *Social Forces* 33:316–21.

Edwards, Christopher. 1979. Crazy for God. Englewood Cliffs: Prentice-Hall.

Hopkins, Hiram. 1830. Renunciation of Free Masonry. Boston.

Kanter, Rosabeth. 1972. Commitment and Community: Communes and Utopias in Sociological Perspective. Cambridge: Harvard.

McHugh, Peter. 1966. "Social disintegration as a requisite of resocialization." *Social Forces* 44:355–63.

Miller, Donald. 1979. "Deprogramming in historical perspective." In James T. Richardson (ed.), *The Deprogramming Controversy: Sociological, Psychological, Legal, and Historical Perspectives.* Transaction Press.

Mills, Jeannie. 1979. Six Years with God. New York: A&W Publishers.

Monk, Maria. 1836 (1962). Awful Disclosures of the Hotel Dieu Nunnery. Handen: Anchor.

Niebuhr, H. Richard. 1929. The Social Sources of Denominationalism. New York: Holt.

Patrick, Ted and Tom Dulack. 1976. Let Our Children Go. New York: E. P. Dutton.

Reed, Rebecca T. 1835. Six Months in a Convent. New York: Arno Press.

Sawatsky, Rodney. 1978. "Moonies, Mormons and Mennonites: Christian heresy and religious toleration." Pp. 20–40 in M. D. Bryant and H. W. Richardson (eds.), *A Time for Consideration: A Scholarly Appraisal of the Unification Church.* New York: Edwin Mellen Press.

Shupe, Anson D., Jr. and David G. Bromley, 1979. "Witches, Moonies and evil." Forthcoming in Thomas Robbins and Dick Anthony (eds.), *In Gods We Trust: New Patterns of American Religious Pluralism.* Transaction Press.

Shupe, Anson D., Jr., Roger Spielmann, and Sam Stigall. 1977. "Deprogramming: the new exorcism." *American Behavioral Scientist* 20:941–56.

Stoner, Carroll and Jo Anne Parke. 1977. All God's Children. Radnor: Chilton.

Thielmann, Bonnie. 1979. The Broken God. Elgin: David C. Cook.

Wallis, Roy. 1977. The Road to Total Freedom: A Sociological Analysis of Scientology. New York: Columbia.

Weber, Max. 1964. The Theory of Social and Economic organization. Translated by A. M. Henderson and T. Parsons (eds.). New York: Free Press.

Wilson, John. 1978. Religion in American Society: The Effective Presence. Englewood Cliffs: Prentice-Hall.

Young, Ann. 1875. Wife No. 19: or, the Story of a Life in Bondage, Being a Complete Expose of Mormonism. Hartford.

Baseball Magic

George Gmelch
Department of Anthropology
Union College

On each pitching day for the first three months of a winning season, Dennis Grossini, a pitcher on a Detroit Tiger farm team, arose from bed at exactly 10:00 a.m. At 1:00 p.m. he went to the nearest restaurant for two glasses of iced tea and a tuna fish sandwich. Although the afternoon was free, he changed into the sweatshirt and supporter he wore during his last winning game, and one hour before the game he chewed a wad of Beech-Nut chewing tobacco. After each pitch during the game he touched the letters on his uniform and straightened his cap after each ball. Before the start of each inning he replaced the pitcher's rosin bag next to the spot where it was the inning before. And after every inning in which he gave up a run, he washed his hands.

When asked which part of the ritual was most important, he said, "You can't really tell what's most important so it all becomes important. I'd be afraid to change anything. As long as I'm winning, I do everything the same."

Trobriand Islanders, according to anthropologist Bronislaw Malinowski, felt the same way about their fishing magic.

Among the Trobrianders, fishing took two forms: in the inner lagoon where fish were plentiful and there was little danger, and on the open sea where fishing was dangerous and yields varied widely. Malinowski found that magic was not used in lagoon fishing, where men could rely solely on their knowledge and skill. But when fishing on the open sea, Trobrianders used a great deal of magical ritual to ensure safety and increase their catch.

Baseball, America's national pastime, is an arena in which players behave remarkably like Malinowski's Trobriand fishermen. To professional baseball players, baseball is more than just a game. It is an occupation. Since their livelihoods depend on how well they perform, many use magic to try to control the chance and uncertainty built into baseball.

To control uncertainty, for example, Tampa's Wade Boggs eats chicken before every game (that's 162 meals of chicken per year), and he has been doing that for eleven years. Jim Leyritz eats turkey, and Dennis Grossini tuna fish. White Sox pitcher Jason Bere listens to the same song on his Walkman on the days he is to pitch. San Francisco Giant pitcher Ron Bryant added a new stick of bubble gum to the collection in his bulging back pocket after each game he won. Jim Ohms, my teammate and pitcher on the Daytona Beach Islanders, put another penny in the pouch of his supporter after each win. Clanging against the hard plastic genital cup, the pennies made an audible sound as he ran the bases toward the end of a winning season.

Whether they are professional baseball players, Trobriand fishermen, soldiers, or even students taking final exams, some people turn to magic in situations of chance, when they believe they have limited control over the success of their activities and the outcome is important. In both technologically advanced societies that pride themselves on a scientific approach to problem solving, as well as in tribal societies, rituals of magic are common. Magic is a human attempt to impose order and certainty on an otherwise uncertain situation. This attempt is irrational in that there is no causal connection between the rituals and instruments of magic and the desired effect. But it is rational in that it creates in the

Revised version of "Superstition and Ritual in American Baseball" from *Elysian Fields Quarterly,* Vol. 11, No. 3, 1992, pp. 25-36. © 1997 by George Gmelch. Reprinted by permission.

practitioner a sense of confidence and control, which in turn helps him execute the activity and achieve the desired result. Put simply, what you believe can have an affect on what happens.

I have long had a close relationship with baseball, first as a participant and then as an observer. I devoted much of my youth to the game and played professionally as first baseman for five teams in the Detroit Tiger organization in the 1960s. It was shortly after the end of my last baseball season, that I took an anthropology course called "Magic, Religion, and Witchcraft." As my professor described the magic practiced by a tribe in Papua New Guinea, it occurred to me that what these so-called "primitive" people did wasn't all that different from what my teammates and I had done to give ourselves luck while playing professional baseball.

In baseball there are three essential activities—pitching, hitting, and fielding. Each varies in the amount of chance and uncertainty associated with it. The pitcher is the player least able to control the outcome of his own efforts. His best pitch may be hit for a home run, while his worst pitch may be hit directly into the hands of a fielder for an out or be swung at and missed for a third strike. He may limit the opposing team to a few hits yet lose the game, or he may give up a dozen hits and still win. One has only to look at the frequency with which pitchers end a season with poor won-lost records but have good earned run averages, or vice versa. For example, in 1990 Dwight Gooden gave up more runs per game than his teammate Sid Fernandez but had a won-lost record nearly twice as good. Gooden won 19 games and lost only 7, while Fernandez won only 9 games while losing 14. They pitched for the same team—the New York Mets—and therefore had the same fielders behind them. Regardless of how well he performs, on every outing the pitcher depends upon the proficiency of his teammates, the ineptitude of the opposition, and caprice.

Hitting is also full of risk and uncertainty—Hall of Famer Ted Williams called it the most difficult single task in the world of sports. Consider the forces and time constraints operating against the batter. A fastball travels from the pitcher's mound to the batter's box, just over sixty feet, in under four-tenths of a second. For only three feet of the journey, an absurdly short two-hundredths of a second, the ball is in a position where it can be hit. And to be hit well the ball must be neither too close to the batter's body nor too far from the "meat" of his bat. Any distraction, any slip of a muscle or change in stance, can throw a swing off. Once the ball is hit chance plays a large role in determining whether it will go into a waiting glove, whistling past a fielder's diving stab, or into the wide open spaces. In a quirky example of luck, some years ago Giant outfielder Willie Mays "dove for the dirt" to avoid being hit in the head by a fastball. While he was falling, the pitch hit his bat and the ball went shooting down the left field line. Mays jumped up and ran, turning the play into a double, while the pitcher looked on in disgust.

The most common form of baseball magic is personal ritual—a prescribed behavior that players scrupulously observe in an effort to ensure that things go their way.

In fielding, on the other hand, the player has almost complete control over the outcome. Once a ball has been hit in his direction, no one can intervene and ruin his chances of catching it for an out. Infielders have approximately three seconds in which to judge the flight of the ball, field it cleanly, and throw it to first base. Outfielders have almost double that amount of time to track down a fly ball. The average fielding percentage (or success rate) of .975, compared with a hitter's success rate or average batting percentage of .250, reflects the degree of certainty in fielding. Compared with the pitcher or the hitter, the fielder has little to worry about. He knows that in better than 9.7 times out of 10 he will execute his task flawlessly.

In sum, pitching and hitting involve a great deal of chance and are comparable to the Trobriand fishermen's open sea. Fielding, on the other hand, involves little uncertainty and is similar to the Trobriander's inner lagoon. In keeping with Malinowski's hypothesis about the relationship between magic and uncertainty, we can expect that baseball players will use magic for hitting and pitching, but not for fielding. Indeed, I observed a wide assortment of magic—rituals, taboos, and fetishes—associated with both hitting and pitching, but never observed the use of any directly connected to fielding. I have known only one player, a shortstop with a weak glove, who practiced any rituals connected with fielding. Let us now turn to the specific kinds of baseball magic used by ballplayers.

Ritual

The most common form of baseball magic is personal ritual—a prescribed behavior that players scrupulously observe in an effort to ensure that things go their way. These personal rituals, like those practiced by Trobriand fishermen, are performed in a routine, unemotional manner, much as players do non-magical things to improve their play such as applying pine tar to their bats to improve the grip, or eye black on their upper cheeks to reduce the sun's glare. Rituals are infinitely varied since a ballplayer may formalize any activity that he considers important or somehow linked to performing well.

Many hitters go through a series of preparatory rituals before stepping into the batter's box. These include tugging on their caps, touching their uniform letters or medallions, crossing themselves, tapping or bouncing the bat on the plate, or swinging the weighted warm-up bat a prescribed number of times. Mike Hargrove, former Cleveland Indians first baseman, had more than a dozen individual elements in his batting ritual, which included grabbing his belt in the middle of his back, pushing down his helmet tight, and pressing the thumb pad on his left hand. And after each pitch he would step out of the batter's box and repeat the entire sequence. His rituals were so time-consuming that he was called "the human rain delay."

Rituals may become so important that they override practicality. Catcher Matt Allen, for example, was wearing a long-sleeve turtleneck shirt on a cool evening in the New York-Penn League when he had a three-hit game. "I kept wearing the shirt and had a good week," he explained. "Then the weather got hot as hell, 85 degrees and muggy, but I would not take that shirt off. I wore it for another ten days—catching—and people thought I was crazy."

One ritual associated with hitting is tagging a base when leaving and returning to the dugout between innings. Mickey Mantle habitually tagged second base on the way to or from the outfield. Dave Jaeger stepped on third base on his way to the dugout after the third, sixth, and ninth innings of each game. Asked if he ever purposely failed to step on the bag, he replied, "Never! I wouldn't dare. It would destroy my confidence to hit." A hitter who is playing poorly may try different combinations of tagging and not tagging particular bases in an attempt to find a successful combination.

When players are not hitting, some managers may rattle the bat bin, as if the bats are in a stupor and can be aroused by a good shaking. Similarly, I have seen hitters rub their hands along the handles of the bats protruding from the bin, presumably in hopes of picking up some power or luck from those bats that are getting hits for their owners.

Rituals usually grow out of exceptionally good performances. When a player does well, he seldom attributes his success to skill alone. Rather he reasons that his skills were no better tonight when he got three hits, than they were last night when he went hitless. Therefore he attributes the inconsistencies in his performance to an object, a food he ate, not having shaved, a new shirt he bought that day, or just about any behavior different from his normal routine. By repeating that behavior, the player seeks to gain control over his performance. Outfielder John White explained how one of his rituals started:

> I was jogging out to centerfield after the national anthem when I picked up a scrap of paper. I got some good hits that night and I guess I decided that the paper had something to do with it. The next night I picked up a gum wrapper and had another good night at the plate. . . . I've been picking up paper every night since.

Like many hitters, John abandoned this ritual and looked for a new one when he stopped hitting.

Most baseball fans observe ritual behavior . . . never realizing that these actions may be as important to the pitcher as actually throwing the ball.

Because most pitchers play only once every four days, they perform rituals less frequently than hitters. But their rituals are just as important, perhaps more so. A starting pitcher cannot make up for a poor performance the next day, and having to wait three days to redeem oneself can be miserable. Moreover, the team's performance depends more on the pitcher than on any other player. Considering the pressures to do well, it is not surprising that pitchers' rituals are often more complex than those of hitters.

Most baseball fans observe ritual behavior, such as pitchers' tugging their caps between pitches, touching the rosin bag after each bad pitch, smoothing the dirt on the mound before each new batter or inning, never realizing that these actions may be as important to the pitcher as actually throwing the ball.

Many other rituals take place off the field, out of public view. On the days they are scheduled to start, many pitchers avoid activities that they believe sap their strength and detract from their effectiveness, or that they otherwise link with poor performance. Some avoid eating certain foods; some will not shave on the day of a game; some pitchers don't shave as long as they are winning. Early in the 1989 season Oakland's Dave Stewart had six consecutive victories and a beard before he finally lost. Ex–St. Louis Cardinal Al Hrabosky took this taboo to extremes: Samsonlike, he refused to cut his hair or beard during the entire season, which was part of the reason for his nickname, the "Mad Hungarian."

Mike Griffin begins his ritual routine a full day before he pitches, by washing his hair. The next day, although he does not consider himself superstitious, he eats bacon for lunch. When Griffin dresses for the game he puts on his clothes in the same order, making certain he puts the slightly longer of his two "stirrup" socks on his right leg. "I just wouldn't feel right mentally if I did it the other way around," he explains. He always wears the same shirt under his uniform on the day he pitches. During the game he takes off his cap after each pitch, and between innings he sits in the same place on the dugout bench. He believes his rituals give him a sense of order which reduce his anxiety about pitching.

Some pitchers even involve their wives or girlfriends in their rituals. One wife reported that her husband insisted that she wash her hair each day he was to pitch. In her memoirs, Danielle Torrez reported that one "rule" she learned as a baseball wife was "to support your husband's superstitions, whether you believe in them or not. I joined the player's wives who ate ice cream in the sixth inning or tacos in the fifth, or who attended games in a pink sweater, a tan scarf, or a floppy hat" (1983:79).

About ball players generally, Marlin coach Rich Donnelly said,

They're like trained animals. They come out here [ballpark] and everything has to be the same, they don't like anything that knocks them of their routine. Just look at the dugout and you'll see every guy sitting in the same spot every night. It's amazing, everybody is in the same spot. And don't you dare take someone's seat.

Taboo

The word taboo comes from a Polynesian term meaning prohibition. Breaking a taboo or prohibition leads to undesirable consequences or bad luck. Most players observe at least a few taboos. Some are careful never to step on the chalk foul lines or lines of the batter's box. One teammate of mine would never watch a movie on a game day, despite the fact that we played nearly every day from April to September. Another teammate refused to read anything before a game because he believed it weakened his batting eye.

Taboos usually grow out of exceptionally poor performances, which players, in search of a reason or cause, attribute to a particular behavior. During my first season of pro ball I ate pancakes before a game in which I struck out four times. A few weeks later I had another terrible game, again after eating pancakes. The result was a pancake taboo: I never ate pancakes during the season from that day on.

Some Latin players have a taboo against crossing bats, against permitting one bat to rest on top of another. One of my Dominican teammates became agitated when another player tossed a bat from the batting cage and it landed on top of his bat. Later he explained that the top bat might steal hits from the lower one. In his view, bats contained a finite number of hits, a sort of baseball "image of limited good." For Hall of Famer Honus Wagner, each bat contained only 100 hits and never more. Regardless of the quality of the bat, he would discard it after its 100th hit. One player told me that many of his teammates on the Class A Asheville Tourists would not let pitchers touch or swing their bats, not even to loosen up. Poor-hitting pitchers were said to pollute or weaken the bats.

Fetishes

Fetishes or charms are material objects believed to embody supernatural power that can aid or protect the owner. Good luck fetishes are standard equipment for some ballplayers. They include a wide assortment of objects from coins, chains, and crucifixes, to a particular baseball hat. Ordinary objects acquire power by being connected to exceptionally hot batting or pitching streaks, especially ones in which players get all the breaks. The object is often a new possession or something a player finds that coincides with the start of the streak and holds responsible for his good fortune. The player attributes the improvement in his performance to the influence of the new object, and comes to regard it as a fetish.

While playing in the Pacific Coast League, Alan Foster forgot his baseball shoes on a road trip and borrowed a pair from a teammate. That night he pitched a no-hitter, which he attributed to the shoes. After he bought them from his teammate, they became a fetish. The prized rock of Expo farmhand Mark LaRosa has a very different origin and use:

> I found it on the field in Elmira after I had gotten bombed [pitching poorly]. It's unusual, perfectly round, and it caught my attention. I keep it to remind me of how important it is to concentrate. When I am going well I look at the rock and remember to keep my focus; the rock reminds me of what can happen when I lose my concentration.

For one season Marge Schott, owner of the Cincinnati Reds, insisted that her field manager rub her St. Bernard "Schotzie" for good luck before each game. When the Reds were on the road, Schott would sometimes send a bag of the dog's hair to the field manager's hotel room.

During World War II American soldiers used fetishes in much same way. Social psychologist Samuel Stouffer and his colleagues found that in the face of great danger and uncertainty, soldiers developed magical practices, particularly the use of protective amulets and good luck charms (crosses, Bibles, rabbits' feet, medals), and jealously guarded articles of clothing they associated with past experiences of escape from danger. Stouffer also found that prebattle preparations were carried out in fixed "ritual" order, much as ballplayers prepare for a game.

Uniform numbers have special significance for some players. Many have a lucky number which they request. Since the choice is usually limited, players may try to get a number that at least contains their lucky number, such as 14, 24, 34, or 54 for the pitcher whose lucky number is four. Oddly enough, there is no consensus about the effect of wearing number 13. Some players will not wear it, others will, and a few like the Yankees David Cone request it.

While most taboos are idiosyncratic, there are a few that all players hold and that do not develop out of individual experience or misfortune.

The way in which number preferences emerge varies. Occasionally a young player requests the number of a former star, hoping that—in a form of imitative magic—it will bring him a similar measure of success. Or he may request a favorite number that he has always associated with good luck. Vida Blue changed his uniform number from 35 to 14, the number he wore as a high-school quarterback. When the new number did not produce the better pitching performance he was looking for, he switched back to his old number.

Clothing, both the choice of colors and the order in which they are put on, combine elements of both ritual and fetish. Some players put on their uniform in a specified order. Expos farmhand Jim Austin always puts on his left sleeve, left pants leg, and left shoe before the right. Most players, however, single out one or two lucky articles or quirks of dress rather than ritualizing all items of clothing. After hitting two home runs in a game, for example, infielder Jim Davenport of the San Francisco Giants discovered that he had missed a buttonhole while dressing for the game. For the remainder of his career he left the same button undone. For Brian Hunter the focus is on his shoes: "I have a pair of high tops and a pair of low tops. Whichever shoes don't get a hit that game, I switch to the other pair." At the same time of our interview, he was struggling at the plate and switching shoes almost every day. For Birmingham Baron pitcher Bo Kennedy the arrangement of the different pairs of baseball shoes in his locker is critical:

I tell the clubies [clubhouse boys] when you hang stuff in my locker don't touch my shoes. If you bump them move them back. I want the Ponys in front, the turfs to the right, and I want them nice and neat with each pair touching each other.... Everyone on the team knows not to mess with my shoes when I pitch.

During streaks—hitting or winning—players may wear the same clothes for each game. Once I changed sweatshirts midway through the game for seven consecutive games to keep a hitting streak going. During a 16-game winning streak, the 1954 New York Giants wore the same clothes in each game and refused to let them be cleaned for fear that their good fortune might be washed away with the dirt. Taking this ritual to the extreme, Leo Durocher, managing the Brooklyn Dodgers to a pennant in 1941, spent three and a half weeks in the same black shoes, gray slacks, blue coat, and knitted blue tie. Conversely, when losing the opposite may occur.

Several of the Oakland A's players, for example, went out and bought new street clothes in an attempt to break a 14-game losing streak.

While most taboos are idiosyncratic, there are a few that all players hold and that do not develop out of individual experience or misfortune. These taboos are learned, some as early as Little League. Mentioning a no-hitter while one is in progress is a widely known example. It is believed that if a pitcher hears the words "no-hitter, the spell will be broken and the no-hitter lost. This taboo is still observed by many sports broadcasters, who use various linguistic subterfuges to inform their listeners that the pitcher has not given up a hit, never mentioning "no-hitter."

Such superstitions, like most everything else, change over time. Many of the rituals and beliefs of early baseball are no longer remembered. In the 1920s and 1930s sportswriters reported that a player who tripped en route to the field would often retrace his steps and carefully walk over the stumbling block for "insurance." A century ago players spent time off the field and on looking for items that would bring them luck. For example, to find a hairpin on the street assured a batter of hitting safely in that day's game (today women don't wear hairpins—a good reason why the belief has died out). To catch sight of a white horse or a wagonload of barrels were also good omens. In 1904 the manager of the New York Giants, John McGraw, hired a driver and a team of white horses to drive past the Polo Grounds around the time his players were arriving at the ballpark. He knew that if his players saw white horses, they'd have more confidence and that could only help them during the game. Belief in the power of white horses survived in a few backwaters until the 1960s. A gray-haired manger of a team I played for in Quebec would drive around the countryside before important games and during the playoffs looking for a white horse. When he was successful, he'd announce it to everyone in the clubhouse before the game.

* * *

B. F. Skinner's early research with pigeons sheds some light on how these rituals, taboos, and fetishes get established in the first place. Like human beings, pigeons quickly learn to associate their behavior with rewards or punishment. By rewarding the birds at the appropriate time, Skinner taught them such elaborate games as table tennis, miniature bowling, and how to play simple tunes on a toy piano.

On one occasion he decided to see what would happen if pigeons were rewarded with food pellets every fifteen seconds, regardless of what they did. He found that the birds tended to associate the arrival of the food with a particular action—tucking the head under a wing, hopping from side to side, or turning in a clockwise direction. About ten seconds after the arrival of the last pellet, a bird would begin doing whatever it had associated with getting the food and keep at it until the next pellet arrived.

Baseball players respond to chance and uncertainty in the same way as people in tribal societies.

In the same way, baseball players tend to believe there is a causal connection between two events that are linked only temporarily. If a superstitious player touches his crucifix and then gets a hit, he may decide the gesture was responsible for his good fortune and follow the same practice the next time he comes to the plate. If he should get another hit, the chances are good that he will begin touching the crucifix each time he bats and that he will do so whether or not he hits safely each time.

The average batter hits safely approximately one quarter of the time.

And if the behavior of Skinner's pigeons or of gamblers at a Las Vegas slot machine is any guide, that is more than enough to keep him believing in a ritual. Skinner found that once a pigeon associated one of its actions with the arrival of food or water, sporadic rewards would keep the connection going. One pigeon, apparently believing that hopping from side to side brought pellets into its feeding cup, hopped ten thousand times without a pellet before finally giving up.

Since the batter associates his hits at least to some degree with his ritual touching of a crucifix, each hit he gets reinforces the strength of the ritual. Even if he falls into a batting slump and the hits temporarily stop, he may con-tinue to touch his crucifix in the hope that it will change his luck. If the slump lasts too long, however, he will soon change his behavior and look for a new practice to bring back his luck.

Skinner and Malinowski's explanations are complementary. Skinner's research throws light on how a ritual develops and why a particular ritual, taboo, or fetish is maintained. Malinowski focuses on why human beings turn to magic in situations of chance and uncertainty. In their attempts to gain greater control over their performance, we saw that baseball players respond to chance and uncertainty in the same way as people in tribal societies. It is wrong to assume that magical practices are a waste of time for either group. The magic in baseball obviously does not make a pitch travel faster or more accurately, or a batted ball seek the gaps between fielders. Nor does the Trobriand brand of magic make the surrounding seas calmer and more abundant with fish. What both kinds of magic do is give their practitioners a sense of control, and with that confidence, and at very little cost.

Bibliography

Malinowski, B. *Magic, Science and Religion and Other Essays* (Glencoe, Ill., 1948).

Skinner, B. F. *Behavior of Organisms: An Experimental Analysis* (D. Appleton-Century Co., 1938).

Skinner, B. F. *Science and Human Behavior* (New York: Macmillan, 1953).

Sociocultural Change: The Impact of the West

The origins of academic anthropology lie in the colonial and imperial ventures of the nineteenth and twentieth centuries. During these periods, many people of the world were brought into a relationship with Europe and the United States that was usually exploitative and often socially and culturally disruptive. For almost a century, anthropologists have witnessed this process and the transformations that have taken place in those social and cultural systems brought under the umbrella of a world economic order. Early anthropological studies—even those widely regarded as pure research—directly or indirectly served colonial interests. Many anthropologists certainly believed that they were extending the benefits of Western technology and society while preserving the cultural rights of those people whom they studied. But representatives of poor nations challenge this view and are far less generous in describing the past role of the anthropologist. Most contemporary anthropologists, however, have a deep moral commitment to defending the legal, political, and economic rights of the people with whom they work.

When anthropologists discuss social change, they usually mean change brought about in preindustrial societies through long-standing interaction with the nation-states of the industrialized world. In early anthropology, contact between the West and the remainder of the world was characterized by the terms "acculturation" and "culture contact." These terms were used to describe the diffusion of cultural traits between the developed and the less developed countries. Often this was analyzed as a one-way process in which cultures of the less developed world were seen, for better or worse, as receptacles for Western

cultural traits. Nowadays, many anthropologists believe that the diffusion of cultural traits across social, political, and economic boundaries was emphasized at the expense of the real issues of dominance, subordinance, and dependence that characterized the colonial experience. Just as importantly, many anthropologists recognize that the present-day forms of cultural, economic, and political interaction between the developed and the so-called underdeveloped world are best characterized as neocolonial.

Most of the authors represented in this unit take the perspective that anthropology should be critical as well as descriptive. They raise questions about cultural contact and subsequent economic and social disruption. (This is demonstrated best in the essays "New Spirits for Old" and "Grounded on Ice.")

In keeping with the notion that the negative impact of the West on traditional cultures began with colonial domination, this unit opens with "Why Can't People Feed Themselves?" and "The Arrow of Disease." These articles show that "progress" for the West has often meant poverty, hunger, and death for traditional peoples.

The following essays emphasize a different aspect of culture affected by the impact of the West. The article "Growing Up as a Fore" points to the problems of maintaining individual identity in a changing society. "Academic Scholarship and Sikhism: Conflict or Legitimization" shows how a whole cultural system may be affected by Western science. "A Pacific Haze: Alcohol and Drugs in Oceania" illustrates the disruptive social and economic changes brought about by the recent introduction of psychoactive drugs.

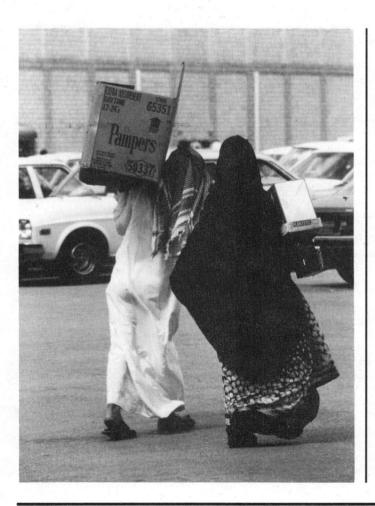

Of course, traditional peoples are not the only losers in the process of cultural destruction. All of humanity stands to suffer as a vast store of human knowledge—embodied in tribal subsistence practices, medicine, and folklore—is obliterated, in a manner not unlike the burning of the library of Alexandria 1,600 years ago. We can only hope that it is not too late to save what is left.

Looking Ahead: Challenge Questions

What is a subsistence system?

What have been the effects of colonialism on formerly subsistence-oriented socioeconomic systems?

How do cash crops inevitably lead to class distinctions and poverty?

How can one nation help another without being ethnocentric?

What was it about their culture that made the Fore people so vulnerable to the harmful effects of the change from a subsistence economy to a cash crop economy?

What ethical obligations do industrial societies have toward respecting the human rights and cultural diversity of traditional communities?

What have been the social, economic, and health consequences of the shift from the use of betel and kava to alcohol, tobacco, and marijuana in Oceania?

Can religion be studied in a university setting without undermining the faith or compromising the science?

Can the Inuit join the modern world and still retain the essence of their traditional culture?

Why Can't People Feed Themselves?

Frances Moore Lappé and Joseph Collins

Frances Moore Lappé and Dr. Joseph Collins are founders and directors of the Institute for Food and Development Policy, located in San Francisco and New York.

Question: You have said that the hunger problem is not the result of overpopulation. But you have not yet answered the most basic and simple question of all: Why can't people feed themselves? As Senator Daniel P. Moynihan put it bluntly, when addressing himself to the Third World, "Food growing is the first thing you do when you come down out of the trees. The question is, how come the United States can grow food and you can't?"

Our Response: In the very first speech I, Frances, ever gave after writing *Diet for a Small Planet*, I tried to take my audience along the path that I had taken in attempting to understand why so many are hungry in this world. Here is the gist of that talk that was, in truth, a turning point in my life:

When I started I saw a world divided into two parts: a *minority* of nations that had "taken off" through their agricultural and industrial revolutions to reach a level of unparalleled material abundance and a *majority* that remained behind in a primitive, traditional, undeveloped state. This lagging behind of the majority of the world's peoples must be due, I thought, to some internal deficiency or even to

several of them. It seemed obvious that the underdeveloped countries must be deficient in natural resources—particularly good land and climate—and in cultural development, including modern attitudes conducive to work and progress.

But when looking for the historical roots of the predicament, I learned that my picture of these two separate worlds was quite false. My two separate worlds were really just different sides of the same coin. One side was on top largely because the other side was on the bottom. Could this be true? How were these separate worlds related?

Colonialism appeared to me to be the link. Colonialism destroyed the cultural patterns of production and exchange by which traditional societies in "underdeveloped" countries previously had met the needs of the people. Many precolonial social structures, while dominated by exploitative elites, had evolved a system of mutual obligations among the classes that helped to ensure at least a minimal diet for all. A friend of mine once said: "Precolonial village existence in subsistence agriculture was a limited life indeed, but it's certainly not Calcutta." The misery of starvation in the streets of Calcutta can only be understood as the end-point of a long historical process—one that has destroyed a traditional social system.

"Underdeveloped," instead of being an adjective that evokes the picture of a static society, became for me a verb (to "underdevelop") meaning the *process* by which the minority of the

world has transformed—indeed often robbed and degraded—the majority.

That was in 1972. I clearly recall my thoughts on my return home. I had stated publicly for the first time a world view that had taken me years of study to grasp. The sense of relief was tremendous. For me the breakthrough lay in realizing that today's "hunger crisis" could not be described in static, descriptive terms. Hunger and underdevelopment must always be thought of as a *process*.

To answer the question "why hunger?" it is counterproductive to simply *describe* the conditions in an underdeveloped country today. For these conditions, whether they be the degree of malnutrition, the levels of agricultural production, or even the country's ecological endowment, are not static factors—they are not "givens." They are rather the *results* of an ongoing historical process. As we dug ever deeper into that historical process for the preparation of this book, we began to discover the existence of scarcity-creating mechanisms that we had only vaguely intuited before.

We have gotten great satisfaction from probing into the past since we recognized it is the only way to approach a solution to hunger today. We have come to see that it is the *force* creating the condition, not the condition itself, that must be the target of change. Otherwise we might change the condition today, only to find tomorrow that it has been recreated—with a vengeance.

Asking the question "Why can't people feed themselves?" carries a sense of bewilderment that there are so many people in the world not able to feed themselves adequately. What astonished us, however, is that there are not *more* people in the world who are hungry— considering the weight of the centuries of effort by the few to undermine the capacity of the majority to feed themselves. No, we are not crying "conspiracy!" If these forces were entirely conspiratorial, they would be easier to detect and many more people would by now have risen up to resist. We are talking about something more subtle and insidious; a heritage of a colonial order in which people with the advantage of considerable power sought their own self-interest, often arrogantly believing they were acting in the interest of the people whose lives they were destroying.

THE COLONIAL MIND

The colonizer viewed agriculture in the subjugated lands as primitive and backward. Yet such a view contrasts sharply with documents from the colonial period now coming to light. For example, A. J. Voelker, a British agricultural scientist assigned to India during the 1890s wrote:

Nowhere would one find better instances of keeping land scrupulously clean from weeds, of ingenuity in device of water-raising appliances, of knowledge of soils and their capabilities, as well as of the exact time to sow and reap, as one would find in Indian agriculture. It is wonderful too, how much is known of rotation, the system of "mixed crops" and of fallowing. . . . I, at least, have never seen a more perfect picture of cultivation."[1]

None the less, viewing the agriculture of the vanquished as primitive and backward reinforced the colonizer's rationale for destroying it. To the colonizers of Africa, Asia, and Latin America, agriculture became merely a means to extract wealth—much as gold from a mine—on behalf of the colonizing power. Agriculture was no longer seen as a source of food for the local population, nor even as their livelihood. Indeed the English economist John Stuart Mill reasoned that colonies should not be thought of as civilizations or countries at all but as "agricultural establishments" whose sole purpose was to supply the "larger community to which they belong." The colonized society's agriculture was only a subdivision of the agricultural system of the metropolitan country. As Mill acknowledged, "Our West India colonies, for example, cannot be regarded as countries. . . . The West Indies are the place where England *finds it convenient* to carry on the production of sugar, coffee and a few other tropical commodities."[2]

Prior to European intervention, Africans practiced a diversified agriculture that included the introduction of new food plants of Asian or American origin. But colonial rule simplified this diversified production to single cash crops— often to the exclusion of staple foods —and in the process sowed the seeds of famine.[3] Rice farming once had been common in Gambia. But with colonial rule so much of the best land was taken over by peanuts (grown for the European market) that rice had to be imported to counter the mounting prospect of famine. Northern Ghana, once famous for its yams and other foodstuffs, was forced to concentrate solely on cocoa. Most of the Gold Coast thus became dependent on cocoa. Liberia was turned into a virtual plantation subsidiary of Firestone Tire and Rubber. Food production in Dahomey and southeast Nigeria was all but abandoned in favor of palm oil; Tanganyika (now Tanzania) was forced to focus on sisal and Uganda on cotton.

The same happened in Indochina. About the time of the American Civil War the French decided that the Mekong Delta in Vietnam would be ideal for producing rice for export. Through a production system based on enriching the large landowners, Vietnam became the world's third largest exporter of rice by the 1930s; yet many landless Vietnamese went hungry.[4]

Rather than helping the peasants, colonialism's public works programs only reinforced export crop production. British irrigation works built in nineteenth-century India did help increase production, but the expansion was for spring export crops at the expense of millets and legumes grown in the fall as the basic local food crops.

Because people living on the land do not easily go against their natural and adaptive drive to grow food for themselves, colonial powers had to force the production of cash crops. The first strategy was to use physical or economic force to get the local population to grow cash crops instead of food on their own plots and then turn them over to the colonizer for export. The second strategy was the direct takeover of the land by large-scale plantations growing crops for export.

FORCED PEASANT PRODUCTION

As Walter Rodney recounts in *How Europe Underdeveloped Africa*, cash crops were often grown literally under threat of guns and whips.[5] One visitor to the Sahel commented in 1928: "Cotton is an artificial crop and one the value of which is not entirely clear to the natives . . ." He wryly noted the "enforced enthusiasm with which the natives . . . have thrown themselves into . . . planting cotton."[6] The forced cultivation of cotton was a major grievance leading to the Maji Maji wars in Tanzania (then Tanganyika) and behind the nationalist revolt in Angola as late as 1960.[7]

Although raw force was used, taxation was the preferred colonial technique to force Africans to grow cash crops. The colonial administrations simply levied taxes on cattle, land, houses, and even the people themselves. Since the tax had to be paid in the coin of the realm, the peasants had either to grow crops to sell or to work on the plantations or in the mines of the Europeans.[8] Taxation was both an effective tool to "stimulate" cash cropping and a source of revenue that the colonial bureaucracy needed to enforce the system. To expand their production of export crops to pay the mounting taxes, peasant producers were forced to neglect the farming of food crops. In 1830, the Dutch administration in Java made the peasants an offer they could not refuse; if they would grow government-owned export crops on one fifth of their land, the Dutch would remit their land taxes.[9] If they refused and thus could not pay the taxes, they lost their land.

Marketing boards emerged in Africa in the 1930s as another technique for getting the profit from cash crop production by native producers into the hands of the colonial government and international firms. Purchases by the marketing boards were well below the world market price. Peanuts bought by the boards from peasant cultivators in West Africa were sold in Britain for more than *seven times* what the peasants received.[10]

The marketing board concept was born with the "cocoa hold-up" in the Gold Coast in 1937. Small cocoa farmers refused to sell to the large cocoa concerns like United Africa Company (a subsidiary of the Anglo-Dutch firm, Unilever—which we know as Lever Brothers) and Cadbury until they got a higher price. When the British government stepped in and agreed to buy the cocoa directly in place of the big business concerns, the smallholders must have thought they had scored at least a minor victory. But had they really? The following year the British formally set up the West African Cocoa Control Board. Theoretically, its purpose was to pay the peasants a reasonable price for their crops. In practice, however, the board, as sole purchaser, was able to hold down the prices paid the peasants for their crops when the world prices were rising. Rodney sums up the real "victory":

> None of the benefits went to Africans, but rather to the British government itself and to the private companies.... Big companies like the United African Company and John Holt were given ... quotas to fulfill on behalf of the boards. As agents of the government, they were no longer exposed to direct attack, and their profits were secure.[11]

These marketing boards, set up for most export crops, were actually controlled by the companies. The chairman of the Cocoa Board was none other than John Cadbury of Cadbury Brothers (ever had a Cadbury chocolate bar?) who was part of a buying pool exploiting West African cocoa farmers.

The marketing boards funneled part of the profits from the exploitation of peasant producers indirectly into the royal treasury. While the Cocoa Board sold to the British Food Ministry at low prices, the ministry upped the price for British manufacturers, thus netting a profit as high as 11 million pounds in some years.[12]

These marketing boards of Africa were only the institutionalized rendition of what is the essence of colonialism—the extraction of wealth. While profits continued to accrue to foreign interests and local elites, prices received by those actually growing the commodities remained low.

PLANTATIONS

A second approach was direct takeover of the land either by the colonizing government or by private foreign interests. Previously self-provisioning farmers were forced to cultivate the plantation fields through either enslavement or economic coercion.

After the conquest of the Kandyan Kingdom (in present day Sri Lanka), in 1815, the British designated all the vast central part of the island as crown land. When it was determined that coffee, a profitable export crop, could be grown there, the Kandyan lands were sold off to British investors and planters at a mere five shillings per acre, the government even defraying the cost of surveying and road building.[13]

Java is also a prime example of a colonial government seizing territory and then putting it into private foreign hands. In 1870, the Dutch declared all uncultivated land—called waste land—property of the state for lease to Dutch plantation enterprises. In addition, the Agrarian Land Law of 1870 authorized foreign companies to lease village-owned land. The peasants, in chronic need of ready cash for taxes and foreign consumer goods, were only too willing to lease their land to the foreign companies for very modest sums and under terms dictated by the firms. Where land was still held communally, the village headman was tempted by high cash commissions offered by plantation companies. He would lease the village land even more cheaply than would the individual peasant or, as was frequently the case, sell out the entire village to the company.[14]

The introduction of the plantation meant the divorce of agriculture from nourishment, as the notion of food value was lost to the overriding claim of "market value" in international trade. Crops such as sugar, tobacco, and coffee were selected, not on the basis of how well they feed people, but for their high price value relative to their weight and bulk so that profit margins could be maintained even after the costs of shipping to Europe.

SUPPRESSING PEASANT FARMING

The stagnation and impoverishment of the peasant food-producing sector was not the mere by-product of benign neglect, that is, the unintended consequence of an overemphasis on export production. Plantations—just like modern "agro-industrial complexes"—needed an abundant and readily available supply of low-wage agricultural workers. Colonial administrations thus devised a variety of tactics, all to undercut self-provisioning agriculture and thus make rural populations dependent on plantation wages. Government services and even the most minimal infrastructure (access to water, roads, seeds, credit, pest and disease control information, and so on) were systematically denied. Plantations usurped most of the good land, either making much of the rural population landless or pushing them onto marginal soils. (Yet the plantations have often held much of their land idle simply to prevent the peasants from using it—even to this day. Del Monte owns 57,000 acres of Guatemala but plants only 9000. The rest lies idle except for a few thousand head of grazing cattle.)[15]

In some cases a colonial administration would go even further to guarantee itself a labor supply. In at least twelve countries in the eastern and southern parts of Africa the exploitation of mineral wealth (gold, diamonds, and copper) and the establishment of cash-crop plantations demanded a continuous supply of low-cost labor. To assure this labor supply, colonial administrations simply expropriated the land of the African communities by violence and drove the people into small reserves.[16] With neither adequate land for their traditional slash-and-burn methods nor access to the means—tools, water, and fertilizer—to make continuous farming of such limited areas viable, the indigenous population could scarcely meet subsistence needs, much less produce surplus to sell in order to cover the colonial taxes. Hundreds of thousands of Africans were forced to become the cheap labor source so "needed" by the colonial plantations. Only by laboring on plantations and in the mines could they hope to pay the colonial taxes.

The tax scheme to produce reserves of cheap plantation and mining labor was particularly effective when the Great Depression hit and the bottom dropped out of cash crop economies. In 1929 the cotton market collapsed, leaving peasant cotton producers, such as those in Upper Volta, unable to pay their colonial taxes. More and more young people, in some years as many as 80,000, were thus forced to migrate to the Gold Coast to compete with each other for low-wage jobs on cocoa plantations.[17]

The forced migration of Africa's most able-bodied workers—stripping village food farming of needed hands—was a recurring feature of colonialism. As late as 1973 the Portuguese "exported" 400,000 Mozambican peasants to work in South Africa in exchange for gold deposited in the Lisbon treasury.

The many techniques of colonialism to undercut self-provisioning agriculture in order to ensure a cheap labor supply are no better illustrated than by the story of how, in the mid-nineteenth century, sugar plantation owners in British Guiana coped with the double blow of the emancipation of slaves and the crash in the world sugar market. The story is graphically recounted by Alan Adamson in *Sugar without Slaves*.[18]

Would the ex-slaves be allowed to take over the plantation land and grow the food they needed? The planters, many ruined by the sugar slump, were determined they would not. The planter-dominated government devised several schemes for thwarting food self-sufficiency. The price of crown land was kept artificially high, and the purchase of land in parcels smaller than 100 acres was outlawed—two measures guaranteeing that newly organized ex-slave cooperatives could not hope to gain access to much land. The government also prohibited cultivation on as much as 400,000 acres—on the grounds of "uncertain property titles." Moreover, although many planters held part of their land out of sugar production due to the depressed world price, they would not allow any alternative production on them. They feared that once the ex-slaves started growing food it would be difficult to return them to sugar production when world market prices began to recover. In addition, the government taxed peasant production, then turned around and used the funds to subsidize the immigration of laborers from India and Malaysia to replace the freed slaves, thereby making sugar production again profitable for the planters. Finally, the government neglected the infrastructure for subsistence agriculture and denied credit for small farmers.

Perhaps the most insidious tactic to "lure" the peasant away from food production—and the one with profound historical consequences—was a policy of keeping the price of imported food low through the removal of tariffs and subsidies. The policy was double-edged: first, peasants were told they need not grow food because they could always buy it cheaply with their plantation wages; second, cheap food imports destroyed the market for domestic food and thereby impoverished local food producers.

Adamson relates how both the Governor of British Guiana and the Secretary for the Colonies Earl Grey favored low duties on imports in order to erode local food production and thereby release labor for the plantations. In 1851 the governor rushed through a reduction of the duty on cereals in order to "divert" labor to the sugar estates. As Adamson comments, "Without realizing it, he [the governor] had put his finger on the most mordant feature of monoculture: . . . its convulsive need to destroy any other sector of the economy which might compete for 'its' labor."[19]

Many colonial governments succeeded in establishing dependence on imported foodstuffs. In 1647 an observer in the West Indies wrote to Governor Winthrop of Massachusetts: "Men are so intent upon planting sugar that they had rather buy foode at very dear rates than produce it by labour, so infinite is the profitt of sugar workes. . . ."[20] By 1770, the West Indies were importing most of the continental colonies' exports of dried fish, grain, beans, and vegetables. A dependence on imported food made the West Indian colonies vulnerable to any disruption in supply. This dependence on imported food stuffs spelled disaster when the thirteen continental colonies gained independence and food exports from the continent to the West Indies were interrupted. With no diversified food system to fall back on, 15,000 plantation workers died of famine between 1780 and 1787 in Jamaica alone.[21] The dependence of the West Indies on imported food persists to this day.

SUPPRESSING PEASANT COMPETITION

We have talked about the techniques by which indigenous populations were forced to cultivate cash crops. In some countries with large plantations, however, colonial governments found it necessary to *prevent* peasants from independently growing cash crops not out of concern for their welfare, but so that they would not compete with colonial interests growing the same crop. For peasant farmers, given a modicum of opportunity, proved themselves capable of outproducing the large plantations not only in terms of output per unit of land but, more important, in terms of capital cost per unit produced.

In the Dutch East Indies (Indonesia and Dutch New Guinea) colonial policy in the middle of the nineteenth century forbade the sugar refineries to buy sugar cane from indigenous growers and imposed a discriminatory tax on rubber produced by native smallholders.[22] A recent unpublished United Nations study of agricultural development in Africa concluded that large-scale agricultural operations owned and controlled by foreign commercial interests (such as the rubber plantations of Liberia, the sisal estates of Tanganyika [Tanzania], and the coffee estates of Angola) only survived the competition of peasant producers because "the authorities actively supported them by suppressing indigenous rural development."[23]

The suppression of indigenous agricultural development served the interests of the colonizing powers in two ways. Not only did it prevent direct competition from more efficient native producers of the same crops, but it also guaranteed a labor force to work on the foreign-owned estates. Planters and foreign investors were not unaware that peasants who could survive economically by their own production would be under less pressure to sell their labor cheaply to the large estates.

The answer to the question, then, "Why can't people feed themselves?" must begin with an understanding of how colonialism actively prevented people from doing just that.

Colonialism

- forced peasants to replace food crops with cash crops that were then expropriated at very low rates;
- took over the best agricultural land for export crop plantations and then forced the most able-bodied workers to leave the village fields to work as slaves or for very low wages on plantations;
- encouraged a dependence on imported food;
- blocked native peasant cash crop production from competing with cash crops produced by settlers or foreign firms.

These are concrete examples of the development of underdevelopment that we should have perceived as such even as we read our history schoolbooks. Why didn't we? Somehow our schoolbooks always seemed to make the flow of history appear to have its own logic—as if it could not have been any other way. I, Frances, recall, in particular, a grade-school, social studies pamphlet on the idyllic life of Pedro, a nine-year-old boy on a coffee plantation in South America. The drawings of lush vegetation and "exotic" huts made his life seem romantic indeed. Wasn't it natural and proper that South America should have plantations to supply my mother and father with coffee? Isn't that the way it was *meant* to be?

Notes

1. Radha Sinha, *Food and Poverty* (New York: Holmes and Meier, 1976), p. 26.
2. John Stuart Mill, *Political Economy*, Book 3, Chapter 25 (emphasis added).
3. Peter Feldman and David Lawrence, "Social and Economic Implications of the Large-Scale Introduction of New Varieties of Foodgrains," Africa Report, preliminary draft (Geneva: UNRISD, 1975), pp. 107–108.
4. Edgar Owens, *The Right Side of History,* unpublished manuscript, 1976.
5. Walter Rodney, *How Europe Underdeveloped Africa* (London: Bogle-L'Ouverture Publications, 1972), pp. 171–172.
6. Ferdinand Ossendowski, *Slaves of the Sun* (New York: Dutton, 1928), p. 276.
7. Rodney, *How Europe Underdeveloped Africa,* pp. 171–172.
8. Ibid., p. 181.
9. Clifford Geertz, *Agricultural Involution* (Berkeley and Los Angeles: University of California Press, 1963), pp. 52–53.
10. Rodney, *How Europe Underdeveloped Africa,* p. 185.
11. Ibid., p. 184.
12. Ibid., p. 186.
13. George L. Beckford, *Persistent Poverty: Underdevelopment in Plantation Economies of the Third World* (New York: Oxford University Press, 1972), p. 99.
14. Ibid., p. 99, quoting from Erich Jacoby, *Agrarian Unrest in Southeast Asia* (New York: Asia Publishing House, 1961), p. 66.
15. Pat Flynn and Roger Burbach, North American Congress on Latin America, Berkely, California, recent investigation.
16. Feldman and Lawrence, "Social and Economic Implications," p. 103.
17. Special Sahelian Office Report, Food and Agriculture Organization, March 28, 1974, pp. 88–89.
18. Alan Adamson, *Sugar Without Slaves: The Political Economy of British Guiana, 1838–1904* (New Haven and London: Yale University Press, 1972).
19. Ibid., p. 41.
20. Eric Williams, *Capitalism and Slavery* (New York: Putnam, 1966), p. 110.
21. Ibid., p. 121.
22. Gunnar Myrdal, *Asian Drama*, vol. 1 (New York: Pantheon, 1966), pp. 448–449.
23. Feldman and Lawrence, "Social and Economic Implications," p. 189.

The Arrow of Disease

When Columbus and his successors invaded the Americas, the most potent weapon they carried was their germs. But why didn't deadly disease flow in the other direction, from the New World to the Old?

Jared Diamond

Jared Diamond is a contributing editor of DISCOVER, *a professor of physiology at the UCLA School of Medicine, a recipient of a MacArthur genius award, and a research associate in ornithology at the American Museum of Natural History. Expanded versions of many of his* DISCOVER *articles appear in his book* The Third Chimpanzee: The Evolution and Future of the Human Animal, *which won Britain's 1992* COPUS *prize for best science book. Not least among his many accomplishments was his rediscovery in 1981 of the long-lost bowerbird of New Guinea. Diamond wrote about pseudohermaphrodites for* DISCOVER'S *special June issue on the science of sex.*

The three people talking in the hospital room were already stressed out from having to cope with a mysterious illness, and it didn't help at all that they were having trouble communicating. One of them was the patient, a small, timid man, sick with pneumonia caused by an unidentified microbe and with only a limited command of the English language. The second, acting as translator, was his wife, worried about her husband's condition and frightened by the hospital environment. The third person in the trio was an inexperienced young doctor, trying to figure out what might have brought on the strange illness. Under the stress, the doctor was forgetting everything he had been taught about patient confidentiality. He committed the awful blunder of requesting the woman to ask her husband whether he'd had any sexual experiences that might have caused the infection.

As the young doctor watched, the husband turned red, pulled himself together so that he seemed even smaller, tried to disappear under his bed sheets, and stammered in a barely audible voice. His wife suddenly screamed in rage and drew herself up to tower over him. Before the doctor could stop her, she grabbed a heavy metal bottle, slammed it onto her husband's head, and stormed out of the room. It took a while for the doctor to elicit, through the man's broken English, what he had said to so enrage his wife. The answer slowly emerged: he had admitted to repeated intercourse with sheep on a recent visit to the family farm; perhaps that was how he had contracted the mysterious microbe.

This episode, related to me by a physician friend involved in the case, sounds so bizarrely one of a kind as to be of no possible broader significance. But in fact it illustrates a subject of great importance: human diseases of animal origins. Very few of us may love sheep in the carnal sense. But most of us platonically love our pet animals, like our dogs and cats; and as a society, we certainly appear to have an inordinate fondness for sheep and other livestock, to judge from the vast numbers of them that we keep.

Some of us—most often our children—pick up infectious diseases from our pets. Usually these illnesses remain no more than a nuisance, but a few have evolved into far more. The major killers of humanity throughout our recent history—smallpox, flu, tuberculosis, malaria, plague, measles, and cholera—are all infectious diseases that arose from diseases of animals. Until World War II more victims of war died of microbes than of gunshot or sword wounds. All those military histories glorifying Alexander the Great and Napoleon ignore the ego-deflating truth: the winners of past wars were not necessarily those armies with the best generals and weapons, but those bearing the worst germs with which to smite their enemies.

The grimmest example of the role of germs in history is much on our minds this month, as we recall the European conquest of the Americas that began with Columbus's voyage of 1492. Numerous as the Indian victims of the murderous Spanish conquistadores were, they were dwarfed in number by the victims of murderous Spanish microbes. These formidable conquerors killed an estimated 95 percent of the New World's pre-Columbian Indian population.

Why was the exchange of nasty germs between the Americas and Europe so unequal? Why didn't the reverse happen instead, with Indian diseases decimating the Spanish invaders, spreading back across the Atlantic, and causing a 95 percent decline in *Europe's* human population?

Similar questions arise regarding the decimation of many other native peoples by European germs, and regarding the decimation of would-be European conquistadores in the tropics of Africa and Asia.

Naturally, we're disposed to think about diseases from our own point of view: What can we do to save ourselves and to kill the microbes? Let's stamp out the scoundrels, and never mind what *their* motives are!

In life, though, one has to understand the enemy to beat him. So for a moment, let's consider disease from the microbes' point of view. Let's look beyond our anger at their making us sick in bizarre ways, like giving us genital sores or diarrhea, and ask why it is that they do such things. After all, microbes are as much a product of natural selection as we are, and so their actions must have come about because they confer some evolutionary benefit.

From our viewpoint, diarrhea and coughing are "symptoms" of disease. From a bug's viewpoint, they're clever evolutionary strategies to broadcast the bug. That's why it's in the bug's interests to make us "sick."

Basically, of course, evolution selects those individuals that are most effective at producing babies and at helping those babies find suitable places to live. Microbes are marvels at this latter requirement. They have evolved diverse ways of spreading from one person to another, and from animals to people. Many of our symptoms of disease actually represent ways in which some clever bug modifies our bodies or our behavior such that we become enlisted to spread bugs.

The most effortless way a bug can spread is by just waiting to be transmitted passively to the next victim. That's the strategy practiced by microbes that wait for one host to be eaten by the next—salmonella bacteria, for example, which we contract by eating already-infected eggs or meat; or the worm responsible for trichinosis, which waits for us to kill a pig and eat it without properly cooking it.

As a slight modification of this strategy, some microbes don't wait for the old host to die but instead hitchhike in the saliva of an insect that bites the old host and then flies to a new one. The free ride may be provided by mosquitoes, fleas, lice, or tsetse flies, which spread malaria, plague, typhus, and sleeping sickness, respectively. The dirtiest of all passive-carriage tricks is perpetrated by microbes that pass from a woman to her fetus—microbes such as the ones responsible for syphilis, rubella (German measles), and AIDS. By their cunning these microbes can already be infecting an infant before the moment of its birth.

Other bugs take matters into their own hands, figuratively speaking. They actively modify the anatomy or habits of their host to accelerate their transmission. From our perspective, the open genital sores caused by venereal diseases such as syphilis are a vile indignity. From the microbes' point of view, however, they're just a useful device to enlist a host's help in inoculating the body cavity of another host with microbes. The skin lesions caused by smallpox similarly spread microbes by direct or indirect body contact (occasionally very indirect, as when U.S. and Australian whites bent on wiping out "belligerent" native peoples sent them gifts of blankets previously used by smallpox patients).

More vigorous yet is the strategy practiced by the influenza, common cold, and pertussis (whooping cough) microbes, which induce the victim to cough or sneeze, thereby broadcasting the bugs toward prospective new hosts. Similarly the cholera bacterium induces a massive diarrhea that spreads bacteria into the water supplies of potential new victims. For modification of a host's behavior, though, nothing matches the rabies virus, which not only gets into the saliva of an infected dog but drives the dog into a frenzy of biting and thereby infects many new victims.

Thus, from our viewpoint, genital sores, diarrhea, and coughing are "symptoms" of disease. From a bug's viewpoint, they're clever evolutionary strategies to broadcast the bug. That's why it's in the bug's interests to make us "sick." But what does it gain by killing us? That seems self-defeating, since a microbe that kills its host kills itself.

Though you may well think it's of little consolation, our death is really just an unintended by-product of host symptoms that promote the efficient transmission of microbes. Yes, an untreated cholera patient may eventually die from producing diarrheal fluid at a rate of several gallons a day. While the patient lasts, though, the cholera bacterium profits from being massively disseminated into the water supplies of its next victims. As long as each victim thereby infects, on average, more than one new victim, the bacteria will spread, even though the first host happens to die.

So much for the dispassionate examination of the bug's interests. Now let's get back to considering our own selfish interests: to stay alive and healthy, best done by killing the damned bugs. One common response to infection is to develop a fever. Again, we consider fever a "symptom" of disease, as if it developed inevitably without serving any function. But regulation of body temperature is under our genetic control, and a fever doesn't just happen by accident. Because some microbes are more sensitive to heat than our own bodies are, by raising our body temperature we in effect try to bake the bugs to death before we get baked ourselves.

Another common response is to mobilize our immune system. White blood cells and other cells actively seek out and kill foreign microbes. The specific antibodies we gradually build up against a particular microbe make us less likely to get reinfected once we are cured. As we all know there are some illnesses, such as flu and the common cold, to which our resistance is only temporary; we can eventually contract the illness again. Against other illnesses, though—including measles, mumps, rubella, pertussis, and the now-defeated menace of smallpox—antibodies stimulated by one infection confer lifelong immunity. That's the principle behind vaccination—to stimulate our antibody production without our having to go through the actual experience of the disease.

We and our pathogens are now locked in an escalating evolutionary contest, with the death of one contestant the price of defeat, and with natural selection playing the role of umpire.

Alas, some clever bugs don't just cave in to our immune defenses. Some have learned to trick us by changing their antigens, those molecular pieces of the microbe that our antibodies recognize. The constant evolution or recycling of new strains of flu, with differing antigens, explains why the flu you got two years ago didn't protect you against the different strain that arrived this year. Sleeping sickness is an even more slippery customer in its ability to change its antigens rapidly.

Among the slipperiest of all is the virus that causes AIDS, which evolves new antigens even as it sits within an individual patient, until it eventually overwhelms the immune system.

Our slowest defensive response is through natural selection, which changes the relative frequency with which a gene appears from generation to generation. For almost any disease some people prove to be genetically more resistant than others. In an epidemic, those people with genes for resistance to that particular microbe are more likely to survive than are people lacking such genes. As a result, over the course of history human populations repeatedly exposed to a particular pathogen tend to be made up of individuals with genes that resist the appropriate microbe just because unfortunate individuals without

those genes were less likely to survive to pass their genes on to their children.

Fat consolation, you may be thinking. This evolutionary response is not one that does the genetically susceptible dying individual any good. It does mean, though, that a human population as a whole becomes better protected.

In short, many bugs have had to evolve tricks to let them spread among potential victims. We've evolved counter-tricks, to which the bugs have responded by evolving counter-counter-tricks. We and our pathogens are now locked in an escalating evolutionary contest, with the death of one contestant the price of defeat, and with natural selection playing the role of umpire.

The form that this deadly contest takes varies with the pathogens: for some it is like a guerrilla war, while for others it is a blitzkrieg. With certain diseases, like malaria or hook-worm, there's a more or less steady trickle of new cases in an affected area, and they will appear in any month of any year. Epidemic diseases, though, are different: they produce no cases for a long time, then a whole wave of cases, then no more cases again for a while.

Among such epidemic diseases, influenza is the most familiar to Americans, this year having been a particularly bad one for us (but a great year for the influenza virus). Cholera epidemics come at longer intervals, the 1991 Peruvian epidemic being the first one to reach the New World during the twentieth century. Frightening as today's influenza and cholera epidemics are, through, they pale beside the far more terrifying epidemics of the past, before the rise of modern medicine. The greatest single epidemic in human history was the influenza wave that killed 21 million people at the end of the First World War. The black death, or bubonic plague, killed one-quarter of Europe's population between 1346 and 1352, with death tolls up to 70 percent in some cities.

The infectious diseases that visit us as epidemics share several characteristics. First, they spread quickly and efficiently from an infected person to

nearby healthy people, with the result that the whole population gets exposed within a short time. Second, they're "acute" illnesses: within a short time, you either die or recover completely. Third, the fortunate ones of us who do recover develop antibodies that leave us immune against a recurrence of the disease for a long time, possibly our entire lives. Finally, these diseases tend to be restricted to humans; the bugs causing them tend not to live in the soil or in other animals. All four of these characteristics apply to what Americans think of as the once more-familiar acute epidemic diseases of childhood, including measles, rubella, mumps, pertussis, and smallpox.

It is easy to understand why the combination of those four characteristics tends to make a disease run in epidemics. The rapid spread of microbes and the rapid course of symptoms mean that everybody in a local human population is soon infected, and thereafter either dead or else recovered and immune. No one is left alive who could still be infected. But since the microbe can't survive except in the bodies of living people, the disease dies out until a new crop of babies reaches the susceptible age—and until an infectious person arrives from the outside to start a new epidemic.

A classic illustration of the process is given by the history of measles on the isolated Faeroe Islands in the North Atlantic. A severe epidemic of the disease reached the Faeroes in 1781, then died out, leaving the islands measles-free until an infected carpenter arrived on a ship from Denmark in 1846. Within three months almost the whole Faeroes population—7,782 people—had gotten measles and then either died or recovered, leaving the measles virus to disappear once again until the next epidemic. Studies show that measles is likely to die out in any human population numbering less than half a million people. Only in larger populations can measles shift from one local area to another, thereby persisting until enough babies have been born in the originally infected area to permit the disease's return.

Rubella in Australia provides a similar example, on a much larger scale. As of 1917 Australia's population was still only 5 million, with most people living in scattered rural areas. The sea voyage to Britain took two months, and land transport within Australia itself was slow. In effect, Australia didn't even consist of a population of 5 million, but of hundreds of much smaller populations. As a result, rubella hit Australia only as occasional epidemics, when an infected person happened to arrive from overseas and stayed in a densely populated area. By 1938, though, the city of Sydney alone had a population of over one million, and people moved frequently and quickly by air between London, Sydney, and other Australian cities. Around then, rubella for the first time was able to establish itself permanently in Australia.

What's true for rubella in Australia is true for most familiar acute infectious diseases throughout the world. To sustain themselves, they need a human population that is sufficiently numerous and densely packed that a new crop of susceptible children is available for infection by the time the disease would otherwise be waning. Hence the measles and other such diseases are also known as "crowd diseases."

Crowd diseases could not sustain themselves in small bands of hunter-gatherers and slash-and-burn farmers. As tragic recent experience with Amazonian Indians and Pacific Islanders confirms, almost an entire tribelet may be wiped out by an epidemic brought by an outside visitor, because no one in the tribelet has any antibodies against the microbe. In addition, measles and some other "childhood" diseases are more likely to kill infected adults than children, and all adults in the tribelet are susceptible. Having killed most of the tribelet, the epidemic then disappears. The small population size explains why tribelets can't sustain epidemics introduced from the outside; at the same time it explains why they could never evolve epidemic diseases of their own to give back to the visitors.

That's not to say that small human populations are free from all infectious diseases. Some of their infections are caused by microbes capable of maintaining themselves in animals or in soil, so the disease remains constantly available to infect people. For example, the yellow fever virus is carried by African wild monkeys and is constantly available to infect rural human populations of Africa. It was also available to be carried to New World monkeys and people by the transatlantic slave trade.

Other infections of small human populations are chronic diseases, such as leprosy and yaws, that may take a very long time to kill a victim. The victim thus remains alive as a reservoir of microbes to infect other members of the tribelet. Finally, small human populations are susceptible to nonfatal infections against which we don't develop immunity, with the result that the same person can become reinfected after recovering. That's the case with hookworm and many other parasites.

All these types of diseases, characteristic of small, isolated populations, must be the oldest diseases of humanity. They were the ones that we could evolve and sustain through the early millions of years of our evolutionary history, when the total human population was tiny and fragmented. They are also shared with, or are similar to the diseases of, our closest wild relatives, the African great apes. In contrast, the evolution of our crowd diseases could only have occurred with the buildup of large, dense human populations, first made possible by the rise of agriculture about 10,000 years ago, then by the rise of cities several thousand years ago. Indeed, the first attested dates for many familiar infectious diseases are surprisingly recent: around 1600 B.C. for smallpox (as deduced from pockmarks on an Egyptian mummy), 400 B.C. for mumps, 1840 for polio, and 1959 for AIDS.

Agriculture sustains much higher human population densities than does hunting and gathering—on average, 10 to 100 times higher. In addition, hunter-gatherers frequently shift camp, leaving behind their piles of feces with their accumulated microbes and worm larvae. But farmers are sedentary and live amid their own sewage, providing microbes with a quick path from one person's body into another person's drinking water. Farmers also become surrounded by disease-transmitting rodents attracted by stored food.

Some human populations make it even easier for their own bacteria and worms to infect new victims, by intentionally gathering their feces and urine and spreading it as fertilizer on the fields where people work. Irrigation agriculture and fish farming provide ideal living conditions for the snails carrying schistosomes, and for other flukes that burrow through our skin as we wade through the feces-laden water.

The explosive increase in world travel by Americans, and in immigration to the United States, is turning us into another melting pot—this time of microbes that we'd dismissed as causing disease in far-off countries.

If the rise of farming was a boon for our microbes, the rise of cities was a veritable bonanza, as still more densely packed human populations festered under even worse sanitation conditions. (Not until the beginning of the twentieth century did urban populations finally become self-sustaining; until then, constant immigration of healthy peasants from the countryside was necessary to make good the constant deaths of city dwellers from crowd diseases.) Another bonanza was the development of world trade routes, which by late Roman times effectively joined the populations of Europe, Asia, and North Africa into one giant breeding ground for microbes. That's when smallpox finally reached Rome as the "plague of Antonius," which killed millions of Roman citizens between A.D. 165 and 180.

Similarly, bubonic plague first appeared in Europe as the plague of Justinian ('sc{a.d.} 542–543). But plague didn't begin to hit Europe with full force, as the black death epidemics, until 1346, when new overland trading with China provided rapid transit for flea-infested furs from plague-ridden areas of Central Asia. Today our jet planes have made even the longest intercontinental flights briefer than the duration of any human infectious disease. That's how an Aerolíneas Argentinas airplane, stopping in Lima, Peru, earlier this year, managed to deliver dozens of cholera-infected people the same day to my city of Los Angles, over 3,000 miles away. The explosive increase in world travel by Americans, and in immigration to the United States, is turning us into another melting pot—this time of microbes that we previously dismissed as just causing exotic diseases in far-off countries.

When the human population became sufficiently large and concentrated, we reached the stage in our history when we could at last sustain crowd diseases confined to our species. But that presents a paradox: such diseases could never have existed before. Instead they had to evolve as new diseases. Where did those new diseases come from?

Evidence emerges from studies of the disease-causing microbes themselves. In many cases molecular biologists have identified the microbe's closest relative. Those relatives also prove to be agents of infectious crowd diseases—but ones confined to various species of domestic animals and pets! Among animals too, epidemic diseases require dense populations, and they're mainly confined to social animals that provide the necessary large populations. Hence when we domesticated social animals such as cows and pigs, they were already afflicted by epidemic diseases just waiting to be transferred to us.

For example, the measles virus is most closely related to the virus causing rinderpest, a nasty epidemic disease of cattle and many wild cud-chewing mammals. Rinderpest doesn't affect humans. Measles, in turn, doesn't affect cattle. The close similarity of the measles and rinderpest viruses suggests that the rinderpest virus transferred from cattle to humans, then became the measles virus by changing its properties to adapt to us. That transfer isn't surprising, considering how closely many peasant farmers live and sleep next to cows and their accompanying feces, urine, breath, sores, and blood. Our intimacy with cattle has been going on for 8,000 years since we domesticated them—ample time for the rinderpest virus to discover us nearby. Other familiar infectious diseases can similarly be traced back to diseases of our animal friends.

Given our proximity to the animals we love, we must constantly be getting bombarded by animal microbes. Those invaders get winnowed by natural selection, and only a few succeed in establishing themselves as human diseases. A quick survey of current diseases lets us trace four stages in the evolution of a specialized human disease from an animal precursor.

In the first stage, we pick up animal-borne microbes that are still at an early stage in their evolution into specialized human pathogens. They don't get transmitted directly from one person to another, and even their transfer from animals to us remains uncommon. There are dozens of diseases like this that we get directly from pets and domestic animals. They include cat scratch fever from cats, leptospirosis from dogs, psittacosis from chickens and parrots, and brucellosis from cattle. We're similarly susceptible to picking up diseases from wild animals, such as the tularemia that hunters occasionally get from skinning wild rabbits.

In the second stage, a former animal pathogen evolves to the point where it does get transmitted directly between people and causes epidemics. However, the epidemic dies out for several reasons—being cured by modern medicine, stopping when everybody has been infected and died, or stopping when everybody has been infected and become immune. For example, a previously unknown disease termed *o'nyong-nyong* fever appeared in East Africa in 1959 and infected several million Africans. It probably arose from a virus of monkeys and was transmitted to humans by mosquitoes. The fact that patients recovered quickly and became immune to further attack helped cause the new disease to die out quickly.

The annals of medicine are full of diseases that sound like no known disease today but that once caused terrifying epidemics before disappearing as mysteriously as they had come. Who alive today remembers the "English sweating sickness" that swept and terrified Europe between 1485 and 1578, or the "Picardy sweats" of eighteenth- and nineteenth-century France?

A third stage in the evolution of our major diseases is represented by former animal pathogens that establish themselves in humans and that do not die out; until they do, the question of whether they will become major killers of humanity remains up for grabs. The future is still very uncertain for Lassa fever, first observed in 1969 in Nigeria and caused by a virus probably derived from rodents. Better established is Lyme disease, caused by a spirochete that we get from the bite of a tick. Although the first known human cases in the United States appeared only as recently as 1962, Lyme disease is already reaching epidemic proportions in the Northeast, on the West Coast, and in the upper Midwest. The future of AIDS, derived from monkey viruses, is even more secure, from the virus's perspective.

The final stage of this evolution is represented by the major, long-established epidemic diseases confined to humans. These diseases must have been the evolutionary survivors of far more pathogens that tried to make the jump to us from animals—and mostly failed.

Diseases represent evolution in progress, as microbes adapt by natural selection to new hosts. Compared with cows' bodies, though, our bodies offer different immune defenses and different chemistry. In that new environment, a microbe must evolve new ways to live and propagate itself.

The best-studied example of microbes evolving these new ways involves myxomatosis, which hit Australian rabbits in 1950. The myxoma virus, native to a wild species of Brazilian rabbit, was known to cause a lethal epidemic in European domestic rabbits, which are a different species. The virus was intentionally introduced to Australia in the hopes of ridding the continent of its plague of European rabbits, foolishly introduced in the nineteenth century. In the first year, myxoma produced a gratifying (to Australian farmers) 99.8 percent mortality in infected rabbits. Fortunately for the rabbits and unfortunately for the farmers, the death rate then dropped in the second year to 90 percent and eventually to 25 percent, frustrating hopes of eradicating rabbits completely from Australia. The problem was that the myxoma virus evolved to serve its own interest, which differed from the farmers' interests and those of the rabbits. The virus changed to kill fewer rabbits and to permit lethally infected ones to live longer before dying. The result was bad for Australian farmers but good for the virus: a less lethal myxoma virus spreads baby viruses to more rabbits than did the original, highly virulent myxoma.

For a similar example in humans, consider the surprising evolution of syphilis. Today we associate syphilis with genital sores and a very slowly developing disease, leading to the death of untreated victims only after many years. However, when syphilis was first definitely recorded in Europe in 1495, its pustules often covered the body from the head to the knees, caused flesh to fall off people's faces, and led to death within a few months. By 1546 syphilis had evolved into the disease with the symptoms known to us today. Apparently, just as with myxomatosis, those syphilis spirochetes evolved to keep their victims alive longer in order to transmit their spirochete offspring into more victims.

How, then, does all this explain the outcome of 1492—that Europeans conquered and depopulated the New World, instead of Native Americans conquering and depopulating Europe?

Part of the answer, of course, goes back to the invaders' technological advantages. European guns and steel swords were more effective weapons than Native American stone axes and wooden clubs. Only Europeans had ships capable of crossing the ocean and horses that could provide a decisive ad-

vantage in battle. But that's not the whole answer. Far more Native Americans died in bed than on the battlefield—the victims of germs, not of guns and swords. Those germs undermined Indian resistance by killing most Indians and their leaders and by demoralizing the survivors.

The role of disease in the Spanish conquests of the Aztec and Inca empires is especially well documented. In 1519 Cortés landed on the coast of Mexico with 600 Spaniards to conquer the fiercely militaristic Aztec Empire, which at the time had a population of many millions. That Cortés reached the Aztec capital of Tenochtitlán, escaped with the loss of "only" two-thirds of his force, and managed to fight his way back to the coast demonstrates both Spanish military advantages and the initial naïveté of the Aztecs. But when Cortés's next onslaught came, in 1521, the Aztecs were no longer naive; they fought street by street with the utmost tenacity.

In the century or two following Columbus's arrival in the New World, the Indian population declined by about 95 percent. The main killers were European germs, to which the Indians had never been exposed.

What gave the Spaniards a decisive advantage this time was smallpox, which reached Mexico in 1520 with the arrival of one infected slave from Spanish Cuba. The resulting epidemic proceeded to kill nearly half the Aztecs. The survivors were demoralized by the mysterious illness that killed Indians and spared Spaniards, as if advertising the Spaniards' invincibility. By 1618 Mexico's initial population of 20 million had plummeted to about 1.6 million.

Pizarro had similarly grim luck when he landed on the coast of Peru in 1531 with about 200 men to conquer the Inca

Empire. Fortunately for Pizarro, and unfortunately for the Incas, smallpox had arrived overland around 1524, killing much of the Inca population, including both Emperor Huayna Capac and his son and designated successor, Ninan Cuyoche. Because of the vacant throne, two other sons of Huayna Capac, Atahuallpa and Huáscar, became embroiled in a civil war that Pizarro exploited to conquer the divided Incas.

When we in the United States think of the most populous New World societies existing in 1492, only the Aztecs and Incas come to mind. We forget that North America also supported populous Indian societies in the Mississippi Valley. Sadly, these societies too would disappear. But in this case conquistadores contributed nothing directly to the societies' destruction; the conquistadores' germs, spreading in advance, did everything. When De Soto marched through the Southeast in 1540, he came across Indian towns abandoned two years previously because nearly all the inhabitants had died in epidemics. However, he was still able to see some of the densely populated towns lining the lower Mississippi. By a century and a half later, though, when French settlers returned to the lower Mississippi, almost all those towns had vanished. Their relics are the great mound sites of the Mississippi Valley. Only recently have we come to realize that the mound-building societies were still largely intact when Columbus arrived, and that they collapsed between 1492 and the systematic European exploration of the Mississippi.

When I was a child in school, we were taught that North America had originally been occupied by about one million Indians. That low number helped justify the white conquest of what could then be viewed as an almost empty continent. However, archeological excavations and descriptions left by the first European explorers on our coasts now suggest an initial number of around 20 million. In the century or two following Columbus's arrival in the New World, the Indian population is estimated to have declined by about 95 percent.

The main killers were European germs, to which the Indians had never been exposed and against which they therefore had neither immunologic nor genetic resistance. Smallpox, measles, influenza, and typhus competed for top rank among the killers. As if those were not enough, pertussis, plague, tuberculosis, diphtheria, mumps, malaria, and yellow fever came close behind. In countless cases Europeans were actually there to witness the decimation that occurred when the germs arrived. For example, in 1837 the Mandan Indian tribe, with one of the most elaborate cultures in the Great Plains, contracted smallpox thanks to a steamboat traveling up the Missouri River from St. Louis. The population of one Mandan village crashed from 2,000 to less than 40 within a few weeks.

The one-sided exchange of lethal germs between the Old and New worlds is among the most striking and consequence-laden facts of recent history. Whereas over a dozen major infectious diseases of Old World origins became established in the New World, not a single major killer reached Europe from the Americas. The sole possible exception is syphilis, whose area of origin still remains controversial.

That one-sidedness is more striking with the knowledge that large, dense human populations are a prerequisite for the evolution of crowd diseases. If recent reappraisals of the pre-Columbian New World population are correct, that population was not far below the contemporaneous population of Eurasia. Some New World cities, like Tenochtitlán, were among the world's most populous cities at the time. Yet Tenochtitlán didn't have awful germs waiting in store for the Spaniards. Why not?

One possible factor is the rise of dense human populations began somewhat later in the New World than in the Old. Another is that the three most populous American centers—the Andes, Mexico, and the Mississippi Valley—were never connected by regular fast trade into one gigantic breeding ground for microbes, in the way that Europe, North Africa, India, and China became connected in late Roman times.

The main reason becomes clear, however, if we ask a simple question: From what microbes could any crowd diseases of the Americas have evolved? We've seen that Eurasian crowd diseases evolved from diseases of domesticated herd animals. Significantly, there were many such animals in Eurasia. But there were only five animals that became domesticated in the Americas: the turkey in Mexico and parts of North America, the guinea pig and llama/alpaca (probably derived from the same original wild species) in the Andes, and Muscovy duck in tropical South America, and the dog throughout the Americas.

That extreme paucity of New World domestic animals reflects the paucity of wild starting material. About 80 percent of the big wild mammals of the Americas became extinct at the end of the last ice age, around 11,000 years ago, at approximately the same time that the first well-attested wave of Indian hunters spread over the Americas. Among the species that disappeared were ones that would have yielded useful domesticates, such as American horses and camels. Debate still rages as to whether those extinctions were due to climate changes or to the impact of Indian hunters on prey that had never seen humans. Whatever the reason, the extinctions removed most of the basis for Native American animal domestication—and for crowd diseases.

The few domesticates that remained were not likely sources of such diseases. Muscovy ducks and turkeys don't live in enormous flocks, and they're not naturally endearing species (like young lambs) with which we have much physical contact. Guinea pigs may have contributed a trypanosome infection like Chagas' disease or leishmaniasis to our catalog of woes, but that's uncertain.

Initially the most surprising absence is of any human disease derived from llamas (or alpacas), which are tempting to consider as the Andean equivalent of Eurasian livestock. However, llamas had three strikes against them as a source of human pathogens: their wild relatives don't occur in big herds as do wild sheep, goats, and pigs; their total numbers were never remotely as large as the Eurasian populations of domestic livestock, since llamas never spread beyond the Andes; and llamas aren't as cuddly as piglets and lambs and aren't kept in such close association with people. (You may not think of piglets as cuddly, but human mothers in the New Guinea highlands often nurse them, and they frequently live right in the huts of peasant farmers.)

The importance of animal-derived diseases for human history extends far beyond the Americas. Eurasian germs played a key role in decimating native peoples in many other parts of the world as well, including the Pacific islands, Australia, and southern Africa. Racist Europeans used to attribute those conquests to their supposedly better brains. But no evidence for such better brains has been forthcoming. Instead, the conquests were made possible by Europeans nastier germs, and by the technological advances and denser populations that Europeans ultimately acquired by means of their domesticated plants and animals.

So on this 500th anniversary of Columbus's discovery, let's try to regain our sense of perspective about his hotly debated achievements. There's no doubt that Columbus was a great visionary, seaman, and leader. There's also no doubt that he and his successors often behaved as bestial murderers. But those facts alone don't fully explain why it took so few European immigrants to initially conquer and ultimately supplant so much of the native population of the Americas. Without the germs Europeans brought with them—germs that were derived from their animals—such conquests might have been impossible.

Article 37

A Pacific Haze:
Alcohol and Drugs in Oceania

Mac Marshall

University of Iowa

All over the world people eat, drink, smoke, or blow substances up their noses in the perennial quest to alter and expand human consciousness. Most of these substances come from psychoactive plants native to different regions—coca, tobacco, and peyote, in the New World; khat, coffee, and marijuana in North Africa and the Middle East; betel and opium in Asia. Some people use hallucinogens from mushrooms or tree bark; others consume more exotic drugs. Produced by fermentation, brewing, or distillation of a remarkable variety of raw materials—ranging from fruits and grains to milk and honey—traditional alcoholic beverages were found almost everywhere before the Age of Exploration.

As European explorers trekked and sailed about the globe between 1500 and 1900, they carried many of these traditional drugs back to their homelands. Different exotic drugs became popular at different times in Europe as the explorers shared their experiences. In this manner, tea, tobacco, coffee, marijuana, and opium gained avid followers in European countries. Today, this worldwide process of drug diffusion continues at a rapid pace, with changes in attitudes toward different drugs and the introduction of new laws governing their use varying accordingly.

Oceanic peoples were no exception to the widespread quest to expand the human mind. From ancient times they used drugs to defuse tense interpersonal or intergroup relations, relax socially, and commune with the spirit world. Betel and kava were far and away the most common traditional drugs used in the Pacific Islands. The geographical distribution of these two drugs was uneven across the islands, and, in a few places (for example, Chuuk [Truk]), no drugs were used at all before the arrival of foreigners. Kava and betel were not only differentially distributed geographically, but they were also differently distributed socially. Every society had rules governing who might take them (and under what circumstances) that limited their consumption, often only to adult men.

In the four-and-a-half centuries since foreign exploration of the Pacific world began, the islanders have been introduced to several new drugs, most notably alcoholic beverages, tobacco, and marijuana. This chapter discusses substance use in the contemporary Pacific Islands by examining the history and patterns of use of the five major drugs found in the islands today: alcohol, betel, kava, marijuana, and tobacco. To the extent that reliable information exists, such recently introduced drugs as cocaine and heroin are also discussed. The primary concern of the chapter is with the negative social, economic, and health consequences that result from consumption of alcohol, tobacco, and marijuana in the contemporary Pacific Islands.

BETEL AND KAVA

"Betel" is a convenient linguistic gloss for a preparation consisting of at least three distinct substances, two of which are pharmacologically active: the nut of the *Areca catechu* palm, the leaves, stems, or catkins of the *Piper betle* vine, and slaked lime from ground seashells or coral. These substances usually are combined into a quid and chewed. In some societies, people swallow the resultant profuse saliva, while in others they spit out the blood red juice. Kava is drunk as a water-based infusion made from the pounded, grated, or chewed root of a shrub, *Piper methysticum.* Whereas betel ingredients can easily be carried on the person and quickly prepared, kava makings are not as portable, and its preparation calls for a more involved procedure. Betel is often chewed individually with little or no ceremony; kava is usually drunk communally, and frequently accompanied by elaborate ceremonial procedures.

Betel chewing appears to have originated long ago in Island Southeast Asia and to have spread into the islands of the Western Pacific from there. While betel use is widespread in Melanesia (including the New Guinea Highlands where it has recently been introduced), it is absent from the Polynesian Triangle, and it is found only on the westernmost Micronesian islands of Palau, Yap, and the Marianas (Marshall 1987a).

In most parts of the Pacific Islands where betel is chewed, its use occupies a social position akin to coffee or tea drinking in Western societies. For example, Iamo (1987) writes that betel is chewed to stimulate social activity, suppress boredom, enhance work, and increase personal enjoyment among the Keakalo people of the south coast of Papua New Guinea. Similarly, Lepowsky (1982) comments that for the people of Vanatinai Island in Papua New Guinea, shared betel symbolizes friendly and peaceful social relations. Iamo notes that betel consumption "is

From *Contemporary Pacific Societies: Studies in Development and Change,* edited by Victoria S. Lockwood and Thomas G. Harding, 1993, Chapter 17, pp. 260-272. © 1993 by Prentice Hall, Inc. Reprinted by permission.

rampant among children, young people, and adults" in Keakalo; that is, it has few social constraints on its use, except in times of scarcity (1987:146). Similarly, "Vanatinai people chew betel many times a day," and they also begin chewing betel early in childhood: "By the age of eight to ten, boys and girls chew whenever they can find the ingredients" (Lepowsky 1982:335).

In those parts of Papua New Guinea where the betel ingredients can be produced in abundance, such as Keakalo and Vanatinai, they figure importantly as items of exchange or for sale as "exports" to surrounding peoples. The enterprising Biwat of East Sepik Province are remarkable in this regard. They trade *Areca* nut, *Piper betle,* and locally grown tobacco with other peoples in the vicinity, carry these products by canoe to the regional market town of Angoram (98 miles away), and occasionally even charter a small airplane to sell as far away as Mount Hagen in the Western Highlands Province (Watson 1987).

Traditionally, kava was drunk only in Oceania, the world region to which the plant appears native. Kava drinking occurred throughout the high islands of Polynesia (except Easter Island, New Zealand, and Rapa), on the two easternmost high islands of Micronesia (Pohnpei and Kosrae), and in various parts of Melanesia, particularly Fiji, Vanuatu, and New Guinea proper. Kava and betel were often in complementary distribution, although there were some societies where both were routinely consumed.

Whereas betel is chewed by males and females, old and young, kava is different. In most Pacific Islands societies, at least traditionally, kava drinking was restricted to men, and often to "fully adult" or high-status men. Although its consumption was thus restricted, young, uninitiated or untitled men, or young women, usually prepared it. These distinctions were notably marked in the elaborate kava ceremonies of Fiji, Tonga, and Samoa. Wherever it was used, however, kava played important parts in pre-Christian religion, political deliberations, ethnomedical systems, and general quiet social interaction among a community's adult men.

On the island of Tanna, Vanuatu, for example, Lindstrom (1987) argues that

getting drunk on and exchanging kava links man to man, separates man from woman, establishes a contextual interpersonal equality among men, and determines and maintains relations of inequality between men and women. Kava is drunk every evening on Tanna at a special kava-drinking ground, separated from the village, and from which women and girls are excluded. Lindstrom argues that kava (which is grown by women) is both itself an important exchange item and symbolically represents male appropriation and control over women and their productive and reproductive capacities. Tannese men fear that women intoxicated on kava would become "crazed" and usurp men's control over them, become sexually wanton, and cease to cook. Lindstrom concludes, "Gender asymmetry in Tannese drunken practice maintains and reproduces social relations of production and exchange" (1987:116).

Among the Gebusi of Papua New Guinea's Western Province, the men of a longhouse community force their male visitors to drink several bowls of kava in rapid succession, usually to the point of nausea. This is done to prevent the chief antagonists at ritual fights or funeral feasts "from disputing or taking retaliatory action against their hosts during a particularly tense moment in the proceedings" (Knauft 1987:85). Forced smoking of home-grown tobacco is used in an analogous manner "to forestall escalation of hostilities" among a people for whom homicide tied to sorcery accusations is a leading cause of male mortality. As on Tanna, Gebusi women never drink kava. Both peoples link kava to sexuality: Lindstrom (1987:112–113) describes a Tannese-origin myth of kava that he calls "kava as dildo"; Knauft (1987:85–88) notes that kava often serves as a metaphor for semen in jokes about heterosexual relations or the ritual homosexuality practiced by the Gebusi.

As is typically the case in human affairs, these long-known and highly valued drug substances were deeply rooted in cultural traditions and patterns of social interaction. Pacific Islands peoples had developed culturally controlled ways of using betel and kava that usually precluded abuse.[1] Users also were unlikely to develop problems because of the relatively benign physiological effects of

these two substances and because neither drug by itself seems to produce serious harmful disease states when consumed in a traditional manner.

Kava drinking leads to a variety of physical effects, perhaps the most pronounced of which are analgesia, muscle relaxation, and a sense of quiet well-being. In addition to its ceremonial and recreational uses, kava is a common drug in Oceanic ethnomedicine, and kava extracts also are employed in Western biomedicine. Of the various drugs discovered by human beings around the world, kava seems to be one of the least problematic. Its physiological effects induce a state of peaceful contemplation and euphoria, with the mental faculties left clear, and it produces no serious pathology unless taken (as by some Australian Aborigines since 1980) at doses far in excess of those consumed by Pacific Islanders. The most prominent effects of prolonged heavy kava consumption among Oceanic peoples are a dry scaly skin, bloodshot eyes, possible constipation and intestinal obstruction, and occasional weight loss (Lemert 1967). Even excessive kava use does not produce withdrawal symptoms, and all of the above conditions are reversible if drinking is discontinued.

The situation with betel is somewhat more complex. The main physical effect obtained by betel chewers is central nervous system stimulation and arousal producing a sense of general well-being (Burton-Bradley 1980). Arecoline, the primary active ingredient in betel, also stimulates various glands, leading to profuse sweating and salivation, among other things. Beginners typically experience such unpleasant symptoms as nausea, diarrhea, and dizziness, and prolonged use leads to physiological addiction. There is some preliminary experimental evidence that arecoline enhances memory and learning, and it is being explored as a possible medicine for patients suffering from Alzheimer's disease (Gilbert 1986).

Considerable controversy surrounds the health risks of betel chewing, particularly as regards its possible role in the development of oral cancer (MacLennan et al. 1985). This debate has been confounded by the fact that many betel chewers in Southeast and South Asia (where most of the clinical data have been collected) add other ingredients to the betel chew, most commonly, and notably, tobacco. A summary of the epidemiological evidence available to date leads to the conclusion that chewing betel using traditional ingredients without the addition of tobacco probably does not carry any significant risk for oral cancer (Gupta et al. 1982).[2] Occasionally, a betel chewer develops what Burton-Bradley (1966) calls "betel nut psychosis," following a period of abstinence and in response to a heavy dose of the drug. This acute reversible toxic psychosis is characterized by delusions and hallucinations in predisposed individuals, but it must be emphasized that its occurrence is rare. There is thus no conclusive evidence that regular betel chewing without the addition of tobacco results in physical or mental health problems for most people. Like kava, betel appears to produce a relatively harmless "high."

As usually taken in Oceania, not only do kava and betel consumption pose few—if any—health risks, but neither drug leads to intoxicated behavior that is socially disruptive (indeed, quite the contrary). The plants from which these substances are derived are locally grown and quite readily available, and the processes for making and taking these two traditional drugs do not require commercial manufacture. In the past twenty years, some cash marketing of both drugs has developed, but this is primarily by smallholders or local concerns, and neither substance is handled by multinational corporations. Thus, kava and betel do not have negative social and economic consequences for the Pacific Islands societies where they are used.

ALCOHOLIC BEVERAGES

Pacific Islanders, like most North American Indians, had no alcoholic beverages until Europeans brought them early in the contact period. Initially, most islanders found alcohol distasteful and spat it out, but eventually they acquired a fondness for what sometimes was called "white man's kava." During the late eighteenth and first half of the nineteenth century, whalers, beachcombers, missionaries, and traders arrived in the

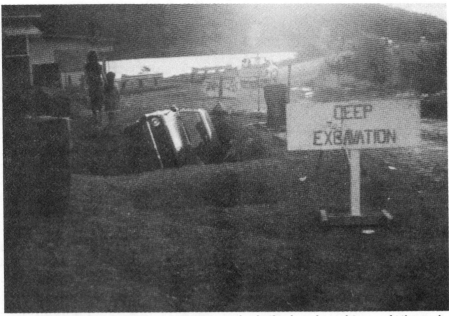

"Driving Under the Influence" Accident, Weno Island, Chuuk, Federated States of Micronesia (1985). (Photo by M. Marshall)

islands in growing numbers. Many of them were drinkers and provided models of drunken behavior for the islanders to copy. Some of them established saloons in the port towns, and alcohol was widely used as an item of trade with the islanders. By at least the 1840s, missionaries to the islands, reflecting temperance politics in the United States and Great Britain, began to speak out forcefully against "the evils of drink" (Marshall and Marshall 1976).

As the European and American powers of the day consolidated colonial control over Oceania in the nineteenth century, they passed laws prohibiting islanders from consuming beverage alcohol. While such laws usually had strong missionary backing, they were also intended to maintain order, protect colonists from the possible "drunken depredations of savages," and serve what were deemed to be the islanders' own best interests. Despite prohibition, production of home brews continued in some areas, theft provided an occasional source of liquor, and the drinking of methylated spirits offered a potentially deadly alcohol alternative in some parts of the Pacific (Marshall 1988:579–582).

Colonially imposed prohibition laws remained in place until the 1950s and 1960s, when they were set aside one after another in the era of decolonization. Since

then, the establishment of new Pacific nations has fostered a maze of legal regulations surrounding alcohol use, and it has also led to the encouragement of alcohol production and marketing. In many different parts of the Pacific Islands, problems have accompanied the relaxation of controls and the expansion of availability.

It is generally true around the world that more men drink alcoholic beverages than women, and that men drink greater quantities than women, but these gender differences are particularly pronounced in most of Oceania. In many of the islands, there are strong social pressures against women drinking, reinforced by church teachings, that effectively keep most women from even tasting alcoholic beverages. With a few exceptions, it is usually only Westernized women in the towns who drink on any sort of a regular basis. Boys below age fourteen or fifteen seldom, if ever, drink, but by the time they are in their late teens or early twenties, nearly all of them partake of alcohol. So much is this the case that in Chuuk (Truk) drinking and drunkenness is called "young men's work" (Marshall 1987b).

These gender differences have resulted in profoundly different attitudes toward alcohol by men and women that sometimes have resulted in outspoken social opposition by women to men's drinking and its attendant social problems (see Marshall and Marshall 1990). Weekend binge drinking by groups of young men—especially in towns—frequently leads to social disruption and confrontations that have been labeled "weekend warfare" in one Micronesian society (Marshall 1979).

For many Pacific Islanders, alcoholic beverages have come to symbolize "the good life" and active participation in a modern, sophisticated lifestyle. Beer is usually the beverage of choice in Oceania, and, in some places, it has been incorporated into ceremonial exchanges surrounding such events as bride price payments, weddings, and funerals. In the Papua New Guinea Highlands' Chuave area, beer is treated as an item of wealth and "has assumed a central role in inter- and intraclan prestations" (Warry 1982:84). Cartons of beer have been endowed with a number of social and symbolic qualities in common with pork, the most highly esteemed traditional valuable. For example, the success of a ceremony is judged, increasingly, by the amount of beer, as well as pork, available for display and distribution; beer in cartons has a known value and the twenty-four bottles are easily divisible; like pigs, the stacked cartons of beer (sometimes as many as 240!) are appropriate items for display; alcohol is a social facilitator in these sometimes tense feast situations; beer—like pork and other foodstuffs—is consumable; and, like pork, beer is used at feasts both as a tool to create relationships and as a weapon to slight rivals (Warry 1982).

The chief problems associated with alcohol use in Oceania are social ones, although it is difficult to divorce these from the interrelated public health and economic costs. Among the more prominent and widespread social problems are domestic strife, particularly wife beating; community fighting and disruption, often with attendant trauma and occasional fatalities; crime, and drunk-driving accidents.

In the post–World War II era, these alcohol-related problems have been a continuing concern of community-based and government agencies in Pacific Islands countries. For example, a seminar was held in 1977 on "Alcohol Problems with the Young People of Fiji" (Fiji National Youth Council 1977), and, in 1986, Catholic youth in the Highlands of Papua New Guinea rallied to oppose alcohol abuse (*The Times of Papua New Guinea 1986a*). Other examples of community-based concerns are church women's groups who championed a legal prohibition against alcohol on Weno, Chuuk (Moen Island, Truk) (Marshall and Marshall 1990), and an ecumenical Christian training center in Papua New Guinea (the Melanesian Institute) that has given voice to village peoples' concerns over abuse of alcohol for many years. Within a decade after it became legal for Papua New Guineans to drink, the government felt it necessary to sponsor an official Commission of Inquiry in 1971 to assess the widely perceived problems that had ensued. Less than ten years later, another investigation of alcohol use and abuse under national government auspices was launched in Papua New Guinea through its Institute for Applied Social and Economic Research (IASER). Such government commissions and groups of concerned citizens usually produce recommendations for action; however, serious and effective alcohol control policies are rarely forthcoming.

Although they have received less attention in the literature, primarily because of the absence of adequate hospital records and autopsy reports for Pacific Islands countries, the physical and mental illnesses linked to either prolonged heavy ethanol intake or binge drinking appear to be considerable. Among these are alcoholic cirrhosis, cancers of the upper respiratory and upper digestive tracts, death from ethanol overdose, alcoholic psychoses, and suicide while under the influence of alcohol.

In recent years, researchers have focused on non-insulin-dependent diabetes mellitus (NIDDM), which has increased in urbanized and migrant Pacific Islands populations (for example, Baker et al. 1986; King et al. 1984). With changes from traditional diets to "modern" diets of refined foods and higher intakes of fats, sugar, sodium, and alcoholic beverages, some Micronesian and Polynesian populations have shown what is thought to be a hereditary susceptibility

Wall Painting (by Robert Suine), Kuglame Taverne, Simbu Province, Papua New Guinea (1980). (Photo by M. Marshall)

to NIDDM, which apparently is only expressed with a change from the traditional rural lifestyle. Urban and migrant islanders typically engage in less physical activity and have higher levels of obesity than their rural nonmigrant counterparts. Given that individuals with diabetes are more vulnerable to the hypoglycemic effects of alcohol because alcohol interferes with hepatic gluconeogenesis (Franz 1983:149; see also Madsen 1974:52–53), heavy drinking that may produce complications for diabetics poses an added health risk.

TOBACCO

Although the Spanish and Portuguese introduced tobacco into the East Indies from the New World in the late sixteenth and early seventeenth centuries, and although this new drug spread rather quickly to the island of New Guinea via traditional trade routes, *Nicotiana tabacum* did not reach most Pacific Islands until the nineteenth century. It became a basic item of trade and even served as a kind of currency during the heyday of European exploration and colonization of Oceania. The first German plantations on the north coast of New Guinea near Madang were tobacco plantations, and the crop continues to be grown commercially in Fiji and Papua New Guinea. In the 1800s, pipe and homemade cigar smoking were quite popular; today manufactured cigarettes dominate the market in most parts of the Pacific Islands. The prevalence of tobacco smoking by both men and women in Pacific Islands populations is much higher than in the developed countries of Australia, New Zealand, and the United States, and higher than in most developing nations elsewhere in the world (Marshall 1991). In some isolated rural parts of Oceania, nearly everyone in a community smokes—including children as young as eight or ten years of age.

With the decline in tobacco use in the developed nations of the West, the multinational corporations that control global production and marketing of this drug have shifted their emphasis to the huge and rapidly growing market in the Third World. Developing countries offer few restrictions to tobacco companies: most such countries have no maximum tar and nicotine levels, no laws restricting sales to minors, no advertising limits, no required health warnings, and no general public awareness of the serious health risks associated with smoking (Stebbins 1990). As a result, tobacco consumption has grown steadily in Third World countries, leading public health experts to predict and document the beginning of a major epidemic of diseases known to be linked to chronic tobacco use. During the 1980s, numerous studies have been published by health care professionals and other concerned individuals noting these alarming trends and calling for action. Studies documenting these problems exist for Africa, Latin America, and Asia, and researchers have begun to chronicle the same sad story for Oceania (Marshall 1991).

As with the upsurge in alcohol use and its aggressive marketing by multinational corporations in Pacific Islands countries, so it is, too, with the produc-

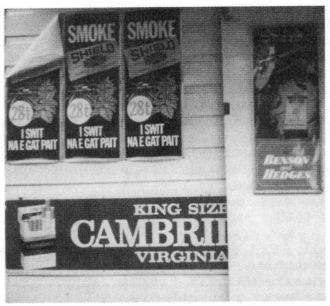

Cigarette advertisements on the outside of a store, Goroka, Eastern Highlands Province, Papua New Guinea (1980). (Photo by M. Marshall)

tion and sale of commercial tobacco products, particularly cigarettes. Almost any store one enters in Oceania today displays tobacco advertisements prominently inside and out, and has numerous tobacco products readily available for sale. Among the many ploys used to push their brands, the tobacco companies sponsor sweepstakes contests with large cash prizes which can be entered by writing one's name and address on an empty cigarette pack and dropping it into a special box for a drawing. Tobacco firms also routinely sponsor sporting events, with trophies and prizes in cash and in kind. In other promotions, those who present fifteen empty packs of the pertinent brands are given "free" T-shirts emblazoned with the cigarette brand name.

The association of tobacco smoking with serious cardiovascular and respiratory diseases—lung cancer, chronic bronchitis, and emphysema—is by now well known. These diseases are particularly linked to the smoking of flue-cured commercial cigarettes, which now have been readily available in Oceania for about thirty years. As the Pacific Islanders who have smoked such cigarettes for many years develop health problems, more suffer from these smoking-related illnesses (Marshall 1991). One New

Zealand study shows that those Maori women who smoke heavily during pregnancy produce infants of a lower average birth weight than those of Europeans or other Pacific Islanders in New Zealand (Hay and Foster 1981). Another study shows Maori women to have a lung cancer rate that is among the world's highest (Stanhope and Prior 1982).

As yet, there have been few efforts to gain control over the smoking epidemic in Pacific Islands countries. In one, the Fiji Medical Association announced a campaign to ban cigarette advertising following a directive from the Fiji Ministry of Health to stop smoking in all patient areas in government hospitals (*Pacific Islands Monthly* 1986). But the most encouraging program has been mounted in Papua New Guinea. In the early 1980s, an antismoking council was established there by members of the medical profession (Smith 1983), and, following several years of public debate, Parliament passed the Tobacco Products (Health Control) Act in November 1987. This law mandates various controls on tobacco advertising, requires health warning labels on cigarette packs and cigarette advertisements, and provides the authority to declare various public places as nonsmoking areas. As of March 1990, these included all national and provincial government offices, the offices and buildings of all educational institutions (other than staff quarters), all hospitals, health centers, clinics and aid posts, cinemas and theatres, public motor vehicles (PMVs), and all domestic flights on scheduled airlines. While there are some enforcement problems, the Department of Health has mounted an aggressive antismoking campaign (tied to the anti-betel-chewing campaign), and this is likely to have a positive impact over the next few years.

Despite the encouraging signs in Papua New Guinea, public-health-oriented antismoking campaigns have met with relatively small success to date in the face of the large sums of money devoted to advertising by the tobacco multinationals. Much more effort is needed in community and public health education if this preventable epidemic is to be brought under control in Oceania.

MARIJUANA

Unlike the use of alcohol, betel, kava, and tobacco, marijuana smoking is uniformly illegal in Oceania. Nonetheless, the plant is now grown quite widely in the islands and has a substantial number of devotees. In part because its cultivation and use is against the law, fewer data are available on marijuana smoking than on the other four common Pacific drugs.

Native to central Asia, marijuana diffused to Oceania much more recently than alcohol or tobacco. While it doubtless was present in such places as Hawaii and New Zealand well before World War II, in other island areas like Micronesia or the New Guinea highlands, it appears to have been introduced only during the 1960s and 1970s.

While considerable controversy surrounds the long-term health effects of marijuana smoking, certain things are by now well known and give cause for concern. Marijuana induces an increased cardiovascular work load, thus posing a potential threat to individuals with hypertension and coronary atherosclerosis. Both of these health problems have been on the rise in Pacific Islands populations, especially in urban areas (Baker et al. 1986; Patrick et al. 1983; Salmond

et al. 1985), and both can only be worsened by marijuana use.

Marijuana smoke is unfiltered and contains about 50 percent more cancer-causing hydrocarbons than tobacco smoke (Maugh 1982). Recent research has shown that "marijuana delivers more particulate matter to the smoker than tobacco cigarettes and with a net four-times greater burden on the respiratory system" (Addiction Research Foundation 1989:3). This same work revealed significant structural changes in the lungs of marijuana smokers, with a higher rate among those who also smoked tobacco. These changes are associated with chronic obstructive lung disease and with lung cancer. Another study has found significant short-term memory impairment in cannabis-dependent individuals that lingers for at least six weeks after use of the drug is stopped (Schwartz et al. 1989). As was discussed above for tobacco, the limited amount of research that has been done shows respiratory illnesses to be major serious diseases in Oceania. Clearly, smoking marijuana will simply raise the incidence of health problems that were already significant in the Pacific Islands even before marijuana gained popularity.

In the Pacific Islands, as in the United States, marijuana growing is attractive because it yields a higher cash return per unit of time per unit of land than other agricultural crops. Even though marijuana is grown as a cash crop and often sold by the "joint," the plant is easy to grow, requires little attention, and thrives in most island environments. As a result, most marijuana consumed in the Pacific Islands, like betel and kava, is locally grown and not imported by drug cartels or multinationals. Even so, marijuana grown in the islands is sometimes exported to larger and more lucrative markets (Nero 1985). This has become the subject of major police concern in Papua New Guinea, where there are some indications that organized crime may be involved in the purchase of marijuana grown in the highlands to be sent overseas (for example, *Niugini Nius* 1990). It will be well nigh impossible to uproot marijuana from Oceania today, but much more

could be done to educate islanders about the health risks associated with its use.

OTHER DRUGS

As of 1989, hard drugs such as cocaine and heroin have made little headway in Pacific Islands communities. The most dramatic example of a place where such penetration has begun is Palau, where heroin first showed up in the early 1970s (Nero 1985:20–23). By 1985, cocaine was being used in Palau as well, and, by then, a number of Palauan heroin addicts had been sent to Honolulu for detoxification and treatment (Polloi 1985).

Although the Palauan case is somewhat unusual for the Pacific Islands at present, there are increased reports of hard drugs being shipped *through* the islands from Asia for metropolitan markets in Australia, New Zealand, and North America. Clearly, given the ease of air travel and relatively lax security and customs checks, more hard drugs will appear in the islands in the coming years.

CONCLUSIONS

Oceania's traditional drugs—betel and kava—create few if any social problems and pose minimal health risks to users. Moreover, these drugs are locally produced, and even when they are sold in the market the profits remain in islanders' hands and enrich the local economy. From an economic perspective, the cropping and selling of marijuana in most of the Pacific Islands operates in much the same way: small growers cultivate the plant for their own use or to sell in local markets. The major differences between marijuana and betel and kava are that marijuana is illegal and that smoking marijuana poses significant health risks. Oceania's other two major drug substances are produced and distributed in a very different manner and pose much more serious social and public health problems.

Over the past decade, an accumulation of studies has shown that alcoholic beverage and tobacco multinational corporations have increasingly targeted developing countries as prime markets for their products (for example, Cavanaugh and Clairmonte 1985; Muller 1978; Stebbins 1990; Wickström 1979). This marketing involves aggressive advertising, often aimed especially at young people and women. Frequently, it takes the form of joint ventures with host governments, on the grounds that large profits can be shared (which ignores the significant health and social costs involved). The multinationals also have become infamous for inducing governments (for example, the United States) to threaten trade embargoes against countries that balk at the unrestrained marketing of alcohol and tobacco products within their borders (*The Nation's Health* 1989).

The developing countries of Oceania have been subject to this "legal pushing" of harmful substances, even though their populations are small and transport poses certain logistical problems. Breweries, ultimately owned by huge overseas corporations, operate in French Polynesia, Western Samoa, Tonga, Fiji, Vanuatu, and Papua New Guinea, and there are distilled beverage producers in Fiji and Papua New Guinea.

For example, domestic production of hard liquor began in Papua New Guinea in 1985 by Fairdeal Liquors Pty. Ltd. Fairdeal imports raw materials (concentrates and ethanol) from its parent corporation based in Malaysia and from other overseas sources. The company then mixes and bottles both its own brands and selected internationally known brands on franchise (for example, Gilbey's gin, Jim Beam whiskey) in its factory in the Port Moresby suburb of Gordons. Initially, Fairdeal was able to market its own product ("Gold Cup") in small, clear plastic sachets for around 35 cents (U.S.) each. These were a marketing success but a social disaster because irresponsible storekeepers sold them to children as well as adults, and because many men drank them to excess. The ensuing public outcry led the Prime Minister to ask the company to withdraw the sachets from the market two months after they were introduced. Following the outcry from concerned citizens, especially in the highlands (*The Times of Papua New Guinea* 1986), Fairdeal briefly closed its Port Moresby factory in December 1986 because the national government also imposed a 1,200 percent increase in the import tax on the concentrate used to produce liquor (*The Times of Papua New Guinea* 1986). But even with this momentary setback, Fairdeal continues to market its own brands in bottles for half the price of comparable imports. This is possible because by bottling locally the company still avoids paying as much excise duty as that paid by importers of alcoholic beverages that are bottled abroad.

It was announced in mid-1989 that new breweries would be built in Papua New Guinea and Western Samoa (*Pacific Islands Monthly* 1989). The Papua New Guinea venture, which since has fallen through, was to be constructed at Kerowagi in Simbu Province, and represented a proposed joint venture among Danbrew Consult of Denmark and the five highlands provincial governments. At least two highlands provincial premiers had to be cajoled into committing their provinces to participation in this scheme, and the highly controversial project was opposed by women's organizations and church groups. Papua New Guinea's major brewery—South Pacific—itself a subsidiary of the Heineken Group, bought out its sole competitor (San Miguel, PNG) early in 1983. San Miguel (PNG) was a subsidiary of "the most successful conglomerate group in the Philippines," a group that held overseas interests in mining, brewing, fishing, finance, and development in nine different countries in Asia and Europe (Krinks 1987).

In 1978, War on Want published a slender volume entitled, *Tobacco and the Third World: Tomorrow's Epidemic?* Just over a decade later, the *question* in that book's title has been answered—a smoking epidemic has swept the Third World, and the Pacific Islands have not been immune to this global trend. While cigarettes and stick tobacco are locally produced in Papua New Guinea and Fiji by subsidiaries of the giant British Tobacco Company, the overwhelming majority of tobacco products sold in Oceania today are commercial cigarettes imported from the developed countries, principally Australia, New Zealand, and the United States. Promotional campaigns continue to have few, if any, restrictions placed upon them, and the costs of sweepstakes and raffle giveaways is small compared to the substantial profits to be earned once new consumers are "hooked."

A haze hangs over the Pacific Islands today, a result of widespread alcohol and tobacco abuse and of the smokescreens put up by multinationals to buy off politicians under the guise that production and marketing of these legal drugs contributes to economic development. In fact, the public health costs of alcohol and tobacco use and the social disruption surrounding alcohol abuse *undermine* economic and social development over the long run. If Pacific Islands governments do not develop more effective systems to prevent and control the aggressive marketing of alcohol and tobacco by multinationals, then the haze in the air and the glazed looks on the faces of island citizens will increase. The resultant social and health costs can only weaken Oceanic communities and make more difficult their dream of building prosperous, healthy, modern societies.

Acknowledgment: I am grateful to Linda A. Bennett for useful comments on an earlier version of this chapter.

Notes

1. This statement remains true for Pacific Islanders; however, Australian Aborigines, to whom kava was introduced in the 1980s, and who consume it in quantities far in excess of those taken by Pacific Islanders, have developed such clinical side effects as weight loss, liver and kidney dysfunction, blood abnormalities, and possible pulmonary hypertension (Mathews et al. 1988; Riley and Mathews 1989).
2. Recently, in Papua New Guinea, and possibly elsewhere in the Pacific Islands, lime manufactured by commercial chemical firms has been substituted for lime produced in the traditional manner from ground seashells or coral. There is some evidence to suggest that the industrially manufactured lime is much more caustic than that traditionally used by Pacific betel chewers, and that this may increase the risk of oral cancer. Although controlled studies to demonstrate this have yet to be done, the Papua New Guinea Department of Health has mounted an active public health campaign advising people that if they chew betel, they run a risk of developing oral cancer.

Growing up as a Fore

E. Richard Sorenson

Dr. Sorenson, director of the Smithsonian's National Anthropological Film Center, wrote The Edge of the Forest *on his Fore studies.*

Untouched by the outside world, they had lived for thousands of years in isolated mountains and valleys deep in the interior of Papua New Guinea. They had no cloth, no metal, no money, no idea that their homeland was an island—or that what surrounded it was salt water. Yet the Fore (for'ay) people had developed remarkable and sophisticated approaches to human relations, and their child-rearing practices gave their young unusual freedom to explore. Successful as hunter-gatherers and as subsistence gardeners, they also had great adaptability, which brought rapid accommodation with the outside world after their lands were opened up.

It was alone that I first visited the Fore in 1963—a day's walk from a recently built airstrip. I stayed six months. Perplexed and fascinated, I returned six times in the next ten years, eventually spending a year and a half living with them in their hamlets.

Theirs was a way of life different from anything I had seen or heard about before. There were no chiefs, patriarchs, priests, medicine men or the like. A striking personal freedom was enjoyed even by the very young, who could move about at will and be where or with whom they liked. Infants rarely cried,

Exploring, two youngsters walk confidently past men's house in hamlet. Smaller women's house is at right.

and they played confidently with knives, axes, and fire. Conflict between old and young did not arise; there was no "generation gap."

Older children enjoyed deferring to the interests and desires of the younger, and sibling rivalry was virtually undetectable. A responsive sixth sense seemed to attune the Fore hamlet mates to each other's interests and needs. They did not have to directly ask, inveigle, bargain or speak out for what they needed or wanted. Subtle, even fleeting expressions of interest, desire, and discomfort were quickly read and helpfully acted on by one's associates. This spontaneous urge to share food, affection, work, trust, tools and pleasure was the social cement that held the Fore hamlets

together. It was a pleasant way of life, for one could always be with those with whom one got along well.

Ranging and planting, sharing and living, the Fore diverged and expanded through high virgin lands in a pioneer region. They hunted out their gardens, tilled them while they lasted, then hunted again. Moving ever away from lands peopled and used they had a self-contained life with its own special ways.

The underlying ecological conditions were like those that must have encompassed the world before agriculture set its imprint so broadly. Abutting the Fore was virtually unlimited virgin land, and they had food plants they could introduce into it. Like hunter-gatherers they sought their sources of sustenance first in one locale and then another, across an extended range, following opportunities provided by a providential nature. But like agriculturalists they concentrated their effort and attention more narrowly on selected sites of production, on their gardens. They were both seekers and producers. A pioneer people in a pioneer land, they ranged freely into a vast territory, but they planted to live.

Cooperative groups formed hamlets and gardened together. When the fertility of a garden declined, they abandoned it. Grass sprung up to cover these abandoned sites of earlier cultivation, and, as the Fore moved on to other parts of the forest, they left uninhabited grasslands to mark their passage.

The traditional hamlets were small, with a rather fluid system of social relations. A single large men's house provided shelter for 10 to 20 men and boys and their visiting friends. The several smaller women's houses each normally sheltered two married women, their unmarried daughters and their sons up to about six years of age. Formal kinship bonds were less important than friendship was. Fraternal "gangs" of youths formed the hamlets; their "clubhouses" were the men's houses.

Learning to be a toddler, a Fore baby takes its first experimental steps. No one urges him on.

In infancy, Fore children begin experimental play with knives and other lethal objects. Sorenson never saw a child warned away or injured by them.

During the day the gardens became the center of life. Hamlets were virtually deserted as friends, relatives and children went to one or more garden plots to mingle their social, economic and erotic pursuits in a pleasant and emotionally filled Gestalt of garden life. The boys and unmarried youths preferred to explore and hunt in the outlying lands, but they also passed through and tarried in the gardens.

Daily activities were not scheduled. No one made demands, and the land was bountiful. Not surprisingly the line between work and play was never clear. The transmission of the Fore behavioral pattern to the young began in early infancy during a period of unceasing human physical contact. The effect of being constantly "in touch" with hamlet mates and their daily life seemed to start a process which proceeded by degrees: close rapport, involvement in regular activity, ability to handle seemingly dangerous implements safely, and responsible freedom to pursue individual interests at will without danger.

While very young, infants remained in almost continuous bodily contact with their mother, her house mates or her gardening associates. At first, mothers' laps were the center of activity, and infants occupied themselves there by nursing, sleeping and playing with their own bodies or those of their caretakers. They were not put aside for the sake of other activities, as when food was being prepared or heavy loads were being carried. Remaining in close, uninterrupted physical contact with those around them, their basic needs such as rest, nourishment, stimulation and security were continuously satisfied without obstacle.

By being physically in touch from their earliest days, Fore youngsters learned to communicate needs, desires and feelings through a body language of touch and response that developed before speech. This opened the door to a much closer rapport with those around them than otherwise would have been possible, and led ultimately to the Fore

Babies have free access to the breast and later, like this toddler being helped to kernels of corn by an older girl, can help themselves to whatever food is around—indulged by children and grown-ups.

brand of social cement and the sixth sense that bound groups together through spontaneous, responsive sharing.

As the infant's awareness increased, his interests broadened to the things his mother and other caretakers did and to the objects and materials they used. Then these youngsters began crawling out to explore things that attracted their attention. By the time they were toddling, their interests continually took them on short sorties to nearby objects and persons. As soon as they could walk well, the excursions extended to the entire hamlet and its gardens, and then beyond with other children. Developing without interference or supervision, this personal exploratory learning quest

freely touched on whatever was around, even axes, knives, machetes, fire, and the like. When I first went to the Fore, I was aghast.

Eventually I discovered that this capability emerged naturally from Fore infant-handling practices in their milieu of close human physical proximity and tactile interaction. Because touch and bodily contact lend themselves naturally to satisfying the basic needs of young children, an early kind of communicative experience fostered cooperative interaction between infants and their caretakers, also kinesthetic contact with the activities at hand. This made it easy for them to learn the appropriate handling of the tools of life.

The early pattern of exploratory activity included frequent return to one of the "mothers." Serving as home base, the bastion of security, a woman might occasionally give the youngster a nod of encouragement, if he glanced in her direction with uncertainty. Yet rarely did the women attempt to control or direct, nor did they participate in the child's quests or jaunts.

As a result Fore children did not have to adjust to rule and schedule in order to find their place in life. They could pursue their interests and whims wherever they might lead and still be part of a richly responsive world of human touch which constantly provided sustenance, comfort, diversion and security.

Close, constant body contact, as between this baby and older girl, creates security in Fore children.

On the way to hunt birds, cuscus (a marsupial) or rats, Fore boys stride through a sweet-potato garden.

Learning proceeded during the course of pursuing interests and exploring. Constantly "in touch" with people who were busy with daily activities, the Fore young quickly learned the skills of life from example. Muscle tone, movement and mood were components of this learning process; formal lessons and commands were not. Kinesthetic skills developed so quickly that infants were able to casually handle knives and similar objects before they could walk.

Even after several visits I continued to be surprised that the unsupervised Fore toddlers did not recklessly thrust themselves into unappreciated dangers, the way our own children tend to do. But then, why should they? From their earliest days, they enjoyed a benevolent sanctuary from which the world could be confidently viewed, tested and appreciated. This sanctuary remained ever available, but did not demand, restrain or impose. One could go and come at will.

In close harmony with their source of life, the Fore young were able confidently, not furtively, to extend their inquiry. They could widen their understanding as they chose. There was no need to play tricks or deceive in order to pursue life.

Emerging from this early childhood was a freely ranging young child rather in tune with his older and younger ham-

let mates, disinclined to act out impulsively, and with a capable appreciation of the properties of potentially dangerous objects. Such children could be permitted to move out on their own, unsupervised and unrestricted. They were safe.

Such a pattern could persist indefinitely, re-creating itself in each new generation. However, hidden within the receptive character it produced was an Achilles heel; it also permitted adoption of new practices, including child-handling practices, which did *not* act to perpetuate the pattern. In only one generation after Western contact, the cycle of Fore life was broken.

Attuned as they were to individual pursuit of economic and social good, it did not take the Fore long to recognize the value of the new materials, practices and ideas that began to flow in. Indeed, change began almost immediately with

efforts to obtain steel axes, salt, medicine and cloth. The Fore were quick to shed indigenous practices in favor of Western example. They rapidly altered their ways to adapt to Western law, government, religion, materials and trade.

Sometimes change was so rapid that many people seemed to be afflicted by a kind of cultural shock. An anomie, even cultural amnesia, seemed to pervade some hamlets for a time. There were individuals who appeared temporarily to have lost memory of recent past events. Some Fore even forgot what type and style of traditional garments they had worn only a few years earlier, or that they had used stone axes and had eaten their dead close relatives.

Remarkably open-minded, the Fore so readily accepted reformulation of identity and practice that suggestion or example by the new government officers, missionaries and scientists could alter tribal affiliation, place names, conduct and hamlet style. When the first Australian patrol officer began to map the region in 1957, an error in communication led him to refer to these people as the "Fore." Actually they had had no name for themselves and the word, Fore, was their name for a quite different group, the Awa, who spoke another language and lived in another valley. They did not correct the patrol officer but adopted his usage. They all now refer to themselves as the Fore. Regional and even personal names changed just as readily.

More than anything else, it was the completion of a steep, rough, always muddy Jeep road into the Fore lands that undermined the traditional life. Almost overnight their isolated region was opened. Hamlets began to move down from their ridgetop sites in order to be nearer the road, consolidating with others.

The power of the road is hard to overestimate. It was a great artery where only restricted capillaries had existed before. And down this artery came a flood of new goods, new ideas and new people. This new road, often impassable even with four-wheel-drive vehicles, was perhaps the single most dramatic stroke wrought by the government. It was to the Fore an opening to a new world. As they began to use the road, they started to shed traditions evolved in the protective insularity of their mountain fastness, to adopt in their stead an emerging market culture.

THE COMING OF THE COFFEE ECONOMY

"Walkabout," nonexistent as an institution before contact, quickly became an accepted way of life. Fore boys began to roam hundreds of miles from their homeland in the quest for new experience, trade goods, jobs and money. Like the classic practice of the Australian aborigine, this "walkabout" took one away from his home for periods of varying length. But unlike the Australian practice, it usually took the boys to jobs and schools rather than a solitary life in traditional lands. Obviously it sprang from the earlier pattern of individual freedom to pursue personal interests and opportunity wherever it might lead. It was a new expression of the old Fore exploratory pattern.

Some boys did not roam far, whereas others found ways to go to distant cities. The roaming boys often sought places where they might be welcomed as visitors, workers or students for a while. Mission stations and schools, plantation work camps, and the servants' quarters of the European population became way-stations in the lives of the modernizing Fore boys.

Some took jobs on coffee plantations. Impressed by the care and attention lavished on coffee by European planters and by the money they saw paid to coffee growers, these young Fore workers returned home with coffee beans to plant.

Coffee grew well on the Fore hillsides, and in the mid-1960s, when the first sizable crop matured, Fore who previously had felt lucky to earn a few dollars found themselves able to earn a few hundred dollars. A rush to coffee ensued, and when the new gardens became productive a few years later, the Fore income from coffee jumped to a quarter of a million dollars a year. The coffee revolution was established.

At first the coffee was carried on the backs of its growers (sometimes for several days) over steep, rough mountain trails to a place where it could be sold to a buyer with a jeep. However, as more and more coffee was produced, the villagers began to turn with efforts to planning and constructing roads in association with neighboring villages. The newly built roads, in turn, stimulated further economic development and the opening of new trade stores throughout the region.

Following European example, the segregated collective men's and women's houses were abandoned. Family houses were adopted. This changed the social and territorial arena for all the young children, who hitherto had been accustomed to living equally with many members of their hamlet. It gave them a narrower place to belong, and it made them more distinctly someone's children. Uncomfortable in the family houses, boys who had grown up in a freer territory began to gather in "boys" houses', away from the adult men who were now beginning to live in family houses with their wives. Mothers began to wear blouses, altering the early freer access to the breast. Episodes of infant and child frustration, not seen in traditional Fore hamlets, began to take place along with repeated incidents of anger, withdrawal, aggressiveness and stinginess.

So Western technology worked its magic on the Fore, its powerful materials and practices quickly shattering their isolated autonomy and life-style. It took only a few years from the time Western intruders built their first grass-thatched patrol station before the Fore way of life they found was gone.

Fortunately, enough of the Fore traditional ways were systematically documented on film to reveal how unique a flower of human creation they were. Like nothing else, film made it possible to see the behavioral patterns of this way of life. The visual record, once made, captured data which was unnoticed and unanticipated at the time of filming and which was simply impossible to study without such records. Difficult-to-spot subtle patterns and fleeting nuances of manner, mood and human relations emerged by use of repeated reexamination of related incidents, sometimes by slow motion and stopped frame. Eventually the characteristic behavioral patterns of Fore life became clear, and an important aspect of human adaptive creation was revealed.

The Fore way of life was only one of the many natural experiments in living that have come into being through thousands of years of independent development in the world. The Fore way is now gone; those which remain are threatened. Under the impact of modern technology and commerce, the entire world is now rapidly becoming one system. By the year 2000 all the independent natural experiments that have come into being during the world's history will be merging into a single world system.

One of the great tragedies of our modern time may be that most of these independent experiments in living are disappearing before we can discover the implication of their special expressions of human possibility. Ironically, the same technology responsible for the worldwide cultural convergence has also provided the means by which we may capture detailed visual records of the yet remaining independent cultures. The question is whether we will be able to seize this never-to-be repeated opportunity. Soon it will be too late. Yet, obviously, increasing our understanding of the behavioral repertoire of humankind would strengthen our ability to improve life in the world.

Academic Scholarship and Sikhism: Conflict or Legitimization

Arthur W. Helweg

OVER THE PAST decade disagreement has developed within the Sikh community of North America. One group supports the goals and results of Sikh scholarship and studies in the universities of Canada and the United States. The other feels that current university scholarship is undermining their faith.[1] The debate has taken on international proportions where Sikhs in England and India are also becoming involved. In fact, some scholars in Sikh studies, who also adhere to the Sikh faith, have been summoned by, appeared before, and tried by the *Akal Takht*[2] in Amritsar.[3] At times, the dispute has taken repulsive proportions where personal safety appears to be at stake and superb and sincere scholars have had their careers put in jeopardy.[4] It has taken on the nature of a Culture War (Hunter 1991) where, on the part of some, reason and the search for truth has been replaced by dogma.

To those who feel Sikh studies programs in universities are undermining their faith, their vehemence is understandable because they perceive, among other things that: (1) some of these programs that were financed by private contributions from the Sikh community have not been supporting their faith, (2) recommendations from the Sikh com-munity have not been followed, even though they were given an advisory role in the development and implementation of these programs, (3) their children will lose their Sikh faith, and (4) Sikhism, in general will be discredited. On the other hand, those for university Sikh studies feel that academic freedom and honesty must be maintained—that trustworthy scholarship should be promoted, no matter what a group believes.

I will argue below that underlying this conflict is an older issue that has plagued South Asia from the time the West started colonizing the region: What criteria should be used to validate a belief system? This problem has been an issue in South Asia ever since western philosophy, religion and scientific methodology challenged the religious and philosophical systems of the subcontinent. In this paper, I will analyse the current Sikh dissension in North America from a social science perspective. In essence, I will argue that the two groups of people are interacting in a context with each behaving and perceiving the situation from different cultural systems. Each is evaluating the other by different criteria, and thus perceiving the other in a derogatory manner, because each is using what they perceive is the true framework for judging the other.

To set forth an analysis of the above situation, this paper will first give brief examples of this type of drama from South Asian history. Then, it will (1) explain the concept of culture, (2) set forth an example of cultural conflict, (3) explain how common concepts have different meaning in eastern and western contexts and (4) show the cultural conflict operating in the Sikh studies debate. Although this is a highly emotional topic, it is my hope that a better understanding and tolerance will develop as parties involved comprehend underlying causes of misunderstanding. . . .

Culture

To understand the current tensions within the North American Sikh community, it is imperative to comprehend the nature of culture. Culture (Kroeber and Parsons 1958; Schneider 1968:1-18) is an abstract symbolic system which is composed of values, meanings, and beliefs.[5] Beliefs may well be the most important element for they are the basic concepts, the foundation on which people interpret the world around them, evaluate themselves, judge others, and develop priorities in their lives. Yet, be-

From *The Transmission of Sikh Heritage in the Diaspora,* edited by Pashaura Singh and N. Gerald Barrier, 1996, pp. 251-268. Published by Manohar Publications, New Delhi. © 1996 by Arthur W. Helweg. Reprinted by permission.

liefs are also concepts that cannot be proved right or wrong.

When we think of beliefs, religion often comes to mind; but there are many beliefs that guide our lives that are not religiously oriented. Examples include capitalism, democracy and gender equality. They are principles that, like all beliefs, cannot be proved or disproved; but they are the foundation that members of a community agree to orient their lives and interpret their experiences and surroundings. Beliefs evoke strong emotions and ideals for which people live and die. All people ascribe to the belief system of their group of identification, whether Sikh or Hungarian. One illustrative example is the American belief in democracy, a concept on which wars have been fought, foreign policy determined and lives lost. It provides for majority rule and helps ensure that a minority can never get their way. This potential difficulty does not shake the faith people have in the democratic way.

Culture also assigns meanings to symbols, provides for a common language, and enables members to interact according to the configurations of their particular culture. However, the same symbols may have different meanings in different contexts and at different times. The United Nations Commission on human rights could not agree on what the term "Human Rights" meant, because people of different cultures had different interpretations. Some people of the Middle East felt that their practice of keeping women isolated was based on high esteem for the female gender and their crucial role in maintaining family honor (Helweg 1986:12–15). To the feminists of the West, this was oppressing or enslaving. The concept "human rights" meant different things in different cultural contexts. The people of each culture know what a particular symbol means and act accordingly. In war, many soldiers have sacrificed their life to keep a national flag flying. In actuality, the flag was a piece of colored cloth. In another place or context, the same cloth may be used for a rag.

Values help establish priorities. When a person is selling a product, that item may have its good and bad points. The sales person, in describing the product to a potential customer, has the option of being honest and possibly losing the sale. Making money and being honest are both values but he must make a choice. The culture sets forth a guide to follow, usually to be honest. The members of a group agree on how values should be prioritized. Thus people generally see themselves in ideal terms, being honest; but, when faced with the actual choice they may behave otherwise, opt for maximizing profit. Thus, how we perceive our selves is known as "ideal culture", but how others see us is "real culture". We generally see ourselves in terms of ideal culture and others see us in terms of real culture.

Cultural Conflict

One example of cultural conflict is the way baseball is played in Japan and the United States.[6] Both countries use similar rules, but the manner, goals, and outcome are very different. Americans play to win, and if they can win by a wide margin, so much the better. The Japanese play for ties, and if a team wins, they attempt to win by a small margin. In Japan teams win a championship, but only by a few games, never by many. The important concept for the Japanese is allowing the opponent to save face. Conversely, Americans attempt to show their superiority over their opponents.

Americans also value individualism and individual effort. In Japan, the guiding principle is that "the nail that stands up must be pounded down." Thus in Japanese baseball, if a player is doing much better than his team mates and starts demonstrating his superiority, the team manager will not play him. Japanese players, like most Japanese, attempt to be anonymous and not stand out. American baseball players in Japan assert their individuality and become noticed. They then are "pounded down" by being placed on the bench, fined or forced to make public apologies. The American baseball players feel this is unfair and become bitter, while Japanese players accept this situation as normal.

The concept of being fair is another difference. An American baseball player in Japan doing very well, will face the "expanding strike zone". In such a situation, umpires call strikes that are outside the normal range. They believe Americans are big, strong and experienced at hitting the ball, while Japanese are not as big, strong or experienced. From the Japanese perspective, fairness demands that the strength of the American be compensated to make things equal. To the Japanese, this practice is fair and helps adjust for differences in size and experience. Americans view the changes in rules as unfair and putting them at a disadvantage.

Americans playing baseball in Japan get very upset because they are not allowed to "show what they can do." They cannot display their superiority or individual effort. Thus, even though they get very high salaries and make much more money than in the States, they are frustrated and unhappy in Japan. Money alone does not provide the personal satisfaction to have a worthwhile life. As one player lamented, "What good is all this money. Am I going to lay down on the floor and roll around in it?" The game is baseball, American players are making a great deal of money, but are often bitter because baseball in Japan has different rules. Americans do not realize that a different "culture" (rules, rewards, meanings, beliefs) of the game prohibits them from obtaining self satisfaction.

Similarly, the game of life is being played by some Sikhs in America according to their cultural beliefs, rules and interpretations; and these differ from the cultural framework on which some universities operate. Because both groups behave differently, each considers the other as being unethical or not living up to their commitments.

Contrasting Cultural Concepts

In the current Sikh studies conflict, there are two sets of opposing systems involved: (1) religion/science and (2) east (Sikh)/west (Judeo-Christian). The following will show that they are not only different systems, but one system is being used to attempt to validate or disprove the other.

Religion/Science

Religion and science[7] are in essence two different systems operating under very different goals and means. First, the purpose of religion is to tell "why," the purpose of science is to explain "how." Our religion tells us why we are here and why we should live the way we are taught. Science tells us how man developed and how the natural world operates. A holy book teaches beliefs and why man should behave in a certain manner. A science book teaches laws and regularities which are found in the dynamics of the natural world.

Second, religious beliefs cannot be proved right or wrong. Evidence may be collected to support a belief, but the belief cannot be proved or disproved. The scientific method is different. Science operates from the assumption of unbroken regularity in the universe. It leaves no room for miracles or divine intervention. Religion allows for miracles and divine intervention. Moreover, scientists observe, and make hypotheses, so that phenomena can be predicted. This brings us to our third point, namely, that the hypothesis must be falsifiable. In other words, the scientific hypothesis must be stated in such a way that if it is wrong, it can be so shown (Ruse nd). Religions allow for miracles and are not formulated in a falsifiable manner. The point is that religion and science operate according to completely different assumptions and goals. One cannot be used to verify the other.

East (Sikh)/West (Christian)

There are many concepts that have the same name in eastern and western contexts, but different meanings. I will explore three, of many, to illustrate. As I set forth the concepts, within each tradition, there is variation. The purpose is not to set forth a theological discourse, but to illustrate a process that is taking place. The three concepts are: the notion of deity, method of achieving goals prescribed by the religion, and the idea of truth.

Deity

Many Christians perceive of their god or deity as a personality, a supreme being that has created man in his own image. Among many Christians, it is a "he" and the relationship is like that of a father to a child. For some, it is a strict father who judges and punishes, for others it is a kind and loving father who helps and guides, sometimes with pain, to improve our character.

On the other hand, for many South Asians, and Sikhs, the deity they worship is an all pervasive force uniting all things of the universe. The purpose of the Guru is to enable one to establish a oneness or relation with the deity. Thus all are united because God is in all of us. Thus harming others also harms oneself, not because it destroys a person's individual character or because the person is committing a sin; but because one is part of the other; and, harming the other is harming oneself. Thus, one Sikh goal in life is to become sensitive to the deity which is inside all of us.[8]

Method

Considering the deity concept for some Christians, they achieve piety in the same way one establishes a relationship with a friend—communicating, which allows one to maintain his or her individuality. This is one of the aspects of prayer, to talk to God on a personal basis. Also, piety is achieved by obeying rules and helping people in this life. The purpose of ritual and worship is to learn or receive encouragement so one will live a correct life in this world. In other words, one's piety is partly determined by the way one lives this life—which means that one is judged by individual achievement.

For many South Asians and some Sikhs, the goal is to lose your individuality and become one with God. To use an analogy, a glass of water is a distinct entity. But, when you take that water and pour it into a lake, the water is still there, but it is indistinguishable from the larger body of water, or lake. Very often what the Sikh and South Asian are trying to do is lose their individuality and become one with God via the Guru. To do this, they want to lose their individuality by becoming one with that spirit. This is often done with the guidance of a guru or sant. For the Sikh, his meditation on the divine Name (*nam*) in the morning is to lose the individual self and become part of the whole.[9] Sikhism is not other worldly to the degree of Hinduism. Guru Nanak was specific about teaching that his followers are to work, do well, and help others in this world. Also, Guru Gobind Singh, in his admonition to take up the sword for justice, also implies the concern of Sikhs with the world.

Truth

The nature of Truth[10] is fundamentally different in South Asian and western cultures and also a major source of the conflict on which this paper is focusing. In the West, Truth is found outside us and is absolute. Often westerners validate by measuring, touching, or applying a code or criteria to the situation. Often, westerners feel that the methodology of science can be applied to validate everything, including religious beliefs. In western Christianity, one learns Truth by reading scriptures, and listening to preachers. These scriptures set forth absolute laws or rules that many perceive as immutable. Again, they are outside the individual.

For the Sikh, and many South Asians, Truth is found inside us. One learns or achieves it by becoming one with the deity through the guidance of the Guru. The Guru and scriptures are certainly important, but in the end, for the Sikh, it is one's relationship with the deity and Guru that reveal Truth. Second, Truth for the Sikh is not necessarily absolute. Truth has many levels and is dependent on context and circumstances.

The difference can be illustrated by the experience of the Muslim saint Kabir. The story goes that one night Kabir heard a knock on his door. When he opened it, there was a thief who said, "I am being chased by the police for stealing this bread, will you hide me?" Kabir replied, "Yes, go and lie in bed with my daughter." Soon, there was a knock on the door and the police standing there said, "We saw the thief we were chasing enter your house, we have come to apprehend him." Kabir replied, "Come in and see for yourself, in bed is my wife and in the other bed is my daughter and her husband." The police left because no man would allow a stranger to be in the same bed with his daughter.

In analysing the story, the question that becomes crucial is: Did Kabir do the right thing by hiding the thief and disobeying the law? From the western perspective, the answer is "no" because the law is an absolute, always to be obeyed. For Kabir, this is not the case. He was in tune or close to the deity that is inside him and the feeling he had was that he should help the thief. Who knows, maybe this was God's way of revealing Truth to the thief. One does not always know the "higher plan", so to speak; but, those who are one with the deity or the Guru are instruments of it and not subject to earthly laws. Truth or right action for Kabir was relative. At another time in another context, it may not be correct to help a thief. But the only way one can tell is by being in tune with the deity that is within all of us.

In thinking through the concepts of deity, method and truth, implications on the cultural level become clear. Both communities, east and west, Christian and Sikh, are evaluating and living life according to different rules and concepts. And although the same words are used, their meanings are different. Thus, each evaluates the other in its own terms of cultural reference. This results in misunderstanding which perceives the behavior of the other as negative. For example, to some Christians, meditation has little value. To a South Asian, the Christian concept of prayer often does not produce what is important. Many Christians consider their faith the only truth. Most Sikhs see their beliefs as being the best, but not the only, way.

Sikhs and Christians may believe they are worshiping the same deity. But what that means differs and how it is done is based on their beliefs, which cannot be proved either right or wrong. Each may collect evidence or make arguments to support their view, but neither can prove their way, or the other, right or wrong. Yet these values, meanings and beliefs influence behavior, perceptions, and evaluation of themselves, others and the world around them. To use the terms of a game analogy, each community of people is playing the game of life according to different cultural rules and concepts; and each is evaluating the other on the basis of its own rules, or cultural system.

Sikh/University Conflict

We come back to the basic issue which is the purpose of this paper. Why do some Sikhs feel that certain Sikh scholars and Sikh studies programs have not upheld their commitment nor doing proper scholarship? The debate and issues are not only old ones in South Asia, but religions, such as fundamentalist Christianity, have had to deal with the same kind of conflict—perceiving scholarship as challenging the validity of their faith.

The debate has been emotional and people have been martyred and careers destroyed on both sides of the issue. The process will probably go on, because what is at the heart of the conflict are beliefs; and, it is beliefs, as I pointed out earlier, that are the principles on which we build our lives, whether in religion or scholarship. Thus I will argue three basic points: (1) misunderstanding arose because American universities and certain Sikh groups are operating within two different cultural systems (2) the validation of the Sikh faith can only be done within an Asian or Sikh cultural system, not that of western science, and (3) developing a university program in Sikh studies gives their religion legitimacy in western society.

Conflict of Two Cultural Systems

Religion and science operate under two systems or orientation. Religion explains the "why," and science the "how." To use one to validate the other is like using oranges to comprehend apples. Each is different in structure and outcome. Although we do not like to admit it, beliefs are not subject to validation by scientific evidence. How can one prove that capitalism is the best for everyone? We think it is best because it is the system we operate by in our culture. But what criteria should be used? Scientific methods only validate scientific theory and processes. Scientific method cannot validate the "why" of life, only the "how". When Sikh scriptures are subjected to study or Sikh history is examined, all that can be determined is a "how" never a "why". Understanding the "how" will never invalidate a belief.

Universities, especially publicly funded universities in the United States, operate under the principle of separation of church and state, as set forth by the Constitution of the United States. This means that publicly funded universities are committed to scientific methodology and not to the validation of any religious belief. In fact, it is unlawful for anyone in the United States, in a publicly funded institution, to advocate a particular religious ideology using state resources. Of course the courts are continually defining what this means and hearing challenges, but separation of church and state is the guiding principle. If a religious community wants to proselytize or set forth a religious ideology, they can do so under the auspices of a privately funded institution.

The state university is obligated to hire a person judged to be the best qualified scholar to serve in the position. In the case of Sikh programs, there may have been an agreement that members of the Sikh community would be an advisory body but that advice does not have to be followed. The final decision lies with the university and they must ensure that the scholar hired has the complete freedom to pursue his scholarship in a manner consistent with the practices of his or her discipline, whether it be a science, social science or humanities. In other words, publicly funded universities must follow scientific principles, not religious dogma.

Validation of Sikhism

As Sikh programs have been established at several universities, Sikh scriptures and society have been subjected to textual, historical, philosophical, social, and in general, scholarly evaluation. The outcome has not always been what some Sikhs would desire. In fact, some feel that the validity of their faith is being undermined by the very institutions to which they have contributed significant financial resources.

The basic issue comes down to the validation of a religion. I would argue that a belief system is validated by its own cultural system. In the case of the Sikhs, the South Asian cultural system defines Truth subjectively and relatively. Kabir knew he was doing the correct thing in aiding the thief because he felt it was proper in these circumstances. Conversely, what should validate Sikhism for a Sikh should not be western science and scholarship but criteria according to their own culture. This, for example, is the experience felt when *gurbani* is recited or the subjective experience of the morning when *nam* is meditated upon. Because the spirit of the deity is inside you, according to Sikh teachings, one goal is to become tuned to that internal spirit. It is by such a method that validation takes place. Western scholarship and methodology does not validate or disprove Sikh beliefs.

Some Sikhs argue that Sikh studies professors do not show what it is like to be a believer from the perspective of the followers of the Gurus. In the past, social sciences have felt that their methodology should follow the physical sciences and be detached and objective. However, current thinking is abandoning that position and considering the subjective perspective of the follower. Yet, even the western trained sociologist and anthropologist realizes and admits that, by not being a follower, they cannot fully understand the subjective perspective of a Sikh or a member of another ethnic group or culture. The limitation is accepted, but the purpose is to analyse and understand, not convert.

One might ask, "Why did or do South Asians feel threatened by western scholarships? They have a history of accomplishment from which to be proud." One cause was the development of a *colonial mentality* under British rule that set forth the western philosophical and religious challenge in South Asia. Second, as one looks at the list of Sikhs who feel that their faith is being eroded by university scholarship, the vast majority are trained in western science or engineering fields. Thus it is no wonder that they think in terms of Truth being outside themselves and Truth being absolute, rather than Truth being inside you and relative. People tend to think in terms of their training. Many who are upset with the treatment of Sikhism by academics are challenging the system using the philosophical criteria of the physical sciences rather than the social sciences or humanities.

I would argue that Sikhs should concentrate on learning their own tradition and validate their faith using the framework of Sikh, Punjabi and South Asian culture, not from the tradition of western oriented Europe or North America.

Legitimizing Sikhism Abroad

Thus comes the final issue. Should Sikhs invest in universities to establish Sikh studies programs? The answer to that question depends on the desired goal. If the goal is to teach and validate the faith, then the Sikhs would be better off creating religious universities as many of the Christian denominations have done. I feel that this is an option that should be taken very seriously.

On the other hand, there are very distinct advantages in establishing Sikh studies programs in state universities. First, it gives Sikhs and their faith a legitimacy in the public perceptions of westerners that will never be achieved otherwise. Without being part of the university curriculum, chances are that Sikhism will remain a strange and exotic creed for most Americans and not taken seriously.

Related to the above, the establishment of Sikh studies programs will make Sikhs an established and recognized feature of the American and western landscape; and that recognition will be present because it offers itself to be challenged by scholarship. Scholarship, again, will not validate or disprove the faith, but by its presence at a university, Sikhism will become legitimized and established in the perception of the general public.

Conclusion

I have tried to show that much of the tension in creating Sikh studies programs in American universities and colleges has resulted in conflicting perceptions between donors and recipients.

Two groups of people are living and evaluating the other according to different cultural systems. As a result, severe misunderstandings develop. Unfortunately, the people most hurt have been the scholars hired to do what they are supposed to do. This is not the fault of any particular people or group, but misperceptions caused by two groups of people dealing with each other on the basis of two cultural systems. As a result, each had different expectations and evaluations of the other which lead to a lot of misunderstanding and conflict. More care should be taken in future on both sides to know exactly the conditions under which money will be given or received for the establishment of Sikh studies.

Second, Sikhs should learn their culture and look to it to validate their faith. They should use the South Asian and Punjabi concept of Truth to evaluate their beliefs, not western science and methodology. Also, Sikhs have nothing to fear by allowing scholars to examine their faith and history. No amount of scholarship can discredit their beliefs. The purpose of the scholarship is to determine how, not understand why; and, beliefs cannot be proved or disproved. If past history is valid, being subject to scholarship will result in a much stronger Sikh community.

Last, in spite of the problems so far, investing in Sikh studies in western universities, is well worth the money for it will make the Sikhs a prominent and established element on the American scene.

Notes

1. It is hard to label these two groups because both comprise university professors, conservatives, liberals, people on the right and people on the left. However, those who attack Sikh studies at the universities, are generally technically trained, i.e. medical people, scientists and engineers. Thus, unlike the Culture Wars, this conflict is not so easy to label.

   Most recently, the anti-university element has focused their attack on, among others, the works of Oberoi (1994), Pashaura Singh (1991) and McLeod (1980, 1984). See Mann and Saraon (1988); Mann, Sandhu, Sidhu, Singh and Sodi (n.d.); Chahal; and Kohli (n.d.) who present the position attacking Sikh studies scholars in American universities.

2. The *Akal Takht* is a multistoried building in the Sikh Golden Temple of Amritsar, Punjab. It is one of the five seats of authority for the

Sikh faith, *takht*. Its *jathedar* (leader) is considered to have authority over the other four, and is the final arbiter in matters relating to the panth. See Cole and Sambhi (1990:35) and Harbans Singh (1992:56–60) for a more complete description.

3. There are many references dealing with the above issue. See *The World Sikh News*, which frequently reported on this issue, and *The Sikh Reformer, Number 5* for a concise summary of the debate. See also Mann and Saraon (1988) for a position challenging the university scholarship in America focusing on Sikh studies.

4. In the social sciences, we realize that it is virtually impossible for an individual to be completely objective. I am not a Sikh. Also, I have a high respect for the scholarship of McLeod, Oberoi and Pashaura Singh. Although I feel I am giving a fair and impartial analysis, I feel that the reader should know possible biases I might have.

5. See Schneider (1968) for a more complete treatment of the concept of culture, on which this article is based.

6. See Whiting (1989) for the study on which this analysis is based.

7. When I use the terms "religion" and "science" here, they are the concepts as set forth in the western tradition. I do this because the Sikh studies conflict is taking place primarily in the west and argued primarily by western oriented and western trained people.

8. I have only focused on a few relevant points here. For a more complete explanation, see Cole and Sambhi (1990:68–9) and Kohli (1873:16–21, 1992a:9–14, 1992b:121–2).

9. See Kohli (1992:61–71) for a fuller explanation.

10. I am not using "truth" meaning deity, I am focusing on determining the validity of one's beliefs or ascertaining proper behavior.

Bibliography

Bharati, Aghenanda. 1990. "Religious Revival in Modern Times," in *The Cambridge Encyclopedia of India, Pakistan, Bangladesh, Sri Lanka*. Francis Robinson, ed., Cambridge, New York, Port Chester, Melbourne, Sydney: Cambridge University Press.

Chahal, Devinder Singh. nd. "The Text and Meaning of the "*Adi Granth*." Xerox copy.

Cole, W. Owen and Piara Singh Sambhi. 1990. *A Popular Dictionary of Sikhism*. London: Curzon Press.

Grewal, J. S. 1990. *The New Cambridge History of India: The Sikhs of Punjab*. Cambridge, New York, Port Chester, Melbourne, Sydney: Cambridge University Press.

Helweg, Arthur. 1986. *Sikhs in England*. Delhi, Bombay, Calcutta: Oxford University Press.

Hunter, James Davison. 1991. *Culture Wars: The Struggle to Define America*. New York: Basic Books.

Kohli, Surinder Singh. nd. "Research Coverage of Blasphemy." Xerox copy.

_____. 1973. *Outlines of Sikh Thought*. New Delhi: Munshiram Manoharlal Publishers Pvt. Ltd.

_____. 1992a. *The Sikh Philosophy*. Amritsar: Singh Brothers.

_____. 1992b. *A Conceptual Encyclopedia of Guru Granth Sahib*. New Delhi: Manohar.

Kroeber, A. L. and T. Parsons. 1958. "The Concepts of Cultural and of Social Systems." *American Sociological Review*, pp. 582–83.

Mann, Jasbir Singh and Harbans Singh Saraon. 1988. *Advanced Studies in Sikhism*. Irvine, CA: Sikh Community of North America.

Mann, Jasbir Singh, Sukhmander Singh Sandhu, Gurmail Singh Sidhu, Surjit Singh, S. S. Sodhi. nd. "The Future of Sikh Studies." Xerox copy.

McLeod, W. H. 1980. *Early Sikh Tradition*. Oxford: Clarendon Press.

_____. 1989. *Who is a Sikh? The Problem of Sikh Identity*. Oxford: Clarendon Press.

Oberoi, Harjot. 1994. *The Construction of Religious Boundaries: Culture, Identity and Diversity in the Sikh Tradition*. Delhi, Oxford, New York: Oxford University Press.

Ruse, Michael. nd. Interview on "God, Darwin and Dinosaurs." A PBS Production. *The Sikh Reformer*. 5 (1994).

Schneider, David M. 1968. *American Kinship: A Cultural Account*. Englewood Cliffs, NJ: Prentice-Hall, Inc.

Singh, Harbans. 1983. *The Heritage of the Sikhs*. Delhi: Manohar

_____. 1992. *The Encyclopedia of Sikhism, Volume I, A–D*, Patiala: Punjabi University Press.

Tinker, Hugh. 1990. *South Asia: A Short History*. Honolulu: University of Hawaii Press.

Whiting, Robert. 1989. *You Gotta Have Wa*. New York: Vintage Books.

Human Nature

New Spirits for Old

By Shoefoot (Bautista Cajicuwa), as told to
Kenneth Good and Mark Ritchie

Until their first contact with outsiders, about fifty years ago, the Yanomami Indians of Venezuela led an isolated existence in the Amazon rain forest. Once these Indians became known to the outside world, anthropologists wanted to study them, and missionaries sought to win their minds and souls. Within a few decades, the Yanomami have been exposed not only to new technologies but also to new "spirits."

Although communal life in the jungle can be pleasant—replete with laughter, friendship, and family—there is also a full measure of paranoia, sickness, and violence. Malaria remains rampant, food is often scarce, and vengeance raids are a fact of life. Shamans often tell their people that the cause of a relative's illness or death is a malevolent spirit sent by someone in a neighboring village. Wars of retaliation are commonly carried out with clubs and bows and arrows. During such tension-filled times, people are afraid to venture out of their villages alone, even to hunt or draw water from the river.

In the early 1960s, a Yanomami shaman and village leader known as Shoefoot, tired of living in fear and seeing people killed, felt betrayed by his spirits. Then he met Joe Dawson and his family, independent Evangelical missionaries from the United States, who convinced him to follow a foreign spirit that would help him find peace. In September 1996, Shoefoot, then sixty-five years old, vis-ited the American Museum of Natural History, along with Joe Dawson's son Gary (Keleewa) and writer Mark Ritchie, who had told Shoefoot's story in his book Spirit of the Rain Forest. *Kenneth Good, an anthropologist who speaks fluent Yanomami, attended as an independent observer for this magazine. During the interview, Good was convinced of the sincerity of Shoefoot's conversion, although it is unique in his twelve years' experience of living with the Yanomami. The following is Shoefoot's statement:*

When I was a little boy, I used to sit in my hammock across from the communal dwelling and listen to the village shamans chant, calling out to the spirits. Everyone held these men in awe: they guided the community, controlled the spirits, and understood all things in life. I watched them blow *ebene* powder into each other's nostrils through long, hollow reeds. This potent drug is made from several jungle plants; it makes strong men's heads snap backward, but then it helps them talk to spirits. One day, I thought, I will become one of the village shamans, as the *hekura* [forest spirits] were already speaking to me.

When I was about fifteen, my father, a shaman himself, called on me to carry on this solemn service to the community. He said the village needed more powerful shamans, because it had so many enemies. Following him and his older brothers, I began to inhale *ebene*

and chant. After several years of training, I was publicly initiated into the world of the *hekura*. Various spirits came to make a home within my chest.

Many sick and dying people were brought to my hearth to be healed. I inhaled the drug, called up the spirits, and tried to drive away those who came to do harm. Some of the sick recovered, but many died, because the spirits of the forest are powerful. When someone died, their relatives would cremate the body and drink the ashes. And they would ask me who was the evil shaman from another village who had caused their misfortune. Sometimes I would understand who it was who had done this, so I would call the men to take up clubs and arrows and raid the village where the evil shaman lived. We would kill as many men as we could, rape the women, and take some back to our village. Then we knew we might be raided ourselves, so I would advise everyone to move out into the forest on a trek of many days to escape the dangers. When a soul was stolen, I would try to send my spirits to retrieve it, but usually without success. I took great amounts of *ebene* so I could see the spirits and magically travel to far places and find them.

When I began my own family, I planted a garden and hunted to feed my children. Many times others would bring sick children, and I would take my drug and chant to cure them. At some times, very many got sick at once, and I was chanting and taking the drug all day and night. But young and old died anyway, and I doubled my efforts to heal until I was exhausted. When food was scarce in the village, I led trekking parties into the forest in search of fruits and berries. I was strong and respected as one who guided his community, and I received the largest portions of meat after a hunt.

As the years went on, the responsibilities of a shaman weighed heavier and heavier upon me. I was tired. So many sick and dying. I could not cure them, no matter how hard I tried. So many threats to my village. People were raiding and killing one another. I could not protect them. Often there were food crises. I took more and more *ebene* to get assistance from the spirits, but my mind began to play tricks. Instead of help, my spirits left me with nothing but worry and fear. Sometimes I was so confused I wanted to escape into the forest, but I never ran off. Some men got lost in the spirit world when they took the drug; many ran into the jungle and were never heard from again. Now and then, one of them was found dead. I was strong, but I was thinking I wasn't strong enough to go on like this.

A visitor from another village told me about foreign people, *nabas*, who had come to live on the river. One older couple had a son called Keleewa, who talks and hunts just like us, because he grew up in a Yanomami village. We call him "the white Yanomami." Keleewa and his father told me of a big spirit that could help us, one that was friendly and not desiring death and destruction. I began to think about this peaceful new spirit, and pretty soon after, my spirits

---

"People were raiding and killing. Many were sick. I could not cure them. When I thought about the new spirit, the forest spirits got jealous. They said if I abandoned them, they would kill me."

---

got jealous and gave me bad dreams. They said they were afraid I would abandon them and that they would kill me if I tried. When I stopped taking *ebene* and turned to the spirit of the *nabas,* I was happy to see that it was stronger than my forest spirits. They became afraid and went away. They didn't tell me to kill people or lead raids anymore. Instead, the new spirit told me to stop fights whenever I could.

I became calm in my mind and my fear went away. I no longer hated anyone or wanted to cause their death. My old spirits were happy whenever someone died, and they kept telling the shamans to stir up more violence. We thought we had power over these spirits, but they really had the power over us—causing our own people to die. Even when we shamans were chanting and taking *ebene* and looking content, there was turmoil inside, for our spirits kept telling us to kill. Some men lost all control when they took the drug, sometimes even killing their own wives and children.

Today I no longer live in fear and I'm a friend to everyone. We have ended our feuds and stopped the killing. Now that we are living in a bigger, more secure village, we are able to devote ourselves to growing more food; we have some cattle, and we have better homes to protect ourselves from the mosquitoes. The *nabas* told us that malaria comes from mosquitoes, not from evil shamans, and we have changed our belief. Some of us have learned to look at blood slides under Keleewa's microscope and tell what kind of malaria someone has. Our population at Honey Village is growing, while many others are decreasing. The new spirit freed me from the fear I had all the time. Today my people are better off and at peace.

Grounded On Ice

The Inuit Struggle to Preserve Their Values

*Written and photographed
by Eric P. Olsen*

The little road to nowhere winds out of the Baffin Island village of Iqaluit into the arctic tundra, a tentative encroachment that quickly surrenders to the frozen wilderness. The treeless hills around the village are pocked by small glacial lakes and softened by robust mosses and patches of brilliant blue flowers hastily celebrating the brief warmth of summer. Underfoot is evidence of recently departed caribou herds, a migration as timeless and portentous for the people of the north as the passage of the seasons. Scanning the terrain from the crest of a low hill one spies the ancient stone inukshuks—cairns often constructed in the form of a man—silhouetted against a gray sky.

Baffin, the fifth-largest island in the world, lies due west of the world's largest, Greenland. The Canadian island is home to some ten thousand people, 80 percent of whom are Inuit populating a handful of inaccessible villages dispersed along the coast. The Inuit existence, perhaps to a greater degree than that of any other people this side of Tierra del Fuego, has been one of physical hardship. Such a contest against nature gives testimony to the resilience, courage, and inventiveness not just of the Inuit but of the human species.

A dream becomes reality

Home to more than four thousand people, Iqaluit has been chosen as the capital of the soon-to-be established territory called Nunavut. Spanning the vast and empty tundra of Canada's eastern Northwest Territories, Nunavut is intended to provide the Inuit with a semiautonomous homeland.

The decision to create Nunavut was approved in a regional plebiscite—held in May 1992—that ratified an earlier agreement between Canadian and Inuit authorities. It is the largest ever settlement of a land-claim suit made by an indigenous people. The plan was voted into law by the Canadian Parliament in 1993 and goes into effect in 1999.

In each of the territory's far-flung villages are a people in the midst of many converging discoveries: spiritual, psychological, and political. But they claim the benefit of hindsight as they prepare to assume control over this new territorial division. "Nunavut will wed traditional knowledge with modern technical know-how in the operation of the government," says Peter Ernerk, a former minister of the Northwest Territories and a commissioner of the Nunavut Implementation Commission. "Once created, Nunavut will, I think, be the envy of the world, a new deal for the people of Canada."

"We're trying on legislation from all over the world," says Caroline Anawak, a longtime resident of Rankin Inlet on the northwest shores of Hudson Bay. She is an activist for Inuit self-determination and wife of the Northwest Territories' sole member of the Canadian Parliament. "Nunavut is more than just a land claim settlement," she says. "It's a dream. I think this is the biggest secret in North America. The world should be following this, cheering this, because if we can pull it off, it will be for everybody."

Visitors may consider this kind of visionary rhetoric an exercise in wishful thinking. Nunavut at present has virtually no economic base. The Canadian government spends an astronomical $15,000 per person to provide services and a veneer of modernity to the lives of the Inuit population. Economic development is currently limited to exploratory mining, a nascent tourist industry, and the export of traditional arts and crafts, which generated an estimated $10 million in retail sales in 1995.

Many Inuit are only too aware of their society's leap into modernity and are guarded in their optimism. "The scary part is that indigenous peoples all over the north are looking to Nunavut

Top: Inukshuks, stone cairns assembled by the Inuit in the "form of a man." Above: A Cape Dorset carver. The sale of arts and crafts provides Nunavut with an estimated $10 million in annual revenue.

to see what we will do," says Eva Adams-Klaassen, the arts and crafts supervisor of Nunavut. "The non-Inuit are in a panic about the transfer, talking about leaving. And if they leave en masse, where will that leave us?"

"Sociologists recognize fifteen steps from the hunter-gatherer stage to the post-technological society of today," another resident told me. "It has taken thousands of years to advance through these stages. It took my father-in-law three weeks."

A reordered life

The fast-forward pace of change in the far north has been particularly pronounced since the Nunavut land claim agreement was voted into law. But this assumption of political sovereignty is the consummation of many changes that have reordered Inuit life since these people first encountered the *quallunaaq* (white race) in the late sixteenth century.

The first recorded contacts appear to have been a result of early European whaling expeditions in the region around 1590. Whaling was discontinued due to worsening climate but resumed more intensively in the early nineteenth century. Upon the beachhead of these early stations followed other commercial interests, most notably the Hudson Bay Trading Company, which expanded contact with the Inuit and introduced the rudiments of a cash economy. And from the beginning of the twentieth century, missionaries, primarily Roman Catholic and Anglican, began the process of displacing traditional shamanistic beliefs. The Christian worldview challenged many seemingly brutal customs that were rooted in the Inuit's bitter struggle for survival.

The interchange with whites was significant for several reasons. First, the Inuit, sharing the grim experience of Native Americans to the south, were exposed to new diseases to which they lacked resistance. Some scholars estimate that nearly one-third of the Inuit population was lost by 1900 through epidemics introduced from outside. Moreover, the depletion of wildlife stocks as a result of commerce with fur traders led the Inuit to abandon their traditional hunting grounds. Perhaps most tellingly, ancient and time-honored relations within the community began to change with the infiltration of foreign commerce, as the exigencies of survival were moderated by the introduction of textiles and manufactured goods.

Yet all these disruptions appear insignificant in the context of the last generation. Canada's living Inuit elders have witnessed a dislocation that has forever altered ancient traditions.

In the 1950s, the Canadian government learned of widespread starvation in the far north. A dog disease had spread across the Arctic, crippling the people's fragile survival strategy. For thousands of years, the Inuit had relief on the Canadian husky as a hunting partner, means of transportation, and as defense against predators.

Compelled to act by this crisis, the government divided the region into districts, assigned each person a number according to the district he resided in, and forcibly relocated the nomadic Inuit into villages. Every Inuk (person) was required to wear a numbered disk to provide ready identification by administrators.

When tuberculosis struck, affected Inuit were removed to the south for treatment. There, they were forced to wear their medical papers around their necks. The numbering system prevailed until Project Surname, initiated by the Inuit themselves, was launched decades later.

It would be difficult to overstate the consequences of the epidemics and the resultant government actions upon a once self-sustaining people. "The government introduced a welfare society," says Adams-Klaassen. "Mostly young,

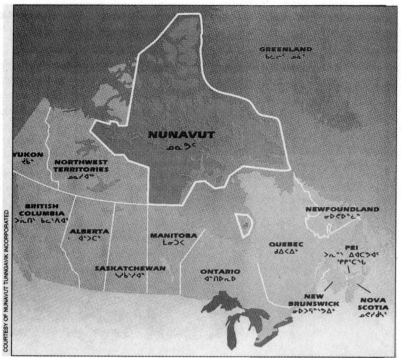

The soon-to-be autonomous territory is roughly four times the size of California.

healthy, capable hunters were selected to relocate first and were loaded on ships. First my brother and uncles were taken to Churchill [Manitoba]. I remember my mother lived in a tar-paper shack with no water or electricity."

For generations, traditional Inuit life had been bracketed by the dictates of climate, and by the belligerence of other native peoples that had prevented migration to the south. By necessity, the Inuit had been obligated to adapt to life in the harshest of environments. Their ability to adapt and survive became a bedrock source of confidence and optimism. This confidence prevails as they contemplate the future confronting their children. It is an ability based, above all, on two factors: an acknowledgment of bitter suffering as part of the fabric of life, and a willingness to subordinate the self to the group in the interests of physical survival.

The struggle for survival in the Arctic was captured in a poignant eyewitness account by an early chronicler of Inuit culture, Diamond Jenness, in 1928:

Permanent homes they had none; life was a perpetual wandering in search of food, a wandering that ended only with death. The winter's twilight had shown me their blurred forms dragging the over-burdened sleds from one sealing ground to another to escape the threat of famine.... Food, clothing and shelter, those primal necessities that generally come so easily to dwellers in more temperate climes, demanded from them ceaseless effort, until the desperate battle to preserve life seemed almost to nullify any purpose for life. Only an invincibly optimistic race, patient, hardy and good tempered, could have wrestled with this environment and survived.

The extraordinary demands of environment likewise engendered strict psychological controls and virtually mandated group harmony. Personal tragedy and emotional trauma, not to mention distraction into melancholy, had to be overcome quickly with a minimum of disruption to the group. In the Canadian Arctic, sociologist Kit Minor wrote, "It would be suicide for a camp to become engrossed in emotional disharmony or to allow a productive camp member to indulge in remorseful seclusion."

Lessons learned

Today, everyone seems to have a story testifying to the near-miraculous power of traditional knowledge to resolve contemporary prob-lems. One account relates that a villager became stranded on the tundra in a disabled snowmobile. Schooled to survive, the resourceful Inuk hunted and killed a fox. He removed a bone from the carcass, carved it to size, and fitted it to the disabled engine. He then drove back to his village with the fox skin to show as reward for his troubles.

Another story, reported in the Rankin Inlet paper last year, related how an Inuk camping with his son accidentally burned down his tent with all of his belongings. This mishap left both of them naked in subzero temperatures. Not to worry. The men proceeded to bag four caribou, skin the animals, and outfit themselves in the hides. Mounting the snowmobile, they drove back to town, where they were treated for frostbite but were otherwise unharmed. Yet another tale related how a man survived on an ice floe for twenty-eight days, living on nothing but ducks and seawater.

Inuit resources of character and experience find modern expression in startling ways. Their acknowledgment of ties beyond the self, for example, is evident in such practices as custom adoption. Every Inuit family seemingly maintains ties with other families through adoption. In each family I encountered, at least one child had been given up for adoption or one or more children had been adopted into the family. Adoption is a cultural norm in Inuit society for any number of incidental reasons—economic, social, or sentimental—and is executed without the burdens and expense and paperwork. The adoptions are carried out when the adoptive parents take possession of the newborn, and the Canadian courts have yet to uphold a single challenge to this Inuit tradition.

The perception that one's family ends at the boundary of one's immediate blood relatives is missing in Inuit culture, where ties of blood and claims of kinship extend into daily life in countless ways.

"If my father says he wants fresh *muktuk* [whale meat], we go out," one young Inuk in Arviat told me. "But almost everything is shared. My brother just killed two caribou. When the elders said they wanted meat, my brother cut some and took it to their homes."

Another experience taken to heart in the far north concerns the availability and consumption of alcohol. Alcohol has been a scourge among Native American populations, and in Nunavut it is subject to varying levels of local control. A number of Inuit communities ban alcohol, while others have adopted strict liquor control boards. In these villages, any person desiring to purchase (import) alcohol must appear before a panel, which will weigh the request and look at the person's history with respect to alcohol consumption. Not surprisingly, a black market for hard liquor has surfaced, but at six hundred dollars for a sixty-ounce bottle, the traffic is unlikely to disrupt territorial policies. The most liberal stance taken by any community is in Iqaluit, recently dubbed "sin city" in the local paper. Alcohol is available in fine restaurants, and a watering hole, the Royal Canadian Legion, stays open Friday night into the early hours.

Looking inward

IF alcohol is not an inordinate problem, other conflicts are challenging communities to look inward for wisdom and resolve. Suicide is not foreign to the Inuit. In the traditional community, old age often came with the acknowledgment that one was becoming an increasing burden, a liability in the group struggle for survival. A responsible and honorable solution, often chosen by the infirm, was suicide. Strangulation by sealskin rope, usually with the assistance of a favored family member, was a common method, as was exposure on the land. The acceptance of suicide even extended to individuals subject to severe depression. But such a step was not taken in desperation or by willful caprice; rather, it was proof of concern that one's personal despair placed an undue burden on the group.

In recent years there has been a shocking incidence of suicide in some Inuit communities. A young Inuk told me that fifteen of his friends had committed suicide over the years, usually over failed relationships or a lack of choices accentuated by boredom. It would be easy to explain this as evidence of a culturally recognized option. Easy but wrong.

"When I was growing up, the ones who committed suicide were the elders," says Peter Ernerk. "Now we have the highest per capita suicide rate in Canada. People think they will come back to life. It's not just an individual problem; it's a community problem.

"To live here you have to be very knowledgeable," Ernerk continued, lamenting the decline of traditional wisdom. "Now we have people falling through the ice, having accidents, because they are not knowledgeable. In the past, elders gave advice and the youth were expected to listen. You were considered a man when you could survive on your own and kill big game. Recently, the elders are getting involved in the schools. They take children on the ice and explain how to hunt and the dangers of ice.

"Thirty-five years ago, I lived in an igloo," he said. "When I grew up, it was a very hard life. We shared. We respected each other. How I long to go back to thirty-five years ago, but I know I can't. But some thoughts we will keep forever."

Prospects

Being "knowledgeable" is perhaps necessary for success in any culture, but as the people of Nunavut prepare to assume their political autonomy, one must ask whether the Inuit survival skills will prove relevant in the coming years and decades. Will the Inuit sense of community, and their knowledge of survival in the Arctic, be

Top: An Inuit woman wearing a traditional caribou-skin parka. Hunting the animal was crucial to the people's survival.
Above: The remains of a supply boat in Arviat.

Top: An Inuit family outing. Nunavut's families are under growing strain as modern forces increasingly disrupt ancient roles and responsibilities. Above: Enjoying the last day of summer vacation.

yet to love and sacrifice unreservedly for one's family and clan: These are cultural values frequently undermined by the messages conveyed through cable transmissions from California and New York.

The insidious assault of Western man's culture on the values and lifestyles of traditional societies like the Inuit is little appreciated in the developed world. But, as we lament the disappearance of the rain forests and endangered species, so we should recognize that the ageless wisdom of indigenous societies—the notion of securing personal benefit through subordination to group welfare—is in danger of passing into history.

The people of the Arctic have been schooled in character-building hardship more strict than the most arduous Marine boot camp. "They are resilient, creative, connected, and resourceful," Anawak told me. And all of their schooling, all of their resources of character, may now be put to the test. For as she fervently asserted, Nunavut *is* more than just a land claim settlement. It is an occasion for a traditional people to embrace modernism yet sustain values that have proven vital over millennia. If the Inuit can successfully integrate the two, Nunavut will offer a lesson other peoples will find well worth learning.

Additional Reading

James Huston, *Confessions of an Igloo Dweller,* Houghton Mifflin, Boston, 1996.

Diamond Jenness, *The People of the Twilight,* University of Chicago, 1928.

_____ and Stuart Jenness, *Arctic Odyssey: The Diary of Diamond Jenness, 1913–16,* University of Washington Press, 1995.

Kit Minor, *Issumatug: Learning from the Traditional Healing Wisdom of the Canadian Inuit,* Fernwood, Halifax, 1992.

Eric P. Olsen, associate executive editor of THE WORLD & I, traveled to Nunavut for two weeks in 1996 as a guest of the national and territorial governments.

relegated to the status of museum exhibit as the people move into the modern world? And will the governing wisdom of today's global popular culture replace their traditions and values?

When I visited Inuit homes that had recently been wired for cable television, and observed women and children watching soap operas, I wondered about the impact of the things they would see. The mantras of self-indulgence and self-gratification commonly promoted by the American media and entertainment industry are in total conflict with every verity of traditional life.

The Inuk "has deep affection for his family," an observer wrote in a 1910 narrative. "He will do and sacrifice more for his children than any people I have ever known, without exception." The fortitude to sit over an ice hole for hours in forty-below temperatures, to disengage emotionally from lifelong bonds of love when the hour of parting comes,

Index

abortion, 134
Achuara people, of Ecuador, 161
Adams-Klaassen, Eva, 221, 222
African Genesis (Ardrey), 74
age-sets, importance of, among Masai people of Tanzania, 76–82
agriculture: colonialism and, 188–195; disease and, 196; and fraternal polyandry in Tibet, 100–103
AIDS, 194, 195, 196, 197
Ainu people, of Japan, 43
alcohol use, in Oceania, 200–206
animals: and skills of Eskimo hunters, 68–70; as source of human diseases, 193–199
apartheid, 33
Appadurai, Ayun, 58
Ardrey, Robert, 74
arranged marriage, in India, 113–116
Australia, 93–97; rubella epidemic in, 195–196; Tiwi people of, 124, 125
ayahuasca, 150–151
Aztec people, of Mexico, 167–172, 198

Barker, James P., 12–13
baseball, ritual in, 180–185
Bellinger, David, 54–55
Berko, Jean, 54–55
betal, 200–202, 205
Boas, Franz, 43
body ritual, among the Nacirema, 173–175
Bonnichsen, Robson, 39, 40, 42
Bradley, Bruce, 41, 42
brainwashing, religious cults and, 176–179
Brazil: infanticide in, 108–112; Mat people of, 160–162
bride price, 62, 78, 80
bride service, 17, 132, 134
bridewealth, 131, 132, 134
brucellosis, 197
bubonic plague, 193, 195, 196–197, 198
Buhl Burial, 44
Bundy, Theodore, 172
bureaucratese, as doublespeak, 49
Burstein, S. R., 153
business, doublespeak in, 50–51

Caesar, Julius, 49
Callatian people, 31–36
Camus, Albert, 167
capital punishment, and rituals of death, 167–172
Carneiro, Robert, 72
Carter, Jimmy, 52
cash crops, colonialism and, 188–192
cat scratch fever, 197
cattle, importance of, to Masai tribesmen of Tanzania, 76–82
Caucasoid race, Kennewick Man and, 37–45
ceremonial exchanges, among the Simbu people of Papua New Guinea, 87–92
Chagas' disease, 199
Chagnon, Napoleon A., 74, 122; on the Yanomamö people of Venezuela, 10–21
Chatters, James 37–45
Cheddar Man, 39
children: of the Fore people of Papua New Guinea, 207–211; of the Mbuti pygmies of

Africa, 157–159; urban, in the United States, 104–107
children of God, 177, 179
cholera, 193, 194, 195, 197
Christmas, among the !Kung people of the Kalahari desert, 27–30
circumcision: female, in Sierra Leone, 137–142; among Masai people of Tanzania, 78, 79–80, 143–149
cities: children of the, in the United States, 104–107; and infanticide in Brazil, 108–112
clothing, as fetishes in baseball, 184
Clovis people, of North America, 40, 41–42, 43
cocoa, 200, 205
coffee, 200
Coimbra, Carlos, 162
colonialism: alcohol use and, 202; as cause of global hunger, 188–192; impact of disease and, on native peoples, 193–199
Conibo people, of Peru, 150–151
Cooper, John, 167
crime, and urban U.S. children, 104–107
crowd diseases, 196, 199
cults, religious, 176–179
cultural relativism, 31–36
culture shock, 12
culture, Sikhism and, 212–217

Darwin, Charles, 45, 83–86
dating, radiocarbon, 38
Davis, Wade, 164
de Sahugun, Fray Bernardino, 171
death, rituals of, 167–172
deity, Sikhism and, 214
Denton, Robert, 122
diabetes, 203
diptheria, 198
disease, evolutionary biology of, 193–199
Divine Light Mission, 176, 177
divorce, in Japan, 117–119
Dobe San, of Kalahari Desert, 123
doublespeak, 48–53
Douglas, Mary, 161
Douyon, Lamarque, 163
dowry, 131, 132, 133, 134
drugs: psychedelic, 150–151; and urban U.S. children, 104–107; use of, in Oceania, 200–206
Duran, Fray Diego, 169

Ecuador, Achuara people of, 161
education: among the Masai people of Tanzania, 80–82; doublespeak in, 49–50; female, in Sierra Leone, 140; postmodernism and, 58–60; Sikhism and, 212–217
Eliot, Charles, 81
epidemics, 195–196, 198, 221–222
Eskimo people, of North America, 31–32, 34, 68–70, 123, 125–126, 220–224
ethnobiology, zombies and, 163–166
euphemisms, as doublespeak, 48
evolution, of diseases, 193–199
exchanges, ceremonial, among the Simbu people of Papua New Guinea, 87–92

fatherhood, virginity and, 134–135

fetishes, in baseball, 183–184
fever, as evolutionary response to disease, 194
Fitzhugh, William, 42
Flannery, Tim F., 96
Folsom people, of North America, 43
food: and Kaliai people of Papua New Guinea, 83–86; and !Kung people of the Kalahari desert, 27–30; and Mat people of Brazil, 160–162; and Yanomamö people of Brazil, 14, 71–75
Fore people, of Papua New Guinea, 207–211
forensic anthropology, Kennewick Man and, 37–45
fraternal polyandry, in Tibet, 100–103
Friedman, Lawrence, 172
fugu fish, in Japan, 165–166

Galaty, John, 78
gangs, youth, and urban U.S. children, 104–107
Gebusi people, of Papua New Guinea, 201
gender issues, 122–126; alcohol issues and, 202–203
Gergen, David, 51
gift exchange, 132, 134
Goode, Arthur, 168
government, U.S., doublespeak in, 48–53
Greenspan, Alan, 49

Hadza, of Tanzania, 125
Haig, Alexander, 51, 52
Haiti, zombies of, 163–166
Haley, Alex, 154
"Hamlet" (Shakespeare), and storytelling among the Tiv people of West Africa, 61–65
Harada, Kunihiko, 55, 57
Hare Krishna, 176, 177, 179
Harris, Marvin, 109, 161, 172
Haynes, C. Vance, 42, 43
Hazda people, of Tanzania, 124, 125
healing, and psychotherapy in Nigeria, 152–156
Herodotus, 31, 32, 35
heroin, 205
Hill, James Douglas, 168
History (Herodotus), 31
hookworm, 196
Horton, Robin, 153, 154
Hourglass Cave skeleton, 44
human sacrifice, and rituals of death, 167–172
hunger, causes of global, 188–192
hunters, skills of Eskimo, 68–70
Hurston, Zora Neale, 164

Ik people, of Kenya, 11
immune system, as evolutionary response to disease, 194
Inca people, of South America, 198
incest taboo, 80
India, arranged marriage in, 113–116
indirect dowry, 132, 134
indirect language, 54–57
infanticide: in Brazil, 108–112; among the Eskimo people of North America, 31–32
infibulation, 142

inflated language, as doublespeak, 49
influenza, 193, 195, 198
Iroquois people, of North America, 123

Jantz, Richard, 40
Japan: Ainu people of, 43; *fugu* fish in, 165–166; marriage in, 117–119
jargon, as doublespeak, 48–49
Jenness, Diamond, 222
Johnson, Floyd, 37, 38

Kalahari Desert, !Kung people of, 27–30
Kaliai people, of Papua New Guinea, 83–86
kava, 200–202, 205
Keen, John, 78
Kennewick Man, 37–45
Kenya: Ik people of, 11; Masai people of, 76–82
khat, 200
Kikuyu people, of Africa, 76, 77
King, Martin Luther, 34
Kingdon, Jonathan, 96
kinship patterns: among Punjabi people of Pakistan, 22–26; among the Yąnomamö people of Venezuela, 10–21
Kline, Nathan, 164
Krantz, Grover S., 38
!Kung people, of the Kalahari desert, 27–30, 123
Kurin, Richard, 23

Laguna Pueblo people, of North America, 127–130
Laird, Charlton, 53
language: doublespeak and, 48–53; indirect, 54–57
Lassa fever, 197
Lebra, Sugiyana, 57
leishmaniansis, 199
leprosy, 196
leptospirosis, 197
Leys, Norman, 77
Linde, Charlotte, 56
Lofland, John, 167
Lovedu people, of Africa, 123, 131
Lyme disease, 197

MacMillan, Catherine J., 38
magic, and ritual in baseball, 180–185
malaria, 193, 198
Malinowski, Bronislaw, 180, 181, 185
Mandan people, of North America, 198–199
Maori people, of New Zealand, 94–95
marijuana, 200, 205
marriage, 131–132; arranged, in India, 113–116; among the Eskimo people of North America, 31; and fraternal polyandry in Tibet, 100–103; in Japan, 117–119; among the Yąnomamö people of Venezuela, 10–11
Masai (Maasai) people, of Tanzania, 76–82, 143–149
Mat people, of Brazil, 160–162
Mbutu pygmies, of Africa, 157–159
McDonald, David, 161
measles, 193, 195, 197, 198
Mende people, of Sierra Leone, 154
Mexico, Aztec people of, 167–172, 198
military, doublespeak in the, 49
Mill, John Stuart, 189
mind control, religious cults and, 176–179
Minor, Kit, 222
Minthorn, Armand, 39–40
Miracle of Language, The (Laird), 53

money, use of, among Simbu people of Papua New Guinea, 87–92
monogamy, 101
morality, cultural relativism and, 31–36
mortal selective neglect, 109
Moynihan, Daniel P., 188
mumps, 196
myxomatosis, 197–198

name taboos, 16
Native Americans: impact of European diseases on, 193–199; Kennewick Man and, 37–45. *See also* Eskimos
natural selection, 45, 94, 195
Ndembu people, of Africa, 153
neglect, and infanticide in Brazil, 108–112
New Zealand, Maori people of, 94–95
Nigeria, psychotherapy and magic in, 152–156
North America: and body ritual among the Nacirema, 173–175; Clovis people of, 40, 41–42, 43; Eskimo people of, 31–32, 34 68–70, 123, 125–126, 218–224; Folsom people of, 43; impact of European diseases on, 193–199; Iroquois people of, 123; Kennewick Man of, 37–45; Laguna Pueblo people of, 127–130; Omaha people of, 133; Solutrean people of, 41–42; Washoe people of, 124, 125

Oceania, alcohol and drug use in, 200–206
Omaha people, of North America, 133
o'nyong-nyong fever, 197
opium, 200
Orwell, George, 51, 53
Owsley, Douglas, 38

Pakistan, Punjabi people of, 22–26
Papua New Guinea, 93–97, 181; food sharing in, 83–86; Fore people of, 207–211; use of betel in, 200–201; use of money among Simbu people of, 87–92
passive infanticide, 109
patriarchy, 123
property, virginity and, 131–136
peasants, global hunger and, 188–192
Pell, Claiborne, 51
Peloponnesian War, The (Thucydides), 49
People's Temple, 179
pertussis, 194, 198
Peru, Conibo people of, 150–151
peyote, 200
physical anthropology, Kennewick Man and, 37–45
plague, 193, 195, 196–197, 198
plantations, colonialism and, 190, 191
plants, psychoactive, use of, in Oceania, 200–206
polar bears, Eskimo hunters and, 68–70
polio, 196
polyandry, fraternal, in Tibet, 100–103
polygamy, 80
postmodernism, education and, 58–60
poverty, and infanticide in Brazil, 108–112
primogeniture, 101
psittacosis, 197
psychedelic drugs: ayahuasca as, 150–151; use of, in Oceania, 200–206
psychotherapy, and magic in Nigeria, 152–156
Punjabi people, of Pakistan, 22–26
pygmies, Mbuti, of Africa, 157–159

rabies, 194

racial issues, Kennewick Man and, 37–45
Radelet, Michael, 168
radiocarbon dating, 38
Rank, Hugh, 50, 51
Rasmussen, Knud, 31
Read, David, 80
Reagan, Ronald, 51, 52
reciprocity, and food sharing in Papua New Guinea, 83–86
religion: and psychotherapy in Nigeria, 152–156; Sikhism and, 212–217; and the Tnevnoc cult, 176–179; and voodoo in Haiti, 163–166
rinderpest, 197
ritual: baseball and, 180–185; body, among the Nacirema, 173–175; death, 167–172; and psychotherapy in Nigeria, 152–156
Rodney, Walter, 189
Ross, Eric, 161
rubella, 194, 195–196

Saitoti, Tepilit Ole, 82; on male circumcision among the Masai people of Tanzania, 143–149
schistosomiosis, 196
Schneider, Alan, 40
Schultes, Richard Evans, 163–166
science, Sikhism and, 214
seals, Eskimo hunters and, 68–70
Semai people, of Venezuela, 122
sexuality, virginity and, 131–136
Shakespeare, William, plays of, and storytelling among the Tiv people of West Africa, 61–65
shame, and divorce in Japan, 119
Sierra Leone: female circumcision in, 137–142; Mende people of, 154
Sikhism, 212–217
Simbu people, of Papua New Guinea, 87–92
Skinner, B. F., 184, 185
smallpox, 193, 194, 195, 196, 198
social pressures, and divorce in Japan, 119
Solutrean people, of North America, 41–42
South Africa, apartheid in, 33
South America, impact of European diseases on, 193–199
Stanford, Dennis, 39, 40, 42
status, virginity and, 131–136
storytelling, among the Tiv people of West Africa, 61–65
Stouffer, Samuel, 183
Straus, Lawrence, 42
suicide, among the Eskimo people, 223
Sumner, William Graham, 32, 33
syphilis, 194, 198

taboos: in baseball, 183, 184; food, 161–162; incest, 80; name, 16
Tanzania: Hazda people of, 124, 125; Masai people of, 76–82, 143–149
television, education and, 58–60
Temne people, of Sierra Leone, 137–142
Thought Women, 128
Thucydides, 49
Tibet, fraternal polyandry in, 100–103
Tiv people, of West Africa, 61–65
Tiwi people, of Australia, 124, 125
Tnevnoc cult, 176–179
tobacco, 200, 203–205
trekking, among the Yąnomamö people of Venezuela, 71–75, 219
Trobriand Island people, 180, 181
truth, Sikhism and, 214–215
tuberculosis, 193, 198, 221

tug of war, among the Mbuti pygmies, 158–159
tularemia, 197
Turnbull, Colin M., 11, 167; on the Mbuti pygmies, 157–159
Turner, Victor, 153
Tiwi, of North Australia, 124, 125
typhus, 198

underdeveloped countries, causes of hunger in, 188–192
Unification Church, 176, 177, 178, 179

United States: and baseball ritual, 180–185; doublespeak and, 48–53; urban children in, 104–107

vaccination, 194
Valero, Helena, 16
Venezuela, Yạnomamö people of, 10–21, 71–75, 122, 218–219
virginity, status, property and, 131–136
Voelker, A. J., 189
voodoo, and zombies of Haiti, 163–166

warriors, Masai, 76–82, 143–149

Washo people, of North America, 124, 125
West Africa, Tiv people of, 61–65
women exchange, 132

Yạnomamö people of Venezuela, 10–21, 71–75, 122, 218–219
yaws, 196
Ye'kwana people, of Venezuela, 10
yellow fever, 196, 198
Yoruba people, of Africa, 154
Yuling Pan, 55

zombies, of Haiti, 163–166

Credits/Acknowledgments

Cover design by Charles Vitelli.

1. Anthropological Perspectives
Facing overview—United Nations photo.

2. Culture and Communication
Facing overview—United Nations photo.

3. The Organization of Society and Culture
Facing overview—United Nations photo by Ray Witlin. 72-73—Photos by Kenneth Good.

4. Other Families, Other Ways
Facing overview—United Nations photo.

5. Gender and Status
Facing overview—United Nations photo.

6. Religion, Belief, and Ritual
Facing overview—American Museum of Natural History, Department of Library Services photo by Captain Hurley.

7. Sociocultural Change: The Impact of the West
Facing overview—Woodfin Camp & Associates photo by Robert Azzi. 207-210—Photos by E. Richard Sorenson. 221, 223-224—Photos by Eric P. Olsen.

ANNUAL EDITIONS ARTICLE REVIEW FORM

■ NAME: _____ DATE: _____

■ TITLE AND NUMBER OF ARTICLE: _____

■ BRIEFLY STATE THE MAIN IDEA OF THIS ARTICLE: _____

_____

■ LIST THREE IMPORTANT FACTS THAT THE AUTHOR USES TO SUPPORT THE MAIN IDEA:

_____

_____

_____

_____

■ WHAT INFORMATION OR IDEAS DISCUSSED IN THIS ARTICLE ARE ALSO DISCUSSED IN YOUR TEXTBOOK OR OTHER READINGS THAT YOU HAVE DONE? LIST THE TEXTBOOK CHAPTERS AND PAGE NUMBERS:

_____

_____

_____

_____

_____

■ LIST ANY EXAMPLES OF BIAS OR FAULTY REASONING THAT YOU FOUND IN THE ARTICLE:

_____

_____

_____

_____

■ LIST ANY NEW TERMS/CONCEPTS THAT WERE DISCUSSED IN THE ARTICLE, AND WRITE A SHORT DEFINITION:

_____

_____

_____

_____

*Your instructor may require you to use this ANNUAL EDITIONS Article Review Form in any number of ways: for articles that are assigned, for extra credit, as a tool to assist in developing assigned papers, or simply for your own reference. Even if it is not required, we encourage you to photocopy and use this page; you will find that reflecting on the articles will greatly enhance the information from your text.

We Want Your Advice

ANNUAL EDITIONS revisions depend on two major opinion sources: one is our Advisory Board, listed in the front of this volume, which works with us in scanning the thousands of articles published in the public press each year; the other is you—the person actually using the book. Please help us and the users of the next edition by completing the prepaid article rating form on this page and returning it to us. Thank you for your help!

ANNUAL EDITIONS: ANTHROPOLOGY 98/99
Article Rating Form

Here is an opportunity for you to have direct input into the next revision of this volume. We would like you to rate each of the 41 articles listed below, using the following scale:

1. **Excellent: should definitely be retained**
2. **Above average: should probably be retained**
3. **Below average: should probably be deleted**
4. **Poor: should definitely be deleted**

Your ratings will play a vital part in the next revision. So please mail this prepaid form to us just as soon as you complete it.
Thanks for your help!

Rating	Article	Rating	Article
	1. Doing Fieldwork among the Yąnomamö		21. Society and Sex Roles
	2. Doctor, Lawyer, Indian Chief		22. Yellow Woman and a Beauty of the Spirit
	3. Eating Christmas in the Kalahari		23. Status, Property, and the Value on Virginity
	4. The Challenge of Cultural Relativism		24. Bundu Trap
	5. The Lost Man		25. The Initiation of a Maasai Warrior
	6. Language, Appearance, and Reality: Doublespeak in 1984		26. A Different Drummer
	7. Why Don't You Say What You Mean?		27. Psychotherapy in Africa
	8. Teaching in the Postmodern Classroom		28. The Mbuti Pygmies: Change and Adaptation
	9. Shakespeare in the Bush		29. *Real* Men *Don't* Eat Deer
	10. Understanding Eskimo Science		30. The Secrets of Haiti's Living Dead
	11. The Yąnomami Keep on Trekking		31. Rituals of Death
	12. Mystique of the Masai		32. Body Ritual among the Nacirema
	13. Too Many Bananas, Not Enough Pineapples, and No Watermelon at All: Three Object Lessons in Living with Reciprocity		33. The Tnevnoc Cult
			34. Baseball Magic
			35. Why Can't People Feed Themselves?
	14. From Shells to Money		36. The Arrow of Disease
	15. Continental Divides		37. A Pacific Haze: Alcohol and Drugs in Oceania
	16. When Brothers Share a Wife		38. Growing Up as a Fore
	17. On the Streets of America		39. Academic Scholarship and Sikhism: Conflict or Legitimization
	18. Death without Weeping		
	19. Arranging a Marriage in India		40. New Spirits for Old
	20. Who Needs Love! In Japan, Many Couples Don't		41. Grounded on Ice

(Continued on next page)

ABOUT YOU

Name _____ Date _____

Are you a teacher? ❑ Or a student? ❑

Your school name _____

Department _____

Address _____

City _____ State _____ Zip _____

School telephone # _____

YOUR COMMENTS ARE IMPORTANT TO US !

Please fill in the following information:

For which course did you use this book? _____

Did you use a text with this *ANNUAL EDITION*? ❑ yes ❑ no

What was the title of the text? _____

What are your general reactions to the *Annual Editions* concept?

Have you read any particular articles recently that you think should be included in the next edition?

Are there any articles you feel should be replaced in the next edition? Why?

Are there any World Wide Web sites you feel should be included in the next edition? Please annotate.

May we contact you for editorial input?

May we quote your comments?

ANNUAL EDITIONS: ANTHROPOLOGY 98/99